KT-376-163

# INTERNATIONAL GUIDE TO LITERATURE ON FILM

Edited by
Tom Costello

**Bowker-Saur**

London • Melbourne • Munich • New Jersey

© 1994 Bowker-Saur, a division of Reed Elsevier (UK) Ltd

All rights reserved. No part of this publication may be reproduced or transmitted in any form or by any means (including photocopying and recording) without the written permission of the copyright holder except in accordance with the provisions of the Copyright, Designs and Patents Act 1988 or under the terms of a licence issued by the Copyright Licensing Agency, 90 Tottenham Court Road, London W1P 9HE. The written permission of the copyright holder must also be obtained before any part of this publication is stored in a retrieval system of any nature. Applications for the copyright holder's written permission to reproduce, transmit or store in a retrieval system any part of this publication should be addressed to the publisher.

Warning: The doing of any unauthorized act in relation to a copyright work may result in both a civil claim for damages and criminal prosecution.

**British Library Cataloguing in Publication Data**
A catalogue record for this title is available from the British Library

**Library of Congress Cataloging-in-Publication Data**
A catalog record for this book is available from the Library of Congress

Published by Bowker-Saur, Maypole House, Maypole Road, East Grinstead, West Sussex RH19 1HU, UK
Tel: +44(0)1342 330100  Fax: +44(0)1342 330191
E-mail: lis@bowker-saur.co.uk
Internet Website: http://www.bowker-saur.co.uk/service/

Reprinted 1995

Bowker-Saur is part of REED REFERENCE PUBLISHING

ISBN 0-86291-595-3

Cover design by Robin Caira
Typesetting by Tradespools Ltd, Frome, Somerset
Printed on acid-free paper
Printed and bound in Great Britain by Antony Rowe Ltd, Chippenham

# CONTENTS

# PREFACE AND USER'S GUIDE

The main purpose of this book is to provide all necessary information to discover if a significant work of literature has been filmed. The volume is arranged alphabetically by author, with literary and film titles (together with their variants) indexed separately. It is hoped that this arrangement will provide users with a quick and easy method of locating film adaptations even when only partial information is at hand.

Beyond this primary purpose other uses (of equal importance) may also be served by the data presented. Because so many of the international classics of literature have been filmed since the advent of sound cinema, the inclusion here of a literary work's first publication date, its original native title and the nationality and language of the author may prove helpful in general bibliographical searches even in the absence of any specific interest in film. Further help is afforded through the classification of literary works according to form – as novels, short stories, or plays.

The decision to include all known adaptations of significant literature filmed during the period 1930–1991 inevitably excludes many important works of silent cinema. It is, however, only their silence which excludes them. The advent of sound in the late 1920s so revolutionized the requirements of film scriptwriting, for example, that judgments about how filmmakers handle a novelist's or playwright's dialogue can only be accurately made when comparison and analysis are conducted with what has become the standard mode of film presentation – the sound movie. The advent of sound, however, was not universal even by 1930. The expense of studio and auditorium equipment could not be as readily met in Tokyo as it was in New York. Some nations lagged behind, while some individual directors continued to prefer the silent to the sound option. In the very few cases where silent film adaptations of significant literature were produced after 1929 these have been included out of respect for the culture of origin.

Which authors to include or exclude has been one of the most taxing problems. Indiscriminate inclusivity would have been easy and might have best served the needs of a certain kind of user. But such an option was never seriously considered. The challenge lay in attempting to do what had not yet been accomplished; to compile a reference work on literature and film which would be primarily literary in its anchorage and selectivity, yet genuinely international in the range of authors, languages and forms of literature it encompassed. Other works have dealt with 'books on film' (Daisne, Enser) and in these less discriminating works (where *The Bible* coexists with Mickey Spillane) no editorial policy appears to govern content. Noticeable too is the general omission in earlier publications of the details of film adaptations made in countries outside the English-speaking world and selected parts of (mostly) western Europe. Given these inadequacies my task lay in defining what constitutes a significant author and in not limiting the cultural boundaries from which s/he derived.

Authors have therefore been included primarily on the basis of literary merit, irrespective of language and without regard to geography. But judgments as to merit have not been based on mere personal whim. Since my own reading is far from global and limited to those few languages I can cope with, it was essential to establish external modes of reference, advice and control if the contents of this book were not to fall victim to my ignorance, or lapse into becoming merely a reflector of personal taste and literary prejudice.

I decided therefore to refer each author under consideration to the judgment of the editors of such standard works as the *Columbia Dictionary of Modern European Literature, The Penguin Companion to Literature* (4 vols), the various Oxford Companions to national literatures and other standard works cited in my bibliography. Advice has also been sought from colleagues at my own and other universities as well as from foreign nationals serving at embassies and institutions in England, Ireland and the United States. Friends or acquaintances with expertise in minority languages have been a very fruitful source of help. This personal rather than printed guidance has been particularly important in relation to recent writers too talented to overlook yet too young when standard literary compendiums went to press to have achieved mention there.

Although the literary merit of writers, as attested by time, consensus and peer evaluation, has been the main criterion for inclusion, it has not been the sole criterion. Filmic merit has also informed decisions. Writers of the second rank whose work has helped produce films of the first rank have been considered. Thus C.S. Forester is listed because of John Huston's rendering of *The African Queen*, Booth Tarkington because of Orson Welles' *The Magnificent Ambersons*, Richard Condon (Frankenheimer's *The Manchurian Candidate*), Barry Hines (Ken Loach's *Kes*), Dorothy M. Johnson (*The Man Who Shot Liberty Valance*), John Ball (*In the Heat of the Night*) and so on. To have excluded such writers from a volume which seeks to encourage the comparative study of literature and film, on the sole grounds that they are not all mentioned within the covers of standard academic reference books, would have been perverse.

Also included, out of respect for their relevance to the development of cinematic narrative style, are genre writers of the calibre of Cornell Woolrich, Raymond Chandler and Patricia Highsmith. 'One book' authors such as Margaret Mitchell (*Gone With the Wind*) have been included for obvious reasons, as have those writers (Conan Doyle, Louisa May Alcott, R.D. Blackmore et al.) whose work is probably more important for the myths and mental landscapes it helped to create than for any advances it offered to the art of prose fiction.

Not all works by a writer (however reputable) are likely to be of equal merit. The rule I have adopted therefore is to include all filmed versions of every work by a writer if any one of their works merits inclusion. Although this creates problems of space in cases of prolific and uneven writers, it has the merit of revealing a profile to enable us to see which particular books most frequently attract the attention and investment of film makers and if such attention changes decade by decade. By extension it also discloses which texts have been overlooked or neglected by the film industry. In the case of several notable authors it is clear that it is not always their best books which repeatedly attract scriptwriters, or indeed, which necessarily produce the best films.

The basic sources for the *International Guide to Literature on Film* are the films themselves plus materials supplied by the institutions and individuals I acknowledge, and the printed sources listed in my bibliography. Most but not all the entries in this volume are documented elsewhere. The exceptions relate to films from east European countries where until recently contemporary writers were paid more for an 'original script' than for an adaptation of one of their own literary works. One consequence of this is that the actual source of some Romanian films, for example, is not mentioned in the official credits. It is the east European writers themselves, and those involved in production, who have been approached to provide the evidence as to which 'original scripts' were (in fact) adaptations of the scriptwriter's own published prose and dramatic fiction.

## Authors' Names

The names of writers are listed in the manner in which they appear in *The British Library General Catalogue* and *The National Union Catalog*. This may cause some problems in cases where pseudonyms have become more widely known than real names – especially if writers publish in both. Thus Hopley-Woolrich, Cornell George (real name), is also George Hopley but is possibly better known as William Irish. The author Evan Hunter publishes often as Ed McBain; Raymond Queneau also gets paid as Sally Mara. All such instances are cross-referenced to lessen difficulty. Civic titles such as Count, Sir, Dr etc. have been omitted. Joint authorship, where known, is acknowledged and cross-referenced. Hungarian, Chinese, Japanese, Spanish and other local modes of naming have been respected. The particular problems associated with the change from the Wade to the Pinyin systems in Chinese has led me to cite all known transliterated forms for each individual name.

*Some conventions:*
**Cao Zhan** ...............name in Pinyin
(Ts'ao Chan) .............name in Wade [*old form*]
(as: Cao Xueqin) ........pseudonym in Pinyin
(Ts'ao Hsüeh ch'in) ....pseudonym in Wade

**Brecht, Bertolt;** ........semi-colon after first author signifies
**Wuolijoki, Hella**        joint authorship

**Murdoch, Iris** – {n}; ....author of a novel which the
**Priestley, J. B.** – {p}....second writer made into a play

**Aytmatov, Chingiz Totekulovich** .... a variant spelling of an author's name
*(see: Aitmatov, Chingiz)*                cross referenced

**Dinesen, Isak** ...........pseudonym followed by real name, where the first
*(Karen Blixen)*            is usual

**Lateur, Frank** ...........real name followed by pseudonym for a
*(as: Stijn Streuvels)*      particular work

## Literary Form

Each literary work has been described as novel (N), play (P), short story (SS) or poetry/verse (V) etc. (The use of 'V' rather than 'P' for poetry is not qualitative, but occasioned by the need to retain unique codes for both plays and poems for the purposes of computer sorting.) Needless to say the lack of any agreed definition as to what constitutes a short story (as distinct from an economical novel) has caused some hesitation. The term 'novella' is still used today, but in view of its important Italian origins, and its rather antique connotations, this use compounds rather than assists the problem of definition. Any work described elsewhere as a novella is therefore classified here as a short story.

*Some conventions:*
**N+P** ..........              a novel and a play
**N-P** ..........              a novel later made into a play
**SS-P(TV)** .....             short story later made into a television play
**F-P** ..........              a play derived from a film
**AUT** ..........             autobiography
**P(R)** ..........            radio play
**N(V)**..........             a novel in verse
**P(K)** ..........            kabuki play
**Rome Haul** *{n}* ..............  The original literary title and form,
*(The Farmer Takes a Wife) {p}* rewritten in another form, with a different title

## Titles: *General note*

Given the international inclusivity I sought there were obvious problems of how best to present the film and literary titles of non-English language works to English readers. It is not uncommon in international film reference works published in Britain or the United States for the language of presentation to be solely English. The world of bibliography, as distinct from filmography, is often more accurate and respectful of the need to present titles in the language of initial publication. For the cineast, therefore, it may be initially disconcerting to discover such well known movies as *Bicycle Thieves*, *Ashes and Diamonds* or *The Wages of Fear* presented in the following pages as *Lardi di biciclette*, *Popiół i diament* and *Le salaire de la peur* respectively. Yet these are the correct and original titles of those movies. Problems of linguistic recognition, pronunciation and cultural alienation are real and are resolved by film distributors who translate, or substitute, English titles for the originals. But a creative writer's or film director's native language is of such fundamental importance that a reference book which seeks to document the relationship between literature and film, rather than to market either, owes a duty to the primary and original identities of these arts and crafts and to their creator's native cultures.

I therefore sought a principle which would be culturally respectful and consistent while not reducing the usefulness of this work to single-language users. Indeed I hope I have increased usefulness by providing, where practicable, both the original language title and any current English translation or transliteration for both literature and film.

## Literary Titles

Literary titles are presented in the language of initial publication (or in a romanized transliteration) and are accompanied (in round parentheses) by the translated English title as published. Where different translations of the same title are known these are cited as 'aka' (also known as). Where no known translation exists an indicative English version of the title is sometimes offered [in square parentheses] if this has been used in the authorities consulted. Both the original title and its English variants are cross-referenced in the index.

## Film Titles

Film titles are a frequent source of confusion. The same film may be known by several different names particularly if it is a joint production involving financial investment from two or more nations. But even unilaterally produced movies are frequently retitled on export, or on re-release. An attempt has been made to list and index all known variants. Film titles are presented in the language of first release in the country of production. Where more than one country has produced the film, an effort has been made to offer the title in the languages of all participating nations. If a distributed English title exists for a non-English film this is quoted in round parentheses. As with literary titles, alternative film titles are indicated by the use of 'aka', and indicative titles appear in square parentheses.

## Indicative Titles

No attempt has been made by the editor to translate to or from any language. The literal or indicative translations offered have been gathered from published sources or from archives. It should be noted that all titles appearing in [ ] represent likely titles, rather than known distributed ones, and are not therefore included in the indexes.

## Literary Dates

The decision to include literary dates as well as film dates was not made for decorative reasons. This labour was forced upon us when we discovered how often primary and secondary filmographic sources were inaccurate in their assumptions regarding the literary origins of films. Credits which include the phrase 'from a story by...' proved to be the most suspect. The 'story' was all too frequently discovered to be an unpublished film script, sometimes less than that – presumably an undeveloped story line. On other occasions one's suspicions were aroused on discovering that the film predated the publication of the alleged literary source by several years. Many of these films also turned out to be based on original film scripts later adapted into other literary forms but retaining the filmed title. Most of these have been excluded. There are however exceptions, the most notable being the 'contes' of the French writer and film director Eric Rohmer whose method of writing short stories based on his own films, which are then published after the film's release, constitute a special case of literary creativity. Special too is the practice of some Hungarian and other writers who deliberately use a completed film as the starting point for a play or piece of impressive prose fiction. In all such interesting cases I indicate that the film has suggested the literature (eg. F-P, F-SS).

It is not uncommon for stage plays to enjoy their first public performance and be filmed before they are published as texts. This tradition has been recognised, with the result that the publication date of some modern plays is later than the release date of their filmed versions.

Short stories have inevitably proved to be the most difficult to verify. Attempting to establish the initial date, place and publisher of short fiction which originally appeared in ephemeral magazines or newspapers in Japan, Poland, Hungary or India has sometimes been – even for helpful librarians in Tokyo, Warsaw, Budapest and Delhi – an impossible task. Consequently many short stories have had to be excluded which could not satisfy our tests. However where the initial publication date could not be proven, but the story later appeared in a collection, the date of this has been cited when we are fairly certain, on other evidence, that the original publication date of the story preceded the film. Sometimes both the initial date and the date of the later collection are cited where these are known.

I have been greatly assisted in this area by Jenny Hughes whose bibliographical skills and persistence have proved invaluable in the verification of literary dates.

*Some conventions:*
**n.d.** ...... no date printed in volume
**c.1150** ..... published in about 1150
**1930(rev.1960)**..published 1930, revised edition 1960
**1920(posth.)** .. published posthumously
**1948(coll.)** ... short story published in a collection
**1930(31)**..... publication date in magazine or journal, followed by date of first book edition

## Film Date

There is, in practice, no common universal standard for dating films. Source material may quote the completion date, the registration date, the date of initial exhibition or the date of first release in the country of origin. Some or all of these may be different. The dating of films is a perennial problem which I cannot claim to have completely resolved. A modern book can be dated, in most cases, from the declarations appearing on the title or copyright pages. Such information can usually be checked in libraries at first hand. Book dates normally correspond to the year the book was actually distributed. Because of the very different modes of production, distribution and access, the world of film is a much less certain sphere. Films too, in many instances, display a copyright date. But they cannot be called-up as readily as books. Such film libraries as exist are of necessity rather inaccessible and limited in the range of material they house and display.

Until the recent advent of home video distribution most films were protected from casual browsers. The sheer cost of producing a single print, the resources needed for projection and viewing, their weight and bulk plus the inherent chemical instability of pre-1950 film stock (which can deteriorate rapidly unless stored under environmentally controlled conditions) have all conspired to make research in the realm of film much more problematical than in the world of books. Consequently the researcher has frequently no choice but to examine the archive records of a film rather than the film itself.

Even where the copyright date of a film can be established this does not necessarily coincide with its date of release or exhibition which can be anything from one to twenty-two (or more) years later. It would be unusual for a publisher to print several thousand copies of a book and then refuse to release these for many years. But this has happened frequently with films. Many films indeed are never released but just lie in vaults – the victims of tantrums, marketing decisions, censorship or suppression. There is generally therefore less problem in ascertaining when a film completed production than in ascertaining the date of first release in the country of origin. Since it is the date of release which corresponds most closely to the publication date of a book, it is this date to which I give priority in my listings. Where the date of completed production is also known this is offered in parenthesis. Parentheses are also used to contain unresolved alternative dates when the evidence conflicts.

### Capitalisation

Effort has been made to avoid giving offence when deploying capital letters in languages other than English. There are however wide inconsistencies in typographical practice in the primary source book material inspected from a number of European and South American countries. *The MLA Style Manual* has been helpful in determining correct and acceptable practice, as indeed has the advice from colleagues and overseas contacts, but in a work as linguistically wide-ranging as this, thoroughgoing correctness may still fall victim to my ignorance – and for this I apologise. Where primary sources are inconsistent in their use of upper or lower case for the same title, I have chosen the lower case option. The titles of films have been presented in the same style as their matching literary sources. Capitals are retained where customary in English and German. They are generally not used in this volume for other languages except for initial letters, proper names and places.

### Accents / Diacritics

Again effort has been made to be exact in the presentation of highly accented languages such as Hungarian, Romanian and Czech but exactitude is made the more difficult by the sheer quantity of otherwise accurate information published in the West which ignores the importance of diacritics and consequently disrespects both the stress and the meaning of non-English names and titles. The parochial limitations of the ASCII and IBM character sets do little to encourage correctness in computer assisted research (and consequently in publishing) since most standard software is unable to generate many basic non-Western characters. A new and revised standard is much needed, one which recognises the equal importance of all natural languages.

## Nationality

The nationality and language of writers is cited for the purposes of making transparent the language in which the writer created the literature. This is particularly important in cases such as Samuel Beckett (Irish nationality, wrote primarily in French), Ben Traven (American [?], wrote in German) and the Spanish-born Arrabal who also writes in French. Dual nationality has been accorded to Americans who took up long-standing residence in England (e.g. T.S. Eliot, Henry James) and to some Europeans who took up residence in the United States, but not to Irish writers who wrote in England. Where nationality is not synonymous with a particular language (e.g. Swiss) the writer's working language is indicated. This is also the practice in relation to writers from multi-lingual communities such as India and Russia. The second abbreviation in the nationality column serves to indicate the culture from which the writer derives.

*Some conventions:*

**British(Scot)** ..... British writer from Scotland
**Russian(Ukr)** ...... Russian writer from the Ukraine
**Greek(anc)**........ Ancient/Classical Greek writer
**Swiss(Fr)** ......... Swiss who writes in French
**Indian(Hin/Urd)** ... Indian who writes in both Hindi and Urdu
**American/British** .. American writer who became a British subject

## Duration

The duration or running-time of films is given in minutes. The duration of 35mm prints may differ from 16mm or video versions, and there may be prints of the same gauge but of different running times in simultaneous circulation. Significant variations are noted in parentheses. Where the length or duration of a film could not be confirmed (following exhaustive searches) it has been excluded from my listings on the grounds that this deficiency raises serious doubts about whether the film was ever actually completed.

*Some conventions:*

**95** .......... running time 95 minutes
**102(95)** ...... some prints 102, others 95
**20(vo)** ....... only available on video
**273** ........ feature film = 273,
**+V(176)** ...... also issued on video at 176

## Video

Where a video version of a film is known to have been distributed in England this is indicated by a '+V' sign. The rapidly changing state of video distribution however makes it impossible to know if a video issued today will still be available in a few months time. It is equally impossible to keep abreast with new releases. Discovering if a film is available on video will usually require a local search for specific titles as and when required.


No work of this nature can pretend to be complete. Limitations of space have forced me to exclude many marginal authors as well as television productions based on the work of some outstanding writers. Intuition and the experience gained during twelve years research provide more than a hint of the many reels of yet undocumented film adaptation awaiting discovery in eastern Europe, China and the Indian continent – as well as closer to home. Opportunities therefore for others to add to my findings will long continue.

I would be most grateful to receive notice of any serious errors or omissions.

**Tom Costello**
Lecturer in Literature
*Department of Continuing Education*
*The University of Liverpool*
*England*

October 1993

# ACKNOWLEDGMENTS

I wish to record my sincere gratitude to the individuals and institutions listed below for their advice and help in improving this book.

Individuals:

**Tessel Andriessen,** (Holland). **A. Angeloglou,** (Greece). **Vladimir Antropov,** (Russia). **Evgenia Ateva,** (Bulgaria). **Michelle Aubert,** (France). **David Barry,** (Ireland). **Brian Birch,** (Hungarian). **Ricardo Braule,** (Brazil). **Rui Santana Brito,** (Portugal). **Prof. Dr. Bucher,** (Germany). **Lourdes Castro,** (Cuba). **Mercedes Certucha Llano,** (Mexico). **Lóránt and Magda Czigány,** (Hungary). **Dolores Devesa,** (Spain). **M. Dogra,** (India). **Jean-Paul Dorchain,** (Belgium). **Barbro Everfjärd,** (Sweden). **Elisabeth Feigl,** (Austria). **Paulina Fernandez Jurado,** (Argentina). **Leonardo Gavina,** (Brazil). **Magdalena Georundova,** (Bulgaria). **Dipali Ghosh,** (India). **Baron Olivier Gillès de Pélichy,** (Belgium). **M. Gladstone,** (Spain). **Julie Harders,** (Australia). **Li Hengji,** (China). **Ma. Araceli Hernández,** (Spain). **Richard Hollingshead,** (Russian). **Jenny Hughes. Mgr. Janina Huppenthal,** (Poland). **Hiroshi Imon,** (Japan). **Joan Ingram. Chen Jingliang,** (China). **Jenő Juhász,** (Hungary). **Hayashi Kanako,** (Japan). **Diana Killen,** (Australia). **Barbara Kościelny,** (Poland). **Branislav Kovačević,** (Yugoslavia). **Eric Le Roy,** (France). **Maria Lewandowska,** (Poland). **Daniela Licurgu,** (Romania). **Eugénio Lisboa,** (Portugal). **Ursula McLean,** (Hungary). **Ronald F. Monteiro,** (Brazil). **Ib Monty,** (Denmark). **José María Moreno,** (Spain). **Colin Morgan. Keith Munro,** (Russian). **P. K. Nair,** (India). **Cristina Neagu,** (Romania). **Maria and Constantin Neagu,** (Romania). **Annie Nickolova,** (Bulgaria). **Lasse Nilsson. Lars Olsson,** (Sweden). **Vladimír Opěla,** (Czechoslovakia). **Lucian Osatiuc,** (Romania). **László Ottovay,** (Hungary). **Tadeusz Pacewicz,** (Poland). **Maria Paldy,** (Hungary). **Arne Pedersen,** (Norway). **Carlos Eduardo Pereira,** (Brazil). **Pat Perilli. Ursula Philips,** (Polish). **Waldemar Piątek,** (Poland). **Esko Rahikainen,** (Finland). **Gabriele Reinsch,** (Germany). **Helga Rolf,** (Germany). **Anita Sandmark,** (Sweden). **Dr. Gunter Schulz,** (Germany). **Irene Scobbie. Milka Staykova,** (Bulgaria). **Kaarle Stewen,** (Finland). **Torbjørn Støverud,** (Norway). **Jørgen Thorning Sørensen,** (Denmark). **B. J. Tasker,** (New Zealand). **Bjarne Thomsen, Jacob Thomsen,** (Denmark). **Hamish Todd,** (Japanese). **Teresa Toledo,** (Cuba). **Dinko Tucaković,** (Yugoslavia). **Hiroshi Utano,** (Japan). **J. A. van Alphen,** (Holland). **Sirpa Vasko,** (Finland). **Joseph Veress,** (Hungary). **Isabel Vilares Cepeda,** (Portugal). **Christina Voigt,** (Germany). **M. I. Waley,** (Turkish). **Paula Weiman-Kelman,** (Israel). **Joaquim A. Whitaker Salles,** (Brazil). **Heloisa Xavier,** (Brazil). **Michiyo Yanase,** (Japan). **Iv. Yankova,** (Bulgaria). **Bánui Zsolt,** (Hungary).

# Acknowledgements

Institutions:
**Ambassade van België,** (Belgium). **Arhiva Naţională de Filme,** (Romania). **Australian High Commission,** London. **Biblioteca Nacional,** (Portugal). **Biblioteca Nacional,** (Spain). **Biblioteka Matice srpske,** (Yugoslavia). **Brazilian Embassy,** London. **British Film Institute,** London. **The British Library,** London. **Bulgarska Nacionalna Filmoteka,** (Bulgaria). **Bundesarchiv - Filmarchiv,** (Germany). **Centre National de la Cinématographie,** (France). **Československý Filmový Ústav,** (Czechoslovakia). **China Film Archive,** Beijing. **Cinemateca Brasileira,** (Brazil). **Cinemateca de Cuba,** Havana. **Cinemateca Museu de Arte Moderna,** (Brazil). **Cinemateca Portuguesa,** (Portugal). **Cinémathèque Suisse,** (Switzerland). **Cineteca Nacional,** (Mexico). **Det Danske Filmmuseum,** (Denmark). **Deutsches Rundfunkarchiv,** (Germany). **Embaixada de Portugal,** London. **Embassy of Greece,** London. **Film Art Research Centre,** (China). **Filmoteka Narodowa w Warszawie,** (Poland). **Fundacion Cinemateca Argentina,** Buenos Aires. **Goethe Institut,** Manchester & London. **Gosfilmofond,** (Russia). **Helsinki University Library,** (Finland). **Hungarian Embassy,** London. **Instituto de la Cinematografia,** (Spain). **Irish Embassy,** London. **Israel Film Archive,** Jerusalem. **Japan Film Library Council,** Tokyo. **Jugoslovenska Kinoteka,** (Yugoslavia). **Keio University Library,** (Japan). **Det kongelige Bibliotek,** (Denmark). **Kungl. Biblioteket,** (Sweden). **Liverpool Public Libraries,** (England). **Magyar Filmintézet,** (Hungary). **Ministerio de Cultura,** (Spain). **National Diet Library,** (Japan). **National Film Archive,** (Australia). **National Film Archive of India,** Pune. **National Institute of Japanese Literature,** Tokyo. **Nederlands Filmmuseum,** (Holland). **New York Public Library,** (U.S.A.). **New Zealand High Commission,** London. **Nihon Bungaku Shinko-kai,** (Japan). **Norsk Filminstitutt,** (Norway). **Országos Idegennyelvü Könyvtár,** (Hungary). **Országos Széchényi Könyvtár,** (Hungary). **Österreichisches Filmmuseum,** (Austria). **Polish Cultural Institute,** London. **Royal Film Archive,** (Belgium). **Royal Netherlands Embassy,** London. **Royal Norwegian Embassy,** London. **Sofia University,** (Bulgaria). **Spanish Embassy,** London. **Staatliches Filmarchiv der DDR.,** (Germany). **State Literature Museum,** (Russia). **Suomalaisen Kirjallisuuden Seura,** (Finland). **Suomen elokuva-arkisto,** (Finland). **Sveriges Television,** (Sweden). **Swedish Film Institute,** Stockholm. **Universitetsbiblioteket Fiolstræde,** (Denmark). **University of California,** (U.S.A.). **University of Edinburgh,** (Scotland). **University of Hull,** (England). **University of Liverpool,** (England). **University of London,** (England). **University of Tokyo Library,** (Japan). **Wojewódzka Biblioteka Publiczna,** (Poland).

Special thanks to **Jenny Hughes** for her patient typing, silent correction of my errors and acute proof-reading.

# Abbreviations

| | | |
|---|---|---|
| aka | .......... | also known as |
| ALG | .......... | Algeria |
| anc | .......... | ancient |
| anon | .......... | anonymous |
| ARG | .......... | Argentine |
| AUST | .......... | Austria |
| AUSTL | .......... | Australia |
| AUT | .......... | autobiography |
| BANG | .......... | Bangladesh |
| BC | .......... | before Christ |
| BEL | .......... | Belgium |
| BEN | .......... | Bengal |
| BER | .......... | Bermuda |
| BIO | .......... | biography |
| Br | .......... | British |
| BRAZ | .......... | Brazil |
| BULG | .......... | Bulgaria |
| c. | .......... | 'about' (circa) |
| CAN | .......... | Canada |
| Cas | .......... | Castilian |
| Cat | .......... | Catalan |
| CB | ........... | Cuba |
| CHL | .......... | Chile |
| CHN | .......... | China |
| COL | .......... | Columbia |
| coll | .......... | collection |
| Cro | .......... | Croat |
| CZ | .......... | Czechoslovakia |
| DEN | .......... | Denmark |
| ed. | .......... | edited by |
| EGY | .......... | Egypt |
| Eng | .......... | English |
| Est | .......... | Est(h)onian |
| et al. | .......... | and others |
| F-N | .......... | novel derived from a film |
| fol | .......... | folio |
| F-P | .......... | play derived from a film |

| | | |
|---|---|---|
| F-SS | .......... | short story derived from a film |
| FD | .......... | fictional diary |
| FIN | .......... | Finland |
| Fle | .......... | Flemish |
| FR | .......... | France |
| GB | .......... | Great Britain |
| GDR | .......... | German Democratic Republic |
| GER | .......... | Germany |
| GR | .......... | Greece |
| HIN | .......... | Hindi |
| HK | .......... | Hong Kong |
| HOLL | .......... | Holland |
| HUNG | .......... | Hungary |
| ICE | .......... | Iceland |
| IND | .......... | India |
| IRE | .......... | Ireland |
| IRN | .......... | Iran |
| IS | .......... | Israel |
| IT | .......... | Italy |
| JAP | .......... | Japan |
| K | .......... | Kabuki |
| Kir | .......... | Kirghiz |
| LIECH | .......... | Liechenstein |
| Mal | .......... | Malayalam |
| Mar | .......... | Marathi |
| MEM | .......... | memoirs |
| MEX | .......... | Mexico |
| MOR | .......... | Morocco |
| N | .......... | novel |
| N(AUT) | .......... | autobiographical novel |
| N(NF) | .......... | non-fictional novel |
| N(V) | .......... | novel in verse |
| N+P | .......... | novel plus a play |
| N+SS | .......... | novel plus a short story |
| N-P | .......... | novel later a play |
| n.d. | .......... | no date |
| NIC | .......... | Nicaragua |
| NIG | .......... | Nigeria |
| NOR | .......... | Norway |
| NZ | .......... | New Zealand |
| P | .......... | play |
| P(K) | .......... | Kabuki play |
| P(R) | .......... | radio play |
| P(R)-P | .......... | radio play later a stage play |
| P(R)-TV | .......... | radio play later a television play |
| P(TV) | .......... | television play |
| P(TV)-N | .......... | television play later a novel |
| P(TV)-P | .......... | television play later a stage play |
| P+SS | .......... | play plus a short story |

## Abbreviations

| | | |
|---|---|---|
| P+V | .......... | play plus a poem |
| P-N | .......... | play later a novel |
| P-SS | .......... | play later a short story |
| P-TVP | .......... | stage play later a television play |
| PAN | .......... | Panama |
| POL | .......... | Poland |
| PORT | .......... | Portugal |
| posth. | .......... | published posthumously |
| Pt. | .......... | Part |
| rev. | .......... | revised |
| ROM | .......... | Romania |
| Russ | .......... | Russian |
| S.AFR | .......... | South Africa |
| Sans | .......... | Sanskrit |
| Scot | .......... | Scottish |
| SEN | .......... | Senegal |
| Serb | .......... | Serbian |
| SL | .......... | Sri Lanka |
| Slov | .......... | Slovak |
| SP | .......... | Spain |
| SS | .......... | short story |
| SS(V) | .......... | short story in verse |
| SS-N | .......... | short story later a novel |
| SS-P | .......... | short story later a play |
| SS-P(TV) | .......... | short story later a television play |
| SWE | .......... | Sweden |
| SWITZ | .......... | Switzerland |
| TAM | .......... | Tamil |
| TEL | .......... | Telepan |
| TUN | .......... | Tunisia |
| TUR | .......... | Turkey |
| Ukr | .......... | Ukrainian |
| Urd | .......... | Urdu |
| USA | .......... | United States of America |
| USSR | .......... | Union of Soviet Socialist Republics |
| V | .......... | verse / poetry |
| +V | .......... | film available on video |
| VEN | .......... | Venezuela |
| vo | .......... | video only |
| vol | .......... | volume |
| YUGO | .......... | Yugoslavia |
| ZAM | .......... | Zambia |

# Literature on Film
## A–Z by Author

| No. | Author | Nationality | Form | Literary Title | Date |
|-----|--------|-------------|------|----------------|------|
| 1 | **Aakjær, Jeppe** | Danish | N | **Jens Langkniv** | 1915 |
| 2 | **Aakjær, Jeppe** | Danish | P | **Livet paa Hegnsgaard** | 1907 |
| 3 | **Aakjær, Jeppe** | Danish | P | **Naar Bønder elsker** | 1911 |
| 4 | **Aanrud, Hans** | Norwegian | SS | **En odelsbonde +** <br> **Mari Smehaugen +** <br> **I bestfars ærend +** <br> **Brødre i Herren+** <br> **Da jeg lå i byen med smør** | 1891+ <br> 1901+ <br> 1923 |
| 5 | **Abe Kōbō** | Japanese | N | **Moetsukita chizu** <br> (The Ruined Map) | 1967 |
| 6 | **Abe Kōbō** | Japanese | P(TV) | **Otoshiana** | 1972 |
| 7 | **Abe Kōbō** | Japanese | N | **Suna no onna** <br> (The Woman in the Dunes) | 1962 |
| 8 | **Abe Kōbō** | Japanese | SS | **Tanin no kao** <br> (The Face of Another) | 1964 |
| 9 | **Abe Tomoji** | Japanese | SS | **Jinko teien** | 1954 |
| 10 | **About, Edmond** | French | SS | **L'homme à l'oreille cassée** <br> (The Man With the Broken Ear) | 1862 |
| 11 | **About, Edmond** | French | SS | **Le roi des montagnes** <br> (The King of the Mountains) | 1857 |
| 12 | **About, Edmond** | French | N | **Trente et quarante** <br> (The Soldier Lover) | 1859 |
| 13 | **Achard, Marcel** | French | P | **La belle marinière** | 1930 |
| 14 | **Achard, Marcel** | French | P | **Domino** | 1932 |
| 15 | **Achard, Marcel** | French | P | **L'idiote** <br> (A Shot in the Dark) | 1960 |
| 16 | **Achard, Marcel** | French | P | **Jean de la lune** | 1929 |
| 17 | **Achard, Marcel** | French | P | **Jean de la lune** | 1929 |
| 18 | **Achard, Marcel** | French | P | **Mistigri** | 1931 |
| 19 | **Achard, Marcel** | French | P | **Noix de coco** | 1936 |
| 20 | **Achard, Marcel** | French | P | **Patate** <br> (Rollo) | 1957 |
| 21 | **Achard, Marcel** | French | P | **Pétrus** | 1934 |
| 22 | **Adams, Samuel Hopkins** | American | N | **The Gorgeous Hussy** | 1934 |
| 23 | **Adams, Samuel Hopkins** | American | N | **The Harvey Girls** | 1942 |
| 24 | **Adams, Samuel Hopkins** | American | SS | **Night Bus** | 1933 |
| 25 | **Adams, Samuel Hopkins** | American | SS | **Night Bus** | 1933 |
| 26 | **Adams, Samuel Hopkins** | American | SS | **Night Bus** | 1933 |
| 27 | **Adams, Samuel Hopkins** | American | N | **The Perfect Specimen** | 1936 |
| 28 | **Adonias Filho** <br> (Adonias Aguiar Filho) | Brazilian | SS | **Um anjo mal** | 1968 |
| 29 | **Adonias Filho** | Brazilian | N | **O forte** <br> [The fortress] | 1965 |
| 30 | **Aeschylus** | Greek(anc) | P | **Prometheus vinctus** <br> (Prometheus Bound) <br> (aka: Prometheus desmotes) | c.468 BC |
| 31 | **Aeschylus - {p}** <br> **Hesiod - {v}** | Greek(anc) | P+V | **Prometheus vinctus** <br> (Prometheus Bound) {p} + <br> **Theogony** {v} + <br> **Bardo Thodal** {v} | c.468+ <br> 770 BC |
| 32 | **Agârbiceanu, Ion** | Romanian | N | **Arhanghelii** <br> [The archangels] | 1914 |
| 33 | **Agârbiceanu, Ion** | Romanian | SS | **Fefeleaga +** <br> **La o nuntă** | 1908+ <br> 1909(10) |
| 34 | **Agârbiceanu, Ion** | Romanian | SS | **Jandarmul** <br> [The gendarme] | 1941 |
| 35 | **Agârbiceanu, Ion** | Romanian | SS | **Lada** <br> [The chest] + <br> **Vîlva băilor** <br> [The fay of the pit] | 1910+ <br> 1909 |

| No | Film Title | Country of Production | Date | Director(s) | Duration of Film |
|----|-----------|----------------------|------|-------------|------------------|
| 1 | Jens Langkniv | DEN | 1940 | Peter Knutzon<br>Peter Lind | 57 |
| 2 | Livet paa Hegnsgaard | DEN | 1938 | Arne Weel | 100 |
| 3 | Naar Bønder elsker | DEN | 1942 | Arne Weel | 88 |
| 4 | Storfolk og småfolk | NOR | 1951 | Tancred Ibsen | 92 |
| 5 | Moetsukita chizu<br>(The Ruined Map)<br>(aka: The Man Without a Map) | JAP | 1968 | Hiroshi Teshigahara | 118 |
| 6 | Kashi to kodomo<br>(aka: Otoshi ana)<br>(The Pitfall) | JAP | 1962 | Hiroshi Teshigahara | 95 |
| 7 | Suna no onna<br>(Woman of the Dunes) | JAP | 1964 | Hiroshi Teshigahara | 127 |
| 8 | Tanin no kao<br>(The Face of Another) | JAP | 1966 | Hiroshi Teshigahara | 121 |
| 9 | Onna no sono<br>(The Garden of Women) | JAP | 1954 | Keisuke Kinoshita | 141 |
| 10 | L'homme à l'oreille cassée | FR | 1935(34) | Robert Boudrioz | 75 |
| 11 | Voleur de femmes | FR | 1964(62) | Willy Rozier | 60 |
| 12 | Trente et quarante | FR | 1945 | Gilles Grangier | 105 |
| 13 | La belle marinière | FR | 1932 | Harry Lachman | 80 |
| 14 | Domino | FR | 1943(42) | Roger Richebé | 100 |
| 15 | A Shot in the Dark | GB | 1964 | Blake Edwards | 100 +V |
| 16 | Jean de la lune | FR | 1931 | Michel Simon<br>Jean Choux | 84 |
| 17 | Jean de la lune | FR | 1948 | Marcel Achard | 94 |
| 18 | Mistigri | FR | 1932 | Harry Lachman | 80 |
| 19 | Noix de coco | FR | 1938 | Jean Boyer | 80 |
| 20 | Patate<br>(IT: L'amico di famiglia)<br>(Friend of the Family) | FR/IT | 1964 | Robert Thomas | 93(90) |
| 21 | Pétrus | FR | 1946 | Marc Allégret | 95 |
| 22 | The Gorgeous Hussy | USA | 1936 | Clarence Brown | 102 |
| 23 | The Harvey Girls | USA | 1946(45) | George Sidney | 101 |
| 24 | It Happened One Night | USA | 1934 | Frank Capra | 107 +V |
| 25 | Eve Knew Her Apples<br>{musical version} | USA | 1945 | Will Jason | 64 |
| 26 | You Can't Run Away From It<br>(aka: It Happened One Night)<br>{musical version} | USA | 1956 | Dick Powell | 95 |
| 27 | The Perfect Specimen | USA | 1937 | Michael Curtiz | 82 |
| 28 | Um anjo mau<br>(Bad Angel) | BRAZ | 1972 | Roberto Santos | 107 |
| 29 | O forte | BRAZ | 1974 | Olney São Paulo | 85 |
| 30 | The Iliac Passion | USA | 1968(67) | Gregory Markopoulos | 90 |
| 31 | Prometheas se deftero prosopo<br>(Prometheus, Second Person Singular) | GR | 1975 | Costas Ferris | 90 |
| 32 | Flăcări pe comori<br>[Flames above treasures] | ROM | 1988 | Nicolae Mărgineanu | 102 |
| 33 | Nunta de piatră<br>(Stone Wedding) | ROM | 1973(72) | Mircea Veroiu<br>Dan Piţa | 88 |
| 34 | Întoarcerea din iad<br>[Coming back from hell] | ROM | 1983 | Nicolae Mărgineanu | 98 |
| 35 | Duhul aurului<br>[Gold's ghost] | ROM | 1974 | Mircea Veroiu<br>Dan Piţa | 96 |

| No. | Author | Nationality | Form | Literary Title | Date |
|-----|--------|-------------|------|----------------|------|
| 36 | Agee, James | American | N | A Death in the Family | 1957 |
| 37 | Agee, James | American | SS | A Mothers Tale | 1952 |
| 38 | Aguiar Filho, Adonias<br>(see: Adonias Filho) | Brazilian | N/SS | | |
| 39 | Agustí, Ignacio | Spanish<br>(Cat/Cas) | N | Mariona Rebull +<br>El viudo Rius | 1944+<br>1945 |
| 40 | Ahcheng<br>(see: Zhong Ahcheng) | Chinese | SS | | |
| 42 | Aho, Juhani<br>(Juhani Brofeldt) | Finnish | N | Juha | 1911 |
| 43 | Aho, Juhani | Finnish | N | Juha | 1911 |
| 44 | Aicard, Jean | French | N | Le diamant noir<br>[The black diamond] | 1895 |
| 45 | Aicard, Jean | French | N | L'illustre Maurin<br>(Maurin the Illustrious) | 1908 |
| 46 | Aicard, Jean | French | N | Maurin des Maures<br>(The Diverting Adventures of Maurin) | 1905 |
| 47 | Aicard, Jean | French | N | Notre-Dame-d'amour | 1896 |
| 48 | Aicard, Jean | French | P | Le père Lebonnard | 1886 |
| 49 | Aicard, Jean | French | N | Le roi de Camargue<br>(King of Camargue) | 1890 |
| 50 | Aiken, Conrad | American | SS | Silent Snow, Secret Snow | 1934 |
| 51 | Aitmatov, Chingiz<br>(Chingiz Torekulovich Aytmatov) | Russian(Kir) | SS | Belyi parokhod<br>(The White Steamship) | 1970 |
| 52 | Aitmatov, Chingiz | Russian | SS | Dzhamilia<br>(Jamila) | 1958 |
| 53 | Aitmatov, Chingiz | Russian | SS | Krasnoe jabloko<br>[Red apples] | 1963 |
| 54 | Aitmatov, Chingiz | Russian | SS | Materinskoe pole<br>[Mother's field] | 1963 |
| 55 | Aitmatov, Chingiz | Russian | SS | Pervyi uchitel | 1963 |
| 56 | Aitmatov, Chingiz | Russian | SS | Proshchay, Gul'sary<br>(Farewell, Gyulsary!) | 1966 |
| 57 | Aitmatov, Chingiz | Russian | SS | Rannie zhuravli<br>(The Cranes Fly Early) | 1975 |
| 58 | Aitmatov, Chingiz | Russian | SS | Topoliok moi v krasnoi kosynke | 1961 |
| 59 | Aitmatov, Chingiz | Russian | SS | Verblyuzhii glaz<br>[Camel's eye] | 1961 |
| 60 | Aitmatov, Chingiz;<br>Mukhamedzhanov, Kaltai | Russian | P | Voskhozhdeniye na Fudziyamu<br>(The Ascent of Mount Fuji) | 1978 |
| 61 | Akins, Zoe | American | P | Daddy's Gone A Hunting | 1923 |
| 62 | Akins, Zoe | American | P | The Greeks Had a Word For It | 1930 |
| 63 | Aksyonov, Vasili | Russian | SS | Papa, slozhi! +<br>Zavtraki sorok tret'ego goda<br>(The Lunches of '43) +<br>Na polputi k lune<br>(Halfway to the Moon) | 1962 |
| 64 | Aksyonov, Vasili | Russian | N | Zvyozdny bilet<br>(A Starry Ticket) | 1961 |
| 65 | Akutagawa Ryūnosuke | Japanese | SS | Rashōmon {ss} +<br>Yabu no naka {ss}<br>(In a Grove) | 1915(17) +<br>1922 |
| 66 | Akutagawa Ryūnosuke | Japanese | SS | Rashōmon {ss} +<br>Yabu no naka {ss} | 1915(17)+<br>1922 |
| 67 | Alain-Fournier | French | N | Le grand Meaulnes<br>(The Lost Domain)<br>(aka: The Wanderer) | 1913 |
| 68 | Alarcón, Pedro Antonio de | Spanish | N | El capitán Veneno<br>(Captain Venom) | 1881 |
| 69 | Alarcón, Pedro Antonio de | Spanish | SS | El clavo<br>(The Nail) | 1854 |
| 70 | Alarcón, Pedro Antonio de | Spanish | N | El escándalo<br>(The Scandal) | 1875 |
| 71 | Alarcón, Pedro Antonio de | Spanish | N | El escándalo | 1875 |

**4**

## FILM

| No | Film Title | Country of Production | Date | Director(s) | Duration of Film |
|---|---|---|---|---|---|
| 36 | All the Way Home | USA | 1963 | Alex Segal | 103 |
| 37 | A Mothers Tale (animation) | USA | 1977 | Rex Goff | 18 +V |
| 38 | | | | | |
| 39 | Mariona Rebull | SP | 1947 | José Luis Sáenz de Heredia | 110(91) |
| 40 | | | | | |
| 42 | Juha | FIN | 1937 | Nyrki Tapiovaara | 100 |
| 43 | Juha | FIN | 1956 | Toivo Särkkä | 115 |
| 44 | Le diamant noir | FR | 1940(39) | Jean Delannoy | 98 |
| 45 | L'illustre Maurin | FR | 1933 | André Hugon | 122 |
| 46 | Maurin des Maures | FR | 1932 | André Hugon | 100 |
| 47 | Notre-Dame-d'amour | FR | 1936 | Pierre Caron | 84 |
| 48 | Le père Lebonnard (IT: Papa' Lebonnard) | FR/IT | 1939(38) | Jean de Limur | 90 |
| 49 | Le roi de Camargue | FR | 1934 | Jacques de Baroncelli | 75 |
| 50 | Silent Snow, Secret Snow | USA | 1966 | Gene Kearney | 17 |
| 51 | Belyi parokhod (The White Boat) | USSR | 1976 | Bolotbek Shamshiev | 101 |
| 52 | Dzhamilia | USSR | 1969 | Irina Poplavskaya | 82 |
| 53 | Krasnoe jabloko | USSR | 1975 | Tolomush Okeev | 83 |
| 54 | Materinskoe pole (aka: Materinskaya polye) (Material Earth) | USSR | 1968(67) | Gennadiy Bazarov | 68 |
| 55 | Pervyi uchitel (The First Teacher) | USSR | 1965 | Andrei Mikhalkov-Konchalovsky | 96 +V |
| 56 | Byeg inokhodsta | USSR | 1969 | Sergei Urusevsky | 71 |
| 57 | Rannie zhuravli | USSR | 1979 | Bolotbek Shamshiev | 95 |
| 58 | Ya-tyan'-shan' | USSR | 1972 | Irina Poplavskaya | Pt.1, 62 Pt.2, 71 |
| 59 | Znoi (Heat) | USSR | 1963 | Larissa Shepitko | 84 |
| 60 | Voskhozhdeniye na Fudziyamu | USSR | 1988 | Bolotbek Shamshiev | 129 |
| 61 | Women Love Once | USA | 1931 | Edward Goodman | 77 |
| 62 | The Greeks Had a Word For Them (aka: Three Broadway Girls) | USA | 1932 | Lowell Sherman | 79 |
| 63 | Puteshestviye [The journey] | USSR | 1967(66) | Inessa Seleznyova | 102 |
| 64 | My Younger Brother | USSR | 1962 | Alexandre Zarkhi | 85 |
| 65 | Rashomon | JAP | 1950 | Akira Kurosawa | 88 |
| 66 | The Outrage | USA | 1964 | Martin Ritt | 96 |
| 67 | Le grand Meaulnes (The Wanderer) | FR | 1967 | Jean-Gabriel Albicocco | 104 |
| 68 | El capitán Veneno | SP | 1951(50) | Luis Marquina | 95(85) |
| 69 | El clavo | SP | 1944 | Rafael Gil | 89(95) |
| 70 | El escándalo | SP | 1943 | José Luis Sáenz de Heredia | 110 |
| 71 | El escándalo | SP | 1964(63) | Javier Setó | 83(88) |

| No. | Author | Nationality | Form | Literary Title | Date |
|-----|--------|-------------|------|----------------|------|
| 72 | Alarcón, Pedro Antonio de | Spanish | N | La pródiga<br>(True to Her Oath) | 1882 |
| 73 | Alarcón, Pedro Antonio de | Spanish | SS | El sombrero de tres picos<br>(The Three-Cornered Hat) | 1874 |
| 74 | Alarcón, Pedro Antonio de | Spanish | SS | El sombrero de tres picos | 1874 |
| 75 | Alarcón, Pedro Antonio de | Spanish | SS | El sombrero de tres picos | 1874 |
| 76 | Alarcón, Pedro Antonio de | Spanish | SS | El sombrero de tres picos | 1874 |
| 77 | Alarcón, Pedro Antonio de | Spanish | SS | El sombrero de tres picos | 1874 |
| 78 | Alarcón y Ariza, Pedro Antonio de<br>(see: Alarcón, Pedro) | Spanish | N/SS | | |
| 79 | Alas, Leopoldo<br>(Leopoldo Alas y Ureña)<br>(Clarín) | Spanish | SS | ¡Adiós, Cordera! | 1892 |
| 80 | Alas, Leopoldo | Spanish | N | La Regenta | 1884 |
| 81 | Alas y Ureña, Leopoldo<br>(see: Alas, Leopoldo) | Spanish | N/SS | | |
| 82 | Albee, Edward | American | P | A Delicate Balance | 1966 |
| 83 | Albee, Edward | American | P | Who's Afraid of Virginia Woolf? | 1962 |
| 84 | Alcott, Louisa May | American | N | An Old Fashioned Girl | 1870 |
| 85 | Alcott, Louisa May | American | N | Little Men | 1871 |
| 86 | Alcott, Louisa May | American | N | Little Men | 1871 |
| 87 | Alcott, Louisa May | American | N | Little Women | 1868 |
| 88 | Alcott, Louisa May | American | N | Little Women | 1868 |
| 89 | Aldecoa, Ignacio | Spanish | N | Con el viento solano<br>[With the easterly wind] | 1956 |
| 90 | Aldecoa, Ignacio | Spanish | SS | Los pájaros de Baden-Baden<br>[The birds of Baden-Baden] | 1965 |
| 91 | Aldecoa, Ignacio | Spanish | SS | Young Sánchez | 1959 |
| 92 | Aldington, Richard | British | N | All Men Are Enemies | 1934 |
| 93 | Alecsandri, Vasile | Romanian | P | Cucoana Chiriţa în Iaşi<br>[Madam Chiriţa in Jassy] | 1852 |
| 94 | Alecsandri, Vasile | Romanian | P | Cucoana Chiriţa în provincie | 1852 |
| 95 | Alencar, José Martiniano de | Brazilian | N | O gaúcho<br>[The gaucho] | 1870 |
| 96 | Alencar, José Martiniano de | Brazilian | N | O guarani<br>[The Guarani Indian] | 1857 |
| 98 | Alencar, José Martiniano de | Brazilian | N | Iracema. Lenda do ceará<br>(Iraçema, the Honey-lips) | 1865 |
| 99 | Alencar, José Martiniano de | Brazilian | SS | Lucíola | 1862 |
| 100 | Alencar, José Martiniano de | Brazilian | SS | Lucíola | 1862 |
| 101 | Alencar, José Martiniano de | Brazilian | N | Ubirajara, lenda Tupi<br>(Ubirajara, a Legend of the Tupy Indians) | 1875 |
| 102 | Algren, Nelson | American | N | The Man With the Golden Arm | 1949 |
| 103 | Algren, Nelson | American | N | A Walk on the Wild Side | 1956 |
| 104 | Allais, Alphonse | French | N | L'affaire Blaireau | 1899 |
| 105 | Allen, William Hervey | American | N | Anthony Adverse | 1933 |
| 106 | Almeida Garrett, João Baptista da<br>Silva Leitão<br>(see: Garrett,) | Portuguese | P | | |
| 107 | Almeida, José Américo de | Brazilian | N | A bagaceira<br>(Trash) | 1928 |
| 108 | Alphonsus, João<br>(João Alphonsus de Guimarães) | Brazilian | N | Totônia Pacheco | 1935 |
| 109 | Amado, Jorge | Brazilian | N | Capitães da areia<br>(Captains of the Sand) | 1937 |
| 110 | Amado, Jorge | Brazilian | N | Donna Flor e seus dois maridos<br>(Dona Flor and Her Two Husbands) | 1966 |
| 111 | Amado, Jorge | Brazilian | N | Gabriela, cravo e canela<br>(Gabriela, Clove and Cinnamon) | 1958 |
| 112 | Amado, Jorge | Brazilian | N | Jubiabá | 1935 |
| 113 | Amado, Jorge | Brazilian | N | Seara vermelha | 1946 |

| No | Film Title | Country of Production | Date | Director(s) | Duration of Film |
|---|---|---|---|---|---|
| 72 | La pródiga | SP | 1946 | Rafael Gil | 95(92) |
| 73 | La traviesa molinera (aka: El sombrero de tres picos) | SP | 1934 | Harry d'Abbadie d'Arrast Ricardo Soriano | 71 |
| 74 | It Happened in Spain (aka: The Three Cornered Hat) | GB/SP | 1934 | Harry d'Abbadie d'Arrast | 65 |
| 75 | Il cappello a tre punte (The Three-Cornered Hat) | IT | 1934 | Mario Camerini | 73 |
| 76 | La bella mugnaia (The Miller's Beautiful Wife) (aka: The Miller's Wife) | IT | 1955 | Mario Camerini | 92 |
| 77 | La picara molinera | SP/FR | 1958(54) | León Klimovsky | 91(80) |
| 78 | | | | | |
| 79 | ¡Adiós, Cordera! | SP | 1966(65) | Pedro Mario Herrero | 85 |
| 80 | La Regenta (Regent's Wife) | SP | 1974 | Gonzalo Suárez | 94(91) |
| 81 | | | | | |
| 82 | A Delicate Balance | USA/GB/CAN | 1973 | Tony Richardson | 134 |
| 83 | Who's Afraid of Virginia Woolf? | USA | 1966 | Mike Nichols | 132 +V |
| 84 | An Old Fashioned Girl | USA | 1948 | Arthur Dreifuss | 80 |
| 85 | Little Men | USA | 1934 | Phil Rosen | 77 |
| 86 | Little Men | USA | 1941(40) | Norman Z. McLeod | 84 |
| 87 | Little Women | USA | 1933 | George Cukor | 115 +V |
| 88 | Little Women | USA | 1949(48) | Mervyn LeRoy | 122 |
| 89 | Con el viento solano | SP | 1965 | Mario Camús | 90(102) |
| 90 | Los pájaros de Baden-Baden | SP | 1975(74) | Mario Camús Manolo Marinero | 124(100) |
| 91 | Young Sánchez | SP | 1963 | Mario Camús | 106(90) |
| 92 | All Men Are Enemies | USA | 1934 | George Fitzmaurice | 78 |
| 93 | Chirița la Iași | ROM | 1988 | Mircea Drăgan | 83 |
| 94 | Cucoana Chirița [Madam Chirița] | ROM | 1987 | Mircea Drăgan | 94 |
| 95 | Paixão de gaúcho | BRAZ | 1958 | Walter George Durst | 100(98) |
| 96 | O guarani | BRAZ | 1979 | Fauzi Mansur | 90 |
| 98 | Iracema, a virgem dos lábios de mel | BRAZ | 1979 | Carlos Coimbra | 95 |
| 99 | Anjo do lodo | BRAZ | 1951 | Luis de Barros | 78(75) |
| 100 | Lucíola, o anjo pecador | BRAZ | 1975 | Alfredo Sternheim | 95 |
| 101 | A lenda de Ubirajara (The Legend of Ubirajara) | BRAZ | 1975 | André Luis de Oliveira | 110 |
| 102 | The Man With the Golden Arm | USA | 1955 | Otto Preminger | 119 +V |
| 103 | Walk on the Wild Side | USA | 1962 | Edward Dmytryk | 114 |
| 104 | Ni vu ni connu | FR | 1958 | Yves Robert | 95 |
| 105 | Anthony Adverse | USA | 1936 | Mervyn LeRoy | 141 |
| 106 | | | | | |
| 107 | Soledade | BRAZ | 1976 | Paulo Thiago | 90 |
| 108 | O predileto | BRAZ | 1975 | Roberto Palmari | 95 |
| 109 | The Wild Pack (aka: The Sandpit Generals) | USA | 1971 | Hall Bartlett | 102 |
| 110 | Dona Flor e seus dois maridos (Dona Flor and Her Two Husbands) | BRAZ | 1976 | Bruno Barreto | 90(105) +V |
| 111 | Gabriela | BRAZ | 1983 | Bruno Barreto | 99 |
| 112 | Jubiabá | BRAZ/FR | 1986 | Nelson Pereira dos Santos | 101 |
| 113 | Seara vermelha (The Violent Land) | BRAZ | 1963 | Alberto d'Aversa | 116 |

| No. | Author | Nationality | Form | Literary Title | Date |
|-----|--------|-------------|------|----------------|------|
| 114 | **Amado, Jorge** | Brazilian | N | **Tenda dos milagres** *(Tent of Miracles)* | 1969 |
| 115 | **Amis, Kingsley** | British | N | **Lucky Jim** | 1953 |
| 116 | **Amis, Kingsley** | British | N | **Take a Girl Like You** | 1960 |
| 117 | **Amis, Kingsley** | British | N | **That Uncertain Feeling** | 1955 |
| 118 | **Amis, Martin** | British | N | **The Rachel Papers** | 1973 |
| 119 | **Anand, Mulk Raj** | Indian(Urd) (Eng) | SS | **Two Leaves and a Bud** | 1937 |
| 120 | **Andersch, Alfred** | German | N | **Die Rote** *(The Redhead)* | 1960 |
| 121 | **Andersch, Alfred** | German | N | **Winterspelt** | 1974 |
| 122 | **Andersen, Benny** | Danish | P | **Orfeus i undergrunden** | 1979 |
| 123 | **Andersen, Benny** | Danish | V | **Svantes viser** *[Svante's songs]* | 1972 |
| 124 | **Andersen, Hans Christian** | Danish | SS | **Fyrtøjet** *(The Tinder Box)* | 1835 |
| 125 | **Andersen, Hans Christian** | Danish | SS | **Der grimme ælling** *(The Ugly Duckling)* | 1844 |
| 126 | **Andersen, Hans Christian** | Danish | SS | **Historien om en moder** *(The Story of a Mother)* | 1848 |
| 127 | **Andersen, Hans Christian** | Danish | SS | **Den lille haufrue** *(The Little Mermaid)* | 1837 |
| 128 | **Andersen, Hans Christian** | Danish | SS | **Den lille haufrue** | 1837 |
| 129 | **Andersen, Hans Christian** | Danish | SS | **Den lille pige med svovlstikkerne** *(The Little Match Girl)* | 1846 |
| 130 | **Andersen, Hans Christian** | Danish | SS | **Den lille pige med svovlstikkerne** | 1846 |
| 131 | **Andersen, Hans Christian** | Danish | SS | **Nattergalen** *(The Nightingale)* | 1844 |
| 132 | **Andersen, Hans Christian** | Danish | SS | **Prinsessen på ærten** *(The Princess on the Pea) (aka: The Princess and the Pea)* | 1835 |
| 133 | **Andersen, Hans Christian** | Danish | SS | **Prinsessen på ærten** | 1835 |
| 134 | **Andersen, Hans Christian** | Danish | SS | **Prinsessen på ærten** | 1835 |
| 135 | **Andersen, Hans Christian** | Danish | SS | **Prinsessen på ærten** | 1835 |
| 136 | **Andersen, Hans Christian** | Danish | SS | **De rode skoe** *(The Red Shoes)* | 1845 |
| 137 | **Andersen, Hans Christian** | Danish | SS | **Skyggen** *(The Shadow)* | 1847 |
| 138 | **Andersen, Hans Christian** | Danish | SS | **Snedronningen** *(The Snow Queen)* | 1845 |
| 139 | **Andersen, Hans Christian** | Danish | SS | **Snedronningen** | 1845 |
| 140 | **Andersen, Hans Christian** | Danish | SS | **Den standhaftige tinsoldat** *(The Steadfast Tin Soldier)* | 1838 |
| 141 | **Andersen, Hans Christian** | Danish | SS | **Den standhaftige tinsoldat** | 1838 |
| 142 | **Andersen, Hans Christian** | Danish | SS | **Svinedrengen** *(The Swineherd)* | 1842 |
| 143 | **Andersen, Hans Christian** | Danish | SS | **Svinedrengen** | 1842 |
| 144 | **Andersen, Hans Christian** | Danish | SS | **De vilde svaner** *(The Wild Swans)* | 1838 |
| 145 | **Anderson, Edward** | American | N | **Thieves Like Us** | 1937 |
| 146 | **Anderson, Edward** | American | N | **Thieves Like Us** | 1937 |
| 147 | **Anderson, Maxwell** | American | P | **Anne of a Thousand Days** | 1948 |
| 148 | **Anderson, Maxwell** | American | P | **Elizabeth The Queen** | 1930 |
| 149 | **Anderson, Maxwell** | American | P | **The Eve of St. Mark** | 1942 |
| 150 | **Anderson, Maxwell** | American | P | **Joan of Lorraine** | 1946 |
| 151 | **Anderson, Maxwell** | American | P | **Key Largo** | 1939 |
| 152 | **Anderson, Maxwell** | American | P | **Knickerbocker Holiday** | 1938 |

**8**

| No | Film Title | Country of Production | Date | Director(s) | Duration of Film |
|----|-----------|----------------------|------|-------------|------------------|
| 114 | Tenda dos milagres (Tent of Miracles) | BRAZ | 1977 | Nelson Pereira dos Santos | 96 |
| 115 | Lucky Jim | GB | 1957 | John Boulting | 95 +V |
| 116 | Take a Girl Like You | GB | 1970(69) | Jonathan Miller | 98 +V |
| 117 | Only Two Can Play | GB | 1962(61) | Sidney Gilliat | 106 +V |
| 118 | The Rachel Papers | GB | 1989 | Damian Harris | 95 |
| 119 | Rahi | IND (HIN) | 1953 | Khvaja Ahmad Abbas | 135 |
| 120 | Die Rote (IT: La rossa) (The Redhead) | GER/IT | 1962 | Helmut Käutner | 100(94) |
| 121 | Winterspelt (aka: Winterspelt 1944) | GER | 1977 | Eberhard Fechner | 111 |
| 122 | Danmark er lukket | DEN | 1980 | Dan Tschernia | 91 |
| 123 | Da Svante forsvandt (When Svante Disappeared) | DEN | 1975 | Henning Carlsen | 86 |
| 124 | Fyrtøjet {animation} | DEN | 1946 | Svend Methling | 70 |
| 125 | Udivitel'naja istozijz pokhozhaja na skazhu | USSR | 1966 | Boris Doline | 69 |
| 126 | Historien om en moder | DEN | 1979 | Claus Weeke | 21 |
| 127 | Rusalotchka (BULG: Malkata rusalka) (The Little Mermaid) | USSR/ BULG | 1976 | Vladimir Bychkov | 82 |
| 128 | The Little Mermaid {animation} | USA | 1989 | John Musker Ron Clements | 83 |
| 129 | Den lille pige med svovlstikkerne | DEN | 1953 | Johan Jacobsen | 14 |
| 130 | Fetiţa cu chibrituri | ROM | 1967 | Aurel Miheleş | 18 |
| 131 | Císaŕuv slavík (The Emperor's Nightingale) {marionettes} | CZ | 1948 | Jiří Trnka | 65 |
| 132 | Svinedrengen og prinsessen på ærten {animation} | DEN | 1962 | Poul Ilsøe | 50 |
| 133 | Printzessa na goroshine | USSR | 1976 | Boris Rytzarev | 89 |
| 134 | The Princess and the Pea | GB | 1979 | Keith Goddard | 10 |
| 135 | The Princess and the Pea | USA | 1983 | Tony Bill | 60 +V |
| 136 | The Red Shoes | GB | 1948 | Michael Powell Emeric Pressburger | 134 +V |
| 137 | The Shadow | USA | 1976 | Don Ham | 27 |
| 138 | Snezhnaya koroleva (Snow Queen) | USSR | 1966 | Gennadi Kazanski | 85 |
| 139 | Lumikuningatar [The snow queen] | FIN | 1986 | Päivi Hartzell | 93 |
| 140 | La petite parade | FR | 1930 | Vladislav Starevitch | 17 |
| 141 | Le petit soldat {animation} | FR | 1948(47) | Paul Grimault | 11 |
| 142 | Svinopas | USSR | 1941 | Alexander Matcheret | 24 |
| 143 | Die Prinzessin und der Schweinehirt (The Princess and the Swineherd) | GER | 1953 | Herbert B. Fredersdorf | 81 |
| 144 | Dikie lebedi | USSR | 1988 | Helle Karis | 86 |
| 145 | They Live by Night (aka: The Twisted Road) | USA | 1948 | Nicholas Ray | 96 |
| 146 | Thieves Like Us | USA | 1974(73) | Robert Altman | 123 |
| 147 | Anne of a Thousand Days | GB | 1970(69) | Charles Jarrott | 146 +V |
| 148 | The Private Lives of Elizabeth and Essex (aka: Elizabeth The Queen) | USA | 1939 | Michael Curtiz | 106 +V(102) |
| 149 | The Eve of St. Mark | USA | 1944 | John M. Stahl | 95 |
| 150 | Joan of Arc | USA | 1948 | Victor Fleming | 145(100) |
| 151 | Key Largo | USA | 1948 | John Huston | 100 +V |
| 152 | Knickerbocker Holiday | USA | 1944 | Harry Joe Brown | 85 |

| No. | Author | Nationality | Form | Literary Title | Date |
|-----|--------|-------------|------|----------------|------|
| 153 | Anderson, Maxwell | American | P | **Mary of Scotland** | 1933 |
| 154 | Anderson, Maxwell | American | P | **Saturday's Children** | 1927 |
| 155 | Anderson, Maxwell | American | P | **Saturday's Children** | 1927 |
| 156 | Anderson, Maxwell | American | P | **Winterset** | 1935 |
| 157 | Anderson, Maxwell - *(p)* March, William - *(n)* | American | N-P | **The Bad Seed** | 1954; 1955 |
| 158 | Anderson, Maxwell; Stallings, L. | American | P | **What Price Glory?** | 1934 |
| 159 | Anderson, Maxwell *(see also: Paton, Alan)* | American | P | | |
| 160 | Anderson, Robert Woodruff | American | P | **I Never Sang For My Father** | 1934 |
| 161 | Anderson, Robert Woodruff | American | P | **Tea and Sympathy** | 1953 |
| 162 | Anderson, Sherwood | American | SS | **I'm a Fool** | 1923 |
| 163 | Andrade, Jorge | Brazilian | P | **Vereda da salvação** *[Path of salvation]* | 1965 |
| 164 | Andrade, Mário de | Brazilian | N | **Amor, verbo intransitivo** *(Fräulein)* | 1927 |
| 165 | Andrade, Mário de | Brazilian | N | **Macunaíma, o herói sem nenhum caráter** | 1928 |
| 166 | Andrade, Oswald de | Brazilian | N | **Os condenados** *(aka: Alma)* | 1922(41) |
| 167 | Andrić, Ivo | Yugoslav(Serb) | SS | **Anikina vremena** *(Anika's Times)* | 1931 |
| 168 | Andrić, Ivo | Yugoslav | N | **Gospodica** *(The Woman From Sarajevo)* | 1945 |
| 169 | Andrić, Ivo | Yugoslav | SS | **Zeko** | 1948 |
| 170 | Andrzejewski, Jerzy | Polish | N | **Bramy raju** *(The Gates of Paradise)* | 1960 |
| 171 | Andrzejewski, Jerzy | Polish | N | **Popiół i diament** *(Ashes and Diamonds)* | 1948 |
| 172 | Angelou, Maya | American(afro) | AUT | **I Know Why the Caged Bird Sings** | 1969 |
| 173 | Anon | Chinese | V | **Ashima** | n.d. |
| 174 | Anon | British | V | **Beowulf** | c.750 |
| 175 | Anon | French | V | **La chanson de Roland** *(The Song of Roland)* | c.1125 |
| 176 | Anon | Dutch | P | **Elckerlijc** *(Everyman)* | c.1485 |
| 177 | Anon | Spanish | N | **Lazarillo de Tormes** | c.1530 |
| 178 | Anon | Dutch | P | **Mariken van Nieumeghen** | c.1485-1510 |
| 179 | Anon | British | V | **Sir Gawain and the Green Knight** | c.1375 |
| 180 | Anouilh, Jean | French | P | **Becket ou l'honneur de Dieu** *(Becket; or the Honour of God)* | 1959 |
| 181 | Anouilh, Jean | French | P | **Ornifle; ou le courant d'air** *(Ornifle)* *(aka: It's Later Than You Think)* | 1956 |
| 182 | Anouilh, Jean | French | P | **Roméo et Jeannette** | 1946 |
| 183 | Anouilh, Jean | French | P | **La valse des toréadors** *(Waltz of the Toreadors)* | 1952 |
| 184 | Anouilh, Jean | French | P | **Le voyageur sans bagage** *(Traveller Without Luggage)* | 1936 |
| 185 | An-Ski, Solomon *(Solomon Rappoport)* *(Shloyme Zanvl Rapoport)* | Russian (Yiddish) | P | **Der Dibuk** *(The Dybbuk)* | 1916 |
| 186 | An-Ski, Solomon | Russian | P | **Der Dibuk** | 1916 |
| 187 | Antônio, João | Brazilian | SS | **Malagueta, Perus e Bacanaço** | 1963 |
| 188 | Anzengruber, Ludwig | Austrian | P | **Doppelselbstmord** *[Double suicide]* | 1876 |
| 189 | Anzengruber, Ludwig | Austrian | P | **Doppelselbstmord** | 1876 |
| 190 | Anzengruber, Ludwig | Austrian | N | **Der G'wissenswurm** *[Pangs of conscience]* | 1905 |
| 191 | Anzengruber, Ludwig | Austrian | P | **Die Kreuzelschreiber** *(The Cross-Makers)* | 1892 |
| 192 | Anzengruber, Ludwig | Austrian | P | **Der Meineidbauer** *(The Farmer Forsworn)* | 1891 |

| No | Film Title | Country of Production | Date | Director(s) | Duration of Film |
|----|-----------|----------------------|------|-------------|------------------|
| 153 | Mary of Scotland | USA | 1936 | John Ford | 123 |
| 154 | Maybe It's Love | USA | 1935(34) | William McGann | 62 |
| 155 | Saturday's Children | USA | 1940 | Vincent Sherman | 101 |
| 156 | Winterset | USA | 1936 | Alfred Santell | 77 |
| 157 | The Bad Seed | USA | 1956 | Mervyn LeRoy | 129 |
| 158 | What Price Glory? | USA | 1952 | John Ford | 111 +V |
| 159 | | | | | |
| 160 | I Never Sang For My Father | USA | 1969 | Gilbert Cates | 92 |
| 161 | Tea and Sympathy | USA | 1956 | Vincente Minnelli | 122 |
| 162 | I'm a Fool | USA | 1977 | Noel Black | 38(vo) |
| 163 | Vereda da salvação | BRAZ | 1965 | Anselmo Duarte | 100 |
| 164 | Lição de amor (Lesson in Love) | BRAZ | 1975 | Eduardo Escorel | 90 |
| 165 | Macunaína (Jungle Freaks) | BRAZ | 1969(68) | Joaquim Pedro de Andrade | 108(95) |
| 166 | Os condenados (Alma) | BRAZ | 1974 | Zelito Viana | 90 |
| 167 | Anikina vremena | YUGO | 1954 | Vladimir Pogačić | 97 |
| 168 | Gospodica (Young Lady) | YUGO/AUST | 1980 | Vojtěch Jasný | 110 |
| 169 | I to će proći (It Will Pass Also) | YUGO | 1985 | Nenad Dizdarević | 99 |
| 170 | Gates to Paradise (YUG: Vrata raja) | GB/YUGO | 1967 | Andrzej Wajda | 89 |
| 171 | Popiół i diament (Ashes and Diamonds) | POL | 1958 | Andrzej Wajda | 106 |
| 172 | I Know Why the Caged Bird Sings | USA | 1978 | Fielder Cook | 110 |
| 173 | Ashima | CHN | 1964 | Liu Qiong | 98 |
| 174 | Beowulf | GB | 1976 | Don Fairservice | 60 |
| 175 | La chanson de Roland | FR | 1978 | Frank Cassenti | 110 |
| 176 | Elckerlijc (Everyman) | HOLL | 1975 | Jos Stelling | 94 |
| 177 | El Lazarillo de Tormes | SP | 1959 | César Fernández Ardavín | 105(87) |
| 178 | Mariken van Nieumeghen | HOLL | 1974 | Jos Stelling | 83(80) |
| 179 | Gawain and the Green Knight | GB | 1973 | Stephen Weeks | 93 |
| 180 | Becket | GB | 1964(63) | Peter Glenville | 148 +V |
| 181 | Ornifle oder der erzürnte Himmel | GER | 1972 | Helmut Käutner | 113 |
| 182 | Monsoon | USA/IND | 1952 | Rodney Amateau | 79 |
| 183 | Waltz of the Toreadors (aka: The Amorous General) | GB | 1962 | John Guillermin | 105 +V |
| 184 | Le voyageur sans bagage | FR | 1944 | Jean Anouilh | 99 |
| 185 | Dybuk (The Dybbuk) | POL | 1938 | Michael Waszinsky | 98 |
| 186 | Hadybbuk (The Dybbuk) | IS/GER | 1968 | Ilan Eldad | 90 |
| 187 | O jogo da vida | BRAZ | 1977 | Maurice Capovilla | 90 |
| 188 | Doppelselbstmord | GER | 1937 | Max W. Kimmich | 21 |
| 189 | Hochzeit im Heu [Wedding in the hay] | GER/AUST | 1951 | Arthur Maria Rabenalt | 91(89) |
| 190 | Die Jugendsünde | GER | 1937 | Franz Seitz | 82 |
| 191 | Die Kreuzelschreiber | GER | 1950(45) | Eduard von Borsody | 95 |
| 192 | Der Meineidbauer | GER | 1941 | Leopold Hainisch | 95 |

| No. | Author | Nationality | Form | Literary Title | Date |
|---|---|---|---|---|---|
| 193 | Anzengruber, Ludwig | Austrian | P | Der Meineidbauer | 1891 |
| 194 | Anzengruber, Ludwig | Austrian | P | Der Pfarrer von Kirchfeld | 1897 |
| 195 | Anzengruber, Ludwig | Austrian | P | Der Pfarrer von Kirchfeld | 1897 |
| 196 | Anzengruber, Ludwig | Austrian | P | Der Pfarrer von Kirchfeld | 1897 |
| 197 | Anzengruber, Ludwig | Austrian | N | Der Schandfleck<br>(The Blot of Shame) | 1904 |
| 198 | Anzengruber, Ludwig | Austrian | N | Der Sternsteinhof<br>(Sternstein Manor) | 185- |
| 199 | Anzengruber, Ludwig | Austrian | P | Das vierte Gebot<br>(The Fourth Commandment) | 1891 |
| 200 | Apṭe, Nārāyan Hari | Indian(Mar) | N | Na paṭanārī goshṭa | 1923 |
| 201 | Aranha, José Pereira da Graça | Brazilian | N | Canaã<br>(Canaan) | 1902 |
| 202 | Arany János | Hungarian | V | Toldi +<br>Toldi estéje +<br>Toldi szerelme<br>(Toldi + Toldi's Eve +Toldi's Love) | 1847+<br>1854+<br>1879 |
| 203 | Arbuzov, Aleksei Nikolaevich | Russian | P | Moy bednyy marat<br>(The Promise) | 1965 |
| 204 | Archer, William | British(Scot) | P | The Green Goddess | 1921 |
| 205 | Archer, William | British | P | The Green Goddess | 1921 |
| 206 | Ardrey, Robert | American | P | Thunder Rock | 1940 |
| 207 | Arène, Paul | French | N | La chèvre d'or<br>(The Golden Goat) | 1888 |
| 208 | Ariosto, Ludovico | Italian | V | Orlando Furioso<br>(aka: The Frenzy of Orlando) | 1516(32) |
| 209 | Aristophanes | Greek(anc) | P | Ekklisiazusai<br>(Women in Parliament)<br>(aka: Woman in Assembly) | c.392 BC |
| 210 | Aristophanes | Greek(anc) | P | Lysistrata | 411 BC |
| 211 | Aristophanes | Greek(anc) | P | Lysistrata | 411 BC |
| 212 | Ariyoshi Sawako | Japanese | N | Fushin no toki | 1968 |
| 213 | Ariyoshi Sawako | Japanese | N | Hanoaka Seishū no tsuma<br>(The Doctor's Wife) | 1966 |
| 214 | Ariyoshi Sawako | Japanese | N | Kōge<br>[Incense and flowers] | 1961-62 |
| 215 | Arlt, Roberto | Argentine | SS | Noche terrible<br>[The terrible night] | 1933 |
| 216 | Arlt, Roberto | Argentine | N | Los siete locos<br>(The Seven Madmen) | 1929 |
| 217 | Armstrong, William | American | N | Sounder | 1969 |
| 218 | Armstrong, William | American | N | Sounder | 1969 |
| 219 | Arnaud, Georges<br>(Henri Georges Girard) | French | N | Le salaire de la peur<br>(The Wages of Fear) | 1950 |
| 220 | Arnaud, Georges | French | N | Le salaire de la peur | 1950 |
| 221 | Arnim, Ludwig Achim von | German | SS | Der tolle Invalide auf dem Fort<br>Ratonneau<br>(The Mad Veteran of Fort<br>Ratonneau) | 1818 |
| 222 | Arrabal, Fernando | Morocco(Fr/Sp) | N | Baal Babylone<br>(Baal Babylon) | 1959 |
| 223 | Arrabal, Fernando | Morocco | P | Fando et Lis<br>(aka: Fando y Lis)<br>(Fando and Lis) | 1958 |
| 224 | Arrabal, Fernando | Morocco | P | Le grand cérémonial<br>(The Grand Ceremonial) | 1965 |

| No | Film Title | Country of Production | Date | Director(s) | Duration of Film |
|---|---|---|---|---|---|
| 193 | Der Meineidbauer (aka: Die Sünderin vom Fernerhof) | GER | 1956 | Rudolf Jugert | 104 |
| 194 | Der Pfarrer von Kirchfeld | AUST | 1937 | Jakob Fleck Luise Fleck | 90 |
| 195 | Der Kirchfeldpfarrer (aka: Das Mädchen vom Pfarrhof) | AUST | 1955 | Alfred Lehner | 94 |
| 196 | Der Pfarrer von Kirchfeld (The Pastor of Kirchfeld) | GER | 1955 | Hans Deppe | 94 |
| 197 | Der Schandfleck | GER/AUST | 1956 | Herbert B. Fredersdorf | 99 |
| 198 | Sternsteinhof (Sternstein Manor) | GER | 1975 | Hans W. Geissendörfer | 125 |
| 199 | Das vierte Gebot (aka: Der Weg abwärts) (aka: Die Kupplerin) | AUST | 1950 | Eduard von Borsody | 99 |
| 200 | Kunku | IND (MAR) | 1937 | V. Shantaram (Venkudre Sântârâm) | 163 |
| 201 | O vale do Canaã (The Valley of Canaan) | BRAZ | 1970 | Jece Valadão | 90 |
| 202 | Daliá idok (Heroic Times) {animation} | HUNG | 1983(82) | József Gémes | 86 |
| 203 | The Promise | GB | 1969 | Michael Hayes | 98 |
| 204 | The Green Goddess | USA | 1930 | Alfred E. Green | 80 |
| 205 | Adventure in Iraq | USA | 1943 | D. Ross Lederman | 65 |
| 206 | Thunder Rock | GB | 1942 | Roy Boulting | 111 |
| 207 | La chèvre d'or | FR | 1943 | René Barberis | 90 |
| 208 | I paladini: storia d'armi ed' amori (aka: Le armi es gli amori) (Hearts and Armour) (aka: Hearts in Armour) | IT/USA | 1982 | Giancomo Battiato | 110 +V(96) |
| 209 | An oles i yinekes tou kosmou [If all the women of the world] | GR | 1967 | Nestor Matsas | 90 |
| 210 | Triumph der Liebe | AUST | 1949 | Alfred Stöger | 88 |
| 211 | Lisistrati (aka: Lycistrata) (Lysistrata) | GR | 1972 | Georges Zervoulakos | 100 |
| 212 | Fushin no toki (The Time of Reckoning) | JAP | 1968 | Tadashi Imai | 119 |
| 213 | Hanaoka Seishū no tsuma (The Wife of Seishu Hanaoka) | JAP | 1967 | Yasuzō Masumura | 100 |
| 214 | Kōge (The Scent of Incense) | JAP | 1964 | Keisuke Kinoshita | 202 |
| 215 | Noche terrible {episode} | ARG | 1967 | Rodolfo Kuhn | 48 |
| 216 | Los siete locos (The Seven Madmen) | ARG | 1973 | Leopoldo Torre Nilsson | 121 |
| 217 | Sounder | USA | 1972 | Martin Ritt | 105 +V |
| 218 | Part 2, Sounder | USA | 1976 | William A. Graham | 98 |
| 219 | Le salaire de la peur (The Wages of Fear) | FR | 1953 | Henri-Georges Clouzot | 144(130) |
| 220 | Sorcerer (aka: The Wages of Fear) | USA | 1977 | William Friedkin | 122(92) |
| 221 | Lebenszeichen (Signs of Life) | GER | 1968 | Werner Herzog | 90 |
| 222 | Viva la muerte | FR/TUN | 1971 | Fernando Arrabal | 90 |
| 223 | Fando y Lis (Fando and Lis) (aka: Tar Babies) | MEX | 1968 | Alejandro Jodorowsky | 98 |
| 224 | Le grand cérémonial | FR | 1969 | Pierre-Alain Jolivet | 105 |

| No. | Author | Nationality | Form | Literary Title | Date |
|---|---|---|---|---|---|
| 225 | **Arrabal, Fernando** | Morocco | P | **Guernica** | 1961 |
| 226 | **Asbjørnsen, Peder Christen** | Norwegian | SS | **Princessen som ingen kunde målbinde følgesvenden** | 1910 |
| 227 | **Ashton, Winifred** (see: Dane, Clemence) | British | P | | |
| 228 | **Ashton-Warner, Sylvia** | New Zealand | N | **Spinster** | 1958 |
| 229 | **Asimov, Isaac** | American | SS | **The Ugly Little Boy** | 1966 |
| 230 | **Assis, Joaquim Maria Machado de** (Machado de Assis) | Brazilian | SS | **O alienista** (The Psychiatrist) | 1881 |
| 231 | **Assis, Joaquim Maria Machado de** | Brazilian | SS | **Um apólogo** | 1885 |
| 232 | **Assis, Joaquim Maria Machado de** | Brazilian | SS | **Um apólogo** | 1885 |
| 233 | **Assis, Joaquim Maria Machado de** | Brazilian | SS | **A cartomante** (The Fortune Teller) | 1884 |
| 234 | **Assis, Joaquim Maria Machado de** | Brazilian | SS | **Confissões de uma viúva moça** | 1870 |
| 235 | **Assis, Joaquim Maria Machado de** | Brazilian | N | **Dom Casmurro** | 1899 |
| 236 | **Assis, Joaquim Maria Machado de** | Brazilian | SS | **Um homem célebre** (A Celebrity) | 1888 |
| 237 | **Assis, Joaquim Maria Machado de** | Brazilian | N | **Memórias póstumas de Brás Cubas** (Epitaph For a Small Winner) | 1881 |
| 238 | **Assis, Joaquim Maria Machado de** | Brazilian | SS | **Noite de Almirante** (Admiral's Night) | 1884 |
| 239 | **Asturias, Miguel Ángel** | Guatemalan | N | **El señor presidente** (The President) | 1946 |
| 240 | **Atwood, Margaret** | Canadian | N | **The Handmaid's Tale** | 1986 |
| 241 | **Auden, W. H.** | British | V | **Night Mail** | 1935 |
| 242 | **Audiberti, Jacques** | French | N-P | **La poupée** | 1956{n} 1959{p} |
| 243 | **Augier, Émile; Sandeau, Jules** | French | P | **Le gendre de Monsieur Poirier** (Monsieur Poirier's Son-in-Law) | 1854 |
| 244 | **Austen, Jane** | British | N | **Pride and Prejudice** | 1813 |
| 245 | **Axelrod, George** | American | P | **Goodbye Charlie** | 1960 |
| 246 | **Axelrod, George** | American | P | **The Seven Year Itch** | 1953 |
| 247 | **Axelrod, George** | American | P | **Will Success Spoil Rock Hunter?** | 1957 |
| 248 | **Ayckbourn, Alan** | British | P | **A Chorus of Disapproval** | 1986 |
| 249 | **Ayckbourn, Alan** | British | P | **Way Upstream** | 1983 |
| 250 | **Aymé, Marcel** | French | N | **La belle image** (The Second Face) (aka: The Grand Seduction) | 1941 |
| 251 | **Aymé, Marcel** | French | N | **Le chemin des écoliers** (The Transient Hour) | 1946 |
| 252 | **Aymé, Marcel** | French | P | **Clérambard** | 1950 |
| 253 | **Aymé, Marcel** | French | N | **La jument verte** (The Green Mare) | 1933 |
| 254 | **Aymé, Marcel** | French | SS | **Le passe-muraille** (The Walker-Through-Walls) | 1943 |
| 255 | **Aymé, Marcel** | French | SS | **Le passe-muraille** | 1943 |
| 256 | **Aymé, Marcel** | French | N | **La table-aux-crevés** (The Hollow Field) | 1929 |
| 257 | **Aymé, Marcel** | French | SS | **La traversée de Paris** (Across Paris) | 1946 |
| 258 | **Aymé, Marcel** | French | N | **Uranus** | 1948 |

| No | Film Title | Country of Production | Date | Director(s) | Duration of Film |
|----|-----------|----------------------|------|-------------|------------------|
| 225 | Guernica - Jede Stunde verletzt und die letzte tötet<br>(aka: Jede Stunde verletzt und die leute tötet) | GER | 1963 | Peter Lilienthal | 30 |
| 226 | Princessen som ingen kunne målbinde | NOR | 1932 | Walter Fyrst | 36 |
| 227 | | | | | |
| 228 | Two Loves<br>(GB: Spinster) | USA | 1961 | Charles Walters | 100 |
| 229 | The Ugly Little Boy | USA | 1978 | Barry Morse | 26 +V |
| 230 | Azyllo muito louca<br>(aka: Um asilo muito louco)<br>(The Alienist) | BRAZ | 1970 | Nelson Pereira dos Santos | 100 |
| 231 | Um apólogo | BRAZ | 1936 | Humberto Mauro<br>Lúcia Miguel Pereira | 07 |
| 232 | Um apólogo | BRAZ | 1939 | Humberto Mauro<br>Roquette Pinto | 15 |
| 233 | A cartomante | BRAZ | 1974 | Marcos Farias | 85 |
| 234 | Confissões de uma viúva moça | BRAZ | 1975 | Adnor Pitanga | 90 |
| 235 | Capitu | BRAZ | 1967 | Paulo César Saraceni | 105 |
| 236 | Um homem célebre | BRAZ | 1974 | Miguel Faria, Jr. | 90 |
| 237 | Viagem ao fim do mundo<br>[Voyage to the end of the world] | BRAZ | 1968 | Fernando Coni Campos | 90 |
| 238 | Esse Rio que eu amo | BRAZ | 1961 | Carlos Hugo Christensen | 104(101) |
| 239 | El señor presidente | CB/FR/NIC | 1983 | Manuel Octavio Gómez | 100 |
| 240 | The Handmaid's Tale<br>(GER: Die Geschichte der Dienerin) | USA/GER | 1990(89) | Volker Schlöndorff | 108 |
| 241 | Nightmail<br>(aka: Night Mail) | GB | 1936 | Harry Watt<br>Basil Wright | 25 |
| 242 | La poupée<br>(He She or It) | FR | 1962 | Jacques Baratier | 95 |
| 243 | Le gendre de Monsieur Poirier | FR | 1934(33) | Marcel Pagnol | 102 |
| 244 | Pride and Prejudice | USA | 1940 | Robert Z. Leonard | 119 +V |
| 245 | Goodbye Charlie | USA | 1964 | Vincente Minnelli | 116 |
| 246 | The Seven Year Itch | USA | 1955(53) | Billy Wilder | 105 +V |
| 247 | Will Success Spoil Rock Hunter?<br>(GB: Oh! For a Man) | USA | 1957 | Frank Tashlin | 95 |
| 248 | A Chorus of Disapproval | GB | 1988 | Michael Winner | 99 +V |
| 249 | Way Upstream | GB | 1986 | Terry Johnson | 100 |
| 250 | La belle image | FR | 1951 | Claude Heymann | 90 |
| 251 | Le chemin des écoliers<br>(IT: Furore di vivere) | FR/IT | 1959 | Michel Boisrond | 81 |
| 252 | Clérambard | FR | 1969 | Yves Robert | 90 |
| 253 | La jument verte<br>(IT: La giumenta verde)<br>(The Green Mare)<br>(aka: The Green Mare's Nest) | FR/IT | 1959 | Claude Autant-Lara | 105(89) |
| 254 | Garou-Garou, le passe-muraille<br>(aka: Le passe-muraille)<br>(aka: Garou-Garou)<br>(Mr Peek-a-Boo) | FR | 1950 | Jean Boyer | 90 |
| 255 | Ein Mann geht durch die Wand<br>(The Man Who Walked Through the Wall) | GER | 1959 | Ladislao Vajda | 99 |
| 256 | La table aux crevés | FR | 1952(51) | Henri Verneuil | 92 |
| 257 | La traversée de Paris<br>(IT: La traversata di Parigi)<br>(A Pig Across Paris)<br>(USA: Four Bags Full) | FR/IT | 1956 | Claude Autant-Lara | 90(84) |
| 258 | Uranus | FR | 1990 | Claude Berri | 99 |

| No. | Author | Nationality | Form | Literary Title | Date |
|-----|--------|-------------|------|----------------|------|
| 259 | **Aytmatov, Chingiz Torekulovich** *(see: Aitmatov, Chingiz)* | Russian(Kir) | SS/P | | |
| 260 | **Azevedo, Aluísio de** | Brazilian | N | **O cortiço** *(A Brazilian Tenement)* | 1890 |
| 261 | **Azevedo, Aluísio de** | Brazilian | N | **O cortiço** | 1890 |
| 262 | **Azorín** *(see: Martínez Ruiz, José)* | Spanish | P | | |
| 263 | **Azuela, Mariano** | Mexican | N | **Mala yerba** *(aka: Marcela)* | 1909 |
| 264 | **Bacchelli, Riccardo** | Italian | N | **Il brigante di Tacca del Lupo** | 1942 |
| 265 | **Bacchelli, Riccardo** | Italian | N | **Il mulino del Po** *(The Mill on the Po)* | 1938-46 |
| 266 | **Bagnold, Enid** | British | P | **The Chalk Garden** | 1956 |
| 267 | **Bagnold, Enid** | British | N | **National Velvet** | 1935 |
| 268 | **Bagnold, Enid** | British | N | **National Velvet** | 1935 |
| 269 | **Bahr, Hermann** | Austrian | P | **Die gelbe Nachtigall** *[The yellow nightingale]* | 1907 |
| 270 | **Bahr, Hermann** | Austrian | N | **Die gelbe Nachtigall** | 1907 |
| 271 | **Bahr, Hermann** | Austrian | P | **Das Konzert** *(The Concert)* | 1909 |
| 272 | **Bahr, Hermann** | Austrian | P | **Das Konzert** | 1909 |
| 273 | **Bahr, Hermann** | Austrian | P | **Das Konzert** | 1909 |
| 274 | **Bahr, Hermann** | Austrian | P | **Der Meister** *(The Master)* | 1904 |
| 275 | **Bailey, Charles W.** *(joint, see: Knebel, Fletcher)* | American | N | | |
| 276 | **Ba Jin** *(see: Li Feigan)* | Chinese | N | | |
| 277 | **Baker, Dorothy** | American | N | **Young Man With a Horn** | 1938 |
| 278 | **Balázs Béla** | Hungarian | N(AUT) | **Álmodó ifjúság** | 1946 |
| 279 | **Balázs Béla** | Hungarian | SS | **Heinrich beginnt den Kampf** *[Henry begins the fight]* | [194-?] |
| 280 | **Balchin, Nigel** | British | N | **Mine Own Executioner** | 1945 |
| 281 | **Balchin, Nigel** | British | N | **The Small Back Room** | 1943 |
| 282 | **Balchin, Nigel** | British | N | **Sort of Traitors** | 1949 |
| 283 | **Baldwin, James** | American(afro) | N | **Go Tell It On The Mountain** | 1953 |
| 284 | **Ball, John Dudley** | American(afro) | N | **In the Heat of the Night** | 1965 |
| 285 | **Ballard, J. G.** | British | N | **Empire of the Sun** | 1984 |
| 286 | **Bałucki, Michał** | Polish | P | **Klub kawalerów** *[Batchelor's club]* | 1890 |
| 287 | **Balzac, Honoré de** | French | SS | **L'auberge rouge** *(The Red Inn)* | 1831 |
| 288 | **Balzac, Honoré de** | French | SS | **Le chef d'oeuvre inconnu** | 1831 |
| 289 | **Balzac, Honoré de** | French | N | **Les Chouans** | 1834 |
| 290 | **Balzac, Honoré de** | French | N | **Les Chouans** | 1834 |
| 291 | **Balzac, Honoré de** | French | SS | **Le colonel Chabert** *(Colonel Chabert)* | 1844 |
| 292 | **Balzac, Honoré de** | French | SS | **Le colonel Chabert** | 1844 |
| 293 | **Balzac, Honoré de** | French | SS | **Le colonel Chabert** | 1844 |
| 294 | **Balzac, Honoré de** | French | SS | **La duchesse de Langeais** *(aka: Ne touchez pas la hache)* | 1839 (aka:1834) |
| 295 | **Balzac, Honoré de** | French | N | **Eugénie Grandet** | 1833 |
| 296 | **Balzac, Honoré de** | French | N | **Eugénie Grandet** | 1833 |
| 297 | **Balzac, Honoré de** | French | N | **Eugénie Grandet** | 1833 |
| 298 | **Balzac, Honoré de** | French | SS | **La fausse maîtresse** *(The Imaginary Mistress)* | 1841 |
| 299 | **Balzac, Honoré de** | French | SS | **La fille aux yeux d'or** *(The Girl With Golden Eyes)* | 1834-35 |
| 300 | **Balzac, Honoré de** | French | SS | **Gobseck** | 1830 |
| 301 | **Balzac, Honoré de** | French | SS | **Gobseck** | 1830 |

| No | Film Title | Country of Production | Date | Director(s) | Duration of Film |
|----|-----------|----------------------|------|-------------|------------------|
| 259 | | | | | |
| 260 | O cortiço | BRAZ | 1945 | Luis de Barros | 111 |
| 261 | O cortiço | BRAZ | 1978 | Francisco Ramalho | 105 |
| 262 | | | | | |
| 263 | Mala yerba | MEX | 1940 | Gabriel Soria | 81 |
| 264 | Il brigante di Tacca del Lupo (The Brigand of Tacca del Lupo) | IT | 1952 | Pietro Germi | 103 |
| 265 | Il mulino del Po (The Mill on the Po) | IT | 1949(48) | Alberto Lattuada | 108(105) |
| 266 | The Chalk Garden | GB | 1963 | Ronald Neame | 106 |
| 267 | National Velvet | USA | 1945 | Clarence Brown | 123 +V |
| 268 | International Velvet | GB | 1978 | Bryan Forbes | 132 +V |
| 269 | Romance in the Dark | USA | 1938 | H. C. Potter | 80 |
| 270 | Das Lied der Nachtigall | GER | 1944(43) | Theo Lingen | 90 |
| 271 | Das Konzert | GER/USA/FR | 1931 | Leo Mittler | 80 |
| 272 | Das Konzert | GER | 1944 | Paul Verhoeven | 86 |
| 273 | Nichts als Ärger mit der Liebe | AUST | 1956 | Thomas Engel | 94 |
| 274 | Skandal in Ischl | AUST | 1957 | Rolf Thiele | 93 |
| 275 | | | | | |
| 276 | | | | | |
| 277 | Young Man With a Horn (GB: Young Man of Music) | USA | 1950 | Michael Curtiz | 112 +V |
| 278 | Álmodo ifjúság (Dreaming Youth) | HUNG | 1974 | János Rózsa | 81 |
| 279 | Veszélyes játékok (Dangerous Games) | HUNG/GER | 1979 | Tamás Fejér | 91 |
| 280 | Mine Own Executioner | GB | 1948 | Anthony Kimmins | 108 |
| 281 | The Small Back Room (aka: Hour of Glory) | GB | 1948 | Michael Powell Emeric Pressburger | 107 |
| 282 | Suspect (USA: The Risk) | GB | 1960 | Roy Boulting John Boulting | 81 |
| 283 | Go Tell It On The Mountain | USA | 1985(84) | Stan Lathan | 97 |
| 284 | In the Heat of the Night | USA | 1967 | Norman Jewison | 109 +V |
| 285 | Empire of the Sun | USA | 1987 | Steven Spielberg | 152 +V |
| 286 | Klub kawalerów | POL | 1962 | Jerzy Zarzycki | 95 |
| 287 | L'auberge rouge (The Red Inn) | FR | 1951 | Claude Autant-Lara | 110 |
| 288 | La belle noiseuse | FR | 1991 | Jacques Rivette | 239 |
| 289 | Les Chouans | FR | 1947 | Henri Calef | 99 |
| 290 | Les révoltés de Lon Manach (aka: Révoltés de Lomanach) (IT: L'eroe della vandea) (The Lon Manach Rebels) | FR/IT | 1954(53) | Richard Pottier | 88 |
| 291 | Un homme sans nom {French version of: Mensch ohne Namen} | FR | 1932 | Roger le Bon Gustav Ucicky | 81 |
| 292 | Mensch ohne Namen | GER | 1932 | Gustav Ucicky | 92 |
| 293 | Le colonel Chabert | FR | 1943 | René le Hénaff | 102 |
| 294 | La duchesse de Langeais (The Wicked Duchess) | FR | 1942 | Jacques de Baroncelli | 99 |
| 295 | Eugenia Grandet | IT | 1946 | Mario Soldati | 100 |
| 296 | Eugénie Grandet | MEX | 1952 | Emilio Gómez Muriel | 117 |
| 297 | Eugene Grande | USSR | 1960 | Sergei Alekseev | 100 |
| 298 | La fausse maîtresse | FR | 1942 | André Cayatte | 85 |
| 299 | La fille aux yeux d'or (The Girl With Golden Eyes) | FR | 1961 | Jean-Gabriel Albicocco | 105 |
| 300 | Gobsek (Gobseck) | USSR | 1936 | Konstantin Eggert | 73 |
| 301 | Gobsek | USSR | 1987 | Alexander Orlov | 100 |

**17**

| No. | Author | Nationality | Form | Literary Title | Date |
|-----|--------|-------------|------|----------------|------|
| 302 | Balzac, Honoré de | French | SS | La Grande Bretèche ou les trois vengeances | 1837 |
| 303 | Balzac, Honoré de | French | N | Un grand homme de province à Paris (Illusions perdues - pt.2) (A Great Man of the Provinces in Paris | 1839 |
| 304 | Balzac, Honoré de | French | P | Mercadet (aka: Le faiseur) | 1851 |
| 305 | Balzac, Honoré de | French | P | Mercadet | 1851 |
| 306 | Balzac, Honoré de | French | N | La peau de chagrin (The Fatal Skin) (aka: The Wild Ass's Skin) | 1831 |
| 307 | Balzac, Honoré de | French | N | La peau de chagrin | 1831 |
| 308 | Balzac, Honoré de | French | N | Le père Goriot (Old Goriot) | 1834(35) |
| 309 | Balzac, Honoré de | French | N | Le père Goriot | 1834(35) |
| 310 | Balzac, Honoré de | French | N | La rabouilleuse (The Black Sheep) (aka: Les deux frères) (aka: Un ménage de garçon en province) | 1845 (aka1841;42) |
| 311 | Balzac, Honoré de | French | N | La rabouilleuse | 1845 |
| 312 | Balzac, Honoré de | French | N | La rabouilleuse | 1845 |
| 313 | Balzac, Honoré de | French | P | Vautrin | 1840 |
| 314 | Balzac, Honoré de | French | P | Vautrin | 1840 |
| 315 | Bandrowski, Juliusz Kaden (see: Kaden Bandrowski, Juliusz) | Polish | N | | |
| 316 | Bandyopādhyāý, Bibhuti Bhushaṇ (Bibhuti Bhushaṇ Banerji) | Indian (Ben) | N | Aparājita (Aparājita: Trumpet Call of Childhood Days) | 1931 |
| 317 | Bandyopādhyāý, Bibhuti Bhushaṇ | Indian | N | Ashāni sanket | 1959 |
| 318 | Bandyopādhyāý, Bibhuti Bhushaṇ | Indian | N | Pather pāñcāli (pt.1) (aka: Song of the Road) | 1929 |
| 319 | Bandyopādhyāý (Banerji), Tārāśaṅkar | Indian (Ben) | N | Abhiyān | 1946 |
| 320 | Bandyopādhyāý (Banerji), Tārāśaṅkar | Indian | SS | Jalsāghar (The Hall of Entertainment) | 1937 |
| 321 | Banerji, Bibhuti Bhusan (see: Bandyopādhyāý, Bibhuti Bhushan) | Indian (Ben) | N | | |
| 322 | Bang, Herman | Danish | SS | Sommerglæder | 1902 |
| 323 | Bang, Herman | Danish | N | Tine | 1889 |
| 324 | Bang, Herman | Danish | N | Ved vejen [By the wayside] | 1886 |
| 325 | Banville, John | Irish | N | The Newton Letter | 1982 |
| 326 | Baraka, Imamu Amiri (see: Jones, Leroi) | American(afro) | P | | |
| 327 | Baranga, Aurel | Romanian | P | Iarbă rea (Ill weed) | 1949 |
| 328 | Baranga, Aurel | Romanian | P | Travesti [Disguise] | 1971 |
| 329 | Barbu, Eugen | Romanian | SS | Domnişoara Aurica [Miss Aurica] | 1962 |
| 330 | Barbu, Eugen | Romanian | N | Facerea lumii [Genesis] | 1964 |
| 331 | Barbu, Eugen | Romanian | SS | Oaie şi ai săi [Oaie and his gentry] | 1958 |
| 332 | Barbu, Eugen | Romanian | N | Şoseaua Nordului [North boulevard] | 1959 |
| 333 | Barker, Howard | British | P | No One Was Saved | 1970 |
| 334 | Barnes, Margaret Ayer | American | N | Westward Passage | 1931 |
| 335 | Barnes, Peter | British | P | Leonardo's Last Supper | 1970 |
| 336 | Barnes, Peter | British | P | The Ruling Class | 1969 |

| No | Film Title | Country of Production | Date | Director(s) | Duration of Film |
|----|-----------|----------------------|------|-------------|-----------------|
| 302 | Un seul amour | FR | 1943 | Pierre Blanchar | 101 |
| 303 | Elveszett illúziók (Lost Illusions) | HUNG | 1983 | Gyula Gazdag | 103 |
| 304 | Le faiseur | FR | 1936 | André Hugon | 66 |
| 305 | The Lovable Cheat | USA | 1949 | Richard Oswald | 75 |
| 306 | Die unheimlichen Wünsche | GER | 1939 | Heinz Hilpert | 98 |
| 307 | Šagrenska koža (animation) | YUGO | 1960 | Ivo Vrbanić Vlado Kristl | 10 |
| 308 | Le père Goriot | FR | 1945(44) | Robert Vernay | 103 |
| 309 | Karriere in Paris [Career in Paris] | GDR | 1951 | Georg C. Klaren | 95 |
| 310 | Honor of the Family | USA | 1931 | Lloyd Bacon | 66 |
| 311 | La rabouilleuse | FR | 1944(43) | Fernand Rivers | 100 |
| 312 | Les arrivistes (GER: Trübe Wasser) | FR/GER | 1960 | Louis Daquin | 112 |
| 313 | Vautrin | FR | 1944(43) | Pierre Billon | 120 |
| 314 | Der Bagnosträfling | GER | 1949 | Gustav Fröhlich | 103 |
| 315 | | | | | |
| 316 | Aparajito (Unvanquished) | IND (BEN) | 1956 | Satyajit Ray | 113 |
| 317 | Ashani sanket (Distant Thunder) | IND (BEN) | 1973 | Satyajit Ray | 99 |
| 318 | Pather Panchali | IND (BEN) | 1955 | Satyajit Ray | 123(115) |
| 319 | Abhiyān (Expedition) | IND (BEN) | 1962 | Satyajit Ray | 150 |
| 320 | Jalsāghar (The Music Room) | IND (BEN) | 1958 | Satyajit Ray | 95 |
| 321 | | | | | |
| 322 | Sommerglæder (Happy Summer) | DEN | 1940 | Svend Methling | 98 |
| 323 | Tine | DEN | 1964 | Knud Leif Thomsen | 137 |
| 324 | Ved vejen (aka: Katinka) | DEN/SWE | 1988 | Max von Sydow | 95 |
| 325 | Reflections | GB | 1983 | Kevin Billington | 100 |
| 326 | | | | | |
| 327 | Viața învinge (Life Triumphs) | ROM | 1951 | Dinu Negreanu | 98 |
| 328 | Premiera [Première] | ROM | 1976 | Mihai Constantinescu | 97 |
| 329 | Domnișoara Aurica | ROM | 1986 | Șerban Marinescu | 98 |
| 330 | Facerea lumii | ROM | 1971 | Gheorghe Vitanidis | 111 |
| 331 | Tatăl risipitor [The prodigal father] | ROM | 1974 | Adrian Petringenaru | 92 |
| 332 | Procesul alb [The white trial] | ROM | 1965 | Iulian Mihu | 127 |
| 333 | Made | GB | 1972 | John Mackenzie | 104 |
| 334 | Westward Passage | USA | 1932 | Robert Milton | 73 +V |
| 335 | Leonardo's Last Supper | GB | 1977(76) | Peter Barnes | 55 |
| 336 | The Ruling Class | GB | 1972 | Peter Medak | 155 |

| No. | Author | Nationality | Form | Literary Title | Date |
|-----|--------|-------------|------|----------------|------|
| 337 | **Baroja y Nessi, Pío** | Spanish | N | **La busca**<br>*(The Quest)* | 1904 |
| 338 | **Baroja y Nessi, Pío** | Spanish | N | **Las inquietudes de Shanti Andía**<br>*(The Restlessness of Shanti Andía)* | 1911 |
| 339 | **Baroja y Nessi, Pío** | Spanish | N | **Zalacaín el aventurero**<br>*[Zalacaín the adventurer]* | 1909 |
| 340 | **Barreto, Afonso Henriques de Lima**<br>*(Afonso Lima Barreto)* | Brazilian | SS | **A Nova California** | 1948 |
| 341 | **Barrie, J. M.** | British(Scot) | P | **The Admirable Crichton** | 1914 |
| 342 | **Barrie, J. M.** | British | P | **The Admirable Crichton** | 1914 |
| 343 | **Barrie, J. M.** | British | P | **Alice Sit By The Fire** | 1919 |
| 344 | **Barrie, J. M.** | British | N | **The Little Minister** | 1891 |
| 345 | **Barrie, J. M.** | British | P | **The Old Lady Shows Her Medals** | 1918 |
| 346 | **Barrie, J. M.** | British | P | **The Old Lady Shows Her Medals** | 1918 |
| 347 | **Barrie, J. M.** | British | N-P | **Peter Pan** *{n-p}*<br>**Peter and Wendy** *{n}* | 1911;<br>1928 |
| 348 | **Barrie, J. M.** | British | N-P | **Peter Pan** *{n-p}*<br>**Peter and Wendy** *{n}* | 1928 |
| 349 | **Barrie, J. M.** | British | P | **Quality Street** | 1913 |
| 350 | **Barrie, J. M.** | British | P | **Rosalind** | 1914 |
| 351 | **Barrie, J. M.** | British | P | **What Every Woman Knows** | 1918 |
| 352 | **Barroso, Maria Alice** | Brazilian | N | **Quem matou Pacífico**<br>*[Who killed Pacifico]* | 1969 |
| 353 | **Barry, Philip** | American | P | **The Animal Kingdom** | 1932 |
| 354 | **Barry, Philip** | American | P | **The Animal Kingdom** | 1932 |
| 355 | **Barry, Philip** | American | P | **Holiday** | 1929 |
| 356 | **Barry, Philip** | American | P | **Holiday** | 1929 |
| 357 | **Barry, Philip** | American | P | **Philadelphia Story** | 1939 |
| 358 | **Barry, Philip** | American | P | **Philadelphia Story** | 1939 |
| 359 | **Barry, Philip** | American | P | **Tomorrow and Tomorrow** | 1931 |
| 360 | **Barry, Philip** | American | P | **Without Love** | 1943 |
| 361 | **Barry, Philip** | American | P | **You and I** | 1923 |
| 362 | **Barstow, Stan** | British | N | **A Kind of Loving** | 1960 |
| 363 | **Bart, Jean** | Romanian | N | **Europolis** | 1933 |
| 364 | **Barth, John** | American | N | **End of the Road** | 1958 |
| 365 | **Bartolini, Luigi** | Italian | N | **Ladri di biciclette**<br>*(Bicycle Thieves)* | 1948 |
| 366 | **Bassani, Giorgio** | Italian | N | **Il giardino dei Finzi-Contini**<br>*(The Garden of the Finzi-Continis)* | 1962 |
| 367 | **Bassani, Giorgio** | Italian | N | **Una notte del '43** | 1960 |
| 368 | **Bassani, Giorgio** | Italian | N | **Gli occhiali d'oro**<br>*(The Gold-Rimmed Spectacles)* | 1956 |
| 369 | **Basso, Hamilton** | American | N | **Days Before Lent** | 1939 |
| 370 | **Basso, Hamilton** | American | N | **The View From Pompey's Head**<br>*(GB: Pompey's Head)* | 1954 |
| 371 | **Bataille, Henry** | French | P | **L'enfant de l'amour**<br>*[Love child]* | 1911 |
| 372 | **Bataille, Henry** | French | P | **La femme nue** | 1908 |
| 373 | **Bataille, Henry** | French | P | **La femme nue** | 1908 |
| 374 | **Bataille, Henry** | French | P | **L'homme à la rose**<br>*[The man with the rose]* | 1921 |
| 375 | **Bataille, Henry** | French | P | **Maman Colibri**<br>*[Mother Hummingbird]* | 1904 |

| No | Film Title | Country of Production | Date | Director(s) | Duration of Film |
|----|-----------|----------------------|------|-------------|------------------|
| 337 | **La busca** <br> *(The Search)* | SP | 1966 | **Angelino Fons** | 94(88) |
| 338 | **Las inquietudes de Shanti-Andía** | SP | 1947(46) | **Arturo Ruiz Castillo** | 121(108) |
| 339 | **Zalacaín el aventurero** | SP | 1954 | **Juan de Orduña** | 90(95) |
| 340 | **Osso, amor e papagaois** <br> *(Bones, Love and Parrots)* | BRAZ | 1957 | **Carlos Alberto de Sousa Barros** <br> **César Mémolo** | 102(95) |
| 341 | **We're Not Dressing** | USA | 1934 | **Norman Taurog** | 77 |
| 342 | **The Admirable Crichton** <br> *(USA: Paradise Lagoon)* | GB | 1957 | **Lewis Gilbert** | 93 |
| 343 | **Darling, How Could You!** | USA | 1951 | **Mitchell Leisen** | 96 |
| 344 | **The Little Minister** | USA | 1934 | **Richard Wallace** | 110 |
| 345 | **Seven Days Leave** <br> *(GB: Medals)* | USA | 1930 | **Richard Wallace** | 83 |
| 346 | **Seven Days Leave** <br> *(GB: Medals)* | USA | 1942 | **Tim Whelan** | 88 |
| 347 | **Peter Pan** <br> *{animation}* | USA | 1952 | **Hamilton Luske** <br> **Clyde Geronimi** <br> **Wilfred Jackson** | 76 |
| 348 | **Hook** | USA | 1991 | **Steven Spielberg** | 141 |
| 349 | **Quality Street** | USA | 1937 | **George Stevens** | 83 |
| 350 | **Forever Female** | USA | 1953 | **Irving Rapper** | 94 |
| 351 | **What Every Woman Knows** | USA | 1934 | **Gregory La Cava** | 90 |
| 352 | **Quem matou Pacífico** | BRAZ | 1977 | **José Renato Santos Pereira** | 90 |
| 353 | **The Animal Kingdom** <br> *(GB: The Woman in His House)* | USA | 1932 | **Edward H. Griffith** | 85 |
| 354 | **One More Tomorrow** | USA | 1946 | **Peter Godfrey** | 88 |
| 355 | **Holiday** | USA | 1930 | **Edward H. Griffith** | 96 |
| 356 | **Holiday** <br> *(GB: Free To Live)* <br> *(aka: Unconventional Linda)* | USA | 1938 | **George Cukor** | 93 |
| 357 | **The Philadelphia Story** | USA | 1940 | **George Cukor** | 112 |
| 358 | **High Society** <br> *{musical version}* | USA | 1956 | **Charles Walters** | 107 <br> +V |
| 359 | **Tomorrow and Tomorrow** | USA | 1932 | **Richard Wallace** | 73 |
| 360 | **Without Love** | USA | 1945 | **Harold S. Bucquet** | 111 |
| 361 | **The Bargain** <br> *(aka: Fame)* <br> *(aka: You and I)* | USA | 1931 | **Robert Milton** | 76 |
| 362 | **A Kind of Loving** | GB | 1962 | **John Schlesinger** | 112 +V |
| 363 | **Porto-Franco** | ROM | 1961 | **Paul Călinescu** | 82 |
| 364 | **End of the Road** | USA | 1970(69) | **Aram Avakian** | 110 |
| 365 | **Ladri di biciclette** <br> *(Bicycle Thieves)* <br> *(aka: The Bicycle Thief)* | IT | 1948 | **Vittorio de Sica** | 90(84) <br> +V |
| 366 | **Il giardino dei Finzi-Contini** <br> *(GER: Der garten der Finzi Contini)* <br> *(The Garden of the Finzi-Continis)* | IT/GER | 1970 | **Vittorio de Sica** | 95(93) |
| 367 | **La lunga notte del '43** | IT | 1960 | **Florestano Vancini** | 100 |
| 368 | **Gli occhiali d'oro** <br> *(FR: Lunettes d'or)* <br> *(Goldrimmed Glasses)* | IT/FR/ YUGO | 1987 | **Giuliano Montaldo** | 110 |
| 369 | **Holiday For Sinners** | USA | 1952 | **Gerald Mayer** | 72 |
| 370 | **The View From Pompey's Head** <br> *(GB: Secret Interlude)* | USA | 1955 | **Philip Dunne** | 97 |
| 371 | **L'enfant de l'amour** | FR | 1944 | **Jean Stelli** | 100 |
| 372 | **La femme nue** | FR | 1932 | **Jean-Paul Paulin** | 91 |
| 373 | **La femme nue** <br> *(The Naked Woman)* | FR | 1949 | **André Berthomieu** | 95 |
| 374 | **The Private Life of Don Juan** | GB | 1934 | **Alexander Korda** | 90 |
| 375 | **Maman Colibri** | FR | 1937 | **Jean Dréville** | 99 |

| No. | Author | Nationality | Form | Literary Title | Date |
|-----|--------|-------------|------|----------------|------|
| 376 | **Bataille, Henry** | French | P | **La marche nuptiale** | 1905 |
| 377 | **Bataille, Henry** | French | P | **Poliche** | 1906 |
| 378 | **Bataille, Henry** | French | P | **Le scandale**<br>(The Scandal) | 1909 |
| 379 | **Bataille, Henry** | French | P | **La tendresse**<br>[Tenderness] | 1921 |
| 380 | **Bataille, Henry** | French | P | **La vierge folle**<br>[The mad virgin] | 1910 |
| 381 | **Bates, H. E.** | British | N | **The Darling Buds of May** | 1958 |
| 382 | **Bates, H. E.** | British | SS | **Dulcima** | 1953 |
| 383 | **Bates, H. E.** | British | N | **The Purple Plain** | 1947 |
| 384 | **Bates, H. E.** | British | N | **The Triple Echo** | 1970 |
| 385 | **Bauer, Wolfgang** | Austrian | P | **Change**<br>(All Change) | 1969 |
| 386 | **Baum, L. Frank** | American | N | **The Land of Oz +**<br>**Ozma of Oz** | 1904+<br>1907 |
| 387 | **Baum, L. Frank** | American | N | **The Land of Oz +**<br>**Ozma of Oz** | 1904+<br>1907 |
| 388 | **Baum, L. Frank** | American | N | **The Wonderful Wizard of Oz** | 1900 |
| 389 | **Baum, L. Frank** | American | N | **The Wonderful Wizard of Oz** | 1900 |
| 390 | **Baxter, James K.** | New Zealand | P(R)-P | **Jack Winter's Dream** | 1959 |
| 391 | **Bazin, Hervé** | French | N | **La tête contre les murs**<br>(Head Against the Wall) | 1949 |
| 392 | **Bazin, René** | French | N | **La terre qui meurt**<br>(Autumn Glory; or, the Toilers<br>of the Field) | 1899 |
| 393 | **Beaumarchais, Pierre-Augustin<br>Caron de** | French | P | **Le barbier de Séville**<br>(aka: Le barbier de Séville, ou la<br>précaution)<br>(The Barber of Seville, or the<br>Useless Precaution) | 1775 |
| 394 | **Beaumarchais, Pierre-Augustin<br>Caron de** | French | P | **Le mariage de Figaro**<br>(The Marriage of Figaro) | 1785 |
| 395 | **Beaumarchais, Pierre-Augustin<br>Caron de** | French | P | **Le mariage de Figaro** | 1785 |
| 396 | **Becher, Johannes R.** | German | N | **Abschied** | 1940 |
| 397 | **Beck, Béatrix** | French | N | **Léon Morin, prêtre**<br>(The Priest)<br>(USA: The Passionate Heart) | 1952 |
| 398 | **Becker, Jurek** | German | N | **Jakob der Lügner**<br>(Jacob the Liar) | 1969 |
| 399 | **Beckett, Samuel** | Irish(Fr) | P | **Acte sans paroles**<br>(Act Without Words) | 1957 |
| 400 | **Beckett, Samuel** | Irish | P | **Acte sans paroles** | 1957 |
| 401 | **Beckett, Samuel** | Irish | P(TV) | **Dis Joe** | 1966 |
| 402 | **Beckett, Samuel** | Irish | P | **Va et vient**<br>(Come and Go) | 1966 |
| 403 | **Becque, Henri** | French | P | **La parisienne**<br>(Parisienne) | 1885 |
| 404 | **Bécquer, Gustavo Adolfo**<br>(G. A. Dominguez Bécquer) | Spanish | SS | **El miserere +**<br>**El monte de las animas +**<br>(The Spirit's Mountain) +<br>**La cruz del diablo**<br>(The Devil's Cross) | 1862+<br>1861+<br>1860 |
| 405 | **Behan, Brendan** | Irish | P | **The Quare Fellow** | 1956 |
| 406 | **Behrman, S. N.** | American | P | **Biography** | 1933 |
| 407 | **Behrman, S. N.** | American | P | **Brief Moment** | 1931 |
| 408 | **Behrman, S. N.** | American | P | **No Time For Comedy** | 1939 |
| 409 | **Behrman, S. N.** | American | P | **The Pirate** | 1943 |
| 410 | **Behrman, S. N.** | American | P | **Second Man** | 1927 |
| 411 | **Bell, Sam Hanna** | Irish | N | **December Bride** | 1951 |
| 412 | **Bellemère, Jean**<br>(see: Sarment, Jean) | French | P | | |

| No | Film Title | Country of Production | Date | Director(s) | Duration of Film |
|---|---|---|---|---|---|
| 376 | La marche nuptiale (IT: Marcia nuziale) | FR/IT | 1935(34) | Mario Bonnard | 95 |
| 377 | Poliche | FR | 1934 | Abel Gance | 90? |
| 378 | Le scandale | FR | 1934 | Marcel L'Herbier | 106 |
| 379 | La tendresse (GER: Zörtlichkert) | FR/GER | 1930 | André Hugon | 89 |
| 380 | La vierge folle | FR | 1938 | Henri Diamant-Berger | 90 |
| 381 | The Mating Game | USA | 1958 | George Marshall | 96 |
| 382 | Dulcima | GB | 1971 | Frank Nesbitt | 98 |
| 383 | The Purple Plain | GB | 1954 | Robert Parrish | 100 +V |
| 384 | The Triple Echo (aka: Soldier in Skirts) | GB | 1972 | Michael Apted | 94 +V |
| 385 | Change | GER | 1974 | Bernd Fischerauer | 101 |
| 386 | Return to Oz {animation} | USA | 1964 | Arthur Rankin | 60 +V(52) |
| 387 | Return to Oz | USA | 1985 | Walter Murch | 109 +V |
| 388 | The Wizard of Oz {musical version} | USA | 1939 | Victor Fleming | 98 +V |
| 389 | The Wiz {musical version} | USA | 1978 | Sidney Lumet | 134 +V(127) |
| 390 | Jack Winter's Dream | NZ | 1980(79) | David Sims | 59 |
| 391 | La tête contre les murs (The Keepers) | FR | 1959 | Georges Franju | 98 |
| 392 | La terre qui meurt | FR | 1936 | Jean Vallée | 88 |
| 393 | El barbero de Sevilla (GER: Der Barbier von Sevilla) | SP/GER | 1938 | Benito Perojo | 106(90) |
| 394 | Ein toller Tag [A crazy day] | GER | 1945 | Oscar Fritz Schuh | 74 |
| 395 | Le mariage de Figaro (The Marriage of Figaro) | FR | 1959 | Jean Meyer | 104 |
| 396 | Abschied (Farewell) | GDR | 1968 | Egon Günther | 106 |
| 397 | Léon Morin, prêtre (IT: Leon Morin, prete) (Leon Morin, Priest) | FR/IT | 1961 | Jean-Pierre Melville | 117(104) |
| 398 | Jakob der Lügner (Jacob the Liar) | GDR | 1974 | Frank Beyer | 95 |
| 399 | Acte sans paroles {puppet version} | FR | 1964 | Bruno Bettiol Guido Bettiol | 11 |
| 400 | Act Without Words | GB | 1983 | Margaret Jordan | 17 +V |
| 401 | Eh Joe! | IRE | 1986 | Alan Gilsenan | 38 |
| 402 | Come and Go | GB | 1986 | Nik Houghton {ed.} | 05 +V |
| 403 | Une parisienne (IT: Una parigina) | FR/IT | 1957 | Michel Boisrond | 86 |
| 404 | La cruz del diablo (Devil's Cross) | SP | 1975(74) | John Gilling | 97 |
| 405 | The Quare Fellow | GB | 1962 | Arthur Dreifuss | 90 +V |
| 406 | Biography (of a Bachelor Girl) | USA | 1934 | Edward H. Griffith | 84 |
| 407 | Brief Moment | USA | 1933 | David Burton | 69 |
| 408 | No Time For Comedy (aka: Guy With a Grin) | USA | 1940 | William Keighley | 98 |
| 409 | The Pirate {musical version} | USA | 1948 | Vincente Minnelli | 102 +V(97) |
| 410 | He Knew Women | USA | 1930 | F. Hugh Herbert | 70 |
| 411 | December Bride | GB | 1990 | Thaddeus O'Sullivan | 88 |
| 412 | | | | | |

| No. | Author | Nationality | Form | Literary Title | Date |
|-----|--------|-------------|------|----------------|------|
| 413 | Bellow, Saul | American | SS | Seize the Day | 1956 |
| 414 | Benavente y Martínez, Jacinto | Spanish | P | Alma triunfante | 1902 |
| 415 | Benavente y Martínez, Jacinto | Spanish | P | La fuerza bruta<br>(Brute Force) | 1908 |
| 416 | Benavente y Martínez, Jacinto | Spanish | P | La hondradez de la cerradura<br>[The secret of the key-hole] | 1943 |
| 417 | Benavente y Martínez, Jacinto | Spanish | P | Lecciones de buen amor | 1924 |
| 418 | Benavente y Martínez, Jacinto | Spanish | P | La malquerida<br>(The Passion Flower)  . | 1913 |
| 419 | Benavente y Martínez, Jacinto | Spanish | P | La malquerida | 1913 |
| 420 | Benavente y Martínez, Jacinto | Spanish | P | La mariposa que voló sobre<br>el mar<br>[The butterfly that flew over the sea] | 1926 |
| 421 | Benavente y Martínez, Jacinto | Spanish | P | Nadie sabe lo que quiere, o, el<br>bailarín y el trabajador | 1925 |
| 422 | Benavente y Martínez, Jacinto | Spanish | P | La noche del sábado<br>(Saturday Night) | 1903 |
| 423 | Benavente y Martínez, Jacinto | Spanish | P | ¡No quiero, No quiero! | 1928 |
| 424 | Benavente y Martínez, Jacinto | Spanish | P | Pepa Doncel | 1928 |
| 425 | Benavente y Martínez, Jacinto | Spanish | P | Rosas de otoño | 1914 |
| 426 | Benavente y Martínez, Jacinto | Spanish | P | Señora ama | 1908 |
| 427 | Benavente y Martínez, Jacinto | Spanish | P | Vidas cruzadas<br>(The Web) | 1929 |
| 428 | Benchley, Nathaniel | American | N | The Off-Islanders<br>(aka: The Russians Are Coming,<br>the Russians Are Coming) | 1961 |
| 429 | Benchley, Nathaniel | American | N | Sail a Crooked Ship | 1960 |
| 430 | Benchley, Nathaniel | American | N | The Visitors | 1964 |
| 431 | Benchley, Peter | American | N | The Deep | 1976 |
| 432 | Benchley, Peter | American | N | The Island | 1979 |
| 433 | Benchley, Peter | American | N | Jaws | 1974 |
| 434 | Benedetti, Mario | Uruguay | N | La tregua | 1960 |
| 435 | Benelli, Sem | Italian | P | La cena delle beffe<br>(The Jest) | 1909 |
| 436 | Benét, Stephen Vincent | American | SS | The Devil and Daniel Webster | 1937 |
| 437 | Benét, Stephen Vincent | American | SS | Everybody Was Very Nice | 1936 |
| 438 | Benét, Stephen Vincent | American | SS | Famous | 1946 |
| 439 | Benét, Stephen Vincent | American | SS | The Sobbin' Women | 1937 |
| 440 | Bengtsson, Frans Gunnar | Swedish | N | Röde Orm, sjöfarara i västerled +<br>Röde Orm, hemma och i österled<br>(The Long Ships)<br>(aka: Red Orm) | 1941+<br>1945 |
| 441 | Bennett, Arnold | British | N+P | Buried Alive {n} +<br>The Great Adventure {p} | 1908+<br>1913 |
| 442 | Bennett, Arnold | British | N | Buried Alive | 1908 |
| 443 | Bennett, Arnold | British | N | The Card | 1912 |
| 444 | Bennett, Arnold | British | N | Mr Prohack | 1922 |
| 445 | Benson, Sally | American | SS | Meet Me in St. Louis | 1942 |
| 446 | Benson, Sally - {n}<br>J. Chodorov & J. Fields - {p} | American | N-P | Junior Miss | 1941{n}<br>1942{p} |
| 447 | Berger, John | British | SS | Play Me Something | 1987 |
| 448 | Berger, Thomas | American | N | Little Big Man | 1964 |
| 449 | Berger, Thomas | American | N | Neighbors | 1980 |
| 450 | Bergman, Hjalmar | Swedish | P | Dollar<br>[Dollars] | 1926 |
| 451 | Bergman, Hjalmar | Swedish | SS | Flickan i frack | 1925 |
| 452 | Bergman, Hjalmar | Swedish | N | Hans nåds testamente<br>(The Baron's Will) | 1910 |
| 453 | Bergman, Hjalmar | Swedish | N | Markurells i Wadköping<br>(Markurells of Wadköping)<br>(aka: God's Orchid) | 1919 |

| No | Film Title | Country of Production | Date | Director(s) | Duration of Film |
|----|-----------|----------------------|------|------------|------------------|
| 413 | Seize the Day | USA | 1986 | Fielder Cook | 94 +V |
| 414 | De mujer a mujer | SP | 1950 | Luis Lucía | 85(93) |
| 415 | La forza bruta (aka: La force brutale) | IT/SP | 1941(40) | Carlo Ludovico Bragaglia | 84 |
| 416 | La hondradez de la cerradura | SP | 1950 | Luis Escobar | 88 |
| 417 | Lecciones de buen amor | SP | 1944(43) | Rafael Gil | 91(86) |
| 418 | La malquerida [The ill-loved] | SP | 1940 | José Lopéz Rubio | 93(94) |
| 419 | La malquerida | MEX | 1949 | Emilio Fernández | 83 |
| 420 | La mariposa que voló sobre el mar | SP | 1951(48) | Antonio de Obregón | 84 |
| 421 | El bailarín y el trabajador | SP | 1936 | Luis Marquina | 94 |
| 422 | La noche del sábado | SP | 1950 | Rafael Gil | 79 |
| 423 | ¡No quiero... No quiero! | SP | 1939(38) | Francisco Elías | 110(106) |
| 424 | Pepa Doncel | SP | 1970(69) | Luis Lucía | 101(97) |
| 425 | Rosas de otoño | SP | 1943 | Juan de Orduña | 72(61) |
| 426 | Señora ama | SP | 1954 | Julio Bracho | 90(82) |
| 427 | Vidas cruzadas | SP | 1942 | Luis Marquina | 70(60) |
| 428 | The Russians Are Coming, the Russians Are Coming | USA | 1966 | Norman Jewison | 125 |
| 429 | Sail a Crooked Ship | USA | 1962 | Irving Brecher | 86 |
| 430 | The Spirit Is Willing | USA | 1967(66) | William Castle | 94 |
| 431 | The Deep | USA/GB | 1977 | Peter Yates | 123 +V |
| 432 | The Island | USA | 1980 | Michael Ritchie | 114 +V |
| 433 | Jaws | USA | 1975 | Steven Spielberg | 125 +V |
| 434 | La tregua (The Truce) | ARG | 1974 | Sergio Renán | 108 |
| 435 | La cena delle beffe (The Jokers Banquet) | IT | 1941 | Alessandro Blasetti | 86 |
| 436 | All That Money Can Buy (aka: The Devil and Daniel Webster) | USA | 1941 | William Dieterle | 106 |
| 437 | Love, Honor and Behave | USA | 1938 | Stanley Logan | 72 |
| 438 | Just For You | USA | 1952 | Elliott Nugent | 104 |
| 439 | Seven Brides For Seven Brothers {musical version} | USA | 1954 | Stanley Donen | 104 +V |
| 440 | The Long Ships (YUGO: Dugi brodovi) | GB/YUGO | 1963 | Jack Cardiff | 124 +V(120) |
| 441 | His Double Life | USA | 1933 | Arthur Hopkins | 63 |
| 442 | Holy Matrimony | USA | 1943 | John M. Stahl | 87 |
| 443 | The Card (USA: The Promoter) | GB | 1952 | Ronald Neame | 91 +V |
| 444 | Dear Mr Prohack | GB | 1949 | Thornton Freeland | 91 |
| 445 | Meet Me in St. Louis {musical version} | USA | 1944 | Vincente Minnelli | 113 +V |
| 446 | Junior Miss | USA | 1945 | George Seaton | 94 |
| 447 | Play Me Something | GB | 1989 | Timothy Neat | 72 |
| 448 | Little Big Man | USA | 1970 | Arthur Penn | 139 +V |
| 449 | Neighbors | USA | 1981 | John G. Avildsen | 94 +V |
| 450 | Dollar | SWE | 1938 | Gustaf Molander | 78 |
| 451 | Flickan i frack (Girl in a Dress-Coat) | SWE | 1956 | Arne Mattsson | 99 |
| 452 | Hans nåds testamente | SWE | 1940 | Per Lindberg | 92 |
| 453 | Markurells i Wadköping (The Markurells of Wadköping) (GER: Väter und Söhne) (Father and Son) | SWE/GER | 1930-31 | Victor Sjöström | 96 |

| No. | Author | Nationality | Form | Literary Title | Date |
|-----|--------|-------------|------|----------------|------|
| 454 | **Bergman, Hjalmar** | Swedish | P | **Swedenhielms** (The Swedenhielms) | 1925 |
| 455 | **Bergman, Hjalmar** | Swedish | P | **Swedenhielms** | 1925 |
| 456 | **Bergman, Hjalmar** | Swedish | P | **Swedenhielms** | 1925 |
| 457 | **Bernanos, Georges** | French | N | **Journal d'un curé de campagne** (The Diary of a Country Priest) | 1936 |
| 458 | **Bernanos, Georges** | French | N | **Nouvelle histoire de Mouchette** (Mouchette) | 1937 |
| 459 | **Bernanos, Georges** | French | N | **Sous le soleil de Satan** (The Star of Satan) | 1926 |
| 460 | **Bersezio, Vittorio** | Italian | P | **Le miserie del signor Travetti** (aka: Le miserie d'Monssù Travet) | 1871 |
| 461 | **Berto, Giuseppe** | Italian | N | **Il brigante** | 1951 |
| 462 | **Berto, Giuseppe** | Italian | N | **Il cielo è rosso** (The Sky Is Red) | 1947 |
| 463 | **Berto, Giuseppe** | Italian | N | **La cosa buffa** (Antonio in Love) | 1966 |
| 464 | **Berto, Giuseppe** | Italian | N | **Oh Serafina!** | 1973 |
| 465 | **Bessa-Luís, Agustina** (Agustina Bessa Luís) | Portuguese | N | **Fanny Owen** | 1979 |
| 466 | **Betjeman, John** | British | V | **Agricultural Caress +** **Invasion Exercise on the Poultry Farm +** **Myfanwy +** **Subaltern's Love Song** | 1966+ 1945+ 1940 |
| 467 | **Betjeman, John** | British | V | **Indoor Games Near Newbury** | 1948 |
| 468 | **Betti, Ugo** | Italian | P | **Delitto all'isola della capre** (Crime on Goat Island) | 1946 |
| 469 | **Beyle, Marie Henri** (see: Stendhal) | French | N/SS | | |
| 470 | **Bieler, Manfred** | German | N | **Der Mädchenkrieg** | 1975 |
| 471 | **Bieler, Manfred** | German | N | **Maria Morzeck oder das Kaninchen bin ich** [Maria Morzeck, or I'm a bunny] | 1965; 1969 |
| 472 | **Bienek, Horst** | German | N | **Die erste Polka** (The First Polka) | 1975 |
| 473 | **Bienek, Horst** | German | N | **Die Zelle** | 1968 |
| 474 | **Bierce, Ambrose** | American | SS | **Boarded Window** | 1891 |
| 475 | **Bierce, Ambrose** | American | SS | **George Thurston** (aka: George Thurston; Three Incidents in the Life of a Man) | 1891 |
| 476 | **Bierce, Ambrose** | American | SS | **The Man and the Snake** | 1891 |
| 477 | **Bierce, Ambrose** | American | SS | **The Mockingbird +** **Chickamauga +** **An Occurrence at Owl Creek Bridge** | 1891 |
| 478 | **Bierce, Ambrose** | American | SS | **Parker Adderson, Philospher** | 1891 |
| 479 | **Binding, Rudolf Georg** | German | SS | **Moselfahrt aus liebeskummer** [Lovesick on the Mosell] | 1932 |
| 480 | **Binding, Rudolf Georg** | German | SS | **Der Opfergang** | 1911 |
| 481 | **Bioy Casares, Adolfo** | Argentine | N | **La invención di Morel** (The Invention of Morel) | 1940 |
| 482 | **Bioy Casares, Adolfo** | Argentine | SS | **Otra esperanza** | 1978 |
| 483 | **Bioy Casares, Adolfo** | Argentine | N | **El perjurio de la nieve** | 1945 |
| 484 | **Bitzius, Albert** (see: Gotthelf, Jeremias) | Swiss(Ger) | N | | |
| 485 | **Bjerke, André** (as: Bernhard Borge) | Norwegian | N | **De dødes tjern** (Death in the Blue Lake) | 1942 |
| 486 | **Bjørneboe, Jens** | Norwegian | N | **Den onde hyrde** [The evil shepherd] | 1960 |

| No | Film Title | Country of Production | Date | Director(s) | Duration of Film |
|---|---|---|---|---|---|
| 454 | **Swedenhielms** | SWE | 1935(34) | **Gustaf Molander** | 92 |
| 455 | **Ein glücklicher Mensch** (aka: Schule des Lebens) | GER | 1943 | **Paul Verhoeven** | 93 |
| 456 | **Familien Swedenhielm** | DEN | 1947(46) | **Lau Lauritzen** | 93 |
| 457 | **Le journal d'un curé de campagne** (Diary of a Country Priest) | FR | 1950 | **Robert Bresson** | 120(110) |
| 458 | **Mouchette** | FR | 1967(66) | **Robert Bresson** | 90 |
| 459 | **Sous le soleil de Satan** (Under Satan's Sun) | FR | 1987 | **Maurice Pialat** | 98 |
| 460 | **Le miserie del signor Travet** (His Young Wife) | IT | 1945 | **Mario Soldati** | 105 |
| 461 | **Il brigante** (The Brigand) | IT | 1961 | **Renato Castellani** | 180(143) |
| 462 | **Il cielo è rosso** (The Sky Is Red) | IT | 1950(49) | **Claudio Gora** | 95 |
| 463 | **La cosa buffa** | IT/FR | 1972 | **Aldo Lado** | 107 |
| 464 | **Bruciati da cocente passione** (Oh Serafina!) | IT | 1976 | **Alberto Lattuada** | 110(100) |
| 465 | **Francisca** | PORT | 1981 | **Manoel de Oliveira** | 166 |
| 466 | **Late Flowering** | GB | 1981 | **Charles Wallace** | 21 |
| 467 | **Indoor Games Near Newbury** | GB | 1976 | **Chris Clough** | 05 |
| 468 | **Les possédées** (The Possessed) (IT: L'isola della donne sole) | FR/IT | 1956(55) | **Charles Brabant** | 90 |
| 469 | | | | | |
| 470 | **Der Mädchenkrieg** (The Girls' War) | GER | 1977 | **Alf Brustellin** **Bernhard Sinker** | 143 |
| 471 | **Maria Morzek** | GER | 1976 | **Horst Flick** | 92 |
| 472 | **Die erste Polka** (The First Polka) | GER | 1978 | **Klaus Emmerich** | 105(96) |
| 473 | **Die Zelle** (The Cell) | GER | 1971 | **Horst Bienek** | 87 |
| 474 | **Boarded Window** | USA | 1973 | **Alan W. Beattie** | 17 +V |
| 475 | **Amerikai anzix** (American Torso) (aka: A View of America) | HUNG | 1976 | **Gábor Bódy** | 104 |
| 476 | **The Man and the Snake** | GB | 1972 | **Sture Rydman** | 26 |
| 477 | **Au coeur de la vie** {The 3 stories as separate episodes} | FR | 1962 | **Robert Enrico** | 95 |
| 478 | **Parker Adderson, Philosopher** | USA | 1977 | **Arthur Barron** | 38 +V |
| 479 | **Moselfahrt aus liebeskummer** | GER | 1953 | **Kurt Hoffmann** | 80 |
| 480 | **Opfergang** (The Great Sacrifice) | GER | 1944 | **Veit Harlan** | 98 |
| 481 | **L'invenzione di Morel** (Morel's Invention) | IT | 1974(73) | **Emidio Greco** | 110 |
| 482 | **Otra esperanza** (Another Hope) | ARG | 1991 | **Mercedes Frutos** | 90 |
| 483 | **El crimen de Oribe** (Oribe's Crime) | ARG | 1950(49) | **Leopoldo Torre Nilsson** **Leopoldo Torres Rios** | 85 |
| 484 | | | | | |
| 485 | **De dødes tjern** | NOR | 1958 | **Kåre Bergstrøm** | 77 |
| 486 | **Tonny** | NOR | 1962 | **Nils R. Müller** | 87 |

| No. | Author | Nationality | Form | Literary Title | Date |
|-----|--------|-------------|------|----------------|------|
| 487 | Bjørnson, Bjørnstjerne | Norwegian | SS | **En glad gutt** <br> *(The Happy Boy)* <br> *(aka: Ovind: a Story of Country Life)* | 1859 |
| 488 | Bjørnson, Bjørnstjerne | Norwegian | N | **Synnøve Solbakken** <br> *(Sunny Hill)* <br> *(aka: Trust and Trial)* | 1857 |
| 489 | Bjørnson, Bjørnstjerne | Norwegian | N | **Synnøve Solbakken** | 1857 |
| 490 | Blackmore, R. D. | British | N | **Lorna Doone** | 1869 |
| 491 | Blackmore, R. D. | British | N | **Lorna Doone** | 1869 |
| 492 | Blackmore, R. D. | British | N | **Lorna Doone** | 1869 |
| 493 | Blake, George | British(Scot) | N | **The Shipbuilders** | 1935 |
| 494 | Blasco Ibáñez, Vicente | Spanish | N | **La barraca** <br> *(The Cabin)* | 1898 |
| 495 | Blasco Ibáñez, Vicente | Spanish | N | **Cañas y barro** <br> *(Reeds and Mud)* | 1902 |
| 496 | Blasco Ibáñez, Vicente | Spanish | N | **Los cuatro jinetes del Apocalipsis** <br> *(The Four Horsemen of the Apocolypse)* | 1916 |
| 497 | Blasco Ibáñez, Vicente | Spanish | N | **Flor de mayo** <br> *(The Mayflower)* | 1895 |
| 498 | Blasco Ibáñez, Vicente | Spanish | N | **Mare nostrum** <br> *(Mare Nostrum - Our Sea)* | 1916 |
| 499 | Blasco Ibáñez, Vicente | Spanish | N | **Sangre y arena** <br> *(Blood and Sand)* <br> *(aka: The Blood of the Arena)* | 1908 |
| 500 | Bleasdale, Alan | British | P(TV) | **Boys From the Blackstuff** | 1983 |
| 501 | Blicher, Steen Steensen | Danish | SS | **Hosekræmmeren** | 1829 |
| 502 | Blicher, Steen Steensen | Danish | SS | **Hosekræmmeren** | 1829 |
| 503 | Blicher, Steen Steensen | Danish | SS | **Præsten i Vejlby** <br> *(The Parson of Vejlby)* | 1829 |
| 504 | Blicher, Steen Steensen | Danish | SS | **Præsten i Vejlby** | 1829 |
| 505 | Blicher, Steen Steensen | Danish | SS | **Sildig Opvaagnen** | 1828 |
| 506 | Blicher, Steen Steensen | Danish | N | **De tre Helligaftener** | 1840 |
| 507 | Blixen, Karen <br> *(see: Dinesen, Isak)* | Danish | SS/MEM | | |
| 508 | Bloch, Pedro | Brazilian | P | **Os pais abstratos** <br> *[The abstract parents]* | 1965 |
| 509 | Bloch, Robert | American | N | **Psycho** | 1959 |
| 510 | Bobrowski, Johannes | German | N | **Levins Mühle** <br> *(Levin's Mill)* | 1964 |
| 511 | Boccaccio, Giovanni | Italian | | **Il decameron** <br> *(The Decameron)* | 1349-50 |
| 512 | Boccaccio, Giovanni | Italian | | **Il decameron** | 1349-50 |
| 513 | Bodelsen, Anders | Danish | N | **Hændeligt uheld** <br> *(Hit and Run, Run, Run)* | 1968 |
| 514 | Bodelsen, Anders | Danish | SS | **Signalet** | 1965 |
| 515 | Bodelsen, Anders | Danish | N | **Tænk på et tal** <br> *(Think of a Number)* | 1968 |
| 516 | Bodelsen, Anders | Danish | N | **Tænk på et tal** | 1968 |
| 517 | Boex, Joseph-Henri <br> *(see: Rosny, J. H.)* | French | N | | |
| 518 | Bogza, Geo | Romanian | SS | **Sfîrşitul lui Iacob Onisia** <br> *(The End of Iacob Onisia)* | 1949 |
| 519 | Böhl von Faber, Cecilia <br> *(see: Caballero, Fernán)* | Spanish | N | | |
| 520 | Boito, Camillo | Italian | SS | **Senso** <br> *(A Thing Apart)* | 1882 |
| 521 | Bojer, Johan | Norwegian | P | **Sigurd Braa** | 1916 |
| 522 | Boland, Bridget | British | P | **Cockpit** | 1948 |
| 523 | Boland, Bridget | British | P | **The Prisoner** | 1954 |
| 524 | Boldrewood, Rolf <br> *(Thomas Alexander Browne)* | Australian | N | **Robbery Under Arms** | 1888(89) |

| No | Film Title | Country of Production | Date | Director(s) | Duration of Film |
|----|-----------|----------------------|------|-------------|-----------------|
| 487 | **En glad gutt** | NOR | 1932 | John W. Brunius | 96 |
| 488 | **Synnöve Solbakken** | SWE | 1935(34) | Tancred Ibsen | 81 |
| 489 | **Synnøve Solbakken** (Girl of Solbakken) | SWE | 1957 | Gunnar Hellström | 90 |
| 490 | **Lorna Doone** | GB | 1935(34) | Basil Dean | 80 |
| 491 | **Lorna Doone** | USA | 1951 | Phil Karlson | 84 |
| 492 | **Lorna Doone** | GB | 1990 | Andrew Grieve | 105 |
| 493 | **The Shipbuilders** | GB | 1943 | John Baxter | 89 |
| 494 | **La barraca** | MEX | 1945(44) | Roberto Gavaldón | 118 |
| 495 | **Cañas y barro** | SP | 1954 | Juan de Orduña | 100 |
| 496 | **Four Horsemen of the Apocalypse** | USA | 1962(61) | Vincente Minnelli | 153 |
| 497 | **Flor de mayo** (USA: Beyond All Limits) (GB: A Mexican Affair) | MEX | 1957 | Roberto Gavaldón | 100(82) |
| 498 | **Mare nostrum** (aka: Du sang à l'aube) | SP | 1948 | Rafael Gil | 90(100) +V |
| 499 | **Blood and Sand** | USA | 1941 | Rouben Mamoulian | 125 +V |
| 500 | **The Blackstuff** | GB | 1980 | Jim Goddard | 107 +V |
| 501 | **Hosekræmmeren** | DEN | 1963 | Max Hellner Johannes Vaabensted | 50 |
| 502 | **Hosekræmmeren** | DEN | 1971 | Knud Leif Thomsen | 84 |
| 503 | **Præsten i Vejlby** | DEN | 1931 | George Schnéevoigt | 107 |
| 504 | **Præsten i Vejlby** | DEN | 1972 | Claus Ørsted | 90 |
| 505 | **Elise** | DEN | 1985 | Claus Ploug | 106 |
| 506 | **Bejleren** | DEN | 1975 | Knud Leif Thomsen | 100 |
| 507 | | | | | |
| 508 | **Até que o casamento nos separe** [Till marriage do us part] | BRAZ | 1968 | Flavio Tambellini | 90 |
| 509 | **Psycho** | USA | 1960 | Alfred Hitchcock | 108 +V |
| 510 | **Levin's Mühle** (Levins Mill) | GDR | 1980 | Horst Seemann | 114 |
| 511 | **Decameron Nights** | GB | 1952 | Hugo Fregonese | 94 |
| 512 | **Il decameron** (The Decameron) | IT/FR/GER | 1971(70) | Pier Paolo Pasolini | 111 +V(107) |
| 513 | **Hændeligt uheld** | DEN | 1970 | Erik Balling | 106 |
| 514 | **Signalet** | DEN | 1966 | Ole Gammeltoft | 29 |
| 515 | **Tænk på et tal** | DEN | 1968 | Palle Kjærulff-Schmidt | 101 |
| 516 | **The Silent Partner** (aka: Double Deadly) | CAN | 1978 | Daryl Duke | 103 +V |
| 517 | | | | | |
| 518 | **Iacob** | ROM | 1987 | Mircea Daneliuc | 115 |
| 519 | | | | | |
| 520 | **Senso** (aka: The Wanton Contessa) | IT | 1954 | Luchino Visconti | 115(90) |
| 521 | **Sangen til livet** | NOR | 1943 | Leif Sinding | 108 |
| 522 | **The Lost People** | GB | 1949 | Bernard Knowles Muriel Box | 88 |
| 523 | **The Prisoner** | GB | 1955 | Peter Glenville | 94 |
| 524 | **Robbery Under Arms** | GB | 1957 | Jack Lee | 99 |

| No. | Author | Nationality | Form | Literary Title | Date |
|-----|--------|-------------|------|----------------|------|
| 525 | Boldrewood, Rolf | Australian | N | Robbery Under Arms | 1888(89) |
| 526 | Böll, Heinrich | German | N | Ansichten eines Clowns<br>(The Clown) | 1963 |
| 527 | Böll, Heinrich | German | N | Billard um halb zehn<br>(Billiards at Half Past Nine) | 1959 |
| 528 | Böll, Heinrich | German | N | Das Brot der frühen Jahre<br>(Bread of Those Early Years)<br>(aka: The Bread of Our Early Years) | 1955 |
| 529 | Böll, Heinrich | German | SS | Dr Murkes gesammeltes<br>Schweigen<br>(Dr Murke's Collected Silences) | 1958 |
| 530 | Böll, Heinrich | German | N | Gruppenbild mit Dame<br>(Group Portrait With Lady) | 1971 |
| 531 | Böll, Heinrich | German | SS | Hauptstädtisches Journal<br>(Bonn Diary) | 1957 |
| 532 | Böll, Heinrich | German | N | Die verlorene Ehre der Katharina<br>Blum<br>(The Lost Honour of Katharina Blum) | 1974 |
| 533 | Bolt, Robert | British | P | A Man For All Seasons | 1960 |
| 534 | Bolt, Robert | British | P | A Man For All Seasons | 1960 |
| 535 | Boothe, Clare<br>(Clare Boothe Luce) | American | P | Kiss the Boys Goodbye | 1939 |
| 536 | Boothe, Clare | American | P | Margin For Error | 1940 |
| 537 | Boothe, Clare | American | P | The Women | 1937 |
| 538 | Boothe, Clare | American | P | The Women | 1937 |
| 539 | Boothe Luce, Clare<br>(see: Boothe, Clare) | American | P | | |
| 540 | Borchert, Wolfgang | German | P | Draußen vor der Tür<br>(The Man Outside) | 1947 |
| 541 | Borge, Bernhard<br>(see: Bjerke, André) | Norwegian | N | | |
| 542 | Borges, Jorge Luis | Argentine | SS | Emma Zunz | 1949 |
| 543 | Borges, Jorge Luis | Argentine | SS | La intrusa | 1952(coll) |
| 544 | Borges, Jorge Luis | Argentine | SS | Tema del traidor y del héroe<br>[Theme of the hero and the traitor] | 1944 |
| 545 | Born, Nicholas | German | N | Die Fälschung | 1979 |
| 546 | Bost, Pierre | French | N | Monsieur Ladmiral va bientôt<br>mourir | 1945 |
| 547 | Boucicault, Dion | Irish | P | The Colleen Bawn<br>(aka: The Colleen Bawn; or,<br>the Brides of Garryowen) | 1864 |
| 548 | Boulle, Pierre | French | N | La planète des singes<br>(Planet of the Apes)<br>(aka: Monkey Planet) | 1963 |
| 549 | Boulle, Pierre | French | N | Le pont de la rivière Kwai<br>(The Bridge Over the River Kwai) | 1952 |
| 550 | Bourdet, Édouard | French | P | Fric-Frac<br>[Burglary] | 1937 |
| 551 | Bourdet, Édouard | French | P | Hyménée<br>[Marriage] | 1941 |
| 552 | Bourdet, Édouard | French | P | Le sexe faible<br>(The Sex Fable) | 1931 |
| 553 | Bourdet, Édouard | French | P | Vient de paraître<br>[Just published] | 1928 |
| 554 | Bowles, Paul | American | N | The Sheltering Sky | 1949 |
| 555 | Boyle, Kay | American | N | Avalanche | 1944 |
| 556 | Boyle, Kay | American | SS | Maiden, Maiden | 1957 |
| 557 | Braaten, Oskar | Norwegian | N+P | Bak høkerens disk {n} +<br>Godvakker - Maren {p} | 1918+<br>1927 |
| 558 | Braaten, Oskar | Norwegian | N+P | Bak høkerens disk {n} +<br>Ungen {p} | 1918+<br>1911 |
| 559 | Braaten, Oskar | Norwegian | N | Bak høkerens disk | 1918 |
| 560 | Braaten, Oskar | Norwegian | P | Bra mennesker<br>[Good people] | 1930 |

| No | Film Title | Country of Production | Date | Director(s) | Duration of Film |
|----|-----------|----------------------|------|-------------|------------------|
| 525 | **Robbery Under Arms** | AUSTL | 1985 | Ken Hannam<br>Donald Crombie | 141<br>+V(105) |
| 526 | **Ansichten eines Clowns**<br>(The Clown) | GER | 1975 | Vojtěch Jasný | 111 |
| 527 | **Nicht versöhnt oder Es hilft nur Gewalt, wo Gewalt herrscht**<br>(aka: Nicht versöhnt)<br>(Not Reconciled) | GER | 1965 | Jean-Marie Straub<br>Danièle Huillet | 55(53) |
| 528 | **Das Brot der frühen Jahre**<br>(The Bread of Our Early Years) | GER | 1962 | Herbert Vesely | 89(84) |
| 529 | **Dr Murkes samlade tystnad**<br>(Dr Murkes Collected Silences) | SWE | 1968 | Per Berglund | 29 |
| 530 | **Gruppenbild mit Dame** | GER/FR | 1976 | Aleksander Petrović | 103 |
| 531 | **Machorka-Muff** | GER | 1963(62) | Jean-Marie Straub<br>Danièle Huillet | 18 |
| 532 | **Die verlorene Ehre der Katharina Blum**<br>(The Lost Honour of Katharina Blum) | GER | 1975 | Volker Schlöndorff<br>Margarethe von Trotta | 105<br>+V |
| 533 | **A Man For All Seasons** | GB | 1966 | Fred Zinnemann | 120 +V |
| 534 | **A Man For All Seasons** | USA | 1988 | Charlton Heston | 150 +V |
| 535 | **Kiss the Boys Goodbye** | USA | 1941 | Victor Schertzinger | 85 |
| 536 | **Margin For Error** | USA | 1943 | Otto Preminger | 74 |
| 537 | **The Women** | USA | 1939 | George Cukor | 132 |
| 538 | **The Opposite Sex** | USA | 1956 | David Miller | 117 |
| 539 | | | | | |
| 540 | **Liebe 47**<br>(Love 47) | GER | 1949(48) | Wolfgang Liebeneiner | 118(110) |
| 541 | | | | | |
| 542 | **Días de odio**<br>(Days of Hate)<br>(aka: Days of Hatred) | ARG | 1954 | Leopoldo Torre Nilsson | 70 |
| 543 | **A intrusa** | BRAZ | 1979 | Carlos Hugo Christensen | 100 |
| 544 | **La strategia del ragno**<br>(The Spider's Strategem) | IT | 1970 | Bernardo Bertolucci | 97<br>+V |
| 545 | **Die Fälschung**<br>(The Forgery) | GER/FR | 1981 | Volker Schlöndorff | 110 |
| 546 | **Un dimanche à la campagne**<br>(A Sunday in the Country) | FR | 1984 | Bertrand Tavernier | 94 |
| 547 | **Lily of Killarney**<br>(USA: Bride of the Lake) | GB | 1934 | Maurice Elvey | 88 |
| 548 | **Planet of the Apes** | USA | 1968(67) | Franklin J. Schaffner | 112<br>+V |
| 549 | **The Bridge on the River Kwai** | GB | 1957 | David Lean | 161<br>+V |
| 550 | **Fric-Frac** | FR | 1939 | Maurice Lehmann<br>Claude Autant-Lara | 120 |
| 551 | **Hyménée** | FR | 1947 | Émile Couzinet | 95 |
| 552 | **Le sexe faible** | FR | 1933 | Robert Siodmak | 95 |
| 553 | **Vient de paraître** | FR | 1949 | Jacques Houssin | 97 |
| 554 | **The Sheltering Sky** | GB/IT | 1990 | Bernardo Bertolucci | 138 +V |
| 555 | **Avalanche** | USA | 1946 | Irving Allen | 70 |
| 556 | **Five Days One Summer** | USA | 1982 | Fred Zinnemann | 108 +V |
| 557 | **Godvakker-Maren** | NOR | 1940 | Knut Hergel | 89 |
| 558 | **Ungen** | NOR | 1974 | Barthold Halle | 122 |
| 559 | **Kjære Maren** | NOR | 1976 | Jan Erik Düring | 91 |
| 560 | **Bra mennesker** | NOR | 1937 | Leif Sinding | 92 |

| No. | Author | Nationality | Form | Literary Title | Date |
|-----|--------|-------------|------|----------------|------|
| 561 | Braaten, Oskar | Norwegian | P | Bra mennesker | 1930 |
| 562 | Braaten, Oskar | Norwegian | P | Den store barnedåpen<br>[The great christening ceremony] | 1925 |
| 563 | Braaten, Oskar | Norwegian | P | Ungen | 1911 |
| 564 | Bracco, Roberto | Italian | P | Sperduti nel buio<br>[Lost in the darkness] | 1906 |
| 565 | Bradbury, Ray | American | SS | Banshee +<br>The Crowd | 1988(coll)+<br>1943 |
| 566 | Bradbury, Ray | American | N | Fahrenheit 451 | 1953 |
| 567 | Bradbury, Ray | American | P | The Foghorn | 1951 |
| 568 | Bradbury, Ray | American | SS | I Sing the Body Electric! | 1969 |
| 569 | Bradbury, Ray | American | SS | The Long Rain +<br>The Veldt +<br>The Last Night of the World | 1950+<br>1951 |
| 570 | Bradbury, Ray | American | SS | The Murderer | 1953 |
| 571 | Bradbury, Ray | American | SS | The Screaming Woman +<br>The Playground | 1951+<br>1953 |
| 572 | Bradbury, Ray | American | N | Something Wicked This Way<br>Comes | 1962 |
| 573 | Braine, John | British | N | Life at the Top | 1962 |
| 574 | Braine, John | British | N | Room at the Top | 1957 |
| 575 | Braithwaite, E. R. | British | N | To Sir, With Love | 1957 |
| 576 | Brancati, Vitaliano | Italian | N | Il bell'Antonio<br>(Antonio, the Great Lover) | 1949 |
| 577 | Brancati, Vitaliano | Italian | N | Don Giovanni in Sicilia<br>[Don Juan in Sicily] | 1941 |
| 578 | Brancati, Vitaliano | Italian | N | Paolo il caldo | 1955 |
| 579 | Brancati, Vitaliano | Italian | SS | Il vecchio con gli stivali<br>[The old man with the boots] | 1944 |
| 580 | Branco, Camilo Castello<br>(see: Castello Branco, Camilo) | Portuguese | N | | |
| 581 | Brandão, Ignácio de Loyola<br>(Ignácio de Loyola) | Brazilian | SS | Ascensão ao mundo de Anuska<br>[Ascension to Anuska's world] | 1965 |
| 582 | Brandão, Ignácio de Loyola | Brazilian | N | Bebel que a cidade comeu<br>[Bebel - girl eaten by the city] | 1968 |
| 583 | Brandys, Kazimierz | Polish | SS | Jak być kochana | 1960 |
| 584 | Brandys, Kazimierz | Polish | N | Matka Królów<br>(Sons and Comrades) | 1957 |
| 585 | Brandys, Kazimierz | Polish | N | Samson | 1948 |
| 586 | Brandys, Kazimierz | Polish | N | Sposób bycia | 1963 |
| 587 | Branner, Hans Christian | Danish | P | Søskende<br>(The Judge) | 1952 |
| 588 | Breban, Nicolae | Romanian | N | Animale bolnave<br>[Sick animals] | 1968 |
| 589 | Brecht, Bertolt | German | SS | Der Arbeitsplatz oder Im<br>Schweisse deines Angesichts<br>sollst du kein Brot essen<br>(The Job...) | 1962 |
| 590 | Brecht, Bertolt | German | P | Baal | 1922 |
| 591 | Brecht, Bertolt | German | P | Die Dreigroschenoper<br>(The Threepenny Opera) | 1928 |
| 592 | Brecht, Bertolt | German | P | Die Dreigroschenoper | 1928 |
| 593 | Brecht, Bertolt | German | P | Furcht und Elend des Dritten<br>Reiches<br>(The Private Life of the Master Race)<br>(aka: Fear and Misery of the Third<br>Reich) | 1941(45) |

| No | Film Title | Country of Production | Date | Director(s) | Duration of Film |
|---|---|---|---|---|---|
| 561 | Det regnar på vår kärlek (It Rains On Our Love) (aka: The Man With an Umbrella) | SWE | 1946 | Ingmar Bergman | 95 |
| 562 | Den store barnedåpen | NOR | 1931 | Einer Sissener Tancred Ibsen | 105 |
| 563 | Ungen (The Child) | NOR | 1938 | Rasmus Breistein | 101 |
| 564 | Sperduti nel buio | IT | 1947 | Camillo Mastrocinque | 105 |
| 565 | Ray Bradbury's Nightmares Volume 2 | USA | 1985 | Douglas Jackson Ralph Thomas | 70 +V(57) |
| 566 | Fahrenheit 451 | GB | 1966 | François Truffaut | 112 |
| 567 | The Beast From 20,000 Fathoms | USA | 1953 | Eugène Lourié | 80 |
| 568 | The Electric Grandmother | USA | 1983 | Noel Black | 48 |
| 569 | The Illustrated Man | USA | 1969 | Jack Smight | 103 +V(94) |
| 570 | The Murderer | USA | 1976 | Andrew Silver | 28 |
| 571 | Ray Bradbury's Nightmares Volume 1 | USA | 1985 | Bruce Pittman William Fruet | 70 +V(57) |
| 572 | Something Wicked This Way Comes | USA | 1983 | Jack Clayton | 95 +V(91) |
| 573 | Life at the Top | GB | 1965 | Ted Kotcheff | 117 |
| 574 | Room at the Top | GB | 1959(58) | Jack Clayton | 117 +V |
| 575 | To Sir, With Love | GB | 1966 | James Clavell | 105 +V |
| 576 | Il bell'Antonio (Handsome Tony) (aka: Handsome Antonio) | IT/FR | 1960 | Mauro Bolognini | 105 |
| 577 | Don Giovanni in Sicilia | IT | 1967 | Alberto Lattuada | 104 |
| 578 | Paolo il caldo (The Sensual Man) (aka: The Sensuous Sicilian) | IT | 1973 | Marco Vicario | 120(124) |
| 579 | Anni difficili (USA: Difficult Years) (GB: The Little Man) | IT | 1948(47) | Luigi Zampa | 90(113) |
| 580 | | | | | |
| 581 | Anuska, manequim e mulher [Anuska, manikin and woman] | BRAZ | 1968 | Francisco Ramalho, Jr. | 95 |
| 582 | Bebel, garota propaganda [Bebel, advertising girl] | BRAZ | 1968 | Maurice Capovilla | 103 |
| 583 | Jak być kochana (How to Be Loved) | POL | 1963(62) | Wojciech Jerzy Has | 101 |
| 584 | Matka Królów [Mother of kings] | POL | 1987(82) | Janusz Zaorski | 126 |
| 585 | Samson | POL | 1961 | Andrzej Wajda | 117 |
| 586 | Sposób bycia (Frame of Mind) | POL | 1966(65) | Jan Rybkowski | 81 |
| 587 | Søskende | DEN | 1966 | Johan Jacobsen | 99 |
| 588 | Printre colinele verzi [In the green hills] | ROM | 1971 | Nicolae Breban | 95 |
| 589 | Tod und Auferstehung des Wilhelm Hausmann (Death and Resurrection of Wilhelm Hausmann) | GDR | 1977 | Christa Mühl | 76 |
| 590 | The Life Story of Baal | GB | 1978 | Edward Bennett | 57 |
| 591 | Die Dreigroschenoper (aka: Die 3 Groschenoper) (The Threepenny Opera) (aka: The Beggar's Opera) | GER | 1931 | G. W. Pabst | 112(100) |
| 592 | Die Dreigroschenoper (FR: L'opera de quat'sous) (The Threepenny Opera) | GER/FR | 1963 | Wolfgang Staudte | 124 |
| 593 | Ubitzi vykhodyat na dorogu (Murderers Are On Their Way) (aka: The Murderers Are Coming) | USSR | 1942 | Vsevolod Pudovkin E. Bolshintsov | 70 |

| No. | Author | Nationality | Form | Literary Title | Date |
|-----|--------|-------------|------|----------------|------|
| 594 | **Brecht, Bertolt** | German | N | **Die Geschäfte des Herrn Julius Caesar** *(The Business Deals of Mr Julius Caesar)* | 1957 |
| 595 | **Brecht, Bertolt** | German | P | **Leben des Galilei** *(The Life of Galileo)* | 1940-55 |
| 596 | **Brecht, Bertolt** | German | P | **Mutter Courage und ihre Kinder** *(Mother Courage and Her Children)* | 1949(41) |
| 597 | **Brecht, Bertolt** | German | SS | **Die unwürdige Greisin** *(The Unseemly Old Lady)* | 1949 |
| 598 | **Brecht, Bertolt; Wuolijoki, Hella** | German | P | **Herr Puntila und sein Knecht Matti** *(Mr Puntila and His Man Matti) (aka: Puntila and Matti, His Hired Man)* | 1948 |
| 599 | **Brecht, Bertolt; Wuolijoki, Hella** | German | P | **Herr Puntila und sein Knecht Matti** | 1948 |
| 600 | **Brickhill, Paul** | Australian | N | **The Great Escape** | 1950 |
| 601 | **Brickhill, Paul** | Australian | N | **Reach For the Sky** | 1954 |
| 602 | **Bridie, James** *(Osborne Henry Mavor)* | British(Scot) | P | **It Depends What You Mean** | 1948 |
| 603 | **Bridie, James** | British | P | **The Golden Legend of Shults** | 1942 |
| 604 | **Bridie, James** | British | P | **A Sleeping Clergyman** | 1933 |
| 605 | **Bridie, James** | British | P | **What Say They?** | 1939 |
| 606 | **Brieux, Eugène** | French | P | **Les avariés** *(Damaged Goods)* | 1902 |
| 607 | **Brieux, Eugène** | French | P | **L'avocat** | 1922 |
| 608 | **Brieux, Eugène** | French | P | **Blanchette** | 1892 |
| 609 | **Brieux, Eugène** | French | P | **La robe rouge** *(The Red Robe)* | 1900 |
| 610 | **Brighouse, Harold** | British | P | **Hobson's Choice** | 1916 |
| 611 | **Brighouse, Harold** | British | P | **Hobson's Choice** | 1916 |
| 612 | **Brink, André** | South African | N | **A Dry White Season** | 1979 |
| 613 | **Bródy Sándor** | Hungarian | P | **A tanítónő** | 1908 |
| 614 | **Brofeldt, Juhani** *(see: Aho, Juhani)* | Finnish | N | | |
| 615 | **Brøgger, Suzanne** | Danish | N | **Fri os fra Kærligheden** *(Deliver Us From Love)* | 1973 |
| 616 | **Bromfield, Louis** | American | SS | **Better Than Life** | 1939 |
| 617 | **Bromfield, Louis** | American | SS | **The Life of Vergie Winters** | 1929 |
| 618 | **Bromfield, Louis** | American | SS | **McLeod's Folly** *(aka: It Takes all Kinds)* | 1939 |
| 619 | **Bromfield, Louis** | American | N | **A Modern Hero** | 1932 |
| 620 | **Bromfield, Louis** | American | N | **Mrs Parkington** | 1943 |
| 621 | **Bromfield, Louis** | American | N | **The Rains Came** | 1937 |
| 622 | **Bromfield, Louis** | American | N | **The Rains Came** | 1937 |
| 623 | **Bromfield, Louis** | American | N | **Twenty-Four Hours** *(aka: Shattered Glass)* | 1930 |
| 624 | **Brontë, Charlotte** | British | N | **Jane Eyre** | 1847 |
| 625 | **Brontë, Charlotte** | British | N | **Jane Eyre** | 1847 |
| 626 | **Brontë, Charlotte** | British | N | **Jane Eyre** | 1847 |
| 627 | **Brontë, Emily Jane** | British | N | **Wuthering Heights** | 1847 |
| 628 | **Brontë, Emily Jane** | British | N | **Wuthering Heights** | 1847 |
| 629 | **Brontë, Emily Jane** | British | N | **Wuthering Heights** | 1847 |
| 630 | **Brontë, Emily Jane** | British | N | **Wuthering Heights** | 1847 |
| 631 | **Brown, Harry Peter M'Nab** | American | P | **A Sound of Hunting** | 1946 |
| 632 | **Brown, Harry Peter M'Nab** | American | N | **The Stars in Their Courses** | 1960 |
| 633 | **Brown, Harry Peter M'Nab** | American | N | **A Walk in the Sun** | 1944 |
| 634 | **Brown, Kenneth H.** | American | P | **The Brig** | 1964 |
| 635 | **Browne, Thomas Alexander** *(see: Boldrewood, Rolf)* | Australian | N | | |
| 636 | **Bruller, Jean** *(see: Vercors)* | French | N | | |

| No | Film Title | Country of Production | Date | Director(s) | Duration of Film |
|----|-----------|----------------------|------|-------------|------------------|
| 594 | **Geschichtsunterricht** (History Lessons) | IT/GER | 1972 | **Jean-Marie Straub** **Danièle Huillet** | 85 |
| 595 | **Galileo** | GB/CAN | 1976(74) | **Joseph Losey** | 145 |
| 596 | **Mutter Courage und ihre Kinder** (Mother Courage and Her Children) | GDR | 1961 | **Peter Palitzsch** **Manfred Wekwerth** {Berliner Ensemble production} | 149 |
| 597 | **La vieille dame indigne** (The Shameless Old Lady) | FR | 1965 | **René Allio** | 90 |
| 598 | **Herr Puntila und sein Knecht Matti** (Mr Puntila and His Servant Matti) | AUST | 1955 | **Alberto Cavalcanti** | 95 |
| 599 | **Herra Puntila ja hänen renkinsä Matti** | FIN | 1979 | **Ralf Långbacka** | 112 |
| 600 | **The Great Escape** | USA | 1963(62) | **John Sturges** | 165 +V |
| 601 | **Reach For the Sky** | GB | 1956 | **Lewis Gilbert** | 136 +V |
| 602 | **Folly To Be Wise** | GB | 1952 | **Frank Launder** | 91 |
| 603 | **There Was a Crooked Man** | GB | 1960 | **Stuart Burge** | 107 |
| 604 | **Flesh and Blood** | GB | 1951 | **Anthony Kimmins** | 102 |
| 605 | **You're Only Young Twice!** | GB | 1952 | **Terry Bishop** | 81 |
| 606 | **Marriage Forbidden** | USA | 1938 | **Phil Stone** | 62 |
| 607 | **Un coup de feu dans la nuit** | FR | 1943 | **Robert Péguy** | 87 |
| 608 | **Blanchette** | FR | 1936 | **Pierre Caron** | 89 |
| 609 | **La robe rouge** | FR | 1933 | **Jean de Marguenat** | 95 |
| 610 | **Hobson's Choice** | GB | 1931 | **Thomas Bentley** | 65 +V |
| 611 | **Hobson's Choice** | GB | 1954(53) | **David Lean** | 107 +V |
| 612 | **A Dry White Season** | USA | 1989 | **Euzhan Palcy** | 107 |
| 613 | **A tanítónő** (The Schoolmistress) | HUNG | 1945 | **Márton Keleti** | 69 |
| 614 | | | | | |
| 615 | **Violer er blå** (Violets Are Blue) | DEN | 1975 | **Peter Refn** | 120 |
| 616 | **It All Came True** | USA | 1940 | **Lewis Seiler** | 97 |
| 617 | **Life of Vergie Winters** | USA | 1934 | **Alfred Santell** | 82 |
| 618 | **Johnny Come Lately** (GB: Johnny Vagabond) | USA | 1943 | **William K. Howard** | 97 |
| 619 | **A Modern Hero** | USA | 1934 | **G. W. Pabst** | 70 |
| 620 | **Mrs Parkington** | USA | 1944 | **Tay Garnett** | 124 |
| 621 | **The Rains Came** | USA | 1939 | **Clarence Brown** | 103 |
| 622 | **The Rains of Ranchipur** | USA | 1955 | **Jean Negulesco** | 104 |
| 623 | **24 Hours** | USA | 1931 | **Marion Gering** | 65 |
| 624 | **Jane Eyre** | USA | 1934 | **Christy Cabanne** | 62 |
| 625 | **Jane Eyre** | USA | 1943 | **Robert Stevenson** | 97 |
| 626 | **Jane Eyre** | GB | 1970 | **Delbert Mann** | 110 |
| 627 | **Wuthering Heights** | USA | 1939 | **William Wyler** | 104 +V |
| 628 | **Abismos de pasión** (aka: Cumbres borrascosas) (Wuthering Heights) | MEX | 1953 | **Luis Buñuel** | 90 |
| 629 | **Wuthering Heights** | GB | 1970 | **Robert Fuest** | 104 +V |
| 630 | **Hurlevent** | FR | 1985 | **Jacques Rivette** | 130 |
| 631 | **Eight Iron Men** | USA | 1952 | **Edward Dmytryk** | 80 |
| 632 | **El Dorado** | USA | 1967(66) | **Howard Hawks** | 126 |
| 633 | **A Walk in the Sun** | USA | 1946(45) | **Lewis Milestone** | 117 |
| 634 | **The Brig** {Living Theatre production} | USA | 1964 | **Jonas Mekas** **Adolfas Mekas** | 68 |
| 635 | | | | | |
| 636 | | | | | |

| No. | Author | Nationality | Form | Literary Title | Date |
|---|---|---|---|---|---|
| 637 | Buchan, John | British(Scot) | N | The Thirty-Nine Steps | 1915 |
| 638 | Buchan, John | British | N | The Thirty-Nine Steps | 1915 |
| 639 | Buchan, John | British | N | The Thirty-Nine Steps | 1915 |
| 640 | Buchholtz, Johannes | Danish | N | Susanne | 1931 |
| 641 | Büchner, Georg | German | SS | Lenz | 1839 |
| 642 | Büchner, Georg | German | SS | Lenz | 1839 |
| 643 | Büchner, Georg | German | SS | Lenz | 1839 |
| 644 | Büchner, Georg | German | P | Woyzeck | 1879 |
| 645 | Büchner, Georg | German | P | Woyzeck | 1879 |
| 646 | Büchner, Georg | German | P | Woyzeck | 1879 |
| 647 | Büchner, Georg | German | P | Woyzeck | 1879 |
| 648 | Buck, Pearl | American | SS | The Big Wave | 1948 |
| 649 | Buck, Pearl | American | N | China Sky | 1942 |
| 650 | Buck, Pearl | American | N | The Dragon Seed | 1942 |
| 651 | Buck, Pearl | American | N | The Good Earth | 1931 |
| 652 | Buck, Pearl | American | N | Satan Never Sleeps (aka: The Devil Never Sleeps) | 1952 (aka:1962) |
| 653 | Buero Vallejo, Antonio | Spanish | P | Historie de una escalera [The story of a stairway] | 1950 |
| 654 | Buero Vallejo, Antonio | Spanish | P | Madrugada | 1954 |
| 655 | Bulgakov, Mikhail | Russian | N | Master i Margarita (The Master and Margarita) | 1966-67 |
| 656 | Bulgakov, Mikhail | Russian | SS | Sobach'e serdtse (Heart of a Dog) | 1968 |
| 657 | Bull, Jacob Breda | Norwegian | N | Jørund Smed | 1924 |
| 658 | Bulwer-Lytton, Edward George (Lytton, Edward Earl) | British | SS | The Haunted and the Haunters; or, The House and the Brain | 1849 |
| 659 | Bulwer-Lytton, Edward George | British | N | The Last Days of Pompeii | 1834 |
| 660 | Bulwer-Lytton, Edward George | British | N | The Last Days of Pompeii | 1834 |
| 661 | Bulwer-Lytton, Edward George | British | P | Richelieu: or, the Conspiracy | 1839 |
| 662 | Burgess, Anthony | British | N | A Clockwork Orange | 1962 |
| 663 | Burnett, Frances Hodgson | American/Br | N | Little Lord Fauntleroy | 1886 |
| 664 | Burnett, Frances Hodgson | American/Br | N | Little Lord Fauntleroy | 1886 |
| 665 | Burnett, Frances Hodgson | American/Br | N-P | A Little Princess {n} The Little Princess {p} | 1905{n}; 1911{p} |
| 666 | Burnett, Frances Hodgson | American/Br | N | The Secret Garden | 1911 |
| 667 | Burnett, William Riley | American | N | Adobe Walls | 1953 |
| 668 | Burnett, William Riley | American | N | Asphalt Jungle | 1949 |
| 669 | Burnett, William Riley | American | N | Asphalt Jungle | 1949 |
| 670 | Burnett, William Riley | American | N | Asphalt Jungle | 1949 |
| 671 | Burnett, William Riley | American | N | Asphalt Jungle | 1949 |
| 672 | Burnett, William Riley | American | N | Captain Lightfoot | 1954 |
| 673 | Burnett, William Riley | American | N | Dark Command; A Kansas Iliad | 1938 |
| 674 | Burnett, William Riley | American | N | Dark Hazard | 1933 |
| 675 | Burnett, William Riley | American | N | Dark Hazard | 1933 |
| 676 | Burnett, William Riley | American | N | Giant Swing | 1932 |
| 677 | Burnett, William Riley | American | N | High Sierra | 1940 |
| 678 | Burnett, William Riley | American | N | High Sierra | 1940 |
| 679 | Burnett, William Riley | American | N | High Sierra | 1940 |
| 680 | Burnett, William Riley | American | N | The Iron Man | 1930 |
| 681 | Burnett, William Riley | American | N | The Iron Man | 1930 |
| 682 | Burnett, William Riley | American | N | The Iron Man | 1930 |
| 683 | Burnett, William Riley | American | N | Little Caesar | 1929 |
| 684 | Burnett, William Riley | American | N | Nobody Lives Forever | 1943 |
| 685 | Burnett, William Riley | American | N | Saint Johnson | 1930 |
| 686 | Burnett, William Riley | American | N | Saint Johnson | 1930 |

| No | Film Title | Country of Production | Date | Director(s) | Duration of Film |
|----|-----------|----------------------|------|-------------|------------------|
| 637 | **The 39 Steps** | GB | 1935 | **Alfred Hitchcock** | 87 +V |
| 638 | **The 39 Steps** | GB | 1959 | **Ralph Thomas** | 93 +V |
| 639 | **The Thirty-Nine Steps** | GB | 1978 | **Don Sharp** | 102 +V |
| 640 | **Susanne** | DEN | 1950 | **Torben Anton Svendsen** | 102 |
| 641 | **Lenz** | GER | 1971(70) | **George Moorse** | 130(125) |
| 642 | **Lenz** | USA | 1981 | **Alexandre Rockwell** | 95 |
| 643 | **Lenz** | HUNG | 1987 | **András Szirtes** | 99 |
| 644 | **Der Fall Wozzeck** (aka: Wozzeck) | GER | 1947 | **Georg C. Klaren** | 97(70) |
| 645 | **Woyzeck** | GER | 1967 | **Rudolf Noelte** | 90 |
| 646 | **Woyzeck** | GER | 1979 | **Werner Herzog** | 82 +V |
| 647 | **Woyzeck** | GER | 1984(83) | **Oliver Herbrich** | 82 |
| 648 | **The Big Wave** | USA/JAP | 1962 | **Tad Danielewski** | 60 |
| 649 | **China Sky** | USA | 1945 | **Ray Enright** | 87 |
| 650 | **The Dragon Seed** | USA | 1944 | **Jack Conway** **Harold S. Bucquet** | 144 |
| 651 | **The Good Earth** | USA | 1937 | **Sidney A. Franklin** | 136 +V |
| 652 | **The Devil Never Sleeps** (USA: Satan Never Sleeps) (aka: China Story) | GB | 1962 | **Leo McCarey** | 126 |
| 653 | **Historie de una escalera** | SP | 1950 | **Ignacio Ferrés Iquino** | 87 |
| 654 | **Madrugada** | SP | 1957 | **Antonio Román** | 85(88) |
| 655 | **Majstor i Margarita** (IT: Maestro i Margherita) (The Master and Margarita) | YUGO/IT | 1972 | **Aleksander Petrović** | 95(100) |
| 656 | **Cuore di cane** (GER: Warum bellt Herr Bobikow?) [Why is Mr Bobikow barking?] | IT/GER | 1976 | **Alberto Lattuada** | 113(110) |
| 657 | **Jørund Smed** (Dit vindarna bär) | NOR | 1948 | **Åke Ohberg** | 88 |
| 658 | **Night Comes Too Soon** | GB | 1948 | **Denis Kavanagh** | 52 |
| 659 | **The Last Days of Pompeii** | USA | 1935 | **Ernest B. Schoedsack** | 96 +V |
| 660 | **Gli ultimi giorni di Pompei** (SP: Los ultimos dias de Pompeya) (GER: Die letzten Tage von Pompeji) (The Last Days of Pompeii) | IT/SP/GER | 1959 | **Mario Bonnard** | 105(98) +V(90) |
| 661 | **Cardinal Richelieu** | USA | 1935 | **Rowland V. Lee** | 83 |
| 662 | **A Clockwork Orange** | GB | 1971 | **Stanley Kubrick** | 136 |
| 663 | **Little Lord Fauntleroy** | USA | 1936 | **John Cromwell** | 98 |
| 664 | **Little Lord Fauntleroy** | GB | 1980 | **Jack Gold** | 103 +V |
| 665 | **The Little Princess** (aka: Sarah Crewe) | USA | 1939 | **Walter Lang** | 93 |
| 666 | **The Secret Garden** | USA | 1949 | **Fred M. Wilcox** | 92 |
| 667 | **Arrowhead** | USA | 1953 | **Charles Marquis Warren** | 105 |
| 668 | **Asphalt Jungle** | USA | 1950 | **John Huston** | 112 |
| 669 | **The Badlanders** | USA | 1958 | **Delmer Daves** | 83 |
| 670 | **Cairo** | GB | 1963 | **Wolf Rilla** | 91 |
| 671 | **Cool Breeze** | USA | 1972 | **Barry Pollack** | 102 +V |
| 672 | **Captain Lightfoot** | USA | 1955 | **Douglas Sirk** | 91 |
| 673 | **Dark Command** | USA | 1940 | **Raoul Walsh** | 92 +V |
| 674 | **Dark Hazard** | USA | 1934 | **Alfred E. Green** | 72 |
| 675 | **Wine, Women and Horses** | USA | 1937 | **Louis King** | 64 |
| 676 | **Dance Hall** | USA | 1941 | **Irving Pichel** | 74 |
| 677 | **High Sierra** | USA | 1941 | **Raoul Walsh** | 100 +V |
| 678 | **Colorado Territory** | USA | 1949 | **Raoul Walsh** | 93 |
| 679 | **I Died a Thousand Times** | USA | 1955 | **Stuart Heisler** | 109 |
| 680 | **The Iron Man** | USA | 1931 | **Tod Browning** | 73 |
| 681 | **Some Blondes Are Dangerous** | USA | 1937 | **Milton Carruth** | 66 |
| 682 | **The Iron Man** | USA | 1951 | **Joseph Pevney** | 81 |
| 683 | **Little Caesar** | USA | 1930 | **Mervyn LeRoy** | 80 +V |
| 684 | **Nobody Lives Forever** | USA | 1946 | **Jean Negulesco** | 100 |
| 685 | **Law and Order** | USA | 1932 | **Edward L. Cahn** | 80(66) |
| 686 | **Law and Order** (aka: The Law) | USA | 1940 | **Ray Taylor** | 57 |

| No. | Author | Nationality | Form | Literary Title | Date |
|-----|--------|-------------|------|----------------|------|
| 687 | **Burnett, William Riley** | American | N | **Saint Johnson** | 1930 |
| 688 | **Burnett, William Riley** | American | N | **Vanity Row** | 1952 |
| 689 | **Burns, Robert E.** | American | N | **I Am a Fugitive From a Georgia Chain Gang!** | 1932 |
| 690 | **Burroughs, Edgar Rice** | American | N | **At the Earth's Core** | 1922 |
| 691 | **Burroughs, Edgar Rice** | American | N | **The Land That Time Forgot** | 1924 |
| 692 | **Burroughs, Edgar Rice** | American | N | **Tarzan of the Apes** | 1914 |
| 693 | **Burroughs, Edgar Rice** | American | N | **Tarzan of the Apes** | 1914 |
| 694 | **Burroughs, Edgar Rice** | American | N | **Tarzan of the Apes** | 1914 |
| 695 | **Burroughs, Edgar Rice** | American | N | **Tarzan of the Apes** | 1914 |
| 696 | **Busch, Wilhelm** | German | SS | **Abenteuer eines Junggesellen** | 1875 |
| 697 | **Busch, Wilhelm** | German | SS(V) | **Die fromme Helene** *(Pious Jemima)* | 1872 |
| 698 | **Busch, Wilhelm** | German | SS(V) | **Max und Moritz: eine Bubengeschicte in sieben Streichen** *(Max and Maurice, a Juvenile History in Seven Tricks)* | 1865 |
| 699 | **Busch, Wilhelm** | German | SS(V) | **Max und Moritz: eine Bubengeschicte in sieben Streichen** | 1865 |
| 700 | **Butor, Michel** | French | N | **La modification** *(Second Thoughts)* | 1957 |
| 701 | **Buzura, Augustin** | Romanian | N | **Orgolii** *[Pride]* | 1977 |
| 702 | **Buzzati, Dino** | Italian | N | **Un amore** *(A Love Affair)* | 1963 |
| 703 | **Buzzati, Dino** | Italian | N | **Il deserto dei Tartari** *(The Tartar Steppe)* | 1940 |
| 704 | **Caballero, Fernán** *(Cecilia Böhl von Faber)* | Spanish | N | **La familia Alvareda** *(Alvareda Family)* | 1856 |
| 705 | **Cahan, Abraham** | American | N | **Yekl** *(aka: Yekl, a Tale of the New York Ghetto)* | 1896 |
| 706 | **Cain, James M.** | American | SS | **Baby in the Icebox** | 1932 |
| 707 | **Cain, James M.** | American | N | **The Butterfly** | 1947 |
| 708 | **Cain, James M.** | American | SS | **Career in C Major** | 1943(coll) |
| 709 | **Cain, James M.** | American | SS | **Career in C Major** | 1943 |
| 710 | **Cain, James M.** | American | N | **Double Indemnity** | 1943 |
| 711 | **Cain, James M.** | American | N | **The Embezzler** | 1943(coll) |
| 712 | **Cain, James M.** | American | N | **Love's Lovely Counterfeit** | 1942 |
| 713 | **Cain, James M.** | American | N | **Mildred Pierce** | 1941 |
| 714 | **Cain, James M.** | American | N | **The Postman Always Rings Twice** | 1934 |
| 715 | **Cain, James M.** | American | N | **The Postman Always Rings Twice** | 1934 |
| 716 | **Cain, James M.** | American | N | **The Postman Always Rings Twice** | 1934 |
| 717 | **Cain, James M.** | American | N | **The Postman Always Rings Twice** | 1934 |
| 718 | **Cain, James M.** | American | N | **Serenade** | 1937 |
| 719 | **Calderón de la Barca, Pedro** | Spanish | P | **El alcalde de Zalamea** *(The Mayor of Zalamea)* *(aka: El garrote más bien dado)* | 1651 |
| 720 | **Calderón de la Barca, Pedro** | Spanish | P | **El alcalde de Zalamea** | 1651 |
| 721 | **Calderón de la Barca, Pedro** | Spanish | P | **La dama duende** *(The Phantom Lady)* | 1647 |
| 722 | **Calderón de la Barca, Pedro** | Spanish | P | **La vida es sueño** *(Life's a Dream)* *(aka: Life Is a Dream)* | 1647 |
| 723 | **Calderón de la Barca, Pedro** | Spanish | P | **La vida es sueño** | 1647 |

| No | Film Title | Country of Production | Date | Director(s) | Duration of Film |
|----|-----------|----------------------|------|-------------|-----------------|
| 687 | Law and Order | USA | 1953 | Nathan Juran | 80 |
| 688 | Accused of Murder | USA | 1956 | Joseph Kane | 76 |
| 689 | I Am a Fugitive From a Chain Gang (aka: I Am a Fugitive) | USA | 1932 | Mervyn LeRoy | 91 |
| 690 | At the Earth's Core | GB | 1976 | Kevin Connor | 90 +V |
| 691 | The Land That Time Forgot | GB | 1975(74) | Kevin Connor | 91 +V |
| 692 | Tarzan, the Ape Man | USA | 1932 | W. S. Van Dyke | 99 |
| 693 | Tarzan, the Ape Man | USA | 1959 | Joseph M. Newman | 82 |
| 694 | Tarzan, the Ape Man | USA | 1981 | John Derek | 112 +V |
| 695 | Greystoke (aka: Greystoke: the Legend of Tarzan, Lord of the Apes) | USA | 1984 | Hugh Hudson | 129 +V |
| 696 | Tobias Knopp - Abenteuer eines Junggesellen | GER | 1949 | Gerhard Fieber Wolfgang Liebeneiner | 76 |
| 697 | Die fromme Helene | GER | 1965 | Axel von Ambesser | 91 |
| 698 | Spuk mit Max und Moritz | GER | 1951 | Ferdinand Diehl | 57 |
| 699 | Max und Moritz {musical version} | GER | 1956 | Norbert Schultze | 73 |
| 700 | La modification (IT: La moglie nuova) | FR/IT | 1970 | Michel Worms | 90 |
| 701 | Orgolii | ROM | 1982 | Manole Marcus | 116 |
| 702 | Un amore | FR/IT | 1965 | Gianni Vernuccio | 97(94) |
| 703 | Il deserto dei Tartari (FR: Le désert des Tartares) (GER: Die Tatarenwüste) (The Desert of the Tartars) | IT/FR/ IRE/GER | 1977(76) | Valerio Zurlini | 148 |
| 704 | Luna de sangre | SP | 1952(50) | Francisco Rovira Beleta | 90(95) |
| 705 | Hester Street | USA | 1974 | Joan Micklin Silver | 86 |
| 706 | She Made Her Bed | USA | 1934 | Ralph Murphy | 70 |
| 707 | Butterfly | USA | 1981 | Matt Cimber | 108 +V |
| 708 | Wife, Husband and Friend | USA | 1939 | Gregory Ratoff | 80 |
| 709 | Everybody Does It | USA | 1949 | Edmund Goulding | 98 |
| 710 | Double Indemnity | USA | 1944 | Billy Wilder | 107 |
| 711 | Money and the Woman | USA | 1940 | William K. Howard | 80 |
| 712 | Slightly Scarlet | USA | 1956(55) | Allan Dwan | 92 |
| 713 | Mildred Pierce | USA | 1945 | Michael Curtiz | 111 |
| 714 | Le dernier tournant (The Postman Always Rings Twice) (aka: The Last Bend) | FR | 1939 | Pierre Chenal | 90 |
| 715 | Ossessione | IT | 1942 | Luchino Visconti | 140 +V |
| 716 | The Postman Always Rings Twice | USA | 1946 | Tay Garnett | 113 |
| 717 | The Postman Always Rings Twice | USA | 1981 | Bob Rafelson | 121 +V |
| 718 | Serenade | USA | 1956 | Anthony Mann | 121 |
| 719 | El alcalde de Zalamea | SP | 1953 | José G. Maesso | 80(84) |
| 720 | Der Richter von Zalamea | GDR | 1956 | Martin Hellberg | 103 |
| 721 | La dama duende (The Phantom Lady) | ARG | 1945 | Luis Saslavsky | 101 |
| 722 | El principe encadenado | SP | 1960 | Luis Lucía | 100 |
| 723 | Memoire des apparences: la vie est un songe (Life Is a Dream) | FR | 1987(86) | Râúl Ruiz | 105 |

| No. | Author | Nationality | Form | Literary Title | Date |
|-----|--------|-------------|------|----------------|------|
| 724 | Caldwell, Erskine | American | N | Claudelle Inglish<br>*(aka: Claudelle)* | 1958<br>(aka:1959) |
| 725 | Caldwell, Erskine | American | N | God's Little Acre | 1933 |
| 726 | Caldwell, Erskine | American | N | Tobacco Road | 1932 |
| 727 | Călinescu, George | Romanian | N | Bietul Ioanide<br>*[The unfortunate Ioanide]* +<br>Scrinul negru<br>*[The black chest of drawers]* | 1953+<br>1960 |
| 728 | Călinescu, George | Romanian | N | Enigma Otiliei<br>*[Otilia's secret]* | 1938 |
| 729 | Callado, Antônio | Brazilian | N | Madona de cedro | 1957 |
| 730 | Callado, Antônio | Brazilian | P | Pedro Mico, zumbi do<br>Catacumba | 1957 |
| 731 | Callado, Antônio | Brazilian | N | Quarup | 1967 |
| 732 | Calvino, Italo | Italian | N | Il cavaliere inesistente<br>*(The Nonexistent Knight)* | 1959 |
| 733 | Calvo Sotelo, Joaquín | Spanish | P | Cartas credenciales +<br>Operación Embajada | 1961+<br>1962 |
| 734 | Calvo Sotelo, Joaquín | Spanish | P | Cuando llegue la noche | 1944 |
| 735 | Calvo Sotelo, Joaquín | Spanish | P | Milagro en la Plaza del Progreso | 1954 |
| 736 | Calvo Sotelo, Joaquín | Spanish | P | Una muchachita de Valladolid | 1957 |
| 737 | Calvo Sotelo, Joaquín | Spanish | P | La muralla<br>*[The wall]* | 1955 |
| 738 | Calvo Sotelo, Joaquín | Spanish | P | Plaza de Oriente | 1947 |
| 739 | Calvo Sotelo, Joaquín | Spanish | P | La visita que no tocó el timbre<br>*[The caller who didn't ring the bell]* | 1951 |
| 740 | Calvo Sotelo, Joaquín;<br>Mihura Santos, Miguel | Spanish | P | ¡Viva lo imposible! | 1951 |
| 741 | Camargo, Joracy | Brazilian | P | O bôbo do rei<br>*[The king's jester]* | 1932 |
| 742 | Camargo, Joracy | Brazilian | P | Deus lhe pague<br>*[May God repay you]* | 193- |
| 743 | Campbell, William March<br>*(joint, see: Anderson, Maxwell)* | American | P | | |
| 744 | Campoamor, Ramón de | Spanish | V | El tren expreso | 1872-74 |
| 745 | Camus, Albert | French | N | La chute<br>*(The Fall)* | 1956 |
| 746 | Camus, Albert | French | N | L'étranger<br>*(The Outsider)*<br>*(USA: The Stranger)* | 1942 |
| 747 | Camus, Albert | French | SS | Les muets | 1957 |
| 748 | Cândido de Carvalho, José<br>*(see: Carvalho, José Cândido de)* | Brazilian | N | | |
| 749 | Cankar, Ivan | Yugoslav(Slov) | N | Martin Kačur | 1906 |
| 750 | Cankar, Ivan | Yugoslav | N | Na klancu<br>*[On the slope]* | 1902 |
| 751 | Cao Xueqin<br>*(see: Cao Zhan)* | Chinese | N | | |
| 752 | Cao Yu<br>*(see: Wan Jiabao)* | Chinese | P | | |
| 753 | Cao Zhan<br>*(Ts'ao Chan)*<br>*(as: Cao Xueqin)*<br>*(Ts'ao Hsüeh ch'in)* | Chinese | N | Hong lou meng<br>*(Dream of the Red Chamber)* | c.1750-92 |
| 754 | Cao Zhan<br>*(as: Cao Xueqin)* | Chinese | N | Hong lou meng | c.1750-92 |
| 755 | Cao Zhan<br>*(as: Cao Xueqin)* | Chinese | N | Hong lou meng | c.1750-92 |
| 756 | Cao Zhan<br>*(as: Cao Xueqin)* | Chinese | N | Hong lou meng | c.1750-92 |
| 757 | Čapek, Karel | Czech | P | Bílá nemoc<br>*(Power and Glory)* | 1937 |

| No | Film Title | Country of Production | Date | Director(s) | Duration of Film |
|----|-----------|----------------------|------|-------------|------------------|
| 724 | Claudelle Inglish (GB: Young and Eager) | USA | 1961 | Gordon Douglas | 99 |
| 725 | God's Little Acre | USA | 1958 | Anthony Mann | 110 +V |
| 726 | Tobacco Road | USA | 1941 | John Ford | 84 |
| 727 | Ioanide | ROM | 1980(79) | Dan Piţa | 121 |
| 728 | Felix şi Otilia (Felix and Otilia) | ROM | 1972 | Iulian Mihu | 146 |
| 729 | A madona de cedro (The Cedar Madona) | BRAZ | 1968(67) | Carlos Coimbra | 106(110) |
| 730 | Pedro Mico [Monkey Pete] | BRAZ | 1985 | Ipojuca Pontes | 99 |
| 731 | Kuarup | BRAZ | 1989 | Rui Guerra | 116 |
| 732 | Il cavaliere inesistente (Nonexistent Knight) (aka: Imaginary Knight) {part animation} | IT | 1970(69) | Pino Zac | 90(97) |
| 733 | Operación Embajada | SP | 1963 | Fernando Palacios | 82(89) |
| 734 | Cuando llegue la noche | SP | 1946 | Jerónimo Mihura | 111(105) |
| 735 | Un angel tuvo la culpa | SP | 1960(59) | Luis Lucía | 100(92) |
| 736 | Una muchachita de Valladolid | SP | 1958 | Luis César Amadori | 95(90) |
| 737 | La muralla | SP | 1958 | Luis Lucía | 80(96) |
| 738 | Plaza de Oriente | SP | 1963(62) | Mateo Cano | 77(92) |
| 739 | La visita que no tocó el timbre (aka: La visita que no llamó al timbre) | SP | 1965 | Mario Camús | 97(96) |
| 740 | ¡Viva lo imposible! | SP | 1958(57) | Rafael Gil | 98(95) |
| 741 | O bôbo do rei | BRAZ | 1936 | Mesquitinha | 92 |
| 742 | Diós se lo pague | ARG | 1948 | Luís César Amadori | 103 |
| 743 | | | | | |
| 744 | El tren expreso | SP | 1955(54) | León Klimovsky | 92(81) |
| 745 | De val | HOLL | 1972 | Adriaan Ditvoorst | 30 |
| 746 | Lo straniero (FR: L'étranger) (The Stranger) (aka: The Outsider) | IT/FR/ALG | 1967 | Luchino Visconti | 104(110) |
| 747 | Le parole a venire | IT | 1970 | Peter del Monte | 54 |
| 748 | | | | | |
| 749 | Idealist | YUGO | 1976 | Igor Pretnar | 121 |
| 750 | Na klancu [At the ravine] | YUGO | 1971 | Vojko Duletič | 100 |
| 751 | | | | | |
| 752 | | | | | |
| 753 | Wang Xifeng danao ning-kuofu [Lady Wang Xifeng makes trouble in the Mansion House] | CHN | 1939 | Yue Feng (Yueh Feng) | 90 |
| 754 | Hong lou meng (Dream of the Red Chamber) | CHN | 1962 | Chen Fan | 169 |
| 755 | You San Jie [The third Lady You] {episode} | CHN | 1963 | Wu Yonggang | 129 |
| 756 | Hong lou meng (Dreams of the Red Chamber) | CHN | 1990 | Xie Tieli | 480 |
| 757 | Bílá nemoc (Skeleton on Horseback) (aka: The White Disease) | CZ | 1937 | Hugo Haas | 78 |

| No. | Author | Nationality | Form | Literary Title | Date |
|-----|--------|-------------|------|----------------|------|
| 758 | Čapek, Karel | Czech | N | Hordubal | 1933 |
| 759 | Čapek, Karel | Czech | N | Krakatit<br>(aka: An Atomic Fantasy) | 1924 |
| 760 | Čapek, Karel | Czech | N | Krakatit | 1924 |
| 761 | Čapek, Karel | Czech | N | První parta<br>(The First Rescue Party) | 1937 |
| 762 | Capote, Truman | American | SS | Among the Paths To Eden +<br>Miriam +<br>A Christmas Memory | 1960+<br>1944+<br>1946 |
| 763 | Capote, Truman | American | SS | Breakfast at Tiffany's | 1958 |
| 764 | Capote, Truman | American | N(NF) | In Cold Blood | 1966 |
| 765 | Capuana, Luigi | Italian | N | Il marchese di Roccaverdina<br>(The Marquis of Roccaverdina) | 1901 |
| 766 | Caragiale, Ion Luca | Romanian | SS | Arendaşul român<br>[The Romanian leaseholder] | 1893 |
| 767 | Caragiale, Ion Luca | Romanian | SS | O conferenţă<br>[Conference] +<br>Diplomaţie<br>[Diplomacy] +<br>C.F.R. + Bubico +<br>Amicii<br>[Friends] +<br>O lacună + Situatiunea | 1899-<br>1909 |
| 768 | Caragiale, Ion Luca | Romanian | P | D'ale carnavalului<br>(Carnival Scenes) +<br>Conul Leonida faţă cu reacţiunea<br>(Master Leonida Versus Reaction) | 1885+<br>1880 |
| 769 | Caragiale, Ion Luca | Romanian | P | D'ale carnavalului | 1885 |
| 770 | Caragiale, Ion Luca | Romanian | SS | Două loturi<br>[Two lottery prizes]<br>(aka: Două bilete pierdute) | 1901<br>(aka:1898) |
| 771 | Caragiale, Ion Luca | Romanian | SS | O făclie de Paşte<br>(The Easter Torch) | 1890 |
| 772 | Caragiale, Ion Luca | Romanian | SS | O făclie de Paşte | 1890 |
| 773 | Caragiale, Ion Luca | Romanian | SS | În vreme de război<br>(In Time of War) | 1898-99 |
| 774 | Caragiale, Ion Luca | Romanian | SS | La hanul lui Mînjoală<br>(At Manjoală's Inn) | 1898 |
| 775 | Caragiale, Ion Luca | Romanian | SS | Lanţul slăbiciunilor<br>[Soft spots] | 1901 |
| 776 | Caragiale, Ion Luca | Romanian | P | Năpasta<br>[The misfortune] | 1890 |
| 777 | Caragiale, Ion Luca | Romanian | P | O noapte furtunoasă<br>[A stormy night]<br>(aka: O noapte furtunoasă sau<br>numărul 9)<br>[A stormy night or number 9] | 1879 |
| 778 | Caragiale, Ion Luca | Romanian | P | O scrisoare pierdută<br>(A Lost Letter) | 1885(89) |
| 779 | Caragiale, Ion Luca | Romanian | SS | Telegrame<br>[Telegrams] | 1899 |
| 780 | Caragiale, Ion Luca | Romanian | SS | Vizită<br>[A visit] | 1901 |
| 781 | Carballido, Emilio | Mexican | N | Las visitaciones del diablo<br>[The visitations of the devil] | 1965 |
| 782 | Carco, Francis<br>(Francis Carcopino-Tusoli) | French | N | L'homme traqué<br>(The Hounded Man)<br>(aka: The Noose of Sin) | 1922 |
| 783 | Carco, Francis | French | N | Jésus la Caille | 1914 |
| 784 | Carco, Francis | French | N | L'ombre | 1933 |
| 785 | Carco, Francis | French | N | Prisons de femmes | 1930 |
| 786 | Carco, Francis | French | N | Prisons de femmes | 1930 |
| 787 | Carco, Francis | French | N | Prisons de femmes | 1930 |
| 788 | Carcopino-Tusoli, Francis<br>(see: Carco, Francis) | French | N | | |

| No | Film Title | Country of Production | Date | Director(s) | Duration of Film |
|----|-----------|----------------------|------|-------------|------------------|
| 758 | Hordubalové<br>(The Brothers Hordubal)<br>(aka: The Hordubals) | CZ | 1937 | Martin Frič | 97 |
| 759 | Krakatit | CZ | 1948 | Otakar Vávra | 104 |
| 760 | Black Sun | SWE/YUGO | 1978 | Arne Mattsson | 100 |
| 761 | První parta<br>(The First Rescue Party) | CZ | 1959 | Otakar Vávra | 95 |
| 762 | Truman Capote's Trilogy<br>(aka: Trilogy) | USA | 1969 | Frank Perry | 99 |
| 763 | Breakfast at Tiffany's | USA | 1961 | Blake Edwards | 115 +V |
| 764 | In Cold Blood | USA | 1967 | Richard Brooks | 134 |
| 765 | Gelosia<br>(Jealousy) | IT | 1953 | Pietro Germi | 95 |
| 766 | Arendaşul român | ROM | 1952 | Jean Georgescu | 07 |
| 767 | Mofturi 1900<br>[Trifles 1900] | ROM | 1965 | Jean Georgescu | 75 |
| 768 | D'ale carnavalului<br>(Carnival Scenes) | ROM | 1959(58) | Gheorghe Naghi<br>Aurel Miheleş | 82 |
| 769 | De ce trag clopotele, Mitică?<br>[Why do the bells toll, Mitică?] | ROM | 1990(81) | Lucian Pintilie | 125 |
| 770 | Două lozuri | ROM | 1957 | Aurel Miheleş<br>Gheorghe Naghi | 63 |
| 771 | Leiba Zibal | ROM | 1930 | Alexandru Stefănescu<br>Ion Brună | 56 |
| 772 | Fürchte dich nicht, Jakob!<br>[Don't be afraid, Jacob!] | GER | 1981 | Radu Gabrea | 101 |
| 773 | Înainte de tăcere<br>[Before silence] | ROM | 1978 | Alexa Visarion | 101 |
| 774 | Hanul dintre dealuri<br>[The inn in the hills] | ROM | 1988 | Cristiana Nicolae | 112 |
| 775 | Lanţul slăbiciunilor | ROM | 1952 | Jean Georgescu | 08 |
| 776 | Năpasta | ROM | 1982 | Alexa Visarion | 98 |
| 777 | O noapte furtunoasă | ROM | 1943 | Jean Georgescu | 68 |
| 778 | O scrisoare pierdută<br>(A Lost Letter) | ROM | 1953 | Sică Alexandrescu<br>Victor Iliu | 138 |
| 779 | Telegrame | ROM | 1960(59) | Gheorghe Naghi<br>Aurel Miheleş | 77 |
| 780 | Vizită | ROM | 1952 | Jean Georgescu | 08 |
| 781 | La visitaciones del diablo | MEX | 1968 | Alberto Isaac | 95 |
| 782 | L'homme traqué | FR | 1947(46) | Robert Bibal | 100 |
| 783 | M'sieur la Caille | FR | 1955 | André Pergament | 82 |
| 784 | L'ombre | FR | 1948 | André Berthomieu | 100 |
| 785 | Prisons de femmes | FR | 1938 | Roger Richebé | 94 |
| 786 | Två kvinnor<br>(Two Women) | SWE | 1947 | Arnold Sjöstrand | 96 |
| 787 | Prisons de femmes | FR | 1958 | Maurice Cloche | 100 |
| 788 | | | | | |

| No. | Author | Nationality | Form | Literary Title | Date |
|-----|--------|-------------|------|----------------|------|
| 789 | Cardoso, Lúcio | Brazilian | N | Crônica da casa assassinada [Chronicle of the assassinated house] | 1959 |
| 790 | Cardoso, Lúcio | Brazilian | SS | O desconhecido | 1940 |
| 791 | Cardoso, Lúcio | Brazilian | SS | Mãos vazias | 1938 |
| 792 | Carette, Louis (see: Marceau, Felicien) | French/ Belgian | P | | |
| 793 | Carpentier, Alejo | Cuban | N | Concierto Barroco | 1974 |
| 794 | Carpentier, Alejo | Cuban | N | El recurso del métodó | 1974 |
| 795 | Carroll, Lewis (Charles Lutwidge Dodgson) | British | SS | Alice's Adventures in Wonderland (aka: Alice in Wonderland) | 1865 |
| 796 | Carroll, Lewis | British | SS | Alice's Adventures in Wonderland | 1865 |
| 797 | Carroll, Lewis | British | SS | Alice's Adventures in Wonderland + Through the Looking Glass | 1865+ 1871 |
| 798 | Carroll, Lewis | British | SS | Alice's Adventures in Wonderland | 1865 |
| 799 | Carroll, Lewis | British | SS | Alice's Adventures in Wonderland + Through the Looking Glass | 1865+ 1871 |
| 800 | Carroll, Lewis | British | SS | Alice's Adventures in Wonderland + Through the Looking Glass | 1865+ 1871 |
| 801 | Carroll, Lewis | British | SS | Alice's Adventures in Wonderland | 1865 |
| 802 | Carroll, Lewis | British | V | Jabberwocky | 1872 |
| 803 | Carter, Angela | British | N | The Magic Toyshop | 1967 |
| 804 | Carvalho, José Cândido de (José Cândido de Carvalho) | Brazilian | N | O coronel e o lobisomem [The colonel and the werewolf] | 1964 |
| 805 | Cary, Joyce | Irish | N | The Horse's Mouth | 1944 |
| 806 | Cary, Joyce | Irish | N | Mister Johnson | 1939 |
| 807 | Casanova, Giacomo | Italian | AUT | Mémoires de Jacques Casanova de Seingalt (The Memoirs of Jacques Casanova) (aka: History of My Life) | 1826-38 |
| 808 | Casanova, Giacomo | Italian | AUT | Mémoires de Jacques Casanova de Seingalt | 1826-38 |
| 809 | Casona, Alejandro (Alejandro Rodríguez Álvarez) | Spanish | P | La barca sin pescador (The Boat Without a Fisherman) | 1945 |
| 810 | Casona, Alejandro | Spanish | P | La dama del alba (Lady of the Dawn) | 1944 |
| 811 | Casona, Alejandro | Spanish | P | Nuestra Natacha [Our Natacha] | 1936 |
| 812 | Casona, Alejandro | Spanish | P | Las tres perfectas casadas | 1941 |
| 813 | Cassola, Carlo | Italian | N | La ragazza di Bube (Bebo's Girl) | 1960 |
| 814 | Cassola, Carlo | Italian | SS | La visita | 1942 |
| 815 | Castello Branco, Camilo (Camilo Castello Branco) | Portuguese | N | Amor de perdição | 1862 |
| 816 | Castello Branco, Camilo | Portuguese | N | Amor de perdição | 1862 |
| 817 | Cather, Willa | American | SS | Jack-A-Boy | 1965(coll) |
| 818 | Cather, Willa | American | N | A Lost Lady | 1924 |
| 819 | Cather, Willa | American | SS | Paul's Case | 1905 |
| 820 | Caṭṭopādhyāý, Śarat Candra (S. Chandra Chatterjee) | Indian(Ben) | N | Baikunṭher uil | 1916 |
| 821 | Caṭṭopādhyāý, Śarat Candra | Indian | N | Biraj bau [Biraj's wife] (HIN: Viraj bahu) | 1914 |
| 822 | Caṭṭopādhyāý, Śarat Candra | Indian | N | Debdās (Devdas) | 1910 |

| No | Film Title | Country of Production | Date | Director(s) | Duration of Film |
|---|---|---|---|---|---|
| 789 | A casa assassinada | BRAZ | 1971 | Paulo César Saraceni | 103 |
| 790 | O desconhecido | BRAZ | 1977 | Ruy Santos | 85 |
| 791 | Mãos vazias | BRAZ | 1971 | Luis Carlos Lacerda de Freitas | 90 |
| 792 | | | | | |
| 793 | Barroco | SP/CB | 1989 | Paul Leduc | 107 |
| 794 | El recurso del métodó (Recourse to the Method) (aka:Viva el Presidente) (aka: Reasons of State) | CB/FR/ MEX | 1978 | Miguel Littin | 109(164) |
| 795 | Alice in Wonderland | USA | 1933 | Norman Z. McLeod | 77 |
| 796 | Alice in Wonderland (FR: Alice au pays des merveilles) {live-action + puppets} | USA/FR/ GB | 1951(48) | Dallas Bower | 75(83) |
| 797 | Alice in Wonderland {animation} | USA | 1951 | Clyde Geronimi Hamilton Luske Wilfred Jackson | 75 +V |
| 798 | Alice's Adventures in Wonderland | GB | 1972 | William Sterling | 101 |
| 799 | Alice {musical version} | BEL/POL/ GB | 1981 | Jerry Gruza Jacek Bromski | 92 +V |
| 800 | Alice in Wonderland | USA | 1985 | Harry Harris | 176 +V |
| 801 | Alice (CZ: Neco z Alenky) {live-action + puppets} | SWITZ | 1988 | Jan Švankmajer | 85 +V |
| 802 | Jabberwocky | GB | 1977 | Terry Gilliam | 101 |
| 803 | The Magic Toyshop | GB | 1986 | David Wheatley | 103 +V |
| 804 | O coronel e o lobisomem | BRAZ | 1978 | Alcino Diniz | 103(118) |
| 805 | The Horse's Mouth | GB | 1959(58) | Ronald Neame | 95 |
| 806 | Mister Johnson | USA | 1990 | Bruce Beresford | 101 +V |
| 807 | Infanzia, vocazione e prime esperienze di Giacomo Casanova veneziano (aka: Casanova) | IT | 1969 | Luigi Comencini | 119(96) |
| 808 | Il Casanova di Federico Fellini (Fellini's Casanova) (aka: Casanova) | IT | 1976 | Federico Fellini | 154(165) |
| 809 | La barca sin pescador | SP | 1965(64) | José María Forn | 83(79) |
| 810 | La dama del alba | SP | 1966(65) | Francisco Rovira Beleta | 105(101) +V |
| 811 | Nuestra Natacha | SP | 1936 | Benito Perojo | 90 |
| 812 | Las tres perfectas casadas | SP/MEX | 1973(72) | Benito Alazraki | 93(89) |
| 813 | La ragazza di Bube (Bebo's Girl) | IT/FR | 1963 | Luigi Comencini | 111 |
| 814 | La visita | IT | 1963 | Antonio Pietrangeli | 100 |
| 615 | Amor de perdição | PORT | 1943 | António Lopes Ribeiro | 128 |
| 816 | Amor de perdição (Ill-Fated Love) | PORT | 1978 | Manoel de Oliveira | 260 |
| 817 | Jack-A-Boy | USA | 1980 | Carl Colby | 28 +V |
| 818 | A Lost Lady | USA | 1934 | Alfred E. Green | 71 |
| 819 | Paul's Case | USA | 1982 | Lamont Jackson | 55 +V |
| 820 | Sautelā bhāī [Step brother] | IND(HIN) | 1962 | Mahesh Kaul | 165 |
| 821 | Biraj bahu | IND | 1955 | Bimal Roy | 150 |
| 822 | Debdās (Devdas) | IND(BEN) | 1935 | P. C. Barua | 137 |

| No. | Author | Nationality | Form | Literary Title | Date |
|-----|--------|-------------|------|----------------|------|
| 823 | Caṭṭopādhyāẏ, Śarat Candra | Indian | N | **Debdās** | 1910 |
| 824 | Caṭṭopādhyāẏ, Śarat Candra | Indian | SS | **Mej-didi** | 1915 |
| 825 | Caṭṭopādhyāẏ, Śarat Candra | Indian | SS | **Parinitā** | 1914 |
| 826 | **Caute, David** | British | N | **Comrade Jacob** | 1961 |
| 827 | **Cela, Camilo José** *(Camilo José Cela Trulock)* | Spanish | N | **La colmena** *(The Hive)* | 1951 |
| 828 | **Cela, Camilo José** | Spanish | N | **La familia de Pascual Duarte** *(The Family of Pascual Duarte) (aka: Pascual Duarte's Family)* | 1945 |
| 829 | **Cela Trulock, Camilo José** *(see: Cela, Camilo José)* | Spanish | N | | |
| 830 | **Cendrars, Blaise** | French | N | **L'or. La merveilleuse histoire du général Johann August Suter** *(Sutter's Gold)* | 1925 |
| 831 | **Cervantes Saavedra, Miguel de** | Spanish | N | **Don Quijote** *(aka: El ingenioso hidalgo Don Quijote de la Mancha) (The History of the Most Ingenious Knight Don Quixote de la Mancha)* | 1605-15 |
| 832 | **Cervantes Saavedra, Miguel de** | Spanish | N | **Don Quijote** | 1605-15 |
| 833 | **Cervantes Saavedra, Miguel de** | Spanish | N | **Don Quijote** *{pt.1, ch. 33-38} (El curioso impertinente) (Story of One Who Was too Curious for His Own Good)* | 1605 |
| 834 | **Cervantes Saavedra, Miguel de** | Spanish | N | **Don Quijote** | 1605-15 |
| 835 | **Cervantes Saavedra, Miguel de** | Spanish | N | **Don Quijote** | 1605-15 |
| 836 | **Cervantes Saavedra, Miguel de** | Spanish | N | **Don Quijote** | 1605-15 |
| 837 | **Cervantes Saavedra, Miguel de** | Spanish | N | **Don Quijote** *{pt.2, ch. 8} (Dulcinea del Toboso)* | 1615 |
| 838 | **Cervantes Saavedra, Miguel de** | Spanish | N | **Don Quijote** *{pt.1, ch. 33-38} (El curioso impertinente)* | 1605 |
| 839 | **Cervantes Saavedra, Miguel de** | Spanish | N | **Don Quijote** | 1605-15 |
| 840 | **Cervantes Saavedra, Miguel de** | Spanish | N | **Don Quijote** | 1605-15 |
| 841 | **Cervantes Saavedra, Miguel de** | Spanish | N | **Don Quijote** | 1605-15 |
| 842 | **Cervantes Saavedra, Miguel de** | Spanish | N | **Don Quijote** | 1605-15 |
| 843 | **Cervantes Saavedra, Miguel de** | Spanish | SS | **La gitanilla** *(The Little Gypsie)* | 1613 |
| 844 | **Cervantes Saavedra, Miguel de; - {n} Wasserman, Dale - {p}** | Spanish | N+P | **Don Quijote {n} + Man of La Mancha {p}** | 1605-15 + 1966{p} |
| 845 | **Chamson, André** | French | N | **L'auberge de l'abîme** *(The Mountain Tavern) (USA: The Fugitive)* | 1933 |
| 846 | **Chamson, André** | French | N | **La crime des justes** *(The Crime of the Just)* | 1928 |
| 847 | **Chamson, André** | French | N | **Tabusse** | 1928 |
| 848 | **Chandler, Raymond** | American | N | **The Big Sleep** | 1939 |
| 849 | **Chandler, Raymond** | American | N | **The Big Sleep** | 1939 |
| 850 | **Chandler, Raymond** | American | N | **Farewell, My Lovely** | 1940 |
| 851 | **Chandler, Raymond** | American | N | **Farewell, My Lovely** | 1940 |
| 852 | **Chandler, Raymond** | American | N | **Farewell, My Lovely** | 1940 |
| 853 | **Chandler, Raymond** | American | N | **The High Window** | 1942 |
| 854 | **Chandler, Raymond** | American | N | **The High Window** | 1942 |
| 855 | **Chandler, Raymond** | American | N | **The Lady in the Lake** | 1943 |
| 856 | **Chandler, Raymond** | American | N | **The Little Sister** | 1949 |
| 857 | **Chandler, Raymond** | American | N | **The Long Goodbye** | 1953 |
| 858 | **Chao P'ing-fu** *(see: Zhao Pingfu)* | Chinese | SS | | |

| No | Film Title | Country of Production | Date | Director(s) | Duration of Film |
|----|-----------|----------------------|------|-------------|------------------|
| 823 | **Debdās**<br>(Devdas) | IND(HIN) | 1955 | **Bimal Roy** | 150(105) |
| 824 | **Majhli didi** | IND(HIN) | 1968 | **Hrishikesh Mukherjee** | 150 |
| 825 | **Parineetā** | IND(HIN) | 1953 | **Bimal Roy** | 150 |
| 826 | **Winstanley** | GB | 1977(75) | **Kevin Brownlow**<br>**Andrew Mollo** | 96 |
| 827 | **La colmena**<br>(The Beehive) | SP | 1982 | **Mario Camús** | 108 |
| 828 | **Pascual Duarte** | SP | 1976(75) | **Ricardo Franco** | 100(105)<br>+V |
| 829 | | | | | |
| 830 | **Sutter's Gold** | USA | 1936 | **James Cruze** | 75 |
| 831 | **Don Quixote**<br>(aka: Adventures of Don Quixote)<br>(FR: Don Quichotte) | GB/FR | 1933(32) | **G. W. Pabst** | 82(78) |
| 832 | **Don Quijote de la Mancha**<br>(aka: Don Quixote) | SP | 1948(47) | **Rafael Gil** | 104(164)<br>(130) |
| 833 | **El curioso impertinente** | SP | 1948 | **Flavio Calzavara** | 85(106) |
| 834 | **Don Kikhot**<br>(aka: Don Quixote) | USSR | 1957 | **Grigori Kozintsev** | 107 |
| 835 | **Don Quijote** | FIN | 1962 | **Eino Ruutsalo** | 08 |
| 836 | **Don Quijote, ayer y hoy** | SP | 1964 | **César Fernández Ardavín** | 58 |
| 837 | **Don Quichotte**<br>(SP: Don Quijote) | FR/SP/<br>GER | 1966(64) | **Carlo Rim**<br>(Carlo-Rim) | 101(97) |
| 838 | **Un diablo bajo la almohada**<br>[A devil under the pillow] | SP | 1968 | **José María Forqué** | 80(101) |
| 839 | **Don Chisciotte e Sancho Panza**<br>(Don Quixote and Sancho Panza) | IT | 1968 | **Giovanni Grimaldi** | 105 |
| 840 | **Don Quijote cabalga de nuevo**<br>(Don Quixote Rides Again) | MEX/SP | 1974(72) | **Roberto Gavaldón** | 125(140) |
| 841 | **As trapalhadas de Dom Quixote**<br>**e Sancho Pança** | BRAZ | 1978 | **Ary Fernandes** | 110 |
| 842 | **Don Chisciotte**<br>(Don Quixote) | IT | 1984 | **Maurizio Scaparro** | 275 |
| 843 | **La gitanilla** | SP | 1940 | **Fernando Delgado** | 86(79) |
| 844 | **Man of La Mancha**<br>(IT: L'uomo della Mancha) | USA/IT | 1972 | **Arthur Hiller** | 132 |
| 845 | **L'auberge de l'abîme** | FR | 1942 | **Willy Rozier** | 99 |
| 846 | **La crime des justes** | FR | 1950(48) | **Jean Gehret** | 90 |
| 847 | **Tabusse** | FR | 1948 | **Jean Gehret** | 95(85) |
| 848 | **The Big Sleep** | USA | 1946(44) | **Howard Hawks** | 114 +V |
| 849 | **The Big Sleep** | GB | 1978 | **Michael Winner** | 99 +V |
| 850 | **The Falcon Takes Over** | USA | 1942 | **Irving Reis** | 66 |
| 851 | **Murder My Sweet**<br>(aka: Farewell, My Lovely) | USA | 1944 | **Edward Dmytryk** | 95<br>+V |
| 852 | **Farewell, My Lovely** | USA | 1975 | **Dick Richards** | 95 +V |
| 853 | **Time to Kill** | USA | 1942 | **Herbert I. Leeds** | 61 |
| 854 | **The Brasher Doubloon**<br>(GB: The High Window) | USA | 1947 | **John Brahm** | 72 |
| 855 | **The Lady in the Lake** | USA | 1947(46) | **Robert Montgomery** | 103 |
| 856 | **Marlowe** | USA | 1969 | **Paul Bogart** | 95 |
| 857 | **The Long Goodbye** | USA | 1973 | **Robert Altman** | 111 +V |
| 858 | | | | | |

| No. | Author | Nationality | Form | Literary Title | Date |
|---|---|---|---|---|---|
| 859 | **Chao Shu-li** (see: Zhao Shuli) | Chinese | SS | | |
| 860 | **Chase, Mary Coyle** | American | P | **Bernadine** | 1953 |
| 861 | **Chase, Mary Coyle** | American | P | **Harvey** (aka: The White Rabbit) | 1944 |
| 862 | **Chase, Mary Coyle** | American | P | **Sorority House** | 1939 |
| 863 | **Châteaubriant, Alphonse de** | French | N | **Monsieur des Lourdines** | 1911 |
| 864 | **Chatterjee, Śarat Chandra** (see: Cattopādhyāẏ, S.C.) | Indian(Ben) | N/SS | | |
| 865 | **Chatwin, Bruce** | British | N | **On the Black Hill** | 1982 |
| 866 | **Chaucer, Geoffrey** | British | V | **The Canterbury Tales** | c.1400 |
| 867 | **Chayefsky, Paddy** | American | N | **Altered States** (aka: The Experiment) | 1978 |
| 868 | **Chayefsky, Paddy** | American | P(TV) | **The Bachelor Party** | 1955 |
| 869 | **Chayefsky, Paddy** | American | P(TV) | **The Catered Affair** | 1955 |
| 870 | **Chayefsky, Paddy** | American | F-P | **The Goddess** | 1971 |
| 871 | **Chayefsky, Paddy** | American | P(TV) | **Marty** | 1955 |
| 872 | **Chayefsky, Paddy** | American | P | **Middle of the Night** | 1957 |
| 873 | **Cheever, John** | American | SS | **The Five Forty-Eight** | 1955 |
| 874 | **Cheever, John** | American | SS | **The Swimmer** | 1964 |
| 875 | **Chekhov, Anton** | Russian | SS | **Anna na shee** (Anna on the Neck) | 1895 |
| 876 | **Chekhov, Anton** | Russian | SS | **Anyuta** | 1886 |
| 877 | **Chekhov, Anton** | Russian | SS | **Baby** (Women) (aka: Peasant Wives) | 1891 |
| 878 | **Chekhov, Anton** | Russian | SS | **Bezzakonie** (A Transgression) | 1887 |
| 879 | **Chekhov, Anton** | Russian | P | **Chayka** (The Seagull) | 1896 |
| 880 | **Chekhov, Anton** | Russian | P | **Chayka** | 1896 |
| 881 | **Chekhov, Anton** | Russian | P | **Chayka** | 1896 |
| 882 | **Chekhov, Anton** | Russian | SS | **Chelovek v futlyare** (The Man in a Shell) (aka: The Man in a Case) | 1898 |
| 883 | **Chekhov, Anton** | Russian | SS | **Chelovek v futlyare** | 1898 |
| 884 | **Chekhov, Anton** | Russian | SS | **Chernyi monakh** (The Black Monk) | 1894 |
| 885 | **Chekhov, Anton** | Russian | SS | **Dama s sobachkoy** (Lady With the Lapdog) (aka: The Lady With the Dog) | 1899 |
| 886 | **Chekhov, Anton** | Russian | SS | **Dama s sobachkoy** | 1899 |
| 887 | **Chekhov, Anton** | Russian | SS | **Damy** (Ladies) | 1886 |
| 888 | **Chekhov, Anton** | Russian | SS | **Dom s mezoninom** (The House With the Mezzanine) (aka: An Artist's Story) | 1896 |
| 889 | **Chekhov, Anton** | Russian | SS | **Drama na okhote** (The Shooting Party) | 1884 |
| 890 | **Chekhov, Anton** | Russian | SS | **Drama na okhote** | 1884 |
| 891 | **Chekhov, Anton** | Russian | SS | **Duel'** (The Duel) | 1891 |
| 892 | **Chekhov, Anton** | Russian | SS | **Duel'** | 1891 |
| 893 | **Chekhov, Anton** | Russian | P | **Dyadya Vanya** (Uncle Vanya) | 1899 |
| 894 | **Chekhov, Anton** | Russian | P | **Dyadya Vanya** | 1899 |
| 895 | **Chekhov, Anton** | Russian | P | **Dyadya Vanya** | 1899 |

| No | Film Title | Country of Production | Date | Director(s) | Duration of Film |
|----|-----------|----------------------|------|-------------|------------------|
| 859 | | | | | |
| 860 | Bernadine | USA | 1957 | Henry Levin | 95 |
| 861 | Harvey | USA | 1950 | Henry Koster | 104 |
| 862 | Sorority House<br>(GB: That Girl From College) | USA | 1939 | John Farrow | 64 |
| 863 | Monsieur des Lourdines | FR | 1943(42) | Pierre de Hérain | 109 |
| 864 | | | | | |
| 865 | On the Black Hill | GB | 1988 | Andrew Grieve | 120(116) |
| 866 | I racconti di Canterbury<br>(The Canterbury Tales) | IT/FR | 1972(71) | Pier Paolo Pasolini | 109(115) |
| 867 | Altered States | USA | 1980(79) | Ken Russell | 102<br>+V |
| 868 | The Bachelor Party | USA | 1957(56) | Delbert Mann | 93 |
| 869 | The Catered Affair<br>(GB: Wedding Breakfast) | USA | 1956 | Richard Brooks | 93 |
| 870 | The Goddess | USA | 1958 | John Cromwell | 105 |
| 871 | Marty | USA | 1955(54) | Delbert Mann | 91 +V |
| 872 | Middle of the Night | USA | 1959 | Delbert Mann | 118 |
| 873 | The Five Forty-Eight<br>(aka: The 5:48) | USA | 1979 | James Ivory | 58 |
| 874 | The Swimmer | USA | 1968 | Frank Perry | 94 |
| 875 | Anna na shee | USSR | 1954 | Isidor Annensky | 86 |
| 876 | Anyuta<br>(Aniuta) | USSR | 1961 | Maria Andjaparidzé | 20 |
| 877 | Glavnye svidetel' | USSR | 1969 | Aida Manasarova | 69 |
| 878 | Bezzakonie | USSR | 1953 | Konstantin Yudin | 15 |
| 879 | The Sea Gull | GB | 1969(68) | Sidney Lumet | 141 |
| 880 | Chayka<br>(The Seagull) | USSR | 1971 | Yuli Karasik | 98 |
| 881 | Il gabbiano<br>(The Seagull) | IT | 1977 | Marco Bellocchio | 125(132) |
| 882 | Chelovek v futlyare | USSR | 1939 | Isidor Annensky | 95 |
| 883 | Chelovek v futlyare<br>{animation} | USSR | 1983 | Leonid Zarubin | 19 |
| 884 | Chernyi monakh | USSR | 1988 | Ivan Dykhovitchny | 87 |
| 885 | Dama s sobachkoy<br>(Lady With the Little Dog)<br>(aka: The Lady With the Dog) | USSR | 1960 | Iosif Heifitz | 88 |
| 886 | Oci ciornie<br>(Dark Eyes) | IT | 1987 | Nikita Mikhalkov | 117<br>+V |
| 887 | Damy<br>(Ladies) | USSR | 1954 | Genrikh Oganisian<br>Lev Kulidzhanov | 18 |
| 888 | Dom s mezoninom | USSR | 1960 | Jakov Bazelian | 84 |
| 889 | Summer Storm | USA | 1944 | Douglas Sirk | 106 |
| 890 | Moi laskovei i nezhnei zver'<br>(aka: Drama na okhote)<br>(The Shooting Party) | USSR | 1978(77) | Emil Loteanu | 105(109) |
| 891 | Duel' | USSR | 1962 | Tatiana Berezantseva<br>Lev Rudnik | 87 |
| 892 | Plokhoy khoroshyi chelovek<br>(The Good Bad Man) | USSR | 1974(73) | Iosif Heifitz | 90 |
| 893 | Uncle Vanya | USA | 1958(56) | Franchot Tone<br>John Goetz | 98 |
| 894 | Uncle Vanya | GB | 1963 | Stuart Burge | 117(90)+V |
| 895 | Dyadya Vanya<br>(Uncle Vanya) | USSR | 1972(71) | Andrei Mikhalkov-Konchalovsky | 102 |

| No. | Author | Nationality | Form | Literary Title | Date |
|-----|--------|-------------|------|----------------|------|
| 896 | **Chekhov, Anton** | Russian | SS | **Ionych**<br>*(Ionitch)* | 1898 |
| 897 | **Chekhov, Anton** | Russian | P | **Iubilei**<br>*(Jubilee)*<br>*(aka: The Anniversary)* | 1891 |
| 898 | **Chekhov, Anton** | Russian | SS | **Kalkhas** | 1896 |
| 899 | **Chekhov, Anton** | Russian | SS | **Kashtanka**<br>*(Bad Conduct)* | 1887 |
| 900 | **Chekhov, Anton** | Russian | SS | **Khirurgia**<br>*(Surgery)* | 1884 |
| 901 | **Chekhov, Anton** | Russian | SS | **Khoristka**<br>*(The Chorus Girl)* | 1886 |
| 902 | **Chekhov, Anton** | Russian | SS | **Khudozhestvo**<br>*(Art)* | 1886 |
| 903 | **Chekhov, Anton** | Russian | P | **Leshii**<br>*(The Wood Demon)* | 1890 |
| 904 | **Chekhov, Anton** | Russian | P | **Medved'**<br>*(The Bear)*<br>*(aka: The Boor)* | 1888 |
| 905 | **Chekhov, Anton** | Russian | P | **Medved'** | 1888 |
| 906 | **Chekhov, Anton** | Russian | SS | **Mest'**<br>*(Vengeance)*<br>*(aka: Revenge)* | 1886 |
| 907 | **Chekhov, Anton** | Russian | SS | **Na dache**<br>*(At a Summer Villa)* | 1886 |
| 908 | **Chekhov, Anton** | Russian | SS | **Nalim**<br>*(The Fish)* | 1885 |
| 909 | **Chekhov, Anton** | Russian | SS | **Nalim** | 1885 |
| 910 | **Chekhov, Anton** | Russian | SS | **Nevesta**<br>*(Betrothed)* | 1902 |
| 911 | **Chekhov, Anton** | Russian | SS | **Ot nechego delat**<br>*[To while away the time]* +<br>**Nervy**<br>*(Nerves)* +<br>**Mstitel'**<br>*(An Avenger)* +<br>**Predloyheniye**<br>*(The Proposal)* | 1886+<br>1885+<br>1887+<br>1888 |
| 912 | **Chekhov, Anton** | Russian | SS | **Palata no.6**<br>*(Ward 6)*<br>*(aka: Ward no. 6)* | 1892 |
| 913 | **Chekhov, Anton** | Russian | SS | **Pari**<br>*(The Bet)*<br>*(aka: Wager)* | 1888 |
| 914 | **Chekhov, Anton** | Russian | SS | **Perepolokh**<br>*(An Upheaval)* | 1886 |
| 915 | **Chekhov, Anton** | Russian | SS | **Peresolil**<br>*(Overdoing It)*<br>*(aka: Overseasoned)* | 1885 |
| 916 | **Chekhov, Anton** | Russian | P | **Platonov**<br>*(aka: Don Juan in the Russian Manner)*<br>*(aka: Wild Honey)* | c.1890 |
| 917 | **Chekhov, Anton** | Russian | SS | **Poprygun'ya**<br>*(The Grasshopper)* | 1892 |
| 918 | **Chekhov, Anton** | Russian | SS | **Proisshestviye**<br>*(An Adventure)* | 1887 |
| 919 | **Chekhov, Anton** | Russian | SS | **Proizvedeniye iskusstva**<br>*(A Work of Art)* | 1886 |
| 920 | **Chekhov, Anton** | Russian | SS | **Rasskaz neizvestnogo cheloveka**<br>*(An Anonymous Story)* | 1893 |
| 921 | **Chekhov, Anton** | Russian | SS | **Roman i kontrabasom**<br>*(Romance With Double Bass)* | 1886 |
| 922 | **Chekhov, Anton** | Russian | SS | **Sapogi**<br>*(Boots)* | 1884-85 |
| 923 | **Chekhov, Anton** | Russian | SS | **Shvedskaya spichka**<br>*(The Swedish Match)*<br>*(aka: Match)* | 1883 |
| 924 | **Chekhov, Anton** | Russian | SS | **Step'**<br>*(The Steppe)* | 1888 |

| No | Film Title | Country of Production | Date | Director(s) | Duration of Film |
|---|---|---|---|---|---|
| 896 | **V gorodye S** (In the Town of S) | USSR | 1967 | **Iosif Heifitz** | 105 |
| 897 | **Iubilei** (Jubilee) (aka: The Anniversary) | USSR | 1944 | **Vladimir Petrov** | 40 |
| 898 | **Lebedinaya pesnya** | USSR | 1966 | **Juri Mogilevtzev** | 18 |
| 899 | **Kashtanka** {animation} | USSR | 1952 | **Mikhail Tzekhanovsky** | 32 |
| 900 | **Khirurgia** | USSR | 1939 | **Jan Frid** | 38 |
| 901 | **Khoristka** | USSR | 1978 | **Alexander Muratov** | 19 |
| 902 | **Khudozhestvo** (A Work of Art: Satirical Shorts) | USSR | 1959 | **M. Kovalev** | 10 |
| 903 | **The Wood Demon** | GB | 1974 | **Donald Mcwhinnie** | 110 |
| 904 | **Medved'** | USSR | 1938 | **Isidor Annensky** | 45 |
| 905 | **The Boor** | USA | 1955(53) | **Nathan Zucker** | 15 |
| 906 | **Vengeance** | USSR | 1960(59) | **Irina Poplavskaya** | 26 |
| 907 | **Na dache** {animation} | USSR | 1954 | **Georgy Lomidze** | 18 |
| 908 | **Nalim** | USSR | 1938 | **Sergei Sploshnov** | 12 |
| 909 | **Nalim** | USSR | 1953 | **Alexei Zolotnitzkie** | 54 |
| 910 | **Nevesta** | USSR | 1956 | **Grigoriy Nikulin** **Vladimir Shredel** | 87 |
| 911 | **Semeinoe schast'e** | USSR | 1969 | **Sergei Solovyov** **Alexander Shein** **Andrei Ladynin** | 89 |
| 912 | **Pavillion V1** | YUGO | 1978 | **Lucian Pintilie** | 97 |
| 913 | **The Bet** | USA | 1969 | **Ron Waller** | 24 +V |
| 914 | **Perepolokh** | USSR | 1954 | **Vassili Ordinskii** **Yakov Segel** | 28 |
| 915 | **Peresolil** {animation} | USSR | 1959 | **Vladimir Degtearyov** | 16 |
| 916 | **Neokončhennaya pyesa dlya mekhanicheskovo pianino** (Unfinished Piece for Mechanical Piano) (aka: The Mechanical Piano) | USSR | 1977 | **Nikita Mikhalkov** | 100 +V |
| 917 | **Poprigun'ya** (The Grasshopper) | USSR | 1955 | **Samson Samsonov** | 90 |
| 918 | **Dogadaj** (An Event) | YUGO | 1969 | **Vatroslav Mimica** | 88 |
| 919 | **Proizvedeniye iskusstva** | USSR | 1959 | **Mark Kovalev** | 10 |
| 920 | **Rasskaz neizvestnogo cheloveka** (Story of an Unknown Man) | USSR | 1980 | **Vitautas Zhalakyavichus** (Vitautas Zalakevicius) | 99 |
| 921 | **Romance With a Double Bass** | GB | 1975(74) | **Robert Young** | 41 +V |
| 922 | **Sapogi** | USSR | 1957 | **Vladimir Niemoliaiev** | 25 |
| 923 | **Svedskaya spichka** (The Safety Match) | USSR | 1954 | **Konstantin Yudin** | 61 |
| 924 | **La steppa** (The Steppe) | IT/FR | 1963(62) | **Alberto Lattuada** | 110(100) |

| No. | Author | Nationality | Form | Literary Title | Date |
|---|---|---|---|---|---|
| 925 | **Chekhov, Anton** | Russian | SS | **Step'** | 1888 |
| 926 | **Chekhov, Anton** | Russian | P | **Svad'ba** <br> (The Wedding) | 1889 |
| 927 | **Chekhov, Anton** | Russian | SS | **Toska** <br> (Grief) <br> (aka: Misery) | 1885 |
| 928 | **Chekhov, Anton** | Russian | SS | **Toska** | 1885 |
| 929 | **Chekhov, Anton** | Russian | P | **Tri sestry** <br> (Three Sisters) | 1901 |
| 930 | **Chekhov, Anton** | Russian | P | **Tri sestry** | 1901 |
| 931 | **Chekhov, Anton** | Russian | P | **Tri sestry** | 1901 |
| 932 | **Chekhov, Anton** | Russian | P | **Tri sestry** | 1901 |
| 933 | **Chekhov, Anton** | Russian | SS | **Tzvety zapozdalye** <br> (Belated Blossom) <br> (aka: Late-Blooming Flowers) | 1882 |
| 934 | **Chekhov, Anton** | Russian | SS | **Van'ka** <br> (Vanka) <br> (aka: Little Jack) | 1886 |
| 935 | **Chekhov, Anton** | Russian | SS | **Van'ka** | 1884 |
| 936 | **Chekhov, Anton** | Russian | SS | **Ved'ma** <br> (The Witch) | 1886 |
| 937 | **Chekhov, Anton** | Russian | SS | **Vint** | 1884 |
| 938 | **Chekhov, Anton** | Russian | SS | **V ovrage** <br> (In the Ravine) | 1900 |
| 939 | **Chekhov, Anton** | Russian | SS | **V ovrage** | 1900 |
| 940 | **Chekhov, Anton** | Russian | SS | **Vragi** <br> (Enemies) <br> (aka: Two Tragedies) | 1887 |
| 941 | **Chekhov, Anton** | Russian | SS | **V sude** <br> (On Trial) | 1886 |
| 942 | **Chen Baichen** | Chinese | P | **Qun mo** <br> [The devils] | 1947 |
| 943 | **Chesterton, G. K.** | British | SS | **Father Brown Stories** | 1929 |
| 944 | **Chesterton, G. K.** | British | N | **Manalive** | 1912 |
| 945 | **Chesterton, G. K.** | British | SS | **The Man Who Knew Too Much** | 1922 |
| 946 | **Chesterton, G. K.** | British | SS | **The Man Who Knew Too Much** | 1922 |
| 947 | **Chesterton, G. K.** | British | SS | **The Wisdom of Father Brown** | 1929 |
| 948 | **Chikamatsu Monzaemon** | Japanese | P | **Daikyoji mukashigoyomi** <br> (aka: Koi hakké hashiragoyomi) <br> (The Almanac of Love) | 1715 |
| 949 | **Chikamatsu Monzaemon** | Japanese | P | **Shinjū ten no Amijima** <br> (The Love Suicides at Amijima) | 1721 |
| 950 | **Chikamatsu Monzaemon** | Japanese | P | **Sonezaki shinjū** | 1703 |
| 951 | **Childers, Erskine** | British | N | **The Riddle of the Sands** | 1903 |
| 952 | **Chilton, Charles;** <br> **Littlewood, Joan** | British | P | **Oh! What a Lovely War** <br> {Littlewood} + <br> **The Long Long Trail** <br> {Chilton} | 1965 |
| 953 | **Chodorov, Edward** <br> (joint, see: Walpole, Hugh) | American | SS-P | | |
| 954 | **Chopin, Kate** | American | N | **The Awakening** | 1899 |
| 955 | **Chopin, Kate** | American | N | **The Awakening** | 1899 |
| 956 | **Chorell, Walentin** | Finnish(Swe) | P | **Kattorna** | 1963 |
| 957 | **Chorell, Walentin** | Finnish | N | **Miriam** | 1954 |
| 958 | **Choromański, Michał** | Polish | N | **Zazdrość i medycyna** <br> (Jealousy and Medecine) | 1932 |
| 959 | **Chou Li-po** <br> (see: Zhou Lipo) | Chinese | N | | |
| 960 | **Chou Shu-jen** <br> (see: Zhou Shuren) | Chinese | SS | | |
| 961 | **Chrétien de Troyes** | French | V | **Conte du Graal** <br> (Perceval) | 1181 |

| No | Film Title | Country of Production | Date | Director(s) | Duration of Film |
|---|---|---|---|---|---|
| 925 | **Step'** (The Steppe) | USSR | 1978 | **Sergei Bondarchuk** | 131 |
| 926 | **Svad'ba** (Wedding) (aka: The Marriage) | USSR | 1944 | **Isidor Annensky** | 47 |
| 927 | **Toska** (Grief) | USSR | 1969 | **Aleksander Blank** | 21 |
| 928 | **The Father** | USA | 1970 | **Mark Fine** | 28 |
| 929 | **Tri sestry** (Three Sisters) | USSR | 1964 | **Samson Samsonov** | 118 |
| 930 | **Three Sisters** | USA | 1966 | **Paul Bogart** | 168 |
| 931 | **Three Sisters** | GB | 1970 | **Laurence Olivier** | 165 +V |
| 932 | **Fürchten und Lieben** | GER | 1987 | **Margarethe von Trotta** | 100 |
| 933 | **Tzvety zapozdalye** (Belated Flowers) | USSR | 1969 | **Abram Room** | 101 |
| 934 | **Van'ka** | USSR | 1961(60) | **Eduard Bocharov** | 32 |
| 935 | **Van'ka zhukov** {animation} | USSR | 1981 | **Leonid Zarubin** | 10 |
| 936 | **Ved'ma** | USSR | 1956 | **Alexander Abramov** | 31 |
| 937 | **Karty** | USSR | 1965 | **Rolan Sergienko** | 18 |
| 938 | **The Beneficiary** | GB | 1979 | **Carlo Gebler** | 47 |
| 939 | **Kasba** | IND | 1990 | **Kumar Shahani** | 121 |
| 940 | **Vragi** | USSR | 1960 | **Yuri Yegorov** | 22 |
| 941 | **Sud** | USSR | 1967 | **David Kocharyan** | 20 |
| 942 | **Qun mo** | CHN | 1948 | **Xu Changlin** | 90 |
| 943 | **Father Brown** (USA: The Detective) | GB | 1954 | **Robert Hamer** | 92 |
| 944 | **Le revolver aux cheveux rouge** | BEL | 1974(73) | **Fréderic Geilfus** **Denise Geilfus** | 90 |
| 945 | **The Man Who Knew Too Much** | GB | 1934 | **Alfred Hitchcock** | 84(75) |
| 946 | **The Man Who Knew Too Much** | USA | 1956(55) | **Alfred Hitchcock** | 120 |
| 947 | **Father Brown, Detective** | USA | 1934 | **Edward Sedgwick** | 67 |
| 948 | **Chikamatsu monogatari** (A Story From Chikamatsu) (aka: The Crucified Lovers) | JAP | 1955(54) | **Kenji Mizoguchi** | 110(102) |
| 949 | **Shinjū ten no Amijima** (Double Suicide) | JAP | 1969 | **Masahiro Shinoda** | 106 |
| 950 | **Sonezaki shinjū** (Double Suicide of Sonezaki) | JAP | 1978 | **Yasuzō Masumura** | 112 |
| 951 | **The Riddle of the Sands** | GB | 1978 | **Tony Maylam** | 102 +V |
| 952 | **Oh! What a Lovely War** | GB | 1969(68) | **Richard Attenborough** | 144 +V(137) |
| 953 | | | | | |
| 954 | **The End of August** | USA | 1981 | **Bob Graham** | 107 +V |
| 955 | **Grand Isle** | USA | 1991 | **Mary Lambert** | 95 |
| 956 | **Kattorna** | SWE | 1965 | **Henning Carlsen** | 91 |
| 957 | **Miriam** | FIN | 1957 | **William Markus** | 88 |
| 958 | **Zazdrość i medycyna** (Jealousy and Medicine) | POL | 1973 | **Janusz Majewski** | 99 |
| 959 | | | | | |
| 960 | | | | | |
| 961 | **Perceval le Gallois** (aka: Perceval) (aka: Perceval 1978) | FR | 1978 | **Eric Rohmer** | 140(135) +V |

| No. | Author | Nationality | Form | Literary Title | Date |
|-----|--------|-------------|------|----------------|------|
| 962 | Christiansen, Sigurd | Norwegian | N | To levende og en død *(Two Living and One Dead)* | 1931 |
| 963 | Christiansen, Sigurd | Norwegian | N | To levende og en død | 1931 |
| 964 | Christiansen, Sigurd | Norwegian | N | To levende og en død | 1931 |
| 965 | Clarín *(see: Alas, Leopoldo)* | Spanish | N | | |
| 966 | Clark, Brian | British | P | Whose Life Is It Anyway? | 1978 |
| 967 | Clark, Walter van Tilberg | American | N | The Ox-Bow Incident | 1940 |
| 968 | Clark, Walter van Tilberg | American | N | The Track of the Cat | 1949 |
| 969 | Clarke, Arthur C. | British | SS-N | The Sentinel *(ss-n)* *(aka: 2001: a Space Odyssey) (n)* | 1967{ss} 1968{n} |
| 970 | Clarke, Arthur C. | British | N | 2010: Odyssey Two *(aka: Two Thousand Ten: Odyssey Two)* | 1982 |
| 971 | Claudel, Paul | French | P | Jeanne d'Arc au bûcher | 1939 |
| 972 | Claus, Hugo Maurice Julien | Belgian(Fle) | P | De dans van de reiger | 1962 |
| 973 | Claus, Hugo Maurice Julien | Belgian | N | Het jaar van de kreeft *[Cancer rising; year of the cancer]* | 1972 |
| 974 | Cleland, John | British | N | Memoirs of a Woman of Pleasure *(aka: Memoirs of Fanny Hill)* | 1749 |
| 975 | Cleland, John | British | N | Memoirs of a Woman of Pleasure | 1749 |
| 976 | Clemens, Samuel *(see: Twain, Mark)* | American | N/SS | | |
| 977 | Coates, Robert M. | American | N | Wisteria Cottage | 1948 |
| 978 | Cobb, Humphrey | American | N | Paths of Glory | 1935 |
| 979 | Cocteau, Jean | French | P | L'aigle à deux têtes *(The Eagle Has Two Heads)* | 1946 |
| 980 | Cocteau, Jean | French | P | L'aigle à deux têtes | 1946 |
| 981 | Cocteau, Jean | French | P | Le bel indifférent | 1949 |
| 982 | Cocteau, Jean | French | N | Les enfants terribles | 1925 |
| 983 | Cocteau, Jean | French | P | Orphée | 1927 |
| 984 | Cocteau, Jean | French | P | Les parents terribles *(Intimate Relations)* | 1938 |
| 985 | Cocteau, Jean | French | P | Les parents terribles | 1938 |
| 986 | Cocteau, Jean | French | N | Thomas l'imposteur *(Thomas the Imposter)* | 1923 |
| 987 | Cocteau, Jean | French | P | La voix humaine *(The Human Voice)* | 1930 |
| 988 | Coelho, Joaquim Guilherme Gomes *(see: Dinis, Julio)* | Portuguese | N | | |
| 989 | Coetzee, J. M. | South African | N | In the Heart of the Country | 1977 |
| 990 | Colette, Sidonie Gabrielle | French | N | Le blé en herbe *(The Ripening Corn)* *(aka: Ripening Seed)* | 1923 |
| 991 | Colette, Sidonie Gabrielle | French | N | Chéri | 1920 |
| 992 | Colette, Sidonie Gabrielle | French | N | Claudine à l'école *(Claudine at School)* | 1900 |
| 993 | Colette, Sidonie Gabrielle | French | N | L'envers du music-hall *(Music-Hall Sidelights)* | 1913 |
| 994 | Colette, Sidonie Gabrielle | French | SS | Gigi | 1945 |

| No | Film Title | Country of Production | Date | Director(s) | Duration of Film |
|---|---|---|---|---|---|
| 962 | To levende og en død | NOR | 1937 | Tancred Ibsen | 83 |
| 963 | Mrtvý mezi živými (Dead Among the Living) | CZ | 1947 | Bořivoj Zeman | 90 |
| 964 965 | Two Living, One Dead | GB/SWE | 1961 | Anthony Asquith | 92 |
| 966 | Whose Life Is It Anyway? | USA | 1981 | John Badham | 119 +V |
| 967 | The Ox-Bow Incident (GB: Strange Incident) | USA | 1943(42) | William A. Wellman | 76 |
| 968 | Track of the Cat | USA | 1954 | William A. Wellman | 102 |
| 969 | 2001: A Space Odyssey | GB | 1968 | Stanley Kubrick | 141 +V |
| 970 | 2010 | USA | 1984 | Peter Hyams | 116 +V |
| 971 | Giovanna d'Arco al rogo (FR: Jeanne d'Arc au bucher) (Joan of Arc at the Stake) | IT/FR | 1954 | Roberto Rossellini | 80 |
| 972 | De dans van de reiger (The Dance of the Heron) | HOLL/GER | 1966(65) | Fons Rademakers | 95 |
| 973 | Het jaar van de kreeft | HOLL | 1975 | Herbert Cureël | 91 |
| 974 | Fanny Hill (aka: Fanny Hill: Memoirs of a Woman of Pleasure) | GER/USA | 1964 | Russ Meyer | 96 +V(86) |
| 975 976 | Fanny Hill | GB | 1983 | Gerry O'Hara | 92 +V(86) |
| 977 | Edge of Fury | USA | 1956 | Irving Lerner Robert J. Gurney | 76 |
| 978 | Paths of Glory | USA | 1957 | Stanley Kubrick | 87 +V |
| 979 | L'aigle à deux têtes (The Eagle Has Two Heads) (USA: The Eagle With Two Heads) | FR | 1948 | Jean Cocteau | 93 |
| 980 | Il mistero di Oberwald (GER: Das Geheimnis von Oberwald) (The Oberwald Mystery) | IT/GER | 1980 | Michelangelo Antonioni | 127 |
| 981 | Le bel indifférent | FR | 1957 | Jacques Demy | 29 |
| 982 | Les enfants terribles (aka: The Strange Ones) | FR | 1949 | Jean-Pierre Melville | 100 |
| 983 | Orphée (Orpheus) | FR | 1950 | Jean Cocteau | 95 +V |
| 984 | Les parents terribles (The Storm Within) | FR | 1948 | Jean Cocteau | 98 |
| 985 | Intimate Relations | GB | 1953 | Charles Frank | 86 |
| 986 | Thomas l'imposteur (Thomas the Imposter) | FR | 1964 | Georges Franju | 94 |
| 987 988 | L'amore (Pt.1: Una voce) (Pt.2: Il miracolo) (aka: L'amore - A Human Voice and a Miracle) (aka: Woman) (aka: Ways of Love) | IT | 1948(47) | Roberto Rossellini | 79(69) |
| 989 | Dust | BEL/FR | 1985 | Marion Hänsel | 87 |
| 990 | Le blé en herbe (Ripening Seed) (USA: The Game of Love) | FR | 1953 | Claude Autant-Lara | 105 |
| 991 | Chéri | FR | 1950 | Pierre Billon | 90 |
| 992 | Claudine à l'école (Claudine) | FR | 1937 | Serge de Poligny | 109 |
| 993 | Divine | FR | 1935 | Max Ophüls | 80 |
| 994 | Gigi | FR | 1949 | Jacqueline Audry | 109 |

| No. | Author | Nationality | Form | Literary Title | Date |
|-----|--------|-------------|------|----------------|------|
| 995 | **Colette, Sidonie Gabrielle** | French | SS | **Gigi** | 1945 |
| 996 | **Colette, Sidonie Gabrielle** | French | N | **L'ingénue libertine** *(The Innocent Libertine) (aka: The Gentle Libertine)* | 1909 |
| 997 | **Colette, Sidonie Gabrielle** | French | N | **Julie de Carneilhan** | 1941 |
| 998 | **Colette, Sidonie Gabrielle** | French | N | **Mitsou; ou, comment l'esprit vient aux filles** *(Mitsou; or How Girls Grow Wise) (aka: Mitsou; or the Education of Young Women)* | 1919 |
| 999 | **Colette, Sidonie Gabrielle** | French | N | **La vagabonde** *(The Vagabond) (aka: Renée the Vagabonde)* | 1910 |
| 1000 | **Collins, Wilkie** | British | N | **Moonstone** | 1868 |
| 1001 | **Collins, Wilkie** | British | N | **The Woman in White** | 1860 |
| 1002 | **Collins, Wilkie** | British | N | **The Woman in White** | 1860 |
| 1003 | **Collodi, Carlo** *(Carlo Lorenzini)* | Italian | SS | **Pinocchio** *(aka: Le avventure di Pinocchio: historia di un burattino) (The Story of a Puppet: or the Adventures of Pinocchio)* | 1890 |
| 1004 | **Collodi, Carlo** | Italian | SS | **Pinocchio** | 1890 |
| 1005 | **Collodi, Carlo** | Italian | SS | **Pinocchio** | 1890 |
| 1006 | **Collodi, Carlo** | Italian | SS | **Pinocchio** | 1890 |
| 1007 | **Collodi, Carlo** | Italian | SS | **Pinocchio** | 1890 |
| 1008 | **Collodi, Carlo** | Italian | SS | **Pinocchio** | 1890 |
| 1009 | **Coloma, Luis** | Spanish | N | **Boy** *(A True Hidalgo)* | 1910 |
| 1010 | **Coloma, Luis** | Spanish | N | **Jeromin** *(The Story of Don Juan of Austria)* | 1905-07 |
| 1011 | **Coloma, Luis** | Spanish | N | **Pequeñeces** *(Currita, Countess of Albornoz)* | 1890 |
| 1012 | **Condé, José** | Brazilian | SS | **Um ramo para Luísa** *[A bouquet for Luísa]* | 1959 |
| 1013 | **Condon, Richard** | American | N | **The Manchurian Candidate** | 1959 |
| 1014 | **Condon, Richard** | American | N | **The Oldest Confession** | 1958 |
| 1015 | **Condon, Richard** | American | N | **Prizzi's Honor** | 1982 |
| 1016 | **Condon, Richard** | American | N | **Winter Kills** | 1974 |
| 1017 | **Connell, Evan S.** | American | N | **Mrs Bridge +** **Mr Bridge** | 1959+ 1969 |
| 1018 | **Connelly, Marc** | American | P | **The Green Pastures** | 1929 |
| 1019 | **Connelly, Marc** *(see also: Kaufman, George S.)* | American | P | | |
| 1020 | **Conrad, Joseph** | British/Polish | SS | **The Duel** *(aka: The Point of Honor)* | 1908 |
| 1021 | **Conrad, Joseph** | British/Polish | N | **Heart of Darkness** | 1899(1902) |
| 1022 | **Conrad, Joseph** | British/Polish | N | **Lord Jim** | 1900 |
| 1023 | **Conrad, Joseph** | British/Polish | N | **An Outcast of the Islands** | 1896 |
| 1024 | **Conrad, Joseph** | British/Polish | N | **The Rover** | 1923 |
| 1025 | **Conrad, Joseph** | British/Polish | N | **The Secret Agent** | 1907 |
| 1026 | **Conrad, Joseph** | British/Polish | SS | **The Secret Sharer** | 1910(12) |
| 1027 | **Conrad, Joseph** | British/Polish | N | **The Shadow Line** | 1916(17) |
| 1028 | **Conrad, Joseph** | British/Polish | SS | **Tomorrow** | 1903 |
| 1029 | **Conrad, Joseph** | British/Polish | N | **Under Western Eyes** | 1911 |
| 1030 | **Conrad, Joseph** | British/Polish | N | **Victory** *(aka: Victory, an Island Tale)* | 1915 |

| No | Film Title | Country of Production | Date | Director(s) | Duration of Film |
|---|---|---|---|---|---|
| 995 | **Gigi** <br> *{musical version}* | USA | 1958 | **Vincente Minnelli** | 115 <br> +V |
| 996 | **L'ingénue libertine** <br> *(aka: Minne, l'ingénue libertine)* <br> *(USA: Minne)* | FR | 1950 | **Jacqueline Audry** | 85 |
| 997 | **Julie de Carneilhan** | FR | 1950(49) | **Jacques Manuel** | 95 |
| 998 | **Mitsou ou comment l'esprit vient aux filles...** <br> *(aka: Mitsou)* | FR | 1956 | **Jacqueline Audry** | 95 |
| 999 | **La vagabonde** | FR | 1931 | **Solange Bussi** | 85 |
| 1000 | **Moonstone** | USA | 1934 | **Reginald Barker** | 60 |
| 1001 | **Crimes at the Dark House** | GB | 1940 | **George King** | 69 |
| 1002 | **The Woman in White** | USA | 1948(47) | **Peter Godfrey** | 109 |
| 1003 | **Pinocchio** <br> *{animation}* | USA | 1940 | **Ben Sharpstein** <br> **Hamilton Luske** | 88 <br> +V(84) |
| 1004 | **Le avventure di Pinocchio** <br> *(Pinocchio)* <br> *(aka: The Adventures of Pinocchio)* <br> *{animation}* | IT | 1967 | **Giuliano Cenci** <br> **Renzo Cenci** | 98 <br> +V |
| 1005 | **Turlis Abenteuer** <br> *[Turli's adventure]* | GDR | 1967 | **Walter Beck** | 75 |
| 1006 | **Le avventure di Pinocchio** <br> *(aka: Pinocchio)* | IT/FR/ GER | 1972(71) | **Luigi Comencini** | 135(92) |
| 1007 | **Pinocchio** <br> *{musical version}* | USA | 1976 | **Sid Smith** <br> **Ron Field** | 76 <br> +V |
| 1008 | **Pinocchio** | USA | 1984 | **Peter Medak** | 50 +V |
| 1009 | **Boy** | SP | 1940 | **Antonio Calvache** | 98(100) |
| 1010 | **Jeromin** | SP | 1953 | **Luis Lucía** | 97(90) |
| 1011 | **Pequeñeces** <br> *[Trifles]* | SP | 1950 | **Juan de Orduña** | 137(98) |
| 1012 | **Um ramo para Luíza** | BRAZ | 1965 | **J. B. Tanko** | 105 |
| 1013 | **The Manchurian Candidate** | USA | 1962 | **John Frankenheimer** | 126 |
| 1014 | **The Happy Thieves** | USA | 1961 | **George Marshall** | 88 |
| 1015 | **Prizzi's Honor** | USA | 1985 | **John Huston** | 129 +V |
| 1016 | **Winter Kills** | USA | 1979 | **William Richert** | 96 |
| 1017 | **Mr and Mrs Bridge** | USA | 1990 | **James Ivory** | 125 <br> +V |
| 1018 | **The Green Pastures** | USA | 1936 | **Marc Connelly** <br> **William Keighley** | 93 |
| 1019 | | | | | |
| 1020 | **The Duellists** | GB | 1977 | **Ridley Scott** | 101 <br> +V |
| 1021 | **Apocalypse Now** | USA | 1979 | **Francis Coppola** | 153 +V |
| 1022 | **Lord Jim** | GB | 1965(64) | **Richard Brooks** | 154 +V |
| 1023 | **Outcast of the Islands** | GB | 1951 | **Carol Reed** | 102 |
| 1024 | **L'avventuriero** <br> *(The Adventurer)* <br> *(aka: The Rover)* | IT | 1967(66) | **Terence Young** | 110(105) <br> +V |
| 1025 | **Sabotage** <br> *(USA: The Woman Alone)* | GB | 1936 | **Alfred Hitchcock** | 76 <br> +V |
| 1026 | **Face to Face** <br> *{Pt.1}* | USA | 1952 | **John Brahm** | 45 (Pt.1) |
| 1027 | **Smuga cienia** <br> *(The Shadow Line)* | POL/GB | 1976 | **Andrzej Wajda** | 109 |
| 1028 | **Naufragio** | MEX | 1977 | **Jaime H. Hermosillo** | 101 |
| 1029 | **Razumov** <br> *(aka: Sous les yeux d'occident)* | FR | 1936 | **Marc Allégret** | 95 |
| 1030 | **Dangerous Paradise** | USA | 1930 | **William A. Wellman** | 57 |

| No. | Author | Nationality | Form | Literary Title | Date |
|-----|--------|-------------|------|----------------|------|
| 1031 | Conrad, Joseph | British/Polish | N | Victory | 1915 |
| 1032 | Conrad, Joseph | British/Polish | N | Victory | 1915 |
| 1033 | Conrad, Joseph | British/Polish | N | Victory | 1915 |
| 1034 | Conscience, Hendrik | Belgian(Fle) | N | De loteling (The Conscript) | 1850 |
| 1035 | Constant de Rebeque, Henri-Benjamin | French | N | Adolphe | 1816 |
| 1036 | Cony, Carlos Heitor | Brazilian | N | Antes, o verão | 1964 |
| 1037 | Cony, Carlos Heitor | Brazilian | N | Matéria de memória | 1962 |
| 1038 | Cooper, James Fenimore | American | N | The Deerslayer (aka: The Deerslayer; or, the First War-Path) | 1841 |
| 1039 | Cooper, James Fenimore | American | N | The Deerslayer | 1841 |
| 1040 | Cooper, James Fenimore | American | N | The Deerslayer | 1841 |
| 1041 | Cooper, James Fenimore | American | N | The Deerslayer | 1841 |
| 1042 | Cooper, James Fenimore | American | N | The Last of the Mohicans (aka: The Last of the Mohicans; or, a Narrative of 1757) | 1826 |
| 1043 | Cooper, James Fenimore | American | N | The Last of the Mohicans | 1826 |
| 1044 | Cooper, James Fenimore | American | N | The Last of the Mohicans | 1826 |
| 1045 | Cooper, James Fenimore | American | N | The Last of the Mohicans | 1826 |
| 1046 | Cooper, James Fenimore | American | N | The Last of the Mohicans | 1826 |
| 1047 | Cooper, James Fenimore | American | N | The Last of the Mohicans | 1826 |
| 1048 | Cooper, James Fenimore | American | N | The Pathfinder (aka: The Pathfinder; or, the Inland Sea) | 1840 |
| 1049 | Cooper, James Fenimore | American | N | The Pathfinder | 1840 |
| 1050 | Cooper, James Fenimore | American | N | The Pathfinder | 1840 |
| 1051 | Cooper, James Fenimore | American | N | The Pioneers (aka: The Pioneers; or, the Sources of the Susquehanna) | 1823 |
| 1052 | Cooper, James Fenimore | American | N | The Prairie | 1827 |
| 1053 | Cooper, James Fenimore | American | N | The Prairie | 1827 |
| 1054 | Ćopić, Branko | Yugoslav(Serb) | SS | Doživljaji Nikoletine Bursaća | 1956 |
| 1055 | Ćopić, Branko | Yugoslav | N | Orlovi rano lete | 1957 |
| 1056 | Corneille, Pierre | French | P | Le Cid | 1637 |
| 1057 | Corneille, Pierre | French | P | Horace | 1641 |
| 1058 | Corneille, Pierre | French | P | Othon | 1665 |
| 1059 | Cortazár, Julio | Argentine | SS | Las babas del Diablo | 1958 |
| 1060 | Ćosić, Dobrica | Yugoslav(Serb) | N | Daleko je sunce (Far Away Is the Sun) | 1951 |
| 1061 | Courteline, Georges | French | P | L'article 330 (Article 330) | 1900 |
| 1062 | Courteline, Georges | French | P | Un client sérieux [A serious customer] | 1897 |
| 1063 | Courteline, Georges | French | P | Le commissaire est bon enfant (The Commissioner) | 1899 |
| 1064 | Courteline, Georges | French | P | Les gaités de l'escadron [The gaieties of the squadron] | 1886 |

| No | Film Title | Country of Production | Date | Director(s) | Duration of Film |
|---|---|---|---|---|---|
| 1031 | **Dans une île perdue** {French version of William Wellman's film:- Dangerous Paradise} | FR | 1930 | **Alberto Cavalcanti** | 73 |
| 1032 | **Tropennächte** {German version of William Wellman's film:- Dangerous Paradise} | GER/USA/ FR | 1931 | **Leo Mittler** | 66 |
| 1033 | **Victory** | USA | 1941(40) | **John Cromwell** | 77 |
| 1034 | **De loteling** (The Conscript) | BEL | 1974 | **Roland Verhavert** | 95 |
| 1035 | **Adolphe, ou l'âge tendre** | FR | 1968 | **Bernard T. Michel** | 103 |
| 1036 | **Antes, o verão** (First, the Summer) (aka: The Summer Before) | BRAZ | 1967 | **Gerson Teveras** | 80 |
| 1037 | **Um homem e sua jaula** | BRAZ | 1969 | **Fernando Coni Campos** | 80(75) |
| 1038 | **The Deerslayer** | USA | 1944(43) | **Lew Landers** | 67 |
| 1039 | **The Deerslayer** | USA | 1957 | **Kurt Neumann** | 77 +V |
| 1040 | **Chingachgock - die grosse Schlange** [Chingachgock - the big snake] | GDR | 1967 | **Richard Grosschopp** | 91 |
| 1041 | **The Deerslayer** | USA | 1978 | **Dick Friedenberg** | 98 +V(74) |
| 1042 | **The Last of the Mohicans** | USA | 1932 | **B. Reeves Eason Ford Beebe** | 50 |
| 1043 | **The Last of the Mohicans** | USA | 1936 | **George B. Seitz** | 91 |
| 1044 | **The Last of the Redmen** | USA | 1947 | **George Sherman** | 78 |
| 1045 | **Der letzte Mohikaner** (The Last of the Mohicans) (IT: La valle della ombre rosse) (SP: El ultimo Mohicano) | GER/IT/ SP | 1965 | **Harald Reinl** | 90(85) |
| 1046 | **Ultimul Mohican** (The Last of the Mohicans) | ROM/FR | 1969(68) | **Jean Dréville Sergiu Nicolaescu** | 82 |
| 1047 | **Last of the Mohicans** | USA | 1977 | **James L. Conway** | 94 +V |
| 1048 | **The Iroquois Trail** (aka: The Tomahawk Trail) | USA | 1950 | **Phil Karlson** | 86 |
| 1049 | **Pathfinder** | USA | 1952 | **Sidney Salkow** | 78 |
| 1050 | **Aventuri in Ontario** | ROM | 1969(68) | **Jean Dréville Sergiu Nicolaescu** | 97 |
| 1051 | **The Pioneers** | USA | 1947 | **Albert Herman** | 60 |
| 1052 | **The Prairie** | USA | 1948 | **Frank Wisbar** | 56 |
| 1053 | **Preeria** | ROM/FR | 1968 | **Pierre Gaspard-Huit Sergiu Nicolaescu** | 95 |
| 1054 | **Doživljaji Nikoletine Bursaća** (aka: Nikoletina Bursać) (Adventures of Nikoletina Bursać) | YUGO | 1964 | **Branko Bauer** | 102 |
| 1055 | **Orlovi rano lete** (The Eagles Fly Early) | YUGO | 1966 | **Soja Jovanovič** | 90 |
| 1056 | **El Cid** | USA/IT | 1961 | **Anthony Mann** | 180 |
| 1057 | **Horace 62** | FR | 1962 | **André Versini** | 90 |
| 1058 | **Othon** (aka: Eyes do not Want to Close at all Times) | GER/IT | 1970(69) | **Jean-Marie Straub Danièle Huillet** | 90(83) |
| 1059 | **Blow-Up** | GB/IT | 1966 | **Michelangelo Antonioni** | 111 +V |
| 1060 | **Daleko je sunce** (The Sun Is Far Away) | YUGO | 1953 | **Radoš Novaković** | 100 |
| 1061 | **L'article 330** | FR | 1934 | **Marcel Pagnol** | 40 |
| 1062 | **Un client sérieux** | FR | 1932 | **Claude Autant-Lara** | 22 |
| 1063 | **Le commissaire est bon enfant, le gendarme est sans pitié** (aka: Pitiless Gendarme) | FR | 1934 | **Pierre Prévert Jacques Becker** | 42 |
| 1064 | **Les gaités de l'escadron** | FR | 1932 | **Maurice Tourneur** | 85 |

| No. | Author | Nationality | Form | Literary Title | Date |
|-----|--------|-------------|------|----------------|------|
| 1065 | **Courteline, Georges** | French | P | **Les gaités de l'escadron** | 1886 |
| 1066 | **Courteline, Georges** | French | P | **Le gendarme est sans pitié** *(The Pitiless Policeman)* | 1899 |
| 1067 | **Courteline, Georges** | French | P | **Lidoire** | 1892 |
| 1068 | **Courteline, Georges** | French | N | **Messieurs les ronds-de-cuir** *(The Bureaucrats)* | 1893 |
| 1069 | **Courteline, Georges** | French | N | **Messieurs les ronds-de-cuir** | 1893 |
| 1070 | **Courteline, Georges** | French | P | **La paix chez soi** *(Peace at Home)* + **La peur des coups** + **Les boulingrin** *(These Cornfields)* | 1903+ 1895+ 1914 |
| 1071 | **Courteline, Georges** | French | N | **Le train de 8h. 47** *[The 8:47 train]* | 1891 |
| 1072 | **Coward, Noël** | British | P | **The Astonished Heart** | 1936 |
| 1073 | **Coward, Noël** | British | P | **Bitter Sweet** | 1929 |
| 1074 | **Coward, Noël** | British | P | **Bitter Sweet** | 1929 |
| 1075 | **Coward, Noël** | British | P | **Blithe Spirit** | 1942 |
| 1076 | **Coward, Noël** | British | P | **Cavalcade** | 1932 |
| 1077 | **Coward, Noël** | British | P | **Cavalcade** | 1932 |
| 1078 | **Coward, Noël** | British | P | **Design For Living** | 1933 |
| 1079 | **Coward, Noël** | British | SS | **Me and the Girls** | 1965 |
| 1080 | **Coward, Noël** | British | SS | **Mister and Mrs Edgehill** | 1951 |
| 1081 | **Coward, Noël** | British | SS | **Mrs Capper's Birthday** | 1965 |
| 1082 | **Coward, Noël** | British | SS | **Pretty Polly Barlow** | 1964 |
| 1083 | **Coward, Noël** | British | P | **Private Lives** | 1930 |
| 1084 | **Coward, Noël** | British | P | **Private Lives** | 1930 |
| 1085 | **Coward, Noël** | British | P | **The Queen Was in the Parlour** | 1926 |
| 1086 | **Coward, Noël** | British | P | **Still Life** | 1938 |
| 1087 | **Coward, Noël** | British | P | **Still Life** | 1938 |
| 1088 | **Coward, Noël** | British | P | **This Happy Breed** | 1943 |
| 1089 | **Coward, Noël** | British | P | **Ways and Means** + **Red Peppers** + **Fumed Oak** | 1936 |
| 1090 | **Coward, Noël** | British | SS | **What Mad Pursuit?** | 1939 |
| 1091 | **Cozzens, James Gould** | American | N | **By Love Possessed** | 1957 |
| 1092 | **Cozzens, James Gould** | American | N | **The Last Adam** *(GB: A Cure of Flesh)* | 1933 |
| 1093 | **Crane, Stephen** | American | SS | **The Blue Hotel** | 1899 |
| 1094 | **Crane, Stephen** | American | SS | **The Bride Comes to Yellow Sky** | 1898 |
| 1095 | **Crane, Stephen** | American | SS | **The Monster** | 1899 |
| 1096 | **Crane, Stephen** | American | N | **The Red Badge of Courage** | 1895 |
| 1097 | **Crane, Stephen** | American | SS | **Three Miraculous Soldiers** | 1896 |
| 1098 | **Creangă, Ion** | Romanian | AUT | **Amintiri din copilărie** *(Recollections)* *(aka: Recollections From Childhood)* | 1881-92 |
| 1099 | **Creangă, Ion** | Romanian | SS | **Capra cu trei iezi** *(The Goat and Her Three Kids)* | 1875 |
| 1100 | **Creangă, Ion** | Romanian | SS | **Povestea lui Harap Alb** *(The Story of Harap Alb)* | 1877 |
| 1101 | **Creangă, Ion** | Romanian | SS | **Povestea porcului** *(The Tale of the Pig)* | 1876 |
| 1102 | **Creangă, Ion** | Romanian | SS | **Punguţa cu doi bani** *(The Purse With Coppers Two)* | 1876 |
| 1103 | **Crommelynck, Fernand** | French | P | **Le cocu magnifique** *(The Magnificent Cuckold)* | 1921 |
| 1104 | **Crommelynck, Fernand** | French | P | **Le cocu magnifique** | 1921 |
| 1105 | **Cronin, A. J.** | British(Scot) | N | **Beyond This Place** | 1953 |

| No | Film Title | Country of Production | Date | Director(s) | Duration of Film |
|---|---|---|---|---|---|
| 1065 | L'allegro squadrone (aka: Alberto il marmittone) (FR: Les gaités de l'escadron) | IT/FR | 1955(54) | Paolo Moffa | 83 |
| 1066 | Le gendarme est sans pitié | FR | 1932 | Claude Autant-Lara | 20 |
| 1067 | Lidoire | FR | 1936(32) | Maurice Tourneur | 20 |
| 1068 | Messieurs les ronds-de-cuir | FR | 1936 | Yves Mirande | 100 |
| 1069 | Messieurs les ronds-de-cuir | FR | 1959 | Henri Diamant-Berger | 85 |
| 1070 | Scènes de ménage | FR | 1954 | André Berthomieu | 80 |
| 1071 | Le train de 8h. 47 | FR | 1935 | Henry Wulschleger | 80 |
| 1072 | The Astonished Heart | GB | 1950 | Terence Fisher Anthony Darnborough | 92 |
| 1073 | Bitter Sweet | GB | 1933 | Herbert Wilcox | 93 |
| 1074 | Bitter Sweet | USA | 1940 | W. S. Van Dyke | 94 |
| 1075 | Blithe Spirit | GB | 1945 | David Lean | 96 +V |
| 1076 | Cavalcade | USA | 1933 | Frank Lloyd | 109 |
| 1077 | Cavalcade | USA | 1955 | Lewis Allen | 44 |
| 1078 | Design For Living | USA | 1933 | Ernst Lubitsch | 95(90) |
| 1079 | Me and the Girls | GB | 1985 | Jack Gold | 54 +V |
| 1080 | Mister and Mrs Edgehill | GB | 1985 | Gavin Millar | 82 +V |
| 1081 | Mrs Capper's Birthday | GB | 1985 | Mike Ockrent | 59 +V |
| 1082 | Pretty Polly (USA: A Matter of Innocence) | GB | 1967 | Guy Green | 102 |
| 1083 | Private Lives | USA | 1931 | Sidney A. Franklin | 82 |
| 1084 | Les amants terribles | FR | 1936 | Marc Allégret | 86 |
| 1085 | Tonight Is Ours | USA | 1933 | Stuart Walker | 76 |
| 1086 | Brief Encounter | GB | 1945 | David Lean | 86 +V |
| 1087 | Brief Encounter | GB | 1974 | Alan Bridges | 103 +V |
| 1088 | This Happy Breed | GB | 1944 | David Lean | 114 +V |
| 1089 | Meet Me Tonight (USA: Tonight at 8.30) | GB | 1952 | Anthony Pélissier | 85 |
| 1090 | What Mad Pursuit? | GB | 1985 | Tony Smith | 55 +V |
| 1091 | By Love Possessed | USA | 1961 | John Sturges | 116 |
| 1092 | Doctor Bull | USA | 1933 | John Ford | 75 |
| 1093 | The Blue Hotel | USA | 1979(77) | Ján Kadár | 54(51) +V |
| 1094 | Face to Face {Pt.2} | USA | 1952 | Bretaigne Windust | 45 (Pt.2) |
| 1095 | Face of Fire (SWE: Mannen utan ansikte) | USA/SWE | 1960(58) | Albert Band | 80 |
| 1096 | The Red Badge of Courage | USA | 1951 | John Huston | 69 +V |
| 1097 | Three Miraculous Soldiers | USA | 1977 | Bernard Selling | 17 +V |
| 1098 | Amintiri din copilărie | ROM | 1965 | Elisabeta Bostan | 59 |
| 1099 | Mama [Mother] | ROM/USSR | 1977(76) | Elisabeta Bostan | 89 |
| 1100 | De-aş fi Harap Alb [If I were Harap Alb] | ROM | 1965 | Ion Popescu Gopo | 82 |
| 1101 | Povestea dragostei [Love's story] {live-action + animation} | ROM | 1977(76) | Ion Popescu Gopo | 83 |
| 1102 | Rămăşagul [The bet] {live-action + animation} | ROM | 1985 | Ion Popescu Gopo | 87 |
| 1103 | Le cocu magnifique | BEL | 1946 | E. G. de Meyst | 90 |
| 1104 | Il magnifico cornuto (FR: Le cocu magnifique) (The Magnificent Cuckold) | IT/FR | 1965(64) | Antonio Pietrangeli | 124 |
| 1105 | Beyond This Place (USA: Web of Evidence) | GB | 1959 | Jack Cardiff | 89 |

| No. | Author | Nationality | Form | Literary Title | Date |
|-----|--------|-------------|------|----------------|------|
| 1106 | Cronin, A. J. | British | N | The Citadel | 1937 |
| 1107 | Cronin, A. J. | British | N | The Grand Canary | 1933 |
| 1108 | Cronin, A. J. | British | N | The Green Years | 1944 |
| 1109 | Cronin, A. J. | British | N | Hatters Castle | 1931 |
| 1110 | Cronin, A. J. | British | P | Jupiter Laughs | 1940 |
| 1111 | Cronin, A. J. | British | P | Jupiter Laughs | 1940 |
| 1112 | Cronin, A. J. | British | N | The Keys of the Kingdom | 1941 |
| 1113 | Cronin, A. J. | British | N | The Spanish Gardener | 1950 |
| 1114 | Cronin, A. J. | British | N | The Stars Look Down | 1935 |
| 1115 | Cronin, A. J. | British | F-N | Vigil in the Night | 1941 |
| 1116 | Cruz, Eddy Dias da (see: Rebelo, Marques) | Brazilian | N | | |
| 1117 | Cseres Tibor | Hungarian | N | Hideg napok | 1965 |
| 1118 | Curel, François de | French | P | Terre inhumaine [Inhuman land] | 1923 |
| 1119 | Curel, François de | French | P | Terre inhumaine | 1923 |
| 1120 | Curtis, Jean-Louis | French | SS | L'éphèbe de Subiaco | 1969 |
| 1121 | Curtis, Jean-Louis | French | N | Gibier de potence (Lucifer's Dream) (aka: Dark Streets of Paris) | 1949 |
| 1122 | Curtis, Jean-Louis | French | N | Un jeune couple | 1967 |
| 1123 | Cusack, Dymphna | Australian | P | Red Sky at Morning | 1942 |
| 1124 | Czeszko, Bohdan | Polish | N | Pokolenie | 1951 |
| 1125 | Dabit, Eugène | French | N | L'Hôtel du Nord (Hotel du Nord) | 1929 |
| 1126 | Dąbrowska, Maria | Polish | N | Noce i dnie [Nights and days] | 1934-35 |
| 1127 | Dagerman, Stig | Swedish | N | Bränt barn (A Burnt Child) | 1948 |
| 1128 | Dagerman, Stig | Swedish | N | Bröllopsbesvär [Wedding worries] | 1949 |
| 1129 | Dagerman, Stig | Swedish | N | Bröllopsbesvär | 1949 |
| 1130 | Dagerman, Stig | Swedish | N | Ormen | 1945 |
| 1131 | Daisne, Johan (Herman Thiery) | Belgian | N | De man die zijn haar kort liet knippen (The Man Who Had His Hair Cut Short) | 1947 |
| 1132 | D'Alton, Louis | Irish | P | This Other Eden | 1954 |
| 1133 | Dana, R. H. | American | | Two Years Before the Mast | 1840 |
| 1134 | Dane, Clemence (Winifred Ashton) | British | P | A Bill of Divorcement | 1921 |
| 1135 | Dane, Clemence | British | P | A Bill of Divorcement | 1921 |
| 1136 | Dane, Clemence; Simpson, Helen | British | P | Enter Sir John | 1928 |
| 1137 | D'Annunzio, Gabriele | Italian | N | Giovanni L'Episcopo (Episcopo and Company) | 1891 |
| 1138 | D'Annunzio, Gabriele | Italian | N | L'innocente (The Intruder) | 1891 |
| 1139 | Dante Alighieri | Italian | V | Divina commedia (Divine Comedy) (aka: Commedia) | c.1306 |
| 1140 | Daudet, Alphonse | French | P | L'arlésienne (L'Arlésienne - the Woman From Arles) | 1872 |

| No | Film Title | Country of Production | Date | Director(s) | Duration of Film |
|----|-----------|----------------------|------|-------------|------------------|
| 1106 | The Citadel | GB | 1938 | King Vidor | 110 |
| 1107 | Grand Canary | USA | 1934 | Irving Cummings | 76 |
| 1108 | The Green Years | USA | 1946 | Victor Saville | 127 |
| 1109 | Hatters Castle | GB | 1941 | Lance Comfort | 100 |
| 1110 | Shining Victory | USA | 1941 | Irving Rapper | 80 |
| 1111 | Ich suche Dich<br>*[I'm looking for you]* | GER | 1953 | Otto Wilhelm Fischer | 95(91) |
| 1112 | The Keys of the Kingdom | USA | 1944 | John M. Stahl | 137 |
| 1113 | The Spanish Gardener | GB | 1956 | Philip Leacock | 97 +V |
| 1114 | The Stars Look Down | GB | 1939 | Carol Reed | 100 +V |
| 1115 | Vigil in the Night | USA | 1940(39) | George Stevens | 97 |
| 1116 | | | | | |
| 1117 | Hideg napok<br>*(Cold Days)* | HUNG | 1966 | András Kovács | 101 |
| 1118 | This Mad World | USA | 1930 | William C. de Mille | 70 |
| 1119 | Le bois des amants<br>*(IT: Il bosco degli amanti)* | FR/IT | 1960 | Claude Autant-Lara | 96(90) |
| 1120 | Chère Louise<br>*(IT: La lunga notte di Louise)*<br>*(Louise)* | FR/IT | 1972 | Philippe de Broca | 105(98) |
| 1121 | Gibier de potence | FR | 1952 | Roger Richebé | 106 |
| 1122 | Un jeune couple | FR | 1969 | René Gainville | 90 |
| 1123 | Red Sky at Morning | AUSTL | 1944 | Hartney Arthur | 55 |
| 1124 | Pokolenie<br>*(A Generation)* | POL | 1955(54) | Andrzej Wajda | 101<br>+V(91) |
| 1125 | Hôtel du Nord | FR | 1938 | Marcel Carné | 110 |
| 1126 | Noce i dnie<br>*(Pt.1: Bogumił i Barbara)*<br>*(Bogumie and Barbara)*<br>*(Pt.2: Wiatr w oczy)*<br>*[Wind blowing in the eyes]* | POL | 1975 | Jerzy Antczak | Pt.1, 141<br>(176)<br>Pt.2, 133<br>(166) |
| 1127 | Bränt barn<br>*(Burnt Child)*<br>*(aka: Sinning Urge)* | SWE | 1968 | Hans Abramson | 103 |
| 1128 | En natt på Glimmingehus | SWE | 1954 | Torgny Wickman | 99 |
| 1129 | Bröllopsbesvär | SWE | 1964 | Åke Falck | 100 |
| 1130 | Ormen<br>*(The Serpent)* | SWE | 1966 | Hans Abramson | 94 |
| 1131 | De man die zijn haar kort liet knippen<br>*(The Man Who Had His Hair Cut Short)* | BEL | 1965 | André Delvaux | 94 |
| 1132 | This Other Eden | GB | 1959 | Muriel Box | 80 |
| 1133 | Two Years Before the Mast | USA | 1946 | John Farrow | 97 |
| 1134 | A Bill of Divorcement | USA | 1932 | George Cukor | 76<br>+V |
| 1135 | A Bill of Divorcement<br>*(GB: Never to Love)* | USA | 1940 | John Farrow | 69 |
| 1136 | Murder<br>*(GER: Mary)*<br>*(aka: Sir John greift ein!)* | GB | 1930 | Alfred Hitchcock | 108<br>+V(92) |
| 1137 | Il delitto di Giovanni Episcopo<br>*(Giovanni Episcopo's Crime)*<br>*(aka: Flesh Will Surrender)* | IT | 1947 | Alberto Lattuada | 94 |
| 1138 | L'innocente<br>*(The Innocent)*<br>*(aka: The Intruder)* | IT/FR | 1976 | Luchino Visconti | 125(135) |
| 1139 | Skärseld<br>*(Dante's A Divine Comedy)*<br>*(aka: Purgatorio)* | SWE | 1975 | Michael Meschke | 86 |
| 1140 | L'arlésienne | FR | 1942 | Marc Allégret | 105 |

| No. | Author | Nationality | Form | Literary Title | Date |
|-----|--------|-------------|------|----------------|------|
| 1141 | **Daudet, Alphonse** | French | N | **Fromont jeune et Risler aîné**<br>*(Fromont the Younger and Risler<br>the Elder)* | 1874 |
| 1142 | **Daudet, Alphonse** | French | N | **Le petit chose**<br>*(The Little Weakling)*<br>*(aka: My Brother Jack)* | 1868 |
| 1143 | **Daudet, Alphonse** | French | N | **Le petit chose** | 1868 |
| 1144 | **Daudet, Alphonse** | French | N | **Sapho**<br>*(Sappho)* | 1884 |
| 1145 | **Daudet, Alphonse** | French | N | **Sapho** | 1884 |
| 1146 | **Daudet, Alphonse** | French | N | **Sapho** | 1884 |
| 1147 | **Daudet, Alphonse** | French | N | **Tartarin de Tarascon, aventures**<br>**prodigieuses de**<br>*(The Prodigious Adventures of<br>Tartarin de Tarascon)* | 1872 |
| 1148 | **Daudet, Alphonse** | French | N | **Tartarin de Tarascon** | 1872 |
| 1149 | **Daudet, Alphonse** | French | SS | **Les trois messes basses**<br>*(The Three Low Masses)* +<br>**L'élixir du père Gaucher** +<br>**Le secret de Maître Cornille** | 1869 |
| 1150 | **Davis, Ossie** | American(afro) | P | **Purlie Victorious** | 1962 |
| 1151 | **Dayton, Katherine**<br>*(joint, see: Kaufman, George S.)* | American | P | | |
| 1152 | **D'Azeglio, Massimo** | Italian | N | **Ettore Fieramosca o la disfida**<br>**di Barletta**<br>*(Ettore Fieramosca, or The<br>Challenge of Barletta)* | 1833 |
| 1153 | **De Filippo, Eduardo** | Italian | P | **Filumena Marturano**<br>*(Filumena)*<br>*(aka: The Best House in Naples)* | 1946 |
| 1154 | **De Filippo, Eduardo** | Italian | P | **Filumena Marturano** | 1946 |
| 1155 | **De Filippo, Eduardo** | Italian | P | **Napoli milionaria!**<br>*[Naples millionaires!]* | 1945 |
| 1156 | **De Filippo, Eduardo** | Italian | P | **Questi fantasmi!**<br>*(Oh, These Ghosts!)* | 1946 |
| 1157 | **De Filippo, Eduardo** | Italian | P | **Questi fantasmi!** | 1946 |
| 1158 | **De Filippo, Eduardo** | Italian | P | **Sabato, domenica e lunedi** | 1959 |
| 1159 | **De Filippo, Eduardo** | Italian | P | **Le voci di dentro**<br>*[The voices from within]* | 1948 |
| 1160 | **Defoe, Daniel** | British | N | **Moll Flanders** | 1722 |
| 1161 | **Defoe, Daniel** | British | N | **Robinson Crusoe**<br>*{pt.1}* | 1719 |
| 1162 | **Defoe, Daniel** | British | N | **Robinson Crusoe** | 1719 |
| 1163 | **Defoe, Daniel** | British | N | **Robinson Crusoe** | 1719 |
| 1164 | **Defoe, Daniel** | British | N | **Robinson Crusoe** | 1719 |
| 1165 | **Defoe, Daniel** | British | N | **Robinson Crusoe** | 1719 |
| 1166 | **Defoe, Daniel** | British | N | **Robinson Crusoe** | 1719 |
| 1167 | **Defoe, Daniel** | British | N | **Robinson Crusoe** | 1719 |
| 1168 | **Defoe, Daniel** | British | N | **Robinson Crusoe** | 1719 |
| 1169 | **Defoe, Daniel** | British | N | **Robinson Crusoe** | 1719 |
| 1170 | **Defoe, Daniel** | British | N | **Robinson Crusoe** | 1719 |
| 1171 | **Defoe, Daniel** | British | N | **Robinson Crusoe** | 1719 |
| 1172 | **De Kruif, Paul**<br>*(joint, see: Howard, Sidney Coe)* | American | P | | |

| No | Film Title | Country of Production | Date | Director(s) | Duration of Film |
|---|---|---|---|---|---|
| 1141 | Fromont jeune et Risler aîné | FR | 1941 | Léon Mathot | 104 |
| 1142 | Le petit chose | FR | 1938 | Maurice Cloche | 95 |
| 1143 | The Last Lesson | USA | 1942 | Allan R. Kenward | 10 |
| 1144 | Inspiration | USA | 1931 | Clarence Brown | 74 |
| 1145 | Sapho | FR | 1934 | Léonce Perret | 90 |
| 1146 | Safo | ARG | 1943 | Carlos Hugo Christensen | 98 |
| 1147 | Tartarin de Tarascon | FR | 1934 | Raymond Bernard | 95 |
| 1148 | Tartarin de Tarascon | FR | 1962 | Francis Blanche | 105 |
| 1149 | Les lettres de mon moulin (Letters From My Windmill) | FR | 1954 | Marcel Pagnol | 120 |
| 1150 1151 | Gone Are The Days | USA | 1963 | Nicholas Webster | 97 |
| 1152 | Ettore Fieramosca | IT | 1938 | Alessandro Blasetti | 114(91) |
| 1153 | Filumena Marturano | IT | 1952(51) | Eduardo de Filippo | 100 |
| 1154 | Matrimonio all'italiana (FR: Mariage à l'italienne) (Marriage Italian Style) | IT/FR | 1964 | Vittorio de Sica | 108(104) +V(96) |
| 1155 | Napoli milionaria (Side Street Story) | IT | 1950 | Eduardo de Filippo | 98 |
| 1156 | Questi fantasmi! | IT | 1954 | Eduardo de Filippo | 90 |
| 1157 | Questi fantasmi! (Ghosts - Italian Style) | IT/FR | 1967 | Renato Castellani | 104 |
| 1158 | Sabato, domenica e lunedi (Saturday, Sunday and Monday) | IT | 1990 | Lina Wertmüller | 115 |
| 1159 | Spara forte...più forte...non capisco! (Shoot Loud... Louder... I Don't Understand) | IT | 1966 | Eduardo de Filippo | 101 |
| 1160 | Molly-Familjeflickan (aka: Molly) | SWE/FR | 1977(76) | Mac Ahlberg (Bert Torn) | 100 |
| 1161 | Robinson Crusoe | USSR | 1947(46) | Alexander Andriyevsky | 74 |
| 1162 | Robinson Crusoé (IT: Il naufragio del Pacifico) | FR/IT | 1951(50) | Jeff Musso | 94 |
| 1163 | Las aventuras de Robinson Crusoe (Robinson Crusoe) (aka: Adventures of Robinson Crusoe) | MEX | 1952 | Luis Buñuel | 90 |
| 1164 | Robinson Crusoe on Mars | USA | 1964 | Byron Haskin | 109 |
| 1165 | Tu imagines Robinson | FR | 1968 | Jean-Daniel Pollet | 87 |
| 1166 | Robinson y viernes en la isla encantada (Robinson Crusoe and the Tiger) (aka: Robinson Crusoe) | MEX | 1969 | Rene Cardona Jn. | 110 +V(105) |
| 1167 | Robinson Crusoe {animation} | AUSTL | 1972 | Gibba | 86 +V(47) |
| 1168 | Zhizn'i udivitel'nye priklutchenija Robinsona Crusoe (Robinson Crusoe) | USSR | 1972 | Stanislas Govorukhin | 92(85) |
| 1169 | As Aventuras de Robinson Crusoe | BRAZ | 1978 | Mozael Silveira | 90 |
| 1170 | Dobrodružství Robinson Crusoe, namornika z Yorku (Adventures of Robinson Crusoe, a Sailor From York) (aka: Robinson Crusoe) | CZ/GER | 1982 | Stanislav Latal | 68 |
| 1171 1172 | Crusoe | USA | 1988 | Caleb Deschanel | 91 |

| No. | Author | Nationality | Form | Literary Title | Date |
|---|---|---|---|---|---|
| 1173 | **Delacour, A.**<br>*(joint, see: Labiche, Eugène)* | French | P | | |
| 1174 | **Delaney, Shelagh** | British | P | **A Taste of Honey** | 1959 |
| 1175 | **Deledda, Grazia** | Italian | N | **La madre**<br>*(The Mother)* | 1920 |
| 1176 | **Delibes, Miguel** | Spanish | N | **El camino**<br>*(The Path)* | 1950 |
| 1177 | **Delibes, Miguel** | Spanish | N | **Mi idolatrado hijo Sisí**<br>*[My adored son, Sisi]* | 1953 |
| 1178 | **Delibes, Miguel** | Spanish | N | **Los santos inocentes** | 1981 |
| 1179 | **Delicado, Francisco** | Spanish | N | **El retrato de la lozana andaluza** | 1528 |
| 1180 | **Denevi, Marco** | Argentine | SS | **Ceremonia secreta** | 1955(61) |
| 1181 | **Denevi, Marco** | Argentine | N | **Rosaura a las diez** | 1955 |
| 1182 | **Déon, Michel** | French | N | **Un taxi mauve** | 1973 |
| 1183 | **De Quincey, Thomas** | British | | **Confessions of an English Opium Eater** | 1822 |
| 1184 | **Déry Tibor** | Hungarian | N | **A befejezetlen mondat**<br>*[The unfinished sentence]* | 1947 |
| 1185 | **Déry Tibor** | Hungarian | SS | **Az óriás**<br>*(The Giant)* | 1948 |
| 1186 | **Déry Tibor** | Hungarian | SS | **Pesti felhőjáték** | 1946 |
| 1187 | **Déry Tibor** | Hungarian | SS | **Szerelem**<br>*(Love)*<br>*(aka: Odysseus) +*<br>**Két asszony** | 1956+<br>1962 |
| 1188 | **Déry Tibor** | Hungarian | SS | **Vidám temetés**<br>*(A Gay Funeral)* | 1963 |
| 1189 | **Descaves, Lucien** | French | P | **Le coeur ébloui** | 1926 |
| 1190 | **Desnoes, Edmundo** | Cuban | N | **Memorias del subdesarrollo**<br>*(Inconsolable Memories)* | 1965 |
| 1191 | **Deval, Jacques** | French | P | **L'amant rêvé** | 1925 |
| 1192 | **Deval, Jacques** | French | P | **Étienne** | 1930 |
| 1193 | **Deval, Jacques** | French | N | **Marie Galante**<br>*(That Girl)* | 1931 |
| 1194 | **Deval, Jacques** | French | P | **Soubrette**<br>*(They Make Good Servants)* | 1938 |
| 1195 | **Deval, Jacques** | French | P | **Tovaritch**<br>*(Tovarich)* | 1934 |
| 1196 | **Desvallières, Maurice**<br>*(joint, see: Feydeau, Goerges)* | French | P | | |
| 1197 | **De Vries, Peter** | American | N | **The Cat's Pajamas +**<br>**Witches Milk** | 1968 |
| 1198 | **De Vries, Peter** | American | N | **Let Me Count the Ways** | 1965 |
| 1199 | **De Vries, Peter** | American | N | **Reuben, Reuben** | 1964 |
| 1200 | **De Vries, Peter** | American | N-P | **Tunnel of Love** | 1954{n}<br>1957{p} |
| 1201 | **Dick, Philip K.** | American | N | **Do Androids Dream of Electric Sheep?** | 1969 |
| 1202 | **Dick, Philip K.** | American | SS | **We Can Remember It For You Wholesale** | 1966 |
| 1203 | **Dickens, Charles** | British | SS | **A Christmas Carol** | 1843 |
| 1204 | **Dickens, Charles** | British | SS | **A Christmas Carol** | 1843 |
| 1205 | **Dickens, Charles** | British | SS | **A Christmas Carol** | 1843 |
| 1206 | **Dickens, Charles** | British | SS | **A Christmas Carol** | 1843 |
| 1207 | **Dickens, Charles** | British | SS | **A Christmas Carol** | 1843 |
| 1208 | **Dickens, Charles** | British | SS | **A Christmas Carol** | 1843 |
| 1209 | **Dickens, Charles** | British | SS | **A Christmas Carol** | 1843 |
| 1210 | **Dickens, Charles** | British | SS | **A Christmas Carol** | 1843 |
| 1211 | **Dickens, Charles** | British | SS | **The Cricket on the Hearth** | 1845 |

| No | Film Title | Country of Production | Date | Director(s) | Duration of Film |
|----|-----------|----------------------|------|-------------|------------------|
| 1173 | | | | | |
| 1174 | A Taste of Honey | GB | 1961 | Tony Richardson | 100 |
| 1175 | Proibito<br>(FR: Du sang dans le soleil)<br>(aka: La madre) | IT/FR | 1955(54) | Mario Monicelli | 90 |
| 1176 | El camino | SP | 1963 | Ana Mariscal | 90(96) |
| 1177 | Retrato de familia<br>(Family Portrait) | SP | 1976 | Antonio Giménez Rico | 99(97) |
| 1178 | Los santos inocentes<br>(The Holy Innocents) | SP | 1984 | Mario Camús | 105(100) |
| 1179 | La lozana andaluza | SP/IT | 1976 | Vicente Escrivá | 97(98) |
| 1180 | Secret Ceremony | GB | 1968 | Joseph Losey | 109 |
| 1181 | Rosaura a las diez | ARG | 1958 | Mario Soffici | 100 |
| 1182 | Un taxi mauve<br>(IT: Un taxi color malva)<br>(The Purple Taxi) | FR/IT/<br>IRE | 1977 | Yves Boisset | 120<br>+V(107) |
| 1183 | Confessions of an Opium Eater<br>(aka: Evils of Chinatown) | USA | 1962 | Albert Zugsmith | 85 |
| 1184 | 141 perc a befejezetlen mondatból<br>(The Unfinished Sentence)<br>(aka: 141 Minutes From the Unfinished Sentence) | HUNG | 1974 | Zoltán Fábri | 128(141) |
| 1185 | Az óriás<br>(The Giant) | HUNG | 1984 | Erika Szántó | 84 |
| 1186 | Felhőjáték<br>(Budapest Cloudplay) | HUNG | 1983 | Gyula Maár | 99 |
| 1187 | Szerelem<br>(Love) | HUNG | 1971 | Károly Makk | 92 |
| 1188 | Az utolsó kézirat<br>(The Last Manuscript) | HUNG | 1988(87) | Károly Makk | 110 |
| 1189 | Le coeur ébloui | FR | 1938 | Jean Vallée | 90 |
| 1190 | Memorias del subdesarrollo<br>(Memories of Underdevelopment) | CB | 1968 | Tomás Gutiérrez Alea<br>(Gutiérrez Alea, Tomás) | 90(97) |
| 1191 | Her Cardboard Lover | USA | 1942 | George Cukor | 93 |
| 1192 | Étienne | FR | 1934 | Jean Tarride | 105 |
| 1193 | Marie Galante | USA | 1934 | Henry King | 90 |
| 1194 | Say It In French | USA | 1938 | Andrew L. Stone | 67 |
| 1195 | Tovaritch | FR | 1935 | Jacques Deval | 100 |
| 1196 | | | | | |
| 1197 | Pete 'n' Tillie | USA | 1972 | Martin Ritt | 100 |
| 1198 | How Do I Love Thee? | USA | 1970 | Michael Gordon | 109 +V |
| 1199 | Reuben, Reuben | USA | 1983 | Robert Ellis Miller | 101 |
| 1200 | The Tunnel of Love | USA | 1958 | Gene Kelly | 98 |
| 1201 | Blade Runner | USA | 1982 | Ridley Scott | 118<br>+V(112) |
| 1202 | Total Recall | USA | 1990 | Paul Verhoeven | 113 |
| 1203 | Scrooge | GB | 1935 | Henry Edwards | 78 |
| 1204 | A Christmas Carol | USA | 1938 | Edwin L. Marin | 69 |
| 1205 | Scrooge<br>(aka: A Christmas Carol) | GB | 1951 | Brian Desmond Hurst | 94<br>+V(86) |
| 1206 | The Stingiest Man in Town<br>{animation} | USA | 1956 | Daniel Petrie | 51<br>+V(47) |
| 1207 | A Christmas Carol | GB | 1960 | Robert Harford-Davis | 28 |
| 1208 | Scrooge<br>{musical version} | GB | 1970 | Ronald Neame | 118<br>+V(115) |
| 1209 | The Passions of Carol | USA | 1975 | Amanda Barton | 76 |
| 1210 | A Christmas Carol | GB | 1984 | Clive Donner | 101 +V |
| 1211 | Le grillon du foyer | FR | 1933 | Robert Boudrioz | 90 |

| No. | Author | Nationality | Form | Literary Title | Date |
|-----|--------|-------------|------|----------------|------|
| 1212 | Dickens, Charles | British | N | David Copperfield (aka: The Personal History of David Copperfield) | 1849 |
| 1213 | Dickens, Charles | British | N | David Copperfield | 1849 |
| 1214 | Dickens, Charles | British | N | David Copperfield | 1849 |
| 1215 | Dickens, Charles | British | N | Dombey and Son | 1848 |
| 1216 | Dickens, Charles | British | N | Great Expectations | 1861 |
| 1217 | Dickens, Charles | British | N | Great Expectations | 1861 |
| 1218 | Dickens, Charles | British | N | Great Expectations | 1861 |
| 1219 | Dickens, Charles | British | N | Great Expectations | 1861 |
| 1220 | Dickens, Charles | British | N | Hard Times (aka: Hard Times. For These Times) | 1854 |
| 1221 | Dickens, Charles | British | N | Little Dorrit | 1857 |
| 1222 | Dickens, Charles | British | N | Little Dorrit | 1857 |
| 1223 | Dickens, Charles | British | N | The Mystery of Edwin Drood | 1870 |
| 1224 | Dickens, Charles | British | N | Nicholas Nickleby | 1838 |
| 1225 | Dickens, Charles | British | N | The Old Curiosity Shop | 1841 |
| 1226 | Dickens, Charles | British | N | The Old Curiosity Shop | 1841 |
| 1227 | Dickens, Charles | British | N | Oliver Twist | 1838 |
| 1228 | Dickens, Charles | British | N | Oliver Twist | 1838 |
| 1229 | Dickens, Charles | British | N | Oliver Twist | 1838 |
| 1230 | Dickens, Charles | British | N | Oliver Twist | 1838 |
| 1231 | Dickens, Charles | British | N | Oliver Twist | 1838 |
| 1232 | Dickens, Charles | British | N | The Pickwick Papers | 1836 |
| 1233 | Dickens, Charles | British | N | A Tale of Two Cities | 1859 |
| 1234 | Dickens, Charles | British | N | A Tale of Two Cities | 1859 |
| 1235 | Dickey, James | American | N | Deliverance | 1970 |
| 1236 | Diderot, Denis | French | N | Jacques le fataliste et son maître (Jacques the Fatalist and His Master) | 1797 |
| 1237 | Diderot, Denis | French | N | La religieuse (The Nun) | 1796 |
| 1238 | Didion, Joan | American | N | Play It As It Lays | 1970 |
| 1239 | Dimitrova, Blaga | Bulgarian | N | Lavina [Avalanche] | 1971 |
| 1240 | Dimitrova, Blaga | Bulgarian | N | Pătuvane kăm sebe si | 1965 |
| 1241 | Dimov, Dimităr | Bulgarian | N | Osădeni dushi | 1945 |
| 1242 | Dimov, Dimităr | Bulgarian | N | Tyutyun | 1951 |
| 1243 | Dinarte, Sylvio (see: Taunay, Alfredo d'Escragnolle) | Brazilian | N | | |
| 1244 | Dinesen, Isak (Karen Blixen) | Danish(Eng) | MEM | Den afrikanske farm (Out of Africa) + Skygger paa græsset (Shadows on the Grass) + Breve fra Africa : 1914-31 (Letters from Africa) | 1937+ 1960+ 1978 |
| 1245 | Dinesen, Isak | Danish | SS | Babette's Feast (Babettes gæstebud) | 1950 |
| 1246 | Dinesen, Isak | Danish | SS | The Immortal Story | 1953 |
| 1247 | Ding Yi (see: He Jingzhi) | Chinese | P | | |

| No | Film Title | Country of Production | Date | Director(s) | Duration of Film |
|----|-----------|----------------------|------|-------------|------------------|
| 1212 | **David Copperfield** *(aka: The Personal History, Adventures, Experience, & Observations of David Copperfield the Younger)* | USA | 1935 | George Cukor | 130 +V |
| 1213 | **David Copperfield** | GB | 1970(69) | Delbert Mann | 118 |
| 1214 | **David Copperfield** *{animation}* | GB | 1984 | Alex Nicholas Ian Mackenzie | 72 +V |
| 1215 | **Rich Man's Folly** | USA | 1931 | John Cromwell | 80 |
| 1216 | **Great Expectations** | USA | 1934 | Stuart Walker | 100 |
| 1217 | **Great Expectations** | GB | 1946 | David Lean | 118 +V |
| 1218 | **Great Expectations** | GB | 1975 | Joseph Hardy | 124 +V |
| 1219 | **Great Expectations** *{animation}* | AUSTL | 1982 | Jean Tych | 72 +V |
| 1220 | **Tempos difíceis** *(Hard Times)* *(aka: Tempos difíceis, este tempo)* | PORT/GB | 1988 | João Botelho | 96 |
| 1221 | **Klein Dorrit** *(Little Dorrit)* | GER | 1934 | Carl Lamac | 93 |
| 1222 | **Little Dorrit** *(Pt.1: Nobody's Fault)* *(Pt.2: Little Dorrit's Story)* | GB | 1988 | Christine Edzard | Pt.1, 176 Pt.2, 181 |
| 1223 | **Mystery of Edwin Drood** | USA | 1935 | Stuart Walker | 85 |
| 1224 | **Nicholas Nickleby** | GB | 1947 | Alberto Cavalcanti | 108 |
| 1225 | **The Old Curiosity Shop** | GB | 1935(34) | Thomas Bentley | 95 |
| 1226 | **Mister Quilp** *(aka: The Old Curiosity Shop)* *{musical version}* | GB | 1975(74) | Michael Tuchner | 119 |
| 1227 | **Oliver Twist** | USA | 1933 | William J. Cowen | 77 |
| 1228 | **Oliver Twist** | GB | 1948 | David Lean | 116 +V |
| 1229 | **Oliver!** *{musical version}* | GB | 1968 | Carol Reed | 146 +V |
| 1230 | **Oliver Twist** | GB | 1983(82) | Clive Donner | 103 +V |
| 1231 | **Oliver & Company** *{animation}* | USA | 1988 | George Scribner | 74 |
| 1232 | **The Pickwick Papers** | GB | 1952 | Noel Langley | 109 +V |
| 1233 | **A Tale of Two Cities** | USA | 1935 | Jack Conway | 128 +V |
| 1234 | **A Tale of Two Cities** | GB | 1958 | Ralph Thomas | 117 +V |
| 1235 | **Deliverance** | USA | 1972 | John Boorman | 109 +V |
| 1236 | **Les dames du Bois de Boulogne** *(The Ladies of the Bois de Boulogne)* *(aka: Ladies of the Park)* | FR | 1945 | Robert Bresson | 90 |
| 1237 | **Suzanne Simonin, la religieuse de Denis Diderot** *(aka: La religieuse)* *(USA: The Nun)* | FR | 1966(65) | Jacques Rivette | 140 |
| 1238 | **Play It As It Lays** | USA | 1972 | Frank Perry | 99 |
| 1239 | **Lavina** | BULG | 1982 | Khristo Khristov Irina Aktasheva | 135 |
| 1240 | **Otklonenie** *[Sidetrack]* | BULG | 1967 | Grisha Ostrovski Todor Stoyanov | 82 |
| 1241 | **Osădeni dushi** *(aka: Ossudeni dushi)* *(Damned Souls)* | BULG | 1975 | Vălo Radev *(Vulo Radev)* | 138 |
| 1242 | **Tyutyun** *(Tobacco)* | BULG | 1962 | Nikolai Korabov | 150 |
| 1243 | | | | | |
| 1244 | **Out of Africa** | USA | 1985 | Sydney Pollack | 161 +V(150) |
| 1245 | **Babettes gæstebud** *(Babettes Feast)* | DEN | 1987 | Gabriel Axel | 103 +V |
| 1246 | **Une histoire immortelle** *(The Immortal Story)* | FR | 1968 | Orson Welles | 60 |
| 1247 | | | | | |

| No. | Author | Nationality | Form | Literary Title | Date |
|---|---|---|---|---|---|
| 1248 | Dinis, Júlio (Joaquim Guilherme Gomes Coelho) | Portuguese | N | **Os Fidalgos da Casa Mourisca** (The Fidalgos of Casa Mourisco) | 1871 |
| 1249 | Dinis, Júlio | Portuguese | N | **A morgadinha dos Canaviais** | 1868 |
| 1250 | Dinis, Júlio | Portuguese | N | **As pupilas do senhor Reitor** | 1867 |
| 1251 | Dinis, Júlio | Portuguese | N | **As pupilas do senhor Reitor** | 1867 |
| 1252 | Ditlevson, Tove | Danish | N | **Barndommens gade** | 1943 |
| 1253 | Ditzen, Rudolf (see: Fallada, Hans) | German | N | | |
| 1254 | Döblin, Alfred | German | N | **Berlin - Alexanderplatz** (Alexanderplatz, Berlin; the Story of Franz Biberkopf) | 1929 |
| 1255 | Doctorow, E. L. | American | N | **Billy Bathgate** | 1989 |
| 1256 | Doctorow, E. L. | American | N | **The Book of Daniel** | 1971 |
| 1257 | Doctorow, E. L. | American | N | **Ragtime** | 1975 |
| 1258 | Doctorow, E. L. | American | N | **Welcome to Hard Times** (aka: Bad Man From Bodie) | 1960 |
| 1259 | Dodgson, Charles Lutwidge (see: Carroll, Lewis) | British | N/V | | |
| 1260 | Domínguez Becquer, Gustavo Adolfo (see: Bécquer, Gustavo) | Spanish | SS | | |
| 1261 | Donato, Hernani | Brazilian | N | **Chão bruto** [Brute ground] | 1956 |
| 1262 | Donato, Hernani | Brazilian | N | **Selva trágica** [Tragic jungle] | 1959 |
| 1263 | Donchev, Anton | Bulgarian | N | **Vreme razdelno** (Time of Parting) | 1964 |
| 1264 | Donnay, Charles Maurice | French | P | **Éducation de prince** | 1895 |
| 1265 | Dorst, Tankred (joint, see: Hamsun, Knut) | German | P | | |
| 1266 | Dostoyevsky, Fyodor | Russian | SS | **Belye nochi** (White Nights) + **Netochka Nezvanova** | 1848+ 1849 |
| 1267 | Dostoyevsky, Fyodor | Russian | SS | **Belye nochi** | 1848 |
| 1268 | Dostoyevsky, Fyodor | Russian | SS | **Belye nochi** | 1848 |
| 1269 | Dostoyevsky, Fyodor | Russian | SS | **Belye nochi** | 1848 |
| 1270 | Dostoyevsky, Fyodor | Russian | N | **Besy** (The Possessed) (aka: The Devils) | 1872 |
| 1271 | Dostoyevsky, Fyodor | Russian | N | **Brat'ya Karamazovy** (The Brothers Karamazov) | 1880 |
| 1272 | Dostoyevsky, Fyodor | Russian | N | **Brat'ya Karamazovy** | 1880 |
| 1273 | Dostoyevsky, Fyodor | Russian | N | **Brat'ya Karamazovy** | 1880 |
| 1274 | Dostoyevsky, Fyodor | Russian | N | **Brat'ya Karamazovy** | 1880 |
| 1275 | Dostoyevsky, Fyodor | Russian | N | **Brat'ya Karamazovy** | 1880 |
| 1276 | Dostoyevsky, Fyodor | Russian | SS | **Dvoynik** (The Double) | 1846 |
| 1277 | Dostoyevsky, Fyodor | Russian | SS | **Dyadyushkin son** (Uncle's Dream) | 1859 |
| 1278 | Dostoyevsky, Fyodor | Russian | N | **Idiot** (The Idiot) | 1868 |
| 1279 | Dostoyevsky, Fyodor | Russian | N | **Idiot** | 1868 |
| 1280 | Dostoyevsky, Fyodor | Russian | N | **Idiot** | 1868 |
| 1281 | Dostoyevsky, Fyodor | Russian | N | **Idiot** | 1868 |
| 1282 | Dostoyevsky, Fyodor | Russian | SS | **Igrok** (The Gambler) (aka: Gambler-Bobok) | 1866 |

| No | Film Title | Country of Production | Date | Director(s) | Duration of Film |
|----|-----------|----------------------|------|-------------|------------------|
| 1248 | Os Fidalgos da Casa Mourisca | PORT | 1938 | Arthur Duarte | 117 |
| 1249 | A morgadinha dos Canaviais | PORT | 1949 | Caetano Bonucci | 93 |
| 1250 | As pupilas do senhor Reitor | PORT | 1935 | José Leitão de Barros | 102 |
| 1251 | As pupilas do senhor Reitor | PORT | 1960 | Perdigão Queiroga | 110 |
| 1252 | Barndommens gade (Street of Childhood) (aka: Early Spring) | DEN | 1986 | Astrid Henning-Jensen | 90 |
| 1253 | | | | | |
| 1254 | Berlin - Alexanderplatz | GER | 1931 | Phil (Piel) Jutzi | 121(89) |
| 1255 | Billy Bathgate | USA | 1991 | Robert Benton | 107 |
| 1256 | Daniel | USA | 1984(83) | Sidney Lumet | 129 +V |
| 1257 | Ragtime | USA | 1981 | Miloš Forman | 155 +V |
| 1258 | Welcome to Hard Times (GB: Killer on a Horse) | USA | 1967(66) | Burt Kennedy | 103 |
| 1259 | | | | | |
| 1260 | | | | | |
| 1261 | Chão bruto | BRAZ | 1959 | Dionízio de Azevedo | 98(100) |
| 1262 | Selva trágica | BRAZ | 1964(62) | Roberto Farias | 95 |
| 1263 | Vreme razdelno (Time of Violence) | BULG | 1988 | Lyudmil Staikov | 164 |
| 1264 | Éducation de prince | FR | 1938 | Alexandre Esway | 95 |
| 1265 | | | | | |
| 1266 | Peterburgskaya noch (Nights of St. Petersburg) (aka: Petersburg Nights) (aka: St. Petersburg) | USSR | 1933 | Grigori Roshal Vera Stroeva | 75 |
| 1267 | Le notti bianche (White Nights) | IT/FR | 1957 | Luchino Visconti | 107(194) |
| 1268 | Belye nochi (White Nights) | USSR | 1960(59) | Ivan Pyriev | 97 |
| 1269 | Quatre nuits d'un rêveur (Four Nights of a Dreamer) | FR/IT | 1971 | Robert Bresson | 87 |
| 1270 | Les possédés (The Possessed) | FR/POL | 1987 | Andrzej Wajda | 116 |
| 1271 | Der Mörder Dimitri Karamasoff (Karamazov) (aka: The Brothers Karamazov) | GER | 1931 | Fedor Ozep | 93 |
| 1272 | I fratelli Karamazoff | IT | 1947 | Giacomo Gentilomo | 112 |
| 1273 | The Brothers Karamazov | USA | 1958 | Richard Brooks | 146 |
| 1274 | Brat'ya Karamazovy (The Brothers Karamazov) (aka: The Murder of Dmitri Karamazov) | USSR | 1969(68) | Ivan Pyriev | Pt.1, 80 Pt.2, 72 Pt.3, 75 |
| 1275 | Mal'tchiki | USSR | 1990 | Yuri Grigorev Renita Grigoreva | 86 |
| 1276 | Partner (aka: Partner F. B.) | IT | 1968 | Bernardo Bertolucci | 105 |
| 1277 | Dyadyushkin son | USSR | 1966 | Konstantin Voinov | 85 |
| 1278 | L'idiot (The Idiot) | FR | 1946 | Georges Lampin | 98 |
| 1279 | Hakuchi (The Idiot) | JAP | 1951 | Akira Kurosawa | 166 |
| 1280 | Idiot (aka: Nastasia Filipovna) (The Idiot) | USSR | 1958 | Ivan Pyriev | 122 |
| 1281 | The Idiot | IND | 1992 | Mani Kaul | 180 |
| 1282 | Le joueur {French version of: Der Spieler} | FR | 1938 | Louis Daquin Gerhard Lamprecht | 95 |

| No. | Author | Nationality | Form | Literary Title | Date |
|-----|--------|-------------|------|----------------|------|
| 1283 | **Dostoyevsky, Fyodor** | Russian | SS | **Igrok** | 1866 |
| 1284 | **Dostoyevsky, Fyodor** | Russian | SS | **Igrok** | 1866 |
| 1285 | **Dostoyevsky, Fyodor** | Russian | SS | **Igrok** | 1866 |
| 1286 | **Dostoyevsky, Fyodor** | Russian | SS | **Igrok** | 1866 |
| 1287 | **Dostoyevsky, Fyodor** | Russian | SS | **Krotkaya** *(Gentle Spirit)* *(aka: The Gentle Maiden)* | 1876 |
| 1288 | **Dostoyevsky, Fyodor** | Russian | SS | **Krotkaya** | 1876 |
| 1289 | **Dostoyevsky, Fyodor** | Russian | N | **Prestupleniye i nakazaniye** *(Crime and Punishment)* | 1867 |
| 1290 | **Dostoyevsky, Fyodor** | Russian | N | **Prestupleniye i nakazaniye** | 1867 |
| 1291 | **Dostoyevsky, Fyodor** | Russian | N | **Prestupleniye i nakazaniye** | 1867 |
| 1292 | **Dostoyevsky, Fyodor** | Russian | N | **Prestupleniye i nakazaniye** | 1867 |
| 1293 | **Dostoyevsky, Fyodor** | Russian | N | **Prestupleniye i nakazaniye** | 1867 |
| 1294 | **Dostoyevsky, Fyodor** | Russian | N | **Prestupleniye i nakazaniye** | 1867 |
| 1295 | **Dostoyevsky, Fyodor** | Russian | N | **Prestupleniye i nakazaniye** | 1867 |
| 1296 | **Dostoyevsky, Fyodor** | Russian | N | **Prestupleniye i nakazaniye** | 1867 |
| 1297 | **Dostoyevsky, Fyodor** | Russian | N | **Prestupleniye i nakazaniye** | 1867 |
| 1298 | **Dostoyevsky, Fyodor** | Russian | SS | **Skverny anekdot** *(A Nasty Story)* | 1862 |
| 1299 | **Dostoyevsky, Fyodor** | Russian | SS | **Vechnyi muzh** *(The Eternal Husband)* | 1870 |
| 1300 | **Dostoyevsky, Fyodor** | Russian | N | **Zapiski iz myortvogo doma** *(House of the Dead)* *(aka: Memoirs From the House of the Dead)* | 1861-62 |
| 1301 | **Dostoyevsky, Fyodor** | Russian | SS | **Zapiski iz podpolya** *(Notes From Underground)* *(aka: Letters From the Underworld)* | 1864 |
| 1302 | **Douwes Dekker, Eduard** *(Multatuli)* | Dutch | N | **Max Havelaar** | 1859 |
| 1303 | **Doyle, Arthur Conan** | British | N | **The Adventures of Sherlock Holmes** | 1892 |
| 1304 | **Doyle, Arthur Conan** | British | N | **The Adventures of Sherlock Holmes** | 1892 |
| 1305 | **Doyle, Arthur Conan** | British | SS | **Charles August Milverton, Adventure of** | 1904 |
| 1306 | **Doyle, Arthur Conan** | British | SS | **The Dancing Men, Adventure of** | 1903 |
| 1307 | **Doyle, Arthur Conan** | British | SS | **The Empty House +** **The Final Problem, Adventure of** | 1903+ 1894 |
| 1308 | **Doyle, Arthur Conan** | British | SS | **The Empty House, Adventure of** | 1903 |
| 1309 | **Doyle, Arthur Conan** | British | N | **The Exploits of Brigadier Gerard** | 1896 |
| 1310 | **Doyle, Arthur Conan** | British | SS | **The Five Orange Pips** | 1892 |
| 1311 | **Doyle, Arthur Conan** | British | SS | **His Last Bow** | 1917 |
| 1312 | **Doyle, Arthur Conan** | British | N | **The Hound of the Baskervilles** | 1902 |
| 1313 | **Doyle, Arthur Conan** | British | N | **The Hound of the Baskervilles** | 1902 |
| 1314 | **Doyle, Arthur Conan** | British | N | **The Hound of the Baskervilles** | 1902 |
| 1315 | **Doyle, Arthur Conan** | British | N | **The Hound of the Baskervilles** | 1902 |
| 1316 | **Doyle, Arthur Conan** | British | N | **The Hound of the Baskervilles** | 1902 |
| 1317 | **Doyle, Arthur Conan** | British | N | **The Hound of the Baskervilles** | 1902 |
| 1318 | **Doyle, Arthur Conan** | British | N | **The Hound of the Baskervilles** | 1902 |
| 1319 | **Doyle, Arthur Conan** | British | N | **The Lost World** | 1912 |

| No | Film Title | Country of Production | Date | Director(s) | Duration of Film |
|----|-----------|----------------------|------|-------------|------------------|
| 1283 | Der Spieler (aka: Roman eines Spielers) | GER | 1938 | Gerhard Lamprecht | 94 |
| 1284 | The Great Sinner | USA | 1949 | Robert Siodmak | 110 |
| 1285 | Le joueur (IT: Il giocatore) (The Gambler) | FR/IT | 1958 | Claude Autant-Lara | 102(96) |
| 1286 | Igrok (The Gambler) | USSR/CZ | 1972 | Alexei Batalov | 95 |
| 1287 | Krotkaya | USSR | 1960 | Alexander Borisov | 71 |
| 1288 | Une femme douce (Gentle Creature) | FR | 1969 | Robert Bresson | 97 |
| 1289 | Crime et châtiment (Crime and Punishment) | FR | 1935 | Pierre Chenal | 98(110) |
| 1290 | Crime and Punishment | USA | 1936 | Josef von Sternberg | 88 |
| 1291 | Brott och straff (Crime and Punishment) | SWE | 1945 | Erik 'Hampe' Faustman | 106(80) |
| 1292 | Crimen y castigo (Crime and Punishment) | MEX | 1950 | Fernando de Fuentes | 120 |
| 1293 | Crime et châtiment (Crime and Punishment) (aka: Most Dangerous Sin) | FR | 1956 | Georges Lampin | 110 |
| 1294 | Crime and Punishment U.S.A | USA | 1959 | Denis Sanders | 96 |
| 1295 | Pickpocket | FR | 1959 | Robert Bresson | 75 |
| 1296 | Prestupleniye i nakazaniye (Crime and Punishment) | USSR | 1970(69) | Lev Kulidzhanov | 200 |
| 1297 | Rikos ja rangaistus (Crime and Punishment) | FIN | 1983 | Aki Kaurismäki | 94 |
| 1298 | Skverny anekdot (A Bad Joke) (aka: The Ugly Story) | USSR | 1987(65) | Alexander Alov Vladimir Naumov | 98 |
| 1299 | L'homme au chapeau rond | FR | 1946 | Pierre Billon | 91 |
| 1300 | Myortvyi dom (House of the Dead) (aka: The Dead House) | USSR | 1932 | Vasiliy Fyodorov | 91 |
| 1301 | El hombre del subsuelo (The Underground Man) | ARG | 1981 | Nicolas Sarquís | 107 |
| 1302 | Max Havelaar | HOLL | 1976 | Fons Rademakers | 170 |
| 1303 | Sherlock Holmes | USA | 1932 | William K. Howard | 68 |
| 1304 | The Adventures of Sherlock Holmes (aka: Sherlock Holmes) | USA | 1939 | Alfred Werker | 85 +V |
| 1305 | The Missing Rembrandt | GB | 1932 | Leslie Hiscott | 84 |
| 1306 | Sherlock Holmes and the Secret Weapon | USA | 1942 | Roy William Neill | 67 +V |
| 1307 | The Sleeping Cardinal (USA: Sherlock Holmes' Fatal Hour) | GB | 1931 | Leslie Hiscott | 84 |
| 1308 | The Woman in Green | USA | 1945 | Roy William Neill | 68 |
| 1309 | The Adventures of Gerard (IT: Le avventure di Gerard) | GB/IT/ SWITZ | 1970 | Jerzy Skolimowski | 91 |
| 1310 | The House of Fear | USA | 1944 | Roy William Neill | 68 |
| 1311 | Sherlock Holmes and the Voice of Terror | USA | 1942 | John Rawlins | 65 +V |
| 1312 | The Hound of the Baskervilles | GB | 1931 | V. Gareth Gundrey | 75 |
| 1313 | Der Hund von Baskerville (The Hound of the Baskervilles) | GER | 1937(36) | Carl Lamac | 82 |
| 1314 | The Hound of the Baskervilles | USA | 1939 | Sidney Lanfield | 80 |
| 1315 | The Hound of the Baskervilles | GB | 1958 | Terence Fisher | 87 +V |
| 1316 | The Hound of the Baskervilles | GB | 1978(77) | Paul Morrissey | 85 +V |
| 1317 | The Hound of the Baskervilles | GB | 1983 | Douglas Hickox | 96 +V |
| 1318 | The Baskerville Curse (aka: Sherlock Holmes: The Baskerville Curse) {animation} | GB | 1983 | Alex Nicholas | 67 +V |
| 1319 | The Lost World | USA | 1960 | Irwin Allen | 98 |

| No. | Author | Nationality | Form | Literary Title | Date |
|-----|--------|-------------|------|----------------|------|
| 1320 | Doyle, Arthur Conan | British | SS | The Man With the Twisted Lip | 1892 |
| 1321 | Doyle, Arthur Conan | British | SS | The Musgrave Ritual, Adventure of | 1893 |
| 1322 | Doyle, Arthur Conan | British | N | The Sign of Four | 1890 |
| 1323 | Doyle, Arthur Conan | British | N | The Sign of Four | 1890 |
| 1324 | Doyle, Arthur Conan | British | SS | The Silver Blaze | 1894 |
| 1325 | Doyle, Arthur Conan | British | SS | The Six Napoleons, Adventure of | 1904(05) |
| 1326 | Doyle, Arthur Conan | British | SS | The Speckled Band | 1892 |
| 1327 | Doyle, Arthur Conan | British | N | A Study in Scarlet | 1887 |
| 1328 | Doyle, Arthur Conan | British | N-P | The Tragedy of the Korosko (USA: A Desert Drama) {n} (USA: The Fires of Fate) {p} | 1897{n} 1898{p} |
| 1329 | Doyle, Arthur Conan | British | N | The Valley of Fear | 1914 |
| 1330 | Drabble, Margaret | British | N | The Millstone | 1964 |
| 1331 | Drachmann, Holger | Danish | P | Der var en gang [Once upon a time] | 1885 |
| 1332 | Drachmann, Holger | Danish | SS | Kirke og orgel | 1904 |
| 1333 | Dreiser, Theodore | American | N | An American Tragedy | 1925 |
| 1334 | Dreiser, Theodore | American | N | An American Tragedy | 1925 |
| 1335 | Dreiser, Theodore | American | N | Jennie Gerhardt | 1911 |
| 1336 | Dreiser, Theodore | American | SS | The Lost Phoebe | 1916 |
| 1337 | Dreiser, Theodore | American | SS | My Brother Paul | 1919 |
| 1338 | Dreiser, Theodore | American | SS | The Prince Who Was a Thief | 1927 |
| 1339 | Dreiser, Theodore | American | N | Sister Carrie | 1900 |
| 1340 | Drieu la Rochelle, Pierre | French | N | Une femme à sa fenêtre (Hotel Acropolis) | 1930 |
| 1341 | Drieu la Rochelle, Pierre | French | N | Le feu follet (Will o' the Wisp) | 1931 |
| 1342 | Drummond de Andrade, Carlos | Brazilian | SS | O índio + Luzia | 1962 |
| 1343 | Drummond de Andrade, Carlos | Brazilian | V | O padre, a môça [The priest and the girl] | 1959-62 |
| 1344 | Druon, Maurice | French | N | Les grandes familles {pt.1} | 1948 |
| 1345 | Druon, Maurice | French | N | La volupté d'être (The Film of Memory) | 1954 |
| 1346 | Drury, Allen | American | N | Advise and Consent | 1959 |
| 1347 | Duhamel, Georges | French | N | Confession de minuit (Confession at Midnight) | 1920 |
| 1348 | Dumarchey, Pierre (see: Mac Orlan, Pierre) | French | N/SS | | |
| 1349 | Dumas, Alexandre (père) | French | N | Le chevalier de Maison-Rouge (Marie Antoinette: or, the Chevalier of the Red House) | 1845 |
| 1350 | Dumas, Alexandre (père) | French | N | Le collier de la reine (The Queen's Necklace) | 1849-50 |
| 1351 | Dumas, Alexandre (père) | French | N | Les compagnons de Jéhu (The Company of Jehu) (aka: Roland of Montreval) | 1857 |
| 1352 | Dumas, Alexandre (père) | French | N | Le comte de Monte-Cristo (The Count of Monte-Cristo) | 1845 |
| 1353 | Dumas, Alexandre (père) | French | N | Le comte de Monte-Cristo | 1845 |
| 1354 | Dumas, Alexandre (père) | French | N | Le comte de Monte-Cristo | 1845 |
| 1355 | Dumas, Alexandre (père) | French | N | Le comte de Monte-Cristo | 1845 |
| 1356 | Dumas, Alexandre (père) | French | N | Le comte de Monte-Cristo | 1845 |
| 1357 | Dumas, Alexandre (père) | French | N | Le comte de Monte-Cristo | 1845 |

| No | Film Title | Country of Production | Date | Director(s) | Duration of Film |
|---|---|---|---|---|---|
| 1320 | The Man With the Twisted Lip | GB | 1951 | Richard M. Grey | 35 |
| 1321 | Sherlock Holmes Faces Death | USA | 1943 | Roy William Neill | 68 |
| 1322 | The Sign of Four | GB | 1932 | Rowland V. Lee Graham Cutts | 75 |
| 1323 | The Sign of Four | GB | 1987 | Peter Hammond | 120 |
| 1324 | Silver Blaze (USA: Murder at the Baskervilles) | GB | 1937 | Thomas Bentley | 70 |
| 1325 | The Pearl of Death | USA | 1944 | William Roy Neill | 69 |
| 1326 | The Speckled Band | GB | 1931 | Jack Raymond | 90 |
| 1327 | A Study in Scarlet | USA | 1933 | Edwin L. Marin | 70 |
| 1328 | Fires of Fate | GB | 1932 | Norman Walker | 74 |
| 1329 | The Triumph of Sherlock Holmes | GB | 1935 | Leslie Hiscott | 84 |
| 1330 | A Touch of Love (USA: Thank You All Very Much) | GB | 1969 | Waris Hussein | 107 |
| 1331 | Der var en gang | DEN | 1966 | John Price | 102 |
| 1332 | Kirke og orgel | DEN | 1932 | George Schnéevoigt | 96 |
| 1333 | An American Tragedy | USA | 1931 | Josef von Sternberg | 100 |
| 1334 | A Place in the Sun | USA | 1951 | George Stevens | 122 |
| 1335 | Jennie Gerhardt | USA | 1933 | Marion Gering | 85 |
| 1336 | The Lost Phoebe | USA | 1983 | Mel Damski | 30 +V |
| 1337 | My Gal Sal | USA | 1942 | Irving Cummings | 103 |
| 1338 | The Prince Who Was a Thief | USA | 1950 | Rudolph Maté | 88 |
| 1339 | Carrie | USA | 1952(51) | William Wyler | 118 |
| 1340 | Une femme à sa fenêtre (IT: Una donna alla finestra) (A Woman at Her Window) | FR/IT | 1976 | Pierre Granier-Deferre | 110(115) |
| 1341 | Le feu follet (IT: Fuoco fatuo) (The Fire Within) (aka: A Time to Live, a Time to Die) | FR/IT | 1963 | Louis Malle | 121 |
| 1342 | Crônica da cidade amada | BRAZ | 1965 | Carlos Hugo Christensen | 116(100) |
| 1343 | O padre e a môça | BRAZ | 1966 | Joaquim Pedro de Andrade | 102 |
| 1344 | Les grandes familles (USA: The Possessors) | FR | 1958 | Denys de la Patellière | 93 |
| 1345 | A Matter of Time (IT: Nina) | USA/IT | 1976 | Vincente Minnelli | 99(105) +V |
| 1346 | Advise and Consent | USA | 1962 | Otto Preminger | 139 |
| 1347 | Les aventures de Salavin (aka: Confession de minuit) | FR | 1964 | Pierre Granier-Deferre | 103 |
| 1348 | | | | | |
| 1349 | Il cavaliere di Maison Rouge | IT | 1953 | Vittorio Cottafavi | 89 |
| 1350 | L'affaire du collier de la reine (The Queen's Necklace) | FR | 1946 | Marcel L'Herbier | 118 |
| 1351 | The Fighting Guardsman | USA | 1945 | Henry Levin | 84 |
| 1352 | Die Gräfin von Monte Christo | GER | 1932 | Karl Hartl | 98 |
| 1353 | The Count of Monte Cristo | USA | 1934 | Rowland V. Lee | 114 |
| 1354 | El conde de Montecristo | MEX | 1941 | Chano Urueta | 193 |
| 1355 | Le comte de Monte-Cristo (IT: Il conte di Montecristo) - {Pt.1} (IT: La rivincita di Montecristo) - {Pt.2} | FR/IT | 1943(42) | Robert Vernay | 94(90) |
| 1356 | Le secret de Monte-Cristo | FR | 1948 | Albert Valentin | 85 |
| 1357 | El conde de Montecristo | ARG | 1953 | León Klimovsky | 103 |

| No. | Author | Nationality | Form | Literary Title | Date |
|-----|--------|-------------|------|----------------|------|
| 1358 | **Dumas, Alexandre** (père) | French | N | **Le comte de Monte-Cristo** | 1845 |
| 1359 | **Dumas, Alexandre** (père) | French | N | **Le comte de Monte-Cristo** | 1845 |
| 1360 | **Dumas, Alexandre** (père) | French | N | **Le comte de Monte-Cristo** | 1845 |
| 1361 | **Dumas, Alexandre** (père) | French | N | **Le comte de Monte-Cristo** | 1845 |
| 1362 | **Dumas, Alexandre** (père) | French | N | **Le comte de Monte-Cristo** | 1845 |
| 1363 | **Dumas, Alexandre** (père) | French | N | **Le comte de Monte-Cristo** | 1845 |
| 1364 | **Dumas, Alexandre** (père) | French | SS | **Les frères corses** (The Corsican Brothers) | 1845 |
| 1365 | **Dumas, Alexandre** (père) | French | SS | **Les frères corses** | 1845 |
| 1366 | **Dumas, Alexandre** (père) | French | SS | **Les frères corses** | 1845 |
| 1367 | **Dumas, Alexandre** (père) | French | SS | **Les frères corses** | 1845 |
| 1368 | **Dumas, Alexandre** (père) | French | N | **Joseph Balsamo** (Memoirs of a Physician) | 1846-48 |
| 1369 | **Dumas, Alexandre** (père) | French | P | **Kean** (Edmund Kean) | 1836 |
| 1370 | **Dumas, Alexandre** (père) | French | P | **Kean** | 1836 |
| 1371 | **Dumas, Alexandre** (père) | French | N | **La reine Margot** (Margaret of Navarre) (aka: Marguerite de Valois) | 1845 |
| 1372 | **Dumas, Alexandre** (père) | French | N | **Le saltéador** (The Brigand) | 1854 |
| 1373 | **Dumas, Alexandre** (père) | French | N | **Les trois mousquetaires** (The Three Musketeers) | 1844 |
| 1374 | **Dumas, Alexandre** (père) | French | N | **Les trois mousquetaires** | 1844 |
| 1375 | **Dumas, Alexandre** (père) | French | N | **Les trois mousquetaires** | 1844 |
| 1376 | **Dumas, Alexandre** (père) | French | N | **Les trois mousquetaires** | 1844 |
| 1377 | **Dumas, Alexandre** (père) | French | N | **Les trois mousquetaires** | 1844 |
| 1378 | **Dumas, Alexandre** (père) | French | N | **Les trois mousquetaires** | 1844 |
| 1379 | **Dumas, Alexandre** (père) | French | N | **Les trois mousquetaires** | 1844 |
| 1380 | **Dumas, Alexandre** (père) | French | N | **Les trois mousquetaires** | 1844 |
| 1381 | **Dumas, Alexandre** (père) | French | N | **Les trois mousquetaires** | 1844 |
| 1382 | **Dumas, Alexandre** (père) | French | N | **Les trois mousquetaires** | 1844 |
| 1383 | **Dumas, Alexandre** (père) | French | N | **Les trois mousquetaires** | 1844 |
| 1384 | **Dumas, Alexandre** (père) | French | N | **Les trois mousquetaires** | 1844 |
| 1385 | **Dumas, Alexandre** (père) | French | N | **La tulipe noire** (The Black Tulip) | 1846 |
| 1386 | **Dumas, Alexandre** (père) | French | N | **La tulipe noire** | 1846 |
| 1387 | **Dumas, Alexandre** (père) | French | N | **Le vicomte de Bragelonne** (The Viscount of Bragelonne) (aka: The Man in the Iron Mask) | 1847 |

| No | Film Title | Country of Production | Date | Director(s) | Duration of Film |
|----|-----------|----------------------|------|-------------|------------------|
| 1358 | Le comte de Monte-Cristo<br>*(IT: Il tesoro di Montecristo) - {Pt.1}*<br>*(IT: La vendetta di Montecristo) - {Pt.2}* | FR/IT | 1955(54) | Robert Vernay | 183 |
| 1359 | The Treasure of Monte Cristo<br>*(USA: The Secret of Monte Cristo)* | GB | 1961(60) | Robert S. Baker<br>Monty Berman | 95 |
| 1360 | Le comte de Monte-Cristo<br>*(IT: Il conte di Montecristo)*<br>*(The Story of the Count of Monte Cristo)* | FR/IT | 1961 | Claude Autant-Lara | 130(90) |
| 1361 | Sous le signe de Monte-Cristo<br>*(IT: Montecristo 70)* | FR/IT | 1969(68) | André Hunebelle | 100(94) |
| 1362 | The Count of Monte Cristo | GB | 1976(74) | David Greene | 104<br>+V |
| 1363 | Uznik zam if | USSR/FR | 1988 | Georgy Jangval'd-Khil'kevitch | Pt.1, 137<br>Pt.2, 97 |
| 1364 | Les frères corses | FR | 1938 | Géo Kelber | 81 |
| 1365 | The Corsican Brothers | USA | 1941 | Gregory Ratoff | 111 |
| 1366 | Los hermanos corsos | ARG | 1955 | Léo Fleider | 94 |
| 1367 | I fratelli corsi<br>*(FR: Les frères corses)*<br>*(The Corsican Brothers)* | IT/FR | 1961 | Anton Giulio Majano | 115 |
| 1368 | Black Magic | USA | 1949 | Gregory Ratoff | 105 |
| 1369 | Kean | IT | 1940 | Guido Brignone | 80 |
| 1370 | Kean<br>*(aka: Kean, genio e sregolatezza)* | IT | 1957(56) | Vittorio Gassman | 98 |
| 1371 | La reine Margot<br>*(IT: La regina Margot)*<br>*(A Woman of Evil)* | FR/IT | 1954 | Jean Dréville | 130 |
| 1372 | Le brigand gentilhomme | FR | 1943(42) | Émile Couzinet | 98 |
| 1373 | Les trois mousquetaires<br>*(Pt.1: Les ferrets de la reine)*<br>*(Pt.2: Milady)* | FR | 1932 | Henri Diamant-Berger | Pt.1, 136<br>Pt.2, 110 |
| 1374 | The Three Musketeers | USA | 1935 | Rowland V. Lee | 97(86) + V |
| 1375 | The Three Musketeers<br>*{musical version}* | USA | 1939 | Allan Dwan | 73 |
| 1376 | Los tres mosquejeros | MEX | 1943(42) | Miguel M. Delgado | 130 |
| 1377 | The Three Musketeers | USA | 1948 | George Sidney | 125 |
| 1378 | Il boia di Lilla<br>*(aka: La vita avventurosa di Milady)*<br>*(Milady and the Musketeers)* | IT | 1952 | Vittorio Cottafavi | 75 |
| 1379 | Les trois mousquetaires<br>*(The Three Musketeers)* | FR | 1953 | André Hunebelle | 120 |
| 1380 | I cavalieri della regina | IT | 1954 | Mauro Bolognini | 79 |
| 1381 | Los tres mosqueteros ... y medio | MEX | 1956 | Gilberto Martínez Solares | 95 |
| 1382 | Les trois mousquetaires<br>*(IT: I tre moschettieri)* | FR/IT | 1961 | Bernard Borderie | 186 |
| 1383 | The Three Musketeers<br>*(aka: The Queen's Diamonds)* | PAN | 1973 | Richard Lester | 107 |
| 1384 | The Four Musketeeres<br>*(aka: The Four Musketeeres: (the Revenge of Milady))*<br>*(SP: Los tres mosqueteros)* | PAN/SP | 1974(73) | Richard Lester | 103(200)<br>+V |
| 1385 | The Black Tulip | GB | 1937 | Alex Bryce | 57 |
| 1386 | La tulipe noire<br>*(IT: Il tulipano nero)*<br>*(SP: El tulipan negro)*<br>*(The Black Tulip)* | FR/IT/<br>SP | 1963 | Christian-Jaque | 115(110)<br>+V(109) |
| 1387 | The Man in the Iron Mask | USA | 1939 | James Whale | 110 |

| No. | Author | Nationality | Form | Literary Title | Date |
|-----|--------|-------------|------|----------------|------|
| 1388 | **Dumas, Alexandre** (*père*) | French | N | **Le vicomte de Bragelonne** | 1847 |
| 1389 | **Dumas, Alexandre** (*père*) | French | N | **Le vicomte de Bragelonne** | 1847 |
| 1390 | **Dumas, Alexandre** (*père*) | French | N | **Le vicomte de Bragelonne** | 1847 |
| 1391 | **Dumas, Alexandre** (*père*) | French | N | **Le vicomte de Bragelonne** | 1847 |
| 1392 | **Dumas, Alexandre** (*père*) | French | N | **Le vicomte de Bragelonne** | 1847 |
| 1393 | **Dumas, Alexandre** (*père*) | French | N | **Le vicomte de Bragelonne** | 1847 |
| 1394 | **Dumas, Alexandre** (*père*); **Gaillardet, Frédéric** | French | P | **La tour de Nesle** (*The Tower of Nesle*) | 1832 |
| 1395 | **Dumas, Alexandre** (*père*); **Gaillardet, Frédéric** | French | P | **La tour de Nesle** | 1832 |
| 1396 | **Dumas, Alexandre** (*père*); **Gaillardet, Frédéric** | French | P | **La tour de Nesle** | 1832 |
| 1397 | **Dumas, Alexandre** (*père*); **Maquet, Auguste** | French | N | **Vingt ans après, suite de trois mousquetaires** (*Twenty Years After*) | 1845 |
| 1398 | **Dumas, Alexandre** (*père*); **Maquet, Auguste** | French | N | **Vingt ans après, suite de trois mousquetaires** | 1845 |
| 1399 | **Dumas, Alexandre** (*fils*) | French | N-P | **La dame aux camélias** (*The Lady of the Camelias*) (*aka: The Lady With the Camelias*) | 1848{n} 1852{p} |
| 1400 | **Dumas, Alexandre** (*fils*) | French | N-P | **La dame aux camélias** | 1848{n} 1852{p} |
| 1401 | **Dumas, Alexandre** (*fils*) | French | N-P | **La dame aux camélias** | 1848{n} 1852{p} |
| 1402 | **Dumas, Alexandre** (*fils*) | French | N-P | **La dame aux camélias** | 1848{n} 1852{p} |
| 1403 | **Dumas, Alexandre** (*fils*) | French | N-P | **La dame aux camélias** | 1848{n} 1852{p} |
| 1404 | **Dumas, Alexandre** (*fils*) | French | N-P | **La dame aux camélias** | 1848{n} 1852{p} |
| 1405 | **Dumas, Alexandre** (*fils*) | French | N-P | **La dame aux camélias** | 1848{n} 1852{p} |
| 1406 | **Dumas, Alexandre** (*fils*) | French | N-P | **La dame aux camélias** | 1848{n} 1852{p} |
| 1407 | **Dumas, Alexandre** (*fils*) | French | N-P | **La dame aux camélias** | 1848{n} 1852{p} |
| 1408 | **Dumas, Alexandre** (*fils*) | French | P | **L'étrangère** (*The Foreigner*) | 1877 |
| 1409 | **Du Maurier, Daphne** | British | SS | **The Birds** | 1952 |
| 1410 | **Du Maurier, Daphne** | British | SS | **Don't Look Now** | 1971 |
| 1411 | **Du Maurier, Daphne** | British | N | **Frenchman's Creek** | 1941 |
| 1412 | **Du Maurier, Daphne** | British | N | **Hungry Hill** | 1943 |
| 1413 | **Du Maurier, Daphne** | British | N | **Jamaica Inn** | 1936 |
| 1414 | **Du Maurier, Daphne** | British | N | **My Cousin Rachel** | 1951 |
| 1415 | **Du Maurier, Daphne** | British | N | **Rebecca** | 1938 |
| 1416 | **Du Maurier, Daphne** | British | N | **Rebecca** | 1938 |
| 1417 | **Du Maurier, Daphne** | British | N | **The Scapegoat** | 1957 |
| 1418 | **Du Maurier, Daphne** | British | P | **The Years Between** | 1945 |
| 1419 | **Du Maurier, George** | British | N | **Peter Ibbetson** | 1892 |
| 1420 | **Du Maurier, George** | British | N | **Trilby** | 1894 |
| 1421 | **Du Maurier, George** | British | N | **Trilby** | 1894 |
| 1422 | **Dunn, Nell** | British | N | **Poor Cow** | 1967 |
| 1423 | **Dunn, Nell** | British | P | **Steaming** | 1981 |

| No | Film Title | Country of Production | Date | Director(s) | Duration of Film |
|----|-----------|----------------------|------|-------------|------------------|
| 1388 | Le vicomte de Bragelonne | FR | 1954 | Fernando Cerchio | 90 |
| 1389 | Le masque de fer<br>(IT: Il prigioniero del re) | FR/IT | 1955(54) | Richard Pottier | 88 |
| 1390 | Vendetta della maschera di ferrola<br>(FR: La vengeance du masque de fer) | IT/FR | 1961 | Silvio Amadio | 89 |
| 1391 | Le masque de fer | FR | 1962 | Henri Decoin | 127 |
| 1392 | The Man in the Iron Mask | USA | 1977(76) | Mike Newell | 120<br>+V |
| 1393 | The Fifth Musketeer | AUST/GB | 1978 | Ken Annakin | 106<br>+V |
| 1394 | La tour de Nesle | FR | 1937 | Gaston Roudès | 95 |
| 1395 | La tour de Nesle<br>(IT: La torre di Nesle)<br>(aka: La torre del piacere)<br>(The Tower of Lust) | FR/IT | 1954 | Abel Gance | 120 |
| 1396 | Der Turm der verbotenen Liebe<br>(IT: Le dolcezze del peccato)<br>(Tower of Screaming Virgins) | GER/IT/<br>FR | 1968 | Franz Antel<br>(François Legrand) | 90(86) |
| 1397 | At Sword's Point | USA | 1952 | Lewis Allen | 81 |
| 1398 | The Return of the Musketeers | GB/FR/<br>SP | 1989(88) | Richard Lester | 101<br>+V(97) |
| 1399 | La dame aux camélias | FR | 1934 | Fernand Rivers<br>Abel Gance | 118 |
| 1400 | Camille | USA | 1937(36) | George Cukor | 109 |
| 1401 | Cha hua nu<br>[The lady with camellias] | CHN | 1938 | Li Pingqian | 98 |
| 1402 | La dame aux camélias<br>(IT: La signora della camelie)<br>(USA: Camille) | FR/IT | 1953(52) | Raymond Bernard | 111 |
| 1403 | Camelia<br>(aka: Passion Sauvage) | MEX | 1953 | Roberto Gavaldón | 110 |
| 1404 | Traviata '53<br>(aka: Fille d'amour) | IT/FR | 1954(53) | Vittorio Cottafavi | 105 |
| 1405 | La bella Lola<br>(FR: La belle Lola)<br>(aka: Une dame aux camélias)<br>(IT: Quel nostro impossible amore) | SP/IT/FR | 1963(62) | Alfonso Balcazar | 125(88) |
| 1406 | Camille 2000 | USA | 1969 | Radley Metzger | 119<br>+V(94) |
| 1407 | La dame aux camélias<br>(GER: Die Kameliendame)<br>(aka: The True Story of Camille) | FR/IT/<br>GER | 1981 | Mauro Bolognini | 115 |
| 1408 | L'étrangère | FR | 1930 | Gaston Ravel | 88 |
| 1409 | The Birds | USA | 1963 | Alfred Hitchcock | 119 +V |
| 1410 | Don't Look Now<br>(IT: A Venezia...un dicembre rosso shocking) | GB/IT | 1973 | Nicolas Roeg | 110<br>+V |
| 1411 | Frenchman's Creek | USA | 1944 | Mitchell Leisen | 112 |
| 1412 | Hungry Hill | GB | 1947(46) | Brian Desmond Hurst | 109(92) |
| 1413 | Jamaica Inn | GB | 1939 | Alfred Hitchcock | 108(98) |
| 1414 | My Cousin Rachel | USA | 1952 | Henry Koster | 98 |
| 1415 | Rebecca | USA | 1940 | Alfred Hitchcock | 130 +V |
| 1416 | Kohra | IND(HIN) | 1964 | Biren Maag | 154 |
| 1417 | The Scapegoat | GB | 1959(58) | Robert Hamer | 92 |
| 1418 | The Years Between | GB | 1946 | Compton Bennett | 100(88) |
| 1419 | Peter Ibbetson | USA | 1935 | Henry Hathaway | 85 |
| 1420 | Svengali | USA | 1931 | Archie Mayo | 81 |
| 1421 | Svengali | GB | 1954 | Noel Langley | 82 |
| 1422 | Poor Cow | GB | 1967 | Ken Loach | 101 +V |
| 1423 | Steaming | GB | 1985 | Joseph Losey | 95 +V |

| No. | Author | Nationality | Form | Literary Title | Date |
|---|---|---|---|---|---|
| 1424 | **Dunn, Nell** | British | SS | **Up the Junction** | 1963 |
| 1425 | **Dunne, John Gregory** | American | N | **True Confessions** | 1977 |
| 1426 | **Duras, Marguerite** | French | N | **Un barrage contre le Pacifique** *(The Sea Wall)* *(aka: A Sea of Troubles)* | 1950 |
| 1427 | **Duras, Marguerite** | French | N | **Détruire, dit-elle** *('Destroy...')* | 1969 |
| 1428 | **Duras, Marguerite** | French | N | **Dix heures et demie du soir en été** *(Ten-thirty on a Summer Night)* | 1960 |
| 1429 | **Duras, Marguerite** | French | N-P | **Des journées entières dans les arbres** *(Days in the Trees) {p}* | 1954{n} 1966{p} |
| 1430 | **Duras, Marguerite** | French | N | **Le marin de Gibraltar** *(The Sailor From Gibraltar)* | 1952 |
| 1431 | **Duras, Marguerite** | French | N | **Moderato cantabile** | 1958 |
| 1432 | **Durrell, Lawrence** | British | N | **Justine +** **Balthazar +** **Mountolive +** **Clea** *(aka: The Alexandria Quartet)* | 1956+ 1958+ 1960 |
| 1433 | **Dürrenmatt, Friedrich** | German | P | **Der Besuch der alten Dame** *(The Visit)* | 1956 |
| 1434 | **Dürrenmatt, Friedrich** | German | P | **Die Ehe des Herrn Mississippi** *(The Marriage of Mr Mississippi)* | 1952 |
| 1435 | **Dürrenmatt, Friedrich** | German | SS | **Grieche sucht Griechin** *(Once a Greek...)* | 1955 |
| 1436 | **Dürrenmatt, Friedrich** | German | SS | **Die Panne** *(USA: Traps)* *(GB: A Dangerous Game)* | 1956 |
| 1437 | **Dürrenmatt, Friedrich** | German | N | **Der Richter und sein Henker** *(The Judge and His Hangman)* | 1950-51 |
| 1438 | **Dürrenmatt, Friedrich** | German | P | **Romulus der Grosse** *(Romulus the Great)* | 1956 |
| 1439 | **Dürrenmatt, Friedrich** | German | N | **Das Versprechen** *(The Pledge)* | 1958 |
| 1440 | **Dürrenmatt, Friedrich** | German | N | **Das Versprechen** | 1958 |
| 1441 | **Dyer, Charles** | British | P | **Rattle of a Simple Man** | 1963 |
| 1442 | **Dyer, Charles** | British | P | **Staircase** | 1966 |
| 1443 | **Dygat, Stanisław** | Polish | N | **Disneyland** *(Cloak of Illusion)* | 1965 |
| 1444 | **Dygat, Stanisław** | Polish | N | **Jezioro Bodeńskie** *[Bodensee] +* **Karnawał** *[Carnival]* | 1946+ 1968 |
| 1445 | **Dygat, Stanisław** | Polish | N | **Pożegnania** | 1948 |
| 1446 | **Eastlake, William** | American | N | **Castle Keep** | 1965 |
| 1447 | **Ebner-Eschenbach, Maria von** | Austrian | SS | **Krambambuli** | 1887 |
| 1448 | **Ebner-Eschenbach, Maria von** | Austrian | SS | **Krambambuli** | 1887 |
| 1449 | **Ebner-Eschenbach, Maria von** | Austrian | SS | **Krambambuli** | 1887 |
| 1450 | **Eça de Queirós, José Maria de** | Portuguese | N | **O primo basílio** | 1878 |
| 1451 | **Echegaray, José** | Spanish | P | **El gran galeoto** *(The Great Galeoto)* | 1881 |
| 1452 | **Eco, Umberto** | Italian | N | **Il nome della rosa** *(The Name of the Rose)* | 1980 |
| 1453 | **Edmonds, Walter D.** | American | N | **Chad Hanna** *(aka: Red Wheels Rolling)* | 1940 |
| 1454 | **Edmonds, Walter D.** | American | N | **Drums Along the Mohawk** | 1936 |
| 1455 | **Edmonds, Walter D.** | American | N-P | **Rome Haul** *{n}* **The Farmer Takes a Wife** *{p}* | 1929{n} 1934{p} |

| No | Film Title | Country of Production | Date | Director(s) | Duration of Film |
|----|-----------|----------------------|------|-------------|------------------|
| 1424 | **Up the Junction** | GB | 1967 | **Peter Collinson** | 119 |
| 1425 | **True Confessions** | USA | 1981 | **Ulu Grosbard** | 108 +V |
| 1426 | **La diga sul Pacifico** <br> *(FR: Barrage contre le Pacifique)* <br> *(This Angry Age)* <br> *(aka: The Sea Wall)* | IT/FR | 1957(56) | **René Clément** | 104(117) |
| 1427 | **Détruire, dit-elle** <br> *(Destroy, She Said)* | FR | 1969 | **Marguerite Duras** | 90 |
| 1428 | **Ten-Thirty p.m. Summer** <br> *(10.30 p.m. Summer)* | USA/FR/ SP | 1966 | **Jules Dassin** | 85 |
| 1429 | **Des journées entières dans les arbres** <br> *(Entire Days Among the Trees)* <br> *(aka: Days in the Trees)* | FR | 1977(76) | **Marguerite Duras** | 95 |
| 1430 | **The Sailor From Gibraltar** | GB | 1967 | **Tony Richardson** | 91 |
| 1431 | **Moderato cantabile** <br> *(aka: Storia di uno strano amore)* | FR/IT | 1960 | **Peter Brook** | 90 |
| 1432 | **Justine** | USA | 1969 | **George Cukor** | 116 +V |
| 1433 | **Der Besuch** <br> *(The Visit)* <br> *(IT: La vendetta della signora)* <br> *(FR: La rancune)* | GER/IT/FR | 1964 | **Bernhard Wicki** | 100 |
| 1434 | **Die Ehe des Herrn Mississippi** | GER/SWITZ | 1961 | **Kurt Hoffmann** | 93 |
| 1435 | **Grieche sucht Griechin** | GER | 1966 | **Rolf Thiele** | 91(89) |
| 1436 | **La più bella serata della mia vita** <br> *(The Most Wonderful Evening of His Life)* | IT/FR | 1972 | **Ettore Scola** | 106 |
| 1437 | **Der Richter und sein Henker** <br> *(IT: Il giudice e i suo boia)* <br> *(The Judge and His Hangman)* <br> *(aka: End of the Game)* | GER/IT | 1975 | **Maximilian Schell** | 96 +V(92) |
| 1438 | **Romulus der Grosse** | GER | 1965 | **Helmut Käutner** | 93 |
| 1439 | **Es geschah am hellichten Tag** <br> *(USA: It Happened in Broad Daylight)* <br> *(aka: Assault in Broad Daylight)* | SWITZ/GER/ SP | 1958 | **Ladislao Vajda** | 101 |
| 1440 | **Das Versprechen** | IT | 1983 | **Alberto Negrin** | 95 |
| 1441 | **Rattle of a Simple Man** | GB | 1964 | **Muriel Box** | 95 +V |
| 1442 | **Staircase** | USA | 1969 | **Stanley Donen** | 101(98) |
| 1443 | **Jowita** <br> *(aka: Jovita)* | POL | 1967 | **Janusz Morgenstern** | 95 |
| 1444 | **Jezioro Bodeńskie** | POL | 1986 | **Janusz Laorski** | 85 |
| 1445 | **Pożegnania** <br> *(Farewells)* | POL | 1958 | **Wojciech Jerzy Has** | 102 |
| 1446 | **Castle Keep** | USA | 1969 | **Sydney Pollack** | 107 +V |
| 1447 | **Krambambuli** <br> *(aka: Die Geschichte eines Hundes)* | GER | 1940 | **Karl Köstlin** | 80 |
| 1448 | **Heimatland** | AUST | 1955 | **Franz Antel** <br> *(François Legrand)* | 99 |
| 1449 | **Sie nanten ihn Krambambuli** <br> *(They Called Him Krambambuli)* | GER | 1972 | **Franz Antel** <br> *(François Legrand)* | 98(94) |
| 1450 | **O primo basílio** | PORT | 1959 | **António Lopes Ribeiro** | 138 |
| 1451 | **El gran galeoto** | SP | 1951(50) | **Rafael Gil** | 78(93) |
| 1452 | **Der Name der Rose** <br> *(The Name of the Rose)* | GER/IT/ FR | 1986 | **Jean-Jacques Annaud** | 129 +V(100) |
| 1453 | **Chad Hanna** | USA | 1940 | **Henry King** | 88(86) |
| 1454 | **Drums Along the Mohawk** | USA | 1939 | **John Ford** | 104 |
| 1455 | **The Farmer Takes a Wife** | USA | 1935 | **Victor Fleming** | 91 |

| No. | Author | Nationality | Form | Literary Title | Date |
|-----|--------|-------------|------|----------------|------|
| 1456 | Edmonds, Walter D. | American | N-P | Rome Haul {n}<br>The Farmer Takes a Wife {p} | 1929{n}<br>1934{p} |
| 1457 | Edqvist, Dagmar Ingeborg | Swedish | N | Fallet Ingegerd Bremssen<br>[The Ingegerd Bremmssen case] | 1937 |
| 1458 | Edqvist, Dagmar Ingeborg | Swedish | N | Kamrathustru<br>(The Marriage of Ebba Garland) | 1932 |
| 1459 | Edqvist, Dagmar Ingeborg | Swedish | N | Musik i mörker | 1937 |
| 1460 | Edqvist, Dagmar Ingeborg | Swedish | N | Musik i mörker | 1937 |
| 1461 | Edqvist, Dagmar Ingeborg | Swedish | N | Rymlingen fast<br>(Brave Fugitive) | 1933 |
| 1462 | Edschmid, Kasimir<br>(Eduard Schmid) | German | N | Wenn es Rosen sind werden<br>sie blühen | 1950 |
| 1463 | Egge, Peter | Norwegian | P | Kjærlighet og vennskap | 1904 |
| 1464 | Eggleston, Edward | American | N | Hoosier Schoolboy | 1883 |
| 1465 | Eichendorff, Joseph von | German | N | Aus dem Leben eines<br>Taugenichts<br>(Memoirs of a Good-for-Nothing) | 1826 |
| 1466 | Eichendorff, Joseph von | German | N | Aus dem Leben eines<br>Taugenichts | 1826 |
| 1467 | Elin Pelin<br>(Dimitâr Ivanov) | Bulgarian | N | Geratsite<br>[The Gerak Family] | 1911 |
| 1468 | Elin Pelin | Bulgarian | N | Yan Bibiyan | 1933 |
| 1469 | Elin Pelin | Bulgarian | N | Zemya | 1922 |
| 1470 | Eliot, George | British | N | The Mill on the Floss | 1860 |
| 1471 | Eliot, T. S. | American/Br | P | Murder in the Cathedral | 1935 |
| 1472 | Elkin, Stanley | American | SS | The Bailbondsman | 1973 |
| 1473 | Elsschot, Willem | Belgian(Fle) | SS | Het dwaallicht<br>(Will-o'-the-Wisp) | 1947 |
| 1474 | Elster, Kristian, Jr. | Norwegian | SS | Den hemmelighetsfulde<br>leilighet | 1928 |
| 1475 | Emerson, John<br>(joint, see: Loos, Anita) | American | P | | |
| 1476 | Eminescu, Mihai | Romanian | V | Fät-Frumos din tei<br>[Lime-tree prince charming] | 1875 |
| 1477 | Ende, Michael | German | N | Die unendliche Geschichte:<br>von A bis Z<br>(The Neverending Story) | 1979 |
| 1478 | Ende, Michael | German | N | Die unendliche Geschichte:<br>von A bis Z | 1979 |
| 1479 | Endō Shūsaku | Japanese | N | Chinmoku<br>(Silence) | 1966 |
| 1480 | Endō Shūsaku | Japanese | N | Dokkoisho | 1967 |
| 1481 | Ercilla y Zúñiga, Alonso de | Spanish | V | La Araucana | 1589 |
| 1482 | Ericson, Walter<br>(see: Fast, Howard) | American | N/SS | | |
| 1483 | Esmann, Gustav | Danish | P | Den kære familie | 1892 |
| 1484 | Espina de Serna, Concha | Spanish | N | Altar Mayor | 1926 |
| 1485 | Espina de Serna, Concha | Spanish | N | Dulce nombre<br>(The Red Beacon) | 1921 |
| 1486 | Espina de Serna, Concha | Spanish | N | La esfinge maragata<br>(Mariflor) | 1914 |
| 1487 | Espina de Serna, Concha | Spanish | N | La niña de Luzmela<br>[The girl from Luzmela] | 1909 |
| 1488 | Euripides | Greek(anc) | P | Bacchae<br>(The Bacchants) | c.405 BC |
| 1489 | Euripides | Greek(anc) | P | Electra | 413 BC |
| 1490 | Euripides | Greek(anc) | P | Hippolytus | 428 BC |

| No | Film Title | Country of Production | Date | Director(s) | Duration of Film |
|----|-----------|----------------------|------|-------------|------------------|
| 1456 | The Farmer Takes a Wife | USA | 1953 | Henry Levin | 81 |
| 1457 | Fallet Ingegerd Bremssen | SWE | 1942 | Anders Henrikson | 87 |
| 1458 | Livet går vidare (Life Goes On) | SWE | 1941 | Anders Henrikson | 81 |
| 1459 | Musik i mörker (Music in Darkness) (GB: Night Is My Future) | SWE | 1948 | Ingmar Bergman | 86 |
| 1460 | Lianbron | SWE | 1965 | Sven Nykvist | 87 |
| 1461 | Kvinna ombord [Woman on-board] | SWE | 1941 | Gunnar Skoglund | 84 |
| 1462 | Eine deutsche Revolution | GER | 1981 | Helmut Herbst | 97 |
| 1463 | Kjærlighet og vennskap | NOR | 1941 | Leif Sinding | 92 |
| 1464 | Hoosier Schoolboy | USA | 1937 | William Nigh | 62 |
| 1465 | Aus dem Leben eines Taugenichts | GDR | 1973 | Celino Bleiweiss | 95 |
| 1466 | Taugenichts (Good For Nothing) | GER | 1978(77) | Bernhard Sinkel Alf Brustellin | 91 +V |
| 1467 | Geratsite | BULG | 1958 | Anton Marinovich | 96 |
| 1468 | Yan Bibiyan | BULG | 1985 | Vasil Apostolov | 84 |
| 1469 | Zemya (Land) | BULG | 1957 | Zahari Zhandov | 99 |
| 1470 | The Mill on the Floss | GB | 1937 | Tim Whelan | 94 |
| 1471 | Murder in the Cathedral | GB | 1952(51) | George Hoellering | 113 |
| 1472 | Alex & the Gypsy (aka: Love and Other Crimes) | USA | 1976 | John Korty | 99 |
| 1473 | Het dwaallicht (Will-o'-the-Wisp) | HOLL | 1973 | Frans Buijens | 91 |
| 1474 | Den hemmelighetsfulle leiligheten | NOR | 1948 | Tancred Ibsen | 75 |
| 1475 | | | | | |
| 1476 | Blanca | ROM | 1955 | Constantin Neagu Mihai Iacob | 29 |
| 1477 | Die unendliche Geschichte (The Never Ending Story) | GER/GB | 1983 | Wolfgang Petersen | 99 +V(90) |
| 1478 | The Neverending Story II, the Next Chapter | GER | 1989 | George Miller | 90 |
| 1479 | Chinmoku (Silence) | JAP/USA | 1971 | Masahiro Shinoda | 126 |
| 1480 | Nippon no seishun (aka: Nihon no seishun) (Hymn to a Tired Man) (aka: The Youth of Japan) | JAP | 1968 | Masaki Kobayashi | 130 |
| 1481 | La Araucana (aka: Conquista de gigantes) (IT: Araucana massacro degli dei) (aka: The Conquest of Chile) | SP/IT/ CHL | 1971 | Julio Coll (Julio Coll Claramount) | 106(84) |
| 1482 | | | | | |
| 1483 | Den kære familie | DEN | 1962 | Erik Balling | 111 |
| 1484 | Altar Mayor | SP | 1944(43) | Gonzalo Delgrás | 103 |
| 1485 | Dulce nombre | SP | 1951 | Enrique Gómez | 84(79) |
| 1486 | La esfinge maragata | SP | 1948 | Antonio de Obregón | 85(79) |
| 1487 | Niña de Luzmela | SP | 1949 | Ricardo Gascón | 87(77) |
| 1488 | Dionysus in 69 | USA | 1970 | Richard Schechner Briand de Palma Robert Fiore Bruce Rubim | 90 |
| 1489 | Elektra (Electra) | GR | 1961 | Michael Cacoyannis | 113 |
| 1490 | Phaedra | USA/GR | 1962(61) | Jules Dassin | 116 |

| No. | Author | Nationality | Form | Literary Title | Date |
|---|---|---|---|---|---|
| 1491 | **Euripides** | Greek(anc) | P | **Iphigenia in Aulis** | c.407 BC |
| 1492 | **Euripides** | Greek(anc) | P | **Medea** | 431 BC |
| 1493 | **Euripides** | Greek(anc) | P | **Medea** | 431 BC |
| 1494 | **Euripides** | Greek(anc) | P | **Medea** | 431 BC |
| 1495 | **Euripides** | Greek(anc) | P | **The Trojan Women** | 415 BC |
| 1496 | **Fabbri, Diego** | Italian | P | **La bugiarda** <br> *[The liar]* | 1964 |
| 1497 | **Fabricius, Sara** <br> *(see: Sandel, Cora)* | Norwegian | N/P | | |
| 1498 | **Fadeev, Alexander** | Russian | N | **Molodaya gvardiya** <br> *(The Young Guard)* | 1945 |
| 1499 | **Falkberget, Johan** | Norwegian | N | **Bør Børson Jr.** | 1920 |
| 1500 | **Falkberget, Johan** | Norwegian | N | **Bør Børson Jr.** | 1920 |
| 1501 | **Falkberget, Johan** | Norwegian | N | **Eli Sjursdotter** <br> *[Eli Sjur's daughter]* | 1913 |
| 1502 | **Falkberget, Johan** | Norwegian | N | **Nattens brød** <br> *[Bread of night]* <br> *(pt.1: An-Magritt)* | 1940 |
| 1503 | **Fallada, Hans** <br> *(Rudolf Ditzen)* | German | N | **Jeder stirbt für sich allein** <br> *[Everyone dies alone]* | 1947 |
| 1504 | **Fallada, Hans** | German | N | **Jeder stirbt für sich allein** | 1947 |
| 1505 | **Fallada, Hans** | German | N | **Kleiner Mann - was nun?** <br> *(Little Man - What Now?)* | 1932 |
| 1506 | **Fallada, Hans** | German | N | **Kleiner Mann - was nun?** | 1932 |
| 1507 | **Farrell, James Thomas** | American | N | **Studs Lonigan** | 1934 |
| 1508 | **Fast, Howard** <br> *(as: Walter Ericson)* | American | N | **Fallen Angel** <br> *(aka: The Darkness Within)* <br> *(aka: Mirage [as Howard Fast])* | 1952 |
| 1509 | **Fast, Howard** <br> *(as: Walter Ericson)* | American | N | **Fallen Angel** | 1952 |
| 1510 | **Fast, Howard** | American | N | **Freedom Road** | 1944 |
| 1511 | **Fast, Howard** | American | SS | **Rachel** | 1945 |
| 1512 | **Fast, Howard** | American | N | **Spartacus** | 1951 |
| 1513 | **Fast, Howard** | American | N | **The Winston Affair** | 1959 |
| 1514 | **Fauchois, René** | French | P | **Boudu sauvé des eaux** | 1932 |
| 1515 | **Fauchois, René** | French | P | **Boudu sauvé des eaux** | 1932 |
| 1516 | **Fauchois, René** | French | P | **Prenez garde à la peinture** <br> *(The Late Christopher Bean)* | 1932 |
| 1517 | **Fauchois, René** | French | P | **Prenez garde à la peinture** | 1932 |
| 1518 | **Fauchois, René** | French | P | **Rêves d'amour** | 1944 |
| 1519 | **Faulkner, William** | American | SS | **Barn Burning** | 1939 |
| 1520 | **Faulkner, William** | American | N+SS | **The Hamlet** *{n}* + <br> **Barn Burning** *{ss}* + <br> **The Spotted Horses** *{ss}* | 1940+ <br> 1939+ <br> 1931 |
| 1521 | **Faulkner, William** | American | N | **Intruder in the Dust** | 1948 |
| 1522 | **Faulkner, William** | American | N | **Pylon** | 1935 |
| 1523 | **Faulkner, William** | American | N | **The Reivers** | 1962 |
| 1524 | **Faulkner, William** | American | SS | **A Rose For Emily** | 1930(31) |
| 1525 | **Faulkner, William** | American | N | **Sanctuary** | 1931 |
| 1526 | **Faulkner, William** | American | N | **Sanctuary** + <br> **Requiem For a Nun** | 1931+ <br> 1951 |
| 1527 | **Faulkner, William** | American | N | **The Sound and the Fury** | 1929 |
| 1528 | **Faulkner, William** | American | SS | **Tomorrow** | 1940(49) |
| 1529 | **Faulkner, William** | American | SS | **Turn About** | 1932 |
| 1530 | **Fazekas Mihály** | Hungarian | V | **Lúdas Matyi** | 1815 |

| No | Film Title | Country of Production | Date | Director(s) | Duration of Film |
|---|---|---|---|---|---|
| 1491 | **Iphigenia** | GR | 1976 | **Michael Cacoyannis** | 129 |
| 1492 | **I epistrofi tis Midias** *[Medea's return]* | GR | 1968 | **Yan Hristian** | 88 |
| 1493 | **Medea** | IT/FR/GER | 1970(69) | **Pier Paolo Pasolini** | 118 +V |
| 1494 | **A Dream of Passion** *{version by Minos Volonakis}* | SWITZ/GR | 1978 | **Jules Dassin** | 110 |
| 1495 | **The Trojan Women** | USA | 1971 | **Michael Cacoyannis** | 111 |
| 1496 | **La bugiarda** *(SP: La mentirosa)* *(Six Days a Week)* | IT/FR/SP | 1965(64) | **Luigi Comencini** | 95(103) +V |
| 1497 | | | | | |
| 1498 | **Molodaya gvardiya** *(The Young Guard)* | USSR | 1948 | **Sergei Gerasimov** | 180 |
| 1499 | **Bør Børson** | NOR | 1938 | **Toralf Sandø** **Knut Hergel** | 113 |
| 1500 | **Bør Børson** | NOR/USA | 1974 | **Jan Erik Düring** | 175 |
| 1501 | **Eli Sjursdotter** | NOR | 1938 | **Leif Sinding** | 80 |
| 1502 | **An-Magritt** | NOR | 1969 | **Arne Skouen** | 101 |
| 1503 | **Jeder stirbt für sich allein** | GER | 1962 | **Falk Harnack** | 106 |
| 1504 | **Jeder stirbt für sich allein** *(Everyone Dies Alone)* | GER | 1975 | **Alfred Vohrer** | 108 |
| 1505 | **Kleiner Mann - was nun?** | GER | 1933 | **Fritz Wendhausen** | 99 |
| 1506 | **Little Man, What Now?** | USA | 1934 | **Frank Borzage** | 90 |
| 1507 | **Studs Lonigan** | USA | 1960 | **Irving Lerner** | 95 |
| 1508 | **Mirage** | USA | 1964 | **Edward Dmytryk** | 109 |
| 1509 | **Jigsaw** | USA | 1968 | **James Goldstone** | 97 |
| 1510 | **Freedom Road** *{tv - 2 parts + feature}* | USA | 1979(78) | **Ján Kadár** | 100 +V |
| 1511 | **Rachel and the Stranger** | USA | 1947 | **Norman Foster** | 93(79)+V |
| 1512 | **Spartacus** | USA | 1960 | **Stanley Kubrick** | 184 +V |
| 1513 | **Man in the Middle** | GB | 1964 | **Guy Hamilton** | 94 |
| 1514 | **Boudu sauvé des eaux** *(Boudu Saved From Drowning)* | FR | 1932 | **Jean Renoir** | 87 |
| 1515 | **Down and Out in Beverly Hills** | USA | 1986(85) | **Paul Mazursky** | 103(97) +V |
| 1516 | **Prenez garde à la peinture** | FR | 1932 | **Henri Chomette** | 86 |
| 1517 | **Christopher Bean** *(aka: Her Sweetheart)* | USA | 1933 | **Sam Wood** | 80 |
| 1518 | **Rêves d'amour** | FR | 1947(46) | **Christian Stengel** | 105 |
| 1519 | **Barn Burning** | USA | 1980 | **Peter Werner** | 41 +V |
| 1520 | **The Long, Hot Summer** | USA | 1958 | **Martin Ritt** | 117 +V |
| 1521 | **Intruder in the Dust** | USA | 1949 | **Clarence Brown** | 86 |
| 1522 | **The Tarnished Angels** | USA | 1957 | **Douglas Sirk** | 91 |
| 1523 | **The Reivers** *(aka: The Yellow Flyer)* | USA | 1970(68) | **Mark Rydell** | 112 +V(90) |
| 1524 | **A Rose For Emily** | USA | 1983 | **John Carradine** | 27 +V |
| 1525 | **The Story of Temple Drake** | USA | 1933 | **Stephen Roberts** | 71 |
| 1526 | **Sanctuary** | USA | 1961(60) | **Tony Richardson** | 90 |
| 1527 | **The Sound and the Fury** | USA | 1959 | **Martin Ritt** | 115 |
| 1528 | **Tomorrow** | USA | 1972(71) | **Joseph Anthony** | 102 +V |
| 1529 | **Today We Live** | USA | 1933 | **Howard Hawks** | 113 |
| 1530 | **Lúdas Matyi** *(Mattie the Gooseboy)* *(aka: Goose Boy)* | HUNG | 1950(49) | **Kálmán Nádasdy** **László Ranódy** | 106(90) |

| No. | Author | Nationality | Form | Literary Title | Date |
|-----|--------|-------------|------|----------------|------|
| 1531 | **Fazekas Mihály** | Hungarian | V | **Lúdas Matyi** | 1815 |
| 1532 | **Fearing, Kenneth** | American | N | **The Big Clock** | 1946 |
| 1533 | **Fearing, Kenneth** | American | N | **The Big Clock** | 1946 |
| 1534 | **Fedin, Konstantin** | Russian | N | **Goroda i gody** (Cities and Years) | 1924 |
| 1535 | **Fedin, Konstantin** | Russian | N | **Goroda i gody** | 1924 |
| 1536 | **Feijóo, Samuel** | Cuban | N | **Juan Quinquin en Pueblo Mocho** | 1964 |
| 1537 | **Fekete Gyula** | Hungarian | N | **Az orvos halála** | 1963 |
| 1538 | **Ferber, Edna** | American | N | **Cimarron** | 1930 |
| 1539 | **Ferber, Edna** | American | N | **Cimarron** | 1930 |
| 1540 | **Ferber, Edna** | American | N | **Come and Get It** | 1935 |
| 1541 | **Ferber, Edna** | American | N | **Giant** | 1952 |
| 1542 | **Ferber, Edna** | American | SS | **Glamour** | 1933 |
| 1543 | **Ferber, Edna** | American | N | **Ice Palace** | 1958 |
| 1544 | **Ferber, Edna** | American | SS | **Old Man Minick** | 1922 |
| 1545 | **Ferber, Edna** | American | SS | **Old Man Minick** | 1922 |
| 1546 | **Ferber, Edna** | American | N | **Saratoga Trunk** | 1941 |
| 1547 | **Ferber, Edna** | American | N | **Showboat** | 1926 |
| 1548 | **Ferber, Edna** | American | N | **Showboat** | 1926 |
| 1549 | **Ferber, Edna** | American | N | **So Big!** | 1924 |
| 1550 | **Ferber, Edna** | American | N | **So Big!** | 1924 |
| 1551 | **Ferber, Edna; Kaufman, George S.** | American | P | **Stage Door** | 1936 |
| 1552 | **Ferber, Edna** (see also: Kaufman, George S.) | American | N/P/ SS | | |
| 1553 | **Fernán Caballero** (see: Caballero, Fernán) | Spanish | N | | |
| 1554 | **Fernandes, Millôr** | Brazilian | P | **Do tamanho de um defunto** | 1957 |
| 1555 | **Fernández Flórez, Wenceslao** | Spanish | N | **El bosque animado** [The lively forest] | 1943 |
| 1556 | **Fernández Flórez, Wenceslao** | Spanish | SS | **La casa de la lluvia** [The house of rain] | 1925 |
| 1557 | **Fernández Flórez, Wenceslao** | Spanish | SS | **Fantasmas** (Laugh and the Ghosts Laugh With You) | 1930 |
| 1558 | **Fernández Flórez, Wenceslao** | Spanish | N | **Ha entrado un ladrón** [A thief has come in] | 1920 |
| 1559 | **Fernández Flórez, Wenceslao** | Spanish | SS | **El hombre que se quiso matar** | 1930 |
| 1560 | **Fernández Flórez, Wenceslao** | Spanish | SS | **El hombre que se quiso matar** | 1930 |
| 1561 | **Fernández Flórez, Wenceslao** | Spanish | SS | **Huella de luz** [Trace of light] | 1925 |
| 1562 | **Fernández Flórez, Wenceslao** | Spanish | N | **Los que no fuimos a la guerra** | 1930 |
| 1563 | **Fernández Flórez, Wenceslao** | Spanish | N | **Luz de luna** [Moonlight] | 1915 |
| 1564 | **Fernández Flórez, Wenceslao** | Spanish | N | **El malvado Carabel** [The wicked Carabel] | 1931 |
| 1565 | **Fernández Flórez, Wenceslao** | Spanish | N | **El malvado Carabel** | 1931 |
| 1566 | **Fernández Flórez, Wenceslao** | Spanish | SS | **Unos pasos de mujer** [A woman's footsteps] | 1934 |
| 1567 | **Fernández Flórez, Wenceslao** | Spanish | SS | **Por qué te engaña tu marido?** | 1940 |
| 1568 | **Fernández Flórez, Wenceslao** | Spanish | N | **El sistema pelegrín** | 1949 |
| 1569 | **Fernández Flórez, Wenceslao** | Spanish | N | **Volvoreta** | 1917 |
| 1570 | **Ferreira, Vergílio** | Portuguese | N | **Cântico final** | 1959 |
| 1571 | **Ferreira, Vergílio** | Portuguese | N | **Manhã submersa** | 1954 |
| 1572 | **Feuchtwanger, Lion** | German | N | **Die Geschwister Oppenheim** (aka: Die Geschwister Oppermann) (The Oppermanns) | 1933 |

| No | Film Title | Country of Production | Date | Director(s) | Duration of Film |
|----|-----------|-----------------------|------|-------------|------------------|
| 1531 | **Lúdas Matyi** (Mattie the Gooseboy) (aka: Goose Boy) {animation} | HUNG | 1977 | **Attila Dargay** | 77 |
| 1532 | **The Big Clock** | USA | 1948(47) | **John Farrow** | 96 |
| 1533 | **No Way Out** | USA | 1987 | **Roger Donaldson** | 115 +V |
| 1534 | **Goroda i gody** | USSR | 1930 | **Yevgeni Chervyakov** | 94 |
| 1535 | **Goroda i gody** (Cities and Years) (aka: Towns and Years) | USSR/ GDR | 1974 | **Alexander Zarkhi** | 110 |
| 1536 | **Aventuras de Juan Quin Quin** (The Adventures of Juan Quinquin) | CB | 1967 | **Julio García Espinosa** | 110(90) |
| 1537 | **Az orvos halála** (Death of a Doctor) | HUNG | 1966(65) | **Frigyes Mamcserov** | 94 |
| 1538 | **Cimarron** | USA | 1931(30) | **Wesley Ruggles** | 130 |
| 1539 | **Cimarron** | USA | 1960 | **Anthony Mann** | 147 |
| 1540 | **Come and Get It** (aka: Roaring Timber) | USA | 1936 | **Howard Hawks** **William Wyler** | 99 +V(95) |
| 1541 | **Giant** | USA | 1956 | **George Stevens** | 197 +V |
| 1542 | **Glamour** | USA | 1934 | **William Wyler** | 74 |
| 1543 | **Ice Palace** | USA | 1960 | **Vincent Sherman** | 143 |
| 1544 | **The Expert** | USA | 1932 | **Archie Mayo** | 69 +V |
| 1545 | **No Place To Go** | USA | 1939 | **Terry Morse** | 54 |
| 1546 | **Saratoga Trunk** | USA | 1945 | **Sam Wood** | 135 |
| 1547 | **Show Boat** {musical version} | USA | 1936 | **James Whale** | 110 |
| 1548 | **Show Boat** {musical version} | USA | 1951 | **George Sidney** | 108 +V |
| 1549 | **So Big** | USA | 1932 | **William A. Wellman** | 80 |
| 1550 | **So Big** | USA | 1953 | **Robert Wise** | 101 |
| 1551 | **Stage Door** | USA | 1937 | **Gregory La Cava** | 92 +V |
| 1552 | | | | | |
| 1553 | | | | | |
| 1554 | **Ladrão em noite de chuva** | BRAZ | 1960 | **Armando Couto** | 80 |
| 1555 | **Fendetestas** | SP | 1975 | **Antonio F. Simón** | 30 |
| 1556 | **La casa de la lluvia** | SP | 1943 | **Antonio Román** | 88(72) |
| 1557 | **El destino se disculpa** | SP | 1944 | **José Luis Sáenz de Heredia** | 110 |
| 1558 | **Ha entrado un ladrón** | SP | 1949 | **Ricardo Gascón** | 99(97) |
| 1559 | **El hombre que se quiso matar** | SP | 1942(41) | **Rafael Gil** | 80(73) |
| 1560 | **El hombre que se quiso matar** (The Man Who Wanted to Kill Himself) | SP | 1971(70) | **Rafael Gil** | 91 |
| 1561 | **Huella de luz** | SP | 1942 | **Rafael Gil** | 77(76) |
| 1562 | **Los que no fuimos a la guerra** | SP | 1962(61) | **Julio Diamante** | 85 |
| 1563 | **Camarote de lujo** | SP | 1958(57) | **Rafael Gil** | 95(93) |
| 1564 | **El malvado Carabel** | SP | 1935 | **Edgar Neville** | 87 +V |
| 1565 | **El malvado Carabel** | SP | 1955 | **Fernando Fernán-Gómez** | 81(82) |
| 1566 | **Unos pasos de mujer** | SP | 1942(41) | **Eusebio Fernández Ardavín** | 80 |
| 1567 | **Por qué te engaña tu marido?** (Why Does Your Husband Deceive You?) | SP | 1969(68) | **Manuel Summers** | 92(88) |
| 1568 | **El sistema pelegrín** | SP | 1951 | **Ignacio Ferrés Iquino** | 96 |
| 1569 | **Volvoreta** | SP | 1976 | **José Antonio Nieves Conde** | 99(100) |
| 1570 | **Cântico final** | PORT | 1975 | **Manuel Guimarães** | 110(106) |
| 1571 | **Manhã submersa** | PORT | 1980 | **Lauro António** | 127 |
| 1572 | **Sem'ya Oppengeim** (The Oppenheim Family) | USSR | 1939 | **Grigori Roshal** | 103 |

| No. | Author | Nationality | Form | Literary Title | Date |
|-----|--------|-------------|------|----------------|------|
| 1573 | **Feuchtwanger, Lion** | German | N | **Goya, oder der arge Weg der Erkenntnis** *(This Is the Hour: a novel about Goya)* | 1951 |
| 1574 | **Feuchtwanger, Lion** | German | N | **Jud Süß** *(Jew Süss)* *(aka: Power)* | 1925 |
| 1575 | **Feuchtwanger, Lion** | German | N | **Jud Süß** | 1925 |
| 1576 | **Feuillet, Octave** | French | N-P | **Roman d'un jeune homme pauvre** *(Romance of a Poor Young Man)* | 1858 |
| 1577 | **Feuillet, Octave** | French | N-P | **Roman d'un jeune homme pauvre** | 1858 |
| 1578 | **Feuillet, Octave** | French | N-P | **Roman d'un jeune homme pauvre** | 1858 |
| 1579 | **Feuillet, Octave** | French | N-P | **Roman d'un jeune homme pauvre** | 1858 |
| 1580 | **Feydeau, Georges** | French | P | **La dame de chez Maxim** *(The Girl From Maxim's)* | 1898 |
| 1581 | **Feydeau, Georges** | French | P | **La dame de chez Maxim** | 1898 |
| 1582 | **Feydeau, Georges** | French | P | **Le dindon** *(Sauce For the Goose)* *(aka: Paying the Piper)* | 1949 |
| 1583 | **Feydeau, Georges** | French | P | **Un fil à la patte** *(Cat Among the Pigeons)* | 1899 |
| 1584 | **Feydeau, Georges** | French | P | **Un fil à la patte** | 1899 |
| 1585 | **Feydeau, Georges** | French | P | **Monsieur Chasse** | 1896 |
| 1586 | **Feydeau, Georges** | French | P | **Occupe-toi d'Amélie** *(Keep an Eye on Amélie)* | 1911 |
| 1587 | **Feydeau, Georges** | French | P | **Occupe-toi d'Amélie** | 1911 |
| 1588 | **Feydeau, Georges** | French | P | **On purge bébé** | 1910 |
| 1589 | **Feydeau, Georges** | French | P | **La puce à l'oreille** *(A Flea in Her Ear)* | 1909 |
| 1590 | **Feydeau, Georges; Desvallières, Maurice** | French | P | **L'Hôtel du Libre-Échange** *(Hotel Paradiso)* | 1894 |
| 1591 | **Feydeau, Georges; Desvallières, Maurice** | French | P | **L'Hôtel du Libre-Échange** | 1894 |
| 1592 | **Feydeau, Georges; Desvallières, Maurice** | French | P | **L'Hôtel du Libre-Échange** | 1894 |
| 1593 | **Fielding, Henry** | British | N | **Joseph Andrews** | 1742 |
| 1594 | **Fielding, Henry** | British | N | **Tom Jones** *(aka: The History of Tom Jones, a Foundling)* | 1749 |
| 1595 | **Fielding, Henry** | British | N | **Tom Jones** | 1749 |
| 1596 | **Figueiredo, Guilherme** | Brazilian | N | **História para se ouvir de noite** *[A story to hear at night]* | 1964 |
| 1597 | **Fischer, Leck** | Danish | P | **Barnet** | 1936 |
| 1598 | **Fischer, Leck** | Danish | P | **Moderhjertet** *[A mother's heart]* | 1943 |
| 1599 | **Fish, Robert** *(see: London, Jack)* | American | N | | |
| 1600 | **Fisher, Vardis** | American | N | **Mountain Man** *(aka: Jeremiah Johnson)* | 1965 |
| 1601 | **Fitch, Clyde** | American | P | **Beau Brummell** | 1908 |
| 1602 | **Fitzgerald, F. Scott** | American | SS | **Babylon Revisited** | 1931 |
| 1603 | **Fitzgerald, F. Scott** | American | SS | **Bernice Bobs Her Hair** | 1920 |
| 1604 | **Fitzgerald, F. Scott** | American | N | **The Great Gatsby** | 1925 |
| 1605 | **Fitzgerald, F. Scott** | American | N | **The Great Gatsby** | 1925 |
| 1606 | **Fitzgerald, F. Scott** | American | N | **The Last Tycoon** | 1941 |
| 1607 | **Fitzgerald, F. Scott** | American | N | **Tender Is the Night** | 1934 |
| 1608 | **Flaubert, Gustave** | French | N | **L'éducation sentimentale** *(Sentimental Education)* | 1869 |

| No | Film Title | Country of Production | Date | Director(s) | Duration of Film |
|----|-----------|----------------------|------|-------------|------------------|
| 1573 | **Goya** {2 - parts} | GDR/ USSR | 1970 | **Konrad Wolf** | 161 |
| 1574 | **Jew Süss** (USA: Power) | GB | 1934 | **Lothar Mendes** | 109(95) |
| 1575 | **Jud Süss** (Jew Suess) {propaganda travesty} | GER | 1940 | **Veit Harlan** | 97(85) |
| 1576 | **A Parisian Romance** | USA | 1932 | **Chester M. Franklin** | 77 |
| 1577 | **Le roman d'un jeune homme pauvre** | FR | 1935 | **Abel Gance** | 120 |
| 1578 | **La novela de un joven pobre** [Story of a poor young man] | ARG | 1942 | **Bayón Herrera** | 98 |
| 1579 | **La novela de un joven pobre** | ARG | 1968 | **Enrique Cahen Salaberry** | 90 |
| 1580 | **The Girl From Maxim's** (FR: La dame de chez Maxim) | GB | 1933 | **Alexander Korda** | 79 |
| 1581 | **La dame de chez Maxim** | FR | 1950 | **Marcel Aboulker** | 92 |
| 1582 | **Le dindon** | FR | 1951 | **Claude Barma** | 85 |
| 1583 | **Un fil à la patte** | FR | 1934(33) | **Karel Anton** | 90 |
| 1584 | **Un fil à la patte** | FR | 1955(54) | **Guy Lefranc** | 86 |
| 1585 | **Monsieur Chasse** | FR | 1947(46) | **Willy Rozier** | 85 |
| 1586 | **Occupe-toi d'Amélie** | FR | 1933(32) | **Richard Weissbach Marguerite Viel** | 107 |
| 1587 | **Occupe-toi d'Amélie** (Keep an Eye on Amelia) (USA: Oh, Amelia!) | FR | 1949 | **Claude Autant-Lara** | 96 |
| 1588 | **On purge bébé** | FR | 1931 | **Jean Renoir** | 62 |
| 1589 | **A Flea in Her Ear** | USA/FR | 1968 | **Jacques Charon** | 94 |
| 1590 | **L'Hôtel du Libre-Échange** | FR | 1934 | **Marc Allégret** | 106 |
| 1591 | **Äktenskapsbrottaren** (The Marriage Wrestler) | SWE | 1964 | **Hasse Ekman** | 93 |
| 1592 | **Hotel Paradiso** | GB | 1966 | **Peter Glenville** | 99 |
| 1593 | **Joseph Andrews** | GB | 1977(76) | **Tony Richardson** | 104 |
| 1594 | **Tom Jones** | GB | 1963 | **Tony Richardson** | 128 +V |
| 1595 | **The Bawdy Adventures of Tom Jones** (aka: The Adventures of Tom Jones) {musical version} | GB | 1976(75) | **Cliff Owen** | 93 |
| 1596 | **Fome de amor** (Lust For Love) (aka: Hunger For Love) | BRAZ | 1968 | **Nelson Pereira dos Santos** | 83(73) |
| 1597 | **Barnet** (Child) | DEN | 1940 | **Benjamin Christensen** | 87 |
| 1598 | **Kris** (Crisis) | SWE | 1946 | **Ingmar Bergman** | 93 |
| 1599 | | | | | |
| 1600 | **Jeremiah Johnson** (aka: The Saga of Jeremiah Johnson) | USA | 1972 | **Sydney Pollack** | 108 +V |
| 1601 | **Beau Brummell** | GB | 1954 | **Curtis Bernhardt** | 111 |
| 1602 | **The Last Time I Saw Paris** | USA | 1954 | **Richard Brooks** | 116 |
| 1603 | **Bernice Bobs Her Hair** | USA | 1977 | **Joan Micklin Silver** | 48 +V |
| 1604 | **The Great Gatsby** | USA | 1949 | **Elliott Nugent** | 90 |
| 1605 | **The Great Gatsby** | USA | 1974 | **Jack Clayton** | 146 +V |
| 1606 | **The Last Tycoon** | USA | 1976 | **Elia Kazan** | 124 +V |
| 1607 | **Tender Is the Night** | USA | 1962(61) | **Henry King** | 146 |
| 1608 | **L'éducation sentimentale** (IT: L'educazione sentimentale) | FR/IT | 1962(61) | **Alexandre Astruc** | 95(90) |

| No. | Author | Nationality | Form | Literary Title | Date |
|-----|--------|-------------|------|----------------|------|
| 1609 | **Flaubert, Gustave** | French | N | **Madame Bovary** | 1857 |
| 1610 | **Flaubert, Gustave** | French | N | **Madame Bovary** | 1857 |
| 1611 | **Flaubert, Gustave** | French | N | **Madame Bovary** | 1857 |
| 1612 | **Flaubert, Gustave** | French | N | **Madame Bovary** | 1857 |
| 1613 | **Flaubert, Gustave** | French | N | **Madame Bovary** | 1857 |
| 1614 | **Flaubert, Gustave** | French | N | **Madame Bovary** | 1857 |
| 1615 | **Flaubert, Gustave** | French | N | **Salammbô** *(Salambo)* | 1863 |
| 1616 | **Fleißer, Marieluise** | German | P | **Pioniere in Ingolstadt** | 1970 |
| 1617 | **Fliegel, Hellmuth** *(see: Heym, Stefan)* | German(Eng) | N | | |
| 1618 | **Flygare-Carlén, Emilie** | Swedish | N | **Rosen på Tistelön** *(The Rose of Tistelön)* *(aka: The Rose of Thistle Isle)* | 1842 |
| 1619 | **Fogazzaro, Antonio** | Italian | N | **Daniele Cortis** | 1885 |
| 1620 | **Fogazzaro, Antonio** | Italian | N | **Malombra** *(The Woman)* | 1881 |
| 1621 | **Fogazzaro, Antonio** | Italian | N | **Malombra** | 1881 |
| 1622 | **Fogazzaro, Antonio** | Italian | N | **Piccolo mondo antico** *(The Little World of the Past)* | 1896 |
| 1623 | **Fonseca, Manuel da** | Portuguese | N | **Cerromaior** | 1943 |
| 1624 | **Fonseca, Rubem** | Brazilian | SS | **Lúcia McCartney +** **O caso de F. A.** | 1969 |
| 1625 | **Fontane, Theodor** | German | N | **Effi Briest** | 1894-95 |
| 1626 | **Fontane, Theodor** | German | N | **Effi Briest** | 1894-95 |
| 1627 | **Fontane, Theodor** | German | N | **Effi Briest** | 1894-95 |
| 1628 | **Fontane, Theodor** | German | N | **Frau Jenny Treibel** | 1892 |
| 1629 | **Fontane, Theodor** | German | N | **Grete Minde** | 1879 |
| 1630 | **Fontane, Theodor** | German | N | **Irrungen, Wirrungen** *(Trials and Tribulations)* *(aka: A Suitable Match)* | 1888 |
| 1631 | **Fontane, Theodor** | German | N | **Mathilde Möhring** | 1907 (rev.1969) |
| 1632 | **Fontane, Theodor** | German | SS | **Stine +** **Irrungen, Wirrungen** | 1890+ 1888 |
| 1633 | **Fontane, Theodor** | German | SS | **Unterm Birnbaum** *[Under the pear tree]* | 1885 |
| 1634 | **Fontane, Theodor** | German | SS | **Unterm Birnbaum** | 1885 |
| 1635 | **Ford, Jesse Hill** | American(afro) | N | **The Liberation of Lord Byron Jones** | 1965 |
| 1636 | **Ford, John** | British | P | **'Tis Pity She's a Whore** | 1633 |
| 1637 | **Forester, C. S.** | British | N | **The African Queen** | 1935 |
| 1638 | **Forester, C. S.** | British | N | **Brown on Resolution** *(aka: Single-Handed)* | 1929 |
| 1639 | **Forester, C. S.** | British | N | **Brown on Resolution** | 1929 |
| 1640 | **Forester, C. S.** | British | N | **Captain Horatio Hornblower** *(GB: Captain Hornblower, R. N.)* | 1939 |
| 1641 | **Forester, C. S.** | British | SS | **Eagle Squadron** | 1942(coll) |
| 1642 | **Forester, C. S.** | British | N | **The Gun** | 1933 |
| 1643 | **Forester, C. S.** | British | N | **Payment Deferred** | 1926 |
| 1644 | **Forster, E. M.** | British | N | **Howards End** | 1910 |
| 1645 | **Forster, E. M.** | British | N | **Maurice** | 1971 |

| No | Film Title | Country of Production | Date | Director(s) | Duration of Film |
|----|-----------|----------------------|------|-------------|------------------|
| 1609 | **Unholy Love** | USA | 1932 | **Albert Ray** | 77 |
| 1610 | **Madame Bovary** | FR | 1934 | **Jean Renoir** | 117(101) |
| 1611 | **Madame Bovary** | GER | 1937 | **Gerhard Lamprecht** | 94 |
| 1612 | **Madame Bovary** | ARG | 1947 | **Carlos Schlieper** | 85 |
| 1613 | **Madame Bovary** | USA | 1949 | **Vincente Minnelli** | 114 |
| 1614 | **Die nackte Bovary** (IT: I peccati di Madame Bovary) | GER/IT | 1967 | **Hans Schott-Schöbinger** | 96 |
| 1615 | **Salammbô** | IT/FR | 1960(59) | **Sergio Grieco** | 106 |
| 1616 | **Pioniere in Ingolstadt** (Pioneers in Ingolstadt) (aka: Recruits in Ingolstadt) | GER | 1971 | **R. W. Fassbinder** | 83 |
| 1617 | | | | | |
| 1618 | **Rosen på Tistelön** | SWE | 1945 | **Åke Ohberg** | 104 |
| 1619 | **Daniele Cortis** | IT | 1947(46) | **Mario Soldati** | 95(61) |
| 1620 | **Malombra** | IT | 1942 | **Mario Soldati** | 130 |
| 1621 | **Malombra** (aka: Malombra, le perversioni sessuali di una adolescente) (Malombra, the Sexual Perversions of an Adolescent) | IT | 1983 | **Bruno Gaburro** | 91 +V |
| 1622 | **Piccolo mondo antico** (Old Fashioned World) | IT | 1941(40) | **Mario Soldati** | 106 |
| 1623 | **Cerromaior** | PORT | 1980 | **Luis Filipe Rocha** | 90 |
| 1624 | **Lúcia McCartney** | BRAZ | 1971 | **David Neves** | 72(84) |
| 1625 | **Der Schritt vom Wege** (A Step Out of Line) (aka: Off the Beaten Track) | GER | 1939 | **Gustaf Gründgens** | 100 |
| 1626 | **Rosen im Herbst** (Roses in Autumn) | GER | 1955 | **Rudolf Jugert** | 107 |
| 1627 | **Fontane Effi Briest** (aka: Effi Briest) | GER | 1974 | **R. W. Fassbinder** | 140 +V |
| 1628 | **Corinna Schmidt** | GDR | 1951 | **Arthur Pohl** | 96 |
| 1629 | **Grete Minde** (aka: Grete Minde - Der Wald ist voller Wölfe) | GER/AUST | 1977(76) | **Heidi Genée** | 100 |
| 1630 | **Ball im Metropol** | GER | 1937 | **Frank Wisbar** | 84 |
| 1631 | **Mein Herz gehört Dir** (aka: Mathilde Möhring) (aka: Erlebnisse einer großen Liebe) (aka: Ich glaube an dich) | GER | 1945 | **Rolf Hansen** | 77(80) |
| 1632 | **Das alte Lied** | GER | 1945 | **Fritz Peter Buch** | 95 |
| 1633 | **Der stumme Gast** (The Silent Guest) | GER | 1945 | **Harald Braun** | 105(100) |
| 1634 | **Unterm Birnbaum** | GDR | 1973 | **Ralf Kirsten** | 90 |
| 1635 | **The Liberation of L. B. Jones** | USA | 1970(69) | **William Wyler** | 102 |
| 1636 | **Addio, fratello crudele** ('Tis Pity She's a Whore) | IT | 1971 | **Giuseppe Patroni Griffi** (Patroni Griffi, Giuseppe) | 102 |
| 1637 | **The African Queen** | GB | 1952(51) | **John Huston** | 103 +V |
| 1638 | **Brown on Resolution** (aka: Forever England) (USA: Born for Glory) | GB | 1935 | **Walter Forde** | 80 |
| 1639 | **Single-Handed** (USA: Sailor of the King) | GB | 1953 | **Roy Boulting** | 85 |
| 1640 | **Captain Horatio Hornblower R. N.** | USA/GB | 1951(50) | **Raoul Walsh** | 118 |
| 1641 | **Eagle Squadron** | USA | 1942 | **Arthur Lubin** | 102 |
| 1642 | **The Pride and the Passion** | USA | 1957 | **Stanley Kramer** | 131 |
| 1643 | **Payment Deferred** | USA | 1932 | **Lothar Mendes** | 75 |
| 1644 | **Howards End** | GB | 1991 | **James Ivory** | 142 |
| 1645 | **Maurice** | GB | 1987 | **James Ivory** | 140 +V |

| No. | Author | Nationality | Form | Literary Title | Date |
|-----|--------|-------------|------|----------------|------|
| 1646 | **Forster, E. M.** | British | N | **A Passage to India** | 1924 |
| 1647 | **Forster, E. M.** | British | N | **A Room With a View** | 1908 |
| 1648 | **Forster, E. M.** | British | N | **Where Angels Fear to Tread** | 1905 |
| 1649 | **Fowler, Gene** *(joint, see: Hecht, Ben)* | American | P | | |
| 1650 | **Fowles, John** | British | N | **The Collector** | 1963 |
| 1651 | **Fowles, John** | British | N | **The French Lieutenant's Woman** | 1959 |
| 1652 | **Fowles, John** | British | N | **The Magus** | 1966 |
| 1653 | **Frame, Janet** | New Zealand | N | **A State of Siege** | 1966 |
| 1654 | **Frame, Janet** | New Zealand | AUT | **To the Is-land +** <br> **Angel at My Table +** <br> **The Envoy from Mirror City** | 1982+ <br> 1984+ <br> 1985 |
| 1655 | **França Júnior, Oswaldo** | Brazilian | N | **Jorge, um brasileiro** *(The Long Haul)* | 1967 |
| 1656 | **France, Anatole** | French | SS | **L'affaire Crainquebille** *(Crainquebille)* | 1901 |
| 1657 | **France, Anatole** | French | SS | **L'affaire Crainquebille** | 1901 |
| 1658 | **France, Anatole** | French | P | **La comédie de celui qui épousa une femme muette** *(The Comedy of the Man Who Married a Dumb Wife)* | 1912 |
| 1659 | **France, Anatole** | French | N | **Le crime de Sylvestre Bonnard** *(The Crime of Sylvestre Bonnard)* | 1881 |
| 1660 | **France, Anatole** | French | N | **Histoire comique** *(A Mummer's Tale)* | 1903 |
| 1661 | **France, Anatole** | French | N | **Thaïs** | 1891 |
| 1662 | **Frank, Bruno** | German | N | **Cervantes** *(A Man Called Cervantes)* | 1934 |
| 1663 | **Frank, Bruno** | German | P | **Perlenkomödie** *[Pearl comedy]* | 1928 |
| 1664 | **Frank, Bruno** | German | P | **Sturm im Wasserglas** *(Storm in a Teacup)* *(USA: Storm Over Patsy)* | 1930 |
| 1665 | **Frank, Bruno** | German | P | **Sturm im Wasserglas** | 1930 |
| 1666 | **Frank, Bruno** | German | P | **Sturm im Wasserglas** | 1930 |
| 1667 | **Frank, Bruno** | German | N | **Trenck** *(Trenck, the Love Story of a Favourite)* | 1926 |
| 1668 | **Frank, Leonhard** | German | N | **Die Jünger Jesu** | 1949 |
| 1669 | **Frank, Leonhard** | German | SS-P | **Karl und Anna** *(Carl and Anna)* *(aka: Beloved Stranger)* *(aka: Desire Me) {ss}* | 1926{ss} <br> 1928{p} |
| 1670 | **Frank, Leonhard** | German | SS-P | **Karl und Anna** | 1926{ss} <br> 1928{p} |
| 1671 | **Franklin, Miles** | Australian | N | **My Brilliant Career** | 1901 |
| 1672 | **Fredro, Alexander** | Polish | P | **Zemsta** *(The Vengeance)* *(aka: Revenge)* | 1833 |
| 1673 | **Fridegård, Jan** | Swedish | N | **Jag, Lars Hård** *(I, Lars Hård)* | 1935 |
| 1674 | **Fridegård, Jan** | Swedish | N | **En natt i juli** | 1933 |
| 1675 | **Frisch, Max** | Swiss(Ger) | N | **Blaubart** *(Bluebeard)* | 1982 |
| 1676 | **Frisch, Max** | Swiss | N | **Homo Faber** | 1957 |
| 1677 | **Fuchs, Daniel** | American | N | **Low Company** | 1937 |
| 1678 | **Fuentes, Carlos** | Mexican (Sp/Eng) | SS | **Aura** | 1966 |
| 1679 | **Fuentes, Carlos** | Mexican (Sp/Eng) | N | **The Old Gringo** *(Gringo viejo)* | 1985 |
| 1680 | **Fugard, Athol** | South African | P | **Boesman and Lena** | 1969 |

| No | Film Title | Country of Production | Date | Director(s) | Duration of Film |
|---|---|---|---|---|---|
| 1646 | A Passage to India | GB | 1985(84) | David Lean | 163 +V |
| 1647 | A Room With a View | GB | 1985 | James Ivory | 117 +V |
| 1648 | Where Angels Fear to Tread | GB | 1991 | Charles Sturridge | 112 +V |
| 1649 | | | | | |
| 1650 | The Collector | USA/GB | 1965 | William Wyler | 120 +V |
| 1651 | The French Lieutenant's Woman | GB | 1981 | Karel Reisz | 123 +V |
| 1652 | Magus | GB | 1968 | Guy Green | 116 |
| 1653 | A State of Siege | NZ | 1978 | Vincent Ward | 52 |
| 1654 | An Angel at My Table | NZ | 1990 | Jane Campion | 160 |
| 1655 | Jorge, um brasileiro (The Long Haul) | BRAZ | 1989 | Paulo Thiago | 113 |
| 1656 | Crainquebille | FR | 1933 | Jacques de Baroncelli | 65 |
| 1657 | Crainquebille (aka: Mort aux vaches) | FR | 1954(53) | Ralph Habib | 87(90) |
| 1658 | Ya qi [The dumb wife] | CHN | 1948 | Wu Renzhi | 98 |
| 1659 | Chasing Yesterday | USA | 1935 | George Nicholls, Jr. | 70 |
| 1660 | Félicie Nanteuil (aka: Histoire comique) | FR | 1943(42) | Marc Allégret | 99 |
| 1661 | Thaïs | POL | 1984 | Ryszard Ber | 104 |
| 1662 | Cervantes (aka: The Young Rebel) | SP/IT/FR | 1968(67) | Vincent Sherman | 120(124) |
| 1663 | Zweierlei Moral (aka: Frau Wera's Schwarze Perlen) | GER | 1931(30) | Gerhard Lamprecht | 84 |
| 1664 | Sturm im Wasserglas (aka: Die Blumenfrau von Lindenau) | AUST/GER | 1931 | Georg Jacoby | 92 |
| 1665 | Storm in a Teacup | GB | 1937 | Victor Saville Ian Dalrymple | 87 |
| 1666 | Sturm im Wasserglas | GER | 1960 | Joseph von Baky | 96 |
| 1667 | Trenck (aka: Trenck, der Roman einer grossen Liebe) (aka: Trenck, der Roman eines Günstlings) | GER | 1932 | Heinz Paul Ernst Neubach | 100 |
| 1668 | Chronik eines Mordes (Chronicle of a Murder) | GDR | 1965 | Joachim Hasler | 91 |
| 1669 | Desire Me | USA | 1947(46) | Arthur Hornblow George Cukor Mervyn LeRoy [uncredited] | 91 |
| 1670 | Die Frau und der Fremde (The Woman and the Stranger) | GDR | 1985 | Rainer Simon | 97 |
| 1671 | My Brilliant Career | AUSTL | 1979 | Gillian Armstrong | 10 +V |
| 1672 | Zemsta (Revenge) | POL | 1957 | Antoni Bohdziewicz Bohdan Korzeniewski | 93(115) |
| 1673 | Lars Hård | SWE | 1948 | Erik 'Hampe' Faustman | 95 |
| 1674 | När ängarna blommar (When Meadows Bloom) | SWE | 1946 | Erik 'Hampe' Faustman | 77 |
| 1675 | Blaubart | GER/SWITZ | 1984 | Krzysztof Zanussi | 92 |
| 1676 | Voyager | GER/FR | 1991 | Volker Schlöndorff | 100 |
| 1677 | The Gangster | USA | 1947 | Gordon Wiles | 84 |
| 1678 | La strega in amore (The Witch in Love) (aka: The Witches) (aka: Strange Obsession) (aka: Aura) | IT | 1966 | Damiano Damiani | 103(110) |
| 1679 | Old Gringo | USA | 1989 | Luis Puenzo | 120 |
| 1680 | Boesman and Lena | S.AFR | 1973 | Ross Devenish | 102 |

| No. | Author | Nationality | Form | Literary Title | Date |
|-----|--------|-------------|------|----------------|------|
| 1681 | Fukazawa Shichirō | Japanese | N | Fuefuki-gawa | 1958-59 |
| 1682 | Fukazawa Shichirō | Japanese | SS | Narayamabushi-kō<br>(The Oak Mountain Song)<br>(aka: The Songs of Oak Mountain) | 1956 |
| 1683 | Fukazawa Shichirō | Japanese | SS | Narayamabushi-kō | 1956 |
| 1684 | Fukazawa Shichirō | Japanese | SS | Tōhoku no jinmutachi | 1957 |
| 1685 | Fuks, Ladislav | Czech | N | Pan Theodor Mundstöck<br>(Mr Theodor Mundstock) | 1963 |
| 1686 | Fuks, Ladislav | Czech | N | Příbeh kriminalniho rady<br>[Adventures of the criminal judge] | 1971 |
| 1687 | Fuks, Ladislav | Czech | N | Spalovač mrtvol | 1967 |
| 1688 | Fulga, Laurenţiu | Romanian | N | Alexandra şi infernul<br>[Alexandra and hell] | 1966 |
| 1689 | Fuller, Charles | American(afro) | P | A Soldier's Play | 1982 |
| 1690 | Furmanov, Dmitriy | Russian | N | Chapayev | 1923 |
| 1691 | Gadda, Carlo Emilio | Italian | N | Quer pasticciaccio brutto de<br>via Merulana<br>(That Awful Mess on Via Merulana) | 1957 |
| 1692 | Gaillardet, F.<br>(joint, see: Dumas, Alexandre, (père)) | French | P | | |
| 1693 | Gaines, Ernest J. | American(afro) | N | The Autobiography of Miss Jane<br>Pittman | 1971 |
| 1694 | Gaines, Ernest J. | American | N | A Gathering of Old Men | 1983 |
| 1695 | Gaines, Ernest J. | American | SS | The Sky Is Gray | 1966 |
| 1696 | Gala, Antonio | Spanish | P | Los buenos dias perdidos | 1973 |
| 1697 | Galaction, Gala<br>(Grigore Pişculescu) | Romanian | SS | Moara lui Călifar<br>(Califar's Mill) | 1902 |
| 1698 | Galgóczi Erzsébet | Hungarian | N | Pókháló | 1972 |
| 1699 | Galgóczi Erzsébet | Hungarian | SS | Törvénten belül<br>[Inside of the law] | 1980 |
| 1700 | Gallegos, Rómulo | Venezuelan | N | Doña Barbara<br>(Dona Barbara) | 1929 |
| 1701 | Gallet, Louis<br>(joint, see: Sardou, Victorien) | French | P | | |
| 1702 | Galsworthy, John | British | SS | The Apple Tree | 1918 |
| 1703 | Galsworthy, John | British | P | Escape | 1926 |
| 1704 | Galsworthy, John | British | P | Escape | 1926 |
| 1705 | Galsworthy, John | British | SS-P | The First and the Last | 1918{ss}<br>1921{p} |
| 1706 | Galsworthy, John | British | SS-P | The First and the Last | 1918{ss}<br>1921{p} |
| 1707 | Galsworthy, John | British | P | Loyalties | 1922 |
| 1708 | Galsworthy, John | British | N | The Man of Property | 1906 |
| 1709 | Galsworthy, John | British | P | Old English | 1924 |
| 1710 | Galsworthy, John | British | N | Over the River<br>(USA: One More River) | 1933 |
| 1711 | Galsworthy, John | British | P | The Skin Game | 1920 |
| 1712 | Gait y Escobar, Alberto<br>(see: Insúa, Alberto) | Spanish | N | | |
| 1713 | Gálvez, Manuel | Argentine | N | La muerte en las calles | 1949 |
| 1714 | Gálvez, Manuel | Argentine | N | Nacha Regules | 1919 |
| 1715 | García Hortelano, Juan | Spanish | N | Nuevas amistades<br>[New friendships] | 1959 |
| 1716 | García Lorca, Federico<br>(Federico García Lorca) | Spanish | P | Bodas de sangre<br>(Blood Wedding) | 1936 |
| 1717 | García Lorca, Federico | Spanish | P | Bodas de sangre | 1936 |

| No | Film Title | Country of Production | Date | Director(s) | Duration of Film |
|---|---|---|---|---|---|
| 1681 | Fuefuki-gawa *(River Fuefuki)* | JAP | 1960 | Keisuke Kinoshita | 117 |
| 1682 | Narayama bushi-kō *(The Ballad of Narayama)* | JAP | 1958 | Keisuke Kinoshita | 98 |
| 1683 | Narayamabushi-kō *(The Ballad of Narayama)* | JAP | 1984 | Shōhei Imamura | 130 |
| 1684 | Tōhoku no jinmutachi *(The Man of Tohoku)* | JAP | 1957 | Kon Ichikawa | 58 |
| 1685 | Kartka z podróży *[Card from the journey]* | POL | 1982 | Waldemar Dziki | 81 |
| 1686 | Wśród nocnej ciszy *[Amidst the night's silence]* | POL | 1978 | Tadeusz Chmielewski | 120 |
| 1687 | Spalovač mrtvol *(The Cremator)* | CZ | 1968 | Juraj Herz | 99 |
| 1688 | Alexandra şi infernul | ROM | 1975 | Iulian Mihu | 101 |
| 1689 | A Soldier's Story | USA | 1984 | Norman Jewison | 101+V |
| 1690 | Chapayev | USSR | 1934 | Georgi Vasiliev Sergei Vasiliev | 90(97) +V |
| 1691 | Un maledetto imbroglio *(The Facts of Murder)* *(aka: A Sordid Affair)* | IT | 1960(59) | Pietro Germi | 114 |
| 1692 | | | | | |
| 1693 | The Autobiography of Miss Jane Pittman *(aka: Fight For Freedom)* | USA | 1974 | John Korty | 109 +V |
| 1694 | A Gathering of Old Men *(GER: Ein Aufstand alter Männer)* | USA/GER | 1987 | Volker Schlöndorff | 120 |
| 1695 | The Sky Is Gray | USA | 1982 | Stan Lathan | 47 +V |
| 1696 | Los buenos dias perdidos | SP | 1975 | Rafael Gil | 99(105) |
| 1697 | Moara lui Călifar | ROM | 1984 | Şerban Marinescu | 70 |
| 1698 | Pókháló *(Cobweb)* | HUNG | 1973 | Imre Mihályfi | 98 |
| 1699 | Egymásra nézve *(Another Way)* | HUNG | 1982 | Károly Makk | 109 |
| 1700 | Doña Barbara | MEX | 1943 | Fernando de Fuentes | 138 |
| 1701 | | | | | |
| 1702 | A Summer Story | GB | 1988(87) | Piers Haggard | 96 +V |
| 1703 | Escape | GB | 1930 | Basil Dean | 69 |
| 1704 | Escape | GB | 1948 | Joseph L. Mankiewicz | 79 |
| 1705 | Twenty-One Days *(USA: 21 Days Together)* | GB | 1939(37) | Basil Dean | 77 |
| 1706 | Die Letzten Werden die Ersten Sein *[Thy last will be the first]* | GER | 1957(56) | Rolf Hansen | 90 |
| 1707 | Loyalties | GB | 1933 | Basil Dean | 74 |
| 1708 | That Forsyte Woman *(aka: The Forsyte Saga)* | USA | 1949 | Compton Bennett | 113 |
| 1709 | Old English | USA | 1930 | Alfred E. Green | 87 |
| 1710 | One More River *(GB: Over the River)* | USA | 1934 | James Whale | 88 |
| 1711 | The Skin Game | GB | 1931 | Alfred Hitchcock | 88 |
| 1712 | | | | | |
| 1713 | La muerte en las calles | ARG | 1957 | Leo Fleider | 80 |
| 1714 | Nacha Regules | ARG | 1950 | Luis César Amadori | 107 |
| 1715 | Nuevas amistades | SP | 1963 | Ramón Comas | 105(85) |
| 1716 | Bodas de sangre | ARG | 1938 | Edmundo Guibourg | 104 |
| 1717 | Bodas de sangre *(Blood Wedding)* *(aka: Blood Honeymoon)* *(aka: Noces de sang)* | MOR | 1977 | Souhel Ben Barka | 85 |

| No. | Author | Nationality | Form | Literary Title | Date |
|-----|--------|-------------|------|----------------|------|
| 1718 | García Lorca, Federico | Spanish | P | Bodas de sangre | 1936 |
| 1719 | García Lorca, Federico | Spanish | P | La casa de Bernarda Alba<br>(The House of Bernarda Alba) | 1945 |
| 1720 | García Lorca, Federico | Spanish | P | Yerma<br>(Yerma) | 1937 |
| 1721 | García Márquez, Gabriel<br>(Gabriel García Márquez) | Colombian | N | Cien años de soledad<br>(A Hundred Years of Solitude) | 1967 |
| 1722 | García Márquez, Gabriel | Colombian | SS | Cronaca di una morte annunciata<br>(Chronicle of a Death Foretold) | 1981 |
| 1723 | García Márquez, Gabriel | Colombian | SS | Cronaca di una morte annunciata | 1981 |
| 1724 | García Márquez, Gabriel | Colombian | SS | Un señor muy viejo con unas<br>alas enormes<br>(A Very Old Man With Enormous<br>Wings) | 1972 |
| 1725 | García Márquez, Gabriel | Colombian | SS | La viuda de Montiel<br>(Montiel's Widow) | 1962 |
| 1726 | García Serrano, Rafael | Spanish | N | La fiel infantería | 1943 |
| 1727 | García Serrano, Rafael | Spanish | N | Los ojos perdidos<br>[Lost eyes] | 1958 |
| 1728 | Gárdonyi Géza | Hungarian | N | Egri csillagok<br>[The stars of Eger] | 1901 |
| 1729 | Garrett, Almeida<br>(Almeida Garrett, Silva Leitao de) | Portuguese | P | Frei Luis de Sousa<br>(Brother Luiz de Souza) | 1859 |
| 1730 | Gautier, Théophile | French | N | Le capitaine Fracasse<br>(Captain Fracasse) | 1863 |
| 1731 | Gautier, Théophile | French | N | Le capitaine Fracasse | 1863 |
| 1732 | Gautier, Théophile | French | N | Mademoiselle de Maupin | 1835-36 |
| 1733 | Gay, John | British | P | The Beggar's Opera | 1728 |
| 1734 | Gay, John | British | P | The Beggar's Opera | 1728 |
| 1735 | Gazzo, Michael V. | American | P | A Hatful of Rain | 1954 |
| 1736 | Geelmuyden, Hans | Norwegian | N | Trine! | 1940 |
| 1737 | Gelber, Jack | American | P | The Connection | 1957 |
| 1738 | Genêt, Jean | French | P | Le balcon<br>(The Balcony) | 1956 |
| 1739 | Genêt, Jean | French | P | Les bonnes<br>(The Maids) | 1948(52) |
| 1740 | Genêt, Jean | French | V | Le condammé à mort<br>(The Man Condemned to Death) | 1942 |
| 1741 | Genet, Jean | French | P | Haute surveillance<br>(Death Watch) | 1949 |
| 1742 | Genêt, Jean | French | N | Querelle de Brest<br>(Querelle of Brest) | 1952 |
| 1743 | George, Peter Bryan | American | N | Red Alert<br>(aka: Two Hours to Dream) | 1958 |
| 1744 | Gevers, Marie | Belgian | N | Paix sur les champs | 1941 |
| 1745 | Giacosa, Giuseppe | Italian | P | Come le foglie<br>(Like Falling Leaves) | 1900 |
| 1746 | Gibson, William | American | N | The Cobweb | 1954 |
| 1747 | Gibson, William | American | P | The Miracle Worker | 1957 |
| 1748 | Gibson, William | American | P | Two For the Seesaw | 1960 |
| 1749 | Gide, André | French | N | La symphonie pastorale<br>(The Pastoral Symphony) | 1919 |
| 1750 | Gide, André | French | N | La symphonie pastorale | 1919 |
| 1751 | Gierow, Karl Ragnar | Swedish | P | Av hjärtans lust | 1944 |
| 1752 | Gierow, Karl Ragnar | Swedish | P | Av hjärtans lust | 1944 |
| 1753 | Gilroy, Frank D. | American | N | From Noon Till Three | 1973 |
| 1754 | Gilroy, Frank D. | American | P | The Only Game in Town | 1967 |

| No | Film Title | Country of Production | Date | Director(s) | Duration of Film |
|---|---|---|---|---|---|
| 1718 | **Bodas de sangre** (Blood Wedding) {ballet version} | SP | 1981(80) | **Carlos Saura** | 72(68) |
| 1719 | **La casa de Bernarda Alba** (The House of Bernarda Alba) | SP | 1987(86) | **Mario Camús** | 104 |
| 1720 | **Yerma** | GER/HUNG | 1984 | **Barna Kabay** **Imre Gyöngyössy** | 111(107) |
| 1721 | **El mar del tiempo perdido** (GER: Das Meer der verlorenen Zeit) (The Sea of Lost Time) | VEN/GER | 1980(78) | **Solveig Hoogestijn** | 82 |
| 1722 | **Cronaca di una morte annunciata** (Chronicle of a Death Foretold) | IT | 1987 | **Francesco Rosi** | 105(110) +V |
| 1723 | **Xuese qingchen** (Bloody Morning) | CHN | 1990 | **Li Shaohong** | 98 |
| 1724 | **Un señor muy viejo con unas alas enormes** | CB/SP | 1988 | **Fernando Birri** | 80 |
| 1725 | **La viuda de Montiel** (Montiel's Widow) (aka: Mrs Montiel, the Widow) | MEX/CB/ VEN/COL | 1979 | **Miguel Littin** | 115(113) |
| 1726 | **La fiel infantería** (Faithful Infantry) | SP | 1959 | **Pedro Lazaga** | 90(113) |
| 1727 | **Los ojos perdidos** | SP | 1966 | **Rafael García Serrano** | 85(96) +V |
| 1728 | **Egri csillagok** (The Lost Talisman) (aka: Stars of Eger) | HUNG | 1968 | **Zoltán Várkonyi** | Pt.1, 71 Pt.2, 86 |
| 1729 | **Frei Luis de Sousa** | PORT | 1950 | **António Lopes Ribeiro** | 118 |
| 1730 | **Le capitaine Fracasse** | FR | 1943(42) | **Abel Gance** | 108 |
| 1731 | **Le capitaine Fracasse** (IT: Capitan Fracassa) | FR/IT | 1961 | **Pierre Gaspard-Huit** | 105 |
| 1732 | **Madamigella di Maupin** (FR: Le chevalier de Maupin) | IT/FR/SP | 1966(65) | **Mauro Bolognini** | 95 |
| 1733 | **The Beggar's Opera** | GB | 1953 | **Peter Brook** | 94 +V |
| 1734 | **The Beggar's Opera** | GB | 1983 | **Richard Eyre** | 140 |
| 1735 | **A Hatful of Rain** | USA | 1957 | **Fred Zinnemann** | 108 |
| 1736 | **Trine** | NOR | 1952 | **Toralf Sandø** | 99 |
| 1737 | **The Connection** | USA | 1961 | **Shirley Clarke** | 110 |
| 1738 | **The Balcony** | USA | 1963(62) | **Joseph Strick** | 84 |
| 1739 | **The Maids** | GB/CAN | 1976(74) | **Christopher Miles** | 95 |
| 1740 | **Possession du condammé** (Condemned and Possessed) | BEL | 1967 | **Albert-André L'Heureux** | 14 |
| 1741 | **Deathwatch** | USA | 1967(65) | **Vic Morrow** | 88 |
| 1742 | **Querelle - Ein Pakt mit dem Teufel** (FR: Querelle de Brest) (aka: Querelle) | GER/FR | 1982 | **R. W. Fassbinder** | 106(120) +V |
| 1743 | **Dr Strangelove** (aka: Dr Strangelove: or How I Learned to Stop Worrying and Love the Bomb) | GB | 1964(63) | **Stanley Kubrick** | 93 +V |
| 1744 | **Paix sur les champs** (Peace Over the Fields) | BEL | 1970 | **Jacques Boigelot** | 90 |
| 1745 | **Come le foglie** | IT | 1935(34) | **Mario Camerini** | 82 |
| 1746 | **The Cobweb** | USA | 1955 | **Vincente Minnelli** | 124 |
| 1747 | **The Miracle Worker** | USA | 1962 | **Arthur Penn** | 106 |
| 1748 | **Two For the Seesaw** | USA | 1962 | **Robert Wise** | 119 |
| 1749 | **Den'en kokyogaku** (La symphonie pastorale) | JAP | 1938 | **Satsuo Yamamoto** | 76 |
| 1750 | **La symphonie pastorale** (Pastoral Symphony) | FR | 1946 | **Jean Delannoy** | 105 |
| 1751 | **Av hjärtans lust** | SWE | 1960 | **Rolf Husberg** | 98 |
| 1752 | **Alt for kvinden** | DEN | 1964 | **Annelise Reenberg** | 99 |
| 1753 | **From Noon Till Three** | USA | 1976(75) | **Frank D. Gilroy** | 99 +V |
| 1754 | **The Only Game in Town** | USA | 1970(69) | **George Stevens** | 113 |

| No. | Author | Nationality | Form | Literary Title | Date |
|---|---|---|---|---|---|
| 1755 | Gilroy, Frank D. | American | P | The Subject Was Roses | 1962 |
| 1756 | Ginzburg, Natalia | Italian | N | Caro Michele<br>(Dear Michael) | 1973 |
| 1757 | Giono, Jean | French | P | Le bout de la route | 1937 |
| 1758 | Giono, Jean | French | N | Le chant du monde<br>(The Song of the World) | 1934 |
| 1759 | Giono, Jean | French | N | Les grands chemins | 1948 |
| 1760 | Giono, Jean | French | N | Jean le bleu<br>(Blue Boy)<br>{ch. VII} | 1932 |
| 1761 | Giono, Jean | French | SS | Jofroi de la Maussan | 1930 |
| 1762 | Giono, Jean | French | N | Regain<br>(Harvest) | 1930 |
| 1763 | Giono, Jean | French | N | Un roi sans divertissement<br>[A king without distractions] | 1947 |
| 1764 | Giono, Jean | French | N | Un de Baumugnes<br>(Lovers Are Never Losers) | 1929 |
| 1765 | Girard, Henri Georges<br>(see: Arnaud, Georges) | French | N | | |
| 1766 | Giraudoux, Jean | French | P | La folle de Chaillot<br>(The Madwoman of Chaillot) | 1945 |
| 1767 | Giraudoux, Jean | French | N-P | Siegfried et le limousin {n}<br>Siegfried {p} | 1922{n}<br>1928{p} |
| 1768 | Glasgow, Ellen | American | N | In This Our Life | 1941 |
| 1769 | Glazarová, Jarmila | Czech | N | Advent | 1950 |
| 1770 | Glazarová, Jarmila | Czech | N | Vlčí jáma<br>(The Wolf Trap) | 1941 |
| 1771 | Goes, Albrecht | German | SS | Unruhige Nacht<br>(Arrow to the Heart)<br>(USA: Unquiet Night) | 1950 |
| 1772 | Goethe, Johann Wolfgang von | German | AUT | Aus meinem Leben. Dichtung<br>und Wahrheit<br>(aka: Dichtung und Wahrhe)<br>(Goethe's Boyhood and Youth) | 1811-33 |
| 1773 | Goethe, Johann Wolfgang von | German | AUT | Aus meinem Leben. Dichtung<br>und Wahrheit | 1811-33 |
| 1774 | Goethe, Johann Wolfgang von | German | AUT | Aus meinem Leben. Dichtung<br>und Wahrheit | 1811-33 |
| 1775 | Goethe, Johann Wolfgang von | German | P | Clavigo | 1774 |
| 1776 | Goethe, Johann Wolfgang von | German | V | Der Erlkönig<br>(Erl-King) | 1782 |
| 1777 | Goethe, Johann Wolfgang von | German | P | Faust<br>(aka: Goethe's Faust)<br>(Faustus) | 1808-32 |
| 1778 | Goethe, Johann Wolfgang von | German | P | Faust | 1808-32 |
| 1779 | Goethe, Johann Wolfgang von | German | P | Faust | 1808-32 |
| 1780 | Goethe, Johann Wolfgang von | German | P | Faust<br>{pt. 1} | 1808 |
| 1781 | Goethe, Johann Wolfgang von | German | P | Faust | 1808-32 |
| 1782 | Goethe, Johann Wolfgang von | German | P | Faust | 1808-32 |
| 1783 | Goethe, Johann Wolfgang von | German | P | Faust | 1808-32 |
| 1784 | Goethe, Johann Wolfgang von | German | P | Götz von Berlichingen mit<br>der eisernen Hand<br>(Goetz of Berlichingen With the<br>Iron Hand) | 1773 |
| 1785 | Goethe, Johann Wolfgang von | German | P | Götz von Berlichingen mit<br>der eisernen Hand | 1773 |
| 1786 | Goethe, Johann Wolfgang von | German | V | Hermann und Dorothea<br>(Herman and Dorothea) | 1798 |
| 1787 | Goethe, Johann Wolfgang von | German | N | Die Leiden des jungen Werthers<br>(The Sufferings of Young Werter)<br>(aka: The Sorrows of Werter) | 1774 |

| No | Film Title | Country of Production | Date | Director(s) | Duration of Film |
|---|---|---|---|---|---|
| 1755 | **The Subject Was Roses** | USA | 1968 | **Ulu Grosbard** | 107 |
| 1756 | **Caro Michele** *(Dear Michael)* | IT | 1976 | **Mario Monicelli** | 108(115) |
| 1757 | **Le bout de la route** | FR | 1948 | **Émile Couzinet** | 85 |
| 1758 | **Le chant du monde** *(IT: Ossessione nuda)* | FR/IT | 1965 | **Marcel Camús** | 95(105) |
| 1759 | **Les grands chemins** *(IT: Il baro)* | FR/IT | 1963 | **Christian Marquand** **Roger Vadim** | 95(90) |
| 1760 | **La femme du boulanger** *(The Baker's Wife)* | FR | 1938 | **Marcel Pagnol** | 116(127) |
| 1761 | **Jofroi** *(aka: Ways of Love)* | FR | 1934(33) | **Marcel Pagnol** | 55 |
| 1762 | **Regain** *(Harvest)* | FR | 1937 | **Marcel Pagnol** | 122(150) |
| 1763 | **Un roi sans divertissement** | FR | 1963 | **François Leterrier** | 85 |
| 1764 | **Angèle** | FR | 1934 | **Marcel Pagnol** | 150(162) |
| 1765 | | | | | |
| 1766 | **The Madwoman of Chaillot** | GB | 1969 | **Bryan Forbes** | 142 |
| 1767 | **Double destin** *(GER: Das zweit Leben)* | FR/GER | 1955(54) | **Victor Vicas** | 90(87) |
| 1768 | **In This Our Life** | USA | 1942 | **John Huston** | 101 |
| 1769 | **Advent** *(The Gates of Dawn)* | CZ | 1956 | **Vladimír Vlček** | 76 |
| 1770 | **Vlči jáma** *(Wolf Trap)* | CZ | 1957 | **Jiří Weiss** | 95 |
| 1771 | **Unruhige Nacht** *(Restless Night)* *(aka: All Night Through)* | GER | 1958 | **Falk Harnack** | 100 |
| 1772 | **Friederike von Sesenheim** *(aka: Die Jugendgeliebte)* *(aka: Goethes Frühlingstraum)* | GER | 1930 | **Hans Tintner** | 88 |
| 1773 | **Friederike** | GER | 1932 | **Fritz Friedmann-Frederich** | 91 |
| 1774 | **Goethe lebt...!** | GER | 1932 | **Eberhard Frowein** | 82 |
| 1775 | **Clavigo** | GER | 1970 | **Marcel Ophüls** | 130 |
| 1776 | **Le roi des aulnes** *(GER: Der Erlkönig)* | FR/GER | 1931 | **Marie-Louise Iribe** **Peter Paul Brauer** | 51 |
| 1777 | **Walpurgis Night** | USA | 1932 | **Howard Higgin** | 20 |
| 1778 | **La leggenda di Faust** *(Faust and the Devil)* *(aka: Faust e Margherita)* | IT | 1948 | **Carmine Gallone** | 87 |
| 1779 | **La beauté du diable** *(IT: La bellezza del diavolo)* *(Beauty and the Devil)* | FR/IT | 1950(49) | **René Clair** | 96(92) |
| 1780 | **Faust** | GER | 1960 | **Peter Gorski** | 128 |
| 1781 | **Faust** | USA | 1964 | **Michael Susman** | 100 |
| 1782 | **Faust XX** | ROM | 1966 | **Ion Popescu Gopo** | 86 |
| 1783 | **Bedazzled** | GB | 1967 | **Stanley Donen** | 103 |
| 1784 | **Götz von Berlichingen** | AUST | 1955 | **Alfred Stöger** **Josef Gielen** | 84 |
| 1785 | **Götz von Berlichingen** *(aka: Götz von Berlichingen mit der eisernen Hand)* *(Man With the Iron Fist)* | GER/YUGO | 1979(78) | **Wolfgang Liebeneiner** | 103(98) |
| 1786 | **Liebesleute** *(aka: Hermann und Dorothea von heute)* | GER | 1935 | **Erich Waschneck** | 96 |
| 1787 | **Le roman de Werther** *(aka: Werther)* | FR | 1938 | **Max Ophüls** | 83 |

| No. | Author | Nationality | Form | Literary Title | Date |
|-----|--------|-------------|------|----------------|------|
| 1788 | Goethe, Johann Wolfgang von | German | N | **Die Leiden des jungen Werthers** | 1774 |
| 1789 | Goethe, Johann Wolfgang von | German | N | **Die Leiden des jungen Werthers** | 1774 |
| 1790 | Goethe, Johann Wolfgang von | German | N | **Die Leiden des jungen Werthers** | 1774 |
| 1791 | Goethe, Johann Wolfgang von | German | V | **Reineke Fuchs** *(Reynard the Fox)* | 1794 |
| 1792 | Goethe, Johann Wolfgang von | German | P | **Satyros** *(Goethe's Satyros)* | 1840 |
| 1793 | Goethe, Johann Wolfgang von | German | N | **Die Wahlverwandtschaften** *(Elective Affinities)* *(aka: Kindred by Choice)* | 1809 |
| 1794 | Goethe, Johann Wolfgang von | German | N | **Die Wahlverwandtschaften** | 1809 |
| 1795 | Goethe, Johann Wolfgang von | German | N | **Die Wahlverwandtschaften** | 1809 |
| 1796 | Goethe, Johann Wolfgang von | German | N | **Die Wahlverwandtschaften** | 1809 |
| 1797 | Goethe, Johann Wolfgang von | German | N | **Wilhelm Meisters Lehrjahre** *(William Meister's Apprenticeship)* *(aka: Wilhem Meister)* | 1795 |
| 1798 | Gogol, Nikolay | Russian(Ukr) | P | **Igroki** *(The Gamblers)* | 1842 |
| 1799 | Gogol, Nikolay | Russian | SS | **Kak possorilis' Ivan Ivanovich s Ivanom Nikiforovitchem** *(Tale of How Ivan Ivanovich Quarrelled With Ivan Nik...)* | 1835 |
| 1800 | Gogol, Nikolay | Russian | SS | **Kak possorilis' Ivan Ivanovich s Ivanom Nikiforovitchem** | 1835 |
| 1801 | Gogol, Nikolay | Russian | SS | **Mayskaya noch'** *(A May Night, or the Drowned Maiden)* *(aka: An Evening in May)* | 1831 |
| 1802 | Gogol, Nikolay | Russian | N | **Myortvye dushi** *(Dead Souls)* *(aka: Home Life in Russia)* *(aka: Tchitchikoff's Journeys)* | 1842 |
| 1803 | Gogol, Nikolay | Russian | SS | **Noch pered rozhdestvom** *(Christmas Eve)* *(aka: The Night of Christmas Eve)* | 1832 |
| 1804 | Gogol, Nikolay | Russian | SS | **Propavshaya gramota** *(The Lost Letter)* | 1831 |
| 1805 | Gogol, Nikolay | Russian | P | **Revizor** *(The Government Inspector)* *(aka: The Inspector General)* | 1836 |
| 1806 | Gogol, Nikolay | Russian | P | **Revizor** | 1836 |
| 1807 | Gogol, Nikolay | Russian | P | **Revizor** | 1836 |
| 1808 | Gogol, Nikolay | Russian | P | **Revizor** | 1836 |
| 1809 | Gogol, Nikolay | Russian | P | **Revizor** | 1836 |
| 1810 | Gogol, Nikolay | Russian | P | **Revizor** | 1836 |
| 1811 | Gogol, Nikolay | Russian | SS | **Shinel'** *(The Overcoat)* *(aka: The Cloak)* | 1842 |
| 1812 | Gogol, Nikolay | Russian | SS | **Shinel'** | 1842 |
| 1813 | Gogol, Nikolay | Russian | SS | **Shinel'** | 1842 |
| 1814 | Gogol, Nikolay | Russian | SS | **Shinel'** | 1842 |
| 1815 | Gogol, Nikolay | Russian | SS | **Sorochinskaya jarmarka** *(The Fair at Sorochintsy)* | 1831 |
| 1816 | Gogol, Nikolay | Russian | SS | **Taras Bulba** | 1835 |
| 1817 | Gogol, Nikolay | Russian | SS | **Taras Bulba** | 1835 |
| 1818 | Gogol, Nikolay | Russian | SS | **Viy** | 1835 |

| No | Film Title | Country of Production | Date | Director(s) | Duration of Film |
|----|-----------|----------------------|------|-------------|------------------|
| 1788 | **Begegnung mit Werther** [Encounter with Werther] | GER | 1949 | Karl Heinz Stroux | 89 |
| 1789 | **Die Leiden des jungen Werther** (The Sorrows of Young Werther) | GDR | 1976 | Egon Günther | 100 |
| 1790 | **Die Leidenschaftlichen** [The passionate ones] | GER/AUST/ SWITZ | 1981 | Thomas Koerfer | 105 |
| 1791 | **The Black Fox** {animation} | USA | 1962 | Louis Clyde Stoumen | 89 |
| 1792 | **Rousseauism and the Young Goethe** | GB | 1972 | Alasdair Clayre | 25 |
| 1793 | **Die Wahlverwandtschaften** (Elective Affinities) | GDR | 1975 | Siegfried Kühn | 101 |
| 1794 | **Tagebuch** (Diary) | GER | 1975 | Rudolf Thome | 146 |
| 1795 | **Le affinita elettive** (Elective Affinities) | IT | 1978 | Gianni Amico | 120 |
| 1796 | **Tarot** | GER | 1986 | Rudolf Thome | 110 |
| 1797 | **Falsche Bewegung** (Wrong Movement) | GER | 1975 | Wim Wenders | 103(74) |
| 1798 | **The Gamblers** | USA | 1969 | Ron Winston | 93 |
| 1799 | **Kak possorilis' Ivan Ivanovich s Ivanom Nikiforovitchem** | USSR | 1941 | Andrei Kustov | 69 |
| 1800 | **Kak possorilis' Ivan Ivanovich s Ivanom Nikiforovitchem** | USSR | 1959 | Vladimir Karasov | 69 |
| 1801 | **Mayskaya noch'** | USSR | 1940 | Nikolay Sadkovitch | 69 |
| 1802 | **Myortvye dushi** (Dead Souls) | USSR | 1961(60) | Léonid Trauberg | 103 |
| 1803 | **Noch pered rozhdestvom** (Christmas Eve) | USSR | 1962 | Alexander Row | 90 |
| 1804 | **Propavshaya gramota** | USSR | 1972 | Boris Ivchenko | 78 |
| 1805 | **Eine Stadt steht Kopf** | GER | 1932 | Gustaf Gründgens | 80 |
| 1806 | **Kuang huan zhi ye** (Mad Night) | CHN | 1936 | Shu Dong-shan (Shin Tung-shan) | 10 |
| 1807 | **The Inspector General** (aka: Happy Times) | USA | 1949 | Henry Koster | 101 +V |
| 1808 | **Revizor** (The Inspector General) | USSR | 1952 | Vladimir Pétrov | 90 |
| 1809 | **Inkognito iz Peterburga** | USSR | 1977 | Leonid Gaidai | 91 |
| 1810 | **Délibábok országa** (The Land of Mirages) | HUNG | 1984 | Márta Mészáros | 83 |
| 1811 | **Il cappotto** (The Overcoat) | IT | 1952 | Alberto Lattuada | 100 |
| 1812 | **The Bespoke Overcoat** | GB | 1955 | Jack Clayton | 32 |
| 1813 | **Garam Coat** (The Overcoat) | IND(HIN) | 1955 | Amar Kumar | 81 |
| 1814 | **Shinel** (The Overcoat) (aka: The Cloak) | USSR | 1959(60) | Alexei Batalov | 78 |
| 1815 | **Sorochinskaya jamarka** (Sorochinsky Fair) | USSR | 1939 | Nikolai Ekk | 96 |
| 1816 | **Tarass Bulba** | FR/GB | 1939(36) | Alexis Granowsky | 105 |
| 1817 | **Taras Bulba** | USA | 1962 | J. Lee Thompson | 124 |
| 1818 | **La maschera del demonio** (Demon's Mask) (aka: Black Sunday) (aka: The House of Fright) | IT | 1960 | Mario Bava | 83 +V |

| No. | Author | Nationality | Form | Literary Title | Date |
|---|---|---|---|---|---|
| 1819 | Gogol, Nikolay | Russian | SS | Viy | 1835 |
| 1820 | Gogol, Nikolay | Russian | SS | Zapiski sumasshedshego (Diary of a Madman) (aka: A Madman's Diary) | 1835 |
| 1821 | Gogol, Nikolay | Russian | P | Zhenit'ba (Marriage) | 1841 |
| 1822 | Gogol, Nikolay | Russian | P | Zhenit'ba | 1841 |
| 1823 | Gojawiczyńska, Apolonia (see: Gojawiczyńska, Pola) | Polish | N | | |
| 1824 | Gojawiczyńska, Pola (Apolonia Gojawiczyńska) | Polish | N | Dziewczęta z Nowolipek [The girls from Nowolipki street] | 1935 |
| 1825 | Gojawiczyńska, Pola | Polish | N | Dziewczęta z Nowolipek | 1935 |
| 1826 | Gojawiczyńska, Pola | Polish | N | Rajska jabłoń [The apple tree of paradise] | 1937 |
| 1827 | Golding, William | British | N | Lord of the Flies | 1954 |
| 1828 | Golding, William | British | N | Lord of the Flies | 1954 |
| 1829 | Goldman, William | American | N | Heat | 1985 |
| 1830 | Goldman, William | American | N | Magic | 1976 |
| 1831 | Goldman, William | American | N | Marathon Man | 1974 |
| 1832 | Goldman, William | American | N | No Way to Treat a Lady | 1964 |
| 1833 | Goldman, William | American | N | Soldier in the Rain | 1960 |
| 1834 | Goldoni, Carlo | Italian | P | La locandiera (Mine Hostess) (aka: Mirandolina) | 1753 |
| 1835 | Goldoni, Carlo | Italian | P | La locandiera | 1753 |
| 1836 | Goldoni, Carlo | Italian | P | I rusteghi (The Boors) | 1761 |
| 1837 | Gomes, Alfredo Dias | Brazilian | P | O pagador de promessas (Journey to Bahia) (aka: Payment as Pledged) | 1961 |
| 1838 | Goncharov, Ivan Aleksandrovich | Russian | N | Oblomov | 1859 |
| 1839 | Goncourt, Edmond | French | N-P | La fille Élisa (Elisa) | 1877{n} 1891{p} |
| 1840 | Goodis, David | American | N | The Burglar | 1953 |
| 1841 | Goodis, David | American | N | The Burglar | 1953 |
| 1842 | Goodis, David | American | N | Dark Passage | 1946 |
| 1843 | Goodis, David | American | N | Down There (aka: Shoot the Piano Player) | 1956 |
| 1844 | Goodis, David | American | N | The Moon in the Gutter | 1954 |
| 1845 | Goodis, David | American | N | Nightfall | 1947 |
| 1846 | Goodis, David | American | N | The Wounded and the Slain | 1959 |
| 1847 | Gordimer, Nadine | South African | N | A World of Strangers | 1958 |
| 1848 | Gorky, Maxim (Alexei Maksimovich Peshkov) | Russian | SS | Chelkash | 1894 |
| 1849 | Gorky, Maxim | Russian | P | Dachniki (Summerfolk) | 1904 |
| 1850 | Gorky, Maxim | Russian | P | Dachniki | 1904 |
| 1851 | Gorky, Maxim | Russian | N | Delo Artamonovykh (The Artamonov Business) (aka: Decadence) (aka: The Artamonovs) | 1925 |
| 1852 | Gorky, Maxim | Russian | AUT | Detstvo (Childhood) (aka: My Childhood) | 1913 |
| 1853 | Gorky, Maxim | Russian | N | Foma Gordeyev (aka: The Man Who Was Afraid) | 1899 |
| 1854 | Gorky, Maxim | Russian | SS | Malva | 1897 |
| 1855 | Gorky, Maxim | Russian | N | Mat' (Mother) (aka: Comrades) | 1906 |

| No | Film Title | Country of Production | Date | Director(s) | Duration of Film |
|---|---|---|---|---|---|
| 1819 | **Viy** | USSR | 1967 | **Konstantin Ershov** **Georgi Kropachev** | 77 |
| 1820 | **Sofi** (aka: Diary of a Madman) | USA | 1967 | **Robert Carlisle** | 92 |
| 1821 | **Zhenit'ba** | USSR | 1937 | **Erast Garin** **Khessia Lokshina** | 98 |
| 1822 1823 | **Zhenit'ba** | USSR | 1977 | **Vitaliy Melnikov** | 97 |
| 1824 | **Dziewczęta z Nowolipek** | POL | 1937 | **Jósef Lejtes** | 101 |
| 1825 | **Dziewczęta z Nowolipek** | POL | 1986 | **Barbara Sass** | 90 |
| 1826 | **Rajska jabłoń** | POL | 1986 | **Barbara Sass** | 106 |
| 1827 | **Lord of the Flies** | GB | 1963 | **Peter Brook** | 91 |
| 1828 | **Lord of the Flies** | USA | 1990 | **Harry Hook** | 90 +V |
| 1829 | **Heat** | USA | 1986 | **R. M. Richards** | 97 +V |
| 1830 | **Magic** | USA | 1978 | **Richard Attenborough** | 106 +V |
| 1831 | **Marathon Man** | USA | 1976 | **John Schlesinger** | 126 +V |
| 1832 | **No Way to Treat a Lady** | USA | 1968(67) | **Jack Smight** | 108 |
| 1833 | **Soldier in the Rain** | USA | 1963 | **Ralph Nelson** | 87 |
| 1834 | **Das Mädchen mit dem guten Ruf** [The girl with the good reputation] | GER | 1938 | **Hans Schweikart** | 79 |
| 1835 | **La locandiera** | IT | 1944(43) | **Luigi Chiarini** | 87 |
| 1836 | **Bădăranii** (The Boors) | ROM | 1960 | **Gheorghe Naghi** **Sică Alexandrescu** | 90 |
| 1837 | **O pagador de promessas** (The Promise) | BRAZ | 1962 | **Anselmo Duarte** | 100 |
| 1838 | **Neskol'ko dnej iz zhizni Oblomova** (aka: Oblomov) | USSR | 1979 | **Nikita Mikhalkov** | 140 +V |
| 1839 | **Élisa** | FR | 1957(56) | **Roger Richebé** | 90 |
| 1840 | **The Burglar** | USA | 1957 | **Paul Wendkos** | 90 |
| 1841 | **Le casse** (IT: Gli scassinatori) (The Burglars) | FR/IT | 1971 | **Henri Verneuil** | 117(127) |
| 1842 | **Dark Passage** | USA | 1947 | **Delmer Daves** | 106 +V |
| 1843 | **Tirez sur le pianiste** (Shoot the Pianist) (aka: Shoot the Piano Player) | FR | 1960 | **François Truffaut** | 80 |
| 1844 | **La lune dans le caniveau** (The Moon in the Gutter) | FR/IT | 1984(83) | **Jean-Jacques Beineix** | 130 |
| 1845 | **Nightfall** | USA | 1957(56) | **Jacques Tourneur** | 78 |
| 1846 | **Descente aux enfers** (Descent into Hell) | FR | 1986 | **Francis Girod** | 90 |
| 1847 | **Dilemma** (aka: World of Strangers) | DEN | 1962 | **Henning Carlsen** | 92 |
| 1848 | **Chelkash** | USSR | 1956 | **Fyodor Filippov** | 46 |
| 1849 | **Dachniki** (Summer Residents in the Countryside) | USSR | 1967 | **Boris Babochkin** | 104 |
| 1850 | **Sommergäste** (Summer Guests) | GER | 1976(75) | **Peter Stein** | 120(115) |
| 1851 | **Delo Artamonovika** (Artamonov and Sons) (aka: The Artamanov Affair) | USSR | 1941 | **Grigori Roshal** | 93(86) |
| 1852 | **Detstvo Gorkovo** (Childhood of Maxim Gorky) | USSR | 1938 | **Mark Donskoi** | 110(100) +V |
| 1853 | **Foma Gordeyev** (The Gordeyev Family) | USSR | 1959 | **Mark Donskoi** | 95 |
| 1854 | **Malva** | USSR | 1957 | **Vladimir Braun** | 85 |
| 1855 | **Mat** (Mother) (aka: 1905) | USSR | 1956 | **Mark Donskoi** | 100 +V |

| No. | Author | Nationality | Form | Literary Title | Date |
|---|---|---|---|---|---|
| 1856 | **Gorky, Maxim** | Russian | AUT | **Moi universitety**<br>*(My Universities)*<br>*(aka: My University Days)* | 1921-22 |
| 1857 | **Gorky, Maxim** | Russian | P | **Na dne**<br>*(The Lower Depths)*<br>*(aka: A Night's Lodging)*<br>*(aka: At the Bottom)*<br>*(aka: Submerged)* | 1903 |
| 1858 | **Gorky, Maxim** | Russian | P | **Na dne** | 1903 |
| 1859 | **Gorky, Maxim** | Russian | P | **Na dne** | 1903 |
| 1860 | **Gorky, Maxim** | Russian | P | **Vassa Zheleznova** | 1910 |
| 1861 | **Gorky, Maxim** | Russian | P | **Vassa Zheleznova** | 1910 |
| 1862 | **Gorky, Maxim** | Russian | AUT | **V lyudyakh**<br>*(My Apprenticeship)*<br>*(aka: In the World)* | 1915 |
| 1863 | **Gorky, Maxim** | Russian | P | **Vragi**<br>*(Enemies)* | 1906 |
| 1864 | **Gorky, Maxim** | Russian | P | **Yegor Bulychov i drugiye**<br>*(Egor Bulyechev and Others)* | 1932 |
| 1865 | **Gotthelf, Jeremias**<br>*(Albert Bitzius)* | Swiss(Ger) | N | **Geld und Geist, oder die Versöhnung**<br>*(Wealth and Welfare)*<br>*(aka: The Soul and Money)* | 1852 |
| 1866 | **Gotthelf, Jeremias** | Swiss | N | **Die Käserei in der Vehfreude** | 1850 |
| 1867 | **Gotthelf, Jeremias** | Swiss | N | **Uli der Knecht**<br>*(Uli, the Farm Servant)* | 1846 |
| 1868 | **Gotthelf, Jeremias** | Swiss | N | **Uli der Pächter**<br>*(aka: Uli de Knecht, 2)* | 1849 |
| 1869 | **Gotthelf, Jeremias** | Swiss | N | **Wie Anne Bäbi Jowäger haushaltet und wie es ihm mit dem doktern geht** | 1843-44 |
| 1870 | **Gracq, Julien** | French | SS | **Le roi Cophétua** | 1970 |
| 1871 | **Graf, Oskar Maria** | German | N | **Das bayrische Dekameron** | 1928 |
| 1872 | **Graf, Oskar Maria** | German | N | **Bolwieser**<br>*(The Station-Master)* | 1931 |
| 1873 | **Grahame, Kenneth** | British | N | **The Wind in the Willows** | 1908 |
| 1874 | **Grahame, Kenneth** | British | N | **The Wind in the Willows** | 1908 |
| 1875 | **Grahame, Kenneth** | British | N | **The Wind in the Willows** | 1908 |
| 1876 | **Grass, Günter** | German | N | **Die Blechtrommel**<br>*(The Tin Drum)* | 1959 |
| 1877 | **Grass, Günter** | German | SS | **Katz und Maus**<br>*(Cat and Mouse)* | 1961 |
| 1878 | **Graves, Robert** | British | SS | **The Shout** | 1929 |
| 1879 | **Gray, Simon** | British | P | **Butley** | 1971 |
| 1880 | **Green, Julien** | French | N | **Léviathan**<br>*(The Dark Journey)* | 1929 |
| 1881 | **Green, Paul** | American | P | **The House of Connelly** | 1931 |
| 1882 | **Greene, Graham** | British | SS | **Across the Bridge** | 1947 |
| 1883 | **Greene, Graham** | British | SS | **The Basement Room**<br>*(aka: The Lost Illusion)* | 1935 |
| 1884 | **Greene, Graham** | British | N | **Brighton Rock** | 1938 |
| 1885 | **Greene, Graham** | British | N | **The Comedians** | 1966 |
| 1886 | **Greene, Graham** | British | N | **The Confidential Agent** | 1939 |
| 1887 | **Greene, Graham** | British | N | **Dr Fischer of Geneva; or, The Bomb Party** | 1980 |
| 1888 | **Greene, Graham** | British | N | **The End of the Affair** | 1951 |
| 1889 | **Greene, Graham** | British | N | **England Made Me**<br>*(aka: The Shipwrecked)* | 1935 |

| No | Film Title | Country of Production | Date | Director(s) | Duration of Film |
|----|-----------|----------------------|------|-------------|-----------------|
| 1856 | **Moi universitety** <br> *(My Universities)* <br> *(aka: University of Life)* | USSR | 1940 | **Mark Donskoi** | 98(104) <br> +V |
| 1857 | **Les bas-fonds** <br> *(The Lower Depths)* <br> *(aka: Underworld)* | FR | 1936 | **Jean Renoir** | 92(89) |
| 1858 | **Ye dian** <br> *(Night Lodging)* | CHN | 1948 | **Tso Lin** | 116 |
| 1859 | **Donzoko** <br> *(The Lower Depths)* | JAP | 1957 | **Akira Kurosawa** | 137(125) |
| 1860 | **Vassa Zheleznova** <br> *(The Mistress)* | USSR | 1953 | **Leonid Lukov** | 95 |
| 1861 | **Vassa** | USSR | 1983(81) | **Gleb Panfilov** | 140 |
| 1862 | **V lyudyakh** <br> *(My Apprenticeship)* <br> *(aka: Among People)* <br> *(aka: Out in the World)* | USSR | 1939 | **Mark Donskoi** | 98 <br> +V |
| 1863 | **Vragi** <br> *(The Enemies)* | USSR | 1938 | **Alexander Ivanovsky** | 80 |
| 1864 | **Yegor Bulychov i drugiye** <br> *(Egor Bulyechev and Others)* | USSR | 1972 | **Sergei Solovyov** | 90 |
| 1865 | **Geld und Geist** | SWITZ | 1964 | **Franz Schnyder** | 121 |
| 1866 | **Annelie vom Berghof** <br> *(aka: Oh diese Weiber)* | SWITZ | 1958 | **Franz Schnyder** | 86 |
| 1867 | **Uli der Knecht** | SWITZ | 1954 | **Franz Schnyder** | 104 |
| 1868 | **Uli der Pächter** <br> *(GER: Und ewig ruft die Heimat)* | SWITZ | 1956 | **Franz Schnyder** | 103 |
| 1869 | **Anne Bäbi Jowäger** <br> *(Pt.1: Wie Jakobli zu einer Frau kommt)* <br> *(Pt.2: Jakobli und Meyeli)* <br> *(aka: Wie Anne Bäbi haushalet und wie es...)* | SWITZ | 1960-61 | **Franz Schnyder** | Pt.1, 102 <br> Pt.2, 104 <br> aka= 147 |
| 1870 | **Rendez-vous à Bray** | FR/BEL/GER | 1971 | **André Delvaux** | 93(89) |
| 1871 | **Das Glöcklein unterm Himmelbett** <br> *(The Bell Beneath the Fourposter)* | GER | 1970 | **Hans Heinrich** | 84 |
| 1872 | **Bolwieser** <br> *{2 parts}* | GER | 1977 | **R. W. Fassbinder** | Pt.1, 104 <br> Pt.2, 96 |
| 1873 | **The Wind in the Willows** <br> *{animation}* | USA | 1949 | **Wolfgang Reitherman** | 75 |
| 1874 | **The Wind in the Willows** <br> *{animation + puppets}* | GB | 1983 | **Brian Cosgrave** <br> **Mark Hall** | 78 <br> +V(75) |
| 1875 | **The Wind in the Willows** <br> *{animation}* | USA/JAP | 1983 | **Arthur Rankin, Jr.** <br> **Jules Bass** | 97 <br> +V(92) |
| 1876 | **Die Blechtrommel** <br> *(The Tin Drum)* | GER/FR | 1979 | **Volker Schlöndorff** | 141 |
| 1877 | **Katz und Maus** <br> *(Cat and Mouse)* | GER/POL | 1967(66) | **Hansjürgen Pohland** | 88 |
| 1878 | **The Shout** | GB | 1978 | **Jerzy Skolimowski** | 86 +V |
| 1879 | **Butley** | GB/USA/CAN | 1974(73) | **Harold Pinter** | 130 |
| 1880 | **Léviathan** | FR | 1962(61) | **Léonard Keigel** | 93 |
| 1881 | **Carolina** <br> *(GB: House of Connelly)* | USA | 1934 | **Henry King** | 85 |
| 1882 | **Across the Bridge** | GB | 1957 | **Ken Annakin** | 103 |
| 1883 | **The Fallen Idol** <br> *(aka: The Lost Illusion)* | GB | 1948 | **Carol Reed** | 94 <br> +V |
| 1884 | **Brighton Rock** <br> *(USA: Young Scarface)* | GB | 1947 | **John Boulting** | 92(86) <br> +V |
| 1885 | **The Comedians** | USA/BER/FR | 1967 | **Peter Glenville** | 147(160) |
| 1886 | **Confidential Agent** | USA | 1945 | **Herman Shumlin** | 122 |
| 1887 | **Dr Fischer of Geneva** | GB | 1984(83) | **Michael Lindsay-Hogg** | 110 |
| 1888 | **The End of the Affair** | GB | 1955(54) | **Edward Dmytryk** | 106 |
| 1889 | **England Made Me** <br> *(aka: The Rape of the Third Reich)* | GB/YUGO | 1972 | **Peter Duffell** | 100 <br> +V(90) |

| No. | Author | Nationality | Form | Literary Title | Date |
|---|---|---|---|---|---|
| 1890 | **Greene, Graham** | British | N | **A Gun For Sale** (USA: This Gun For Hire) | 1936 |
| 1891 | **Greene, Graham** | British | N | **A Gun For Sale** | 1936 |
| 1892 | **Greene, Graham** | British | N | **The Heart of the Matter** | 1948 |
| 1893 | **Greene, Graham** | British | N | **The Honorary Consul** | 1973 |
| 1894 | **Greene, Graham** | British | N | **The Human Factor** | 1978 |
| 1895 | **Greene, Graham** | British | SS | **The Lieutenant Died Last** | 1940 |
| 1896 | **Greene, Graham** | British | N | **Loser Takes All** | 1955 |
| 1897 | **Greene, Graham** | British | N | **Loser Takes All** | 1955 |
| 1898 | **Greene, Graham** | British | N | **The Man Within** (aka: The Smugglers) | 1929 |
| 1899 | **Greene, Graham** | British | N | **The Ministry of Fear** | 1943 |
| 1900 | **Greene, Graham** | British | N | **Monsignor Quixote** | 1982 |
| 1901 | **Greene, Graham** | British | N | **Our Man in Havana** | 1958 |
| 1902 | **Greene, Graham** | British | N | **The Power and the Glory** (USA: The Labyrinthine Ways) | 1940 |
| 1903 | **Greene, Graham** | British | N | **The Power and the Glory** | 1940 |
| 1904 | **Greene, Graham** | British | N | **The Quiet American** | 1955 |
| 1905 | **Greene, Graham** | British | SS | **A Shocking Accident** | 1967 |
| 1906 | **Greene, Graham** | British | N | **Stamboul Train** (USA: Orient Express) | 1932 |
| 1907 | **Greene, Graham** | British | F-N | **The Third Man** | 1950 |
| 1908 | **Greene, Graham** | British | N | **Travels With My Aunt** | 1969 |
| 1909 | **Grevenius, Herbert** | Swedish | P | **Krigsmans erinran** | 1947 |
| 1910 | **Grevenius, Herbert** | Swedish | P | **Lunchrasten** [The lunch break] | 1952 |
| 1911 | **Grevenius, Herbert** | Swedish | P | **Sonja** | 1928 |
| 1912 | **Griffin, John Howard** | American | N | **Black Like Me** | 1960 |
| 1913 | **Griffiths, Trevor** | British | P | **Comedians** | 1976 |
| 1914 | **Griffiths, Trevor** | British | P | **Country: a Tory Story** | 1981 |
| 1915 | **Grimm, Jacob Ludwig; Grimm, Wilhelm Karl** | German | SS | **Daumesdick** (Thumbling) | 1812 |
| 1916 | **Grimm, Jacob Ludwig; Grimm, Wilhelm Karl** | German | SS | **Der Froschkonig oder der eiserne Heinrich** (The Frog-King, or Iron Henry) (aka: The Frog Prince) | 1812 |
| 1917 | **Grimm, Jacob Ludwig; Grimm, Wilhelm Karl** | German | SS | **Der Froschkonig oder der eiserne Heinrich** | 1812 |
| 1918 | **Grimm, Jacob Ludwig; Grimm, Wilhelm Karl** | German | SS | **Die Gänsemagd** (The Goose-Girl) | 1812 |
| 1919 | **Grimm, Jacob Ludwig; Grimm, Wilhelm Karl** | German | SS | **Die goldene Gans** (The Golden Goose) | 1812 |
| 1920 | **Grimm, Jacob Ludwig; Grimm, Wilhelm Karl** | German | SS | **Hänsel und Gretel** (Hansel and Gretel) | 1812 |
| 1921 | **Grimm, Jacob Ludwig; Grimm, Wilhelm Karl** | German | SS | **Hänsel und Gretel** | 1812 |
| 1922 | **Grimm, Jacob Ludwig; Grimm, Wilhelm Karl** | German | SS | **Hänsel und Gretel** | 1812 |
| 1923 | **Grimm, Jacob Ludwig; Grimm, Wilhelm Karl** | German | SS | **Hänsel und Gretel** | 1812 |
| 1924 | **Grimm, Jacob Ludwig; Grimm, Wilhelm Karl** | German | SS | **Hänsel und Gretel** | 1812 |
| 1925 | **Grimm, Jacob Ludwig; Grimm, Wilhelm Karl** | German | SS | **Hans im Glück** (Hans in Luck) | 1812 |
| 1926 | **Grimm, Jacob Ludwig; Grimm, Wilhelm Karl** | German | SS | **Die kluge Bauerntochter** (The Peasant's Wise Daughter) | 1812 |
| 1927 | **Grimm, Jacob Ludwig; Grimm, Wilhelm Karl** | German | SS | **König Drosselbart** (King Thrushbeard) | 1812 |
| 1928 | **Grimm, Jacob Ludwig; Grimm, Wilhelm Karl** | German | SS | **Rumpelstilzchen** (Rumpelstiltskin) | 1812 |
| 1929 | **Grimm, Jacob Ludwig; Grimm, Wilhelm Karl** | German | SS | **Schneeweisschen und Rosenrot** (Snow-White and Rose-Red) | 1812 |
| 1930 | **Grimm, Jacob Ludwig; Grimm, Wilhelm Karl** | German | SS | **Schneewittchen** (Snow-White) | 1812 |
| 1931 | **Grimm, Jacob Ludwig; Grimm, Wilhelm Karl** | German | SS | **Schneewittchen** | 1812 |

| No | Film Title | Country of Production | Date | Director(s) | Duration of Film |
|----|-----------|----------------------|------|-------------|------------------|
| 1890 | This Gun For Hire | USA | 1942 | Frank Tuttle | 81 +V |
| 1891 | Short Cut to Hell | USA | 1957 | James Cagney | 89 |
| 1892 | The Heart of the Matter | GB | 1953 | George More O'Ferrall | 105 |
| 1893 | The Honorary Consul (USA: Beyond the Limit) | GB | 1983 | John Mackenzie | 103 +V(99) |
| 1894 | The Human Factor | GB/USA | 1980(79) | Otto Preminger | 114 +V |
| 1895 | Went the Day Well? (USA: Forty-Eight Hours) | GB | 1942 | Alberto Cavalcanti | 92 |
| 1896 | Loser Takes All | GB | 1956 | Ken Annakin | 88 |
| 1897 | Loser Takes All | GB | 1990 | James Scott | 100 |
| 1898 | The Man Within (USA: The Smugglers) | GB | 1947 | Bernard Knowles | 90 |
| 1899 | Ministry of Fear | USA | 1944(43) | Fritz Lang | 87 |
| 1900 | Monsignor Quixote | GB | 1985 | Rodney Bennett | 135 |
| 1901 | Our Man in Havana | GB | 1960(59) | Carol Reed | 112 |
| 1902 | The Fugitive | USA | 1947 | John Ford | 104 +V |
| 1903 | The Power and the Glory | USA | 1961 | Marc Daniels | 98 |
| 1904 | The Quiet American | USA | 1958(57) | Joseph L. Mankiewicz | 121 |
| 1905 | A Shocking Accident | GB | 1983 | James Scott | 25 |
| 1906 | Orient Express | USA | 1934 | Paul Martin | 71 |
| 1907 | The Third Man | GB | 1949 | Carol Reed | 103 +V |
| 1908 | Travels With My Aunt | USA | 1972 | George Cukor | 109 |
| 1909 | Krigsmans erinran (A Soldier's Duties) | SWE | 1947 | Erik 'Hampe' Faustman | 84 |
| 1910 | Café Lunchrasten | SWE | 1954 | Erik 'Hampe' Faustman | 79 |
| 1911 | Sonja | SWE | 1943 | Erik 'Hampe' Faustman | 79 |
| 1912 | Black Like Me | USA | 1964 | Carl Lerner | 107 |
| 1913 | Comedians | GB | 1979 | Richard Eyre | 90 +V |
| 1914 | Country | GB | 1981 | Richard Eyre | 80 +V |
| 1915 | Tom Thumb | GB | 1958 | George Pal | 92(98) |
| 1916 | The Tale of the Frog Prince | USA | 1984 | Eric Idle | 54 +V |
| 1917 | The Frog Prince | USA | 1987 | Jackson Hunsicker | 83 +V |
| 1918 | Die Gänsemagd | GER | 1957 | Fritz Genschow | 77 |
| 1919 | Die goldene Gans | GER | 1953 | W. Oehmichen | 75 |
| 1920 | Hänsel und Gretel | GER | 1954 | Fritz Genschow | 87 |
| 1921 | Hänsel und Gretel | GER | 1954 | Walter Janssen | 55 |
| 1922 | Hansel and Gretel {puppets} | USA | 1954 | John Paul | 75 |
| 1923 | Hansel and Gretel | USA | 1982 | James Frawley | 51(vo) |
| 1924 | Hansel and Gretel | IS/GB | 1987 | Len Talan | 82 +V |
| 1925 | Hans im Glück | GER | 1949 | Peter Hamel | 75 |
| 1926 | Wie Heiratet man einen König? | GDR | 1968 | Rainer Simon | 79 |
| 1927 | König Drosselbart | CZ/GER | 1984 | Miloslav Luther | 95 |
| 1928 | Rumpelstiltskin {musical version} | USA | 1987(86) | David Irving | 85 +V(81) |
| 1929 | Schneeweisschen und Rosenrot | GER | 1955 | Erich Kobler | 60 |
| 1930 | Snow White and the Seven Dwarfs {animation} | USA | 1937 | David Hand | 82 |
| 1931 | Schneewittchen und die sieben Zwerge | GER | 1955 | Erich Kobler | 75 |

| No. | Author | Nationality | Form | Literary Title | Date |
|-----|--------|-------------|------|----------------|------|
| 1932 | Grimm, Jacob Ludwig; Grimm, Wilhelm Karl | German | SS | **Schneewittchen** | 1812 |
| 1933 | Grimm, Jacob Ludwig; Grimm, Wilhelm Karl | German | SS | **Schneewittchen** | 1812 |
| 1934 | Grin, Aleksandr *(Aleksandr Stepanovich Grinevsky)* | Russian | N | **Dzhessi i Morgiana** *(Jessie and Morgiana)* | 1928 |
| 1935 | Grinevsky, Aleksandr Stepanovich *(see: Grin, Aleksandr)* | Russian | N | | |
| 1936 | Grossman, Vasily | Russian | SS | **V gorode Berdicheve** *[In the town of Berdicheve]* | 1934 |
| 1937 | Grün, Max von der | German | N | **Vorstad krokodile** *[Crocodiles in the suburbs]* | 1976 |
| 1938 | Guan Hanqing *(Kuan Han-ch'ing)* | Chinese | P | **Dou er yuan** *(aka: Tou O yüan)* *[The wrongs of Tou O]* | c.1230 |
| 1939 | Guan Hanqing | Chinese | P | **San kan hu die meng** *(aka: Hu-tieh meng)* *[The butterfly dream]* | c.1230 |
| 1940 | Guan Hanqing | Chinese | P | **Wang jiang ting** *(aka: Wang-chiang-t'ing)* *(The Riverside Pavilion)* | c.1230 |
| 1941 | Gu Hua *(Ku Hua)* | Chinese | N | **Fu rong zhen** *(aka: Fu-jung chen)* *[Peony town]* | 1979 |
| 1942 | Guarnieri, Gianfrancesco | Brazilian | P | **Gimba: Presidente dos Valentes** *[Gimba: president of the valiant ones]* | 1959 |
| 1943 | Guimarães, Bernardo | Brazilian | N | **O seminarista** | 1895 |
| 1944 | Guimarães, João Alphonsus de *(see: Alphonsus, João)* | Brazilian | N | | |
| 1945 | Guimerà, Àngel | Spanish(Cat) | P | **La filla del mar** *[The daughter of the sea]* | 1900 |
| 1946 | Guimerà, Àngel | Spanish | P | **Maria Rosa** | 1894 |
| 1947 | Güiraldes, Ricardo | Argentine | N | **Don Segundo Sombra** *(Don Segundo Sombra: Shadows on the Pampas)* | 1926 |
| 1948 | Guthrie, A. B. | American | N | **The Big Sky** | 1947 |
| 1949 | Guthrie, A. B. | American | N | **These Thousand Hills** | 1956 |
| 1950 | Guthrie, A. B. | American | N | **The Way West** | 1949 |
| 1951 | Gutiérrez, Eduardo | Argentine | N | **Juan Moreira** | 1879 |
| 1952 | Gutiérrez, Eduardo | Argentine | N | **Juan Moreira** | 1879 |
| 1953 | Gyurkó László | Hungarian | P | **Szerelmem, Elektra** | 1968 |
| 1954 | Haggard, H. Rider | British | N | **Allan Quatermain** *(aka: Allan Quartermain)* | 1887 |
| 1955 | Haggard, H. Rider | British | N | **Allan Quatermain** | 1887 |
| 1956 | Haggard, H. Rider | British | N | **King Solomon's Mines** | 1885 |
| 1957 | Haggard, H. Rider | British | N | **King Solomon's Mines** | 1885 |
| 1958 | Haggard, H. Rider | British | N | **King Solomon's Mines** | 1885 |
| 1959 | Haggard, H. Rider | British | N | **King Solomon's Mines** | 1885 |
| 1960 | Haggard, H. Rider | British | N | **She** | 1886 |
| 1961 | Haggard, H. Rider | British | N | **She** | 1886 |
| 1962 | Haggard, H. Rider | British | N | **She** | 1886 |
| 1963 | Haitov, Nikolai *(Nikolai Khaitov)* | Bulgarian | SS | **Măzhki vremena** *[Manly times]* + **Svatba** | 1967 |
| 1964 | Haitov, Nikolai | Bulgarian | SS | **Koziyat rog** | 1967 |
| 1965 | Halbe, Max | German | P | **Jugend** *(Youth)* *(aka: When Love Is Young)* | 1893 |
| 1966 | Halbe, Max | German | P | **Mutter Erde** *(Mother Earth)* | 1898 |

| No | Film Title | Country of Production | Date | Director(s) | Duration of Film |
|---|---|---|---|---|---|
| 1932 | **Snow White and the Seven Dwarfs** | USA | 1983 | **Peter Medak** | 53 +V |
| 1933 | **Snow White and the Seven Dwarfs** (aka: Snow White) | USA | 1987 | **Michael Berz** | 85 +V |
| 1934 | **Morgiana** | CZ | 1972 | **·Juraj Herz** | 95 |
| 1935 | | | | | |
| 1936 | **Komissar** (The Commissar) | USSR | 1967 | **Alexander Askoldov** | 110 |
| 1937 | **Vorstadtkrokodile** | GER | 1978 | **Wolfgang Becker** | 88 |
| 1938 | **Dou er yuan** | CHN | 1959 | **Zhang Xinshi** | 129 |
| 1939 | **San kan hu die meng** | CHN | 1958 | **Cai Zhenya** | 110 |
| 1940 | **Wang jiang ting** | CHN | 1958 | **Zhou Feng** | 90 |
| 1941 | **Fu rong zhen** | CHN | 1986 | **Xie Jin** | 140 |
| 1942 | **Gimba** | BRAZ | 1962 | **Flávio Rangel** | 80 |
| 1943 | **O seminarista** (The Seminarist) | BRAZ | 1976 | **José Geraldo Santos Pereira** | 103 |
| 1944 | | | | | |
| 1945 | **La hija del mar** (aka: La filla del mar) | SP | 1953(52) | **Antonio Momplet** | 77(85) |
| 1946 | **Maria Rosa** | SP | 1965(64) | **Armando Moreno** | 127(97) |
| 1947 | **Don Segundo Sombra** | ARG | 1969 | **Manuel Artín** | 100 |
| 1948 | **The Big Sky** | USA | 1952 | **Howard Hawks** | 122 +V |
| 1949 | **These Thousand Hills** | USA | 1959(58) | **Richard Fleischer** | 96 |
| 1950 | **The Way West** | USA | 1967 | **Andrew V. McLaglen** | 122 |
| 1951 | **Juan Moreira** | ARG | 1936 | **Nelo Cosimi** | 89 |
| 1952 | **Juan Moreira** | ARG | 1948 | **Luis J. Moglia Barth** | 86 |
| 1953 | **Elektreia** (aka: Szerelmem, Elektra) (Electra, My Love) | HUNG | 1974 | **Miklós Jancsó** | 76 |
| 1954 | **King Solomon's Treasure** | GB/CAN | 1979 | **Alvin Rakoff** | 88 +V(84) |
| 1955 | **Allan Quartermain and the Lost City of Gold** | USA | 1987 | **Gary Nelson** | 99 |
| 1956 | **King Solomon's Mines** | GB | 1937 | **Robert Stevenson** | 80 +V |
| 1957 | **King Solomon's Mines** | USA | 1950 | **Compton Bennett Andrew Marton** | 102 |
| 1958 | **Watusi** (aka: The Quest For King Solomon's Mines) | USA | 1958 | **Kurt Neumann** | 85 +V(80) |
| 1959 | **King Solomon's Mines** | USA | 1985 | **J. Lee Thompson** | 100 +V |
| 1960 | **She** | USA | 1935 | **Irving Pichel Lansing C. Holden** | 89 |
| 1961 | **She** | GB | 1965 | **Robert Day** | 105 |
| 1962 | **She** | IT | 1985(82) | **Avi Nesher** | 104 +V |
| 1963 | **Măzhki vremena** | BULG | 1967 | **Eduard Zahariev** | 134 |
| 1964 | **Koziyat rog** (The Goat Horn) | BULG | 1972 | **Metodi Andonov** | 100 |
| 1965 | **Jugend** (Youth) | GER | 1938 | **Veit Harlan** | 93 |
| 1966 | **Das Leben ruft** | GER | 1944 | **Arthur Maria Rabenalt** | 81 |

**109**

| No. | Author | Nationality | Form | Literary Title | Date |
|---|---|---|---|---|---|
| 1967 | Halbe, Max | German | P | Der Strom<br>*[The stream]* | 1903(04) |
| 1968 | Hall, James N.<br>*(joint, see: Nordhoff, Charles)* | American | N | | |
| 1969 | Hall, Oakley | American | N | Downhill Racers | 1963 |
| 1970 | Hall, Oakley | American | N | Warlock | 1958 |
| 1971 | Hall, Willis | British | P | The Long the Short and the Tall | 1959 |
| 1972 | Hall, Willis<br>*(see also: Waterhouse Keith)* | British | N-P | | |
| 1973 | Hamilton, Patrick | British | P | Gaslight | 1939 |
| 1974 | Hamilton, Patrick | British | P | Gaslight | 1939 |
| 1975 | Hamilton, Patrick | British | P | Hangover Square<br>*(aka: Hangover Square; or, the Man With Two Minds; a Story of Darkest Earl's Court in the Year 1939)* | 1941 |
| 1976 | Hamilton, Patrick | British | P | Rope | 1929 |
| 1977 | Hamilton, Patrick | British | P(R) | To the Public Danger | 1939 |
| 1978 | Hamilton, Patrick | British | N | Twenty Thousand Streets Under the Sky; a London Trilogy | 1935 |
| 1979 | Hammett, Dashiell | American | N | The Glass Key | 1931 |
| 1980 | Hammett, Dashiell | American | N | The Glass Key | 1931 |
| 1981 | Hammett, Dashiell | American | N | The Maltese Falcon | 1930 |
| 1982 | Hammett, Dashiell | American | N | The Maltese Falcon | 1930 |
| 1983 | Hammett, Dashiell | American | N | The Maltese Falcon | 1930 |
| 1984 | Hammett, Dashiell | American | N | Red Harvest | 1929 |
| 1985 | Hammett, Dashiell | American | N | The Thin Man | 1934 |
| 1986 | Hamsun, Knut | Norwegian | N | Landstrykere<br>*(Vagabonds)* | 1927 |
| 1987 | Hamsun, Knut | Norwegian | N | Mysterier | 1892 |
| 1988 | Hamsun, Knut | Norwegian | N | Pan<br>*(aka: Pan; af Løjnant Thomas Glahns papirer)*<br>*(Pan; from Lieutenant Thomas Glahn's Papers)* | 1894 |
| 1989 | Hamsun, Knut | Norwegian | N | Pan | 1894 |
| 1990 | Hamsun, Knut | Norwegian | N | Siste kapitel<br>*(Chapter the Last)* | 1923 |
| 1991 | Hamsun, Knut | Norwegian | N | Sult<br>*(Hunger)* | 1890 |
| 1992 | Hamsun, Knut | Norwegian | N | Victoria<br>*(aka: Victoria, en kærligheds historie)*<br>*(Victoria, a Love Story)* | 1898 |
| 1993 | Hamsun, Knut | Norwegian | N | Victoria | 1898 |
| 1994 | Hamsun, Knut; - {n}<br>Dorst, Tankred - {p} | Norwegian/<br>German | N-P | På gjengrodde stier {n}<br>*(On Overgrown Paths)*<br>Eiszeit {p} | 1949{n}<br>1973{p} |
| 1995 | Handke, Peter | German | N | Die Angst des Tormanns beim Elfmeter<br>*(The Goalie's Anxiety at the Penalty Kick)* | 1970 |
| 1996 | Handke, Peter | German | N | Der kurze Brief zum langen Abschied<br>*(Short Letter, Long Farewell)* | 1972 |
| 1997 | Handke, Peter | German | N | Die linkshändige Frau<br>*(The Left-Handed Woman)* | 1976 |
| 1998 | Hansberry, Lorraine | American(afro) | P | A Raisin in the Sun | 1959 |
| 1999 | Hansen, Martin A. | Danish | N | Løgneren<br>*(The Liar)* | 1950 |
| 2000 | Hardy, Thomas | British | N | Far From the Madding Crowd | 1874 |
| 2001 | Hardy, Thomas | British | SS | Our Exploits at West Poley | 1892-93 |
| 2002 | Hardy, Thomas | British | SS | Our Exploits at West Poley | 1892-93 |

| No | Film Title | Country of Production | Date | Director(s) | Duration of Film |
|---|---|---|---|---|---|
| 1967 | **Der Strom** | GER | 1942 | **Günther Rittau** | 89 |
| 1968 | | | | | |
| 1969 | **Downhill Racer** | USA | 1969 | **Michael Ritchie** | 102 +V |
| 1970 | **Warlock** | USA | 1959 | **Edward Dmytryk** | 121 |
| 1971 | **The Long the Short and the Tall** (aka: Jungle Fighters) | GB | 1960 | **Leslie Norman** | 105 +V |
| 1972 | | | | | |
| 1973 | **Gaslight** (USA: Angel Street) | GB | 1940 | **Thorold Dickinson** | 88 |
| 1974 | **Gaslight** (aka: The Murder in Thornton Square) | USA | 1944 | **George Cukor** | 114 +V(110) |
| 1975 | **Hangover Square** | USA | 1945 | **John Brahm** | 77 |
| 1976 | **Rope** | USA/GB | 1948 | **Alfred Hitchcock** | 81 +V |
| 1977 | **To the Public Danger** | GB | 1948 | **Terence Fisher** | 44 |
| 1978 | **Bitter Harvest** | GB | 1963 | **Peter Graham Scott** | 96 |
| 1979 | **The Glass Key** | USA | 1935 | **Frank Tuttle** | 87 |
| 1980 | **The Glass Key** | USA | 1942 | **Stuart Heisler** | 85 |
| 1981 | **The Maltese Falcon** (aka: The Dangerous Female) | USA | 1931 | **Roy Del Ruth** | 80 |
| 1982 | **Satan Met a Lady** (aka: Men on Her Mind) | USA | 1936 | **William Dieterle** | 74 |
| 1983 | **The Maltese Falcon** | USA | 1941 | **John Huston** | 100 +V |
| 1984 | **Roadhouse Nights** | USA | 1930 | **Hobart Henley** | 80 |
| 1985 | **The Thin Man** | USA | 1934 | **W. S. Van Dyke** | 93 |
| 1986 | **Landstrykere** | NOR | 1989 | **Ola Solum** | 138 |
| 1987 | **Mysteries** | HOLL/FR | 1978 | **Paul de Lussanet** | 103 |
| 1988 | **Pan** (aka: Das Schicksal des Leutnants Thomas Glahn) | GER | 1937 | **Olaf Fjord** | 93(86) |
| 1989 | **Kort är sommaren** (NOR: Du kom en sommar) (Short Is the Summer) | SWE | 1962 | **Astrid Henning-Jensen** **Bjarne Henning-Jensen** | 110 |
| 1990 | **Das letzte Kapitel** (The Last Chapter) | GER | 1961 | **Wolfgang Liebeneiner** | 109 |
| 1991 | **Sult** (aka: Svält) (Hunger) | DEN/NOR/ SWE | 1966 | **Henning Carlsen** | 111 |
| 1992 | **Viktoria** | GER | 1935 | **Carl Hoffmann** | 91 |
| 1993 | **Victoria** | SWE/GER | 1979(78) | **Bo Widerberg** | 89(107) |
| 1994 | **Eiszeit** (NOR: Istid) (Ice Age) | GER/NOR | 1975(74) | **Peter Zadek** | 115 |
| 1995 | **Die Angst des Tormanns beim Elfmeter** (The Goalkeeper's Fear of the Penalty) | GER/AUST | 1971 | **Wim Wenders** | 100 +V |
| 1996 | **Der kurze Brief zum langen Abschied** | GER | 1978(77) | **Herbert Vesely** | 97 |
| 1997 | **Die linkshändige Frau** (The Left-Handed Woman) | GER | 1978(77) | **Peter Handke** | 119(116) |
| 1998 | **A Raisin in the Sun** | USA | 1961 | **Daniel Petrie** | 128 |
| 1999 | **Løgneren** | DEN | 1970 | **Knud Leif Thomsen** | 106 |
| 2000 | **Far From the Madding Crowd** | GB | 1967 | **John Schlesinger** | 167 +V |
| 2001 | **The Secret Cave** | GB | 1953 | **John Durst** | 62 |
| 2002 | **Exploits at West Poley** | GB | 1985 | **Diarmuid Lawrence** | 63 |

| No. | Author | Nationality | Form | Literary Title | Date |
|---|---|---|---|---|---|
| 2003 | **Hardy, Thomas** | British | N | **Tess of the D'Urbervilles** *(aka: Tess of the D'Urbervilles: a Pure Woman)* | 1891 |
| 2004 | **Hardy, Thomas** | British | N | **Tess of the D'Urbervilles** | 1891 |
| 2005 | **Hare, David** | British | P(TV) | **Licking Hitler** | 1978 |
| 2006 | **Hare, David** | British | P | **Plenty** | 1978 |
| 2007 | **Harris, John Beynon** *(see: Wyndham, John)* | British | N/SS | | |
| 2008 | **Harris, Mark** | American | N | **Bang the Drum Slowly** | 1956 |
| 2009 | **Harrison, Harry** | American | N | **Make Room! Make Room!** | 1966 |
| 2010 | **Hart, Moss** | American | P | **Act One** | 1959 |
| 2011 | **Hart, Moss** | American | P | **Christopher Blake** | 1947 |
| 2012 | **Hart, Moss** | American | P | **Lady in the Dark** | 1941 |
| 2013 | **Hart, Moss** | American | P | **Winged Victory** | 1943 |
| 2014 | **Hart, Moss** *(see also: Kaufman, George S.)* | American | P | | |
| 2015 | **Harte, Bret** | American | SS | **The Luck of Roaring Camp** | 1869 |
| 2016 | **Harte, Bret** | American | SS | **Mliss, an Idyll of Red Mountain** | 1869 |
| 2017 | **Harte, Bret** | American | SS | **The Outcasts of Poker Flat** | 1868 |
| 2018 | **Harte, Bret** | American | SS | **The Outcasts of Poker Flat** | 1868 |
| 2019 | **Harte, Bret** | American | SS | **Salomy Jane's Kiss** | 1898 |
| 2020 | **Harte, Bret** | American | SS | **Tennessee's Partner** | 1907 |
| 2021 | **Hartley, L. P.** | British | N | **The Go-Between** | 1953 |
| 2022 | **Hartley, L. P.** | British | N | **The Hireling** | 1957 |
| 2023 | **Hartley, L. P.** | British | SS | **The Island** | 1948 |
| 2024 | **Hašek, Jaroslav** | Czech | N | **Osudy dobrého vojáka Švejka za světové války** *(The Good Soldier Svejk and his Fortunes in the World War)* | 1920-23 |
| 2025 | **Hašek, Jaroslav** | Czech | N | **Osudy dobrého vojáka Švejka za světové války** | 1920-23 |
| 2026 | **Hašek, Jaroslav** | Czech | N | **Osudy dobrého vojáka Švejka za světové války** | 1920-23 |
| 2027 | **Hašek, Jaroslav** | Czech | N | **Osudy dobrého vojáka Švejka za světové války** | 1920-23 |
| 2028 | **Hašek, Jaroslav** | Czech | N | **Osudy dobrého vojáka Švejka za světové války** | 1920-23 |
| 2029 | **Hauff, Wilhelm** | German | SS | **Die Geschichte von dem kleinen Muck** *(The Story of Little Muck)* *(aka: Story of a Manikin)* | 1826 |
| 2030 | **Hauff, Wilhelm** | German | SS | **Die Geschichte von dem kleinen Muck** | 1826 |
| 2031 | **Hauff, Wilhelm** | German | SS | **Der junge Engländer** *(The Young Foreigner)* | 1905 |
| 2032 | **Hauff, Wilhelm** | German | SS | **Das kalte Herz** *(The Cold Heart)* *(aka: The Marble Heart)* | 1828 |
| 2033 | **Hauff, Wilhelm** | German | SS | **Das Märchen vom falschen Prinzen** *(The False Prince)* | 1826 |
| 2034 | **Hauff, Wilhelm** | German | SS | **Das Wirtshaus im Spessart** *(The Inn in the Spessart)* | 1828 |
| 2035 | **Hauff, Wilhelm** | German | SS | **Der Zwerg Nase** *(The Dwarf Nose)* *(aka: Dwarf Long Nose)* | 1827 |
| 2036 | **Hauptmann, Gerhart** | German | SS | **Bahnwärter Thiel** *(Flagman Thiel)* | 1888 |
| 2037 | **Hauptmann, Gerhart** | German | P | **Der Biberpelz** *(The Beaver Coat)* | 1893 |
| 2038 | **Hauptmann, Gerhart** | German | P | **Der Biberpelz** | 1893 |
| 2039 | **Hauptmann, Gerhart** | German | P | **Dorothea Angermann** | 1926 |
| 2040 | **Hauptmann, Gerhart** | German | P | **Fuhrmann Henschel** *(Drayman Henschel)* | 1898(99) |

| No | Film Title | Country of Production | Date | Director(s) | Duration of Film |
|---|---|---|---|---|---|
| 2003 | **Dulhan ek raat ki** <br>*[Bride for a single night]* | IND | 1967 | **Dharm Dev Kashyap** | 170 |
| 2004 | **Tess** | FR/GB | 1979 | **Roman Polanski** | 171 +V(164) |
| 2005 | **Licking Hitler** | GB | 1978 | **David Hare** | 64 +V |
| 2006 | **Plenty** | USA | 1985 | **Fred Schepisi** | 124 +V |
| 2007 | | | | | |
| 2008 | **Bang the Drum Slowly** | USA | 1973 | **John Hancock** | 97 +V |
| 2009 | **Soylent Green** | USA | 1973 | **Richard Fleischer** | 100 +V |
| 2010 | **Act One** | USA | 1963 | **Dore Schary** | 110 |
| 2011 | **The Decision of Christopher Blake** | USA | 1948 | **Peter Godfrey** | 75 |
| 2012 | **Lady in the Dark** | USA | 1944 | **Mitchell Leisen** | 100 |
| 2013 | **Winged Victory** | USA | 1944 | **George Cukor** | 130 |
| 2014 | | | | | |
| 2015 | **Luck of Roaring Camp** | USA | 1937 | **I. V. Willat** | 60 |
| 2016 | **M'Liss** | USA | 1936 | **George Nicholls, Jr.** | 66 |
| 2017 | **The Outcasts of Poker Flat** | USA | 1937 | **Christy Cabanne** | 68 |
| 2018 | **The Outcasts of Poker Flat** | USA | 1952 | **Joseph M. Newman** | 80 |
| 2019 | **Wild Girl** <br>*(GB: Salomy Jane)* | USA | 1932 | **Raoul Walsh** | 79 |
| 2020 | **Tennessee's Partner** | USA | 1955(54) | **Allan Dwan** | 87 |
| 2021 | **The Go-Between** | GB | 1971 | **Joseph Losey** | 116 +V |
| 2022 | **The Hireling** | GB | 1973 | **Alan Bridges** | 108 +V |
| 2023 | **The Island** | USA | 1977 | **Robert Fuest** | 30 +V |
| 2024 | **Dobrý voják Švejk** <br>*(The Good Soldier Schweik)* | CZ | 1931 | **Martin Frič** | 86 |
| 2025 | **Noviye pokhozdeniya Shveika** <br>*(New Adventures of Schweik)* <br>*(aka: The Good Soldier Schweik)* | USSR | 1943 | **Sergei Yutkevich** | 72 |
| 2026 | **Dobrý voják Švejk** <br>*(The Good Soldier Schweik)* | CZ | 1956 | **Karel Steklý** | 108 |
| 2027 | **Der brave Soldat Schwejk** <br>*(The Good Soldier Schweik)* | GER | 1960 | **Axel von Ambesser** | 96 |
| 2028 | **Schwejks Flegeljahre** | GER | 1963 | **Wolfgang Liebeneiner** | 89 |
| 2029 | **Der kleine Muck** | GER | 1944 | **Franz Fiedler** | 82(78) |
| 2030 | **Die Geschichte vom kleinen Muck** <br>*(aka: Ein Abenteuer aus 1001 Nacht)* <br>*(aka: Die Abenteuer des kleinen Muck)* <br>*(Little Mook)* | GDR | 1953 | **Wolfgang Staudte** | 100(75) |
| 2031 | **Der junge Engländer** | GDR | 1958 | **Gottfried Kolditz** | 48 |
| 2032 | **Das kalte Herz** <br>*(The Cold Heart)* | GDR | 1950 | **Paul Verhoeven** | 106(104) |
| 2033 | **Labakan** | CZ/BULG | 1956 | **Václav Krška** | 75 |
| 2034 | **Das Wirtshaus im Spessart** <br>*(The Inn at Spessart)* | GER | 1958 | **Kurt Hoffmann** | 99 |
| 2035 | **Zwerg Nase** | GER | 1953(52) | **Francesco Stephani** | 82 |
| 2036 | **Bahnwärter Thiel** | GDR | 1982 | **Hans Joachim Kasprzik** | 78 |
| 2037 | **Der Biberpelz** | GER | 1937 | **Jürgen von Alten** | 98 |
| 2038 | **Der Biberpelz** | GDR | 1949 | **Erich Engel** | 96 |
| 2039 | **Dorothea Angermann** | GER | 1959(58) | **Robert Siodmak** | 105 |
| 2040 | **Fuhrmann Henschel** | AUST | 1956 | **Josef von Baky** | 104 |

| No. | Author | Nationality | Form | Literary Title | Date |
|-----|--------|-------------|------|----------------|------|
| 2041 | Hauptmann, Gerhart | German | P | Hanneles Himmelfahrt<br>(Hannele)<br>(aka: The Assumption of Hannele) | 1893 |
| 2042 | Hauptmann, Gerhart | German | P | Die Jungfern vom Bischofsberg<br>(Maidens of the Mount) | 1907 |
| 2043 | Hauptmann, Gerhart | German | P | Die Ratten<br>(The Rats) | 1911 |
| 2044 | Hauptmann, Gerhart | German | P | Rose Bernd | 1903 |
| 2045 | Hauptmann, Gerhart | German | P | Vor Sonnenaufgang<br>(Before Dawn) | 1889 |
| 2046 | Hauptmann, Gerhart | German | P | Vor Sonnenuntergang<br>[Before sunset] | 1932 |
| 2047 | Hauptmann, Gerhart | German | P | Vor Sonnenuntergang | 1932 |
| 2048 | Hauptmann, Gerhart | German | N | Wanda<br>(aka: Der Dämon) | 1928 |
| 2049 | Havrevold, Finn | Norwegian | N | Marens lille ugle<br>(Maren's Little Owl) | 1957 |
| 2050 | Hawkins, Anthony Hope<br>(see: Hope, Anthony) | British | N/P | | |
| 2051 | Hawthorne, Nathaniel | American | N | The House of the Seven Gables | 1851 |
| 2052 | Hawthorne, Nathaniel | American | N+SS | The House of the Seven Gables<br>(n) +<br>Rappaccini's Daughter (ss) +<br>Dr Heideggers Experiment (ss) | 1851+<br><br>1846+<br>1837 |
| 2053 | Hawthorne, Nathaniel | American | N | The Scarlet Letter | 1850 |
| 2054 | Hawthorne, Nathaniel | American | N | The Scarlet Letter | 1850 |
| 2055 | Hawthorne, Nathaniel | American | SS | Young Goodman Brown | 1846 |
| 2056 | Hayashi Fumiko | Japanese | SS | Bangiku<br>(Late Chrysanthemum)+<br>Suisen +<br>Shirasagi | 1948+<br>1949 |
| 2057 | Hayashi Fumiko | Japanese | N | Chairo no me | 1950 |
| 2058 | Hayashi Fumiko | Japanese | N | Hōrōki<br>(Journal of a Vagabond)<br>(aka: A Roving Record) | 1928-29 |
| 2059 | Hayashi Fumiko | Japanese | N | Inazuma | 1935 |
| 2060 | Hayashi Fumiko | Japanese | N | Inazuma | 1935 |
| 2061 | Hayashi Fumiko | Japanese | N | Meshi<br>[Rice] | 1951 |
| 2062 | Hayashi Fumiko | Japanese | N | Ukigumo<br>(Floating Cloud) | 1935 |
| 2063 | Haycox, Ernest | American | N | Bugles in the Afternoon | 1944 |
| 2064 | Haycox, Ernest | American | N | Canyon Passage | 1945 |
| 2065 | Haycox, Ernest | American | N | The Man in the Saddle | 1938 |
| 2066 | Haycox, Ernest | American | SS | Stage to Lordsburg | 1937 |
| 2067 | Haycox, Ernest | American | SS | Stage to Lordsburg | 1937 |
| 2068 | Haycox, Ernest | American | SS | Stage to Lordsburg | 1937 |
| 2069 | Haycox, Ernest | American | N | Sundown Jim | 1940 |
| 2070 | Haycox, Ernest | American | N | Trail Town | 1941 |
| 2071 | Haycox, Ernest | American | N | Trouble Shooter | 1937 |
| 2072 | Hebbel, Christian Friedrich | German | P | Agnes Bernauer | 1852 |
| 2073 | Hebbel, Christian Friedrich | German | V | Mutter und Kind | 1859 |
| 2074 | Hebbel, Christian Friedrich | German | P | Der Rubin | 1851 |
| 2075 | Hecht, Ben | American | SS | Actor's Blood +<br>Concerning a Woman of Sin | 1936+<br>1945 |
| 2076 | Hecht, Ben | American | SS | Crime Without Passion | 1945(coll) |
| 2077 | Hecht, Ben | American | N | The Florentine Dagger | 1923 |
| 2078 | Hecht, Ben | American | N | I Hate Actors<br>(aka: Hollywood Mystery) | 1944<br>(aka:1946) |
| 2079 | Hecht, Ben | American | SS | Miracle in the Rain | 1943 |
| 2080 | Hecht, Ben | American | SS | Specter of the Rose | 1945 |

| No | Film Title | Country of Production | Date | Director(s) | Duration of Film |
|---|---|---|---|---|---|
| 2041 | Hanneles Himmelfahrt | GER | 1934 | Thea von Harbou | 64 |
| 2042 | Die Jungfern vom Bischofsberg | GER | 1943 | Peter Paul Brauer | 97 |
| 2043 | Die Ratten (The Rats) | GER | 1955 | Robert Siodmak | 91(97) |
| 2044 | Rose Bernd (aka: The Sins of Rose Bernd) | GER | 1957 | Wolfgang Staudte | 98(110) |
| 2045 | Vor Sonnenaufgang | GER | 1976 | Oswald Döpke | 104 |
| 2046 | Der Herrscher (The Ruler) | GER | 1937 | Veit Harlan | 106 |
| 2047 | Vor Sonnenuntergang (Before Sunset) | GER | 1956 | Gottfried Reinhardt | 103 |
| 2048 | Königin der Arena [Queen of the Big Top] | GER | 1952 | Rolf Meyer | 82 |
| 2049 | Ugler i mosen | NOR | 1959 | Ivo Caprino | 94 |
| 2050 | | | | | |
| 2051 | The House of the Seven Gables | USA | 1940 | Joe May | 89 |
| 2052 | Twice-Told Tales | USA | 1963 | Sidney Salkow | 119 |
| 2053 | The Scarlet Letter | USA | 1934 | Robert G. Vignola | 70 |
| 2054 | Der scharlachrote Buchstabe (SP: La letra escarlata) (The Scarlet Letter) | GER/SP | 1973 | Wim Wenders | 94(90) |
| 2055 | Young Goodman Brown | USA | 1973 | Donald Fox | 30 +V |
| 2056 | Bangiku (Late Chrysanthemums) | JAP | 1954 | Mikio Naruse | 117 |
| 2057 | Tsuma (Wife) | JAP | 1953 | Mikio Naruse | 89 |
| 2058 | Hōrōki (A Wanderer's Notebook) (aka: Lonely Lane) | JAP | 1962 | Mikio Naruse | 124 |
| 2059 | Inazuma (Lightning) | JAP | 1952 | Mikio Naruse | 93 |
| 2060 | Inazuma | JAP | 1967 | Hideo Ōba | 85 |
| 2061 | Meshi (Repast) | JAP | 1951 | Mikio Naruse | 97 |
| 2062 | Ukigumo (Floating Clouds) | JAP | 1955 | Mikio Naruse | 123 |
| 2063 | Bugles in the Afternoon | USA | 1951 | Roy Rowland | 84 |
| 2064 | Canyon Passage | USA | 1946 | Jacques Tourneur | 92 |
| 2065 | Man in the Saddle (aka: The Outcast) | USA | 1951 | André de Toth | 87 |
| 2066 | Stagecoach | USA | 1939 | John Ford | 96 +V |
| 2067 | Stagecoach | USA | 1966 | Gordon Douglas | 114 |
| 2068 | Stagecoach | USA | 1986 | Ted Post | 100 +V |
| 2069 | Sundown Jim | USA | 1942 | James Tinling | 53 |
| 2070 | Abilene Town | USA | 1946 | Edwin L. Marin | 89 +V |
| 2071 | Union Pacific | USA | 1939 | Cecil B. DeMille | 130 |
| 2072 | Le jugement de Dieu | FR | 1952 | Raymond Bernard | 98 |
| 2073 | Mutter und Kind | GER | 1933 | Hans Steinhoff | 91 |
| 2074 | Die verzauberte Prinzessin | GER | 1939 | Alf Zengerling | 55 |
| 2075 | Actors and Sin | USA | 1951 | Ben Hecht Lee Garmes | 91 |
| 2076 | Crime Without Passion | USA | 1934 | Ben Hecht Charles MacArthur | 82 |
| 2077 | The Florentine Dagger | USA | 1935 | Robert Florey | 69 |
| 2078 | Je hais les acteurs (I Hate Actors) | FR | 1986 | Gérard Krawczyk | 95 |
| 2079 | Miracle in the Rain | USA | 1956(55) | Rudolph Maté | 107 |
| 2080 | Specter of the Rose | USA | 1946 | Ben Hecht | 90 |

| No. | Author | Nationality | Form | Literary Title | Date |
|---|---|---|---|---|---|
| 2081 | Hecht, Ben; Fowler, Gene | American | P | The Great Magoo | 1933 |
| 2082 | Hecht, Ben; Fowler, Gene | American | P | The Great Magoo | 1933 |
| 2083 | Hecht, Ben; MacArthur, Charles | American | P | The Front Page | 1928 |
| 2084 | Hecht, Ben; MacArthur, Charles | American | P | The Front Page | 1928 |
| 2085 | Hecht, Ben; MacArthur, Charles | American | P | The Front Page | 1928 |
| 2086 | Hecht, Ben; MacArthur, Charles | American | P | The Front Page | 1928 |
| 2087 | Hecht, Ben; MacArthur, Charles | American | P | Jumbo | 1935 |
| 2088 | Hecht, Ben; MacArthur, Charles | American | P | Twentieth Century | 1932 |
| 2089 | Hedberg, Olle | Swedish | N | Iris och löjtnantshjärta [Iris and the lieutenant's heart] | 1934 |
| 2090 | Hedberg, Olle | Swedish | N | Stopp! Tänk på något annat [Stop! think of something else!] | 1939 |
| 2091 | Hedberg, Tor | Swedish | P | Johan Ulfstjerna | 1907 |
| 2092 | Hedberg, Tor | Swedish | P | Nationalmonumentet | 1923 |
| 2093 | Heggen, Thomas | American | N-P | Mister Roberts | 1946{n} 1948{p} |
| 2094 | Heiberg, Johan Ludvig | Danish | P | Elverhøj | 1828 |
| 2095 | Heijermans, Herman | Dutch | P | Op hoop van zegen (Good Hope) | 1901 |
| 2096 | Heijermans, Herman | Dutch | P | Op hoop van zegen | 1901 |
| 2098 | Heinlein, Robert A. | American | N | The Puppet Masters | 1951 |
| 2100 | Heinlein, Robert A. | American | N | Rocket Ship Galileo | 1947 |
| 2101 | He Jingzhi; Ting Yi (Ding Yi) | Chinese | P | Bai mao nu (aka: Bai-mao nü) [The white haired girl] | 1944 |
| 2102 | Heller, Joseph | American | N | Catch 22 | 1961 |
| 2103 | Hellman, Lillian | American | P | Another Part of the Forest | 1947 |
| 2104 | Hellman, Lillian | American | P | The Children's Hour | 1934 |
| 2105 | Hellman, Lillian | American | P | The Children's Hour | 1934 |
| 2106 | Hellman, Lillian | American | P | The Little Foxes | 1939 |
| 2107 | Hellman, Lillian | American | SS | Pentimento | 1973 |
| 2108 | Hellman, Lillian | American | P | The Searching Wind | 1944 |
| 2109 | Hellman, Lillian | American | P | Toys in the Attic | 1960 |
| 2110 | Hellman, Lillian | American | P | Watch on the Rhine | 1941 |
| 2111 | Hellström, Gustav | Swedish | N | Storm över Tjurö | 1942 |
| 2112 | Heltai Jenő | Hungarian | N | Jaguár | 1914 |
| 2113 | Hemingway, Ernest | American | N | A Farewell to Arms | 1929 |
| 2114 | Hemingway, Ernest | American | N | A Farewell to Arms | 1929 |
| 2115 | Hemingway, Ernest | American | N | For Whom the Bell Tolls | 1940 |
| 2116 | Hemingway, Ernest | American | N | Islands in the Stream | 1970 |
| 2117 | Hemingway, Ernest | American | SS | The Killers | 1927 |
| 2118 | Hemingway, Ernest | American | SS | The Killers | 1927 |
| 2119 | Hemingway, Ernest | American | SS | My Old Man | 1923 |
| 2120 | Hemingway, Ernest | American | SS | The Old Man and the Sea | 1952 |
| 2121 | Hemingway, Ernest | American | SS | The Short Happy Life of Francis Macomber | 1938 |
| 2122 | Hemingway, Ernest | American | SS | The Snows of Kilimanjaro | 1938 |
| 2123 | Hemingway, Ernest | American | SS | Soldier's Home | 1930 |
| 2124 | Hemingway, Ernest | American | N | The Sun Also Rises (GB: Fiesta) | 1926 |
| 2125 | Hemingway, Ernest | American | N | To Have and Have Not | 1937 |
| 2126 | Hemingway, Ernest | American | N | To Have and Have Not | 1937 |
| 2127 | Hemingway, Ernest | American | N | To Have and Have Not | 1937 |

| No | Film Title | Country of Production | Date | Director(s) | Duration of Film |
|----|-----------|----------------------|------|-------------|------------------|
| 2081 | Shoot the Works | USA | 1934 | Wesley Ruggles | 82 |
| 2082 | Some Like It Hot (aka: Rhythm Romance) | USA | 1939 | George Archainbaud | 64 |
| 2083 | The Front Page | USA | 1931 | Lewis Milestone | 101 |
| 2084 | His Girl Friday | USA | 1940(39) | Howard Hawks | 92 |
| 2085 | The Front Page | USA | 1974 | Billy Wilder | 105 |
| 2086 | Switching Channels | USA | 1987 | Ted Kotcheff | 105 +V |
| 2087 | Jumbo (aka: Billy Rose's Jumbo) {musical version} | USA | 1962 | Charles Walters | 125 |
| 2088 | Twentieth Century | USA | 1934 | Howard Hawks | 91 |
| 2089 | Iris och löjtnantshjärta (Iris and the Lieutenant) (GB: Iris) | SWE | 1946 | Alf Sjöberg | 85 |
| 2090 | Stopp! Tänk på något annat | SWE | 1944 | Åke Ohberg | 106 |
| 2091 | Johan Ulfstjerna | SWE | 1936 | Gustaf Edgren | 77 |
| 2092 | Det är min modell (It's My Model) (aka: Affairs of a Model) | SWE | 1946 | Gustaf Molander | 104 |
| 2093 | Mister Roberts | USA | 1955 | John Ford Mervyn LeRoy | 120 +V |
| 2094 | Elverhøj | DEN | 1939 | Svend Methling | 93 |
| 2095 | Op hoop van zegen (The Good Hope) | HOLL | 1934 | Alex Benno | 99 |
| 2096 | Op hoop van zegen | HOLL | 1986 | Guido Pieters | 102 |
| 2098 | The Brain Eaters | USA | 1958 | Bruno Ve Sota | 60 |
| 2100 | Destination Moon | USA | 1950 | Irving Pichel | 91 +V |
| 2101 | Bai mao nu | CHN | 1950 | Wan Bin Zhang Shuihua | 109 |
| 2102 | Catch-22 | USA | 1970 | Mike Nichols | 122 +V |
| 2103 | Another Part of the Forest | USA | 1948 | Michael Gordon | 107 |
| 2104 | These Three | USA | 1936 | William Wyler | 93 |
| 2105 | The Children's Hour (GB: The Loudest Whisper) | USA | 1962(61) | William Wyler | 107 |
| 2106 | The Little Foxes | USA | 1941 | William Wyler | 116 +V |
| 2107 | Julia | USA | 1977 | Fred Zinnemann | 117 +V |
| 2108 | The Searching Wind | USA | 1946 | William Dieterle | 107 |
| 2109 | Toys in the Attic | USA | 1963 | George Roy Hill | 90 |
| 2110 | Watch on the Rhine | USA | 1943 | Herman Shumlin | 114 +V |
| 2111 | Storm över Tjurö | SWE | 1954 | Arne Mattsson | 109 |
| 2112 | Jaguár | HUNG | 1967 | János Dömölky | 86 |
| 2113 | A Farewell to Arms | USA | 1932 | Frank Borzage | 78 +V |
| 2114 | A Farewell to Arms | USA | 1958(57) | Charles Vidor | 149 +V |
| 2115 | For Whom the Bell Tolls | USA | 1943 | Sam Wood | 125 +V |
| 2116 | Islands in the Stream | USA | 1977(76) | Franklin J. Schaffner | 105 |
| 2117 | The Killers (aka: A Man Alone) | USA | 1946 | Robert Siodmak | 105 |
| 2118 | The Killers | USA | 1964 | Don Siegel | 95 +V |
| 2119 | Under My Skin | USA | 1950 | Jean Negulesco | 86 |
| 2120 | The Old Man and the Sea | USA | 1958 | John Sturges | 89 |
| 2121 | The Macomber Affair | USA | 1947(46) | Zoltan Korda | 89 |
| 2122 | The Snows of Kilimanjaro | USA | 1952 | Henry King | 117 |
| 2123 | Soldier's Home | USA | 1977 | Robert Young | 42 +V |
| 2124 | The Sun Also Rises | USA | 1957 | Henry King | 129 . |
| 2125 | To Have and Have Not | USA | 1944 | Howard Hawks | 100 +V |
| 2126 | The Breaking Point | USA | 1950 | Michael Curtiz | 97 |
| 2127 | The Gun Runners | USA | 1958 | Don Siegel | 82 |

**117**

| No. | Author | Nationality | Form | Literary Title | Date |
|-----|--------|-------------|------|----------------|------|
| 2128 | Hemmer, Jarl | Finnish | P+SS | Anna Ringars *(p)* + Fattiggubbens brud *(ss)* | 1925+ 1926 |
| 2129 | Hemmer, Jarl | Finnish | SS | Den blå veckan | 1928 |
| 2130 | Hemmer, Jarl | Finnish | N | En man och hans samvete *(A Fool of Faith)* | 1931 |
| 2131 | Hémon, Louis | French | N | Maria Chapdelaine; récit du Canada français *(Maria Chapdelaine, a Romance of French Canada)* | 1916 (1914) |
| 2132 | Hémon, Louis | French | N | Maria Chapdelaine | 1916 (1914) |
| 2133 | Hémon, Louis | French | N | Monsieur Ripois and Nemesis *(aka: Monsieur Ripois et la Némésis)* | 1925 (aka:1950) |
| 2134 | Henley, Beth | American | P | Crimes of the Heart | 1982 |
| 2135 | Henley, Beth | American | P | The Miss Firecracker Contest | 1985 |
| 2136 | Henry, O. *(William Sydney Porter)* | American | SS | The Badge of Policeman O'Roon | 1910 |
| 2137 | Henry, O. | American | SS | Caballero's Way | 1904 |
| 2138 | Henry, O. | American | SS | The Clarion Call + Last Leaf + Ransom of Red Chief + Gift of the Magi + Cop and the Anthem | 1908+ 1910+ 1907+ 1906 |
| 2139 | Henry, O. | American | SS | The Cop and the Anthem | 1906 |
| 2140 | Henry, O. | American | SS | A Double-Dyed Deceiver | 1909 |
| 2141 | Henry, O. | American | SS | The Passing of Black Eagle | 1909 |
| 2142 | Herández, José | Argentine | V | Martín Fierro *(Pt.1: El gaucho Martín Fierro Pt.2: La vuelta de Martín Fierro)* | 1872-79 |
| 2143 | Herbert, Frank | American | N | Dune | 1965 |
| 2144 | Herburger, Günter | German | SS | Die Eroberung der Zitadelle | 1972 |
| 2145 | Herburger, Günter | German | SS | Hauptlehrer Hofer | 1975 |
| 2146 | Herculano, Alexandre | Portuguese | N | O bobo | 1884 |
| 2147 | Herczeg Ferenc | Hungarian | P | A dolovai nábob leánya *[The daughter of the nabob of Dolova]* | 1894 |
| 2148 | Herczeg Ferenc | Hungarian | P | A kék róka *[Blue fox]* | 1917 |
| 2149 | Hergesheimer, Joseph | American | N | Java Head | 1919 |
| 2150 | Hergesheimer, Joseph | American | N | Tampico | 1926 |
| 2151 | Hergesheimer, Joseph | American | N | Tol'able David | 1923 |
| 2152 | Hériat, Raymond Payelle | French | P | Les joies de la famille *(A Very Rich Woman)* | 1950 |
| 2153 | Herlihy, James Leo | American | N | All Fall Down | 1960 |
| 2154 | Herlihy, James Leo | American | N | Midnight Cowboy | 1965 |
| 2155 | Herlihy, James Leo; Noble, W. | American | P | Blue Denim | 1958 |
| 2156 | Hermans, Willem Frederik | Dutch | N | De donkere kamer van Damocles *(The Dark Room of Damocles)* | 1958 |
| 2157 | Hermans, Willem Frederik | Dutch | SS | Paranoia | 1953 |
| 2158 | Hernádi Gyula | Hungarian | SS | Kiáltás *[Cry]* | 1967 |
| 2159 | Hernádi Gyula | Hungarian | N | Kiáltás és kiáltás | 1981 |
| 2160 | Hernádi Gyula | Hungarian | N | Sirokkó | 1969 |
| 2161 | Hernádi Gyula | Hungarian | F-SS | Vörös rekviem *[Red requiem]* | 1975 |
| 2162 | Hersey, John | American | N | A Bell For Adano | 1944 |

| No | Film Title | Country of Production | Date | Director(s) | Duration of Film |
|----|-----------|----------------------|------|-------------|------------------|
| 2128 | **Vaivaisukon morsian** <br> *[The wooden pauper's bride]* | FIN | 1944 | **Toivo Särkkä** | 113 |
| 2129 | **Sininen viikko** <br> *(Blue Week)* | FIN | 1954 | **Matti Kassila** | 79 |
| 2130 | **1918 - mies ja hänen omatumtonsa** <br> *(aka: 1918)* | FIN | 1957 | **Toivo Särkkä** | 100 |
| 2131 | **Maria Chapdelaine** <br> *(The Naked Heart)* | FR | 1934 | **Julien Duvivier** | 120 |
| 2132 | **The Naked Heart** <br> *(aka: Maria Chapdelaine)* | GB/FR | 1950 | **Marc Allégret** | 96 |
| 2133 | **Knave of Hearts** <br> *(USA: Lovers, Happy Lovers)* <br> *(aka: Monsieur Ripois)* | GB | 1954 | **René Clément** | 103 |
| 2134 | **Crimes of the Heart** | USA | 1987 | **Bruce Beresford** | 101 +V |
| 2135 | **Miss Firecracker** | USA | 1989 | **Thomas Schlamme** | 103 |
| 2136 | **Doctor Rhythm** | USA | 1938 | **Frank Tuttle** | 80 |
| 2137 | **The Return of the Cisco Kid** | USA | 1939 | **Herbert I. Leeds** | 70 |
| 2138 | **O. Henry's Full House** <br> *(aka: Full House)* | USA | 1952 | **Henry Koster** <br> **Henry Hathaway** <br> **Howard Hawks** <br> **Henry King** *(et al)* | 117 |
| 2139 | **A la belle étoile** | FR | 1966 | **Pierre Prévert** | 60 |
| 2140 | **The Texan** | USA | 1930 | **John Cromwell** | 79 |
| 2141 | **Black Eagle** | USA | 1948 | **Robin Cohn** | 76 |
| 2142 | **Martín Fierro** | ARG | 1968 | **Leopoldo Torre Nilsson** | 135 |
| 2143 | **Dune** | USA | 1984 | **David Lynch** | 131 +V |
| 2144 | **Die Eroberung der Zitadelle** <br> *(The Conquest of the Citadel)* | GER | 1977 | **Bernhard Wicki** | 151 |
| 2145 | **Hauptlehrer Hofer** <br> *(Schoolmaster Hofer)* | GER | 1975 | **Peter Lilienthal** | 111 |
| 2146 | **O bobo** <br> *(The Jester)* | PORT | 1987 | **José Álvaro Morais** | 123(127) |
| 2147 | **Rakoczy-Marsch** <br> *(HUNG: Rakoczi induló)* | GER/HUNG/ AUST | 1933 | **István Szekely** <br> *(Steve Sekely)* <br> **Gustav Fröhlich** | 101 |
| 2148 | **Der Blaufuchs** <br> *(The Blue Fox)* | GER | 1938 | **Viktor Tourjansky** | 96 |
| 2149 | **Java Head** | GB | 1934 | **J. Walter Ruben** | 85 |
| 2150 | **The Woman I Stole** | USA | 1933 | **Irving Cummings** | 67 |
| 2151 | **Tol'able David** | USA | 1930 | **John Blystone** | 85 |
| 2152 | **Rosie!** | USA | 1968(67) | **David Lowell Rich** | 98 |
| 2153 | **All Fall Down** | USA | 1962 | **John Frankenheimer** | 110 |
| 2154 | **Midnight Cowboy** | USA | 1969 | **John Schlesinger** | 113 +V |
| 2155 | **Blue Denim** <br> *(GB: Blue Jeans)* | USA | 1959 | **Philip Dunne** | 89 |
| 2156 | **Als twee druppels water** <br> *(Spitting Image)* <br> *(aka: Dark Room of Damocles)* <br> *(aka: Like Two Drops of Water)* | HOLL | 1963(62) | **Fons Rademakers** | 119(121) |
| 2157 | **Paranoia** | HOLL | 1967 | **Adriaan Ditvoorst** | 102 |
| 2158 | **Csend és kiáltás** <br> *(Silence and Cry)* | HUNG | 1968(67) | **Miklós Jancsó** | 85 |
| 2159 | **Kiáltás és kiáltás** <br> *(Cry and Cry Again)* | HUNG | 1988(87) | **Zsolt Kézdi-Kovács** | 86 |
| 2160 | **Sirokkó** <br> *(aka: Teli sirokkó lek)* <br> *(FR: Sirocco d'hiver)* <br> *(Winter Wind)* | HUNG/FR | 1969 | **Miklós Jancsó** | 79 |
| 2161 | **Még kér a nép** <br> *(Red Psalm)* <br> *(aka: Red Song)* <br> *(aka: People Still Ask)* | HUNG | 1971 | **Miklós Jancsó** | 88 |
| 2162 | **A Bell For Adano** | USA | 1945 | **Henry King** | 104 |

| No. | Author | Nationality | Form | Literary Title | Date |
|-----|--------|-------------|------|----------------|------|
| 2163 | Hersey, John | American | N | The War Lover | 1959 |
| 2164 | Hesse, Hermann | German | N | Siddhartha: Eine indische Dichtung (Siddhartha) | 1922 |
| 2165 | Hesse, Hermann | German | N | Der Steppenwolf (Steppenwolf) | 1927 |
| 2166 | Heym, Stefan (Hellmuth Fliegel) | German(Eng) | N | Hostages (aka: Der Fall Glasenapp) (The Glasenapp Case) | 1942 |
| 2167 | Hibberd, Jack | Australian | P | Dimboola | 1974 |
| 2168 | Highsmith, Patricia | American | N | The Blunderer | 1954 |
| 2169 | Highsmith, Patricia | American | N | Edith's Diary | 1977 |
| 2170 | Highsmith, Patricia | American | N | The Glass Cell | 1964 |
| 2171 | Highsmith, Patricia | American | N | Ripley's Game | 1974 |
| 2172 | Highsmith, Patricia | American | N | Strangers on a Train | 1950 |
| 2173 | Highsmith, Patricia | American | N | Strangers on a Train | 1950 |
| 2174 | Highsmith, Patricia | American | N | The Talented Mr Ripley | 1955 |
| 2175 | Highsmith, Patricia | American | N | This Sweet Sickness | 1960 |
| 2176 | Higuchi Ichiyo | Japanese | N | Takekurabe (They Compare Heights) (aka: Growing Up) (aka: Teenagers Vying for Tops) | 1896 |
| 2177 | Hilton, James | British | N | Dawn of Reckoning | 1925 |
| 2178 | Hilton, James | British | N | Goodbye, Mr Chips | 1934 |
| 2179 | Hilton, James | British | N | Goodbye, Mr Chips | 1934 |
| 2180 | Hilton, James | British | N | Knight Without Armour (USA: Without Armor) | 1933 |
| 2181 | Hilton, James | British | N | Lost Horizon | 1933 |
| 2182 | Hilton, James | British | N | Lost Horizon | 1933 |
| 2183 | Hilton, James | British | N | Random Harvest | 1941 |
| 2184 | Hilton, James | British | N | So Well Remembered | 1947 |
| 2185 | Hilton, James | British | SS | The Story of Dr Wassell | 1943 |
| 2186 | Hilton, James | British | N | We Are Not Alone | 1937 |
| 2187 | Himes, Chester | American(afro) | N | Cotton Comes to Harlem | 1965 |
| 2188 | Himes, Chester | American | N | For Love of Imabelle (aka: A Rage in Harlem) | 1957 (aka:1965) |
| 2189 | Himes, Chester | American | N | The Heat's On | 1966 |
| 2190 | Hines, Barry | British | N | The Gamekeeper | 1975 |
| 2191 | Hines, Barry | British | N | A Kestrel For a Knave | 1968 |
| 2192 | Hiraoka Kimatake (joint, see: Mishima Yukio) | Japanese | N | | |
| 2193 | Hłasko, Marek | Polish | SS | Następny do raju (Next Stop - Paradise) | 1958 |
| 2194 | Hłasko, Marek | Polish | N | Ósmy dzień tygodnia (The Eighth Day of the Week) | 1957 |
| 2195 | Hłasko, Marek | Polish | SS | Pętla | 1956 |
| 2196 | Hochhuth, Rolf | German | P | Ärztinnen | 1980 |
| 2197 | Hochhuth, Rolf | German | N | Eine Liebe in Deutschland (A German Love Story) | 1978 |
| 2198 | Hochwalder, Fritz | Austrian | P | Der Flüchtling | 1945 |
| 2199 | Hodson, James (joint, see: Wilson, John) | British | N | | |
| 2200 | Hoel, Sigurd | Norwegian | N | En dag i oktober (One Day in October) | 1931 |

| No | Film Title | Country of Production | Date | Director(s) | Duration of Film |
|---|---|---|---|---|---|
| 2163 | **The War Lover** | GB | 1962 | **Philip Leacock** | 105 |
| 2164 | **Siddhartha** | USA | 1973(72) | **Conrad Rooks** | 89 |
| 2165 | **Steppenwolf** | USA/SWITZ | 1974 | **Fred Haines** | 106 |
| 2166 | **Hostages** | USA | 1943 | **Frank Tuttle** | 88 |
| 2167 | **Dimboola** | AUSTL | 1979 | **John Duigan** | 94 |
| 2168 | **Le meurtrier** <br> *(IT: L'omicida)* <br> *(GER: Der Mörder)* <br> *(Enough Rope)* | FR/IT/GER | 1963(62) | **Claude Autant-Lara** | 107(110) |
| 2169 | **Ediths Tagebuck** <br> *(Edith's Diary)* | GER | 1983 | **Hans W. Geissendörfer** | 108 |
| 2170 | **Die gläserne Zelle** <br> *(The Glass Cell)* | GER | 1977 | **Hans W. Geissendörfer** | 90 |
| 2171 | **Der amerikanische Freund** <br> *(The American Friend)* | GER/FR | 1977 | **Wim Wenders** | 127 +V(123) |
| 2172 | **Strangers on a Train** | USA | 1951 | **Alfred Hitchcock** | 100 +V |
| 2173 | **Once You Kiss a Stranger** <br> *(aka: You Can't Win 'Em All)* | USA | 1969 | **Robert Sparr** | 106 |
| 2174 | **Plein soleil** <br> *(IT: Delitto in pieno sole)* <br> *(aka: In pieno solo)* <br> *(USA: Purple Noon)* <br> *(aka: Lust For Evil)* | FR/IT | 1959 | **René Clément** | 115(120) |
| 2175 | **Dites-lui que je l'aime** <br> *(This Sweet Sickness)* | FR | 1977 | **Claude Miller** | 106 |
| 2176 | **Takekurabe** <br> *(Growing Up)* <br> *(aka: Comparison of Heights)* <br> *(aka: Daughters of Yoshiwara)* | JAP | 1955 | **Heinosuke Gosho** | 95 |
| 2177 | **Rage in Heaven** | USA | 1941 | **W. S. Van Dyke** | 82 |
| 2178 | **Goodbye, Mr Chips** | GB | 1939 | **Sam Wood** | 114 |
| 2179 | **Goodbye, Mr Chips** | GB | 1969 | **Herbert Ross** | 147 |
| 2180 | **Knight Without Armour** | GB | 1937 | **Jacques Feyder** | 109 +V(96) |
| 2181 | **Lost Horizon** | USA | 1937 | **Frank Capra** | 120 +V |
| 2182 | **Lost Horizon** | USA | 1972 | **Charles Jarrott** | 143 |
| 2183 | **Random Harvest** | USA | 1942 | **Mervyn LeRoy** | 126 |
| 2184 | **So Well Remembered** | GB | 1947 | **Edward Dmytryk** | 114 |
| 2185 | **The Story of Dr Wassell** | USA | 1944 | **Cecil B. DeMille** | 104 |
| 2186 | **We Are Not Alone** | USA | 1939 | **Edmund Goulding** | 112 |
| 2187 | **Cotton Comes to Harlem** | USA | 1970 | **Ossie Davis** | 97 |
| 2188 | **A Rage in Harlem** | GB | 1991 | **Bill Duke** | 108 +V |
| 2189 | **Come Back Charleston Blue** | USA | 1972 | **Mark Warren** | 101 |
| 2190 | **The Gamekeeper** | GB | 1978 | **Ken Loach** | 84 |
| 2191 | **Kes** | GB | 1969 | **Ken Loach** | 113 +V |
| 2192 | | | | | |
| 2193 | **Baza ludzi umarłych** <br> *[Base of dead people]* | POL | 1959(58) | **Czesław Petelski** | 108 |
| 2194 | **Ósmy dzień tygodnia** <br> *(GER: Achte Wochentag)* <br> *(The Eighth Day of the Week)* | POL/GER | 1983(58) | **Aleksander Ford** | 85(89) |
| 2195 | **Pętla** <br> *(The Noose)* | POL | 1958(57) | **Wojciech Jerzy Has** | 104 |
| 2196 | **Ärztinnen** <br> *(Lady Doctors)* | GDR/SWE/ GER/SWITZ | 1984 | **Horst Seemann** | 106 |
| 2197 | **Eine Liebe in Deutschland** <br> *(A Love in Germany)* | GER/FR | 1983 | **Andrzej Wajda** | 115(107) |
| 2198 | **Die Frau am Weg** <br> *(aka: Der Grenzjäger vom wilden Karst)* | AUST | 1948 | **Eduard von Borsody** | 82 |
| 2199 | | | | | |
| 2200 | **Egen ingång** <br> *(Private Entrance)* | SWE | 1956 | **Hasse Ekman** | 93 |

| No. | Author | Nationality | Form | Literary Title | Date |
|---|---|---|---|---|---|
| 2201 | Hoel, Sigurd | Norwegian | N | Fjorten dager før frostnettene<br>*[Fourteen days before the frost nights]* | 1935 |
| 2202 | Hoel, Sigurd | Norwegian | N | Stevnemøte med glemte ar | 1954 |
| 2203 | Hoel, Sigurd | Norwegian | N | Syndere i sommersol<br>*(Sinners in Summertime)* | 1928 |
| 2204 | Hoffenberg, M.<br>*(joint, see: Southern, Terry)* | American | N | | |
| 2205 | Hoffmann, Ernst Theodor Amadeus | German | N | Die Elixiere des Teufels<br>*(The Devils Elixirs)* | 1815-16 |
| 2206 | Hoffmann, Ernst Theodor Amadeus | German | N | Die Elixiere des Teufels | 1815-16 |
| 2207 | Hoffmann, Ernst Theodor Amadeus | German | SS | Das Fräulein von Scudéri<br>*(Mademoiselle de Scuderi)*<br>*(aka: Cardillac, the Jeweler)* | 1819 |
| 2208 | Hoffmann, Ernst Theodor Amadeus | German | SS | Das Fräulein von Scudéri | 1819 |
| 2209 | Hoffmann, Ernst Theodor Amadeus | German | SS | Das Fräulein von Scudéri | 1819 |
| 2210 | Hoffmann, Ernst Theodor Amadeus | German | SS | Das Fräulein von Scudéri | 1819 |
| 2211 | Hoffmann, Ernst Theodor Amadeus | German | SS | Nußknacker und Mausekönig<br>*(Nutcracker and Mouse-King)* | 1816 |
| 2212 | Hofmannsthal, Hugo von | Austrian | P | Jedermann: Das Spiel von Sterben des reichen Mannes<br>*(The Salzberg Everyman)* | 1911 |
| 2213 | Holberg, Ludvig | Danish(Nor) | P | Erasmus Montanus | 1731 |
| 2214 | Holberg, Ludvig | Danish | P | Jeppe paa bjerget<br>*(Jeppe of the Hill)* | 1858 |
| 2215 | Holberg, Ludvig | Danish | P | Jeppe paa bjerget | 1858 |
| 2216 | Holberg, Ludvig | Danish | P | Jeppe paa bjerget | 1858 |
| 2217 | Hölderlin, Friedrich | German | N | Hyperion; oder, Der Eremit in Griechenland | 1797-99 |
| 2218 | Hölderlin, Friedrich | German | P | Der Tod des Empedokles<br>*(The Death of Empedocles)* | 1826 |
| 2219 | Holz, Arno;<br>Jerschke, Oskar | German | P | Traumulus | 1904 |
| 2220 | Homer | Greek(anc) | V | Iliad | n.d. |
| 2221 | Homer | Greek(anc) | V | Iliad | n.d. |
| 2222 | Homer | Greek(anc) | V | Odyssey | n.d. |
| 2223 | Hope, Anthony<br>*(Anthony Hope Hawkins)* | British | N | The Prisoner of Zenda | 1894 |
| 2224 | Hope, Anthony | British | N | The Prisoner of Zenda | 1894 |
| 2225 | Hope, Anthony | British | N | The Prisoner of Zenda | 1894 |
| 2226 | Hopkins, John | British | P | This Story of Yours | 1969 |
| 2227 | Hopley, George<br>*(see: Hopley-Woolrich, Cornell George)* | American | N/SS | | |
| 2228 | Hopley-Woolrich, Cornell George<br>*(as: Cornell Woolrich)* | American | N | Black Alibi | 1942 |
| 2229 | Hopley-Woolrich, Cornell George<br>*(ditto)* | American | N | The Black Angel | 1943 |
| 2230 | Hopley-Woolrich, Cornell George<br>*(ditto)* | American | N | The Black Curtain | 1941 |
| 2231 | Hopley-Woolrich, Cornell George<br>*(ditto)* | American | N | The Black Path of Fear | 1944 |
| 2232 | Hopley-Woolrich, Cornell George<br>*(ditto)* | American | SS | The Boy Cried Murder | 1947 |
| 2233 | Hopley-Woolrich, Cornell George<br>*(ditto)* | American | SS | The Boy Cried Murder | 1947 |

| No | Film Title | Country of Production | Date | Director(s) | Duration of Film |
|---|---|---|---|---|---|
| 2201 | **Før frostnettene** | NOR | 1966 | **Arnljot Berg** | 94 |
| 2202 | **Stevnemøte med glemte ar** *(Rendezvous With Forgotten Years)* | NOR | 1957 | **Jon Lennart Mjøen** | 90 |
| 2203 | **Syndere i sommersol** | NOR | 1934 | **Einer Sissener** | 104 |
| 2204 | | | | | |
| 2205 | **Die Elixiere des Teufels** *(The Devils Elixirs)* | GDR | 1973 | **Ralf Kirsten** | 105 |
| 2206 | **Die Elixiere des Teufels** *(The Elixirs of the Devil)* | GER | 1976 | **Manfred Purzer** | 113 |
| 2207 | **Juwelen** | AUST | 1930 | **Hans Brückner** | 87 |
| 2208 | **Die tödlichen Träume** *[Deadly dreams]* *(aka: Liebestraum)* | GER | 1951 | **Paul Martin** | 80 |
| 2209 | **Das Fräulein von Scudéri** *(aka: Die Schätze des Teufels)* | GER/SWE | 1955 | **Eugen York** | 94 |
| 2210 | **Cardillac** | GER | 1969 | **Edgar Reitz** | 110(97) |
| 2211 | **Nutcracker Fantasy** *(aka: Nutcracker)* *{puppet version}* | USA/JAP | 1979 | **Takeo Nakamura** | 81 +V(79) |
| 2212 | **Jedermann** *(Everyman)* | AUST | 1961 | **Gottfried Reinhardt** | 98(96) |
| 2213 | **Jorden er flad** | DEN | 1976 | **Henrik Stangerup** | 116 |
| 2214 | **Jeppe paa bjerget** | NOR | 1933 | **Harry Ivarson** **Per Aabel** | 80 |
| 2215 | **Loffe som miljonär** *[Loffe as a millionaire]* | SWE | 1948 | **Gösta Bernhard** | 89 |
| 2216 | **Jeppe på bjerget** *(aka: Konge for en dag)* *(Jeppe of the Hill)* | DEN | 1981 | **Kasper Rostrup** | 106 |
| 2217 | **Winterreise im Olympiastadion** *[Winter journey in the Olympic stadium]* | GER | 1980(79) | **Klaus Michael Gruber** | 70 |
| 2218 | **Der Tod des Empedokles** *(The Death of Empedocles)* | GER/FR | 1986 | **Jean-Marie Straub** **Danièle Huillet** | 132 |
| 2219 | **Traumulus** | GER | 1936 | **Carl Froelich** | 98 |
| 2220 | **Helen of Troy** | USA | 1955 | **Robert Wise** | 114 |
| 2221 | **La guerra di Troia** *(FR: La guerre de Troie)* *(The Trojan War)* *(aka: The Wooden Horse of Troy)* | IT/FR | 1961 | **Giorgio Ferroni** | 105 +V |
| 2222 | **Ulisse** *(Ulysses)* | IT | 1954(53) | **Mario Camerini** | 104 +V(99) |
| 2223 | **The Prisoner of Zenda** | USA | 1937 | **John Cromwell** | 101 |
| 2224 | **The Prisoner of Zenda** | USA | 1952 | **Richard Thorpe** | 101 +V |
| 2225 | **The Prisoner of Zenda** | USA | 1979 | **Richard Quine** | 108 |
| 2226 | **The Offence** *(aka: The Offense)* | GB | 1973(72) | **Sidney Lumet** | 113 +V |
| 2227 | | | | | |
| 2228 | **The Leopard Man** | USA | 1943 | **Jacques Tourneur** | 59(70) |
| 2229 | **The Black Angel** | USA | 1946 | **Roy William Neill** | 80 |
| 2230 | **Street of Chance** | USA | 1942 | **Jack Hively** | 74 |
| 2231 | **The Chase** | USA | 1946 | **Arthur Ripley** | 86 |
| 2232 | **The Window** | USA | 1949 | **Ted Tetzlaff** | 73 |
| 2233 | **The Boy Cried Murder** | GB/GER/ YUGO | 1966 | **George Breakston** | 86 |

| No. | Author | Nationality | Form | Literary Title | Date |
|-----|--------|-------------|------|----------------|------|
| 2234 | Hopley-Woolrich, Cornell George (ditto) | American | SS | The Boy Cried Murder | 1947 |
| 2235 | Hopley-Woolrich, Cornell George (ditto) | American | N | The Bride Wore Black | 1940 |
| 2236 | Hopley-Woolrich, Cornell George (as: William Irish) | American | N | Deadline at Dawn | 1944 |
| 2237 | Hopley-Woolrich, Cornell George (ditto) | American | N | I Married a Dead Man | 1948 |
| 2238 | Hopley-Woolrich, Cornell George (ditto) | American | N | I Married a Dead Man | 1948 |
| 2239 | Hopley-Woolrich, Cornell George (ditto) | American | N | I Wouldn't Be In Your Shoes | 1943 |
| 2240 | Hopley-Woolrich, Cornell George (as: Cornell Woolrich) | American | SS | I'm Dangerous Tonight | 1981 (coll) |
| 2241 | Hopley-Woolrich, Cornell George (ditto) | American | N | Manhattan Love Song | 1932 |
| 2242 | Hopley-Woolrich, Cornell George (as: George Hopley) | American | N | Night Has a Thousand Eyes | 1945 |
| 2243 | Hopley-Woolrich, Cornell George (as: William Irish) | American | SS | Nightmare | 1943 |
| 2244 | Hopley-Woolrich, Cornell George (ditto) | American | SS | Nightmare | 1943 |
| 2245 | Hopley-Woolrich, Cornell George (ditto) | American | N | Phantom Lady | 1942 |
| 2246 | Hopley-Woolrich, Cornell George (ditto) | American | SS | Rear Window | 1944 |
| 2247 | Hopley-Woolrich, Cornell George (ditto) | American | SS | Two Fellows in a Furnished Room | 1946 |
| 2248 | Hopley-Woolrich, Cornell George (ditto) | American | N | Waltz into Darkness | 1947 |
| 2249 | Horváth, Ödön von | German(Yugo) | P | Geschichten aus dem Wiener Wald (Tales From the Vienna Woods) | 1931 |
| 2250 | Horváth, Ödön von | German(Yugo) | N | Jugend ohne Gott (Youth Without God) | 1938 |
| 2251 | Hostrup, Jens Christian | Danish | P | Gjenboerne (aka: Genboerne) [The neighbors] | 1844 |
| 2252 | Howard, Sidney Coe | American | P | Half Gods | 1930 |
| 2253 | Howard, Sidney Coe | American | P | The Silver Cord | 1926 |
| 2254 | Howard, Sidney Coe | American | P | They Knew What They Wanted | 1924 |
| 2255 | Howard, Sidney Coe | American | P | They Knew What They Wanted | 1924 |
| 2256 | Howard, Sidney Coe; De Kruif, Paul | American | P | Yellow Jack | 1934 |
| 2257 | Hrabal, Bohumil | Czech | N | Ostře sledované vlaky (A Close Watch on the Trains) (aka: Closely Watched Trains) | 1965 |
| 2258 | Hrabal, Bohumil | Czech | SS | Postřižiny [The shorn] | 1976 |
| 2259 | Hsü Ti-shan (see: Xu Dishan) | Chinese | SS | | |
| 2260 | Huch, Ricarda | German | N | Der Fall Deruga (The Deruga Trial) | 1917 |
| 2261 | Huch, Ricarda | German | N | Der Fall Deruga | 1917 |
| 2262 | Huch, Ricarda | German | N | Der letzte Sommer | 1902 |
| 2263 | Hughes, Langston | American(afro) | SS | Thank You, M'am | 1963 |
| 2264 | Hughes, Richard | British | N | A High Wind in Jamaica (USA: The Innocent Voyage) | 1929 |
| 2265 | Hughes, Thomas | British | N | Tom Brown's Schooldays | 1857 |
| 2266 | Hughes, Thomas | British | N | Tom Brown's Schooldays | 1857 |

| No | Film Title | Country of Production | Date | Director(s) | Duration of Film |
|---|---|---|---|---|---|
| 2234 | **Cloak and Dagger** | USA | 1984 | **Richard Franklin** | 101 |
| 2235 | **La mariée était en noir** (IT: La sposa in nero) (The Bride Wore Black) | FR/IT | 1967 | **François Truffaut** | 107 |
| 2236 | **Deadline at Dawn** | USA | 1946 | **Harold Clurman** | 83 +V |
| 2237 | **No Man of Her Own** | USA | 1950 | **Mitchell Leisen** | 98 |
| 2238 | **J'ai épousé une ombre** (I Married a Shadow) (aka: I Married a Dead Man) | FR | 1983 | **Robin Davis** | 110 |
| 2239 | **I Wouldn't Be In Your Shoes** | USA | 1948 | **William Nigh** | 71 |
| 2240 | **I'm Dangerous Tonight** | USA | 1990 | **Tobe Hooper** | 88 +V |
| 2241 | **Manhattan Love Song** | USA | 1934 | **Leonard Fields** | 69 |
| 2242 | **Night Has a Thousand Eyes** | USA | 1948(47) | **John Farrow** | 80 |
| 2243 | **Fear in the Night** | USA | 1947 | **Maxwell Shane** | 72 |
| 2244 | **Nightmare** | USA | 1956 | **Maxwell Shane** | 89 |
| 2245 | **Phantom Lady** | USA | 1944 | **Robert Siodmak** | 87 |
| 2246 | **Rear Window** | USA | 1954 | **Alfred Hitchcock** | 112 +V |
| 2247 | **The Guilty** | USA | 1947 | **John Reinhardt** | 70 |
| 2248 | **La sirène du Mississipi** (Mississippi Mermaid) (IT: La mia droga si chiama Julie) | FR/IT | 1969 | **François Truffaut** | 109(122) |
| 2249 | **Geschichten aus dem Wiener Wald** (Tales From the Vienna Woods) | GER/AUST | 1979 | **Maximilian Schell** | 95 |
| 2250 | **Wie ich ein Neger wurde** (How I Became Black) | GER | 1970 | **Roland Gall** | 97 |
| 2251 | **Genboerne** | DEN | 1939 | **Arne Weel** | 100 |
| 2252 | **Free Love** (GB: Blind Wives) | USA | 1930 | **Hobart Henley** | 70 |
| 2253 | **The Silver Cord** | USA | 1933 | **John Cromwell** | 74 |
| 2254 | **A Lady To Love** (GER: Die Sehnsucht jeder Frau) | USA | 1930 | **Victor Sjöström** | 92 |
| 2255 | **They Knew What They Wanted** | USA | 1940 | **Garson Kanin** | 96 |
| 2256 | **Yellow Jack** | USA | 1938 | **George B. Seitz** | 83 |
| 2257 | **Ostře sledované vlaky** (Closely Observed Trains) (aka: Closely Watched Trains) | CZ | 1966 | **Jiří Menzel** | 92 |
| 2258 | **Postřižiny** (Cutting It Short) (aka: Short Cut) (aka: Cuttings) (aka: Tonsure) | CZ | 1980 | **Jiří Menzel** | 98 |
| 2259 | | | | | |
| 2260 | **Der Fall Deruga** | GER | 1938 | **Fritz Peter Buch** | 104(83) |
| 2261 | **... und nichts als die Wahrheit** (And Nothing But the Truth) | GER | 1958 | **Franz Peter Wirth** | 96 |
| 2262 | **Der letzte Sommer** (The Last Summer) | GER | 1954 | **Harald Braun** | 109 |
| 2263 | **Thank You, M'am** | USA | 1976 | **Andrew Sugerman** | 12 +V |
| 2264 | **A High Wind in Jamaica** | GB | 1965 | **Alexander Mackendrick** | 103 |
| 2265 | **Tom Brown's School Days** (aka: Adventures at Rugby) | USA | 1940 | **Robert Stevenson** | 86 |
| 2266 | **Tom Brown's Schooldays** | GB | 1951(50) | **Gordon Parry** | 96 +V |

| No. | Author | Nationality | Form | Literary Title | Date |
|-----|--------|-------------|------|----------------|------|
| 2267 | **Hugo, Victor** | French | N | **L'homme qui rit**<br>(The Laughing Man)<br>(aka: By Order of the King) | 1869 |
| 2268 | **Hugo, Victor** | French | P | **Lucrèce Borgia** | 1833 |
| 2269 | **Hugo, Victor** | French | P | **Lucrèce Borgia** | 1833 |
| 2270 | **Hugo, Victor** | French | P | **Lucrèce Borgia** | 1833 |
| 2271 | **Hugo, Victor** | French | P | **Lucrèce Borgia** | 1833 |
| 2272 | **Hugo, Victor** | French | P | **Lucrèce Borgia** | 1833 |
| 2273 | **Hugo, Victor** | French | N | **Les misérables** | 1862 |
| 2274 | **Hugo, Victor** | French | N | **Les misérables** | 1862 |
| 2275 | **Hugo, Victor** | French | N | **Les misérables** | 1862 |
| 2276 | **Hugo, Victor** | French | N | **Les misérables** | 1862 |
| 2277 | **Hugo, Victor** | French | N | **Les misérables** | 1862 |
| 2278 | **Hugo, Victor** | French | N | **Les misérables** | 1862 |
| 2279 | **Hugo, Victor** | French | N | **Les misérables** | 1862 |
| 2280 | **Hugo, Victor** | French | N | **Les misérables** | 1862 |
| 2281 | **Hugo, Victor** | French | N | **Les misérables** | 1862 |
| 2282 | **Hugo, Victor** | French | N | **Les misérables** | 1862 |
| 2283 | **Hugo, Victor** | French | N | **Les misérables** | 1862 |
| 2284 | **Hugo, Victor** | French | N | **Les misérables** | 1862 |
| 2285 | **Hugo, Victor** | French | N | **Notre-Dame de Paris**<br>(The Hunchback of Notre-Dame) | 1831 |
| 2286 | **Hugo, Victor** | French | N | **Notre-Dame de Paris** | 1831 |
| 2287 | **Hugo, Victor** | French | V | **Les pauvres gens**<br>(in: Légende des siècles XIII) | 1859 |
| 2288 | **Hugo, Victor** | French | P | **Ruy Blas** | 1838 |
| 2289 | **Hugo, Victor** | French | N | **Les travailleurs de la mer**<br>(Toilers of the Sea) | 1866 |
| 2290 | **Hugo, Victor** | French | N | **Les travailleurs de la mer** | 1866 |
| 2291 | **Humphrey, William** | American | N | **Home from the Hill** | 1958 |
| 2292 | **Hunter, Evan** | American | N | **The Blackboard Jungle** | 1954 |
| 2293 | **Hunter, Evan**<br>(as: Ed McBain) | American | N | **Blood Relatives** | 1975 |
| 2294 | **Hunter, Evan** | American | N | **Buddwing** | 1964 |
| 2295 | **Hunter, Evan**<br>(as: Ed McBain) | American | N | **Cop Hater** | 1956 |
| 2296 | **Hunter, Evan** | American | N | **Every Little Crook and Nanny** | 1972 |
| 2297 | **Hunter, Evan**<br>(as: Ed McBain) | American | N | **Fuzz** | 1968 |
| 2298 | **Hunter, Evan** | American | N | **A Horses Head** | 1967 |
| 2299 | **Hunter, Evan**<br>(as: Ed McBain) | American | N | **Killer's Wedge** | 1959 |
| 2300 | **Hunter, Evan**<br>(as: Ed McBain) | American | N | **King's Ransom** | 1959 |
| 2301 | **Hunter, Evan**<br>(as: Ed McBain) | American | N | **Lady, Lady, I Did It!** | 1961 |
| 2302 | **Hunter, Evan** | American | N | **Last Summer** | 1968 |
| 2303 | **Hunter, Evan** | American | N | **A Matter of Conviction** | 1959 |

| No | Film Title | Country of Production | Date | Director(s) | Duration of Film |
|---|---|---|---|---|---|
| 2267 | L'uomo che ride<br>(FR: L'homme qui rit)<br>(The Man With the Golden Mask) | IT/FR | 1965 | **Sergio Corbucci** | 94(86) |
| 2268 | Lucrèce Borgia | FR | 1935 | **Abel Gance** | 95 |
| 2269 | Lucrezia Borgia | IT | 1940 | **Hans Heinrich** | 78 |
| 2270 | Lucrecia Borgia | ARG | 1947 | **Luis Bayón Herrera** | 90 |
| 2271 | Le notti di Lucrezia Borgia<br>(aka: Lucrèce Borgia)<br>(Nights of Temptation) | IT/FR | 1959 | **Sergio Grieco** | 120(92) |
| 2272 | Lucrezia<br>(aka: Lucrèce Borgia, l'amante del diavolo)<br>(Lucrèce Borgia, the Devil's Lover) | IT/AUST | 1968 | **Osvaldo Civirani** | 102(85) |
| 2273 | Jan Barujan<br>(Jean Valjean) | JAP | 1931 | **Tomu Uchida** | Pt.1, 72<br>Pt.2, 91 |
| 2274 | Les misérables<br>(Pt.1: Une tempête sous une crâne)<br>(aka: Jean Valjean)<br>(Pt.2: Les Thémardier)<br>(Pt.3: Liberté, liberté cherie) | FR | 1934(33) | **Raymond Bernard** | Pt.1, 120<br>Pt.2, 90<br>Pt.3, 95 |
| 2275 | Les misérables | USA | 1935 | **Richard Boleslavsky** | 109 |
| 2276 | Gavrosh | USSR | 1937 | **Tatiana Lukashevitch** | 75 |
| 2277 | Los miserables | MEX | 1944 | **Fernando A. Rivero** | 103 |
| 2278 | El Bouassa<br>(aka: Les misérables) | EGY | 1944 | **Kamal Selim** | 120[?] |
| 2279 | I miserabili<br>(Pt.1: Caccia all'uomo)<br>(Pt.2: Tempesta su Parigi)<br>(aka: Les misérables) | IT | 1947 | **Riccardo Freda** | 93(103) |
| 2280 | Re-Mizeraburu<br>(Les misérables)<br>{2 - parts} | JAP | 1950 | **Daisuke Itō<br>Masahiro Makino** | 112 |
| 2281 | Ezhai padum padu | IND(TAM) | 1950 | **K. Ramnath** | 198 |
| 2282 | Les misérables | USA | 1952 | **Lewis Milestone** | 106 |
| 2283 | Les misérables<br>(IT: I miserabili) | FR/IT | 1958(57) | **Jean-Paul le Chanois** | Pt.1, 97<br>Pt.2, 120 |
| 2284 | Les misérables | FR | 1982 | **Robert Hossein** | 187(180) |
| 2285 | The Hunchback of Notre Dame | USA | 1939 | **William Dieterle** | 116<br>+V |
| 2286 | Notre-Dame de Paris<br>(The Hunchback of Notre-Dame) | FR/IT | 1956 | **Jean Delannoy** | 100 |
| 2287 | Les pauvres gens | FR | 1937 | **Antoine Mourre** | 29 |
| 2288 | Ruy Blas | FR | 1948 | **Pierre Billon** | 92(114) |
| 2289 | Toilers of the Sea | GB | 1936 | **Selwyn Jepson<br>Ted Fox** | 83 |
| 2290 | Sea Devils | GB | 1953(52) | **Raoul Walsh** | 90 |
| 2291 | Home From the Hill | USA | 1960 | **Vincente Minnelli** | 132 |
| 2292 | The Blackboard Jungle | USA | 1955 | **Richard Brooks** | 101 |
| 2293 | Blood Relatives | CAN/FR | 1978(77) | **Claude Chabrol** | 90<br>+V |
| 2294 | Mister Buddwing<br>(aka: Woman Without a Face) | USA | 1966(65) | **Delbert Mann** | 95(100) |
| 2295 | Cop Hater | USA | 1958(57) | **William Berke** | 73 |
| 2296 | Every Little Crook and Nanny | USA | 1972 | **Cy Howard** | 92 |
| 2297 | Fuzz | USA | 1972 | **Richard A. Colla** | 92(98)<br>+V |
| 2298 | Le cri du cormoran le soir au-dessus des jongues | FR | 1971 | **Michel Audiard** | 85 |
| 2299 | La soupe aux poulets | FR | 1963 | **Philippe Agostini** | 90 |
| 2300 | Tengoku to jigoku<br>(High and Low)<br>(aka: The Ransom)<br>(aka: Heaven and Hell) | JAP | 1963(62) | **Akira Kurosawa** | 142<br>+V |
| 2301 | Kofuku<br>(Lonely Heart)<br>(aka: Happiness) | JAP | 1982 | **Kon Ichikawa** | 106 |
| 2302 | Last Summer | USA | 1969 | **Frank Perry** | 97 |
| 2303 | The Young Savages | USA | 1961 | **John Frankenheimer** | 103(110) |

| No. | Author | Nationality | Form | Literary Title | Date |
|-----|--------|-------------|------|----------------|------|
| 2304 | Hunter, Evan (as: Ed McBain) | American | N | **The Mugger** | 1956 |
| 2305 | Hunter, Evan (as: Ed McBain) | American | N | **The Pusher** | 1956 |
| 2306 | Hunter, Evan | American | N | **Strangers When We Meet** | 1958 |
| 2307 | Hunter, Evan (as: Ed McBain) | American | N | **Ten Plus One** | 1963 |
| 2308 | Hunter, Evan | American | F-N | **Walk Proud** | 1979 |
| 2309 | Hunter, Kristin | American(afro) | N | **The Landlord** | 1966 |
| 2310 | Hunyady Sándor | Hungarian | SS | **Bakaruhában** (Adventure in Uniform) | 1935 |
| 2311 | Hunyady Sándor | Hungarian | SS | **Bakaruhában** | 1935 |
| 2312 | Hunyady Sándor | Hungarian | N | **A vöröslámpás ház** [The house with the red light] | 1937 |
| 2313 | Huxley, Aldous | British | SS | **The Gioconda Smile** | 1922 |
| 2314 | Huxley, Aldous | British | SS | **Young Archimedes** | 1924 |
| 2315 | Ibrăileanu, Garabet | Romanian | N | **Adela. Fragment din jurnalul lui Emil Codrescu** (Iulie-August 189...) [Adela. A fragment from Emil Codrescu's diary...] | 1933 |
| 2316 | Ibsen, Henrik | Norwegian | P | **Et dukkehjem** (A Doll's House) (aka: Nora) | 1879 |
| 2317 | Ibsen, Henrik | Norwegian | P | **Et dukkehjem** | 1879 |
| 2318 | Ibsen, Henrik | Norwegian | P | **Et dukkehjem** | 1879 |
| 2319 | Ibsen, Henrik | Norwegian | P | **Et dukkehjem** | 1879 |
| 2320 | Ibsen, Henrik | Norwegian | P | **En folkefiende** (An Enemy of the People) (aka: An Enemy of Society) | 1882 |
| 2321 | Ibsen, Henrik | Norwegian | P | **En folkefiende** {version by Arthur Miller} | 1882 |
| 2322 | Ibsen, Henrik | Norwegian | P | **En folkefiende** | 1882 |
| 2323 | Ibsen, Henrik | Norwegian | P | **Fru Inger til Østraad** (Lady Inger of Østrat) (aka: Lady Inger) | 1857 |
| 2324 | Ibsen, Henrik | Norwegian | P | **Hedda Gabler** | 1890 |
| 2325 | Ibsen, Henrik | Norwegian | P | **Hedda Gabler** | 1890 |
| 2326 | Ibsen, Henrik | Norwegian | P | **Lille Eyolf** (Little Eyolf) | 1894 |
| 2327 | Ibsen, Henrik | Norwegian | P | **Peer Gynt** | 1867 |
| 2328 | Ibsen, Henrik | Norwegian | P | **Peer Gynt** | 1867 |
| 2329 | Ibsen, Henrik | Norwegian | P | **Samfundets støtter** (The Pillars of Society) (aka: The Pillars of the Community) | 1877 |
| 2330 | Ibsen, Henrik | Norwegian | P | **Samfundets støtter** | 1877 |
| 2331 | Ibsen, Henrik | Norwegian | P | **Vildanden** (The Wild Duck) | 1884 |
| 2332 | Ibsen, Henrik | Norwegian | P | **Vildanden** | 1884 |
| 2333 | Ibsen, Henrik | Norwegian | P | **Vildanden** | 1884 |
| 2334 | Ibuse Masuji | Japanese | N | **Kuroi ame** (Black Rain) | 1965-66 |
| 2335 | Ibuse Masuji | Japanese | N | **Okomasan** | 1941 |
| 2336 | Ihara Saikaku | Japanese | N | **Kōshoku ichidai onna** (Life of an Amorous Woman) | 1686 |
| 2337 | Ilf, Ilya; Petrov, Evgeny | Russian | N | **Dvenadtsat' stul'yev** (Twelve Chairs) | 1928 |
| 2338 | Ilf, Ilya; Petrov, Evgeny | Russian | N | **Dvenadtsat' stul'yev** | 1928 |
| 2339 | Ilf, Ilya; Petrov, Evgeny | Russian | N | **Dvenadtsat' stul'yev** | 1928 |
| 2340 | Ilf, Ilya; Petrov, Evgeny | Russian | N | **Dvenadtsat' stul'yev** | 1928 |

| No | Film Title | Country of Production | Date | Director(s) | Duration of Film |
|----|-----------|----------------------|------|-------------|-----------------|
| 2304 | **The Mugger** | USA | 1958 | **William Berke** | 74 |
| 2305 | **The Pusher** | USA | 1960 | **Gene Milford** | 82 |
| 2306 | **Strangers When We Meet** | USA | 1960 | **Richard Quine** | 117 +V |
| 2307 | **Sans mobile apparent** (IT: Senza movente) (Without Apparent Motive) | FR/IT | 1971 | **Philippe Labro** | 105(100) |
| 2308 | **Walk Proud** | USA | 1979 | **Robert Collins** | 102 |
| 2309 | **The Landlord** | USA | 1970 | **Hal Ashby** | 110 |
| 2310 | **The Girl Downstairs** | USA | 1938 | **Norman Taurog** | 77 |
| 2311 | **Bakaruhában** (A Sunday Romance) | HUNG | 1957 | **Imre Fehér** | 92(98) |
| 2312 | **Egy erkölcsös éjszaka** (A Very Moral Night) | HUNG | 1979(77) | **Károly Makk** | 92(103) |
| 2313 | **A Woman's Vengeance** | USA | 1947 | **Zoltan Korda** | 96 |
| 2314 | **Prelude to Fame** | GB | 1950 | **Fergus McDonell** | 88 |
| 2315 | **Adela** | ROM | 1985 | **Mircea Veroiu** | 82 |
| 2316 | **Casa de muñecas** (A Doll's House) | ARG | 1943 | **Ernesto Arancibia** | 95 |
| 2317 | **Nora** | GER | 1944 | **Harald Braun** | 102 |
| 2318 | **A Doll's House** | GB | 1973 | **Patrick Garland** | 95 |
| 2319 | **A Doll's House** | GB/FR | 1973 | **Joseph Losey** | 106 +V |
| 2320 | **Ein Volksfeind** | GER | 1937 | **Hans Steinhoff** | 102 +V |
| 2321 | **An Enemy of the People** | USA | 1978(77) | **George Schaefer** | 103 +V |
| 2322 | **Ganashatru** (An Enemy of the People) | IND(HIN) | 1989 | **Satyajit Ray** | 100 |
| 2323 | **Fru Inger til Østråt** (Lady Inger of Østrat) | NOR | 1975 | **Sverre Udnæs** | 97 |
| 2324 | **Hedda** | GB | 1977(75) | **Trevor Nunn** | 102 +V |
| 2325 | **Hedda Gabler** | BEL/HOLL | 1979 | **Jan Decorte** | 113 |
| 2326 | **Jazeere** | IND(HIN) | 1989 | **Govind Nihalani** | 144 |
| 2327 | **Peer Gynt** | GER | 1934 | **Fritz Wendhausen** | 119 |
| 2328 | **Peer Gynt** | USA | 1965 | **David Bradley** | 85 |
| 2329 | **Stützen der Gesellschaft** (Pillars of Society) | GER | 1935 | **Detlef Sierck** (Douglas Sirk) | 81 |
| 2330 | **Dharamveer** | IND(MAR) | 1937 | **Master Vinayak** | 157 |
| 2331 | **Vildanden** (The Wild Duck) | NOR | 1963 | **Tancred Ibsen** | 105 |
| 2332 | **Die Wildente** (The Wild Duck) | GER/AUST | 1976 | **Hans W. Geissendörfer** | 105 |
| 2333 | **The Wild Duck** | AUSTL | 1984 | **Henri Safran** | 96 |
| 2334 | **Kuroi ame** (Black Rain) | JAP | 1988 | **Shōhei Imamura** | 123 |
| 2335 | **Hideko no shasho-san** (Hideko the Bus Conductor) | JAP | 1941 | **Mikio Naruse** | 70 |
| 2336 | **Saikaku ichidai onna** (The Life of Oharu) | JAP | 1952 | **Kenji Mizoguchi** | 133 |
| 2337 | **Keep Your Seats Please** | GB | 1936 | **Monty Banks** | 82 |
| 2338 | **Dreizehn Stühle** (aka: 13 Stühle) | GER | 1938 | **E. W. Emo** | 92 |
| 2339 | **It's in the Bag** (GB: The Fifth Chair) | USA | 1945 | **Richard Wallace** | 87 |
| 2340 | **Las doce sillas** (The Twelve Chairs) | CB | 1962 | **Tomás Gutiérrez Alea** (Gutiérrez Alea, Tomás) | 91(97) |

| No. | Author | Nationality | Form | Literary Title | Date |
|-----|--------|-------------|------|----------------|------|
| 2341 | Ilf, Ilya;<br>Petrov, Evgeny | Russian | N | Dvenadtsat' stul'yev | 1928 |
| 2342 | Ilf, Ilya;<br>Petrov, Evgeny | Russian | N | Dvenadtsat' stul'yev | 1928 |
| 2343 | Ilf, Ilya;<br>Petrov, Evgeny | Russian | N | Dvenadtsat' stul'yev | 1928 |
| 2344 | Ilf, Ilya;<br>Petrov, Evgeny | Russian | N | Zolotoy telyonok<br>(The Golden Calf) | 1931 |
| 2345 | Inge, William | American | P | Bus Stop | 1955 |
| 2346 | Inge, William | American | P | Come Back, Little Sheba | 1950 |
| 2347 | Inge, William | American | P | The Dark at the Top of the Stairs | 1957 |
| 2348 | Inge, William | American | N | Good Luck, Miss Wyckoff | 1970 |
| 2349 | Inge, William | American | P | A Loss of Roses | 1960 |
| 2350 | Inge, William | American | P | Picnic | 1952 |
| 2351 | Inoue Yasushi | Japanese | N | Kaseki | 1967 |
| 2352 | Insúa, Alberto<br>(Alberto Galt y Escobar) | Spanish | N | La mujer, el torero y el toro | 1926 |
| 2353 | Insúa, Alberto | Spanish | N | El negro que tenía el alma blanca | 1922 |
| 2354 | Insúa, Alberto | Spanish | N | El negro que tenía el alma blanca | 1922 |
| 2355 | Ionesco, Eugène | French | P | Le nouveau locataire<br>(The New Tenant) | 1958 |
| 2356 | Ionesco, Eugène | French | P | Le rhinocéros<br>(Rhinoceros) | 1959 |
| 2357 | Ionesco, Eugène | French | P | Le rhinocéros | 1959 |
| 2358 | Iovkov, Iordan<br>(see: Yovkov, Yordan) | Bulgarian | N/SS | | |
| 2359 | Irish, William<br>(see: Hopley-Woolrich, Cornell George) | American | N/SS | | |
| 2360 | Irving, John | American | N | The Hotel New Hampshire | 1981 |
| 2361 | Irving, John | American | N | The World According to Garp | 1978 |
| 2362 | Irving, Washington | American | SS | The Legend of Sleepy Hollow | 1819-20 |
| 2363 | Irwin, Wallace | American | N | North Shore | 1932 |
| 2364 | Isaković, Antonije | Yugoslav(Serb) | SS | Paprat i vatra | 1962 |
| 2365 | Isherwood, Christopher - {ss}<br>Van Druten, John - {p} | British/<br>American | SS+P | The Berlin Stories {ss} +<br>I Am a Camera {p} | 1945+<br>1952 |
| 2366 | Isherwood, Christopher - {ss}<br>Van Druten, John - {p} | British/<br>American | SS+P | The Berlin Stories {ss} +<br>I Am a Camera {p} | 1945+<br>1952 |
| 2367 | Ishihara Shintarō | Japanese | N | Aoi satsujinsha | 1966 |
| 2368 | Ishihara Shintarō | Japanese | N | Kaseki no mori | 1970 |
| 2369 | Ishihara Shintarō | Japanese | SS | Kawaita hana | 1958 |
| 2370 | Ishihara Shintarō | Japanese | SS | Shokei no heya<br>(The Punishment Room) | 1956 |
| 2371 | Ishikawa Tatsuzo | Japanese | N | Aoiro kakumei | 1952-53 |
| 2372 | Ishizaka Yōjirō | Japanese | N | Hi no ataru sakamichi<br>[A slope in the sun] | 1958 |
| 2373 | Ishizaka Yōjirō | Japanese | N | Ishinaka-sensei gyōjōki<br>(Mr Ishinaka Tells Tales of Rural<br>Drollery) | 1948-49 |
| 2374 | Ishizaka Yōjirō | Japanese | SS | Kuchizuke +<br>Kiri no naka no shojo<br>[The girl in the mist] +<br>Onna doshi | 1954+<br>1955 |
| 2375 | Ishizaka Yōjirō | Japanese | SS | Magokoro | 1939 |
| 2376 | Ishizaka Yōjirō | Japanese | N | Wakai hito<br>(Young People) | 1933-36 |

| No | Film Title | Country of Production | Date | Director(s) | Duration of Film |
|----|-----------|----------------------|------|-------------|------------------|
| 2341 | **Twelve Plus One** (aka: Twelve + One) (IT: Una su 13) (aka: 12 piú 1) | USA/FR/IT | 1970(69) | **Luciano Lucignani** | 94 +V(90) |
| 2342 | **The Twelve Chairs** | USA | 1970 | **Mel Brooks** | 94 +V(89) |
| 2343 | **Dvenadtsat stulyev** (Twelve Chairs) | USSR | 1971 | **Leonid Gaidai** | 160 |
| 2344 | **Zolotoy telyonok** {2 - parts} | USSR | 1968 | **Mikhail Shveytzer** | Pt.1, 75 Pt.2, 98 |
| 2345 | **Bus Stop** (aka: The Wrong Kind of Girl) | USA | 1956 | **Joshua Logan** | 90 +V |
| 2346 | **Come Back, Little Sheba** | USA | 1953(52) | **Daniel Mann** | 99 |
| 2347 | **The Dark at the Top of the Stairs** | USA | 1960 | **Delbert Mann** | 123 |
| 2348 | **Good Luck, Miss Wyckoff** (aka: The Shaming) (aka: The Sin) | USA | 1979 | **Marvin J. Chomsky** | 105 +V(90) |
| 2349 | **The Stripper** (GB: Woman of Summer) | USA | 1963 | **Franklin J. Schaffner** | 94 |
| 2350 | **Picnic** | USA | 1955 | **Joshua Logan** | 113 |
| 2351 | **Kaseki** (Fossils) | JAP | 1975(74) | **Masaki Kobayashi** | 217 |
| 2352 | **La mujer, el torero y el toro** | SP | 1950(49) | **Fernando Butragueño** | 95(82) |
| 2353 | **El negro que tenía el alma blanca** | SP | 1934 | **Benito Perojo** | 83 |
| 2354 | **El negro que tenía el alma blanca** | SP | 1951 | **Hugo del Carril** | 87(94) |
| 2355 | **The New Tenant** | GB | 1964 | **George Brandt** | 30 |
| 2356 | **Die Nashörner** (Rhinoceros) {animation} | POL | 1963 | **Jan Lenica** | 11 |
| 2357 | **Rhinoceros** | USA | 1974 | **Tom O'Horgan** | 101 |
| 2358 | | | | | |
| 2359 | | | | | |
| 2360 | **The Hotel New Hampshire** | USA | 1984 | **Tony Richardson** | 110 +V |
| 2361 | **The World According to Garp** | USA | 1982 | **George Roy Hill** | 136 |
| 2362 | **The Legend of Sleepy Hollow** (aka: Adventures of Ichabod and Mr Toad) | USA | 1980 | **Henning Schellerup** | 98 +V |
| 2363 | **The Woman in Red** | USA | 1935 | **Robert Florey** | 68 |
| 2364 | **Tri** (Three) | YUGO | 1965 | **Aleksander Petrović** | 80 |
| 2365 | **I Am a Camera** | GB | 1955 | **Henry Cornelius** | 99 +V |
| 2366 | **Cabaret** {musical version} | USA | 1972 | **Bob Fosse** | 128(123) +V |
| 2367 | **Fukushu no uta ga kikoeru** [Song of vengeance] | JAP | 1968 | **Masahisa Sadanaga** **Shigeyuki Yamane** | 90 |
| 2368 | **Kaseki no mori** (The Petrified Forest) | JAP | 1973 | **Masahiro Shinoda** | 118 |
| 2369 | **Kawaita hana** (Pale Flower) | JAP | 1964 | **Masahiro Shinoda** | 98 |
| 2370 | **Shokei no heya** (Punishment Room) | JAP | 1956 | **Kon Ichikawa** | 96 |
| 2371 | **Aoiro kakumei** (The Blue Revolution) | JAP | 1953 | **Kon Ichikawa** | 108 |
| 2372 | **Hi no ataru sakamichi** | JAP | 1967 | **Katsumi Nishikawa** | 105 |
| 2373 | **Ishinaka-sensei gyōjōki** (Conduct Report On Professor Ishinaka) | JAP | 1950 | **Mikio Naruse** | 96 |
| 2374 | **Kuchizuke, III: onna doshi** (The Kiss, Part III: Woman's Ways) | JAP | 1955 | **Masanori Kakei** **Hideo Suzuki** **Mikio Naruse** | 115 |
| 2375 | **Magokoro** (Sincerity) | JAP | 1939 | **Mikio Naruse** | 80 |
| 2376 | **Wakai hito** (Young People) | JAP | 1937 | **Shirō Toyoda** | 81 |

| No. | Author | Nationality | Form | Literary Title | Date |
|---|---|---|---|---|---|
| 2377 | Ishizaka Yōjirō | Japanese | N | **Wakai hito** | 1933-36 |
| 2378 | Istrati, Panait | Romanian(Fr) | N | **Les chardons du Baragan** (ROM: Ciulinii Bărăganului) (The Thistles of the Baragan) | 1928{Fr} 1942{Rom} |
| 2379 | Istrati, Panait | Romanian | N | **Codin** (aka: Enfance d'Adrien Zograffi; Codine) | 1926{Fr} 1935{Rom} |
| 2380 | Itō Sachio | Japanese | N | **Nogiku no haka** [The grave in the wild chrysanthemums] | 1906 |
| 2381 | Ivanov, Dimitur (see: Elin Pelin) | Bulgarian | N | | |
| 2382 | Ivanov, Vsevolod | Russian | P | **Bronepoezd No 14-69** (Armoured Train) | 1922 |
| 2383 | Ivasiuc, Alexandru | Romanian | N | **Apa** [The water] | 1973 |
| 2384 | Iwaszkiewicz, Jarosław | Polish | SS | **Brzezina** | 1933 |
| 2385 | Iwaszkiewicz, Jarosław | Polish | SS | **Kochankowie z Marony** [Lovers from Marona] | 1961 |
| 2386 | Iwaszkiewicz, Jarosław | Polish | SS | **Kościół w Skaryszewie** [Church at Skaryszew] | 1967 |
| 2387 | Iwaszkiewicz, Jarosław | Polish | SS | **Matka Joanna od Aniołów** (Mother Joan of the Angels) | 1946 |
| 2388 | Iwaszkiewicz, Jarosław | Polish | SS | **Panny z Wilka** | 1933 |
| 2389 | Iwaszkiewicz, Jarosław | Polish | SS | **Róża** [Rose] | 1936 |
| 2390 | Izumi Kyōka | Japanese | N | **Baishoku kamonanban** | 1920 |
| 2391 | Izumi Kyōka | Japanese | N | **Nihonbashi** | 1914 |
| 2392 | Izumi Kyōka | Japanese | N | **Shirasagi** | 1909 |
| 2393 | Izumi Kyōka | Japanese | N | **Uta andon** | 1910 |
| 2394 | Izumi Kyōka | Japanese | N | **Uta andon** | 1910 |
| 2395 | Izumi Kyōka | Japanese | P | **Yashagaike** | 1913 |
| 2396 | Jackson, Charles Reginald | American | N | **The Lost Weekend** | 1944 |
| 2397 | Jackson, Helen Hunt | American | N | **Ramona** | 1884 |
| 2398 | Jackson, Shirley | American | N | **The Bird's Nest** | 1954 |
| 2399 | Jackson, Shirley | American | N | **The Haunting of Hill House** | 1959 |
| 2400 | Jacobsen, Jørgen-Frantz | Danish | N | **Barbara** | 1939 |
| 2401 | James, Henry | American/Br | SS | **The Altar of the Dead +** **The Beast in the Jungle** | 1895+ 1903 |
| 2402 | James, Henry | American/Br | SS | **The Aspern Papers** | 1888 |
| 2403 | James, Henry | American/Br | SS | **The Aspern Papers** | 1888 |
| 2404 | James, Henry | American/Br | SS | **The Bench of Desolation** | 1910 |
| 2405 | James, Henry | American/Br | N | **The Bostonians** | 1886 |
| 2406 | James, Henry | American/Br | SS | **Daisy Miller** | 1877 |
| 2407 | James, Henry | American/Br | N | **The Europeans** | 1878 |
| 2408 | James, Henry | American/Br | SS | **The Jolly Corner** | 1908 |
| 2409 | James, Henry | American/Br | N | **The Sense of the Past** | 1917 |
| 2410 | James, Henry | American/Br | N | **The Sense of the Past** | 1917 |
| 2411 | James, Henry | American/Br | SS | **The Turn of the Screw** | 1898 |

| No | Film Title | Country of Production | Date | Director(s) | Duration of Film |
|----|-----------|----------------------|------|-------------|------------------|
| 2377 | **Wakai hito** *(Young People)* *(aka: The Young Generation)* | JAP | 1952 | **Kon Ichikawa** | 113 |
| 2378 | **Ciulinii Bărăganului** *(FR: Les chardons du Baragan)* *(The Thistles of the Baragan)* | ROM/FR | 1958(57) | **Louis Daquin** | 113 |
| 2379 | **Codin** *(FR: Codine)* | ROM/FR | 1963 | **Henri Colpi** | 97 |
| 2380 | **Nogiku no gotoki kimi nariki** *(You Were Like a Wild Chrysanthemum)* | JAP | 1955 | **Keisuke Kinoshita** | 92 |
| 2381 | | | | | |
| 2382 | **Tommy** *(aka: Siberian Patrol)* | USSR | 1931 | **Yakov Protazanov** | 63 |
| 2383 | **Trei zile şi trei nopţi** *[Three days and three nights]* | ROM | 1976 | **Dinu Tănase** | 113 |
| 2384 | **Brzezina** *(The Birch Wood)* | POL | 1970 | **Andrzej Wajda** | 99 |
| 2385 | **Kochankowie z Marony** | POL | 1966 | **Jerzy Larzycki** | 102 |
| 2386 | **Ryś** *[The lynx]* | POL | 1982 | **Stanisław Różewicz** | 84 |
| 2387 | **Matka Joanna od Aniołów** *(Mother Joan of the Angels)* *(aka: The Devil and the Nun)* | POL | 1961(60) | **Jerzy Kawalerowicz** | 109 |
| 2388 | **Panny z Wilka** *(FR: Les Demoiselles de Wilko)* *(The Young Ladies of Wilko)* *(aka: Girls From Wilko)* | POL/FR | 1979 | **Andrzej Wajda** | 115 |
| 2389 | **Ubranie prawie nowe** *(The Suit Almost New)* | POL | 1964 | **Włodzimierz Haupe** | 95 |
| 2390 | **Orizuru Osen** *(The Downfall)* *(aka: The Downfall of Osen)* | JAP | 1935(34) | **Kenji Mizoguchi** | 91 |
| 2391 | **Nihonbashi** *(Bridge of Japan)* | JAP | 1956 | **Kon Ichikawa** | 112 |
| 2392 | **Shirasagi** *(The White Heron)* *(aka: The Snowy Heron)* | JAP | 1958 | **Teinosuke Kinugasa** | 97 |
| 2393 | **Uta andon** *(The Song Lantern)* *(aka: Song of the Lantern)* | JAP | 1943 | **Mikio Naruse** | 93 |
| 2394 | **Uta andon** *(The Lantern)* *(aka: The Old Lantern)* | JAP | 1960 | **Teinosuke Kinugasa** | 114 |
| 2395 | **Yashagaike** *(Demon Pond)* | JAP | 1979 | **Masahiro Shinoda** | 124 |
| 2396 | **The Lost Weekend** | USA | 1945 | **Billy Wilder** | 101 |
| 2397 | **Ramona** | USA | 1936 | **Henry King** | 90 |
| 2398 | **Lizzie** | USA | 1957 | **Hugo Haas** | 81 |
| 2399 | **The Haunting** | GB/USA | 1963 | **Robert Wise** | 112 |
| 2400 | **Barbara** | GER | 1961 | **Frank Wisbar** | 96 |
| 2401 | **La chambre verte** *(The Green Room)* | FR | 1978 | **François Truffaut** | 94 |
| 2402 | **The Lost Moment** | USA | 1947 | **Martin Gabel** | 89 +V |
| 2403 | **Les papiers d'Aspern** *(aka: Aspern)* | PORT | 1982 | **Eduardo de Gregorio** | 96 |
| 2404 | **Le banc de la désolation** *(The Bench of Desolation)* | FR | 1974(73) | **Claude Chabrol** | 52 |
| 2405 | **The Bostonians** | GB | 1984 | **James Ivory** | 122 +V |
| 2406 | **Daisy Miller** | USA | 1974 | **Peter Bogdanovich** | 92 +V |
| 2407 | **The Europeans** | GB | 1979 | **James Ivory** | 83 +V |
| 2408 | **The Jolly Corner** | USA | 1979(77) | **Arthur Barron** | 43 +V |
| 2409 | **Berkeley Square** | USA | 1933 | **Frank Lloyd** | 84 |
| 2410 | **The House in the Square** *(USA: I'll Never Forget You)* | GB | 1951 | **Roy Ward Baker** | 91 |
| 2411 | **The Innocents** *(aka: The Turn of the Screw)* | GB | 1961 | **Jack Clayton** | 90(100) +V |

| No. | Author | Nationality | Form | Literary Title | Date |
|-----|--------|-------------|------|----------------|------|
| 2412 | James, Henry | American/Br | SS | The Turn of the Screw | 1898 |
| 2413 | James, Henry | American/Br | N | Washington Square | 1881 |
| 2414 | James, Henry | American/Br | N | What Maisie Knew | 1897 |
| 2415 | James, M. R. | British | SS | Casting the Runes | 1911 |
| 2416 | Janson, Kristofer | Norwegian | SS | Liv | 1866 |
| 2417 | Jardiel Poncela, Enrique | Spanish | P | Un adulterio decente | 1935 |
| 2418 | Jardiel Poncela, Enrique | Spanish | P | Blanca por fuera y rosa por dentro [Blanca on the outside and Rosa within] | 1943 |
| 2419 | Jardiel Poncela, Enrique | Spanish | P | Las cinco advertencias de Satanás | 1938 |
| 2420 | Jardiel Poncela, Enrique | Spanish | P | Las cinco advertencias de Satanás | 1938 |
| 2421 | Jardiel Poncela, Enrique | Spanish | P | Eloísa está debajo de un almendro | 1943 |
| 2422 | Jardiel Poncela, Enrique | Spanish | P | Es peligroso asomarse al exterior | 1944 |
| 2423 | Jardiel Poncela, Enrique | Spanish | P | Los ladrones somos gente honrada | 1941 |
| 2424 | Jardiel Poncela, Enrique | Spanish | P | Los ladrones somos gente honrada | 1941 |
| 2425 | Jardiel Poncela, Enrique | Spanish | P | Margarita, Armando y su padre | 1931 |
| 2426 | Jardiel Poncela, Enrique | Spanish | P | Un marido de ida y vuelta | 1939 |
| 2427 | Jardiel Poncela, Enrique | Spanish | P | Tu y yo somos tres | 1946 |
| 2428 | Jardiel Poncela, Enrique | Spanish | P | Usted tiene ojos de mujer fatal | 1926 |
| 2429 | Jarry, Alfred | French | P | Ubu Roi | 1896 |
| 2430 | Jékely Zoltán | Hungarian | V | A 272. tágy leírása [The description of the art piece No.272] | 1975 |
| 2431 | Jellicoe, Ann | British | P | The Knack | 1962 |
| 2432 | Jensen, Erik Aalbæk | Danish | N | Gertrud | 1956 |
| 2433 | Jensen, Erik Aalbæk | Danish | N | Kridtstregen | 1976 |
| 2434 | Jensen, Johannes V. | Danish | SS | De naaede Forgen (aka: Nåede de forgen?) [Did they catch the ferry?] | 1925(28) |
| 2435 | Jensen, Johannes V. | Danish | N | Gudrun | 1936 |
| 2436 | Jerome, Jerome K. | British | P-N | The Passing of the Third Floor Back | 1905{p} 1907{n} |
| 2437 | Jerome, Jerome K. | British | N | Three Men in a Boat (to say nothing of the dog) | 1889 |
| 2438 | Jerome, Jerome K. | British | N | Three Men in a Boat (to say nothing of the dog) | 1889 |
| 2439 | Jerome, Jerome K. | British | N | Three Men in a Boat (to say nothing of the dog) | 1889 |
| 2440 | Jerschke, Oskar (joint, see: Holz, Arno) | German | P | | |
| 2441 | Jhabvala, Ruth Prawer | Indian(Eng) | N | Heat and Dust | 1975 |
| 2442 | Jhabvala, Ruth Prawer | Indian | N | The Householder | 1960 |
| 2443 | Jiménez, Juan Ramón | Spanish | AUT | Platero y yo (Platero and I) | 1914 |
| 2444 | Jirásek, Alois | Czech | P | Jan Roháč | 1922 |
| 2445 | Johnson, Dorothy M. | American | SS | The Hanging Tree | 1957 |
| 2446 | Johnson, Dorothy M. | American | SS | A Man Called Horse | 1953 |
| 2447 | Johnson, Dorothy M. | American | SS | The Man Who Shot Liberty Valance | 1953 |
| 2448 | Johnson, Eyvind | Swedish | N | Här har du ditt liv! | 1935 |
| 2449 | Johnson, James Weldon | American(afro) | V | Go Down Death - a Funeral Sermon | 1927 |
| 2450 | Johnson, Terry | British | P | Insignificance | 1982 |
| 2451 | Johnston, Jennifer | Irish | N | The Old Jest | 1979 |

| No | Film Title | Country of Production | Date | Director(s) | Duration of Film |
|---|---|---|---|---|---|
| 2412 | **The Nightcomers** | GB | 1972(71) | **Michael Winner** | 96 |
| 2413 | **The Heiress** | USA | 1949 | **William Wyler** | 115 |
| 2414 | **What Maisie Knew** | USA | 1976 | **Babette Mangolte** | 55 |
| 2415 | **Night of the Demon** *(USA: Curse of the Demon)* | GB | 1957 | **Jacques Tourneur** | 82 |
| 2416 | **Liv** | NOR | 1934 | **Rasmus Breistein** | 92 |
| 2417 | **Un adulterio decente** *(A Decent Adultery)* | SP | 1970(69) | **Rafael Gil** | 99(95) |
| 2418 | **Blanca por fuera, rosa por dentro** | SP | 1972(71) | **Pedro Lázaga** | 109(89) |
| 2419 | **Las cinco advertencias de Satanás** | SP | 1938(37) | **Isidro Socías** | 90(86) |
| 2420 | **Las cinco advertencias de Satanás** | SP/PORT | 1969 | **José Luis Merino** | 102 +V |
| 2421 | **Eloísa está debajo de un almendro** *(Eloisa Is Underneath an Almond Tree)* | SP | 1943 | **Rafael Gil** | 109(80) |
| 2422 | **Es peligroso asomarse al exterior** | SP | 1945 | **Alejandro Ulloa** | 87(83) |
| 2423 | **Los ladrones somos gente honrada** | SP | 1942(41) | **Ignacio Ferrés Iquino** | 102(99) |
| 2424 | **Los ladrones somos gente honrada** | SP | 1956 | **Pedro L. Ramírez** | 89(83) |
| 2425 | **Margarita, Armando y su padre** | ARG | 1939 | **Francisco Mugica** | 90 |
| 2426 | **Un marido de ida y vuelta** | SP | 1957 | **Luis Lucía** | 96(88) +V |
| 2427 | **Tu y yo somos tres** | SP | 1963(62) | **Rafael Gil** | 89 |
| 2428 | **Usted tiene ojos de mujer fatal** | SP | 1962 | **José Maria Elorrieta** | 86 |
| 2429 | **Ubu** *{animation}* | GB | 1978 | **Geoff Dunbar** | 20 |
| 2430 | **A kard** *(The Sword)* *(aka: En vagyok a falu rossza egyedül)* | HUNG | 1977 | **János Dömölky** | 80 |
| 2431 | **The Knack...and how to get it** *(aka: The Knack)* | GB | 1965 | **Richard Lester** | 84 |
| 2432 | **Ekko af et skud** | DEN | 1970 | **Erik Frohn Nielsen** | 99 |
| 2433 | **Forræderne** | DEN | 1983 | **Ole Roos** | 113 |
| 2434 | **De naaede Færgen** *(They Caught the Ferry)* | DEN | 1948 | **Carl Th. Dreyer** | 12 |
| 2435 | **Gudrun** *(Suddenly, A Woman!)* | DEN | 1963 | **Anker Sørensen** | 102 |
| 2436 | **The Passing of the Third Floor Back** | GB | 1935 | **Berthold Viertel** | 90 |
| 2437 | **Three Men in a Boat** | GB | 1933 | **Graham Cutts** | 60 |
| 2438 | **Three Men in a Boat** | GB | 1956 | **Ken Annakin** | 94 |
| 2439 | **Drei Mann in einen Boot** *[Three men in a boat]* | GER | 1961 | **Helmut Weiß** | 93 |
| 2440 | | | | | |
| 2441 | **Heat and Dust** | GB | 1983(82) | **James Ivory** | 133 +V |
| 2442 | **Gharbar** *(The Householder)* | IND | 1963 | **James Ivory** | 101 |
| 2443 | **Platero y yo** *(Platero and I)* | SP | 1965(64) | **Alfredo Castellón** | 95(85) |
| 2444 | **Jan Roháč z Dubé** | CZ | 1947(46) | **Vladimír Borský** | 85 |
| 2445 | **The Hanging Tree** | USA | 1959 | **Delmer Daves** | 107 |
| 2446 | **A Man Called Horse** | USA | 1970 | **Elliot Silverstein** | 114 +V |
| 2447 | **The Man Who Shot Liberty Valance** | USA | 1962 | **John Ford** | 121 |
| 2448 | **Här har du ditt liv** *(Here Is Your Life)* | SWE | 1966 | **Jan Troell** | 149 |
| 2449 | **Go Down Death** | USA | 1941 | **Spencer Williams** | 63 |
| 2450 | **Insignificance** | GB | 1985(84) | **Nicolas Roeg** | 109 +V |
| 2451 | **The Dawning** | GB | 1988 | **Robert Knights** | 94 +V |

| No. | Author | Nationality | Form | Literary Title | Date |
|-----|--------|-------------|------|----------------|------|
| 2452 | **Jókai Mór** | Hungarian | N | **Az aranyember** <br> *(The Man With the Golden Touch)* <br> *(aka: Timar's Two Worlds)* | 1872 |
| 2453 | **Jókai Mór** | Hungarian | N | **Fekete gyémántok** <br> *(The Dark Diamonds)* <br> *(aka: Black Diamonds)* | 1870 |
| 2454 | **Jókai Mór** | Hungarian | N | **Kárpáthy Zoltán** <br> *[Nabob, Zoltán Kárpáthy]* | 1854 |
| 2455 | **Jókai Mór** | Hungarian | N | **A kőszívű ember fiai** <br> *(The Baron's Sons)* | 1869 |
| 2456 | **Jókai Mór** | Hungarian | N | **Egy magyar nábob** <br> *(An Hungarian Nabob)* | 1853 |
| 2457 | **Jókai Mór** | Hungarian | N | **Névtelen vár** <br> *(The Nameless Castle)* | 1877 |
| 2458 | **Jókai Mór** | Hungarian | N | **Rab Ráby** <br> *(The Strange Story of Rab Ráby)* | 1879 |
| 2459 | **Jókai Mór** | Hungarian | N | **Szegény gazdagok** <br> *(The Poor Plutocrats)* | 1860 |
| 2460 | **Jolley, Elizabeth** | Australian | SS | **The Last Crop** | 1983 |
| 2461 | **Jones, James** | American | N | **From Here to Eternity** | 1951 |
| 2462 | **Jones, James** | American | N | **Some Came Running** | 1957 |
| 2463 | **Jones, James** | American | N | **The Thin Red Line** | 1962 |
| 2464 | **Jones, Leroi** <br> *(Amiri Imamu Baraka)* | American(afro) | P | **Dutchman** | 1964 |
| 2465 | **Jones, Leroi** | American | P | **Slave** | 1964 |
| 2466 | **Jonson, Ben** | British | P | **Volpone** <br> *(aka: Volpone, or the Fox)* | 1607 |
| 2467 | **Josephson, Ragnar** | Swedish | P | **Kanske en diktare** <br> *(Perhaps a Poet)* | 1932 |
| 2468 | **Josephson, Ragnar** | Swedish | P | **Kanske en diktare** | 1932 |
| 2469 | **Jou Shih** <br> *(see: Zhao Pingfu)* | Chinese | SS | | |
| 2470 | **Jouve, Pierre-Jean** | French | N | **Paulina 1880** | 1925 |
| 2471 | **Joyce, James** | Irish | SS | **The Dead** <br> *(from: Dubliners)* | 1914 |
| 2472 | **Joyce, James** | Irish | N | **Finnegan's Wake** | 1939 |
| 2473 | **Joyce, James** | Irish | N | **A Portrait of the Artist As a Young Man** | 1916 |
| 2474 | **Joyce, James** | Irish | N | **Ulysses** | 1922 |
| 2475 | **Kaden-Bandrowski, Juliusz** <br> *(Juliusz Kaden Bandrowski)* | Polish | N | **Czarne skrzydła** <br> *[Black wings]* | 1928-29 |
| 2476 | **Kaffka Margit** | Hungarian | N | **Hangyaboly** | 1917 |
| 2477 | **Kafka, Franz** | Austrian | N | **Amerika** <br> *(America)* <br> *(aka: Der Verschollene)* <br> *[The lost one]* | 1927 |
| 2478 | **Kafka, Franz** | Austrian | SS | **Ein Brudermord** <br> *(A Fratricide)* | 1919 |
| 2479 | **Kafka, Franz** | Austrian | SS | **Ein Hungerkünstler** <br> *(A Hunger Artist)* | 1924 |
| 2480 | **Kafka, Franz** | Austrian | SS | **In der Strafkolonie** <br> *(In the Penal Settlement)* <br> *(aka: In the Penal Colony)* | 1919 |
| 2481 | **Kafka, Franz** | Austrian | N | **Der Prozeß** <br> *(The Trial)* | 1925 |
| 2482 | **Kafka, Franz** | Austrian | N | **Das Schloß** <br> *(The Castle)* | 1926 |
| 2483 | **Kafka, Franz** | Austrian | N | **Das Schloß** | 1926 |

| No | Film Title | Country of Production | Date | Director(s) | Duration of Film |
|----|-----------|----------------------|------|-------------|------------------|
| 2452 | **Az aranyember** <br> *(The Man With the Golden Touch)* | HUNG | 1962 | **Viktor Gertler** | 116 |
| 2453 | **Fekete gyémántok** <br> *(Black Diamonds)* | HUNG | 1977(76) | **Zoltán Várkonyi** | 166 |
| 2454 | **Zoltán Kárpáthy** <br> *(aka: Kárpáthy Zoltán)* <br> *(The Last of the Nabobs)* <br> *{Pt.2}* | HUNG | 1966 | **Zoltán Várkonyi** | 87 |
| 2455 | **A kőszívű ember fiai** <br> *(Men and Banners)* | HUNG | 1965 | **Zoltán Várkonyi** | Pt.1, 86 <br> Pt.2, 88 |
| 2456 | **Egy magyar nábob** <br> *(The Last of the Nabobs)* <br> *{Pt.1}* | HUNG | 1966 | **Zoltán Várkonyi** | 104 |
| 2457 | **Névtelen vár** <br> *(The Nameless Castle)* | HUNG | 1982 | **Éva Zsurzs** | 121 |
| 2458 | **Rab Ráby** <br> *(Captive Raby)* | HUNG | 1965 | **György Hintsch** | 106 |
| 2459 | **Szegény gazdagok** <br> *(aka: Fatia Negra)* <br> *(Poor Rich)* | HUNG | 1959 | **Frigyes Bán** | 102 |
| 2460 | **The Last Crop** | GB/AUSTL | 1990 | **Sue Clayton** | 58 |
| 2461 | **From Here to Eternity** | USA | 1953 | **Fred Zinnemann** | 114 +V |
| 2462 | **Some Came Running** | USA | 1959(58) | **Vincente Minnelli** | 136 |
| 2463 | **The Thin Red Line** | USA | 1964 | **Andrew Marton** | 72 |
| 2464 | **Dutchman** | GB | 1967(66) | **Anthony Harvey** | 56 |
| 2465 | **A Fable** | USA | 1971 | **Al Freeman** | 80 |
| 2466 | **Volpone** | FR | 1941(40) | **Maurice Tourneur** | 98 |
| 2467 | **Kanske en diktare** | SWE | 1933 | **Lorens Marmstedt** | 78 |
| 2468 | **Farliga vägar** <br> *(Dangerous Roads)* | SWE | 1942 | **Anders Henrikson** | 86 |
| 2469 | | | | | |
| 2470 | **Paulina 1880** <br> *(aka: La novice de Mantoue)* | FR/GER | 1972 | **Jean-Louis Bertuccelli** | 110 |
| 2471 | **The Dead** | GB/USA/ GER | 1987 | **John Huston** | 83 <br> +V(79) |
| 2472 | **Passages From 'Finnegan's Wake'** <br> *(aka: Finnegan's Wake)* <br> *(aka: Passages From James Joyce's Finnegan's Wake)* | USA | 1965 | **Mary Ellen Bute** | 97(88) |
| 2473 | **A Portrait of the Artist As a Young Man** | GB | 1977 | **Joseph Strick** | 92 |
| 2474 | **Ulysses** | USA/GB | 1967 | **Joseph Strick** | 132 |
| 2475 | **Czarne skrzydła** | POL | 1963 | **Ewa Petelska** <br> **Czesław Petelski** | 104 |
| 2476 | **Hangyaboly** <br> *(Ants' Nest)* | HUNG | 1972(71) | **Zoltán Fábri** | 104 |
| 2477 | **Klassenverhältnisse** <br> *(Class Relations)* | GER/FR | 1984 | **Jean-Marie Straub** <br> **Danièle Huillet** | 127 |
| 2478 | **Ein Brudermord** <br> *{puppets}* | GB | 1981 | **Brothers Quay** | 05 |
| 2479 | **The Hunger Artist** | USA | 1976 | **Fred Smith** | 10 |
| 2480 | **La colonia penal** <br> *(The Penal Colony)* | CHL | 1971 | **Râúl Ruiz** | 68 |
| 2481 | **Le procès** <br> *(IT: Il processo)* <br> *(GER: Der Prozeß)* <br> *(The Trial)* | FR/IT/GER | 1963(62) | **Orson Welles** | 118(100) <br> +V |
| 2482 | **Das Schloß** <br> *(The Castle)* | GER/SWITZ | 1968 | **Rudolf Noelte** | 91 |
| 2483 | **Linna** <br> *(The Castle)* | FIN | 1986 | **Jaakko Pakkasvirta** | 99 |

**137**

| No. | Author | Nationality | Form | Literary Title | Date |
|---|---|---|---|---|---|
| 2484 | Kafka, Franz | Austrian | SS | Die Verwandlung<br>(Metamorphosis)<br>(aka: The Transformation) | 1912 |
| 2485 | Kaiser, Georg | German | P | Der Brand im Opernhaus<br>(Fire in the Opera House) | 1919 |
| 2486 | Kaiser, Georg | German | P | Der mutige Seefahrer | 1926 |
| 2487 | Kaiser, Georg | German | P | Der mutige Seefahrer | 1926 |
| 2488 | Kaiser, Georg | German | P | Zwei Krawatten | 1930 |
| 2489 | Kaleb, Vjekoslav | Yugoslav(Cro) | N | Divota prašine<br>(Glorious Dust) | 1954 |
| 2490 | Kantor, Mackinlay | American | N | Arouse and Beware | 1936 |
| 2491 | Kantor, Mackinlay | American | N | Gentle Annie<br>(aka: The Goss Boys) | 1942 |
| 2492 | Kantor, Mackinlay | American | N(V) | Glory For Me<br>{novel in verse} | 1945 |
| 2493 | Kantor, Mackinlay | American | N | God and My Country | 1954 |
| 2494 | Kantor, Mackinlay | American | SS | Gun Crazy | 1940 |
| 2495 | Kantor, Mackinlay | American | N | Happy Land | 1943 |
| 2496 | Kantor, Mackinlay | American | SS | Mountain Music | 1944(coll) |
| 2497 | Kantor, Mackinlay | American | N | The Romance of Rosy Ridge | 1937 |
| 2498 | Kantor, Mackinlay | American | N | The Voice of Bugle Ann | 1935 |
| 2499 | Kantor-Berg, Friedrich<br>(see: Torberg, Friedrich) | Austrian | N | | |
| 2500 | Karaslavov, Georgi | Bulgarian | N | Selkor<br>[Village correspondent] | 1933 |
| 2501 | Karaslavov, Georgi | Bulgarian | N | Snakha<br>[Daughter-in-law] | 1942 |
| 2502 | Karaslavov, Georgi | Bulgarian | N | Tango | 1948 |
| 2503 | Karaslavov, Georgi | Bulgarian | N | Tatul<br>[Thorn apple] | 1938 |
| 2504 | Karavelov, Lyuben | Bulgarian | N | Bălgari ot staro vreme | 1867 |
| 2505 | Karinthy Ferenc | Hungarian | N | Budapesti tavasz<br>(Spring Comes to Budapest) | 1953 |
| 2506 | Karinthy Ferenc | Hungarian | SS | Házszentelő<br>[House-warming] | 1977 |
| 2507 | Karinthy Ferenc | Hungarian | SS | Ifjuság, szerelem | 1957 |
| 2508 | Karinthy Frigyes | Hungarian | SS | Tanár úr, kérem!<br>(Please Sir!) | 1916 |
| 2509 | Karinthy Frigyes | Hungarian | N | Utazás a koponyám körül<br>(A Journey Round My Skull) | 1937 |
| 2510 | Kaschnitz, Marie-Luise | German | SS | Popp und Mingel | 1960 |
| 2511 | Kassák Lajos | Hungarian | N | Angyalföld<br>[Angel's land] | 1929 |
| 2512 | Kästner, Erich | German | N | Das doppelte Lottchen<br>(Lottie and Lisa) | 1949 |
| 2513 | Kästner, Erich | German | N | Das doppelte Lottchen | 1949 |
| 2514 | Kästner, Erich | German | N | Das doppelte Lottchen | 1949 |
| 2515 | Kästner, Erich | German | N | Drei Männer im Schnee<br>(Three Men in the Snow) | 1934 |
| 2516 | Kästner, Erich | German | N | Drei Männer im Schnee | 1934 |
| 2517 | Kästner, Erich | German | N | Drei Männer im Schnee | 1934 |
| 2518 | Kästner, Erich | German | N | Drei Männer im Schnee | 1934 |
| 2519 | Kästner, Erich | German | N | Emil und die Detektive<br>(Emil and the Detectives) | 1928 |
| 2520 | Kästner, Erich | German | N | Emil und die Detektive | 1928 |
| 2521 | Kästner, Erich | German | N | Emil und die Detektive | 1928 |
| 2522 | Kästner, Erich | German | N | Emil und die Detektive | 1928 |

| No | Film Title | Country of Production | Date | Director(s) | Duration of Film |
|----|-----------|----------------------|------|-------------|------------------|
| 2484 | **Förvandlingen** *(Metamorphosis)* | SWE | 1976(75) | Ivo Dvorák | 88 |
| 2485 | **Brand in der Oper** *(aka: Barcarole)* *(The Love Duet)* *(aka: Fire in the Opera)* | GER | 1930 | Carl Froelich | 83 |
| 2486 | **Der mutige Seefahrer** | GER | 1935 | Hans Deppe | 89 |
| 2487 | **The Ghost Comes Home** | USA | 1940 | William Thiele | 79 |
| 2488 | **Zwei Krawatten** | GER | 1930 | Felix Basch<br>Richard Weichert | 89 |
| 2489 | **Čudoviti prah** *(Glorious Dust)* | YUGO | 1975 | Milan Ljubić | 90 |
| 2490 | **The Man From Dakota** *(GB: Arouse and Beware)* | USA | 1940 | Leslie Fenton | 75 |
| 2491 | **Gentle Annie** | USA | 1944 | Andrew Marton | 80 |
| 2492 | **The Best Years of Our Lives** | USA | 1946 | William Wyler | 182 +V(159) |
| 2493 | **Follow Me, Boys!** | USA | 1966 | Norman Tokar | 131 +V |
| 2494 | **Gun Crazy** *(aka: Deadly Is the Female)* | USA | 1949 | Joseph H. Lewis | 87 |
| 2495 | **Happy Land** | USA | 1943 | Irving Pichel | 75 |
| 2496 | **Mountain Music** | USA | 1937 | Robert Florey | 76 |
| 2497 | **The Romance of Rosy Ridge** | USA | 1947 | Roy Rowland | 103 |
| 2498 | **The Voice of Bugle Ann** | USA | 1936 | Richard Thorpe | 70 |
| 2499 | | | | | |
| 2500 | **Selkor** | BULG | 1974 | Atanas Traikov | 87 |
| 2501 | **Snakha** | BULG | 1954 | Anton Marinovich | 113 |
| 2502 | **Tango** | BULG | 1969 | Vasil Mirchev | 78 |
| 2503 | **Tatul** | BULG | 1979 | Atanas Traikov | 91 |
| 2504 | **Bǎlgari ot staro vreme** *(Bulgarians of Olden Times)* | BULG | 1945 | Dimitǎr Minkov | 71 |
| 2505 | **Budapesti tavasz** *(Springtime in Budapest)* *(aka: Spring Comes to Budapest)* | HUNG | 1955 | Félix Máriássy | 98 |
| 2506 | **Gyertek el a névnapomra** | HUNG | 1984 | Zoltán Fábri | 122 |
| 2507 | **Bolond április** *(Summer Clouds)* | HUNG | 1957 | Zoltán Fábri | 84 |
| 2508 | **Tanár úr, kérem!** *(Professor, please...)* | HUNG | 1956 | Frigyes Mamcserov | 70 |
| 2509 | **Utazás a koponyám körül** *(A Journey Around My Skull)* *(aka: A Trip Around My Cranium)* | HUNG | 1971(70) | György Révész | 84 |
| 2510 | **Popp und Mingel** | GER | 1975 | Ula Stöckl | 53 |
| 2511 | **Az Angyalok földje** *(Land of Angels)* | HUNG | 1962 | György Révész | 98 |
| 2512 | **Das doppelte Lottchen** *(Two Times Lottie)* | GER | 1950 | Josef von Baky | 99 |
| 2513 | **Twice Upon a Time** | GB | 1953 | Emeric Pressburger | 75 |
| 2514 | **The Parent Trap** | USA | 1961 | David Swift | 129 +V |
| 2515 | **Stackars miljonärer** *[Poor millionaires]* | SWE | 1936 | Tancred Ibsen<br>Ragnar Arvedson | 99 |
| 2516 | **Paradise For Three** | USA | 1938 | Edward Buzzell | 75 |
| 2517 | **Drei Männer im Schnee** | AUST | 1955 | Kurt Hoffmann | 93 |
| 2518 | **Drei Männer im Schnee** | GER | 1973 | Alfred Vohrer | 92 |
| 2519 | **Emil und die Detektive** *(Emil and the Detectives)* | GER | 1931 | Gerhard Lamprecht | 74 |
| 2520 | **Emil and the Detectives** *(USA: Emil)* | GB | 1935 | Milton Rosmer | 70 |
| 2521 | **Emil und die Detektive** | GER | 1954 | Robert A. Stemmle | 95(90) |
| 2522 | **Emil and the Detectives** | USA | 1964 | Peter Tewksbury | 100 +V |

| No. | Author | Nationality | Form | Literary Title | Date |
|---|---|---|---|---|---|
| 2523 | **Kästner, Erich** | German | N | **Fabian. Die Geschicte eines Moralisten** *(Fabian; the Story of a Moralist)* | 1931 |
| 2524 | **Kästner, Erich** | German | N | **Das fliegende Klassenzimmer** *(The Flying Classroom)* | 1933 |
| 2525 | **Kästner, Erich** | German | N | **Das fliegende Klassenzimmer** | 1933 |
| 2526 | **Kästner, Erich** | German | N | **Georg und die Zwischenfälle** *(aka: Der kleine Grenzverkehr) (A Salzburg Comedy)* | 1938 |
| 2527 | **Kästner, Erich** | German | N | **Georg und die Zwischenfälle** | 1938 |
| 2528 | **Kästner, Erich** | German | SS | **Die Konferenz der Tiere** *(The Animals' Conference)* | 1949 |
| 2529 | **Kästner, Erich** | German | N | **Pünktchen und Anton** *(Annaluise and Anton)* | 1930 |
| 2530 | **Kästner, Erich** | German | N | **Die verschwundene Miniatur** *(The Missing Miniature; or, the Adventures of a Sensitive Butcher)* | 1935 |
| 2531 | **Kataev, Valentin** | Russian | N | **Beleyet parus odinokiy** *(Lonely White Sail) (aka: A White Sail Gleams)* | 1936 |
| 2532 | **Kataev, Valentin** | Russian | N | **Khutorok v stepi** *(The Small Farm in the Steppe) (aka: The Cottage in the Steppe)* | 1956 |
| 2533 | **Kataev, Valentin** | Russian | N | **Za vlast Sovetov** *[For the powers of the Soviets] (aka: Katacomby) (Catacombs)* | 1949(51) |
| 2534 | **Kaufman, George S.** | American | P | **The Butter-and-Egg Man** | 1926 |
| 2535 | **Kaufman, George S.** | American | P | **The Butter-and-Egg Man** | 1926 |
| 2536 | **Kaufman, George S.** | American | P | **The Butter-and-Egg Man** | 1926 |
| 2537 | **Kaufman, George S.** | American | P | **The Butter-and-Egg Man** | 1926 |
| 2538 | **Kaufman, George S.** | American | P | **The Butter-and-Egg Man** | 1926 |
| 2539 | **Kaufman, George S.; Connelly, Marc** | American | P | **Dulcy** | 1921 |
| 2540 | **Kaufman, George S.; Connelly, Marc** | American | P | **To The Ladies** | 1923 |
| 2541 | **Kaufman, George S.; Dayton, Katharine** | American | P | **First Lady** | 1935 |
| 2542 | **Kaufman, George S.; Ferber, Edna** | American | P | **Dinner at Eight** | 1932 |
| 2543 | **Kaufman, George S.; Ferber, Edna** | American | P | **The Royal Family** | 1928 |
| 2544 | **Kaufman, George S.; Hart, Moss** | American | P | **George Washington Slept Here** | 1941 |
| 2545 | **Kaufman, George S.; Hart, Moss** | American | P | **The Man Who Came to Dinner** | 1939 |
| 2546 | **Kaufman, George S.; Hart, Moss** | American | P | **Once in a Lifetime** | 1932 |
| 2547 | **Kaufman, George S.; Hart, Moss** | American | P | **You Can't Take It With You** | 1937 |
| 2548 | **Kaufman, George S.; Mankiewicz, Herman J.** | American | P | **The Good Fellow** | 1931 |
| 2549 | **Kaufman, George S.; Teichmann, Howard** | American | P | **The Solid Gold Cadillac** | 1954 |
| 2550 | **Kaufman, George S.** *(see also: Ferber, Edna)* | American | P | | |
| 2551 | **Kaufman, George S.** *(see also: Lardner, Ring)* | American | P | | |
| 2552 | **Kawabata Yasunari** | Japanese | SS | **Asakusa no shimai** | 1932(34) |
| 2553 | **Kawabata Yasunari** | Japanese | SS | **Izu no odoriko** *(The Izu Dancer) (aka: The Dancing Girl of Izu)* | 1925 |
| 2554 | **Kawabata Yasunari** | Japanese | SS | **Izu no odoriko** | 1925 |
| 2555 | **Kawabata Yasunari** | Japanese | N | **Izu no odoriko** | 1925 |

| No | Film Title | Country of Production | Date | Director(s) | Duration of Film |
|----|-----------|----------------------|------|-------------|------------------|
| 2523 | **Fabian** | GER | 1980 | **Wolf Gremm** | 116 |
| 2524 | **Das fliegende Klassenzimmer** | GER | 1954 | **Kurt Hoffmann** | 92 |
| 2525 | **Das fliegende Klassenzimmer** | GER | 1973 | **Werner Jacobs** | 92 |
| 2526 | **Der kleine Grenzverkehr** (Small Border Traffic) | GER | 1943 | **Hans Deppe** | 82 |
| 2527 | **Salzburger G'schichten** (Salzburg Tales) | GER | 1956 | **Kurt Hoffmann** | 91 |
| 2528 | **Die Konferenz der Tiere** {animation} | GER | 1969 | **Curt Linda** | 92(82) |
| 2529 | **Pünktchen und Anton** | GER/AUST | 1953 | **Thomas Engel** | 90 |
| 2530 | **Die verschwundene Miniatur** | GER | 1954 | **Karl Heinz Schroth** | 87 |
| 2531 | **Byeleyet parus odinky** (Lone White Sail) (aka: Lonely White Sail) | USSR | 1938 | **Vladimir Legoshin** | 92 |
| 2532 | **Khutorok v stepi** (The Cottage in the Steppe) (aka: Small Farm in the Steppe) | USSR | 1971 | **Boris Buneev** | 94 |
| 2533 | **Za vlast Sovetov** | USSR | 1956 | **Boris Buneev** | 99 |
| 2534 | **The Tenderfoot** | USA | 1932 | **Ray Enright** | 73 |
| 2535 | **Hello Sweetheart** | GB | 1935 | **Monty Banks** | 70 |
| 2536 | **Dance, Charlie, Dance** | USA | 1937 | **Frank McDonald** | 65 |
| 2537 | **An Angel From Texas** | USA | 1940 | **Ray Enright** | 69 |
| 2538 | **Three Sailors and a Girl** | USA | 1953 | **Roy Del Ruth** | 95 |
| 2539 | **Dulcy** | USA | 1940 | **S. Sylvan Simon** | 64 |
| 2540 | **Elmer and Elsie** | USA | 1934 | **Gilbert (Gil) Pratt** | 65 |
| 2541 | **First Lady** | USA | 1937 | **Stanley Logan** **Arthur Ripley** | 82 |
| 2542 | **Dinner at Eight** | USA | 1933 | **George Cukor** | 113 +V(107) |
| 2543 | **The Royal Family of Broadway** (GB: Theatre Royal) | USA | 1931 | **George Cukor** **Cyril Gardner** | 82 |
| 2544 | **George Washington Slept Here** | USA | 1942 | **William Keighley** | 93 |
| 2545 | **The Man Who Came to Dinner** | USA | 1941 | **William Keighley** | 112 |
| 2546 | **Once in a Lifetime** | USA | 1932 | **Russell Mack** | 75 |
| 2547 | **You Can't Take It With You** | USA | 1938 | **Frank Capra** | 126 +V(121) |
| 2548 | **Good Fellows** | USA | 1943 | **Jo Graham** | 70 |
| 2549 | **The Solid Gold Cadillac** | USA | 1956 | **Richard Quine** | 99 |
| 2550 | | | | | |
| 2551 | | | | | |
| 2552 | **Otome-gokoro sannin shimai** (Three Sisters With Maiden Hearts) | JAP | 1935 | **Mikio Naruse** | 75 |
| 2553 | **Izu no odoriko** (Dancing Girls of Izu) (aka: Dancer of Izu) | JAP | 1933 | **Heinosuke Gosho** | 93 |
| 2554 | **Izu no odoriko** (Dancing Girls of Izu) (aka: Dancing Girl) | JAP | 1961(60) | **Yoshirō Kawazu** | 88 |
| 2555 | **Izu no odoriko** | JAP | 1967 | **Hideo Onchi** | 85 |

**141**

| No. | Author | Nationality | Form | Literary Title | Date |
|-----|--------|-------------|------|----------------|------|
| 2556 | **Kawabata Yasunari** | Japanese | N | **Koto** | 1962 |
| 2557 | **Kawabata Yasunari** | Japanese | SS | **Maihime** | 1951 |
| 2558 | **Kawabata Yasunari** | Japanese | N | **Nemureru bijo** <br> (House of the Sleeping Beauties) | 1960-61 |
| 2559 | **Kawabata Yasunari** | Japanese | N | **Utsukushisa to kanashim' to** <br> (Beauty and Sadness) | 1961-64 |
| 2560 | **Kawabata Yasunari** | Japanese | N | **Yama-no oto** <br> (The Sound of the Mountain) | 1954 |
| 2561 | **Kawabata Yasunari** | Japanese | N | **Yukiguni** <br> (Snow Country) | 1935 |
| 2562 | **Kazakevich, Emmanuil** | Russian | N | **Vesna na Odere** <br> (Spring on the Oder) | 1950 |
| 2563 | **Kazantzakis, Nikos** | Greek | N | **O Christos Xanastavronetai** <br> (Christ Recrucified) <br> (aka: The Greek Passion) | 1948 |
| 2564 | **Kazantzakis, Nikos** | Greek | N | **O teleftaios peirasmos** <br> (The Last Temptation) | 1955 |
| 2565 | **Kazantzakis, Nikos** | Greek | N | **Vios kai politeia tou Alexi Zobra** <br> (Zorba the Greek) | 1946 |
| 2566 | **Keane, John B.** | Irish | P | **The Field** | 1966 |
| 2567 | **Keller, Gottfried** | Swiss(Ger) | SS | **Das Fähnlein der sieben Aufrechten** <br> (The Company of the Upright Seven) | 1861(78) |
| 2568 | **Keller, Gottfried** | Swiss | SS | **Kleider machen Leute** <br> (Clothes Make the Man) | 1873 |
| 2569 | **Keller, Gottfried** | Swiss | SS | **Der Landvogt von Griefensee** | 1877(78) |
| 2570 | **Keller, Gottfried** | Swiss | SS | **Die mißbrauchten Liebesbriefe** <br> (The Abused Love Letters) | 1873 |
| 2571 | **Keller, Gottfried** | Swiss | SS | **Die mißbrauchten Liebesbriefe** | 1873 |
| 2572 | **Keller, Gottfried** | Swiss | SS | **Regine** | 1872 |
| 2573 | **Keller, Gottfried** | Swiss | SS | **Regine** | 1872 |
| 2574 | **Keller, Gottfried** | Swiss | SS | **Romeo und Julia auf dem Dorfe** <br> (A Village Romeo and Juliet) | 1876 |
| 2575 | **Keller, Gottfried** | Swiss | SS | **Romeo und Julia auf dem Dorfe** | 1876 |
| 2576 | **Keller, Gottfried** | Swiss | SS | **Romeo und Julia auf dem Dorfe** | 1876 |
| 2577 | **Keller, Gottfried** | Swiss | SS | **Romeo und Julia auf dem Dorfe** | 1876 |
| 2578 | **Kember, Paul** | British | P | **Not Quite Jerusalem** | 1982 |
| 2579 | **Kempinski, Tom** | British | P | **Duet For One** | 1981 |
| 2580 | **Keneally, Thomas** | Australian | N | **The Chant of Jimmie Blacksmith** | 1972 |
| 2581 | **Kennaway, James Pebles Ewing** | British(Scot) | N | **Tunes of Glory** | 1956 |
| 2582 | **Kennedy, Margaret** | British | N | **The Constant Nymph** | 1924 |
| 2583 | **Kennedy, Margaret** | British | N | **The Constant Nymph** | 1924 |
| 2584 | **Kennedy, Margaret** | British | P | **Escape Me Never** | 1934 |
| 2585 | **Kennedy, Margaret** | British | P | **Escape Me Never** | 1934 |
| 2586 | **Kerouac, Jack** | American | N | **The Subterraneans** | 1958 |
| 2587 | **Kertész Ákos** | Hungarian | N | **Makra** | 1971 |
| 2588 | **Kertész Ákos** | Hungarian | N | **Sikátor** <br> [Alley] | 1965 |
| 2589 | **Kesey, Ken** | American | N | **One Flew Over the Cuckoo's Nest** | 1962 |
| 2590 | **Kesey, Ken** | American | N | **Sometimes a Great Notion** | 1966 |
| 2591 | **Kessel, Joseph** | French | N | **Les amants du Tage** | 1954 |
| 2592 | **Kessel, Joseph** | French | N | **L'armée des ombres** <br> (Army of Shadows) | 1943 |

| No | Film Title | Country of Production | Date | Director(s) | Duration of Film |
|---|---|---|---|---|---|
| 2556 | **Koto** <br>(Twin Sisters of Kyoto) <br>(aka: The Old Capital) | JAP | 1963 | Noboru Nakamura | 107 |
| 2557 | **Maihime** <br>(Dancing Girl) <br>(aka: The Dancer) | JAP | 1951 | Mikio Naruse | 85 |
| 2558 | **Nemureru bijo** <br>(The House of the Sleeping Virgins) <br>(aka: Sleeping Beauty) | JAP | 1968 | Kōzaburō Yoshimura | 96 |
| 2559 | **Utsukushisa to kanashimi to** <br>(With Beauty and Sorrow) | JAP | 1965 | Masahiro Shinoda | 106 |
| 2560 | **Yama no oto** <br>(Sound of the Mountain) <br>(aka: Sounds From the Mountains) | JAP | 1954 | Mikio Naruse | 94 |
| 2561 | **Yukiguni** <br>(Snow Country) | JAP | 1958(57) | Shirō Toyoda | 134 |
| 2562 | **Vesna na Odere** | USSR | 1968 | Leon Saakov | 102 |
| 2563 | **Celui qui doit mourir** <br>(IT: Colui che deve morire) <br>(He Who Must Die) | FR/IT | 1957 | Jules Dassin | 126(131) |
| 2564 | **The Last Temptation of Christ** | USA/CAN | 1988 | Martin Scorsese | 163 +V(157) |
| 2565 | **Zorba the Greek** | USA/GR | 1965(64) | Michael Cacoyannis | 141 +V |
| 2566 | **The Field** | GB | 1990 | Jim Sheridan | 110 +V |
| 2567 | **Hermine und die sieben Aufrechten** | GER | 1935 | Frank Wisbar | 111 |
| 2568 | **Kleider machen Leute** <br>(Clothes Make People) | GER | 1940 | Helmut Käutner | 106 |
| 2569 | **Der Landvogt von Griefensee** <br>(The Bailiff of Griefensee) | GER/SWITZ | 1979 | Wilfried Bolliger | 100 |
| 2570 | **Die mißbrauchten Liebesbriefe** | SWITZ | 1940 | Leopold Lindtberg | 92(117) |
| 2571 | **Die mißbrauchten Liebesbriefe** <br>(The Abused Love Letters) | GER | 1969 | Hans Dieter Schwarze | 91 |
| 2572 | **Regine** | GER | 1935 | Erich Waschneck | 95 |
| 2573 | **Regine** | GER | 1956 | Harald Braun | 105 |
| 2574 | **Romeo und Julia auf dem Dorfe** | SWITZ | 1941 | Valérian Schmidely <br>Hans Trommer | 94(102) |
| 2575 | **Espoir** | FR | 1941 | Willy Rozier | 92 |
| 2576 | **Jungenliebe** <br>(aka: Übers Jahr, wenn die Kornblumen blühen) | GER | 1947(44) | Eduard von Borsody | 88 |
| 2577 | **Romeo und Julia auf dem Dorfe** | GDR | 1984 | Siegfried Kühn | 91 |
| 2578 | **Not Quite Jerusalem** <br>(aka: Not Quite Paradise) | GB | 1984 | Lewis Gilbert | 114 +V(110) |
| 2579 | **Duet For One** | USA | 1986 | Andrei Mikhalkov-Konchalovsky | 107 +V |
| 2580 | **The Chant of Jimmie Blacksmith** | AUSTL | 1978 | Fred Schepisi | 122 +V |
| 2581 | **Tunes of Glory** | GB | 1960 | Ronald Neame | 106 +V |
| 2582 | **The Constant Nymph** | USA | 1933 | Basil Dean | 98 |
| 2583 | **The Constant Nymph** | USA | 1943 | Edmund Goulding | 112 |
| 2584 | **Escape Me Never** | GB | 1935 | Paul Czinner | 95 |
| 2585 | **Escape Me Never** | USA | 1947 | Peter Godfrey | 104 |
| 2586 | **The Subterraneans** | USA | 1960 | Ranald MacDougall | 89 |
| 2587 | **Makra** | HUNG | 1974(72) | Tamás Rényi | 104 |
| 2588 | **Sikátor** <br>(Deadlock) | HUNG | 1966 | Tamás Rényi | 89 |
| 2589 | **One Flew Over the Cuckoo's Nest** | USA | 1975 | Miloš Forman | 134 +V |
| 2590 | **Sometimes a Great Notion** <br>(GB: Never Give an Inch) | USA | 1971 | Paul Newman | 114 +V(110) |
| 2591 | **Les amants du Tage** <br>(aka: Lovers of Lisbon) <br>(USA: Lovers' Net) | FR | 1955(54) | Henri Verneuil | 123(112) |
| 2592 | **L'armée des ombres** <br>(IT: L'armata degli eroi) <br>(Army in the Shadows) <br>(aka: The Shadow Army) | FR/IT | 1969 | Jean-Pierre Melville | 143(107) |

**143**

| No. | Author | Nationality | Form | Literary Title | Date |
|-----|--------|-------------|------|----------------|------|
| 2593 | **Kessel, Joseph** | French | N | **Le bataillon du ciel** | 1947 |
| 2594 | **Kessel, Joseph** | French | N | **Belle de jour** | 1928 |
| 2595 | **Kessel, Joseph** | French | N | **Les cavaliers**<br>(The Horsemen) | 1967 |
| 2596 | **Kessel, Joseph** | French | N | **Le coup de grace** | 1931 |
| 2597 | **Kessel, Joseph** | French | N | **L'équipage**<br>[The crew] | 1923 |
| 2598 | **Kessel, Joseph** | French | N | **L'équipage** | 1923 |
| 2599 | **Kessel, Joseph** | French | N | **Le lion**<br>(The Lion) | 1958 |
| 2600 | **Kessel, Joseph** | French | N | **Nuits des princes**<br>(Princes of the Night) | 1927 |
| 2601 | **Kessel, Joseph** | French | N | **Nuits des princes** | 1927 |
| 2602 | **Khaitov, Nikolal**<br>(see: Haitov, Nikolai) | Bulgarian | SS | | |
| 2603 | **Kielland, Alexander** | Norwegian | N | **Jacob** | 1891 |
| 2604 | **Kielland, Alexander** | Norwegian | N | **Jacob** | 1891 |
| 2605 | **Kielland, Alexander** | Norwegian | SS | **Sankt Hans fest**<br>[The feast of St. John] | 1887 |
| 2606 | **Kielland, Axel** | Norwegian | P | **Herren og hans tjenere**<br>(The Lord and His Servants) | 1955 |
| 2607 | **Kikuchi Kan** | Japanese | N | **Kafuku** | 1936-37 |
| 2608 | **Kikuchi Kan** | Japanese | P | **Toki no ujigami** | 1924 |
| 2609 | **Kingsley, Charles** | British | N | **The Water-Babies**<br>(aka: The Water-Babies: a fairy tale<br>for a land-baby) | 1863 |
| 2610 | **Kingsley, Sidney** | American | P | **Dead End** | 1935 |
| 2611 | **Kingsley, Sidney** | American | P | **Detective Story** | 1949 |
| 2612 | **Kingsley, Sidney** | American | P | **Men in White** | 1933 |
| 2613 | **Kipling, Rudyard** | British | N | **Captains Courageous** | 1897 |
| 2614 | **Kipling, Rudyard** | British | V | **Gunga Din** | 1890 |
| 2615 | **Kipling, Rudyard** | British | V | **His Apologies** | 1932 |
| 2616 | **Kipling, Rudyard** | British | N | **Kim** | 1901 |
| 2617 | **Kipling, Rudyard** | British | SS | **The King's Ankus** | 1895 |
| 2618 | **Kipling, Rudyard** | British | N | **The Light that Failed** | 1890 |
| 2619 | **Kipling, Rudyard** | British | SS | **The Man Who Would Be King** | 1888 |
| 2620 | **Kipling, Rudyard** | British | SS | **Soldiers Three** | 1888 |
| 2621 | **Kipling, Rudyard** | British | SS | **Toomai of the Elephants** | 1894 |
| 2622 | **Kipling, Rudyard** | British | SS | **Wee Willie Winkie** | 1888 |
| 2623 | **Kishida Kunio** | Japanese | N | **Izumi** | 1939 |
| 2624 | **Kishida Kunio** | Japanese | P | **Shu-u** | 1926 |
| 2625 | **Kishida Kunio** | Japanese | N | **Zenma** | 1951 |
| 2626 | **Kivi, Aleksis**<br>(Aleksis Stenvall) | Finnish | P | **Kihlaus** | 1866 |
| 2627 | **Kivi, Aleksis** | Finnish | P | **Nummisuutarit** | 1864 |
| 2628 | **Kivi, Aleksis** | Finnish | P | **Nummisuutarit** | 1864 |
| 2629 | **Kivi, Aleksis** | Finnish | N | **Seitsemän veljestä**<br>(Seven Brothers) | 1870 |
| 2630 | **Kleist, Heinrich von** | German | P | **Amphitryon** | 1807 |
| 2631 | **Kleist, Heinrich von** | German | P | **Amphitryon** | 1807 |
| 2632 | **Kleist, Heinrich von** | German | SS | **Der Findling**<br>(The Foundling) | 1811 |

| No | Film Title | Country of Production | Date | Director(s) | Duration of Film |
|---|---|---|---|---|---|
| 2593 | Le bataillon du ciel | FR | 1946(45) | Alexandre Esway | 100 |
| 2594 | Belle de jour<br>(IT: Bella di giorno) | FR/IT | 1967 | Luis Buñuel | 100 |
| 2595 | The Horsemen | USA | 1970 | John Frankenheimer | 109 |
| 2596 | Sirocco | USA | 1951 | Curtis Bernhardt | 98 |
| 2597 | L'équipage<br>(Flight Into Darkness) | FR | 1935 | Anatole Litvak | 111 |
| 2598 | The Woman I Love | USA | 1937 | Anatole Litvak | 85 |
| 2599 | The Lion | GB | 1962 | Jack Cardiff | 96 |
| 2600 | Nuit des prince | FR | 1938(37) | Wladimir von Strijewsky | 102 |
| 2601<br>2602 | Ab Mitternacht | FR/GER | 1938 | Carl Hoffmann | 78 |
| 2603 | Torres Snørtevold | NOR | 1940 | Tancred Ibsen | 102 |
| 2604 | Jacobs stege<br>(Jacob's Ladder) | SWE | 1942 | Gustaf Molander | 104 |
| 2605 | Sankt Hans fest | NOR | 1947 | Toralf Sandø | 88 |
| 2606 | Herren og hans tjenere<br>(The Master and His Servants) | NOR | 1959 | Arne Skouen | 84 |
| 2607 | Kafuku<br>(Learn From Experience) | JAP | 1937 | Mikio Naruse | Pt.1, 90<br>Pt.2, 90 |
| 2608 | Toki no ujigami<br>(The Man of the Moment) | JAP | 1932 | Kenji Mizoguchi | 60 |
| 2609 | The Water Babies<br>{live-action + animation} | GB/POL | 1978 | Lionel Jeffries | 92<br>+V(88) |
| 2610 | Dead End<br>(aka: Dead End: Cradle of Crime) | USA | 1937 | William Wyler | 92<br>+V(88) |
| 2611 | Detective Story | USA | 1951 | William Wyler | 103 |
| 2612 | Men in White | USA | 1934 | Richard Boleslavsky | 80 |
| 2613 | Captains Courageous | USA | 1937 | Victor Fleming | 116 +V |
| 2614 | Gunga Din | USA | 1939 | George Stevens | 114 |
| 2615 | His Apologies | GB | 1935 | Widgey R. Newman | 18 |
| 2616 | Kim | USA | 1950 | Victor Saville | 112 |
| 2617 | Jungle Book<br>(aka: Rudyard Kipling's Jungle Book) | USA | 1942 | Zoltan Korda | 115<br>+V(109) |
| 2618 | The Light that Failed | USA | 1939 | William A. Wellman | 97 |
| 2619 | The Man Who Would Be King | GB/USA | 1975 | John Huston | 129 +V |
| 2620 | Soldiers Three | USA | 1951 | Tay Garnett | 87 |
| 2621 | Elephant Boy | GB | 1937 | Robert Flaherty<br>Zoltan Korda | 84<br>+V(76) |
| 2622 | Wee Willie Winkie | USA | 1937 | John Ford | 99 |
| 2623 | Izumi<br>(The Spring)<br>(aka: The Fountainhead) | JAP | 1956 | Masaki Kobayashi | 129 |
| 2624 | Shu-u<br>(Sudden Rain) | JAP | 1956 | Mikio Naruse | 91 |
| 2625 | Zenma<br>(The Good Fairy)<br>(aka: The Good Demon) | JAP | 1951 | Keisuke Kinoshita | 108 |
| 2626 | Kihlaus<br>(The Betrothal) | FIN | 1955 | Erik Blomberg | 78 |
| 2627 | Nummisuutarit<br>(The Village Shoemakers) | FIN | 1938 | Wilho Ilmari | 117 |
| 2628 | Nummisuutarit<br>(The Village Shoemakers) | FIN | 1957 | Valentin Vaala | 93 |
| 2629 | Seitsemän veljestä<br>(Seven Brothers) | FIN | 1939 | Wilho Ilmari | 108 |
| 2630 | Amphitryon<br>(aka: Aus den Wolken kommt das Glück) | GER | 1935 | Reinhold Schünzel | 93 |
| 2631 | Amphitryon | GER | 1981 | Michael de Groot | 28 |
| 2632 | Der Findling<br>(The Foundling) | GER | 1967(66) | George Moorse | 74 |

| No. | Author | Nationality | Form | Literary Title | Date |
|-----|--------|-------------|------|----------------|------|
| 2633 | Kleist, Heinrich von | German | SS | Die Marquise von O-- <br> (The Marquise of O--) | 1810 |
| 2634 | Kleist, Heinrich von | German | SS | Michael Kohlhaas | 1810 |
| 2635 | Kleist, Heinrich von | German | P | Penthesilea | 1808 |
| 2636 | Kleist, Heinrich von | German | SS | Die Verlobung von San Domingo <br> (The Engagement in Santo Domingo) | 1811 |
| 2637 | Kleist, Heinrich von | German | P | Der zerbrochene Krug <br> (The Broken Jug) | 1811 |
| 2638 | Kleist, Heinrich von | German | P | Der zerbrochene Krug | 1811 |
| 2639 | Klitgaard, Mogens | Danish | N | Elly Petersen | 1941 |
| 2640 | Kluge, Alexander | German | SS | Anita G | 1962 |
| 2641 | Kluge, Kurt | German | N | Die Zaubergeige | 1940 |
| 2642 | Knebel, Fletcher; <br> Bailey, Charles W. | American | N | Seven Days in May | 1962 |
| 2643 | Knudsen, Jakob | Danish | N | Den gamle Præst <br> [The old clergyman] | 1899 |
| 2644 | Kobayashi Takiji | Japanese | N | Kani-kōsen <br> (The Cannery Boat) | 1929 |
| 2645 | Kober, Arthur | American | P | Having Wonderful Time | 1937 |
| 2646 | Koch, Christopher <br> (see: Koch, C. J.) | Australian | N | | |
| 2647 | Koch, C. J. <br> (Christopher Koch) | Australian | N | The Year of Living Dangerously | 1978 |
| 2648 | Kolar, Slavko | Yugoslav(Cro) | P | Svoga tela gospodar <br> [Master of his own body] | 1942 |
| 2649 | Kolozsvári Grandpierre Emil | Hungarian | N | A csillagszemű | 1953 |
| 2650 | Kong Shangren | Chinese | P | Tao hua shan <br> [Peach blossom fan] | c.1690 |
| 2651 | Konopnicka, Maria | Polish | SS | O krasnoludkach i o sierotce Marysi <br> (The Brownie Scouts) | 1896 |
| 2652 | Kon Tōkō | Japanese | N | Tento gekijō | 1957 |
| 2653 | Kopit, Arthur | American | P | Indians | 1969 |
| 2654 | Kopit, Arthur | American | P | Oh Dad, Poor Dad, Mamma's Hung You in the Closet and I'm Feelin' So Sad | 1960 |
| 2655 | Korniychuk, Aleksander | Russian(Ukr) | P | Bogdan Khmel'nyts'ky | 1939 |
| 2656 | Korniychuk, Aleksander | Russian | P | Front <br> (The Front) | 1942 |
| 2657 | Korniychuk, Aleksander | Russian | P | Partizany v stepyakh Ukrayiny <br> (Guerillas of the Ukrainian Steppes) | 1941 |
| 2658 | Korniychuk, Aleksander | Russian | P | Stranitsa dnevnika <br> [Pages from a diary] | 1965 |
| 2659 | Korniychuk, Aleksander | Russian | P | V stepyakh Ukrayiny <br> [In the steppes of the Ukraine] | 1941 |
| 2660 | Kosinski, Jerzy | American | N | Being There | 1970 |
| 2661 | Kostov, Stefan | Bulgarian | P | Golemanov | 1928 |
| 2662 | Kosztolányi Dezső | Hungarian | N | Aranysárkány | 1925 |
| 2663 | Kosztolányi Dezső | Hungarian | N | Édes Anna <br> (Wonder Maid) | 1926 |
| 2664 | Kosztolányi Dezső | Hungarian | SS | A kulcs <br> [The key] + <br> Fűrdés <br> [Bathing] + <br> Kinai kancsó <br> [Chinese vase] | 1943 |
| 2665 | Kosztolányi Dezső | Hungarian | N | Pacsirta | 1924 |

| No | Film Title | Country of Production | Date | Director(s) | Duration of Film |
|----|-----------|----------------------|------|-------------|------------------|
| 2633 | **Die Marquise von O...** (FR: La Marquise d'O) (The Marquise von O...) | GER/FR | 1976 | **Eric Rohmer** | 107 |
| 2634 | **Michael Kohlhaas - der Rebell** (aka: Michael Kohlhaas) | GER | 1969(68) | **Volker Schlöndorff** | 100(95) |
| 2635 | **Heinrich Penthesilea von Kleist** (aka: Träumereien über eine Inszenierung) | GER | 1983(82) | **Hans Neuenfels** | 144 |
| 2636 | **San Domingo** | GER | 1970 | **Hans-Jürgen Syberberg** | 138(128) |
| 2637 | **Der zerbrochene Krug** (The Broken Jug) | GER | 1937 | **Gustav Ucicky** | 85 +V |
| 2638 | **Jungfer, Sie gefällt mir** [The maid pleases me] | GDR | 1969 | **Günther Reisch** | 104 |
| 2639 | **Elly Petersen** | DEN | 1944 | **Alice O'Fredericks Jon Iversen** | 104 |
| 2640 | **Abschied von gestern** (Yesterday Girl) | GER | 1966 | **Alexander Kluge** | 88 |
| 2641 | **Die Zaubergeige** | GER | 1944 | **Herbert Maisch** | 103 |
| 2642 | **Seven Days in May** | USA | 1964(63) | **John Frankenheimer** | 118 |
| 2643 | **Den gamle Præst** | DEN | 1939 | **Jon Iversen** | 86 |
| 2644 | **Kanikōsen** (The Crab-Canning Ship) | JAP | 1953 | **Sō Yamamura** | 112 |
| 2645 2646 | **Having Wonderful Time** | USA | 1938 | **Alfred Santell** | 71 |
| 2647 | **The Year of Living Dangerously** | AUSTL | 1983 | **Peter Weir** | 110 +V |
| 2648 | **Svoga tela gospodar** | YUGO | 1957 | **Fedor Hanžeković** | 109 |
| 2649 | **A csillagszemű** (Starry-Eye) | HUNG | 1977 | **Miklós Markos** | 94 |
| 2650 | **Li xiangjun** [Tragedy of a patriot courtesan] | CHN | 1940 | **Wu Cun** | 98 |
| 2651 | **Marysia i krasnoludki** (Orphan Mary and the Dwarfs) | POL | 1961(60) | **Jerzy Szeski Konrad Paradowski** | 79 |
| 2652 | **Nusumareta yokujō** (Stolen Desire) | JAP | 1958 | **Shōhei Imamura** | 92 |
| 2653 | **Buffalo Bill and the Indians, or Sitting Bull's History Lesson** (aka: Buffalo Bill) | USA | 1976 | **Robert Altman** | 135 +V(123) |
| 2654 | **Oh Dad, Poor Dad, Mamma's Hung You in the Closet and I'm Feeling So Sad** | USA | 1966(65) | **Richard Quine** | 86 |
| 2655 | **Bogdan Khmelnitskii** | USSR | 1941 | **Igor Savchenko** | 114 |
| 2656 | **Front** (The Front) | USSR | 1943 | **Georgi Vasiliev Sergei Vasiliev** | 116 |
| 2657 | **Partizany v stepyakh Ukrayiny** | USSR | 1942 | **Igor Savchenko** | 78 |
| 2658 | **A tepyer sudi...** [And now pass judgement] | USSR | 1967 | **Vladimir Dovgan** | 92 |
| 2659 | **V stepyakh Ukrayiny** | USSR | 1952 | **Timofiéi Lievtchouk** | 108 |
| 2660 | **Being There** | USA | 1979 | **Hal Ashby** | 130 +V |
| 2661 | **Golemanov** | BULG | 1958 | **Kiril Ilinchev** | 82 |
| 2662 | **Aranysárkány** (The Golden Kite) | HUNG | 1966 | **László Ranódy** | 93 |
| 2663 | **Édes Anna** (aka: Anna) | HUNG | 1958 | **Zoltán Fábri** | 87 |
| 2664 | **Színes tintákról álmodom** (Colours) | HUNG | 1980 | **László Ranódy** | 91 |
| 2665 | **Pacsirta** (Skylark) | HUNG | 1964 | **László Ranódy** | 106 |

| No. | Author | Nationality | Form | Literary Title | Date |
|-----|--------|-------------|------|----------------|------|
| 2666 | **Krag, Vilhelm** | Norwegian | P | **Baldevins bryllup** <br> *[Baldevin's wedding]* | 1900 |
| 2667 | **Kraszewski, Jószef Ignacy** | Polish | N | **Hrabina Cosel** <br> *(The Countess Cosel)* | 1874 |
| 2668 | **Kristensen, Tom** | Danish | N | **Hærværk** <br> *(Havoc)* | 1930 |
| 2669 | **Krleža, Miroslav** | Yugoslav(Cro) | SS | **Cvrćak pod vodopadom** <br> *(The Cricket Beneath the Waterfall)* | 1937 |
| 2670 | **Krleža, Miroslav** | Yugoslav | P | **Vučjak** | 1925 |
| 2671 | **Kroetz, Franz Xaver** | German | P | **Wildwechsel** <br> *[Deer crossing]* | 1968 |
| 2672 | **Krog, Helge** | Norwegian | P | **På solsiden** <br> *(On Life's Sunny Side)* | 1927 |
| 2673 | **Krúdy Gyula** | Hungarian | N | **Szindbád ifjúsága** <br> *[Sindbad's youth]* + <br> **Szindbád utazásai** <br> *[Sindbad's voyages]* | 1911+ <br> 1912 |
| 2674 | **Krusenstjerna, Agnes von** | Swedish | N | **Fröknarna von Pahlen** <br> *[The Misses von Pahlen]* | 1930-35 |
| 2675 | **Kuan Han-ch'ing** <br> *(see: Guan Hanqing)* | Chinese | P | | |
| 2676 | **Kubin, Alfred** | Austrian | N | **Die andere Seite** <br> *(The Other Side)* | 1908 |
| 2677 | **Ku Hua** <br> *(see: Gu Hua)* | Chinese | N | | |
| 2678 | **Kuncewiczowa, Maria** | Polish | N | **Cudzoziemka** <br> *(The Stranger)* | 1935(36) |
| 2679 | **Kundera, Milan** | Czech | SS | **Já, truchlivý bůh** <br> *[I the sad god]* | 1963 |
| 2680 | **Kundera, Milan** | Czech | SS | **Nikdo se nebude smát** <br> *(Nobody Will Laugh)* | 1963 |
| 2681 | **Kundera, Milan** | Czech | N | **Wesnesitelná lehkost byti** <br> *(The Unbearable Lightness of Being)* | 1985 |
| 2682 | **Kundera, Milan** | Czech | N | **Žert** <br> *(The Joke)* | 1967 |
| 2683 | **Kuprin, Aleksander Ivanovich** | Russian | SS | **Granatovyi braslet** <br> *(The Garnet Bracelet)* <br> *(aka: The Bracelet of Garnets)* | 1911 |
| 2684 | **Kuprin, Aleksander Ivanovich** | Russian | SS | **Oleissa** <br> *(aka: Olesja)* | 1898 |
| 2685 | **Kuprin, Aleksander Ivanovich** | Russian | SS | **Poyedinok** <br> *(The Duel)* | 1905 |
| 2686 | **Labiche, Eugène;** <br> **Delacour, A.** | French | P | **La cagnotte** <br> *(Three Cheers For Paris)* | 1864 |
| 2687 | **Labiche, Eugène;** <br> **Marc-Michel** | French | P | **Un chapeau de paille d'Italie** <br> *(An Italian Straw Hat)* | 1847 |
| 2688 | **Labiche, Eugène;** <br> **Marc-Michel** | French | P | **Un chapeau de paille d'Italie** | 1847 |
| 2689 | **Labiche, Eugène;** <br> **Marc-Michel** | French | P | **Un chapeau de paille d'Italie** | 1847 |
| 2690 | **Labiche, Eugène;** <br> **Marc-Michel** | French | P | **Les deux timides** <br> *(The Two Cowards)* | 1860 |
| 2691 | **Labiche, Eugène;** <br> **Martin, Eduard** | French | P | **Le voyage de Monsieur Perrichon** <br> *(Monsieur Perrichon's Holiday)* <br> *(aka: Mr Perrichon Goes Abroad)* | 1860 |
| 2692 | **Labiche, Eugène;** <br> **Monnier, A.;** <br> **Martin, Eduard** | French | P | **L'affaire de la rue de Lourcine** | 1857 |
| 2693 | **Labiche, Eugène;** <br> **Marc-Michel;** <br> **Martin, Eduard** | French | P | **La poudre aux yeux** <br> *(Throwing Dust in People's Eyes)* | 1861 |
| 2694 | **Laclos, Choderlos de** | French | N | **Les liaisons dangereuses** <br> *(Dangerous Liaisons)* <br> *(aka: Dangerous Acquaintances)* | 1782 |
| 2695 | **Laclos, Choderlos de** | French | N | **Les liaisons dangereuses** | 1782 |

| No | Film Title | Country of Production | Date | Director(s) | Duration of Film |
|---|---|---|---|---|---|
| 2666 | **Baldevins bröllop** | SWE | 1938 | **Gideon Wahlberg** **Emil A. Pehrsson** | 104 |
| 2667 | **Hrabina Cosel** (Countess Cosel) | POL | 1968 | **Jerzy Antczak** | 152(125) |
| 2668 | **Hærværk** | DEN | 1977 | **Ole Roos** | 132 |
| 2669 | **Put u raj** (Way to Paradise) | YUGO | 1970 | **Mario Fanelli** | 90 |
| 2670 | **Horvatov izbor** (Horvat's Choice) | YUGO | 1985 | **Eduard Galić** | 113 |
| 2671 | **Wildwechsel** (Wild Game) (aka: Jailbait) | GER | 1972 | **R. W. Fassbinder** | 102 |
| 2672 | **På solsiden** | NOR | 1956 | **Edith Carlmar** | 81 |
| 2673 | **Szindbád** (Sindbad) | HUNG | 1972(71) | **Zoltán Huszárik** | 98 |
| 2674 | **Älskande par** (Loving Couples) | SWE | 1964 | **Mai Zetterling** | 118 |
| 2675 | | | | | |
| 2676 | **Traumstadt** | GER | 1973 | **Johannes Schaaf** | 124 |
| 2677 | | | | | |
| 2678 | **Cudzoziemka** | POL | 1986 | **Ryszard Ber** | 105 |
| 2679 | **Já, truchlivý bůh** | CZ | 1969 | **Antonín Kachlík** | 85 |
| 2680 | **Nikdo se nebude smát** (Nobody Will Laugh) (aka: Nobody Gets the Last Laugh) | CZ | 1965 | **Hynek Bočan** | 80 |
| 2681 | **The Unbearable Lightness of Being** | USA | 1987 | **Philip Kaufman** | 172 +V(165) |
| 2682 | **Žert** (The Joke) | CZ | 1969 | **Jaromil Jireš** | 81 |
| 2683 | **Granatovyy braslet** (The Garnet Bracelet) | USSR | 1965 | **Abram Room** | 94 |
| 2684 | **La sorcière** (SWE: Häxan) (The Sorcerers) | FR/SWE | 1956(55) | **André Michel** | 97 |
| 2685 | **Shurochka** | USSR | 1982 | **Iosif Heifitz** | 98 |
| 2686 | **Trois jours de bringue à Paris** | FR | 1954(53) | **Émile Couzinet** | 84 |
| 2687 | **Der Florentiner Hut** [The florentine hat] | GER | 1939 | **Wolfgang Liebeneiner** | 91 |
| 2688 | **Un chapeau de paille d'Italie** | FR | 1944(40) | **Maurice Cammage** | 85 |
| 2689 | **Slaměný klobouk** | CZ | 1971 | **Oldřich Lipský** | 88 |
| 2690 | **Les deux timides** (aka: Jeunes timides) | FR | 1942 | **Yves Allégret** (as: Yves Champlain) | 83 |
| 2691 | **Le voyage de Monsieur Perrichon** | FR | 1934 | **Jean Tarride** | 90 |
| 2692 | **L'affaire de la rue de Lourcine** | FR | 1933(30) | **Marcel Dumont** | 45 |
| 2693 | **Huan tian xi di** [Hilarity] | CHN | 1949 | **Zheng Xiaoqiu** | 90 |
| 2694 | **Les liaisons dangereuses** | FR | 1959 | **Roger Vadim** | 106 |
| 2695 | **Une femme fidèle** (When a Woman in Love) | FR | 1976 | **Roger Vadim** | 90(86) +V(81) |

| No. | Author | Nationality | Form | Literary Title | Date |
|-----|--------|-------------|------|----------------|------|
| 2696 | Laclos, Choderlos de | French | N | Les liaisons dangereuses (Christopher Hampton's stage adaptation) | 1782 |
| 2697 | Laclos, Choderlos de | French | N | Les liaisons dangereuses | 1782 |
| 2698 | La Farge, Oliver | American | N | Laughing Boy | 1929 |
| 2699 | La Fayette, Marie- Madeleine Pioche de la Vergne | French | N | La princesse de Clèves (The Princess of Clèves) | 1678 |
| 2700 | Laforet Diáz, Carmen | Spanish | N | Nada (aka: Andrea) | 1945 |
| 2701 | Laforet Diáz, Carmen | Spanish | N | Nada | 1945 |
| 2702 | Lagerkvist, Pär | Swedish | N-P | Barabbas | 1950{n} 1953{p} |
| 2703 | Lagerkvist, Pär | Swedish | N-P | Barabbas | 1950{n} 1953{p} |
| 2704 | Lagerlöf, Selma | Swedish | N | Löwenskölda ringen (vol 2: Charlotte Löwensköld) (The Ring of the Löwenskölds) | 1925 |
| 2705 | Lagerlöf, Selma | Swedish | N | Charlotte Löwensköld | 1925 |
| 2706 | Lagerlöf, Selma | Swedish | SS | Dunungen [Downy] | 1894 |
| 2707 | Lagerlöf, Selma | Swedish | N | Herr Arnes penningar (Herr Arne's Hoard) | 1903 |
| 2708 | Lagerlöf, Selma | Swedish | N | Kejseren af Portugallien (The Emperor of Portugallia) | 1914 |
| 2709 | Lagerlöf, Selma | Swedish | N | Körkarlen (Thy Soul Shall Bear Witness) | 1912 |
| 2710 | Lagerlöf, Selma | Swedish | N | Körkarlen | 1912 |
| 2711 | Lagerlöf, Selma | Swedish | N | Nils Holgerssons underbara resa (The Wonderful Adventures of Nils) | 1906-07 |
| 2712 | Lagerlöf, Selma | Swedish | N | Nils Holgerssons underbara resa | 1906-07 |
| 2713 | Lagerlöf, Selma | Swedish | SS | Tösen från stormyrtorpet (The Girl From the Marsh Croft) | 1908 |
| 2714 | Lagerlöf, Selma | Swedish | SS | Tösen från stormyrtorpet | 1908 |
| 2715 | Lagerlöf, Selma | Swedish | SS | Tösen från stormyrtorpet | 1908 |
| 2716 | Lagerlöf, Selma | Swedish | SS | Tösen från stormyrtorpet | 1908 |
| 2717 | Lagerlöf, Selma | Swedish | SS | Tösen från stormyrtorpet | 1908 |
| 2718 | Lalić, Mihailo | Yugoslav(Serb) | N | Hajka | 1960 |
| 2719 | Lalić, Mihailo | Yugoslav | N | Lelejska gora (The Wailing Mountain) | 1957 |
| 2720 | Lalić, Mihailo | Yugoslav | N | Svadba | 1962(50) |
| 2721 | Lamartine, Alphonse de | French | V | Jocelyn | 1836 |
| 2722 | Lamartine, Alphonse de | French | V | Jocelyn | 1836 |
| 2723 | Lampedusa, Giuseppe di | Italian | N | Il gattopardo (The Leopard) | 1958 |
| 2724 | Lampo, Hubert | Belgian(Fle) | N | Kasper in de onderwereld (aka: De goden moeten hun getal hebben) | 1974 (aka:1969) |
| 2725 | Lao She (see: Shu Qingchun) | Chinese | P | | |
| 2726 | Lardner, Ring | American | SS | Alibi Ike | 1929 |
| 2727 | Lardner, Ring | American | SS | The Big Town | 1938 |
| 2728 | Lardner, Ring | American | SS | Champion | 1929 |
| 2729 | Lardner, Ring | American | SS | The Golden Honeymoon | 1929 |
| 2730 | Lardner, Ring; Kaufman, George S. | American | P | June Moon | 1929 |
| 2731 | Lardner, Ring; Kaufman, George S. | American | P | June Moon | 1929 |
| 2732 | Larner, Jeremy | American | N | Drive, He Said | 1964 |
| 2733 | Larsen, Gunnar | Norwegian | N | To mistenkelige personer | 1933 |
| 2734 | Laski, Marghanita | British | N | Little Boy Lost | 1949 |
| 2735 | Lateur, Frank (as: Stijn Streuvels) | Belgian(Fle) | N | De Teleurgang van de Waterhoek | 1927 |

| No | Film Title | Country of Production | Date | Director(s) | Duration of Film |
|----|-----------|----------------------|------|-------------|-----------------|
| 2696 | Dangerous Liaisons | USA | 1988 | Stephen Frears | 120 +V(115) |
| 2697 | Valmont | FR/GB | 1989 | Milos Forman | 137 |
| 2698 | Laughing Boy | USA | 1934 | W. S. Van Dyke | 80 |
| 2699 | La princesse de Clèves (IT: La principessa di Clèves) | FR/IT | 1961 | Jean Delannoy | 110 |
| 2700 | Nada | SP | 1947 | Edgar Neville | 120(87) |
| 2701 | Graciela | ARG | 1956 | Leopoldo Torre Nilsson | 87 |
| 2702 | Barabbas | SWE | 1953 | Alf Sjöberg | 105 |
| 2703 | Barabba (Barabbas) | IT | 1961 | Richard Fleischer | 144(134) +V |
| 2704 | Charlotte Löwensköld (aka: Charlotte Löwenskjöld) | SWE | 1930 | Gustaf Molander | 93 |
| 2705 | Charlotte Löwensköld | SWE | 1979 | Jackie Söderman | 124 |
| 2706 | Dunungen | SWE | 1941 | Weyler Hildebrand | 90 |
| 2707 | Herr Arnes penningar (aka: Herr Arnes pengar) (Sir Arne's Treasure) | SWE | 1954 | Gustaf Molander | 88 |
| 2708 | Kejsarn av Portugallien (The Emperor of Portugal) | SWE | 1944 | Gustaf Molander | 116 |
| 2709 | La charrette fantôme (The Phantom Chariot) | FR | 1939 | Julien Duvivier | 93 |
| 2710 | Körkarlen (The Phantom Carriage) | SWE | 1958 | Arne Mattsson | 108 |
| 2711 | Zakoldovanny malchik (animation) | USSR | 1956(55) | [Soyuzmultfilm Studio] | 48 |
| 2712 | Nils Holgerssons underbara resa (The Wonderful Adventures of Nils) | SWE | 1962 | Kenne Fant | 96 |
| 2713 | Das Mädchen vom Moorhof | GER | 1935 | Detlef Sierck (Douglas Sirk) | 82 |
| 2714 | Suotorpan tyttö | FIN | 1940 | Toivo Särkkä | 71 |
| 2715 | Tösen från stormyrtorpet | SWE | 1947 | Gustaf Edgren | 94 |
| 2716 | Husmandstøsen | DEN | 1952 | Alice O'Fredericks | 103 |
| 2717 | Das Mädchen vom Moorhof | GER | 1958 | Gustav Ucicky | 88 |
| 2718 | Hajka (Manhunt) (aka: Pursuit) | YUGO | 1977 | Živojin Pavlović | 93 |
| 2719 | Lelejska gora (The Mountain of Horror) | YUGO | 1968 | Zdravko Velimirović | 95 |
| 2720 | Svadba (The Wedding) | YUGO/USSR | 1973 | Radomir Šaranović | 92 |
| 2721 | Jocelyn | FR | 1933 | Pierre Guerlais | 86 |
| 2722 | Jocelyn | FR | 1952 | Jacques de Casembroot | 92 |
| 2723 | Il gattopardo (The Leopard) | IT/FR | 1963(62) | Luchino Visconti | 161(205) |
| 2724 | Kasper in de onderwereld (Kasper in the Underworld) | BEL | 1978(77) | Jef van der Heyden | 93 |
| 2725 | | | | | |
| 2726 | Alibi Ike | USA | 1935 | Ray Enright | 73 |
| 2727 | So This Is New York | USA | 1948 | Richard Fleischer | 78 |
| 2728 | Champion | USA | 1949 | Mark Robson | 97 +V |
| 2729 | The Golden Honeymoon | USA | 1980 | Noel Black | 52 |
| 2730 | June Moon | USA | 1931 | A. Edward Sutherland | 71 |
| 2731 | Blonde Trouble | USA | 1937 | George Archainbaud | 67 |
| 2732 | Drive, He Said | USA | 1970 | Jack Nicholson | 90 |
| 2733 | To mistenkelige personer | NOR | 1950 | Tancred Ibsen | 101 |
| 2734 | Little Boy Lost | USA | 1953 | George Seaton | 95 |
| 2735 | Mira | HOLL | 1971 | Fons Rademakers | 93 |

| No. | Author | Nationality | Form | Literary Title | Date |
|-----|--------|-------------|------|----------------|------|
| 2736 | **Lateur, Frank** *(as: Stijn Streuvels)* | Belgian | N | **De Vlaschaard** | 1908 |
| 2737 | **Lateur, Frank** *(as: Stijn Streuvels)* | Belgian | N | **De Vlaschaard** | 1908 |
| 2738 | **Laurent, Jacques** *(Saint-Laurent, Cécil)* *(see: Stendhal)* | French | N | | |
| 2739 | **Laurents, Arthur** | American | P | **Home of the Brave** *(aka: The Way Back)* | 1946 |
| 2740 | **Laurents, Arthur** | American | P | **The Time of the Cuckoo** | 1953 |
| 2741 | **Laurents, Arthur** | American | N | **The Turning Point** | 1977 |
| 2742 | **Laurents, Arthur** | American | N | **The Way We Were** | 1972 |
| 2743 | **Laurents, Arthur** | American | P | **West Side Story** | 1959 |
| 2744 | **Lau Shaw** *(see: Shu Qingchun)* | Chinese | P | | |
| 2745 | **Lavedan, Henri** | French | P | **Le duel** | 1905 |
| 2746 | **Lawler, Ray** | Australian | P | **The Summer of the Seventeenth Doll** | 1957 |
| 2747 | **Lawrence, D. H.** | British | SS | **The Captain's Doll** | 1923 |
| 2748 | **Lawrence, D. H.** | British | SS | **The Fox** | 1923 |
| 2749 | **Lawrence, D. H.** | British | N | **Kangaroo** | 1923 |
| 2750 | **Lawrence, D. H.** | British | N | **Lady Chatterley's Lover** *(aka: The First Lady Chatterley)* | 1928(44) |
| 2751 | **Lawrence, D. H.** | British | N | **Lady Chatterley's Lover** | 1928(44) |
| 2752 | **Lawrence, D. H.** | British | N | **The Rainbow** *{pt.2}* | 1915 |
| 2753 | **Lawrence, D. H.** | British | SS | **The Rocking Horse Winner** | 1932 |
| 2754 | **Lawrence, D. H.** | British | SS | **The Rocking Horse Winner** | 1932 |
| 2755 | **Lawrence, D. H.** | British | SS | **The Rocking Horse Winner** | 1932 |
| 2756 | **Lawrence, D. H.** | British | N | **Sons and Lovers** | 1913 |
| 2757 | **Lawrence, D. H.** | British | N | **The Trespasser** | 1912 |
| 2758 | **Lawrence, D. H.** | British | N | **The Virgin and the Gypsy** | 1930 |
| 2759 | **Lawrence, D. H.** | British | N | **Women in Love** | 1920 |
| 2760 | **Lawrence, T. E.** | British | | **Seven Pillars of Wisdom** | 1926(35) |
| 2761 | **Lawson, John Howard** | American | P | **Success Story** | 1932 |
| 2762 | **Laxness, Halldór** | Icelandic | N | **Þu vínviður hreini** *[You pure vine]* + **Fuglinn í fjörunni** *[The bird in the shore]* *(Salka valka)* | 1931-32 |
| 2763 | **Le Carré, John** *(David John Moore Cornwell)* | British | N | **Call For the Dead** | 1961 |
| 2764 | **Le Carré, John** | British | N | **The Little Drummer Girl** | 1983 |
| 2765 | **Le Carré, John** | British | N | **The Looking Glass War** | 1965 |
| 2766 | **Le Carré, John** | British | N | **The Russia House** | 1989 |
| 2767 | **Le Carré, John** | British | N | **The Spy Who Came In From The Cold** | 1963 |
| 2768 | **Lee, Harper** | American | N | **To Kill a Mockingbird** | 1960 |
| 2769 | **Le Fanu, Sheridan** | Irish | SS | **Carmilla** + **Room in the Dragon Volant** | 1872 |
| 2770 | **Le Fanu, Sheridan** | Irish | SS | **Carmilla** | 1872 |
| 2771 | **Le Fanu, Sheridan** | Irish | SS | **Carmilla** | 1872 |
| 2772 | **Le Fanu, Sheridan** | Irish | SS | **Carmilla** | 1872 |
| 2773 | **Le Fanu, Sheridan** | Irish | SS | **Carmilla** | 1872 |

| No | Film Title | Country of Production | Date | Director(s) | Duration of Film |
|----|-----------|----------------------|------|-------------|------------------|
| 2736 | **Wenn die Sonne wieder scheint** [When the sun shines again] (aka: Der Flachsacker) | GER | 1943 | **Boleslav Barlog** | 87 |
| 2737 | **De Vlaschaard** (aka: Le champ de lin) (Flax Field) | BEL/HOLL | 1983 | **Jan Gruyaert** | 90 |
| 2738 | | | | | |
| 2739 | **Home of the Brave** | USA | 1949 | **Mark Robson** | 83 |
| 2740 | **Summer Madness** (USA: Summertime) | GB/USA | 1955 | **David Lean** | 100 |
| 2741 | **The Turning Point** | USA | 1977 | **Herbert Ross** | 119 +V |
| 2742 | **The Way We Were** | USA | 1973 | **Sydney Pollack** | 118 +V |
| 2743 | **West Side Story** | USA | 1961 | **Robert Wise** **Jerome Robbins** | 151 +V(115) |
| 2744 | | | | | |
| 2745 | **Le duel** | FR | 1939 | **Pierre Fresnay** | 84 |
| 2746 | **The Summer of the Seventeenth Doll** (aka: Season of Passion) | AUSTL/GB | 1959 | **Leslie Norman** | 94 |
| 2747 | **The Captain's Doll** | GB | 1983(82) | **Claude Whatham** | 110 |
| 2748 | **The Fox** | USA/CAN | 1967 | **Mark Rydell** | 110 |
| 2749 | **Kangaroo** | AUSTL | 1986 | **Tim Burstall** | 110 +V |
| 2750 | **L'amant de Lady Chatterley** (Lady Chatterley's Lover) | FR | 1955 | **Marc Allégret** | 98 |
| 2751 | **Lady Chatterley's Lover** (FR: L'amant de Lady Chatterley) | GB/FR | 1981 | **Just Jaeckin** | 103 +V(99) |
| 2752 | **The Rainbow** | GB | 1989(88) | **Ken Russell** | 111 +V |
| 2753 | **The Rocking Horse Winner** | GB | 1949 | **Anthony Pélissier** | 90 +V |
| 2754 | **The Rocking Horse Winner** | GB | 1977 | **Peter Medak** | 30 |
| 2755 | **The Rocking Horse Winner** | GB | 1983 | **Robert Bierman** | 33 |
| 2756 | **Sons and Lovers** | GB | 1960 | **Jack Cardiff** | 100 |
| 2757 | **The Trespasser** | USA | 1981 | **Colin Gregg** | 90 +V |
| 2758 | **The Virgin and the Gypsy** | GB | 1970(69) | **Christopher Miles** | 95 +V |
| 2759 | **Women in Love** | GB | 1969 | **Ken Russell** | 130 +V |
| 2760 | **Lawrence of Arabia** | GB | 1962 | **David Lean** | 222 |
| 2761 | **Success At Any Price** | USA | 1934 | **J. Walter Ruben** | 74 |
| 2762 | **Salka Valka** | SWE | 1954 | **Arne Mattsson** | 131 |
| 2763 | **The Deadly Affair** | GB | 1966 | **Sidney Lumet** | 107 +V |
| 2764 | **The Little Drummer Girl** | USA | 1984 | **George Roy Hill** | 130 +V |
| 2765 | **The Looking Glass War** | GB | 1969 | **Frank R. Pierson** | 107 +V |
| 2766 | **The Russia House** | USA | 1990 | **Fred Schepisi** | 123 +V |
| 2767 | **The Spy Who Came In From The Cold** | GB | 1966(65) | **Martin Ritt** | 112 |
| 2768 | **To Kill a Mockingbird** | USA | 1962 | **Robert Mulligan** | 129 +V |
| 2769 | **Vampyr der Traum des Allan Gray** (FR: Vampyr, ou l'étrange aventure de David Gray) (USA: Castle of Doom) (aka: Not Against Flesh) | GER/FR | 1932 | **Carl Th. Dreyer** | 83(99) |
| 2770 | **Terror in the Crypt** (GB: Crypt of Terror) | USA | 1960 | **Thomas Miller** | 84 |
| 2771 | **Et mourir de plaisir** (IT: Il sangue e la rosa) (Blood and Roses) | FR/IT | 1961(60) | **Roger Vadim** | 87(74) |
| 2772 | **Lust For a Vampire** (aka: To Love a Vampire) | GB | 1970 | **Jimmy Sangster** | 95 +V(85) |
| 2773 | **The Vampire Lovers** | GB | 1970 | **Roy Ward Baker** | 91(88) +V |

**153**

| No. | Author | Nationality | Form | Literary Title | Date |
|-----|--------|-------------|------|----------------|------|
| 2774 | Le Fanu, Sheridan | Irish | SS | Carmilla | 1872 |
| 2775 | Le Fanu, Sheridan | Irish | N | Uncle Silas | 1864 |
| 2776 | Le Fort, Gertrud von | German | SS | Die Letzte am Schafott (The Song at the Scaffold) | 1931 |
| 2777 | Lehmann, Rosamond | British | N | The Weather in the Streets | 1936 |
| 2778 | Lem, Stanisław | Polish | N | Astronauci [The Astronauts] | 1951 |
| 2779 | Lem, Stanisław | Polish | N | Solaris | 1961 |
| 2780 | Lemonnier, Camille | Belgian | N | Le mort [Death] | 1882 |
| 2781 | Lengyel József | Hungarian | SS | Oldás és kötés | 1964 (coll) |
| 2782 | Lenormand, Henri-René | French | P | Le simoun | 1921 |
| 2783 | Lenz, Siegfried | German | N | Deutschstunde (The German Lesson) | 1968 |
| 2784 | Lenz, Siegfried | German | SS | Das Feuerschiff (The Lightship) | 1960 |
| 2785 | Lenz, Siegfried | German | SS | Das Feuerschiff | 1960 |
| 2786 | Lenz, Siegfried | German | N | Der Mann im Strom | 1957 |
| 2787 | Lenz, Siegfried | German | P(R)-P | Zeit der Schuldlosen | 1961{pR} 1962{p} |
| 2789 | Leonov, Leonid Maksimovich | Russian | P | Nashestviye (Invasion) | 1942 |
| 2790 | Leonov, Leonid Maksimovich | Russian | N | Russkiy les (The Russian Forest) | 1953 |
| 2791 | León y Román, Ricardo | Spanish | N | El amor de los amores (The Wisdom of Sorrow) | 1912 |
| 2792 | Leprince de Beaumont, Marie | French | SS | La belle et la bête (Beauty and the Beast) | 1785-89 |
| 2793 | Lera, Ángel María de | Spanish | SS | Bochorno | 1960 |
| 2794 | Lera, Ángel María de | Spanish | N | La boda (The Wedding) | 1959 |
| 2795 | Lera, Ángel María de | Spanish | N | Los clarines del miedo (The Horns of Fear) | 1958 |
| 2796 | Lermontov, Mikhail | Russian | SS | Ashik Kerib | 1837 |
| 2797 | Lermontov, Mikhail | Russian | N | Geroi nashego vremeni (A Hero of Our Time) (aka: A Hero of Our Own Times) (aka: The Hero of Our Days) | 1840 |
| 2798 | Lermontov, Mikhail | Russian | N | Geroi nashego vremeni {ch.2, Maksim Maksimich, ch.5, Taman; ch.1, Bela} | 1840 |
| 2799 | Lermontov, Mikhail | Russian | N | Geroi nashego vremeni (ch.1, Bela) | 1840 |
| 2800 | Lermontov, Mikhail | Russian | N | Geroi nashego vremeni (ch.2, Maksim Maksimich, ch.5, Taman) | 1840 |
| 2801 | Lermontov, Mikhail | Russian | P | Maskarad | 1836 |
| 2802 | Lermontov, Mikhail | Russian | N | Vadim | 1832-34 |
| 2803 | Lesage, Alain-René | French | N | Gil Blas (aka: Histoire de Gil Blas de Santillane) (Adventure of Gil Blas de Santillane) | 1715-35 |
| 2804 | Leskov, Nikolay Semyonovich | Russian | SS | Kotin and Platonida | 1867 |
| 2805 | Leskov, Nikolay Semyonovich | Russian | SS | Ledi Makbet Mtenskogo uezda (Lady Macbeth of the Mtsensk District) | 1865 |

| No | Film Title | Country of Production | Date | Director(s) | Duration of Film |
|---|---|---|---|---|---|
| 2774 | **La novia ensangrentada** (The Blood-Splattered Bride) (aka: Til Death Do Us Part) (aka: Bloody Fiancee) | SP | 1972(69) | **Vicente Aranda** | 96(90) +V(83) |
| 2775 | **Uncle Silas** (USA: The Inheritance) | GB | 1947 | **Charles Frank** | 103(98) |
| 2776 | **Le dialogue des Carmélites** (IT: I dialoghi delle Carmelitane) (The Carmelites) | FR/IT | 1960 | **Raymond-Léopold Bruckberger Philippe Agostini** | 106 |
| 2777 | **The Weather in the Streets** | GB | 1984(83) | **Gavin Millar** | 125(130) |
| 2778 | **Der Schweigende Stern** (First Spaceship on Venus) | GER/POL | 1960 | **Kurt Maetzig** | 78 |
| 2779 | **Solaris** | USSR | 1972 | **Andrei Tarkovsky** | 165 +V |
| 2780 | **Le mort** | BEL/FR | 1936 | **E. G. De Meyst** | 67 |
| 2781 | **Oldás és kötés** (Cantata) (aka: Loosening and Tightening) | HUNG | 1963(62) | **Miklós Jancsó** | 100(98) |
| 2782 | **Le simoun** | FR | 1933 | **Firmin Gémier** | 70 |
| 2783 | **Deutschstunde** (German Lesson) {2 - parts} | GER | 1971 | **Peter Beauvais** | 220 |
| 2784 | **Das Feuerschiff** | GER | 1963(62) | **Ladislao Vajda** | 84 |
| 2785 | **The Lightship** | USA | 1985 | **Jerzy Skolimowski** | 88 +V |
| 2786 | **Der Mann im Strom** | GER | 1958 | **Eugen York** | 91 |
| 2787 | **Zeit der Schuldlosen** (Time of the Innocent) | GER | 1964 | **Thomas Fantl** | 95(97) |
| 2789 | **Nashestviye** (Invasion) | USSR | 1944 | **Abram Room** | 100 |
| 2790 | **Russkiy les** (The Russian Forest) | USSR | 1964 | **Vladimir Petrov** | Pt.1, 86 Pt.2, 85 |
| 2791 | **El amor de los amores** [The love of loves] | SP | 1962(60) | **Juan de Orduña** | 114(93) |
| 2792 | **La belle et la bête** (Beauty and the Beast) | FR | 1946 | **Jean Cocteau** | 92 +V |
| 2793 | **Bochorno** | SP | 1964(63) | **Juan de Orduña** | 112(83) |
| 2794 | **La boda** | ARG/SP | 1964(63) | **Lucas Demare** | 88(85) |
| 2795 | **Los clarines del miedo** | SP | 1958 | **Antonio Román** | 80(91) |
| 2796 | **Ashik Kerib** | USSR | 1988 | **David Abashidze Sergei Paradzhanov** | 77 |
| 2797 | **Knjazhna Mary** (The Princess Mary) | USSR | 1955 | **Isidor Annensky** | 101 |
| 2798 | **Geroi nashego vremeni** (Pt.1: Maxim Maximych. Taman) (Pt.2: Bela) | USSR | 1965 | **Stanislav Rostotsky** | Pt.1, 103 Pt.2, 141 |
| 2799 | **Bela** | USSR | 1967 | **Stanislav Rostotsky** | 114 |
| 2800 | **Maxim Maximych. Taman** | USSR | 1967 | **Stanislav Rostotsky** | 103 |
| 2801 | **Maskarad** (Masquerade) | USSR | 1941 | **Sergei Gerasimov** | 110 |
| 2802 | **Il giorno del furore** (Fury) (aka: One Russian Summer) (aka: Days of Fury) (aka: Fury Rides the Wind) | IT/GB | 1973 | **Antonio Calenda** | 118(112) |
| 2803 | **Les aventures de Gil Blas Santillane** (SP: Una aventura de Gil Blas) | FR/SP | 1955 | **René Jolivet** | 95 |
| 2804 | **Coilin and Platonida** | GB/GER | 1976 | **James Scott** | 85 |
| 2805 | **Sibirska Ledi Magbet** (Siberian Lady Macbeth) (aka: Lady Macbeth of Mtsensk) (aka: Fury Is a Woman) | YUGO | 1962 | **Andrzej Wajda** | 92 |

| No. | Author | Nationality | Form | Literary Title | Date |
|-----|--------|-------------|------|----------------|------|
| 2806 | **Leskov, Nikolay Semyonovich** | Russian | SS | **Ledi Makbet Mtenskogo uezda** | 1865 |
| 2807 | **Leskov, Nikolay Semyonovich** | Russian | N | **Pavlin** <br>*[Peacock]* | 1874 |
| 2808 | **Leskov, Nikolay Semyonovich** | Russian | SS | **Tupeinyi khudozhnik** <br>*(The Toupee Artist)* | 1883 |
| 2809 | **Lessing, Doris** | British | N | **The Grass Is Singing** | 1950 |
| 2810 | **Lessing, Doris** | British | N | **Memoirs of a Survivor** | 1974 |
| 2811 | **Lessing, Gotthold Ephraim** | German | P | **Emilia Galotti** | 1772 |
| 2812 | **Lessing, Gotthold Ephraim** | German | P | **Emilia Galotti** | 1772 |
| 2813 | **Lessing, Gotthold Ephraim** | German | P | **Minna von Barnhelm** <br>*(aka: A Soldier's Fortune)* | 1767 |
| 2814 | **Lessing, Gotthold Ephraim** | German | P | **Minna von Barnhelm** | 1767 |
| 2815 | **Lessing, Gotthold Ephraim** | German | P | **Minna von Barnhelm** | 1767 |
| 2816 | **Lessing, Gotthold Ephraim** | German | P | **Minna von Barnhelm** | 1767 |
| 2817 | **Lessing, Gotthold Ephraim** | German | P | **Minna von Barnhelm** | 1767 |
| 2818 | **Lessing, Gotthold Ephraim** | German | P | **Nathan der Weise** <br>*(Nathan the Wise)* | 1779 |
| 2819 | **Levi, Carlo** | Italian | N | **Cristo si è fermato a Eboli** <br>*(Christ Stopped at Eboli)* | 1945 |
| 2820 | **Levin, Meyer** | American | N-P | **Compulsion** | 1956{n} <br>1959{p} |
| 2821 | **Levin, Meyer** | American | N | **My Father's House** | 1947 |
| 2822 | **Lewis, Sinclair** | American | N | **Ann Vickers** | 1933 |
| 2823 | **Lewis, Sinclair** | American | N | **Babbitt** | 1922 |
| 2824 | **Lewis, Sinclair** | American | N | **Cass Timberlane** | 1945 |
| 2825 | **Lewis, Sinclair** | American | N | **Dodsworth** | 1929 |
| 2826 | **Lewis, Sinclair** | American | N | **Elmer Gantry** | 1927 |
| 2827 | **Lewis, Sinclair** | American | SS | **Let's Play King** | 1931 |
| 2828 | **Lewis, Sinclair** | American | SS | **Let's Play King** | 1931 |
| 2829 | **Lewis, Sinclair** | American | N | **Main Street** | 1920 |
| 2830 | **Lewis, Sinclair** | American | N | **Mantrap** | 1926 |
| 2831 | **Lewis, Sinclair** | American | N | **Martin Arrowsmith** <br>*(aka: Arrowsmith)* | 1925 |
| 2832 | **Liang Bin** <br>*(Liang Pin)* | Chinese | N | **Hongqi pu** <br>*(aka: Hung-ch'i p'u)* <br>*(Keep the Red Flag Flying)* | 1958 <br>(rev.1959) |
| 2833 | **Liang Pin** <br>*(see: Liang Bin)* | Chinese | N | | |
| 2834 | **Li Fei-kan** <br>*(see: Li Feigan)* | Chinese | N | | |
| 2835 | **Li Feigan** <br>*(Li Fei-kan)* <br>*(as: Ba Jin)* <br>*(Pa Chin)* | Chinese | N | **Han ye** <br>*(aka: Han-yeh)* <br>*[Cold nights]* | 1944 |
| 2836 | **Li Feigan** <br>*(as: Ba Jin)* | Chinese | N | **Jia** <br>*(aka: Chia)* <br>*(The Family)* | 1933 |
| 2837 | **Li Feigan** <br>*(as: Ba Jin)* | Chinese | N | **Jia** | 1931(33) |
| 2838 | **Li Feigan** <br>*(as: Ba Jin)* | Chinese | SS | **Tuan yuan** <br>*[Reunion]* | 1956 |
| 2839 | **Lima Barreto, Afonso Henrique de** <br>*(see: Barreto, Afonso)* | Brazilian | SS | | |
| 2840 | **Lindau, Paul** | German | P | **Der Andere** | 1893 |
| 2841 | **Lindsay, H.** <br>*(joint, see: Runyon, Damon)* | American | P | | |
| 2842 | **Lindsay, Joan** | Australian | N | **Picnic at Hanging Rock** | 1967 |
| 2843 | **Lindsay, Norman** | Australian | N | **Age of Consent** | 1938 |

| No | Film Title | Country of Production | Date | Director(s) | Duration of Film |
|----|-----------|----------------------|------|-------------|------------------|
| 2806 | Katerina Izmailova (Lady Macbeth of Mtsensk) | USSR | 1967 | Mikhail Shapiro | 149 |
| 2807 | Tragödie einer Leidenschaft [A tragedy of passion] | GER | 1949 | Kurt Meisel | 89 |
| 2808 | Drama iz starinnoi zhizni (Drama From Olden Times) | USSR | 1971 | Ilya Averbakh | 90 |
| 2809 | The Grass Is Singing (SWE: Graset sjunger) (aka: The Killing Heat) | GB/SWE/ ZAM | 1981 | Michael Raeburn | 109 +V |
| 2810 | Memoirs of a Survivor | GB | 1981 | David Gladwell | 115 +V |
| 2811 | Emilia Galotti | GER | 1958 | Martin Hellberg | 97 |
| 2812 | Emilia Galotti | GER | 1968 | Franz Peter Wirth Ludwig Cremer | 110 |
| 2813 | Das Fräulein von Barnhelm | GER | 1940 | Hans Schweikart | 98 |
| 2814 | Heldinnen [Heroines] {musical version} | GER | 1960 | Dietrich Haugk | 97 |
| 2815 | Minna von Barnhelm | GDR | 1962 | Martin Hellberg | 107 |
| 2816 | Minna von Barnhelm | GER | 1966 | Ludwig Cremer | 105 |
| 2817 | Minna von Barnhelm | GER | 1976 | Franz Peter Wirth | 114 +V |
| 2818 | Nathan der Weise | GER | 1967 | Franz Peter Wirth | 160(148) |
| 2819 | Cristo si è fermato a Eboli (FR: Le Christ s'est arrêté à Eboli) (Christ Stopped at Eboli) (aka: Eboli) | IT/FR | 1979 | Francesco Rosi | 152(150) |
| 2820 | Compulsion | USA | 1959 | Richard Fleischer | 103 |
| 2821 | Beit Avi (My Father's House) | IS | 1947 | Herbert Kline | 85 |
| 2822 | Ann Vickers | USA | 1933 | John Cromwell | 72 |
| 2823 | Babbitt | USA | 1934 | William Keighley | 74 |
| 2824 | Cass Timberlane | USA | 1947 | George Sidney | 119 |
| 2825 | Dodsworth | USA | 1936 | William Wyler | 101 |
| 2826 | Elmer Gantry | USA | 1960 | Richard Brooks | 146 +V |
| 2827 | Forbidden Adventure (aka: Newly Rich) | USA | 1931 | Norman Taurog | 77 |
| 2828 | Majestät auf Abwegen [His Majesty on the wrong path] | GER | 1958 | Robert A. Stemmle | 92 |
| 2829 | I Married a Doctor | USA | 1936 | Archie Mayo | 87 |
| 2830 | Untamed | USA | 1940 | George Archainbaud | 83 |
| 2831 | Arrowsmith | USA | 1931 | John Ford | 99(108) |
| 2832 | Hongqi pu | CHN | 1960 | Ling Zifeng | 147 |
| 2833 | | | | | |
| 2834 | | | | | |
| 2835 | Han ye | CHN | 1984 | Qiu Wen | 105 |
| 2836 | Jia (Family) | CHN | 1941 | Pu Wan-chang Hsu Hsin-fu et al | 197 |
| 2837 | Jia (Family) | CHN | 1957(56) | Chen Xihe Ye Ming | 128 |
| 2838 | Yingxiong ernu [The heroic son and daughter] | CHN | 1964 | Wu Zhaodi | 117 |
| 2839 | | | | | |
| 2840 | Der Andere (FR: Le procureur Hallers) | GER | 1930 | Robert Wiene | 104 |
| 2841 | | | | | |
| 2842 | Picnic at Hanging Rock | AUSTL | 1975 | Peter Weir | 115 +V |
| 2843 | Age of Consent | AUSTL | 1969 | Michael Powell | 103 +V |

| No. | Author | Nationality | Form | Literary Title | Date |
|---|---|---|---|---|---|
| 2844 | **Linklater, Eric** | British(Scot) | N | **Laxdale Hall** | 1951 |
| 2845 | **Linklater, Eric** | British | N | **Poet's Pub** | 1929 |
| 2846 | **Linklater, Eric** | British | N | **Private Angelo** | 1946 |
| 2847 | **Linna, Väinö** | Finnish | N | **Musta rakkaus** | 1948 |
| 2848 | **Linna, Väinö** | Finnish | N | **Täällä pohjantähden alla** {pts.1-2} (Here Under the North Star) | 1959-60 |
| 2849 | **Linna, Väinö** | Finnish | N | **Täällä pohjantähden alla** {pt.3} | 1962 |
| 2850 | **Linna, Väinö** | Finnish | N | **Tuntematon sotilas** (The Unknown Soldier) | 1954 |
| 2851 | **Linna, Väinö** | Finnish | N | **Tuntematon sotilas** | 1954 |
| 2852 | **Linnankoski, Johannes** (Vihtori Peltonen) | Finnish | SS | **Hilja, maitotyttö** | 1913 |
| 2853 | **Linnankoski, Johannes** | Finnish | N | **Laulu tulipunaisesta kukasta** (The Song of the Blood-Red Flower) | 1905 |
| 2854 | **Linnankoski, Johannes** | Finnish | N | **Laulu tulipunaisesta kukasta** | 1905 |
| 2855 | **Linnankoski, Johannes** | Finnish | N | **Laulu tulipunaisesta kukasta** | 1905 |
| 2856 | **Linnankoski, Johannes** | Finnish | N | **Laulu tulipunaisesta kukasta** | 1905 |
| 2857 | **Lispector, Clarice** | Brazilian | SS | **O corpo** [The body] | 1974 |
| 2858 | **Lispector, Clarice** | Brazilian | N | **A hora da estrela** (The Hour of the Star) | 1977 |
| 2859 | **Lispector, Clarice** | Brazilian | N | **Perto do coração selvagem** [Close to the savage heart] | 1943 |
| 2860 | **Littlewood, Joan** (joint, see: Chilton, Charles) | British | N-P | | |
| 2861 | **Livings, Henry** | British | P | **Eh?** | 1965 |
| 2862 | **Ljungquist, Walter** | Swedish | N | **Nycklar till okänt rum** | 1950 |
| 2863 | **Ljungquist, Walter** | Swedish | N | **Ombyte av tåg** | 1933 |
| 2864 | **Ljungquist, Walter** | Swedish | N | **Vandring med månen** | 1941 |
| 2865 | **Llewellyn, Richard** | British(Welsh) | N | **How Green Was My Valley** | 1939 |
| 2866 | **Llewellyn, Richard** | British | N | **None But the Lonely Heart** | 1943 |
| 2867 | **Llewellyn, Richard** | British | P | **The Noose** | 1947 |
| 2868 | **Llewellyn, Richard** | British | P | **Poison Pen** | 1938 |
| 2869 | **Lobato, Monteiro** (Monteiro Lobato) | Brazilian | SS | **O comprador de fazendas** | 1918 |
| 2870 | **Lobato, Monteiro** | Brazilian | SS | **O comprador de fazendas** | 1918 |
| 2871 | **Lobato, Monteiro** | Brazilian | SS | **O saci** | 1921 |
| 2872 | **Lobato, Monteiro** | Brazilian | SS | **O sítio do picapau amarelo** [Yellow woodpecker farm] | 1939 |
| 2873 | **Lockridge, Ross** | American | N | **Raintree County** | 1948 |
| 2874 | **Lo Hua-sheng** (see: Xu Dishan) | Chinese | SS | | |
| 2875 | **Lo-Johansson, Ivar** | Swedish | N | **Bara en mor** | 1939 |
| 2876 | **Lo-Johansson, Ivar** | Swedish | N | **Kungsgatan** [King's street] | 1935 |
| 2877 | **Lo Kuan-chung** (see: Luo Guanzhong) | Chinese | N | | |
| 2878 | **London, Jack** | American | SS | **The Abysmal Brute** | 1913 |
| 2879 | **London, Jack** | American | SS | **Brown Wolf** | 1906 |
| 2880 | **London, Jack** | American | N | **Call of the Wild** | 1903 |
| 2881 | **London, Jack** | American | N | **Call of the Wild** | 1903 |
| 2882 | **London, Jack** | American | SS | **Flush of Gold** | 1910 |

| No | Film Title | Country of Production | Date | Director(s) | Duration of Film |
|----|-----------|----------------------|------|-------------|------------------|
| 2844 | **Laxdale Hall** (USA: Scotch on the Rocks) | GB | 1953(52) | **John Eldridge** | 77 |
| 2845 | **Poet's Pub** | GB | 1949 | **Frederick Wilson** | 79 |
| 2846 | **Private Angelo** | GB | 1949 | **Peter Ustinov** **Michael Anderson** | 106 |
| 2847 | **Musta rakkaus** (Black Love) | FIN | 1957 | **Edvin Laine** | 100 |
| 2848 | **Täällä pohjantähden alla** (Here Beneath the North Star) | FIN | 1968 | **Edvin Laine** | 102(186) |
| 2849 | **Akseli ja Elina** (Akseli and Elina) | FIN | 1970 | **Edvin Laine** | 93 |
| 2850 | **Tuntematon sotilas** (The Unknown Soldier) | FIN | 1955(54) | **Edvin Laine** | 132 |
| 2851 | **Tuntematon sotilas** (The Unknown Soldier) | FIN | 1985 | **Rauni Mollberg** | 193(210) |
| 2852 | **Hilja, maitotyttö** (Hilja the Milkmaid) | FIN | 1953 | **Toivo Särkkä** | 87 |
| 2853 | **Sången om den eldröda blomman** (FIN: Laulu tulipunaisesta kukasta) | SWE | 1934 | **Per-Axel Branner** | 97 |
| 2854 | **Laulu tulipunaisesta kukasta** (The Song of the Blood-Red Flower) | FIN | 1938 | **Teuvo Tulio** | 110 |
| 2855 | **Sången om den eldröda blommen** (Song of the Scarlet Flower) | SWE | 1956 | **Gustaf Molander** | 104 |
| 2856 | **Laulu tulipunaisesta kukasta** (The Song of the Blood-Red Flower) | FIN | 1971 | **Mikko Niskanen** | 98 |
| 2857 | **O corpo** | BRAZ | 1991 | **José Antônio Garcia** | 78 |
| 2858 | **A hora da estrela** (The Hour of the Star) | BRAZ | 1985 | **Suzana Amaral** | 96 |
| 2859 | **Perto do coração selvagem** | BRAZ | 1966 | **Maurício Rittner** | 08 |
| 2860 | | | | | |
| 2861 | **Work Is a Four Letter Word** | GB | 1967 | **Peter Hall** | 93 |
| 2862 | **Den vita katten** (The White Cat) | SWE | 1950 | **Hasse Ekman** | 92 |
| 2863 | **Ombyte av tåg** (Changing Trains) (aka: Unexpected Meeting) | SWE | 1943 | **Hasse Ekman** | 92 |
| 2864 | **Vandring med månen** (Wandering With the Moon) | SWE | 1945 | **Hasse Ekman** | 105 |
| 2865 | **How Green Was My Valley** | USA | 1941 | **John Ford** | 118 |
| 2866 | **None But the Lonely Heart** | USA | 1944 | **Clifford Odets** | 113 |
| 2867 | **Noose** (USA: The Silk Noose) | GB | 1948 | **Edmond T. Gréville** | 95 |
| 2868 | **Poison Pen** | GB | 1939 | **Paul L. Stein** | 79 |
| 2869 | **O comprador de fazendas** | BRAZ | 1951 | **Alberto Pieralisi** | 89(96) |
| 2870 | **O comprador de fazendas** | BRAZ | 1974 | **Alberto Pieralisi** | 87(106) |
| 2871 | **O saci** | BRAZ | 1953(52) | **Rudolfo Nanni** | 65 |
| 2872 | **O picapau amarelo** | BRAZ | 1974 | **Geraldo Sarno** | 85 |
| 2873 | **Raintree County** | USA | 1957 | **Edward Dmytryk** | 166 |
| 2874 | | | | | |
| 2875 | **Bara en mor** (Only a Mother) | SWE | 1949 | **Alf Sjöberg** | 100 |
| 2876 | **Kungsgatan** | SWE | 1943 | **Gösta Cederlund** | 96 |
| 2877 | | | | | |
| 2878 | **Conflict** | USA | 1936 | **David Howard** | 63 |
| 2879 | **Brown Wolf** | CAN | 1972 | **George Kaczender** | 25 |
| 2880 | **The Call of the Wild** | USA | 1935 | **William A. Wellman** | 81 |
| 2881 | **Call of the Wild** (GER: Ruf der wildnis) (IT: Il richiamo della foresta) | GB/SP/GER/ IT/FR | 1973(72) | **Ken Annakin** | 105 +V(100) |
| 2882 | **Alaska** | USA | 1944 | **George Archainbaud** | 76 |

| No. | Author | Nationality | Form | Literary Title | Date |
|-----|--------|-------------|------|----------------|------|
| 2883 | London, Jack | American | N | Martin Eden | 1906 |
| 2884 | London, Jack | American | SS | The Mexican | 1913 |
| 2885 | London, Jack | American | SS | The Mexican | 1913 |
| 2886 | London, Jack | American | SS | The Mexican | 1913 |
| 2887 | London, Jack | American | N | The Mutiny of the Elsinore | 1915 |
| 2888 | London, Jack | American | N | The Mutiny of the Elsinore | 1915 |
| 2889 | London, Jack | American | N | The Sea Wolf | 1904 |
| 2890 | London, Jack | American | N | The Sea Wolf | 1904 |
| 2891 | London, Jack | American | N | The Sea Wolf | 1904 |
| 2892 | London, Jack | American | N | The Sea Wolf | 1904 |
| 2893 | London, Jack | American | N | The Sea Wolf | 1904 |
| 2894 | London, Jack | American | N | The Sea Wolf | 1904 |
| 2895 | London, Jack | American | SS | That Spot | 1910 |
| 2896 | London, Jack | American | SS | To Build a Fire | 1910 |
| 2897 | London, Jack | American | SS | To Build a Fire | 1910 |
| 2898 | London, Jack | American | N | White Fang | 1905 |
| 2899 | London, Jack | American | N | White Fang | 1905 |
| 2900 | London, Jack | American | N | White Fang | 1905 |
| 2901 | London, Jack | American | N | White Fang | 1905 |
| 2902 | London, Jack | American | SS | White Silence | 1930 |
| 2903 | London, Jack; Fish, Robert | American | N | The Assassination Bureau Ltd | 1963 |
| 2904 | Longfellow, Henry Wadsworth | American | V | The Song of Hiawatha | 1855 |
| 2905 | Longfellow, Henry Wadsworth | American | V | The Wreck of the Hesperus | 1841 |
| 2906 | Longus | Greek(anc) | N | Daphnis and Chloe | c.200 |
| 2907 | Longus | Greek(anc) | N | Daphnis and Chloe | c.200 |
| 2908 | Lönnrot, Elias (ed.) | Finnish | V | Kalevala (The Kalevala, the Epic Poem of Finland) | 1835 |
| 2909 | Loos, Anita | American | N | But Gentlemen Marry Brunettes | 1928 |
| 2910 | Loos, Anita | American | N | Gentlemen Prefer Blondes | 1925 |
| 2911 | Loos, Anita; Emerson, John | American | P | The Social Register | 1931 |
| 2912 | Loos, Anita; Emerson, John | American | P | The Whole Town's Talking | 1925 |
| 2913 | Lope de Vega Carpio (see: Vega, Lope de) | Spanish | P | | |
| 2914 | López Rubio, José | Spanish | P | Una madeja de lana azul celeste [A ball of sky-blue yarn] | 1952 |
| 2915 | López Rubio, José | Spanish | P | La otra orilla [The other shore] | 1955 |
| 2916 | López Rubio, José | Spanish | P | Un trono para Cristy | 1957 |
| 2917 | Lorca, Federico García (see: García Lorca, Federico) | Spanish | P | | |
| 2918 | Lorenzini, Carlo (see: Collodi, Carlo) | Italian | SS | | |
| 2919 | Loti, Pierre | French | N-P | Madame Chrysanthème | 1888{n} 1893{p} |
| 2920 | Loti, Pierre | French | N | Pêcheur d'islande (An Iceland Fisherman) | 1886 |
| 2921 | Loti, Pierre | French | N | Pêcheur d'islande | 1886 |
| 2922 | Loti, Pierre | French | N-P | Ramuntcho (A Tale of the Pyrenees) | 1896{n} 1908{p} |
| 2923 | Loti, Pierre | French | N-P | Ramuntcho | 1896{n} 1908{p} |

| No | Film Title | Country of Production | Date | Director(s) | Duration of Film |
|----|-----------|----------------------|------|-------------|------------------|
| 2883 | **Adventures of Martin Eden** (aka: Martin Eden) | USA | 1942 | **Sidney Salkow** | 87 |
| 2884 | **El mexicano** (The Mexican) | MEX | 1944 | **Augustin P. Delgado** | 87 |
| 2885 | **The Fighter** | USA | 1952 | **Herbert Kline** | 78 +V |
| 2886 | **The Mexican** | USSR | 1956 | **Vladimir Kaplunovski** | 82 |
| 2887 | **Les mutinés de l'Elseneur** | FR | 1936 | **Pierre Chenal** | 90 |
| 2888 | **The Mutiny of the Elsinore** | GB | 1937 | **Roy Lockwood** | 79 |
| 2889 | **The Sea Wolf** | USA | 1930 | **Alfred Santell** | 89 |
| 2890 | **The Sea Wolf** | USA | 1941 | **Michael Curtiz** | 90 |
| 2891 | **Barricade** | USA | 1949 | **Peter Godfrey** | 75 |
| 2892 | **Wolf Larsen** | USA | 1958 | **Harmon Jones** | 83 |
| 2893 | **Der Seewolf** (ROM: Lupul mărilor) | GER/ROM | 1973(72) | **Wolfgang Staudte** | 96 |
| 2894 | **Il lupo dei mari** (Wolf Larsen) (aka: The Legend of the Sea Wolf) (aka: Wolf of the Seven Seas) | IT | 1975 | **Giuseppi Vari** | 92 +V |
| 2895 | **Sign of the Wolf** | USA | 1941 | **Howard Bretherton** | 80 |
| 2896 | **To Build a Fire** | GB | 1970(69) | **David Cobham** | 56 +V |
| 2897 | **To Build a Fire** | USA | 1975 | **Robert Stitzel** | 15 |
| 2898 | **White Fang** | USA | 1936 | **David Butler** | 74 |
| 2899 | **Belyi klyk** | USSR | 1946 | **Alexander Zguridi** | 84 |
| 2900 | **Zanna bianca** (SP: Comillo blanco) (White Fang) (aka: Challenge to White Fang) | IT/SP/FR | 1974(73) | **Lucio Fulci** | 101(105) |
| 2901 | **White Fang** | USA | 1990 | **Randal Kleiser** | 109 |
| 2902 | **Romance of the Redwoods** | USA | 1939 | **Charles Vidor** | 67 |
| 2903 | **The Assasssination Bureau** | GB | 1969(68) | **Basil Dearden** | 110 |
| 2904 | **Hiawatha** | USA | 1952 | **Kurt Neumann** | 80 |
| 2905 | **The Wreck of the Hesperus** | USA | 1948 | **John Hoffman** | 70 |
| 2906 | **Mikres Aphrodites** (Young Aphrodites) | GR | 1962 | **Nikos Koundouros** | 88 |
| 2907 | **Dhafnis ke Hloi 66** (Daphnis and Chloe 66) | GR | 1967(66) | **Mika Zaharopoulou** | 82 |
| 2908 | **Sampo** (The Day the Earth Froze) (aka: The Magic Sampo) | USSR/FIN | 1959 | **Aleksander Ptushko** | 91 |
| 2909 | **Gentlemen Marry Brunettes** | USA | 1955 | **Richard Sale** | 97 |
| 2910 | **Gentlemen Prefer Blondes** {musical version} | USA | 1953 | **Howard Hawks** | 91 +V(89) |
| 2911 | **The Social Register** | USA | 1934 | **Marshall Neilan** | 71 |
| 2912 | **Ex-Bad Boy** | USA | 1931 | **Vin Moore** | 68 |
| 2913 | | | | | |
| 2914 | **Una madeja de lana azul celeste** | SP | 1964 | **José Luis Madrid** | 68 |
| 2915 | **La otra orilla** | SP | 1966(64) | **José Luis Madrid** | 96(76) |
| 2916 | **Eine Thron für Christine** (SP: Un trono para Cristy) | GER/SP | 1960(59) | **Luis César Amadori** | 84(98) |
| 2917 | | | | | |
| 2918 | | | | | |
| 2919 | **Il songo di Butterfly** (GER: Premiere der Butterfly) (The Dream of Butterfly) | IT/GER | 1939 | **Carmine Gallone** | 95 |
| 2920 | **Pêcheur d'islande** (An Iceland Fisherman) | FR | 1933 | **Pierre Guerlais** | 75 |
| 2921 | **Pêcheur d'islande** | FR | 1959 | **Pierre Schoendoerffer** | 87 |
| 2922 | **Ramuntcho** | FR | 1937 | **René Barberis** | 90 |
| 2923 | **Le mariage de Ramuntcho** | FR | 1947(46) | **Max de Vaucorbeil** | 80 |

| No. | Author | Nationality | Form | Literary Title | Date |
|-----|--------|-------------|------|----------------|------|
| 2924 | **Loti, Pierre** | French | N-P | **Ramuntcho** | 1896{n}<br>1908{p} |
| 2925 | **Loti, Pierre** | French | N | **Le roman d'un Spahi**<br>(The Romance of a Spahi) | 1881 |
| 2926 | **Louÿs, Pierre** | French | N | **Les aventures du Roi Pausole**<br>(The Adventures of King Pausole) | 1901 |
| 2927 | **Louÿs, Pierre** | French | N | **La femme et le pantin**<br>(The Woman and the Puppet) | 1898 |
| 2928 | **Louÿs, Pierre** | French | N | **La femme et le pantin** | 1898 |
| 2929 | **Louÿs, Pierre** | French | N | **La femme et le pantin** | 1898 |
| 2930 | **Louzeiro, José** | Brazilian | N | **Infância dos mortos**<br>[Infancy of the dead] | 1977 |
| 2931 | **Louzeiro, José** | Brazilian | N | **Lúcio Flávio, o passageiro da agonia**<br>[Lucio Flavio, the passenger of agony] | 1975 |
| 2932 | **Lovinescu, Horia** | Romanian | P | **Citadela sfărîmată**<br>[The destroyed citadel] | 1955 |
| 2933 | **Lovinescu, Horia** | Romanian | P | **Febre**<br>[Fever] | 1963 |
| 2934 | **Lovinescu, Horia** | Romanian | P | **Moartea unui artist**<br>[Death of an artist] | 1965 |
| 2935 | **Lovinescu, Horia** | Romanian | P | **Surorile Boga**<br>[The Boga sisters] | 1959(63) |
| 2936 | **Lowry, Malcolm** | British | N | **Under the Volcano** | 1947 |
| 2937 | **Loyola, Ignácio de**<br>(see: Brandão, Ignácio de Loyola) | Brazilian | SS/N | | |
| 2938 | **Lucas, Victoria**<br>(see: Plath, Sylvia) | American | N | | |
| 2939 | **Luce, Clare Boothe**<br>(see: Boothe, Clare) | American | P | | |
| 2940 | **Ludwig, Otto** | German | P | **Der Erbförster**<br>(The Forest Warden) | 1853 |
| 2941 | **Ludwig, Otto** | German | N | **Zwischen Himmel und Erde**<br>(Between Heaven and Earth) | 1856 |
| 2942 | **Ludwig, Otto** | German | N | **Zwischen Himmel und Erde** | 1856 |
| 2943 | **Lu Hsün**<br>(see: Zhou Shuren) | Chinese | SS | | |
| 2944 | **Luís, Agustina Bessa**<br>(see: Bessa-Luis, Agustina) | Portuguese | N | | |
| 2946 | **Lundkvist, Nils Artur** | Swedish | SS | **Hästhandlarens flickor** | 1935 |
| 2947 | **Lundkvist, Nils Artur** | Swedish | N | **Komedi i Hägerskog**<br>[Comedy in Hägerskog] | 1959 |
| 2948 | **Lundkvist, Nils Artur** | Swedish | N | **Vindingevals**<br>[Vindinge waltz] | 1956 |
| 2949 | **Luo Guanzhong**<br>(Lo Kuan-chung) | Chinese | N | **San Guo yanyi**<br>(aka: San-kuo-chih-yen-i)<br>(San Kuo, or Romance of the Three Kingdoms) | 1522 |
| 2950 | **Luo Huasheng**<br>(see: Xu Dishan) | Chinese | SS | | |
| 2951 | **Lu Xun**<br>(see: Zhou Shuren) | Chinese | SS | | |
| 2952 | **Lynch, Benito** | Argentine | N | **Los caranchos de la Florida** | 1916 |
| 2953 | **Lynch, Benito** | Argentine | N | **El inglés de los güesos** | 1924 |
| 2954 | **Lytton, Edward Earle Lytton Bulwer-Lytton**<br>(see: Bulwer-Lytton) | British | N | | |
| 2955 | **MacArthur, Charles;**<br>**Sheldon, Edward Brewster** | American | P | **My Lulu Belle** | 1925 |
| 2956 | **MacArthur, Charles**<br>(see also: Hecht, Ben) | American | P/SS | | |
| 2957 | **McBain, Ed**<br>(see Hunter, Evan) | American | N | | |

| No | Film Title | Country of Production | Date | Director(s) | Duration of Film |
|---|---|---|---|---|---|
| 2924 | Ramuntcho | FR | 1958 | Pierre Schoendoerffer | 90 |
| 2925 | Le roman d'un Spahi | FR | 1936 | Michel Bernheim | 82 |
| 2926 | Les aventures du Roi Pausole | FR | 1933 | Alexis Granowsky | 75 |
| 2927 | The Devil Is a Woman | USA | 1935 | Josef von Sternberg | 82 |
| 2928 | La femme et le pantin<br>(IT: Femmina)<br>(A Woman Like Satan)<br>(aka: The Female) | FR/IT | 1959(58) | Julien Duvivier | 100(120) |
| 2929 | Cet obscur objet du désir<br>(SP: Ese oscuro objeto del deseo)<br>(That Obscure Object of Desire) | FR/SP | 1977 | Luis Buñuel | 103(96)<br>+V |
| 2930 | Pixote | BRAZ | 1981(80) | Hector Babenco | 125 |
| 2931 | Lúcia Flávio, o passageiro da agonia | BRAZ | 1977 | Hector Babenco | 92 |
| 2932 | Citadela sfărîmată | ROM/FR | 1957 | Marc Maurette | 107 |
| 2933 | Poveste sentimentală<br>[A sentimental story] | ROM | 1961 | Iulian Mihu | 94 |
| 2934 | Moartea unui artist | ROM | 1991 | Horea Popescu | 113 |
| 2935 | Surorile<br>[The sisters] | ROM | 1984 | Iulian Mihu | 119 |
| 2936 | Under the Volcano | USA | 1984 | John Huston | 112 +V |
| 2937 | | | | | |
| 2938 | | | | | |
| 2939 | | | | | |
| 2940 | Der Erbförster | GER | 1945 | Alois Johannes Lippl | 80 |
| 2941 | Zwischen Himmel und Erde<br>(aka: Liebe läßt sich nicht erzwingen) | GER | 1934 | Franz Seitz | 92 |
| 2942 | Zwischen Himmel und Erde | GER | 1942 | Harald Braun | 101 |
| 2943 | | | | | |
| 2944 | | | | | |
| 2946 | Hästhandlarens flickor<br>(Time of Desire) | SWE | 1954 | Egil Holmsen | 87 |
| 2947 | Komedi i Hägerskog | SWE | 1968 | Torgny Anderberg | 100 |
| 2948 | Vindingevals<br>(Waltz of Sex) | SWE | 1968 | Åke Falck | 99 |
| 2949 | Diao chan<br>[The sex trap]<br>{episode} | CHN | 1938 | Pu Wancang | 90 |
| 2950 | | | | | |
| 2951 | | | | | |
| 2952 | Los caranchos de la Florida | ARG | 1938 | Alberto de Zavalía | 78 |
| 2953 | El inglés de los güesos | ARG | 1940 | Carlos Hugo Christensen | 79 |
| 2954 | | | | | |
| 2955 | Lulu Belle | USA | 1948 | Leslie Fenton | 87 |
| 2956 | | | | | |
| 2957 | | | | | |

| No. | Author | Nationality | Form | Literary Title | Date |
|-----|--------|-------------|------|----------------|------|
| 2958 | McCarthy, Mary | American | N | The Group | 1963 |
| 2959 | McCoy, Horace | American | N | Kiss Tomorrow Goodbye | 1948 |
| 2960 | McCoy, Horace | American | N | Scalpel | 1952 |
| 2961 | McCoy, Horace | American | N | They Shoot Horses, Don't They? | 1935 |
| 2962 | McCullers, Carson | American | SS | The Ballad of the Sad Café | 1951 |
| 2963 | McCullers, Carson | American | N | The Heart is a Lonely Hunter | 1940 |
| 2964 | McCullers, Carson | American | N-P | The Member of the Wedding | 1946{n} 1951{p} |
| 2965 | McCullers, Carson | American | N | Reflections in a Golden Eye | 1941 |
| 2966 | Macedo, Joaquim Manuel de | Brazilian | N | A moreninha | 1844 |
| 2967 | McEwan, Ian | British | N | The Comfort of Strangers | 1981 |
| 2968 | McEwan, Ian | British | P(TV) | The Imitation Game | 1981 |
| 2969 | McGahern, John | Irish | SS | Wheels | 1970 |
| 2970 | McGough, Roger | British | V | After the Merrymaking | 1971 |
| 2971 | McGrath, John | British | P(TV) | The Cheviot, the Stag and the Black, Black Oil | 1974 |
| 2972 | McGrath, John | British | P | Events While Guarding the Bofors Gun | 1966 |
| 2973 | McGuane, Thomas | American | N | Ninety-Two in the Shade | 1973 |
| 2974 | McGuane, Thomas | American | N | The Sporting Club | 1968 |
| 2975 | Machado, Aníbal | Brazilian | SS | O iniciado do vento [The wind's initiate] | 1959 |
| 2976 | Machado, Aníbal | Brazilian | SS | Tati, a garôta | 1959 |
| 2977 | Machado, Aníbal | Brazilian | SS | Viagem aos seios de Duília | 1959 |
| 2978 | Machado, Maria Clara | Brazilian | P | A bruxinha que era boa [A good little witch] | 1957 |
| 2979 | Machado, Maria Clara | Brazilian | P | O cavalinho azul [The little blue horse] | 1960 |
| 2980 | Machado, Maria Clara | Brazilian | P | Pluft, o fantasminha | 1957 |
| 2981 | Machado de Assis (see: Assis, Joaquim Maria Machado de) | Brazilian | SS/N | | |
| 2982 | Machado y Ruiz, Antonio | Spanish | V | La tierra de Alvar González (The House of Alvar González) | 1939 |
| 2983 | Machado y Ruiz, Manuel; Machado y Ruiz, Antonio | Spanish | P | La duquesa de Benameji | 1932 |
| 2984 | Machado y Ruiz, Manuel; Machado y Ruiz, Antonio | Spanish | P | La Lola se va a los puertos [Lola heads for the ports] | 1929 |
| 2985 | Machiavelli, Niccolò | Italian | P | La mandragola (The Mandrake) (aka: Mandragola) | 1519 |
| 2986 | Mackenzie, Compton | British | N | Carnival | 1912 |
| 2987 | Mackenzie, Compton | British | N | Carnival | 1912 |
| 2988 | Mackenzie, Compton | British | N | Rockets Galore | 1957 |
| 2989 | Mackenzie, Compton | British | N | Sylvia Scarlett | 1918-19 |
| 2990 | Mackenzie, Compton | British | N | Whisky Galore! (USA: Tight Little Island) | 1947 |
| 2991 | Maclaren, Ian (see: Watson, John) | British | N | | |
| 2992 | McLaverty, Michael | Irish | SS | The Schooner | 1978 |
| 2993 | McLeish, Archibald | American | V | Epistle To Be Left in the Earth | 1930 |
| 2994 | McMurtry, Larry | American | N | Horseman, Pass By | 1961 |
| 2995 | McMurtry, Larry | American | N | The Last Picture Show | 1966 |
| 2996 | McMurtry, Larry | American | N | Leaving Cheyenne | 1963 |
| 2997 | McMurtry, Larry | American | N | Terms of Endearment | 1975 |
| 2998 | McMurtry, Larry | American | N | Texasville | 1990 |
| 2999 | Mac Orlan, Pierre (Pierre Dumarchey) | French | N | La bandera | 1931 |
| 3000 | Mac Orlan, Pierre | French | SS | Marguerite de la nuit | 1925 |
| 3001 | Mac Orlan, Pierre | French | N | Le quai des brumes | 1927 |
| 3002 | Mac Orlan, Pierre | French | N | La tradition de minuit (One Floor Up) | 1930 |

| No | Film Title | Country of Production | Date | Director(s) | Duration of Film |
|---|---|---|---|---|---|
| 2958 | The Group | USA | 1966 | Sidney Lumet | 152 |
| 2959 | Kiss Tomorrow Goodbye | USA | 1950 | Gordon Douglas | 101 |
| 2960 | Bad For Each Other | USA | 1953 | Irving Rapper | 83 |
| 2961 | They Shoot Horses, Don't They? | USA | 1969 | Sydney Pollack | 120 +V(108) |
| 2962 | The Ballad of the Sad Café | USA | 1990 | Simon Callow | 101 |
| 2963 | The Heart is a Lonely Hunter | USA | 1968 | Robert Ellis Miller | 123 +V |
| 2964 | The Member of the Wedding | USA | 1953 | Fred Zinnemann | 91 |
| 2965 | Reflections in a Golden Eye | USA | 1967 | John Huston | 107 |
| 2966 | A moreninha {musical version} | BRAZ | 1970 | Glauco Mirko Laurelli | 96 |
| 2967 | Cortesie per gli ospiti (The Comfort of Strangers) | IT/GB | 1990 | Paul Schrader | 104 |
| 2968 | The Imitation Game | GB | 1980 | Richard Eyre | 95 +V |
| 2969 | Wheels | IRE | 1976 | Cathal Black | 18 |
| 2970 | Plod | GB | 1972 | Michael Cort | 20 |
| 2971 | The Cheviot, the Stag and the Black, Black Oil | GB | 1974 | John MacKenzie | 90 +V |
| 2972 | The Bofors Gun | GB | 1968 | Jack Gold | 105 |
| 2973 | Ninety-Two in the Shade (aka: 92 in the Shade) | USA | 1975 | Thomas McGuane | 93 +V |
| 2974 | The Sporting Club | USA | 1971 | Larry Peerce | 105 +V |
| 2975 | O menino e o vento [The boy and the wind] | BRAZ | 1967 | Carlos Hugo Christensen | 104 |
| 2976 | Tati, a garôta | BRAZ | 1973 | Bruno Barreto | 100 |
| 2977 | Viagem aos seios de Duília | BRAZ | 1963 | Carlos Hugo Christensen | 104(85) |
| 2978 | A danca das bruxas [Dance of witches] | BRAZ | 1970 | Francisco Dreux | 100 |
| 2979 | O cavalinho azul | BRAZ | 1985 | Eduardo Escorel | 82 |
| 2980 | Pluft, o fantasminha | BRAZ | 1962 | Romain Lésage | 95 |
| 2981 | | | | | |
| 2982 | La laguna negra | SP | 1952 | Arturo Ruiz Castillo | 100(79) |
| 2983 | La duquesa de Benameji | SP | 1949(48) | Luis Lucía | 103(97) |
| 2984 | La Lola se va a los puertos | SP | 1947 | Juan de Orduña | 120 |
| 2985 | La mandragola (The Mandrake) (aka: The Love Root) | IT/FR | 1965 | Alberto Lattuada | 99(103) |
| 2986 | Dance Pretty Lady | GB | 1932 | Anthony Asquith | 64 |
| 2987 | Carnival | GB | 1946 | Stanley Haynes | 93 |
| 2988 | Rockets Galore (USA: Mad Little Island) | GB | 1958 | Michael Relph | 94 |
| 2989 | Sylvia Scarlett | USA | 1936(35) | George Cukor | 94 +V |
| 2990 | Whisky Galore! (USA: Tight Little Island) | GB | 1949(48) | Alexander Mackendrick | 82 +V |
| 2991 | | | | | |
| 2992 | The Schooner | IRE | 1983 | Bill Miskelly | 53 |
| 2993 | Epistle To Be Left in the Earth | CAN | 1973 | John Saxton | 20 |
| 2994 | Hud | USA | 1962 | Martin Ritt | 112 |
| 2995 | The Last Picture Show | USA | 1971 | Peter Bogdanovich | 118 |
| 2996 | Lovin' Molly | USA | 1973 | Sidney Lumet | 98 |
| 2997 | Terms of Endearment | USA | 1983 | James L. Brooks | 132 +V |
| 2998 | Texasville | USA | 1990 | Peter Bogdanovich | 125 |
| 2999 | La bandera (aka: Escape From Yesterday) | FR | 1935 | Julien Duvivier | 100 |
| 3000 | Marguerite de la nuit (IT: Margherita della notte) | FR/IT | 1955 | Claude Autant-Lara | 126(100) |
| 3001 | Le quai des brumes (Port of Shadows) | FR | 1938 | Marcel Carné | 91 |
| 3002 | La tradition de minuit | FR | 1939 | Roger Richebé | 105 |

| No. | Author | Nationality | Form | Literary Title | Date |
|---|---|---|---|---|---|
| 3003 | **Madách Imre** | Hungarian | V | **Az ember tragédiája**<br>(The Tragedy of Man) | 1863 |
| 3004 | **Maeterlinck, Maurice** | Belgian | P | **La mort de Tintagiles**<br>(The Death of Tintagiles) | 1894 |
| 3005 | **Maeterlinck, Maurice** | Belgian | P | **L'oiseau bleu**<br>(The Blue Bird) | 1909 |
| 3006 | **Maeterlinck, Maurice** | Belgian | P | **L'oiseau bleu** | 1909 |
| 3007 | **Mahfūz, Najib** | Egyptian | N | **Quasr al-Shauq**<br>(aka: Qasr Ash-Shauq)<br>(Palace of Desire) | 1957 |
| 3008 | **Mailer, Norman** | American | N | **An American Dream** | 1965 |
| 3009 | **Mailer, Norman** | American | | **The Executioner's Song** | 1979 |
| 3010 | **Mailer, Norman** | American | N | **The Naked and the Dead** | 1948 |
| 3011 | **Mailer, Norman** | American | N | **Tough Guys Don't Dance** | 1984 |
| 3012 | **Majerová, Maria** | Czech | N | **Siréna**<br>(The Strike) | 1935 |
| 3013 | **Malamud, Bernard** | American | SS | **The Angel Levine** | 1955 |
| 3014 | **Malamud, Bernard** | American | N | **The Fixer** | 1966 |
| 3015 | **Malamud, Bernard** | American | N | **The Natural** | 1952 |
| 3016 | **Mallet-Joris, Françoise** | Belgian | N | **La chambre rouge**<br>(The Red Room) | 1955 |
| 3017 | **Mallet-Joris, Françoise** | Belgian | SS | **Les poubelles**<br>(The Garbage Men) | 1956 |
| 3018 | **Mallet-Joris, Françoise** | Belgian | N | **Le rempart des Béguines**<br>(Into the Labyrinth) | 1951 |
| 3019 | **Malory, Sir Thomas** | British | V | **Le Morte D'Arthur**<br>(aka: La Mort Darthur) | 1485 |
| 3020 | **Malory, Sir Thomas** | British | V | **Le Morte D'Arthur** | 1485 |
| 3021 | **Malraux, André** | French | N | **L'éspoir**<br>(Man's Hope) | 1937 |
| 3022 | **Mamet, David** | American | P | **Sexual Perversity in Chicago** | 1978 |
| 3023 | **Mándy Iván** | Hungarian | SS | **Borika vendégei** | 1965 |
| 3024 | **Mándy Iván** | Hungarian | SS | **Ciklon**<br>[Cyclone] | 1966<br>(coll) |
| 3025 | **Mándy Iván** | Hungarian | N | **Csutak és a szürke ló** | 1959 |
| 3026 | **Mándy Iván** | Hungarian | N | **A locsolókocsi** | 1965 |
| 3027 | **Mándy Iván** | Hungarian | SS+N | **Régi idők mozija** {ss}<br>(The Movie of Old Times) +<br>**A pálya szélén** {n}<br>(On the Touch Lines) | 1967+<br>1963 |
| 3028 | **Manev, Todor Sŭbev**<br>(see: Zidarov, Kamen) | Bulgarian | P | | |
| 3029 | **Mankiewicz, Herman J.**<br>(joint, see: Kaufman, George S.) | American | P | | |
| 3030 | **Mann, Heinrich** | German | N | **Empfang bei der Welt** | 1956<br>(posth.) |
| 3031 | **Mann, Heinrich** | German | N | **Professor Unrat**<br>(aka: Der blaue Engel)<br>(The Blue Angel)<br>(USA: Small Town Tyrant) | 1905<br>(aka:1947) |
| 3032 | **Mann, Heinrich** | German | N | **Professor Unrat** | 1905 |
| 3033 | **Mann, Heinrich** | German | N | **Der Untertan**<br>(The Patrioteer)<br>(aka: Man of Straw)<br>(USA: Little Superman) | 1914-18 |
| 3034 | **Mann, Klaus** | German | N | **Flucht in den Norden**<br>(Journey Into Freedom) | 1934 |
| 3035 | **Mann, Klaus** | German | N | **Mephisto** | 1936 |
| 3036 | **Mann, Thomas** | German | N | **Bekenntnisse des Hochstaplers**<br>**Felix Krull**<br>(Confessions of Felix Krull,<br>Confidence Man) | 1922(54) |

| No | Film Title | Country of Production | Date | Director(s) | Duration of Film |
|---|---|---|---|---|---|
| 3003 | Angyali üdvözlet (The Annunciation) | HUNG | 1984 | András Jeles | 100 |
| 3004 | The Death of Tintagiles | GB | 1977 | Malcolm Edwards | 37(vo) |
| 3005 | The Blue Bird | USA | 1940 | Walter Lang | 98(88) |
| 3006 | The Blue Bird | USA/USSR | 1976 | George Cukor | 83(99) |
| 3007 | Qasr al-Shauq (aka: Kasr el shawk) | EGY | 1967 | Hassan el Emam | 130 |
| 3008 | An American Dream (GB: See You in Hell, Darling) | USA | 1966 | Robert Gist | 103 |
| 3009 | The Executioner's Song | USA | 1982 | Lawrence Schiller | 135(200) +V |
| 3010 | The Naked and the Dead | USA | 1958 | Raoul Walsh | 131 +V |
| 3011 | Tough Guys Don't Dance | USA | 1987 | Norman Mailer | 109 +V |
| 3012 | Siréna (The Strike) | CZ | 1947 | Karel Steklý | 83 |
| 3013 | The Angel Levine | USA | 1970 | Ján Kadár | 105 |
| 3014 | The Fixer | USA | 1968 | John Frankenheimer | 130 |
| 3015 | The Natural | USA | 1984 | Barry Levinson | 122 +V |
| 3016 | La chambre rouge | BEL/FR | 1972 | Jean-Pierre Berckmans | 99 |
| 3017 | Le travail c'est la liberté | FR | 1959 | Louis Grospierre | 87 |
| 3018 | Le rempart des Béguines (The Beguines) | FR | 1972 | Guy Casaril | 90 |
| 3019 | Knights of the Round Table | GB | 1953 | Richard Thorpe | 115 |
| 3020 | Excalibur | USA | 1981 | John Boorman | 140 +V |
| 3021 | L'éspoir (SP: Sierra de teruel) (Man's Hope) (aka: Days of Hope) | FR/SP | 1945(39) | André Malraux Max Aub Denis Marion | 78(73) |
| 3022 | About Last Night... | USA | 1986 | Edward Zwick | 113 +V |
| 3023 | Lányarcok tükörben (Parallel Faces) | HUNG | 1973(72) | Róbert Bán | 91 |
| 3024 | Ketten haltak meg (Two Have Died) | HUNG | 1966(65) | György Palásthy | 77 |
| 3025 | Csutak é a szürke ló (Csutak and the Grey Horse) | HUNG | 1960 | Zoltán Várkonyi | 78 |
| 3026 | A locsolókocsi (The Orange Watering Truck) | HUNG | 1974(73) | Zsolt Kézdi-Kovács | 89 |
| 3027 | Régi idők focija (Football of the Good Old Days) | HUNG | 1973 | Pál Sándor | 85 |
| 3028 | | | | | |
| 3029 | | | | | |
| 3030 | Belcanto oder Darf eine Nutte schluchzen? (aka: Belcanto) | GER | 1977 | Robert van Ackeren | 94 |
| 3031 | Der blaue Engel (The Blue Angel) | GER | 1930 | Josef von Sternberg | 103 +V |
| 3032 | The Blue Angel | USA | 1959 | Edward Dmytryk | 107 |
| 3033 | Der Untertan (The Underdog) (aka: The Submissive) | GDR | 1951 | Wolfgang Staudte | 90(106) +V |
| 3034 | Pako pohjoiseen | FIN/GER | 1985 | Ingemo Engström | 118 |
| 3035 | Mephisto | HUNG/GER | 1981 | István Szabó | 144 +V |
| 3036 | Die Bekenntnisse des Hochstaplers Felix Krull (The Confessions of Felix Krull) | GER | 1957 | Kurt Hoffmann | 107 |

| No. | Author | Nationality | Form | Literary Title | Date |
|-----|--------|-------------|------|----------------|------|
| 3037 | **Mann, Thomas** | German | N | **Buddenbrooks** {pts.1-2} | 1901 |
| 3038 | **Mann, Thomas** | German | N | **Doktor Faustus** (Doctor Faustus) | 1947 |
| 3039 | **Mann, Thomas** | German | N | **Königliche Hoheit** (Royal Highness) | 1909 |
| 3040 | **Mann, Thomas** | German | N | **Lotte in Weimar** (USA: The Beloved Returns) | 1939 |
| 3041 | **Mann, Thomas** | German | SS | **Der Tod in Venedig** (Death in Venice) | 1912 |
| 3042 | **Mann, Thomas** | German | SS | **Tonio Kröger** | 1903 |
| 3043 | **Mann, Thomas** | German | SS | **Unordnung und frühes Leid** (Disorder and Early Sorrow) | 1925 |
| 3044 | **Mann, Thomas** | German | SS | **Wälsungenblut** (The Blood of the Walsungs) + **Ein Glück** (A Gleam) | 1921+ 1904 |
| 3045 | **Mann, Thomas** | German | N | **Der Zauberberg** (The Magic Mountain) | 1924 |
| 3046 | **Manov, Emil** | Bulgarian | N | **Pleneno yato** [Captured squadron] | 1947 |
| 3047 | **Manzoni, Alessandro** | Italian | N | **I promessi sposi** (The Betrothed) | 1842 |
| 3048 | **Manzoni, Alessandro** | Italian | N | **I promessi sposi** | 1842 |
| 3049 | **Mao Dun** (see: Shen Yanbing) | Chinese | N/SS | | |
| 3050 | **Mao Tun** (see: Shen Yanbing) | Chinese | N/SS | | |
| 3051 | **Maquet, Auguste** (joint, see: Dumas, Alexandre (père)) | French | N | | |
| 3052 | **Mara, Sally** (see: Queneau, Raymond) | French | N | | |
| 3053 | **Marceau, Félicien** (Louis Carette) | French/ Belgian | P | **La bonne soupe** | 1958 |
| 3054 | **Marceau, Félicien** | French/ Belgian | P | **L'oeuf** (The Egg) | 1957 |
| 3055 | **March, Joseph Moncure** | American | V | **The Set-Up** | 1928 |
| 3056 | **March, Joseph Moncure** | American | V | **The Wild Party** | 1928 |
| 3057 | **Marc-Michel** (joint, see: Labiche, Eugène) | French | P | | |
| 3058 | **Marcos, Plínio** | Brazilian | P | **Navalha na carne** (Razor in the Flesh) | 1968 |
| 3059 | **Marcos, Plínio** | Brazilian | SS | **Quebradas da vida** | 1973 |
| 3060 | **Margueritte, Victor** | French | N | **La garçonne** (The Batchelor Girl) | 1922 |
| 3061 | **Margueritte, Victor** | French | N | **La garçonne** | 1922 |
| 3062 | **Marinković, Ranko** | Yugoslav(Cro) | N | **Kiklop** | 1966(52) |
| 3063 | **Marivaux, Pierre de** | French | P | **Le jeu de l'amour et du hasard** (The Game of Love and Chance) (aka: Love in Livery) | 1730 |
| 3064 | **Marlowe, Christopher** | British | P | **Doctor Faustus** (aka: The Tragicall History of D. Faustus) | 1604 1616 |
| 3065 | **Marlowe, Christopher** | British | P | **Edward II** | 1594 |
| 3066 | **Marmol, José Pedro Cristólogo** | Argentine | N | **Amalia** | 1851 |
| 3067 | **Marquand, John Phillips** | American | N | **B. F.'s Daughter** (GB: Polly Fulton) | 1946 |
| 3068 | **Marquand, John Phillips** | American | N | **H. M. Pulham, Esquire** (aka: Gone Tomorrow) | 1941 |
| 3069 | **Marquand, John Phillips** | American | N | **The Late George Apley** | 1937 |
| 3070 | **Marquand, John Phillips** | American | N | **Melville Goodwin, U.S.A.** | 1951 |
| 3071 | **Marquand, John Phillips** | American | N | **Stopover Tokyo** | 1957 |
| 3072 | **Marquand, John Phillips** | American | N | **Thank You, Mr Moto** | 1936 |
| 3073 | **Marquand, John Phillips** | American | N | **Think Fast, Mr Moto** | 1937 |
| 3074 | **Márquez, Gabriel García** (see: García Márquez, Gabriel) | Colombian | SS/N | | |

| No | Film Title | Country of Production | Date | Director(s) | Duration of Film |
|----|-----------|----------------------|------|------------|------------------|
| 3037 | **Die Buddenbrooks** *(2 - parts)* | GER | 1959 | **Alfred Weidenmann** | Pt.1, 99 Pt.2, 106 |
| 3038 | **Doktor Faustus** *(Doctor Faustus)* | GER | 1982 | **Franz Seitz** | 137 |
| 3039 | **Königliche Hoheit** | GER | 1953 | **Harald Braun** | 106 |
| 3040 | **Lotte in Weimar** | GDR | 1975 | **Egon Günther** | 124 |
| 3041 | **Morte a Venezia** *(FR: Mort à Venise) (Death in Venice)* | IT/FR | 1971 | **Luchino Visconti** | 128(135) +V |
| 3042 | **Tonio Kröger** | GER/FR | 1964 | **Rolf Thiele** | 90 |
| 3043 | **Unordnung und frühes Leid** *(Disorder and Early Suffering)* | GER | 1977(76) | **Franz Seitz** | 90(86) |
| 3044 | **Wälsungenblut** *(Blood of the Walsungs)* | GER | 1964 | **Rolf Thiele** | 85 |
| 3045 | **Der Zauberberg** *(The Magic Mountain)* | GER/FR/IT | 1982(81) | **Hans W. Geissendörfer** | 153 |
| 3046 | **Pleneno yato** | BULG | 1962 | **Ducho Mundrov** | 90 |
| 3047 | **I promessi sposi** *(The Spirit and the Flesh)* | IT | 1941 | **Mario Camerini** | 115 |
| 3048 | **I promessi sposi** *(SP: Promesa sagrada)* | IT/SP | 1964(63) | **Mario Maffei** | 110(102) |
| 3049 | | | | | |
| 3050 | | | | | |
| 3051 | | | | | |
| 3052 | | | | | |
| 3053 | **La bonne soupe** *(IT: La pappa reale)* | FR/IT | 1963 | **Robert Thomas** | 97 |
| 3054 | **L'oeuf** | FR | 1972(71) | **Jean Herman** | 90 |
| 3055 | **The Set-Up** | USA | 1949 | **Robert Wise** | 72 |
| 3056 | **The Wild Party** | USA | 1974 | **James Ivory** | 100 +V |
| 3057 | | | | | |
| 3058 | **A navalha na carne** | BRAZ | 1970 | **Braz Chediak** | 90 |
| 3059 | **Barra pesada** | BRAZ | 1977 | **Reginaldo Faria** | 95 |
| 3060 | **La garçonne** | FR | 1936 | **Jean de Limur** | 95 |
| 3061 | **La garçonne** | FR | 1957 | **Jacqueline Audry** | 97 |
| 3062 | **Kiklop** *(Cyclops)* | YUGO | 1982 | **Antun Vrdoljak** | 137 |
| 3063 | **Les amoureux du 'France'** *(IT: Il gioco degli innamorati)* | FR/IT | 1965(64) | **Pierre Grimblat** **François Reichenback** | 96 |
| 3064 | **Doctor Faustus** *(IT: Il dottor Faustus)* | GB/IT | 1967 | **Richard Burton** **Nevill Coghill** | 93 |
| 3065 | **Edward II** | GB | 1991 | **Derek Jarman** | 90 |
| 3066 | **Amalia** | ARG | 1936 | **Luis J. Moglia Barth** | 104 |
| 3067 | **B. F.'s Daughter** *(GB: Polly Fulton)* | USA | 1948 | **Robert Z. Leonard** | 106 |
| 3068 | **H. M. Pulham Esquire** | USA | 1941 | **King Vidor** | 120 |
| 3069 | **The Late George Apley** | USA | 1947 | **Joseph L. Mankiewicz** | 96 |
| 3070 | **Top Secret Affair** *(GB: Their Secret Affair)* | USA | 1957 | **H. C. Potter** | 100 |
| 3071 | **Stopover Tokyo** | USA | 1957 | **Richard L. Breen** | 101 +V |
| 3072 | **Thank You, Mr Moto** | USA | 1937 | **Norman Foster** | 67 |
| 3073 | **Think Fast, Mr Moto** | USA | 1937 | **Norman Foster** | 66 |
| 3074 | | | | | |

**169**

| No. | Author | Nationality | Form | Literary Title | Date |
|---|---|---|---|---|---|
| 3075 | Marquina, Eduardo | Spanish | P | Doña María la Brava | 1909 |
| 3076 | Marryat, Frederick | British | N | The Little Savage | 1848-49 |
| 3077 | Marryat, Frederick | British | N | Mr Midshipman Easy | 1836 |
| 3078 | Marsé, Juan | Spanish | SS | Libertad provisional | 1976 |
| 3079 | Marsé, Juan | Spanish | N | La muchacha de las brages de oro | 1978 |
| 3080 | Marsé, Juan | Spanish | N | Si te dicen que caí | 1973 |
| 3081 | Martin, Eduard (joint, see: Labiche, Eugène) | French | P | | |
| 3082 | Martín Gaite, Carmen | Spanish | SS | Las ataduras | 1960 |
| 3083 | Martín Recuerda, José | Spanish | P | Las salvajes en Puente San Gil [The savages of San Gil bridge] | 1963 |
| 3084 | Martínez Ruiz, José (Azorin) | Spanish | P | La guerrilla | 1936 |
| 3085 | Martínez Sierra, Gregorio | Spanish | P | El amor brujo (Love Magic) | 1915 |
| 3086 | Martínez Sierra, Gregorio | Spanish | P | Canción de cuna (The Cradle Song) | 1911 |
| 3087 | Martínez Sierra, Gregorio | Spanish | N | Tú eres la paz (Ana María) | 1906 |
| 3088 | Martinson, Harry | Swedish | N | Vägen till Klockrike (The Road) | 1948 |
| 3089 | Mason, A. E. W. | British | N | At the Villa Rose | 1910 |
| 3090 | Mason, A. E. W. | British | N | At the Villa Rose | 1910 |
| 3091 | Mason, A. E. W. | British | N | The Drum | 1937 |
| 3092 | Mason, A. E. W. | British | N | Fire Over England | 1936 |
| 3093 | Mason, A. E. W. | British | N | The Four Feathers | 1902 |
| 3094 | Mason, A. E. W. | British | N | The Four Feathers | 1902 |
| 3095 | Mason, A. E. W. | British | N | The Four Feathers | 1902 |
| 3096 | Mason, A. E. W. | British | N | The Four Feathers | 1902 |
| 3097 | Mason, A. E. W. | British | P | Green Stockings (aka: Colonel Smith) | 1909 |
| 3098 | Mason, A. E. W. | British | P | Green Stockings | 1909 |
| 3099 | Mason, A. E. W. | British | N | The House of the Arrow | 1924 |
| 3100 | Mason, A. E. W. | British | N | The House of the Arrow | 1924 |
| 3101 | Mason, A. E. W. | British | N | The House of the Arrow | 1924 |
| 3102 | Mason, A. E. W. | British | N | The House of the Arrow | 1924 |
| 3103 | Matavulj, Simō | Yugoslav(Serb) | N | Bakonja fra Brne | 1892 |
| 3104 | Maugham, Robin | British | N | Line on Ginger (aka: The Intruder) | 1949 (aka:1960) |
| 3105 | Maugham, Robin | British | N | The Rough and the Smooth | 1951 |
| 3106 | Maugham, Robin | British | SS | The Servant | 1948 |
| 3107 | Maugham, W. Somerset | British | SS | The Ant and the Grasshopper + Winter Cruise + Gigolo and Gigolette | 1936+ 1947+ 1940 |
| 3108 | Maugham, W. Somerset | British | SS | The Beachcomber (aka: The Vessel of Wrath) | 1931 |
| 3109 | Maugham, W. Somerset | British | SS | The Beachcomber | 1931 |
| 3110 | Maugham, W. Somerset | British | N | Christmas Holiday | 1939 |
| 3111 | Maugham, W. Somerset | British | P | The Circle | 1921 |
| 3112 | Maugham, W. Somerset | British | SS | The Colonel's Lady + The Kite + The Alien Corn + The Facts of Life | 1947+ 1931+ 1940 |
| 3113 | Maugham, W. Somerset | British | P | The Constant Wife | 1926 |
| 3114 | Maugham, W. Somerset | British | SS | The Hairless Mexican + Triton | 1928 |

**170**

| No | Film Title | Country of Production | Date | Director(s) | Duration of Film |
|----|-----------|----------------------|------|-------------|------------------|
| 3075 | **Doña María la Brava** | SP | 1948(47) | **Luis Marquina** | 90(105) |
| 3076 | **The Little Savage** | USA/MEX | 1959 | **Byron Haskin** | 72 |
| 3077 | **Midshipman Easy** (USA: Men of the Sea) | GB | 1935 | **Carol Reed** | 77 |
| 3078 | **Libertad provisional** (Out on Parole) | SP | 1976 | **Roberto Bodegas** | 98(94) +V |
| 3079 | **La muchacha de las brages de oro** (The Golden Girl) | SP/VEN | 1980 | **Vicente Aranda** | 101 |
| 3080 | **Si te dicen que caí** (If They Tell You I Fell) | SP | 1989 | **Vicente Aranda** | 120 |
| 3081 | | | | | |
| 3082 | **Emilia... parada y fonda** | SP | 1976 | **Angelino Fons** | 103(94) |
| 3083 | **Las salvajes en Puente San Gil** [The wild women on San Gil bridge] | SP | 1967(66) | **Antoni Ribas** | 90(85) +V |
| 3084 | **La guerrilla** | SP/IT | 1972 | **Rafael Gil** | 95(90) |
| 3085 | **El amor brujo** | SP | 1967 | **Francisco Rovira Beleta** | 90(99) |
| 3086 | **Canción de cuna** | SP | 1961(60) | **José María Elorrieta** | 93(83) |
| 3087 | **Tú eres la paz** | ARG | 1942 | **Gregorio Martínez Sierra** | 74 |
| 3088 | **Vägen till Klockrike** (The Road to Klockrike) | SWE | 1953 | **Gunnar Skoglund** | 102 |
| 3089 | **At the Villa Rose** (USA: Mystery at the Villa Rose) | GB | 1930 | **Leslie Hiscott** | 100 |
| 3090 | **At the Villa Rose** (USA: House of Mystery) | GB | 1939 | **Walter Summers** | 74 |
| 3091 | **The Drum** (aka: The Drums) | GB | 1938 | **Zoltan Korda** | 90 +V |
| 3092 | **Fire Over England** | GB | 1937(36) | **William K. Howard** | 92 +V |
| 3093 | **The Four Feathers** | USA | 1930(29) | **Lothar Mendes** | 83 |
| 3094 | **The Four Feathers** | GB | 1939 | **Zoltan Korda** | 126 +V |
| 3095 | **Storm Over the Nile** (aka: The Four Feathers) | GB | 1955 | **Terence Young** **Zoltan Korda** | 107 +V |
| 3096 | **The Four Feathers** | GB | 1978(77) | **Don Sharp** | 110 +V |
| 3097 | **The Flirting Widow** | USA | 1930 | **William A. Seiter** | 70 |
| 3098 | **Her Imaginary Lover** | GB | 1933 | **George King** | 65 |
| 3099 | **The House of the Arrow** | GB | 1930 | **Leslie Hiscott** | 76 |
| 3100 | **La maison de la flèche** | FR | 1930 | **Henri Fescourt** | 82 |
| 3101 | **The House of the Arrow** (aka: Castle of Crimes) | GB | 1940 | **Harold French** | 66 |
| 3102 | **The House of the Arrow** | GB | 1953 | **Michael Anderson** | 72 |
| 3103 | **Bakonja fra Brne** | YUGO | 1951 | **Fedor Hanžeković** | 104 |
| 3104 | **The Intruder** | GB | 1953 | **Guy Hamilton** | 84 |
| 3105 | **The Rough and the Smooth** (USA: Portrait of a Sinner) | GB | 1959 | **Robert Siodmak** | 99 |
| 3106 | **The Servant** | GB | 1963 | **Joseph Losey** | 115 +V |
| 3107 | **Encore** | GB | 1951 | **Harold French** **Pat Jackson** **Anthony Pélissier** | 88 |
| 3108 | **Vessel of Wrath** (aka: The Beachcomber) | GB | 1938 | **Erich Pommer** | 93 |
| 3109 | **The Beachcomber** | GB | 1954 | **Muriel Box** | 90 |
| 3110 | **Christmas Holiday** | USA | 1944 | **Robert Siodmak** | 93 |
| 3111 | **Strictly Unconventional** (aka: The Circle) | USA | 1930 | **David Burton** | 60 |
| 3112 | **Quartet** (aka: Somerset Maugham's Quartet) | GB | 1948 | **Ken Annakin** **Arthur Crabtree** **Harold French** **Ralph Smart** | 120 +V |
| 3113 | **Finden sie, daß Constanze sich richtig verhält?** (The Constant Wife) | GER | 1962 | **Tom Pevsner** | 81 |
| 3114 | **The Secret Agent** | GB | 1936 | **Alfred Hitchcock** | 85 +V |

| No. | Author | Nationality | Form | Literary Title | Date |
|---|---|---|---|---|---|
| 3115 | Maugham, W. Somerset | British | N | The Hour Before the Dawn | 1942 |
| 3116 | Maugham, W. Somerset | British | SS-P | The Letter | 1926{ss}<br>1927{p} |
| 3117 | Maugham, W. Somerset | British | SS-P | The Letter | 1926{ss}<br>1927{p} |
| 3118 | Maugham, W. Somerset | British | SS-P | The Letter | 1926{ss}<br>1927{p} |
| 3119 | Maugham, W. Somerset | British | SS-P | The Letter | 1926{ss}<br>1927{p} |
| 3120 | Maugham, W. Somerset | British | SS-P | The Letter | 1926{ss}<br>1927{p} |
| 3121 | Maugham, W. Somerset | British | N | The Moon and Sixpence | 1919 |
| 3122 | Maugham, W. Somerset | British | N | The Narrow Corner | 1932 |
| 3123 | Maugham, W. Somerset | British | N | The Narrow Corner | 1932 |
| 3124 | Maugham, W. Somerset | British | N | Of Human Bondage | 1915 |
| 3125 | Maugham, W. Somerset | British | N | Of Human Bondage | 1915 |
| 3126 | Maugham, W. Somerset | British | N | Of Human Bondage | 1915 |
| 3127 | Maugham, W. Somerset | British | P | Our Betters | 1921 |
| 3128 | Maugham, W. Somerset | British | N | The Painted Veil | 1925 |
| 3129 | Maugham, W. Somerset | British | N | The Painted Veil | 1925 |
| 3130 | Maugham, W. Somerset | British | SS | Rain | 1921 |
| 3131 | Maugham, W. Somerset | British | SS | Rain | 1921 |
| 3132 | Maugham, W. Somerset | British | SS | Rain | 1921 |
| 3133 | Maugham, W. Somerset | British | N | The Razor's Edge | 1944 |
| 3134 | Maugham, W. Somerset | British | N | The Razor's Edge | 1944 |
| 3135 | Maugham, W. Somerset | British | P | The Sacred Flame | 1928 |
| 3136 | Maugham, W. Somerset | British | P | The Sacred Flame | 1928 |
| 3137 | Maugham, W. Somerset | British | P | The Tenth Man | 1913 |
| 3138 | Maugham, W. Somerset | British | N | Theatre | 1937 |
| 3139 | Maugham, W. Somerset | British | P | Too Many Husbands<br>(GB: Home and Beauty) | 1919 |
| 3140 | Maugham, W. Somerset | British | P | Too Many Husbands | 1919 |
| 3141 | Maugham, W. Somerset | British | SS | The Verger +<br>Mr Knowall +<br>Sanatorium | 1947 |
| 3142 | Maupassant, Guy de | French | N | Bel-Ami | 1885 |
| 3143 | Maupassant, Guy de | French | N | Bel-Ami | 1885 |
| 3144 | Maupassant, Guy de | French | N | Bel-Ami | 1885 |
| 3145 | Maupassant, Guy de | French | N | Bel-Ami | 1885 |
| 3146 | Maupassant, Guy de | French | SS | Les bijoux<br>(The Jewels) | 1884 |
| 3147 | Maupassant, Guy de | French | SS | Boule de suif<br>(Ball-of-fat)<br>(aka: Ball-of-tallow) | 1880 |
| 3148 | Maupassant, Guy de | French | SS | Boule de suif | 1880 |
| 3149 | Maupassant, Guy de | French | SS | Boule de suif +<br>Mademoiselle Fifi | 1880+<br>1881 |
| 3150 | Maupassant, Guy de | French | SS | Boule de suif +<br>Mademoiselle Fifi | 1880+<br>1881 |
| 3151 | Maupassant, Guy de | French | SS | Ce cochon de Morin<br>(That Pig, Morin) | 1883 |
| 3152 | Maupassant, Guy de | French | SS | Ce cochon de Morin | 1883 |
| 3153 | Maupassant, Guy de | French | SS | La chevelure<br>(Woman's Hair) | 1885 |
| 3154 | Maupassant, Guy de | French | SS | La chevelure | 1885 |
| 3155 | Maupassant, Guy de | French | SS | Deux amis<br>(Two Friends) | 1883 |

**172**

| No | Film Title | Country of Production | Date | Director(s) | Duration of Film |
|---|---|---|---|---|---|
| 3115 | The Hour Before the Dawn | USA | 1944 | Frank Tuttle | 75 |
| 3116 | The Letter | USA | 1930(29) | Jean de Limur | 61 |
| 3117 | La lettre (The Letter) | FR | 1930 | Louis Mercanton | 70 |
| 3118 | Weib im Dschungel | GER/FR/USA | 1931(30) | Dimitri Buchowetzki | 63 |
| 3119 | The Letter | USA | 1940 | William Wyler | 95 +V |
| 3120 | The Unfaithful | USA | 1947 | Vincent Sherman | 109 |
| 3121 | The Moon and Sixpence | USA | 1942 | Albert Lewin | 85 |
| 3122 | The Narrow Corner | USA | 1933 | Alfred E. Green | 71 |
| 3123 | Isle of Fury | USA | 1936 | Frank McDonald | 60 |
| 3124 | Of Human Bondage | USA | 1934 | John Cromwell | 83 |
| 3125 | Of Human Bondage | USA | 1946 | Edmund Goulding | 105 |
| 3126 | Of Human Bondage | GB | 1964 | Ken Hughes Henry Hathaway | 99 |
| 3127 | Our Betters | USA | 1933 | George Cukor | 83 |
| 3128 | The Painted Veil | USA | 1934 | Richard Boleslavsky | 84 |
| 3129 | The Seventh Sin | USA | 1957 | Ronald Neame | 94 |
| 3130 | Rain | USA | 1932 | Lewis Milestone | 92 |
| 3131 | Miss Sadie Thompson | USA | 1953 | Curtis Bernhardt | 91 |
| 3132 | Sadie | USA | 1980 | Bob C. Chinn | 88 +V |
| 3133 | The Razor's Edge | USA | 1946 | Edmund Goulding | 146 |
| 3134 | The Razor's Edge | USA | 1984 | John Byrum | 128 +V |
| 3135 | Die heilige Flamme (The Sacred Flame) | GER/USA | 1930 | Berthold Viertel | 86 |
| 3136 | The Right to Live (GB: The Sacred Flame) | USA | 1935 | William Keighley | 75 |
| 3137 | The Tenth Man | GB | 1936 | Brian Desmond Hurst | 68 |
| 3138 | Julia, du bist zauberhaft (The Seduction of Julia) (USA: Adorable Julia) | AUST/FR | 1962 | Alfred Weidenmann | 97 |
| 3139 | Too Many Husbands (GB: My Two Husbands) | USA | 1940 | Wesley Ruggles | 84 |
| 3140 | Three For The Show | USA | 1954 | H. C. Potter | 93 |
| 3141 | Trio | GB | 1950 | Ken Annakin Harold French | 91 |
| 3142 | Bel-Ami | GER | 1939 | Willi Forst | 100 |
| 3143 | The Private Affairs of Bel-Ami | USA | 1946 | Albert Lewin | 112 |
| 3144 | Bel-Ami | AUST | 1954 | Louis Daquin | 100 |
| 3145 | Bel-Ami | SWE/FR | 1976(75) | Mac Ahlberg (Bert Torn) | 104 |
| 3146 | Romanze in Moll (Romance in a Minor Key) | GER | 1943 | Helmut Käutner | 98 |
| 3147 | Pyshka (aka: Boule de suif) | USSR | 1934 | Mikhail Romm | 69 |
| 3148 | Maria no Oyuki (Oyuki the Virgin) (aka: Oyuki the Madonna) (aka: The Virgin From Oyuki) | JAP | 1935 | Kenji Mizoguchi | 80 |
| 3149 | Mademoiselle Fifi | USA | 1944 | Robert Wise | 69 |
| 3150 | Boule de suif (aka: Madame Fifi) (Angel and Sinner) | FR | 1945 | Christian-Jaque | 100 |
| 3151 | Ce cochon de Morin | FR | 1933 | Georges Lacombe | 87 |
| 3152 | La terreur des dames | FR | 1956 | Jean Boyer | 93 |
| 3153 | La chevelure | FR | 1961 | Ado Kyrou | 19 |
| 3154 | Golden Braid | AUSTL | 1990 | Paul Cox | 91 |
| 3155 | Deux amis | FR | 1946 | Dimitri Kirsanoff | 25 |

| No. | Author | Nationality | Form | Literary Title | Date |
|-----|--------|-------------|------|----------------|------|
| 3156 | **Maupassant, Guy de** | French | SS | **La femme de Paul** *(Paul's Mistress)* + **Le signe** *(The Sign)* *(aka: The Signal)* | 1881+ 1887 |
| 3157 | **Maupassant, Guy de** | French | SS | **Histoire d'une fille de ferme** *(Story of a Farm Girl)* | 1881 |
| 3158 | **Maupassant, Guy de** | French | SS | **Le horla** *(The Horla)* | 1887 |
| 3159 | **Maupassant, Guy de** | French | SS | **Le masque** *(The Mask)* + **La maison Tellier** + **La modéle** *(Model)* *(aka: The Artist's Wife)* | 1890+ 1881+ 1888 |
| 3160 | **Maupassant, Guy de** | French | SS | **L'ordonnance** | 1889 |
| 3161 | **Maupassant, Guy de** | French | SS | **Une partie de campagne** *(Country Excursion)* | 1881 |
| 3162 | **Maupassant, Guy de** | French | N | **Pierre et Jean** *(Pierre and Jean)* | 1888 |
| 3163 | **Maupassant, Guy de** | French | N | **Pierre et Jean** | 1888 |
| 3164 | **Maupassant, Guy de** | French | SS | **La question du latin** *(Question of Latin)* *(aka: Are We to Teach Latin?)* | 1900 |
| 3165 | **Maupassant, Guy de** | French | SS | **Le rosier de Madame Husson** *(Madame Husson's 'rosier')* | 1888 |
| 3166 | **Maupassant, Guy de** | French | SS | **Le rosier de Madame Husson** | 1888 |
| 3167 | **Maupassant, Guy de** | French | SS | **Le signe** *(The Sign)* *(aka: The Signal)* *(aka: Playing With Fire)* | 1887 |
| 3168 | **Maupassant, Guy de** | French | N | **Une vie: l'humble verité** *(A Woman's Life)* *(aka: Life)* | 1883 |
| 3169 | **Maupassant, Guy de** | French | N | **Une vie: l'humble verité** | 1883 |
| 3170 | **Maupassant, Guy de** | French | N | **Une vie: l'humble verité** | 1883 |
| 3171 | **Maupassant, Guy de** | French | SS | **Yvette** | 1885 |
| 3172 | **Mauriac, François** | French | N | **Les anges noirs** *(The Dark Angels)* | 1936 |
| 3173 | **Mauriac, François** | French | N | **Thérèse Desqueyroux** *(Thérèse)* | 1927 |
| 3174 | **Maurois, André** | French | N | **Climats** *(The Climates of Love)* *(aka: Whatever Gods May Be)* | 1928 |
| 3175 | **Maurois, André** | French | N | **Édouard VII et son temps** *(King Edward and his Times)* | 1933 |
| 3176 | **Maurois, André** | French | SS | **Thanatos Palace Hôtel** | 1951 |
| 3177 | **Mavor, Osborne Henry** *(see: Bridie, James)* | British | P | | |
| 3178 | **Meckel, Christoph** | German | N | **Bockshorn** *[Goat's horn]* | 1973 |
| 3179 | **Medoff, Mark** | American | P | **Children of a Lesser God** | 1980 |
| 3180 | **Meinel, Valério** | Brazilian | N | **Porque Claúdia Lessin vai morrer** | 1978 |
| 3181 | **Melo Neto, João Cabral de** | Brazilian | V | **O Rio** *[The river]* + **Morte e vida Severina** *[Death and life Severina]* | 1954(53)+ 1955 |
| 3182 | **Melville, Herman** | American | SS | **Bartleby** | 1853 |
| 3183 | **Melville, Herman** | American | SS | **Benito Cereno** | 1855 |
| 3184 | **Melville, Herman** | American | SS | **Billy Budd** | 1924 |

| No | Film Title | Country of Production | Date | Director(s) | Duration of Film |
|---|---|---|---|---|---|
| 3156 | **Masculin féminin: 15 faits précis** *(aka: Masculin - féminin)* *(SWE: Maskulinum - femininum)* | FR/SWE | 1966 | **Jean-Luc Godard** | 104 |
| 3157 | **Am Anfang war es Sünde** *(At First it Was Sin)* *(YUGO: Greh)* | GER/YUGO | 1954 | **František Čáp** | 96 |
| 3158 | **Diary of a Madman** | USA | 1962 | **Reginald Le Borg** | 96 |
| 3159 | **Le plaisir** *(House of Pleasure)* | FR | 1952(51) | **Max Ophüls** | 95 |
| 3160 | **L'ordonnance** | FR | 1933 | **Viktor Tourjansky** | 76 |
| 3161 | **Partie de campagne** *(A Day in the Country)* *(aka: Country Excursion)* | FR | 1946(36) | **Jean Renoir** | 40(45) |
| 3162 | **Pierre et Jean** | FR | 1943 | **André Cayatte** | 72 |
| 3163 | **Una mujer sin amor** *(aka: Cuando los hijos nos juzgan)* *(A Woman Without Pity)* | MEX | 1951 | **Luis Buñuel** | 90 |
| 3164 | **Le petit Prof** | FR | 1958 | **Carlo Rim** *(Carlo-Rim)* | 88 |
| 3165 | **Le rosier de Madame Husson** *(The Virtuous Isidore)* | FR | 1932(31) | **Bernard Deschamps** | 80 |
| 3166 | **Le rosier de Madame Husson** *(aka: The Prize)* | FR | 1950 | **Jean Boyer** | 84(100) |
| 3167 | **Une femme coquette** | SWITZ | 1955 | **Jean-Luc Godard** *(as Hans Lucas)* | 10 |
| 3168 | **Naiskohtaloita** *(aka: Une vie)* | FIN | 1947 | **Toivo Särkkä** | 95 |
| 3169 | **Une vie** *(IT: Una vita (il dramma di una sposa))* *(One Life)* | FR/IT | 1958 | **Alexandre Astruc** | 91(88) |
| 3170 | **Onno no isshō** *[One life]* | JAP | 1967 | **Yoshitarō Nomura** | 138 |
| 3171 | **Yvette** *(aka: Die Tochter einer Kurtisane)* | GER | 1938 | **Wolfgang Liebeneiner** | 98 |
| 3172 | **Les anges noirs** | FR | 1937 | **Willy Rozier** | 95 |
| 3173 | **Thérèse Desqueyroux** *(aka: Thérèse)* | FR | 1962 | **Georges Franju** | 109 |
| 3174 | **Climats** *(Climates of Love)* | FR | 1961 | **Stellio Lorenzi** | 143 |
| 3175 | **Entente cordiale** | FR | 1939 | **Marcel L'Herbier** | 110 |
| 3176 | **Sursis pour un vivant** *(IT: Pensione Edelweiss)* | FR/IT | 1959 | **Victor Merenda** | 88(95) |
| 3177 | | | | | |
| 3178 | **Bockshorn** | GDR | 1984 | **Frank Beyer** | 102 |
| 3179 | **Children of a Lesser God** | USA | 1986 | **Randa Haines** | 119 +V |
| 3180 | **A caso Claudia** | BRAZ | 1979 | **Miguel H. Borges** | 90 |
| 3181 | **Morte e vida Severina** | BRAZ | 1977 | **Zelito Viana** | 85 |
| 3182 | **Bartleby** | GB | 1970 | **Anthony Friedmann** | 79 |
| 3183 | **Benito Cereno** | FR/IT/BRAZ | 1969 | **Serge Roullet** | 75 |
| 3184 | **Billy Budd** | GB | 1962 | **Peter Ustinov** | 125(112) |

| No. | Author | Nationality | Form | Literary Title | Date |
|-----|--------|-------------|------|----------------|------|
| 3185 | **Melville, Herman** | American | SS | **The Encantades** <br> *(aka: The Encantades, or Enchanted Isles)* | 1854 |
| 3186 | **Melville, Herman** | American | SS | **The Lightning-Rod Man** | 1854 |
| 3187 | **Melville, Herman** | American | N | **Moby Dick** <br> *(aka: The Whale)* | 1851 |
| 3188 | **Melville, Herman** | American | N | **Moby Dick** | 1851 |
| 3189 | **Melville, Herman** | American | N | **Omoo** | 1847 |
| 3190 | **Melville, Herman** | American | N | **Typee** | 1846 |
| 3191 | **Menander** | Greek(anc) | P | **Dyscolus** <br> *(Misanthrope)* <br> *(aka: The Bad-Tempered Man)* | 316 BC |
| 3192 | **Mendès, Catulle** | French | N | **Grande-Maguet** | 1888 |
| 3193 | **Mercer, David** | British | P(TV) | **In Two Minds** | 1967 |
| 3194 | **Mercer, David** | British | P(TV) | **A Suitable Case For Treatment** | 1966 |
| 3195 | **Mérimée, Prosper** | French | SS | **Carmen** | 1846 |
| 3196 | **Mérimée, Prosper** | French | SS | **Carmen** | 1846 |
| 3197 | **Mérimée, Prosper** | French | SS | **Carmen** | 1846 |
| 3198 | **Mérimée, Prosper** | French | SS | **Carmen** | 1846 |
| 3199 | **Mérimée, Prosper** | French | SS | **Carmen** | 1846 |
| 3200 | **Mérimée, Prosper** | French | SS | **Carmen** | 1846 |
| 3201 | **Mérimée, Prosper** | French | SS | **Carmen** | 1846 |
| 3202 | **Mérimée, Prosper** | French | SS | **Carmen** | 1846 |
| 3203 | **Mérimée, Prosper** | French | SS | **Carmen** | 1846 |
| 3204 | **Mérimée, Prosper** | French | SS | **Carmen** | 1846 |
| 3205 | **Mérimée, Prosper** | French | SS | **Carmen** | 1846 |
| 3206 | **Mérimée, Prosper** | French | SS | **Carmen** | 1846 |
| 3207 | **Mérimée, Prosper** | French | SS | **Carmen** | 1846 |
| 3208 | **Mérimée, Prosper** | French | P | **Le carrosse du Saint-Sacrement** <br> *(The Coach of the Holy Sacrament)* | 1829 |
| 3209 | **Mérimée, Prosper** | French | SS | **Colomba** <br> *(Columba, a Corsican Story)* | 1841 |
| 3210 | **Mérimée, Prosper** | French | SS | **Colomba** | 1841 |
| 3211 | **Mérimée, Prosper** | French | SS | **Colomba** | 1841 |
| 3212 | **Mérimée, Prosper** | French | SS | **Lokis** | 1869 |
| 3213 | **Mérimée, Prosper** | French | SS | **Tamango** <br> *(The Slave Ship)* | 1829 |
| 3214 | **Mészöly Miklós** | Hungarian | SS | **Magasiskola** <br> *(The Falcons)* | 1967 |
| 3215 | **Meyer, Conrad Ferdinand** | Swiss(Ger) | SS | **Gustav Adolfs Page** | 1882 |
| 3216 | **Meyer, Conrad Ferdinand** | Swiss | SS | **Die Richterin** | 1885 |
| 3217 | **Meyer, Conrad Ferdinand** | Swiss | SS | **Der Schuß von der Kanzel** <br> *(The Shot From the Pulpit)* | 1879 |
| 3218 | **Meyer, G.** <br> *(see: Meyrink, Gustav)* | Austrian/ German | N | | |
| 3219 | **Meyer-Förster, Wilhelm** | German | N-P | **Karl Heinrich** {n} <br> **Alt-Heidelberg** {p} <br> [Old Heidelberg] | 1899{n} <br> 1902{p} |
| 3220 | **Meyer-Förster, Wilhelm** | German | N-P | **Karl Heinrich** {n} <br> **Alt-Heidelberg** {p} | 1899{n} <br> 1902{p} |
| 3221 | **Meyrink, Gustav** <br> *(Meyer, G.)* | Austrian/ German | N | **Der Golem** <br> *(The Golem)* | 1915 |
| 3222 | **Meyrink, Gustav** | Austrian/ German | N | **Der Golem** | 1915 |
| 3223 | **Michener, James A.** | American | N | **The Bridges at Toko-Ri** | 1953 |
| 3224 | **Michener, James A.** | American | N | **Caravans** | 1963 |

| No | Film Title | Country of Production | Date | Director(s) | Duration of Film |
|---|---|---|---|---|---|
| 3185 | As ilhas encantadas<br>(FR: Les îles enchantées) | PORT/FR | 1966(65) | Carlos Vilardebo | 90 |
| 3186 | The Lightning-Rod Man | USA | 1975 | John de Chancie | 16 +V |
| 3187 | Moby Dick | USA/GER | 1930 | Lloyd Bacon | 75 |
| 3188 | Moby Dick | GB/USA | 1956 | John Huston | 115 +V |
| 3189 | Omoo, Omoo the Shark God | USA | 1949 | Leon Leonard | 58 |
| 3190 | Enchanted Island | USA | 1958 | Allan Dwan | 94 +V |
| 3191 | O parthenos<br>[The virgin] | GR | 1967 | Dimis Dadiras | 90 |
| 3192 | La Grande Maguet | FR | 1947 | Roger Richebé | 95 |
| 3193 | Family Life<br>(USA: Wednesday's Child) | GB | 1971 | Ken Loach | 108<br>+V |
| 3194 | Morgan - A Suitable Case For Treatment<br>(aka: Morgan!) | GB | 1966 | Karel Reisz | 97(93)<br>+V |
| 3195 | Gipsy Blood<br>(USA: Carmen) | GB | 1931 | Cecil Lewis | 79 |
| 3196 | Andalusische Nächte | GER/SP | 1938 | Herbert Maisch | 95 |
| 3197 | Carmen | ARG | 1943 | Luís César Amadori | 96 |
| 3198 | Carmen | FR/IT | 1945(42) | Christian-Jaque | 100 |
| 3199 | The Loves of Carmen | USA | 1948 | Charles Vidor | 99 |
| 3200 | Carmen proibita<br>(SP: Siempre Carmen) | IT/SP | 1952 | Giuseppe M. Scotese<br>Alejandro Perla | 85(93) |
| 3201 | Carmen Jones<br>{musical version} | USA | 1954 | Otto Preminger | 104 |
| 3202 | Carmen de la Ronda<br>(aka: La Carmen de Grenada) | SP | 1959 | Tulio Demicheli | 98(83) |
| 3203 | Carmen de Trastevere | IT/FR | 1962 | Carmine Gallone | 105(94) |
| 3204 | Carmen, Baby | USA/HOLL | 1967 | Radley Metzger | 82 +V |
| 3205 | L'uomo, l'orgoglio, la vendetta<br>[Man, pride, revenge]<br>(GER: Mit django kam der Tod)<br>[With Django came death] | IT/GER | 1968(67) | Luigi Bazzoni | 91(99) |
| 3206 | La tragédie de Carmen<br>(The Tragedy of Carmen) | FR | 1983 | Peter Brook | 85 |
| 3207 | Carmen | SP | 1983 | Carlos Saura | 101(90)+V |
| 3208 | La carrozza d'oro<br>(FR: La carrosse d'or)<br>(The Golden Coach) | IT/FR | 1953 | Jean Renoir | 100 |
| 3209 | Colomba | FR | 1949(48) | Émile Couzinet | 94 |
| 3210 | Vendetta | USA | 1950 | Mel Ferrer | 84 |
| 3211 | Colomba | FR | 1953 | Jacques Séverac | 80 |
| 3212 | Lokis<br>(The Bear) | POL | 1970 | Janusz Majewski | 97 |
| 3213 | Tamango | FR/IT | 1957 | John Berry | 98 |
| 3214 | Magasiskola<br>(The Falcons) | HUNG | 1970 | István Gaál | 90(88) |
| 3215 | Gustav Adolfs Page | AUST | 1960 | Rolf Hansen | 93(81) |
| 3216 | Violanta | SWITZ/GER | 1978 | Daniel Schmid | 95 |
| 3217 | Der Schuß von der Kanzel | SWITZ | 1942 | Leopold Lindtberg | 102 |
| 3218 | | | | | |
| 3219 | The Student Prince<br>{musical version} | USA | 1954 | Richard Thorpe | 107 |
| 3220 | Alt-Heidelberg | GER | 1959 | Ernst Marischka | 105 |
| 3221 | Golem<br>(FR: Le golem) | CZ/FR | 1936 | Julien Duvivier | 83 |
| 3222 | Golem | POL | 1980 | Piotr Szulkin | 92 |
| 3223 | The Bridges at Toko-Ri | USA | 1954 | Mark Robson | 104 +V |
| 3224 | Caravans | USA/IRN | 1978 | James Fargo | 129 +V |

| No. | Author | Nationality | Form | Literary Title | Date |
|-----|--------|-------------|------|----------------|------|
| 3225 | Michener, James A. | American | N | Hawaii | 1959 |
| 3226 | Michener, James A. | American | N | Hawaii | 1959 |
| 3227 | Michener, James A. | American | SS | Return to Paradise | 1951 |
| 3228 | Michener, James A. | American | N | Sayonara | 1954 |
| 3229 | Michener, James A. | American | SS | Tales of the South Pacific | 1947 |
| 3230 | Michener, James A. | American | SS | Until They Sail | 1951 |
| 3231 | Mihailović, Dragoslav | Yugoslav(Serb) | SS | Lilika | 1967 |
| 3232 | Mihailović, Dragoslav | Yugoslav | N | Petrijin venac | 1975 |
| 3233 | Mihura Santos, Miguel | Spanish | P | Carlota | 1958 |
| 3234 | Mihura Santos, Miguel | Spanish | P | La decente | 1969 |
| 3235 | Mihura Santos, Miguel | Spanish | P | Las entretenidas | 1963 |
| 3236 | Mihura Santos, Miguel | Spanish | P | Maribel y la extraña familia | 1960 |
| 3237 | Mihura Santos, Miguel | Spanish | P | Melocotón en almíbar [Peaches and syrup] | 1959 |
| 3238 | Mihura Santos, Miguel | Spanish | P | ¡Sublime desísíon! | 1960 |
| 3239 | Mihura Santos, Miguel (see also: Calvo Sotelo, Joaquin) | Spanish | P | | |
| 3240 | Mikszáth Kálmán | Hungarian | N | Akli Miklós es. kir. udv. mulattató története | 1903 |
| 3241 | Mikszáth Kálmán | Hungarian | N | A beszélő köntös (The Magic Caftan) | 1889 |
| 3242 | Mikszáth Kálmán | Hungarian | N | Beszterce ostroma | 1896 |
| 3243 | Mikszáth Kálmán | Hungarian | N | A fekete város | 1911 |
| 3244 | Mikszáth Kálmán | Hungarian | N | Kísértet lublón | 1896 |
| 3245 | Mikszáth Kálmán | Hungarian | N | Különös házasság (A Strange Marriage) | 1901 |
| 3246 | Mikszáth Kálmán | Hungarian | N | A Noszty fiú esete Tóth Marival [The young Noszty's affair with Mary Tóth] | 1908 |
| 3247 | Mikszáth Kálmán | Hungarian | N | A Noszty fiú esete Tóth Marival | 1908 |
| 3248 | Mikszáth Kálmán | Hungarian | N | A szelistyei asszonyok [The women of Szelistye] | 1901 |
| 3249 | Mikszáth Kálmán | Hungarian | N | Szent Péter esernyője (St. Peter's Umbrella) | 1895 |
| 3250 | Milankov, Momčilo | Yugoslav(Serb) | SS | Neznanka | 1964 |
| 3251 | Miller, Arthur | American | P | All My Sons | 1947 |
| 3252 | Miller, Arthur | American | P | The Crucible | 1953 |
| 3253 | Miller, Arthur | American | P | Death of a Salesman | 1949 |
| 3254 | Miller, Arthur | American | P | Death of a Salesman | 1949 |
| 3255 | Miller, Arthur | American | P | Death of a Salesman | 1949 |
| 3256 | Miller, Arthur | American | SS | The Misfits | 1961 |
| 3257 | Miller, Arthur | American | P | A View From the Bridge | 1955 |
| 3258 | Miller, Henry | American | N | Quiet Days in Clichy | 1956 |
| 3259 | Miller, Henry | American | N | Tropic of Cancer | 1935 |
| 3260 | Miller, Warren | American | N | The Cool World | 1959 |
| 3261 | Mirbeau, Octave | French | P | Les affaires sont les affaires [Business is business] | 1903 |

**178**

| No | Film Title | Country of Production | Date | Director(s) | Duration of Film |
|---|---|---|---|---|---|
| 3225 | **Hawaii** | USA | 1966 | **George Roy Hill** | 186(171) |
| 3226 | **The Hawaiians** (GB: Master of the Islands) | USA | 1970 | **Tom Gries** | 132 |
| 3227 | **Return to Paradise** | USA | 1953 | **Mark Robson** | 109 |
| 3228 | **Sayonara** | USA | 1957 | **Joshua Logan** | 147 +V |
| 3229 | **South Pacific** {musical version} | USA | 1958 | **Joshua Logan** | 170 +V |
| 3230 | **Until They Sail** | USA | 1957 | **Robert Wise** | 95 |
| 3231 | **Lilika** | YUGO | 1970 | **Branko Pleša** | 100 |
| 3232 | **Petrijin venac** (Petrija's Wreath) | YUGO | 1980 | **Srdan Karanović** | 97 |
| 3233 | **Carlota** | SP | 1958 | **Enrique Cahen Salaberry** | 100(79) |
| 3234 | **La decente** (The Decent One) | SP | 1971(70) | **José Luis Sáenz de Heredia** | 98(94) +V |
| 3235 | **Las panteras se comen a los ricos** (The Panthers Eat the Rich) | SP | 1970(69) | **Ramón Fernández** | 83(79) +V |
| 3236 | **Maribel y la extraña familia** (Maribel and the Strange Family) | SP | 1960 | **José María Forqué** | 110(95) |
| 3237 | **Melocóton en almíbar** | SP | 1960 | **Antonio del Amo** | 82(88) |
| 3238 | **Solo para hombres** [For men only] | SP | 1960 | **Fernando Fernán-Gómez** | 85(90) |
| 3239 | | | | | |
| 3240 | **Akli Miklós** (aka: Miklós Akli) | HUNG | 1986 | **György Révész** | 90(93) |
| 3241 | **A beszélő köntös** (Talking Caftan) | HUNG | 1969(68) | **Tamás Fejér** | 84 |
| 3242 | **Beszterce ostroma** (Siege of Beszterce) | HUNG | 1948 | **Márton Keleti** | 98 |
| 3243 | **A fekete város** (The Black Town) (aka: Town in Mourning) | HUNG | 1972(71) | **Éva Zsurzs** | Pt.1, 91 Pt.2, 95 |
| 3244 | **Kísértet lublón** (The Phantom On Horseback) | HUNG | 1976 | **Róbert Bán** | 86 |
| 3245 | **Különös házasság** (Strange Marriage) | HUNG | 1951 | **Márton Keleti** | 111 |
| 3246 | **1 hr Leibhusar** | GER/CZ/ HUNG | 1938(37) | **Hubert Marischka** | 94 |
| 3247 | **A Noszty fiú esete Tóth Marival** (Love and Money) (aka: Affair Between the Noszty Boy and Mari Tóth) | HUNG | 1960 | **Viktor Gertler** | 102 |
| 3248 | **Mit csinált Felséged 3-5-ig?** (Where Was Your Majesty Between 3 and 5?) (aka: His Majesty's Dates) | HUNG | 1965(64) | **Károly Makk** | 87 |
| 3249 | **Szent Péter esernyője** (St. Peter's Umbrella) | HUNG/CZ | 1958 | **Frigyes Bán** | 93 |
| 3250 | **Budenje pacova** | YUGO | 1967 | **Živojin Pavlović** | 79 |
| 3251 | **All My Sons** | USA | 1948 | **Irving Reis** | 94 |
| 3252 | **Les sorcières de Salem** (The Witches of Salem) | FR/GDR | 1957 | **Raymond Rouleau** | 140 |
| 3253 | **Death of a Salesman** | USA | 1951 | **Laslo Benedek** | 112 |
| 3254 | **Most pereyti nelzja** (aka: Most pereyti nelieya) (The Bridge Cannot be Crossed) (aka: Death of a Salesman) | USSR | 1960 | **Teodor Vulfovitch Nikita Kurikhin** | 97 |
| 3255 | **Death of a Salesman** | USA | 1985 | **Volker Schlöndorff** | 150 +V |
| 3256 | **The Misfits** | USA | 1961 | **John Huston** | 124 +V |
| 3257 | **Vu du pont** (IT: Uno sguardo dal ponte) (A View From the Bridge) | FR/IT | 1961 | **Sidney Lumet** | 117 |
| 3258 | **Quiet Days at Clichy** (Stille dage i Clichy) | DEN | 1970 | **Jens-Jørgen Thorsen** | 96 |
| 3259 | **Tropic of Cancer** | USA | 1970(69) | **Joseph Strick** | 88 |
| 3260 | **The Cool World** | USA | 1963 | **Shirley Clarke** | 106 |
| 3261 | **Les affaires sont les affaires** | FR | 1942 | **Jean Dréville** | 82 |

| No. | Author | Nationality | Form | Literary Title | Date |
|-----|--------|-------------|------|----------------|------|
| 3262 | **Mirbeau, Octave** | French | N | **Le jardin des supplices**<br>*(The Garden of Tortures)*<br>*(aka: Torture Garden)* | 1899 |
| 3263 | **Mirbeau, Octave** | French | N | **Le journal d'une femme de chambre**<br>*(The Diary of a Chambermaid)* | 1900 |
| 3264 | **Mirbeau, Octave** | French | N | **Le journal d'une femme de chambre** | 1900 |
| 3265 | **Mishev, Georgi** | Bulgarian | N | **Matriarkhat** | 1967 |
| 3266 | **Mishima Yukio**<br>*(Hiraoka Kimatake)* | Japanese | N | **Ai no kawaki**<br>*(Thirst For Love)* | 1950 |
| 3267 | **Mishima Yukio** | Japanese | N | **Gogo no eikō**<br>*(The Sailor Who Fell From Grace With the Sea)* | 1963 |
| 3268 | **Mishima Yukio** | Japanese | N | **Kinkaku-ji**<br>*(The Temple of the Golden Pavilion)* | 1956 |
| 3269 | **Mishima Yukio** | Japanese | N | **Kinkaku-ji**<br>*(The Temple of the Golden Pavilion)* +<br>**Kyoko no Ie**<br>*[Kyoko's house]* +<br>**Homba** *(Runaway Horses)* | 1956+<br>1959+<br>1969 |
| 3270 | **Mishima Yukio** | Japanese | P | **Kurotokage** | 1962 |
| 3271 | **Mishima Yukio** | Japanese | N | **Shiosai**<br>*(The Sound of Waves)* | 1954 |
| 3272 | **Mitchell, Adrian** | British | P(TV)-N | **Men Friday** *{tvp}*<br>**Man Friday** *{n}* | 1974{pTV}<br>1975{n} |
| 3273 | **Mitchell, Julian** | British | P | **Another Country** | 1982 |
| 3274 | **Mitchell, Margaret** | American | N | **Gone With the Wind** | 1936 |
| 3275 | **Mitford, Nancy** | British | N | **The Blessing** | 1951 |
| 3276 | **Mitra, Narendranāth** | Indian(Ben) | SS | **Mahānagar**<br>*(aka: Abataranikē)*<br>*[Foreward]* | 1949 |
| 3277 | **Mňačko, Ladislav** | Czech | N | **Smrt' sa volá Engelchen**<br>*(Death Is Called Engelchen)* | 1959 |
| 3278 | **Mo, Timothy** | British | N | **Sour Sweet**<br>*(USA: Soursweet)* | 1982 |
| 3279 | **Moberg, Vilhelm** | Swedish | P | **Änkeman Jarl** | 1940 |
| 3280 | **Moberg, Vilhelm** | Swedish | P | **Domaren** | 1957 |
| 3281 | **Moberg, Vilhelm** | Swedish | N | **Invandrarna**<br>*(Unto a Good Land)* +<br>**Nybyggarna** +<br>**Sista brevet till Sverige**<br>*(The Last Letter)* | 1952+<br>1956+<br>1959 |
| 3282 | **Moberg, Vilhelm** | Swedish | P | **Kassabrist** | 1925 |
| 3283 | **Moberg, Vilhelm** | Swedish | N-P | **Mans kvinna**<br>*[Man's woman]*<br>*(Fulfilment)* *{p}* | 1933{n}<br>1943{p} |
| 3284 | **Moberg, Vilhelm** | Swedish | N-P | **Rid i natt!**<br>*(Ride This Night!)* | 1941{n}<br>1942{p} |
| 3285 | **Moberg, Vilhelm** | Swedish | N | **Sänkt sedebetyg** | 1935 |
| 3286 | **Moberg, Vilhelm** | Swedish | N | **Utvandrarna**<br>*(The Emigrants)* +<br>**Invandrarna**<br>*(Unto a Good Land)* | 1949+<br>1952 |
| 3287 | **Moldova György** | Hungarian | N | **Malom a pokolban** | 1968 |
| 3288 | **Molière**<br>*(Jean-Baptiste Poquelin)* | French | P | **Le bourgeois gentilhomme**<br>*(The Would-Be Gentleman)*<br>*(aka: Middle-Class Gentleman)* | 1670 |
| 3289 | **Molière** | French | P | **Les femmes savantes**<br>*(The Learned Ladies)*<br>*(aka: The Bluestockings)* | 1673 |

| No | Film Title | Country of Production | Date | Director(s) | Duration of Film |
|---|---|---|---|---|---|
| 3262 | Le jardin des supplices<br>*(The Garden of Torture)* | FR | 1976 | Christian Gion | 90 |
| 3263 | Diary of a Chambermaid | USA | 1946 | Jean Renoir | 98<br>+V(86) |
| 3264 | Le journal d'une femme de chambre<br>*(IT: Il diario di una cameriera)*<br>*(The Diary of a Chambermaid)* | FR/IT | 1964(63) | Luis Buñuel | 98 |
| 3265 | Matriarkhat<br>*[Matriarchate]* | BULG | 1977 | Lyudmil Staikov | 104 |
| 3266 | Ai no kawaki<br>*(Longing For Love)*<br>*(aka: Thirst For Love)* | JAP | 1967(66) | Koreyoshi Kurahara | 98 |
| 3267 | The Sailor Who Fell From Grace<br>With the Sea | GB | 1976 | Lewis John Carlino | 105<br>+V |
| 3268 | Enjo<br>*(Conflagration)*<br>*(aka: Flame of Torment)* | JAP | 1958 | Kon Ichikawa | 96 |
| 3269 | Mishima: a Life in Four Chapters | USA/JAP | 1985 | Paul Schrader | 120<br>+V(116) |
| 3270 | Kurotokage<br>*(Black Lizard)* | JAP | 1968 | Kinji Fukasaku | 86 |
| 3271 | Shiosai<br>*(The Sound of Waves)* | JAP | 1954 | Senkichi Taniguchi | 96 |
| 3272 | Man Friday | GB | 1975 | Jack Gold | 115<br>+V(104) |
| 3273 | Another Country | GB | 1984 | Marek Kanievska | 90 +V |
| 3274 | Gone With the Wind | USA | 1939 | Victor Fleming | 222 +V |
| 3275 | Count Your Blessings | USA | 1959 | Jean Negulesco | 102 |
| 3276 | Mahānagar<br>*(The Big City)* | IND(BEN) | 1963 | Satyajit Ray | 131 |
| 3277 | Smrt si říká Engelchen<br>*(Death Is Called Engelchen)* | CZ | 1963 | Ján Kadár<br>Elmar Klos | 134 |
| 3278 | Soursweet | GB | 1989(88) | Mike Newell | 111<br>+V |
| 3279 | Änkeman Jarl | SWE | 1945 | Sigurd Wallén | 97 |
| 3280 | Domaren<br>*(The Judge)* | SWE | 1960 | Alf Sjöberg | 109 |
| 3281 | Nybyggarna<br>*(The New Land)* | SWE | 1972 | Jan Troell | 161(205) |
| 3282 | Kärlek och kassabrist<br>*(Love and Deficit)* | SWE | 1932 | Gustaf Molander | 71 |
| 3283 | Mans kvinna | SWE | 1945 | Gunnar Skoglund | 88 |
| 3284 | Rid i natt!<br>*(Ride Tonight!)* | SWE | 1942 | Gustaf Molander | 106 |
| 3285 | Gläd dig i din ungdom<br>*(Rejoice While You Are Young)* | SWE | 1939 | Per Lindberg | 88 |
| 3286 | Utvandrarna<br>*(The Emigrants)* | SWE | 1971(70) | Jan Troell | 151(192) |
| 3287 | Malom a pokolban<br>*(Mills of Hell)* | HUNG | 1987 | Gyula Maár | 100 |
| 3288 | Le bourgeois gentilhomme<br>*{Comédie Française production}* | FR | 1958 | Jean Meyer | 97 |
| 3289 | Les femmes savantes<br>*{Comédie Française production}* | FR | 1965 | Jean Meyer | 100 |

| No. | Author | Nationality | Form | Literary Title | Date |
|-----|--------|-------------|------|----------------|------|
| 3290 | **Molière** | French | P | **Les fourberies de Scapin**<br>*(The Cheats of Scapin)* | 1671 |
| 3291 | **Molière** | French | P | **George Dandin, ou le mari**<br>**confondu**<br>*(The Amorous Widow, or, The*<br>*Wanton Wife)* | 1669 |
| 3292 | **Molière** | French | P | **Monsieur de Pourceaugnac**<br>*(Monsieur de Pourceaugnac, or*<br>*Squire Trelooby)* | 1670 |
| 3293 | **Molière** | French | P | **Les précieuses ridicules**<br>*(Pretentious Young Ladies)*<br>*(aka: The Affected Young Ladies)* | 1660 |
| 3294 | **Molière** | French | P | **Tartuffe**<br>*(Tartuffe, or the Imposter)* | 1669 |
| 3295 | **Molière** | French | P | **Tartuffe** | 1669 |
| 3296 | **Molin, Pelle** | Swedish | SS | **Kärnfolk** | 1897 |
| 3297 | **Molnár Ferenc** | Hungarian | P | **Delila**<br>*(Delilah)* | 1937 |
| 3298 | **Molnár Ferenc** | Hungarian | P | **Egy, kettő, harom**<br>*[One, two, three]* | 1929 |
| 3299 | **Molnár Ferenc** | Hungarian | P | **A hattyú**<br>*(The Swan)* | 1921 |
| 3300 | **Molnár Ferenc** | Hungarian | P | **A hattyú** | 1921 |
| 3301 | **Molnár Ferenc** | Hungarian | P | **Az ismeretlen lány**<br>*[The unknown girl]* | 1934 |
| 3302 | **Molnár Ferenc** | Hungarian | P | **A jó tünder**<br>*(The Good Fairy)* | 1930 |
| 3303 | **Molnár Ferenc** | Hungarian | P | **A jó tünder** | 1930 |
| 3304 | **Molnár Ferenc** | Hungarian | P | **Liliom** | 1910 |
| 3305 | **Molnár Ferenc** | Hungarian | P | **Liliom** | 1910 |
| 3306 | **Molnár Ferenc** | Hungarian | P | **Liliom** | 1910 |
| 3307 | **Molnár Ferenc** | Hungarian | P | **Nagy szerelem**<br>*[A great love]* | 1935 |
| 3308 | **Molnár Ferenc** | Hungarian | P | **Olympia** | 1928 |
| 3309 | **Molnár Ferenc** | Hungarian | N | **A Pál-utcai fiúk**<br>*(The Paul Street Boys)* | 1907 |
| 3310 | **Molnár Ferenc** | Hungarian | N | **A Pál-utcai fiúk** | 1907 |
| 3311 | **Molnár Ferenc** | Hungarian | P | **A testőr**<br>*(The Guardsman)* | 1910 |
| 3312 | **Molnár Ferenc** | Hungarian | P | **A testőr** | 1910 |
| 3313 | **Molnár Ferenc** | Hungarian | P | **A testőr** | 1910 |
| 3314 | **Monnier, A.**<br>*(joint, see: Labiche, Eugène)* | French | P | | |
| 3315 | **Monsarrat, Nicholas** | British | N | **The Cruel Sea** | 1951 |
| 3316 | **Monsarrat, Nicholas** | British | SS | **The Ship That Died of Shame** | 1952 |
| 3317 | **Monsarrat, Nicholas** | British | N | **Something to Hide** | 1966 |
| 3318 | **Monsarrat, Nicholas** | British | N | **The Story of Esther Costello** | 1953 |
| 3319 | **Monteiro Lobato**<br>*(see: Lobato, Monteiro)* | Brazilian | SS | | |
| 3320 | **Montello, Josué** | Brazilian | SS | **O monstro** | 1966 |
| 3321 | **Montello, Josué** | Brazilian | N | **Uma tarde, outra tarde** | 1968 |
| 3322 | **Moody, William Vaughan** | American | P | **A Sabine Woman**<br>*(aka: The Great Divide)* | 1906;<br>1909 |
| 3323 | **Moore, Brian** | Irish/Canadian | N | **Black Robe** | 1985 |
| 3324 | **Moore, Brian** | Irish/Canadian | N | **Cold Heaven** | 1983 |
| 3325 | **Moore, Brian** | Irish/Canadian | N | **The Lonely Passion of Judith**<br>**Hearne**<br>*(aka: Judith Hearne)* | 1955 |

| No | Film Title | Country of Production | Date | Director(s) | Duration of Film |
|---|---|---|---|---|---|
| 3290 | Les fourberies de Scapin (The Trickeries of Scapin) | FR | 1981 | Roger Coggio | 107 |
| 3291 | Dandin György (George Dandin) | HUNG | 1955 | Zoltán Várkonyi | 87 |
| 3292 | Monsieur de Pourceaugnac | FR | 1932 | Gaston Ravel Tony Lekain | 84 |
| 3293 | Les précieuses ridicules | FR | 1935(34) | Léonce Perret | 30 |
| 3294 | Tartuffe {Comédie Française production} | FR | 1963 | Jean Meyer | 98 |
| 3295 | Tartuffe | FR | 1984 | Gérard Depardieu | 140 |
| 3296 | Ådalens poesi [The poetry of Ådelen] | SWE | 1947 | Ivar Johansson | 94 |
| 3297 | Blond Fever | USA | 1944 | Richard Whorf | 69 |
| 3298 | One, Two, Three | USA | 1961 | Billy Wilder | 115 +V |
| 3299 | One Romantic Night | USA | 1930 | Paul L. Stein | 71 |
| 3300 | The Swan | USA | 1956 | Charles Vidor | 108 |
| 3301 | The Bride Wore Red | USA | 1937 | Dorothy Arzner | 103 |
| 3302 | The Good Fairy | USA | 1935 | William Wyler | 90 |
| 3303 | I'll Be Yours | USA | 1947 | William A. Seiter | 93 |
| 3304 | Liliom | USA | 1930 | Frank Borzage | 94 |
| 3305 | Liliom | FR | 1934(33) | Fritz Lang | 120 |
| 3306 | Carousel {musical version} | USA | 1956 | Henry King | 129 |
| 3307 | Double Wedding | USA | 1937 | Richard Thorpe | 87 |
| 3308 | A Breath of Scandal (IT: Olympia) | USA/IT | 1960 | Michael Curtiz | 98 |
| 3309 | No Greater Glory | USA | 1934 | Frank Borzage | 78 |
| 3310 | The Boys of Paul Street (HUNG: A Pál utcai fiúk) | USA/HUNG | 1969(68) | Zoltán Fábri | 108 |
| 3311 | The Guardsman | USA | 1931 | Sidney A. Franklin | 83 |
| 3312 | The Chocolate Soldier | USA | 1941 | Roy Del Ruth | 102 |
| 3313 | Jatszani kell (Double Play) (aka: Fitz and Lily) (aka: Lily in Love) (aka: The Players) (aka: Playing For Keeps) | HUNG/USA | 1984 | Karoly Makk | 108 +V |
| 3314 | | | | | |
| 3315 | The Cruel Sea | GB | 1952 | Charles Frend | 126 +V |
| 3316 | The Ship That Died of Shame (USA: PT Raiders) | GB | 1955 | Basil Dearden | 91 |
| 3317 | Something to Hide (aka: Shattered) | GB | 1973(71) | Alastair Reid | 99 +V(92) |
| 3318 | The Story of Esther Costello (aka: The Golden Virgin) | GB | 1957 | David Miller | 104 |
| 3319 | | | | | |
| 3320 | O monstro de Santa Tereza | BRAZ | 1975 | William Cobbett | 90 |
| 3321 | Uma tarde outra tarde | BRAZ | 1975 | William Cobbett | 85 |
| 3322 | Woman Hungry (aka: The Challenge) | USA | 1930 | Clarence Badger | 66 |
| 3323 | Black Robe | CAN/AUSTL | 1991 | Bruce Beresford | 100 |
| 3324 | Cold Heaven | USA | 1990 | Nicolas Roeg | 105 |
| 3325 | The Lonely Passion of Judith Hearne | GB | 1988 | Jack Clayton | 116 +V |

| No. | Author | Nationality | Form | Literary Title | Date |
|---|---|---|---|---|---|
| 3326 | Moore, Brian | Irish/Canadian | N | The Luck of Ginger Coffey | 1960 |
| 3327 | Moore, David John Cornwell<br>(see: Le Carré, John) | British | N | | |
| 3328 | Moore, George | Irish | N | Esther Waters | 1894 |
| 3329 | Moraes, Vinícius de | Brazilian | V | Balada das duas mocinhas de Botafogo | 1959 |
| 3330 | Moraes, Vinícius de | Brazilian | P | Orfeu da conceição | 1956 |
| 3331 | Móra Ferenc | Hungarian | N | Ének a búzamezőkről<br>(Song of the Wheatfields) | 1927 |
| 3332 | Móra Ferenc | Hungarian | N | Hannibál föltámasztása<br>[Hannibal's resurrection] | 1949 |
| 3333 | Móra Ferenc | Hungarian | N | Kincskereső kisködmön | 1918 |
| 3334 | Morante, Elsa | Italian | N | L'isola di Arturo<br>(Arthur's Island) | 1957 |
| 3335 | Morante, Elsa | Italian | N | La storia<br>(History: a Novel) | 1974 |
| 3336 | Moravia, Alberto<br>(Alberto Pincherle) | Italian | SS | Agostino | 1944 |
| 3337 | Moravia, Alberto | Italian | N | L'amore coniugale<br>(Conjugal Love) | 1949 |
| 3338 | Moravia, Alberto | Italian | SS | Appuntamento al mare<br>(Appointment at the Beach) | 1962 |
| 3339 | Moravia, Alberto | Italian | N | La ciociara<br>(Two Women) | 1957 |
| 3340 | Moravia, Alberto | Italian | N | Il conformista<br>(The Conformist) | 1951 |
| 3341 | Moravia, Alberto | Italian | SS | Delitto al circolo del tennis<br>(Crime at the Tennis Club) | 1952 |
| 3342 | Moravia, Alberto | Italian | N | Il disprezzo<br>(A Ghost at Noon) | 1954 |
| 3343 | Moravia, Alberto | Italian | SS | Donna invisibile<br>(Invisible Woman) | 1970<br>(coll) |
| 3344 | Moravia, Alberto | Italian | SS | Faccia di mascalzone | 1954 |
| 3345 | Moravia, Alberto | Italian | N | Gli indifferenti<br>(The Time of Indifference)<br>(aka: The Indifferent Ones) | 1929 |
| 3346 | Moravia, Alberto | Italian | N | La noia<br>(The Empty Canvas) | 1960 |
| 3347 | Moravia, Alberto | Italian | SS | Gli ordini sono ordini<br>(Orders Are Orders) | 1970 |
| 3348 | Moravia, Alberto | Italian | SS | La provinciale<br>(The Wayward Wife) | 1952 |
| 3349 | Moravia, Alberto | Italian | N | La romana<br>(Woman of Rome) | 1947 |
| 3350 | Mørch, Dea Trier | Danish | N | Vinterbørn | 1976 |
| 3351 | Moreau, Émile<br>(joint, see: Sardou, Victorien) | French | P | | |
| 3352 | Morgan, Charles | British | N | The Fountain | 1932 |
| 3353 | Morgan, Charles | British | N-P | The River Line | 1949{n}<br>1952{p} |
| 3354 | Móricz Zsigmond | Hungarian | N | Árvácska<br>[Little orphan] | 1941 |
| 3355 | Móricz Zsigmond | Hungarian | SS | Égi madár<br>(Celestial Bird) | 1935 |
| 3356 | Móricz Zsigmond | Hungarian | N | Légy jó mindhalálig<br>(Be Faithful Unto Death) | 1921 |
| 3357 | Móricz Zsigmond | Hungarian | N | Nem élhetek muzsikaszó nélkül | 1916 |

| No | Film Title | Country of Production | Date | Director(s) | Duration of Film |
|---|---|---|---|---|---|
| 3326 3327 | The Luck of Ginger Coffey | CAN/USA | 1964 | Irvin Kershner | 100 |
| 3328 | Esther Waters | GB | 1948 | Ian Dalrymple Peter Proud | 109 |
| 3329 | Marília e Marina | BRAZ | 1976 | Luiz Fernando Goulart | 90 |
| 3330 | Orfeu negro (IT: Orfeo negro) (Black Orpheus) | FR/IT/BRAZ | 1958 | Marcel Camús | 106 |
| 3331 | Ének a búzamezőkről (Song of the Cornfields) | HUNG | 1947 | István Szőts | 84 |
| 3332 | Hannibál tanár úr (Professor Hannibal) | HUNG | 1956 | Zoltán Fábri | 91 |
| 3333 | A kincskereső kisködmön (The Magic Jacket) | HUNG | 1973(72) | Mihály Szemes | 98 |
| 3334 | L'isola di Arturo (Arturo's Island) | IT | 1962(61) | Damiano Damiani | 93 |
| 3335 | La storia (History) (aka: The Story) | IT/FR | 1986(85) | Luigi Comencini | 251 |
| 3336 | Agostino | IT | 1962 | Mauro Bolognini | 90 |
| 3337 | L'amore coniugale | IT | 1971(70) | Dacia Maraini | 100(102) |
| 3338 | Le ore nude (The Naked Hours) | IT | 1964 | Marco Vicario | 87(90) |
| 3339 | La ciociara (Two Women) | IT/FR | 1960 | Vittorio de Sica | 100 |
| 3340 | Il conformista (The Conformist) | IT/FR/GER | 1970 | Bernardo Bertolucci | 107(117) |
| 3341 | Delitto al circolo del tennis (GB: The Rage Within) | IT/YUGO | 1970(69) | Franco Rossetti | 95(91) |
| 3342 | Le mépris (IT: Il disprezzo) (Contempt) | FR/IT | 1963 | Jean-Luc Godard | 100(90) +V |
| 3343 | La donna invisibile | IT | 1969 | Paolo Spinola | 94 |
| 3344 | Peccato che sia una canaglia (Too Bad She's Bad) | IT | 1955 | Alessandro Blasetti | 95 |
| 3345 | Gli indifferenti (Time of Indifference) (aka: Time For Indifference) | IT/FR | 1964(63) | Francesco Maselli | 100(115) |
| 3346 | La noia (The Empty Canvas) | IT/FR | 1964(63) | Damiano Damiani | 118(100) |
| 3347 | Gli ordini sono ordini | IT | 1972 | Franco Giraldi | 100 |
| 3348 | La provinciale (Wayward Wife) | IT | 1952 | Mario Soldati | 92 |
| 3349 | La romana (Woman of Rome) | IT/FR | 1954 | Luigi Zampa | 93(110) |
| 3350 3351 | Vinterbørn (Winter-Born) (aka: Winter Children) | DEN | 1978 | Astrid Henning-Jensen | 100 |
| 3352 | The Fountain | USA | 1934 | John Cromwell | 84 |
| 3353 | Kennwort: Reiher [Password: Reiher] | GER | 1963 | Rudolf Jugert | 95 |
| 3354 | Árvácska (No Man's Daughter) | HUNG | 1976 | László Ranódy | 92(87) |
| 3355 | Égi madár (Bird of Heaven) | HUNG | 1958 | Imre Fehér | 101 |
| 3356 | Légy jó mindhalálig (Be Good Until Death) (aka: Be Faithful Unto Death) (aka: Be Good For Ever) | HUNG | 1960 | László Ranódy | 90 |
| 3357 | Nem élhetek muzsikaszó nélkül (The Music's the Thing) (aka: I Can't Live Without Music) | HUNG | 1978 | Ferenc Sik | 88 |

| No. | Author | Nationality | Form | Literary Title | Date |
|-----|--------|-------------|------|----------------|------|
| 3358 | **Móricz Zsigmond** | Hungarian | N | **Rokonok** | 1930 |
| 3359 | **Móricz Zsigmond** | Hungarian | P | **Úri muri** | 1928 |
| 3360 | **Mörike, Eduard** | German | SS | **Mozart auf der Reise nach Prag** (Mozart on the Way to Prague) | 1855 |
| 3361 | **Mori Ōgai** | Japanese | N | **Gan** (The Wild Goose) (aka: The Wild Geese) | 1911-13 |
| 3362 | **Mori Ōgai** | Japanese | N | **Sanshō dayu** (Sansho-Dayu) (aka: Sansho the Steward) | 1915 |
| 3363 | **Morley, Christopher** | American | N | **Kitty Foyle** | 1939 |
| 3364 | **Mortimer, John** | British | P | **The Dock Brief** | 1958 |
| 3365 | **Mortimer, Penelope** | British | N | **The Pumpkin Eater** | 1962 |
| 3366 | **Mosley, Nicholas** | British | N | **Accident** | 1965 |
| 3367 | **Mosley, Nicholas** | British | N | **Impossible Object** | 1968 |
| 3368 | **Motley, Willard** | American(afro) | N | **Knock On Any Door** | 1947 |
| 3369 | **Motley, Willard** | American | N | **Let No Man Write My Epitaph** | 1958 |
| 3370 | **Mo Yan** (Mo Yen) | Chinese | SS | **Hong gao liang** (aka: Hung kao liang chia tsu) [Red sorghum] | 1985 |
| 3371 | **Mo Yen** (see: Mo Yan) | Chinese | SS | | |
| 3372 | **Mukhamedzhanov, Kaltai** (joint, see: Aitmatov, Chingiz) | Russian(Kir) | P | | |
| 3373 | **Mukka, Timo K.** | Finnish | N | **Maa on syntinen laulu** | 1964 |
| 3374 | **Mukka, Timo K.** | Finnish | N | **Tabu** | 1965 |
| 3375 | **Mulisch, Harry** | Dutch | N | **De aanslag** (The Assault) | 1982 |
| 3376 | **Mulisch, Harry** | Dutch | N | **Twee vrouwen** (Two Women) | 1975 |
| 3377 | **Multatuli** (see: Douwes Dekker, Eduard) | Dutch | N | | |
| 3378 | **Muniz, Lauro César** | Brazilian | P | **O santo milagroso** [The miraculous saint] | 1967 |
| 3379 | **Munk, Kaj** | Danish | P | **Havet og menneskene** | 1948 |
| 3380 | **Munk, Kaj** | Danish | P | **Kærlighed** (Love) | 1948 |
| 3381 | **Munk, Kaj** | Danish | P | **Ordet** (The Word) (aka: I begynnelsen var ordet) | 1932 |
| 3382 | **Munk, Kaj** | Danish | P | **Ordet** | 1932 |
| 3383 | **Murasaki Shikibu** | Japanese | N | **Genji monogatari** (The Tale of Genji) | c.1001-1005 |
| 3384 | **Murdoch, Iris - {n}; Priestly, J. B. - {p}** | British | N-P | **A Severed Head** | 1961{n} 1964{p} |
| 3385 | **Murger, Henri** | French | P-N | **La vie de Bohème {p}** (Scènes de la Bohème) {n} (aka: Scènes de la vie de Bohème) (Bohemians of the Latin Quarter) | 1848(51); 1849{n} |
| 3386 | **Murger, Henri** | French | P-N | **La vie de Bohème {p}** (Scènes de la Bohème) {n} | 1848(51); 1849{n} |
| 3387 | **Murger, Henri** | French | P-N | **La vie de Bohème {p}** (Scènes de la Bohème) {n} | 1848(51); 1849{n} |
| 3388 | **Musil, Robert** | Austrian | P | **Die Schwärmer** | 1921 |
| 3389 | **Musil, Robert** | Austrian | N | **Die Verwirrungen des Zöglings Törless** (Young Törless) | 1906 |
| 3390 | **Musset, Alfred de** | French | P | **Les caprices de Marianne** | 1834 |

| No | Film Title | Country of Production | Date | Director(s) | Duration of Film |
|----|-----------|----------------------|------|-------------|------------------|
| 3358 | **Rokonok** (Relatives) | HUNG | 1954 | **Félix Máriássy** | 100 |
| 3359 | **Úri muri** (Gentry Skylarking) | HUNG | 1950(49) | **Frigyes Bán** | 99 |
| 3360 | **Eine kleine Nachtmusik** | GER | 1939 | **Leopold Hainisch** | 93 |
| 3361 | **Gan** (Wild Geese) (aka: The Mistress) | JAP | 1953 | **Shirō Toyoda** | 104 |
| 3362 | **Sanshō dayu** (Sansho the Bailiff) (aka: The Bailiff) | JAP | 1954 | **Kenji Mizoguchi** | 123 |
| 3363 | **Kitty Foyle** | USA | 1940 | **Sam Wood** | 108 |
| 3364 | **The Dock Brief** (aka: A Case For the Jury) (aka: Trial and Error) | GB | 1962 | **James Hill** | 88 |
| 3365 | **The Pumpkin Eater** | GB | 1964 | **Jack Clayton** | 110 |
| 3366 | **Accident** | GB | 1967 | **Joseph Losey** | 105 +V |
| 3367 | **L'impossible objet** (USA: Story of a Love Story) (aka: Impossible Object) | FR | 1973 | **John Frankenheimer** | 110 |
| 3368 | **Knock On Any Door** | USA | 1949 | **Nicholas Ray** | 100 |
| 3369 | **Let No Man Write My Epitaph** (Reach For Tomorrow) | USA | 1959 | **Philip Leacock** | 106 |
| 3370 | **Hong gao liang** | CHN | 1987 | **Zhang Yimou** | 93 |
| 3371 | | | | | |
| 3372 | | | | | |
| 3373 | **Maa on syntinen laulu** (Earth Is a Sinful Song) | FIN | 1973 | **Rauni Mollberg** | 108 |
| 3374 | **Milka** | FIN | 1980 | **Rauni Mollberg** | 109 |
| 3375 | **De aanslag** (The Assault) | HOLL | 1986 | **Fons Rademakers** | 149 +V(120) |
| 3376 | **Twee vrouwen** (Two Women) | HOLL | 1979 | **George Sluizer** | 89(113) |
| 3377 | | | | | |
| 3378 | **O santo milagroso** | BRAZ | 1966 | **Carlos Coimbra** | 105 |
| 3379 | **Havet og menneskene** | DEN | 1970 | **Sigfred Aagaard** | 91 |
| 3380 | **Kärlek** (DEN: Kærlighed) (Love) | SWE | 1952 | **Gustaf Molander** | 107 |
| 3381 | **Ordet** (The Word) | SWE | 1943 | **Gustaf Molander** | 108 |
| 3382 | **Ordet** (The Word) | DEN | 1955 | **Carl Th. Dreyer** | 125 |
| 3383 | **Genji monogatari** (The Tale of Genji) | JAP | 1951 | **Kōzaburō Yoshimura** | 124 |
| 3384 | **A Severed Head** | GB | 1970 | **Dick Clement** | 98 +V |
| 3385 | **Mimi** | GB | 1935 | **Paul L. Stein** | 94 |
| 3386 | **La vie de bohème** | FR | 1945(43) | **Marcel L'Herbier** | 120 |
| 3387 | **La bohème** | FR/IT | 1988 | **Luigi Comencini** | 107 |
| 3388 | **Die Schwärmer** (Dreamers) | GER | 1985 | **Hans Neuenfels** | 116 |
| 3389 | **Der junge Törless** (Young Törless) | GER/FR | 1966 | **Volker Schlöndorff** | 87 |
| 3390 | **La règle du jeu** (Rules of the Game) | FR | 1939 | **Jean Renoir** | 110 |

**187**

| No. | Author | Nationality | Form | Literary Title | Date |
|---|---|---|---|---|---|
| 3391 | **Musset, Alfred de** | French | N | **La confession d'un enfant du siècle** (Confessions of a Child of the Century) | 1836 |
| 3392 | **Musset, Alfred de** | French | P | **Il faut qu'une porte soit ouverte ou fermée** (A Door Should Be Either Open or Shut) | 1848 |
| 3393 | **Musset, Alfred de** | French | SS | **Mademoiselle Mimi Pinson** (aka: Mimi Pinson) | 1853 (aka:1866) |
| 3394 | **Musset, Alfred de** | French | SS | **La mouche** | 1854 |
| 3395 | **Musset, Alfred de** | French | P | **On ne badine pas avec l'amour** (Love Is Not To Be Trifled With) | 1834 |
| 3396 | **Nabl, Franz** | German | N | **Das Grab des Lebendigen** (aka: Die Ortliebschen Frauen) | 1917 (aka:1936) |
| 3397 | **Nabokov, Vladimir** (as: Vladimir Sirin) | Russian/ American | N | **Kamera Obscura** (Laughter in the Dark) (aka: Camera Obscura) | 1932 |
| 3398 | **Nabokov, Vladimir** (as: Vladimir Sirin) | Russian/ American | N | **Korol, Dama, Valet** (King, Queen, Knave) | 1928 |
| 3399 | **Nabokov, Vladimir** | Russian/ American | N | **Lolita** | 1955 |
| 3400 | **Nabokov, Vladimir** (as: Vladimir Sirin) | Russian/ American | N | **Otchayanie** (Despair) | 1937 |
| 3401 | **Nagai Kafū** | Japanese | N | **Bokutō kidan** (A Strange Tale From East of the River) | 1937 |
| 3402 | **Nagai Kafū** | Japanese | N | **Odoriko** (The Dancing Girl) | 1944 |
| 3403 | **Nagy Lajos** | Hungarian | SS | **Razzia** | 1929 |
| 3404 | **Najac, Emile de** (joint, see: Sardou, Victorien) | French | P | | |
| 3405 | **Nakatsuka Takashi** | Japanese | N | **Tsuchi** | 1910 |
| 3406 | **Nałkowska, Zofia** | Polish | N | **Granica** [The boundary] | 1936(35) |
| 3407 | **Nałkowska, Zofia** | Polish | N | **Granica** | 1936(35) |
| 3408 | **Nałkowska, Zofia** | Polish | N | **Romans Teresy Hennert** | 1927(24) |
| 3409 | **Namiki Gohei III** | Japanese | P(K) | **Kanjinchō** | 1840 |
| 3410 | **Namora, Fernando** | Portuguese | N | **Domingo à tarde** | 1961 |
| 3411 | **Namora, Fernando** | Portuguese | N | **A noite e a madrugada** [Night and dawn] | 1950 |
| 3412 | **Namora, Fernando** | Portuguese | SS | **Retalhos da vida de um médico** (Mountain Doctor) | 1949 |
| 3413 | **Narayan, R. K.** | Indian(Eng) | N | **The Guide** | 1958 |
| 3414 | **Narayan, R. K.** | Indian | N | **The Guide** | 1958 |
| 3415 | **Narayan, R. K.** | Indian | N | **Swamy and Friends** | 1935 |
| 3416 | **Nash, N. Richard** | American | P | **The Rainmaker** | 1955 |
| 3417 | **Nash, Ogden** (joint, see: Perelman, S. J.) | American | P | | |
| 3418 | **Nathan, Robert** | American | N | **The Bishop's Wife** | 1928 |
| 3419 | **Nathan, Robert** | American | N | **The Enchanted Voyage** | 1936 |
| 3420 | **Nathan, Robert** | American | SS | **One More Spring** | 1933 |
| 3421 | **Nathan, Robert** | American | N | **Portrait of Jennie** | 1940 |
| 3422 | **Natsume Sōseki** | Japanese | N | **Gubijinsō** (Red Poppy) | 1908 |
| 3423 | **Natsume Sōseki** | Japanese | N | **Kokoro** (The Heart) | 1914 |

| No | Film Title | Country of Production | Date | Director(s) | Duration of Film |
|---|---|---|---|---|---|
| 3391 | Spowiedź dziecięcia w eku | POL | 1986 | Marek Nowicki | 100 |
| 3392 | Il faut qu'une porte soit ouverte ou fermée | FR | 1949 | Louis Cuny | 19 |
| 3393 | Mimi Pinson | FR | 1958 | Robert Darène | 95 |
| 3394 | Das Schonheitsfleckchen | GER | 1936 | Rolf Hansen | 30 |
| 3395 | On ne badine pas avec l'amour | FR | 1961 | Jean Desailly | 87 |
| 3396 | Die Ortliebschen Frauen [The Ortlieb family woman] | GER | 1979 | Luc Bondy | 113 |
| 3397 | Laughter in the Dark (FR: La chambre obscure) | GB/FR | 1969 | Tony Richardson | 104 |
| 3398 | Herzbube (USA: King, Queen, Knave) | GER/USA | 1972 | Jerzy Skolimowski | 92 |
| 3399 | Lolita | GB | 1962(61) | Stanley Kubrick | 153 |
| 3400 | Despair (aka: Eine Reise ins Licht - Despair) | GER/FR | 1978 | R. W. Fassbinder | 119 +V |
| 3401 | Bokutō kidan (Twilight Story) (aka: A Strange Story of East of the River Sumida) | JAP | 1960 | Shirō Toyoda | 120 |
| 3402 | Odoriko (Dancing Girl) (aka: Chorus Girl) | JAP | 1957 | Hiroshi Shimizu | 96 |
| 3403 | Razzia (Raid) | HUNG | 1958 | László Nádasy | 100 |
| 3404 | | | | | |
| 3405 | Tsuchi (Earth) | JAP | 1939 | Tomu Uchida | 92 |
| 3406 | Granica | POL | 1938 | Jósef Lejtes | 87 |
| 3407 | Granica | POL | 1978 | Jan Rybkowski | 93 |
| 3408 | Romans Teresy Hennert (The Romance of Teresy Hennert) | POL | 1978 | Ignacy Gogolewski | 86 |
| 3409 | Tora no o o fumu otokotachi (They Who Step on the Tiger's Tail) | JAP | 1952(45) | Akira Kurosawa | 57 |
| 3410 | Domingo à tarde (Sunday Afternoon) | PORT | 1966(64) | António de Macedo | 90 |
| 3411 | A noite e a madrugada | PORT | 1983 | Artur Ramos | 108 |
| 3412 | Retalhos da vida de um médico | PORT | 1962 | Jorge Brum do Canto | 93 |
| 3413 | The Guide | USA/IND | 1964 | Tad Danielewski | 120 |
| 3414 | Guide | IND(HIN) | 1965 | Vijay Anand | 179 |
| 3415 | Swamy (aka: Malgudi Days) | IND(HIN) | 1987 | Shankar Nag | 118(100) |
| 3416 | The Rainmaker | USA | 1956 | Joseph Anthony | 121 |
| 3417 | | | | | |
| 3418 | The Bishop's Wife | USA | 1948(47) | Henry Koster | 108 |
| 3419 | Wake Up and Dream | USA | 1946 | Lloyd Bacon | 92 |
| 3420 | One More Spring | USA | 1935 | Henry King | 87 |
| 3421 | The Portrait of Jennie (GB: Jennie) (aka: Tidal Wave) | USA | 1949(48) | William Dieterle | 86 +V |
| 3422 | Gubijinsō (aka: Gubigin-sō) (Poppy) (aka: The Field Poppy) | JAP | 1935 | Kenji Mizoguchi | 73 |
| 3423 | Kokoro (The Heart) | JAP | 1955(54) | Kon Ichikawa | 122 |

| No. | Author | Nationality | Form | Literary Title | Date |
|-----|--------|-------------|------|----------------|------|
| 3424 | **Natsume Sōseki** | Japanese | N | **Sore kara**<br>*(And Then)* | 1910 |
| 3425 | **Natsume Sōseki** | Japanese | N | **Wagahai wa neko de aru**<br>*(I Am a Cat)* | 1905 |
| 3426 | **Navarro Villoslada, Francisco** | Spanish | N | **Amaya: o, los vascos en el siglo VIII**<br>*[Amayo, or the Basques of the eighth century]* | 1879 |
| 3427 | **Neagu, Fănuş** | Romanian | SS-N | **Dincolo de nisipuri** *(ss)*<br>*[Beyond the sands]* ·<br>*(Îngerul a strigat) {n}*<br>*[The angel shouted]* | 1962{ss}<br>1968{n} |
| 3428 | **Neagu, Fănuş** | Romanian | SS | **Lişca** | 1960 |
| 3429 | **Nedelcovici, Bujor** | Romanian | N | **Zile de nisip**<br>*[Days of sand]* | 1979 |
| 3430 | **Němcová, Božena** | Czech | N | **Babička**<br>*(The Grandmother)* | 1846 |
| 3431 | **Németh Lászlo** | Hungarian | N | **Iszony**<br>*(Revulsion)* | 1947 |
| 3432 | **Nenadić, Dobrilo** | Yugoslav(Serb) | N | **Dorotej** | 1977 |
| 3433 | **Nerval, Gérard de** | French | SS | **La main de gloire**<br>*(aka: La main enchantée)* | 1832<br>(aka:1852) |
| 3434 | **Nesbit, E.** | British | N | **The Railway Children** | 1906 |
| 3435 | **Nestroy, Johann** | Austrian | P | **Der böse Geist Lumpazivagabundus** | 1835 |
| 3436 | **Nestroy, Johann** | Austrian | P | **Der böse Geist Lumpazivagabundus** | 1835 |
| 3437 | **Nestroy, Johann** | Austrian | P | **Der Färber und sein Zwillingsbruder** | 1890 |
| 3438 | **Nestroy, Johann** | Austrian | P | **Hinüber - herbüer** | 1844 |
| 3439 | **Nestroy, Johann** | Austrian | P | **Einen Jux will er sich machen**<br>*(The Matchmaker)* | 1844 |
| 3440 | **Nestroy, Johann** | Austrian | P | **Einen Jux will er sich machen** | 1844 |
| 3441 | **Nestroy, Johann** | Austrian | P | **Einen Jux will er sich machen** | 1844 |
| 3442 | **Nestroy, Johann** | Austrian | P | **Der Zerrissene** | 1845 |
| 3443 | **Neumann, Alfred** | German | SS-P | **Der patriot**<br>*(The Patriot)*<br>*(aka: Such Men Are Dangerous) {p}* | 1925{ss}<br>1927{p} |
| 3444 | **Neumann, Alfred** | German | SS | **Viele heißen Kain** | 1950 |
| 3445 | **Neumann, Robert** | Austrian(Eng) | N | **Struensee**<br>*(aka: Der Favorit der Königin)*<br>*(The Queen's Doctor)* | 1935<br>(aka:1953) |
| 3446 | **Neveux, Georges** | French | P | **Juliette ou la clé des songes** | 1930 |
| 3447 | **Nexø, Martin Andersen** | Danish | N | **Ditte Menneskebarn**<br>*(Ditte: Daughter of Man)* | 1917-21 |
| 3448 | **Nexø, Martin Andersen** | Danish | SS | **Lotterisvensken** | 1919 |
| 3449 | **Nexø, Martin Andersen** | Danish | N | **Pelle Erobrenen**<br>*(vol 1: Barndom)*<br>*(Pelle the Conqueror)* | 1906-10 |
| 3450 | **Nezval, Vítĕzslav** | Czech | SS | **Valerie a týden divů** | 1945 |
| 3451 | **Niccodemi, Dario** | Italian(Sp/Fr) | P | **Scampolo** | 1916 |
| 3452 | **Nichols, Peter** | British | P | **A Day in the Death of Joe Egg**<br>*(aka: Joe Egg)* | 1967 |
| 3453 | **Nichols, Peter** | British | P | **The National Health;**<br>**or, Nurse Norton's Affair** | 1970 |
| 3454 | **Nichols, Peter** | British | P | **Privates on Parade** | 1977 |
| 3455 | **Nikolaeva, Galina** | Russian | N | **Zhatva**<br>*[Harvest]* | 1950 |
| 3456 | **Nilin, Pavel** | Russian | N | **Chelovek idyot v goru**<br>*[Man goes uphill]* | 1936 |

| No | Film Title | Country of Production | Date | Director(s) | Duration of Film |
|----|-----------|----------------------|------|-------------|------------------|
| 3424 | **Sore kara** <br> *(And Then)* | JAP | 1986(85) | **Yoshimitsu Morita** | 130 |
| 3425 | **Wagahai wa neko de aru** <br> *(I Am a Cat)* | JAP | 1975 | **Kon Ichikawa** | 116 |
| 3426 | **Amaya** | SP | 1953(52) | **Luis Marquina** | 110(92) |
| 3427 | **Dincolo de nisipuri** | ROM | 1973 | **Radu Gabrea** | 107 |
| 3428 | **Lişca** | ROM | 1984 | **Ion Cărmăzan** | 99 |
| 3429 | **Faleze de nisip** <br> *[Cliffs of sand]* | ROM | 1983(82) | **Dan Piţa** | 102 |
| 3430 | **Babička** | CZ | 1940 | **František Čáp** | 92(99) |
| 3431 | **Iszony** <br> *(Abhorrence)* | HUNG | 1965 | **György Hintsch** | 113 |
| 3432 | **Dorotej** | YUGO | 1981 | **Zdravko Velimirović** | 97 |
| 3433 | **La main du diable** <br> *(aka: Carnival of Sinners)* | FR | 1942 | **Maurice Tourneur** | 82 |
| 3434 | **The Railway Children** | GB | 1970 | **Lionel Jeffries** | 108 |
| 3435 | **Lumpazivagabundus** | AUST | 1937 | **Geza von Bolvary** | 90 |
| 3436 | **Lumpazivagabundus** | GER | 1956 | **Franz Antel** <br> *(François Legrand)* | 99 |
| 3437 | **Wenn Poldi ins Manöver zieht** | AUST | 1956 | **Hans Quest** | 90 |
| 3438 | **Glück im Winkel** <br> *[Happiness in a small corner]* | GER | 1937 | **Alfred Stöger** | 22 |
| 3439 | **Das Einmaleins der Liebe** | GER | 1935 | **Carl Hoffmann** | 95 |
| 3440 | **Einmal keine Sorgen haben** <br> *(aka: Einen Jux will er sich machen)* | AUST/GER | 1953 | **Georg Marischka** | 92 |
| 3441 | **Einen Jux will er sich machen** | AUST | 1958 | **Alfred Stöger** <br> **Leopold Lindtberg** | 104 |
| 3442 | **Die goldene Fessel** | GER | 1944 | **Hans Thimig** | 91 |
| 3443 | **Le patriote** <br> *(aka: The Mad Emperor)* | FR | 1938 | **Maurice Tourneur** | 113 |
| 3444 | **Das Haus des Schweigens** <br> *(aka: Jahre des Schweigens)* | GER | 1951 | **Hans Heinrich** | 101 |
| 3445 | **Herrscher ohne Krone** | GER | 1957 | **Harald Braun** | 104 |
| 3446 | **Juliette ou la clé des songes** <br> *(US: Juliette or the Dream Book)* | FR | 1951(50) | **Marcel Carné** | 93 |
| 3447 | **Ditte Menneskebarn** <br> *(Ditta: Child of Man)* | DEN | 1946 | **Bjärne Henning-Jensen** <br> **Astrid Henning-Jensen** | 103 |
| 3448 | **Der lotterieschwede** <br> *[The lottery Swede]* | GDR | 1958 | **Joachim Kunert** | 71 |
| 3449 | **Pelle Erobrenen** <br> *(Pelle the Conqueror)* | DEN/SWE | 1988(87) | **Bille August** | 149 +V |
| 3450 | **Valerie a týden divů** <br> *(Valerie and Her Week of Wonders)* | CZ | 1970(69) | **Jaromil Jireš** | 77 |
| 3451 | **Scampolo** | GER | 1957 | **Alfred Weidenmann** | 109 |
| 3452 | **A Day in the Death of Joe Egg** | GB | 1972(70) | **Peter Medak** | 106 |
| 3453 | **The National Health** <br> *(aka: The National Health or Nurse Norton's Affair)* | GB | 1973 | **Jack Gold** | 97 +V(93) |
| 3454 | **Privates on Parade** | GB | 1982 | **Michael Blakemore** | 112 +V |
| 3455 | **Vozvrashchenie Vasilya Bortnikova** <br> *(The Return of Vassily Bortnikov)* <br> *(aka: Vasili's Return)* | USSR | 1953 | **Vsevolod Pudovkin** | 90 |
| 3456 | **Bolshaya zhizn** <br> *(A Great Life)* <br> *(aka: Big Life)* | USSR | 1939/58 (46) | **Leonid Lukov** | Pt.1, 98 <br> Pt.2, 95 |

**191**

| No. | Author | Nationality | Form | Literary Title | Date |
|-----|--------|-------------|------|----------------|------|
| 3457 | **Nilin, Pavel** | Russian | SS | **Vpervye zamuzhem**<br>(First Married) | 1978 |
| 3458 | **Nilsson Piraten, Fritiof** | Swedish | SS | **Bock i Örtagård** | 1933 |
| 3459 | **Nilsson Piraten, Fritiof** | Swedish | N | **Bokhandlaren som slutade bada** | 1937 |
| 3460 | **Nilsson Piraten, Fritiof** | Swedish | N | **Bombi Bitt och jag**<br>(Bombi Bitt) | 1932 |
| 3461 | **Nin, Anais** | American | MEM | **Henry and June: From the<br>Unexpurgated Diary** | 1986 |
| 3462 | **Niwa Fumio** | Japanese | N | **Bara gassen** | 1937(38) |
| 3463 | **Niwa Fumio** | Japanese | N | **Ikari no machi** | 1949 |
| 3464 | **Noble, W.**<br>(joint, see: Herlihy, James Leo) | American | P | | |
| 3465 | **Nogami Yaeko** | Japanese | N | **Machiko** | 1928 |
| 3466 | **Noma Hiroshi** | Japanese | N | **Shinkū-chitai**<br>(Zone of Emptiness) | 1952 |
| 3467 | **Nordhoff, Charles;<br>Hall, James N.** | American | N | **Botany Bay** | 1941 |
| 3468 | **Nordhoff, Charles;<br>Hall, James N.** | American | N | **High Barbaree** | 1945 |
| 3469 | **Nordhoff, Charles;<br>Hall, James N.** | American | N | **The Hurricane** | 1936 |
| 3470 | **Nordhoff, Charles;<br>Hall, James N.** | American | N | **The Hurricane** | 1936 |
| 3471 | **Nordhoff, Charles;<br>Hall, James N.** | American | N | **Men Without Country** | 1944 |
| 3472 | **Nordhoff, Charles;<br>Hall, James N.** | American | N | **Mutiny on the Bounty +<br>Men Against the Sea +<br>Pitcairn's Island** | 1932+<br>1934 |
| 3473 | **Nordhoff, Charles;<br>Hall, James N.** | American | N | **Mutiny on the Bounty** | 1932 |
| 3474 | **Nordhoff, Charles;<br>Hall, James N.** | American | N | **No More Gas**<br>(aka: Out of Gas) | 1940 |
| 3475 | **Norway, Nevil Shute**<br>(see: Shute, Nevil) | British | N/SS | | |
| 3476 | **Noyes, Alfred** | British | V | **The Highwayman** | 1907 |
| 3477 | **Nugent, Eliot**<br>(joint, see: Thurber, James) | American | P | | |
| 3478 | **Nušić, Branislav** | Yugoslav(Serb) | P | **Gospoda ministarka**<br>[The cabinet minister's wife] | 1929 |
| 3479 | **Nušić, Branislav** | Yugoslav | P | **Sumnjivo lice** | 1887 |
| 3480 | **Oakley, Barry** | Australian | N | **A Salute to the Great McCarthy** | 1970 |
| 3481 | **Oates, Joyce Carol** | American | SS | **Where Are You Going, Where<br>Have You Been?** | 1967 |
| 3482 | **O'Brien, Edna** | Irish | N | **The Country Girls** | 1960 |
| 3483 | **O'Brien, Edna** | Irish | N | **The Lonely Girl** | 1962 |
| 3484 | **Obstfelder, Sigbjørn** | Norwegian | N | **Korset**<br>[The cross] | 1896 |
| 3485 | **O'Casey, Sean** | Irish | P | **Bedtime Story** | 1951 |
| 3486 | **O'Casey, Sean** | Irish | P | **Juno and the Paycock** | 1928 |
| 3487 | **O'Casey, Sean** | Irish | P | **Juno and the Paycock** | 1928 |
| 3488 | **O'Casey, Sean** | Irish | AUT | **Mirror in My House** | 1956 |
| 3489 | **O'Casey, Sean** | Irish | P | **The Plough and the Stars** | 1926 |
| 3490 | **O'Connor, Edwin** | American | N | **The Last Hurrah** | 1956 |
| 3491 | **O'Connor, Flannery** | American | SS | **A Circle in the Fire** | 1955 |
| 3492 | **O'Connor, Flannery** | American | SS | **Comforts of Home** | 1965 |
| 3493 | **O'Connor, Flannery** | American | SS | **The Displaced Person** | 1955 |
| 3494 | **O'Connor, Flannery** | American | SS | **Good Country People** | 1955 |
| 3495 | **O'Connor, Flannery** | American | SS | **The River** | 1955 |
| 3496 | **O'Connor, Flannery** | American | N | **Wise Blood** | 1955 |

| No | Film Title | Country of Production | Date | Director(s) | Duration of Film |
|---|---|---|---|---|---|
| 3457 | **Vpervye zamuzhem** <br> (Married For the First Time) | USSR | 1980 | Iosif Heifitz | 99(92) |
| 3458 | **Bock i Örtagård** <br> (A Goat in the Garden) | SWE | 1958 | Gösta Folke | 101 |
| 3459 | **Bokhandlaren som slutade bada** <br> (The Bookseller Who Gave Up Bathing) | SWE | 1968 | Jarl Kulle | 99 |
| 3460 | **Bombi Bitt och jag** <br> [Bombi Bitt and I] | SWE | 1936 | Gösta Rodin | 76 |
| 3461 | **Henry & June** | USA | 1990 | Philip Kaufman | 136 |
| 3462 | **Bara gassen** <br> (The Battle of Roses) | JAP | 1950 | Mikio Naruse | 98 |
| 3463 | **Ikari no machi** <br> (The Angry Street) | JAP | 1950 | Mikio Naruse | 105 |
| 3464 | | | | | |
| 3465 | **Hana hiraku** <br> (A Flower Blooms) | JAP | 1948 | Kon Ichikawa | 85 |
| 3466 | **Shinkū chitai** <br> (Vacuum Zone) | JAP | 1952 | Satsuo Yamamoto | 129 |
| 3467 | **Botany Bay** | USA | 1952 | John Farrow | 94 |
| 3468 | **High Barbaree** | USA | 1947 | Jack Conway | 91 |
| 3469 | **The Hurricane** | USA | 1937 | John Ford | 110 <br> +V(99) |
| 3470 | **Hurricane** <br> (aka: Forbidden Paradise) | USA | 1979 | Jan Troell | 119 <br> +V |
| 3471 | **Passage to Marseille** | USA | 1944 | Michael Curtiz | 110 |
| 3472 | **Mutiny on the Bounty** | USA | 1935 | Frank Lloyd | 135 |
| 3473 | **Mutiny on the Bounty** | USA | 1962 | Lewis Milestone | 185(179) <br> +V |
| 3474 | **The Tuttles of Tahiti** | USA | 1942 | Charles Vidor | 91 |
| 3475 | | | | | |
| 3476 | **The Highwayman** | USA | 1951 | Lesley Selander | 82 |
| 3477 | | | | | |
| 3478 | **Gospoda ministarka** | YUGO | 1958 | Žorž Skrigin | 90 |
| 3479 | **Sumnjivo lice** <br> (A Suspicious Character) | YUGO | 1954 | Soja Jovanović <br> Predrag Dinulović | 80 |
| 3480 | **The Great McCarthy** | AUSTL | 1975 | David Baker | 98 |
| 3481 | **Smooth Talk** | USA | 1985 | Joyce Chopra | 91 <br> +V |
| 3482 | **The Country Girls** | GB | 1984(83) | Desmond Davis | 108 +V |
| 3483 | **Girl With Green Eyes** | GB | 1964(63) | Desmond Davis | 91 +V |
| 3484 | **Den evige Eva** | NOR | 1953 | Rolf Randall | 77 |
| 3485 | **Pension pro svobodné pány** | CZ | 1967 | Jiří Krejčík | 90 |
| 3486 | **Juno and the Paycock** <br> (aka: The Shame of Mary Boyle) | GB | 1930(29) | Alfred Hitchcock | 99(85) |
| 3487 | **Yao qian shu** <br> (Money Tree) | CHN | 1937 | Tan You-liu | 91 |
| 3488 | **Young Cassidy** | GB/USA | 1965(64) | Jack Cardiff <br> John Ford | 110 |
| 3489 | **The Plough and the Stars** | USA | 1936 | John Ford | 78 |
| 3490 | **The Last Hurrah** | USA | 1958 | John Ford | 122 |
| 3491 | **A Circle in the Fire** | USA | 1975 | Victor Nunez | 50 +V |
| 3492 | **Comforts of Home** | USA | 1974 | Jerome Shore | 40 +V |
| 3493 | **The Displaced Person** | USA | 1977 | Glenn Jordan | 58 +V |
| 3494 | **Good Country People** | USA | 1975 | Jeff Jackson | 32 |
| 3495 | **The River** | USA | 1978 | Barbara Noble | 29 +V |
| 3496 | **Wise Blood** <br> (GER: Die Weisheit des Blutes) | USA/GER | 1979 | John Huston | 108 <br> +V(102) |

| No. | Author | Nationality | Form | Literary Title | Date |
|-----|--------|-------------|------|----------------|------|
| 3497 | O'Connor, Frank (Michael O'Donovan) | Irish | SS | Guests of the Nation | 1931 |
| 3498 | Odets, Clifford | American | P | The Big Knife | 1949 |
| 3499 | Odets, Clifford | American | P | Clash by Night | 1942 |
| 3500 | Odets, Clifford | American | P | The Country Girl (GB: Winter Journey) | 1951 |
| 3501 | Odets, Clifford | American | P | Golden Boy | 1937 |
| 3502 | O'Donovan, Michael (see: O'Connor, Frank) | Irish | SS | | |
| 3503 | Ōe Kenzaburō | Japanese | SS | Shiiku (Prize Stock) (aka: The Catch) | 1958 |
| 3504 | O'Faolain, Sean | Irish | SS | The Woman Who Married Clark Gable | 1948 |
| 3505 | O'Flaherty, Liam | Irish | N | The Informer | 1925 |
| 3506 | O'Flaherty, Liam | Irish | N | The Informer | 1925 |
| 3507 | O'Flaherty, Liam | Irish | N | Mr Gilhooley | 1926 |
| 3508 | O'Flaherty, Liam | Irish | N | The Puritan | 1931 |
| 3509 | O'Hara, John | American | N | Butterfield 8 | 1935 |
| 3510 | O'Hara, John | American | N | From the Terrace | 1958 |
| 3511 | O'Hara, John | American | SS-P | Pal Joey | 1939{ss} 1940{p} |
| 3512 | O'Hara, John | American | N | A Rage to Live | 1949 |
| 3513 | O'Hara, John | American | N | Ten North Frederick | 1955 |
| 3514 | Olesha, Yury Karlovich | Russian | SS-P | Tri tolstyaka (The Three Fat Men) | 1928{ss} 1930{p} |
| 3515 | Oliveira, Carlos (Albert Serra de) | Portuguese | N | Uma abelha na chuva [A bee in the rain] | 1953 |
| 3516 | Oliveira, José Carlos de | Brazilian | N | Terror e êxtase [Terror and ecstasy] | 1978 |
| 3517 | Olujić, Grozdana | Yugoslav(Serb) | N | Glasam za ljubav [I vote for love] | 1953 |
| 3518 | Olujić, Grozdana | Yugoslav | N | Izlet u nebo (An Excursion to Heaven) | 1958 |
| 3519 | Omre, Arthur | Norwegian | N | Flukten (Flight) | 1936 |
| 3520 | Omre, Arthur | Norwegian | N | Smuglere [The smugglers] | 1935 |
| 3521 | O'Neill, Eugene | American | P | Ah Wilderness! | 1933 |
| 3522 | O'Neill, Eugene | American | P | Ah Wilderness! | 1933 |
| 3523 | O'Neill, Eugene | American | P | Anna Christie | 1922 |
| 3524 | O'Neill, Eugene | American | P | Anna Christie | 1922 |
| 3525 | O'Neill, Eugene | American | P | Desire Under the Elms | 1923 |
| 3526 | O'Neill, Eugene | American | P | The Emperor Jones | 1920 |
| 3527 | O'Neill, Eugene | American | P | The Hairy Ape | 1922 |
| 3528 | O'Neill, Eugene | American | P | The Iceman Cometh | 1946 |
| 3529 | O'Neill, Eugene | American | P | Long Day's Journey into Night | 1955 |
| 3530 | O'Neill, Eugene | American | P | The Moon of the Caribbees + In the Zone + Bound East For Cardiff + The Long Voyage Home | 1918+ 1916+ 1919 |
| 3531 | O'Neill, Eugene | American | P | Mourning Becomes Electra | 1931 |
| 3532 | O'Neill, Eugene | American | P | Recklessness | 1914 |
| 3533 | O'Neill, Eugene | American | P | Strange Interlude | 1928 |
| 3534 | Ōoka Shōhei | Japanese | N | Musashino fujin | 1951 |
| 3535 | Ōoka Shōhei | Japanese | N | Nobi (Fires on the Plain) | 1954 |
| 3536 | Örkény István | Hungarian | N-P | Macskajáték (Catsplay) | 1963{n} 1969{p} |

| No | Film Title | Country of Production | Date | Director(s) | Duration of Film |
|---|---|---|---|---|---|
| 3497 | **Guests of the Nation** | IRE | 1936 | **Denis Johnston** | 50 |
| 3498 | **The Big Knife** | USA | 1955 | **Robert Aldrich** | 111 |
| 3499 | **Clash by Night** | USA | 1952 | **Fritz Lang** | 105 +V |
| 3500 | **The Country Girl** | USA | 1954 | **George Seaton** | 104 |
| 3501 3502 | **Golden Boy** | USA | 1939 | **Rouben Mamoulian** | 91(101) |
| 3503 | **Shiiku** (The Catch) | JAP | 1961 | **Nagisa Ōshima** | 105 |
| 3504 | **The Woman Who Married Clark Gable** | IRE/GB | 1985 | **Thaddeus O'Sullivan** | 28 |
| 3505 | **The Informer** | USA | 1935 | **John Ford** | 91 |
| 3506 | **Uptight** | USA | 1968 | **Jules Dassin** | 104 |
| 3507 | **Dernière jeunesse** (Last Desire) | FR | 1939 | **Jeff Musso** | 88 |
| 3508 | **Le puritain** (The Puritan) | FR | 1937 | **Jeff Musso** | 87(97) |
| 3509 | **Butterfield 8** | USA | 1960 | **Daniel Mann** | 108 |
| 3510 | **From the Terrace** | USA | 1960 | **Mark Robson** | 144 |
| 3511 | **Pal Joey** {musical version} | USA | 1957 | **George Sidney** | 112 +V |
| 3512 | **A Rage to Live** | USA | 1965 | **Walter Grauman** | 101 |
| 3513 | **Ten North Frederick** | USA | 1958 | **Philip Dunne** | 102 |
| 3514 | **Tri tolstyaka** (Three Fat Men) | USSR | 1967(66) | **Alexei Batalov Iosif Shapiro** | 114 |
| 3515 | **Uma abelha na chuva** | PORT | 1971(69) | **Fernando Lopes** | 75 |
| 3516 | **Terror e êxtase** | BRAZ | 1980 | **Antônio Calmon** | 95 |
| 3517 | **Glasam za ljubav** | YUGO | 1965 | **Svetomir Janić** | 89 |
| 3518 | **Čudna devojka** (Strange Girl) | YUGO | 1962 | **Jovan Živanović** | 100 |
| 3519 | **Ukjent mann** (Unknown Man) | NOR | 1952(51) | **Astrid Henning-Jensen** | 104 |
| 3520 | **Smuglere** | NOR | 1968 | **Rolf Clemens** | 108 |
| 3521 | **Ah, Wilderness!** | USA | 1935 | **Clarence Brown** | 101 |
| 3522 | **Summer Holiday** {musical version} | USA | 1947 | **Rouben Mamoulian** | 92 |
| 3523 | **Anna Christie** | USA | 1930 | **Clarence Brown** | 90 |
| 3524 | **Anna Christie** {German version of Clarence Brown's film} | USA/GER | 1930 | **Jacques Feyder** | 90 |
| 3525 | **Desire Under the Elms** | USA | 1958(57) | **Delbert Mann** | 111(114) |
| 3526 | **The Emperor Jones** | USA | 1933 | **Dudley Murphy** | 72 |
| 3527 | **The Hairy Ape** | USA | 1944 | **Alfred Santell** | 90 |
| 3528 | **The Iceman Cometh** | USA | 1973 | **John Frankenheimer** | 239 |
| 3529 | **Long Day's Journey into Night** | USA | 1962 | **Sidney Lumet** | 136(174) +V |
| 3530 | **The Long Voyage Home** | USA | 1940 | **John Ford** | 104 |
| 3531 | **Mourning Becomes Electra** | USA | 1947 | **Dudley Nichols** | 173 |
| 3532 | **The Constant Woman** (aka: Auction in Souls) | USA | 1933 | **Victor Schertzinger** | 73 |
| 3533 | **Strange Interlude** (GB: Strange Interval) | USA | 1932 | **Robert Z. Leonard** | 110 |
| 3534 | **Musashino fujin** (The Lady of Musashino) (aka: Woman of Musashino) | JAP | 1951 | **Kenji Mizoguchi** | 92 |
| 3535 | **Nobi** (Fires on the Plain) | JAP | 1959 | **Kon Ichikawa** | 108 |
| 3536 | **Macskajáték** (Catsplay) (aka: Cats Game) | HUNG | 1974 | **Károly Makk** | 123(115) |

| No. | Author | Nationality | Form | Literary Title | Date |
|-----|--------|-------------|------|----------------|------|
| 3537 | Örkény István | Hungarian | N-P | **Macskajáték** | 1963{n}<br>1969{p} |
| 3538 | Örkény István | Hungarian | SS | **Rekviem** | 1957-58 |
| 3539 | Örkény István | Hungarian | N-P | **Tóték** | 1964{n}<br>1967{p} |
| 3540 | Orton, Joe | British | P | **Entertaining Mr Sloane** | 1964 |
| 3541 | Orton, Joe | British | P | **Loot** | 1967 |
| 3542 | Ørum, Poul | Danish | N | **Kun sandheden** | 1974 |
| 3543 | Orwell, George | British | N | **Animal Farm** | 1945 |
| 3544 | Orwell, George | British | N | **Nineteen Eighty-Four** | 1949 |
| 3545 | Orwell, George | British | N | **Nineteen Eighty-Four** | 1949 |
| 3546 | Orzeszkowa, Eliza | Polish | N | **Cham**<br>*[The boor]* | 1888(89) |
| 3547 | Orzeszkowa, Eliza | Polish | N | **Nad Niemnem**<br>*[On the banks of the Niemen]* | 1888(87) |
| 3548 | Osaragi Jirō | Japanese | N | **Munakata shimai** | 1949 |
| 3549 | Osaragi Jirō | Japanese | N | **Nadare** | 1937 |
| 3550 | Osborne, John | British | P | **The Entertainer** | 1957 |
| 3551 | Osborne, John | British | P | **The Entertainer** | 1957 |
| 3552 | Osborne, John | British | P | **Inadmissible Evidence** | 1965 |
| 3553 | Osborne, John | British | P | **Look Back in Anger** | 1957 |
| 3554 | Osborne, John | British | P | **Luther** | 1961 |
| 3555 | Osbourne, Lloyd<br>*(joint, see: Stevenson, Robert Louis)* | British | N | | |
| 3556 | Ostrovsky, Alexander | Russian | P | **Beshennye den'gi**<br>*(Easy Money)* | 1870 |
| 3557 | Ostrovsky, Alexander | Russian | P | **Bespridannitsa** | 1878 |
| 3558 | Ostrovsky, Alexander | Russian | P | **Bespridannitsa** | 1878 |
| 3559 | Ostrovsky, Alexander | Russian | P | **Bez vini vinovatiye**<br>*(More Sinned Against Than Sinning)* | 1884 |
| 3560 | Ostrovsky, Alexander | Russian | P | **Dokhodnoe mesto**<br>*[A profitable post]* | 1857 |
| 3561 | Ostrovsky, Alexander | Russian | P | **Goriachee serdtse**<br>*[An ardent heart]* | 1869 |
| 3562 | Ostrovsky, Alexander | Russian | P | **Groza**<br>*(The Storm)*<br>*(aka: The Thunderstorm)* | 1859 |
| 3563 | Ostrovsky, Alexander | Russian | P | **Les**<br>*(The Forest)* | 1871 |
| 3564 | Ostrovsky, Alexander | Russian | P | **Les** | 1871 |
| 3565 | Ostrovsky, Alexander | Russian | P | **Na boikom meste**<br>*(At the Jolly Spot)* | 1865 |
| 3566 | Ostrovsky, Alexander | Russian | P | **Na vsyakogo mudretsa dovol'no prostoty**<br>*(Even a Wise Man Stumbles)*<br>*(aka: Too Clever by Half; or, Diary of a Scoundrel)* | 1868 |
| 3567 | Ostrovsky, Alexander | Russian | P | **Poslednaya zhertva**<br>*(A Last Sacrifice)* | 1878 |
| 3568 | Ostrovsky, Alexander | Russian | P | **Pravda khorosho, a schaste luchshe**<br>*[Truth is good, but happiness is better]* | 1877 |
| 3569 | Ostrovsky, Alexander | Russian | P | **Puchina**<br>*[The Abyss]* | 1866 |
| 3570 | Ostrovsky, Alexander | Russian | P | **Snegurochka**<br>*[The snow maiden]* | 1873 |
| 3571 | Ostrovsky, Alexander | Russian | P | **Talanty i poklonniki**<br>*(Artistes and Admirers)* | 1882 |

| No | Film Title | Country of Production | Date | Director(s) | Duration of Film |
|---|---|---|---|---|---|
| 3537 | **Katzenspiel** (Catsplay) | GER | 1983 | István Szabó | 83 |
| 3538 | **Reqiem** | HUNG | 1982(81) | Zoltán Fábri | 97 |
| 3539 | **Isten hozta,őrnagy úr!** (The Toth Family) (aka: The Tot Family) | HUNG | 1969 | Zoltán Fábri | 106 |
| 3540 | **Entertaining Mr Sloane** | GB | 1970(69) | Douglas Hickox | 94 +V(90) |
| 3541 | **Loot** (aka: Loot...Give Me Money, Honey!) | GB | 1970 | Silvio Narizzano | 101 +V(96) |
| 3542 | **Kun sandheden** | DEN | 1975 | Henning Ørnbak | 95 |
| 3543 | **Animal Farm** {animation} | GB | 1954 | John Halas Joy Batchelor | 73 +V |
| 3544 | **1984** | GB | 1955 | Michael Anderson | 90 |
| 3545 | **Nineteen Eighty-Four** (aka: 1984) | GB | 1984 | Michael Radford | 110 +V |
| 3546 | **Cham** | POL | 1931 | Jan-Nowina Przybylski | 94 |
| 3547 | **Nad Niemnem** | POL | 1987(86) | Zbigniew Kuźminski | 177 |
| 3548 | **Munekata shimai** (The Munekata Sisters) | JAP | 1950 | Yasujirō Ozu | 112 |
| 3549 | **Nadare** (Avalanche) | JAP | 1937 | Mikio Naruse | 70 |
| 3550 | **The Entertainer** | GB | 1960 | Tony Richardson | 96 |
| 3551 | **The Entertainer** | USA | 1975 | Donald Wrye | 105 |
| 3552 | **Inadmissible Evidence** | GB | 1968 | Anthony Page | 96 |
| 3553 | **Look Back in Anger** | GB | 1959 | Tony Richardson | 101 +V |
| 3554 | **Luther** | GB/CAN/USA | 1976(73) | Guy Green | 112 |
| 3555 | | | | | |
| 3556 | **Beshenye den'gi** | USSR | 1981 | Yevgeny Matveyev | 86 |
| 3557 | **Bespridannitsa** (Without Dowry) | USSR | 1937 | Yakov Protazanov | 80 |
| 3558 | **Zhestokij romans** (Cruel Romance) (aka: Ruthless Romance) (aka: Dowerless Bride) | USSR | 1984 | Eldar Ryazanov | 140 |
| 3559 | **Bez vini vinovatiye** (Innocent Though Guilty) (aka: Guilty Though Innocent) | USSR | 1946(45) | Vladimir Petrov | 100 |
| 3560 | **Vankansya** | USSR | 1981 | Margarita Mikaelyan | 77 |
| 3561 | **Goriachee serdtse** {2 - parts} | USSR | 1953 | Gennadi Kazanski | Pt.1, 102 Pt.2, 77 |
| 3562 | **Groza** (The Storm) (aka: Thunderstorm) | USSR | 1934(33) | Vladimir Petrov | 85 |
| 3563 | **Les** {2 - parts} | USSR | 1953 | Vladimir Vengerov Semen Timoshenko | Pt.1, 93 Pt.2, 76 |
| 3564 | **Les** | USSR | 1980 | Vladimir Motil | 121 |
| 3565 | **Na boikom meste** | USSR | 1955 | Vladimir Sukhobokov Elena Skatchko | 101 |
| 3566 | **Na vsyakogo mudretsa dovol'no prostoty** {2 - parts} | USSR | 1952 | A. Dormenko | Pt.1, 103 Pt.2, 75 |
| 3567 | **Poslednaya zhertva** (The Last Victim) | USSR | 1976 | Pyotr Todorovsky | 99 |
| 3568 | **Pravda khorosho, a schaste luchshe** {2 - parts} | USSR | 1951 | Sergei Alekseev | Pt.1, 82 Pt.2, 67 |
| 3569 | **Puchina** | USSR | 1958 | Antonin Dawson Yuri Muzykant | 99 |
| 3570 | **Snegurochka** | USSR | 1969(68) | Pavel Kadochnikov | 92 |
| 3571 | **Talanty i poklonniki** | USSR | 1955 | Andrey Apsolon Boris Dmokhovski | 89 |

| No. | Author | Nationality | Form | Literary Title | Date |
|-----|--------|-------------|------|----------------|------|
| 3572 | **Ostrovsky, Alexander** | Russian | P | **Talanty i poklonniki** | 1882 |
| 3573 | **Ostrovsky, Alexander** | Russian | P | **Volki i ovsty** *(Wolves and Sheep)* | 1875 |
| 3574 | **Ostrovsky, Nikolay** | Russian | N | **Kak zakalyalas stal** *(How the Steel Was Tempered)* *(aka: The Making of a Hero)* | 1932-34 |
| 3575 | **Ostrovsky, Nikolay** | Russian | N | **Kak zakalyalas stal** | 1932-34 |
| 3576 | **Otčenášek, Jan** | Czech | N | **Občan Brych** | 1955 |
| 3577 | **Otčenášek, Jan** | Czech | N | **Romeo, Julie a tma** *(Romeo and Juliet and the Darkness)* | 1960 |
| 3578 | **Ousmane Sembène** *(Sembène, Ousmane)* | Senegalese(Fr) | SS | **Le mandat** *(The Money Order)* | 1965 |
| 3579 | **Ousmane Sembène** | Senegalese | SS | **La noire de...** | 1962 |
| 3580 | **Ousmane Sembène** | Senegalese | N | **Xala** | 1973 |
| 3581 | **Øverland, Arnulf** | Norwegian | P | **Venner** | 1917 |
| 3582 | **Ovid** *(Publius Ovidius Naso)* | Latin(anc) | V | **Metamorphoses** | c.2-8 |
| 3583 | **Oz, Amos** | Israeli | N | **Michael sheli** *(My Michael)* | 1968 |
| 3584 | **Paasilinna, Arto** | Finnish | N | **Hirtettyjen kettujen metsä** *[Forest of hanged foxes]* | 1983 |
| 3585 | **Paasilinna, Arto** | Finnish | N | **Jäniksen vuosi** | 1975 |
| 3586 | **Paasilinna, Arto** | Finnish | N | **Ulvova mylläri** *[The howling miller]* | 1981 |
| 3587 | **Pa Chin** *(see: Li Feigan)* | Chinese | N | | |
| 3588 | **Pagnol, Marcel** | French | F-P | **César** | 1937 |
| 3589 | **Pagnol, Marcel** | French | N | **L'eau des collines** *(vol 1: Jean de Florette)* | 1963 |
| 3590 | **Pagnol, Marcel** | French | N | **L'eau des collines** *(vol 2: Manon des sources)* | 1963 |
| 3591 | **Pagnol, Marcel** | French | P | **Fanny** | 1932 |
| 3592 | **Pagnol, Marcel** | French | P | **Fanny** | 1932 |
| 3593 | **Pagnol, Marcel** | French | P | **Fanny** | 1932 |
| 3594 | **Pagnol, Marcel** | French | P | **Fanny +** **Marius** | 1932+ 1931 |
| 3595 | **Pagnol, Marcel** | French | F-N | **Manon des sources** | 1962-63 |
| 3596 | **Pagnol, Marcel** | French | P | **Marius** | 1931 |
| 3597 | **Pagnol, Marcel** | French | P | **Marius** | 1931 |
| 3598 | **Pagnol, Marcel** | French | P | **Marius +** **Fanny +** **César** | 1931+ 1932+ 1937 |
| 3599 | **Pagnol, Marcel** | French | AUT | **Souvenirs d'enfance** *(vol 1: La gloire de mon père)* *(The Days Were Too Short)* | 1957 |
| 3600 | **Pagnol, Marcel** | French | AUT | **Souvenirs d'enfance** *(vol 2: Le château de ma mère)* *(The Days Were Too Short)* | 1957 |
| 3601 | **Pagnol, Marcel** | French | P | **Topaze** | 1930 |
| 3602 | **Pagnol, Marcel** | French | P | **Topaze** | 1930 |
| 3603 | **Pagnol, Marcel** | French | P | **Topaze** | 1930 |
| 3604 | **Pagnol, Marcel** | French | P | **Topaze** | 1930 |
| 3605 | **Pagnol, Marcel** | French | P | **Topaze** | 1930 |
| 3606 | **Pagnol, Marcel** | French | P | **Topaze** | 1930 |

| No | Film Title | Country of Production | Date | Director(s) | Duration of Film |
|----|-----------|----------------------|------|-------------|------------------|
| 3572 | **Talanty i poklonniki** | USSR | 1973 | **Isidor Annensky** | 90 |
| 3573 | **Volki i ovsty** *{2 - parts}* | USSR | 1952 | **Vladimir Sukhobokov** | Pt.1, 86 Pt.2, 95 |
| 3574 | **Kak zakalyalas stal** *(How the Steel Was Tempered)* *(aka: Heroes Are Made)* | USSR | 1943 | **Mark Donskoi** | 78 |
| 3575 | **Pavel Korchagin** | USSR | 1957 | **Alexander Alov** **Vladimir Naumov** | 95 |
| 3576 | **Občan Brych** *(Citizen Brych)* | CZ | 1958 | **Otakar Vávra** | 102 |
| 3577 | **Romeo, Julie a tma** *(Romeo, Juliet and Darkness)* *(aka: Sweet Light in a Dark Room)* | CZ | 1960 | **Jiří Weiss** | 96 |
| 3578 | **Mandabi** *(aka: Le mandat)* *(The Money Order)* | SEN/FR | 1968 | **Ousmane Sembène** | 90 |
| 3579 | **La noire de...** *(Black Girl)* *(aka: The Black Girl From...)* | SEN/FR | 1965 | **Ousmane Sembène** | 60 |
| 3580 | **Xala** *(Impotence)* *(aka: The Curse)* | SEN | 1974 | **Ousmane Sembène** | 123 |
| 3581 | **Venner** *(Friends)* | NOR | 1960 | **Tancred Ibsen** | 91 |
| 3582 | **Winds of Change** *(aka: Metamorphoses)* *{animation}* | USA | 1978 | **Takashi** | 89(82) |
| 3583 | **Michael sheli** *(My Michael)* | IS | 1974 | **Dan Wolman** | 90 |
| 3584 | **Hirtettyjen kettujen metsä** | FIN | 1986 | **Jouko Suikkari** | 98 |
| 3585 | **Jäniksen vuosi** *(The Year of the Hare)* | FIN | 1977 | **Risto Jarva** | 129 |
| 3586 | **Ulvova mylläri** | FIN | 1982 | **Jaakko Pakkasvirta** | 100 |
| 3587 | | | | | |
| 3588 | **César** | FR | 1936 | **Marcel Pagnol** | 121(160) |
| 3589 | **Jean de Florette** | FR/IT | 1986 | **Claude Berri** | 122 +V |
| 3590 | **Manon des sources** *(Manon of the Spring)* | FR/IT/ SWITZ | 1986 | **Claude Berri** | 114 +V |
| 3591 | **Fanny** | FR | 1932 | **Marc Allégret** | 126(142) |
| 3592 | **Fanny** | IT | 1933 | **Mario Almirante** | 96 |
| 3593 | **Zum schwarzen Walfisch** | GER | 1934 | **Fritz Wendhausen** | 99 |
| 3594 | **Port of Seven Seas** | USA | 1938 | **James Whale** | 81 |
| 3595 | **Manon des sources** *(Manon of the Springs)* | FR | 1952 | **Marcel Pagnol** | 190(240) |
| 3596 | **Marius** *(GER: Zum goldenen Anker)* | FR | 1931 | **Alexander Korda** | 130(108) |
| 3597 | **Längtan till havet** *(Longing For the Sea)* | SWE | 1931 | **John W. Brunius** **Alexander Korda** | 112 |
| 3598 | **Fanny** | USA | 1961(60) | **Joshua Logan** | 133(110) |
| 3599 | **La gloire de mon père** *(My Father's Glory)* | FR | 1990 | **Yves Robert** | 111 +V |
| 3600 | **Le château de ma mère** *(My Mother's Castle)* | FR | 1990 | **Yves Robert** | 98 +V |
| 3601 | **Topaze** | FR | 1932 | **Louis J. Gasnier** | 103 |
| 3602 | **Topaze** | USA | 1933 | **Harry D'Abbadie D'Arrast** | 78 |
| 3603 | **Topaze** | FR | 1936 | **Marcel Pagnol** | 110 |
| 3604 | **Jin yin shi jie** *(Gold and Silver World)* | CHN | 1939 | **Li Pin-chian** | 100 |
| 3605 | **Topaze** | FR | 1951 | **Marcel Pagnol** | 135 |
| 3606 | **Mr Topaze** *(USA: I Like Money)* | GB | 1961 | **Peter Sellers** | 97 |

| No. | Author | Nationality | Form | Literary Title | Date |
|---|---|---|---|---|---|
| 3607 | **Paiva, Marcelo Rubens** | Brazilian | N | **Feliz ano velho**<br>*[Happy old year]* | 1982 |
| 3608 | **Palacio Valdés, Armando** | Spanish | N | **La aldea perdida**<br>*[The lost village]* | 1903 |
| 3609 | **Palacio Valdés, Armando** | Spanish | N | **La fe**<br>*(Faith)* | 1892 |
| 3610 | **Palacio Valdés, Armando** | Spanish | N | **La hermana San Sulpicio**<br>*(Sister St. Sulpice)* | 1889 |
| 3611 | **Palacio Valdés, Armando** | Spanish | N | **La hermana San Sulpicio** | 1889 |
| 3612 | **Palacio Valdés, Armando** | Spanish | N | **La hermana San Sulpicio** | 1889 |
| 3613 | **Palacio Valdés, Armando** | Spanish | N | **Santa Rogelia** | 1926 |
| 3614 | **Palacio Valdés, Armando** | Spanish | N | **El señorito Octavio** | 1881 |
| 3615 | **Palacio Valdés, Armando** | Spanish | N | **Sinfonia pastoral** | 1931 |
| 3616 | **Palazzeschi, Aldo** | Italian | N | **Sorelle Materassi**<br>*(The Sisters Materassi)* | 1934 |
| 3617 | **Panduro, Leif** | Danish | N | **Rend mig i traditionerne**<br>*(Kick Me in the Traditions)* | 1958 |
| 3618 | **Panduro, Leif** | Danish | N | **De uanstændige** | 1960 |
| 3619 | **Panduro, Leif** | Danish | N | **Den ubetænksomme elsker**<br>*[The thoughtless lover]* | 1973 |
| 3620 | **Panfyorov, Fyodor** | Russian | N | **Bruski**<br>*(Brusski. A Story of Peasant Life in Soviet Russia)* | 1928-37 |
| 3621 | **Panova, Vera Fyodorovna** | Russian | N | **Sentimental'nyj roman** | 1958 |
| 3622 | **Panzini, Alfredo** | Italian | N | **Il padrone sono me**<br>*[The boss is me]* | 1925 |
| 3623 | **Pardo Bazán, Emilia** | Spanish | SS | **El indulto**<br>*(The Pardon)* | 1885 |
| 3624 | **Pardo Bazán, Emilia** | Spanish | N | **La sirena negra**<br>*[The black mermaid]* | 1908 |
| 3625 | **Pardo Bazán, Emilia** | Spanish | N | **Un viaje de novios**<br>*(A Wedding Trip)* | 1881 |
| 3626 | **Parker, Dorothy** | American | SS | **Horsie** | 1933 |
| 3627 | **Parks, Gordon** | American(afro) | N | **The Learning Tree** | 1963 |
| 3628 | **Páskándi Géza** | Hungarian | SS | **Weiskopf úr, hány óra?**<br>*[Mr Weisskopf, what's the time?]* | 1968 |
| 3629 | **Paskov, Viktor** | Bulgarian | N | **Balada za Georg Henig** | 1987 |
| 3630 | **Pasolini, Pier Paolo** | Italian | N | **Ragazzi di Vita**<br>*(The Ragazzi)* | 1955 |
| 3631 | **Pasolini, Pier Paolo** | Italian | N | **Teorema**<br>*(Theorem)* | 1968 |
| 3632 | **Pasolini, Pier Paolo** | Italian | N | **Una vita violente**<br>*(A Violent Life)* | 1959 |
| 3633 | **Pasolini, Pier Paolo** | Italian | N | **Una vita violenta** | 1959 |
| 3634 | **Pasternak, Boris** | Russian | N | **Doktor Zhivago**<br>*(Doctor Zhivago)* | 1957 |
| 3635 | **Paterson, Andrew Barton**<br>*(Banjo Paterson)* | Australian | V | **The Man From Snowy River** | 1895 |
| 3636 | **Paterson, Banjo**<br>*(see: Paterson, Andrew Barton)* | Australian | V | | |
| 3637 | **Paton, Alan** | South African | N | **Cry, the Beloved Country** | 1948 |
| 3638 | **Paton, Alan -** *{n}*<br>**Anderson, Maxwell -** *{p}* | South African | N-P | **Cry, the Beloved Country** *{n}*<br>**Lost in the Stars** *{p}* | 1948{n}<br>1950{p} |
| 3639 | **Patrick, John** | American | P | **The Hasty Heart** | 1945 |
| 3640 | **Patrick, John -** *{p}*<br>**Sneider, Vern -** *{n}* | American | N-P | **Teahouse of the August Moon** | 1951{n}<br>1952{p} |
| 3641 | **Pavese, Cesare** | Italian | SS+N | **Dialoghi con Leucò** *{ss}*<br>*(Dialogues with Leucò)* +<br>**La luna e i falò** *{n}*<br>*(The Moon and the Bonfire)* | 1947+<br>1950 |
| 3642 | **Pavese, Cesare** | Italian | SS | **Tra donne sole**<br>*(Among Women Only)* | 1949 |

| No | Film Title | Country of Production | Date | Director(s) | Duration of Film |
|---|---|---|---|---|---|
| 3607 | **Feliz ano velho** | BRAZ | 1988 | **Roberto Gervitz** | 105 |
| 3608 | **Las aguas bajan negras** | SP | 1948(47) | **José Luis Sáenz de Heredia** | 100(96) |
| 3609 | **La fe** | SP | 1947 | **Rafael Gil** | 102 |
| 3610 | **La hermana San Sulpicio** | SP | 1934 | **Florián Rey** | 90 |
| 3611 | **La hermana San Sulpicio** | SP | 1952 | **Luis Lucía** | 88(92) |
| 3612 | **La novicia rebelde** | SP | 1972(71) | **Luis Lucía** | 106(96) |
| 3613 | **Rogelia** | SP | 1962 | **Rafael Gil** | 98(96) |
| 3614 | **El señorito Octavio** | SP | 1950 | **Jerónimo Mihura** | 75(95) |
| 3615 | **Bajo el cielo de Asturias** | SP | 1950 | **Gonzalo Delgrás** | 78(87) |
| 3616 | **Sorelle Materassi** (The Materassi Sisters) | IT | 1943 | **Ferdinando Maria Poggioli** | 98 |
| 3617 | **Rend mig i traditionerne** | DEN | 1979 | **Edward Fleming** | 106 |
| 3618 | **De uanstændige** | DEN | 1983 | **Edward Fleming** | 85 |
| 3619 | **Den ubetænksomme elsker** | DEN | 1982 | **Claus Ploug** | 96 |
| 3620 | **V poiskakh radosti** (In Search of Happiness) | USSR | 1940 | **Vera Stroyeva** **Grigori Roshal** | 114 |
| 3621 | **Sentimentalnyi roman** (A Sentimental Story) | USSR | 1976 | **Igor Maslennikov** | 90 |
| 3622 | **Il padrone sono me** | IT/FR | 1956(55) | **Franco Brusati** | 100 |
| 3623 | **El indulto** | SP | 1960 | **José Luis Sáenz de Heredia** | 105(90) |
| 3624 | **La sirena negra** | SP | 1947 | **Carlos Serrano de Osma** | 77(71) |
| 3625 | **Un viaje de novios** | SP | 1947 | **Gonzalo Delgrás** | 94 |
| 3626 | **Queen For a Day** | USA | 1951 | **Arthur Lubin** | 107 |
| 3627 | **The Learning Tree** | USA | 1969 | **Gordon Parks** | 107 |
| 3628 | **Hány az óra, vekker úr?** (What's the Time, Mr Clock?) | HUNG | 1985 | **Péter Bacsó** | 109 |
| 3629 | **Ti, koito si na nebeto** [Thou, which art in heaven] | BULG | 1990 | **Docho Bodzhakov** | 102 |
| 3630 | **La notte brava** (Night Heat) (aka: Bad Girls Don't Cry) (aka: On Any Street) | IT/FR | 1959 | **Mauro Bolognini** | 95 |
| 3631 | **Teorema** (Theorem) | IT | 1968 | **Pier Paolo Pasolini** | 98 |
| 3632 | **Accattone** | IT | 1961 | **Pier Paolo Pasolini** | 120 |
| 3633 | **Una vita violenta** (A Violent Life) | IT/FR | 1962 | **Paolo Heusch** **Brunello Rondi** | 100(115) |
| 3634 | **Dr Zhivago** | USA | 1965 | **David Lean** | 193 +V |
| 3635 | **The Man From Snowy River** | AUSTL | 1982 | **George Miller** | 104 +V |
| 3636 | | | | | |
| 3637 | **Cry, the Beloved Country** (aka: African Fury) | GB | 1951 | **Zoltan Korda** | 103(96) |
| 3638 | **Lost in the Stars** {musical version} | USA | 1974 | **Daniel Mann** | 114 |
| 3639 | **The Hasty Heart** | GB | 1949 | **Vincent Sherman** | 110 |
| 3640 | **The Teahouse of the August Moon** | USA | 1956 | **Daniel Mann** | 123 |
| 3641 | **Dalla nube alla resistenza** (GER: Von der Wolke zum Wilderstand) (From the Cloud to the Resistance) | IT/FR/GER/ GB | 1979 | **Jean-Marie Straub** **Danièle Huillet** | 103 |
| 3642 | **Le amiche** (Girl Friends) | IT | 1955 | **Michelangelo Antonioni** | 104 |

| No. | Author | Nationality | Form | Literary Title | Date |
|---|---|---|---|---|---|
| 3643 | Pavlović, Živojin | Yugoslav(Serb) | N | Zadah tela | 1982 |
| 3644 | Peixoto, Júlio Afrânio | Brazilian | N | Bugrinha | 1922 |
| 3645 | Peixoto, Júlio Afrânio | Brazilian | N | Maria Bonita | 1914 |
| 3646 | Peltonen, Vihtori (see: Linnankoski, Johannes) | Finnish | N/SS | | |
| 3647 | Peṇḍse, Śhrīpād Nārāyaṇ | Indian(Mar) | N | Gārambica Bāpū (Wild Bapu of Garambi) | 1952 |
| 3648 | Penzoldt, Ernst | German | SS | Korporal Mombour | 1941 |
| 3649 | Perelman, Laura (joint, see: Perelman, S. J.) | American | P | | |
| 3650 | Perelman, S. J.; Nash, Odgen | American | P | One Touch of Venus | 1944 |
| 3651 | Perelman, S. J.; Perelman, Laura | American | P | The Night Before Christmas | 1942 |
| 3652 | Pérez Galdós, Benito | Spanish | N-P | El abuelo (The Grandfather) | 1897{n} 1904{p} |
| 3653 | Pérez Galdós, Benito | Spanish | N | Fortunata y Jacinta (Fortunata and Jacinta) | 1887 |
| 3654 | Pérez Galdós, Benito | Spanish | N | Marianela | 1878 |
| 3655 | Pérez Galdós, Benito | Spanish | N | Marianela | 1878 |
| 3656 | Pérez Galdós, Benito | Spanish | N | Nazarín | 1895 |
| 3657 | Pérez Galdós, Benito | Spanish | N | Tormento (Torment) | 1884 |
| 3658 | Pérez Galdós, Benito | Spanish | N | Tristana | 1892 |
| 3659 | Perrault, Charles | French | SS | Barbe-bleue (Bluebeard) | 1697 |
| 3660 | Perrault, Charles | French | SS | La belle au bois dormant (Sleeping Beauty) | 1697 |
| 3661 | Perrault, Charles | French | SS | La belle au bois dormant | 1697 |
| 3662 | Perrault, Charles | French | SS | La belle au bois dormant | 1697 |
| 3663 | Perrault, Charles | French | SS | Cendrillon (aka: Cendrillon, ou la petite pantoufle de verre) (Cinderella) | 1697 |
| 3664 | Perrault, Charles | French | SS | Cendrillon | 1697 |
| 3665 | Perrault, Charles | French | SS | Cendrillon | 1697 |
| 3666 | Perrault, Charles | French | SS | Cendrillon | 1697 |
| 3667 | Perrault, Charles | French | SS | Cendrillon | 1697 |
| 3668 | Perrault, Charles | French | SS | Cendrillon | 1697 |
| 3669 | Perrault, Charles | French | SS | Cendrillon | 1697 |
| 3670 | Perrault, Charles | French | SS | Cendrillon | 1697 |
| 3671 | Perrault, Charles | French | SS | Cendrillon | 1697 |
| 3672 | Perrault, Charles | French | SS | Cendrillon | 1697 |
| 3673 | Perrault, Charles | French | SS | Le maistre chat, ou le chat botté (Puss in Boots) (aka: The Master Cat: or Puss in Boots) | 1697 |
| 3674 | Perrault, Charles | French | V | Peau d'âne (The Donkey-skin Girl) | 1697 |
| 3675 | Perrault, Charles | French | SS | Le petit poucet (Tom Thumb) | 1697 |
| 3676 | Perret, Jacques | French | N | Le caporal épinglé | 1947 |

| No | Film Title | Country of Production | Date | Director(s) | Duration of Film |
|----|-----------|----------------------|------|-------------|------------------|
| 3643 | **Zadah tela** <br> *(Body Scent)* <br> *(aka: Body Smell)* | YUGO | 1983 | **Živojin Pavlović** | 98 |
| 3644 | **Diamante bruto** <br> *(Uncut Diamond)* | BRAZ | 1977 | **Orlando Senna** | 90 |
| 3645 | **Maria Bonita** | BRAZ | 1936 | **Julien Mandel** | 76 |
| 3646 | | | | | |
| 3647 | **Gãrambica Bãpũ** <br> *(aka: Gârambicha Bãpũ)* | IND(MAR) | 1980 | **Baba Mazgonkar** | 119 |
| 3648 | **Es kommt ein Tag** <br> *[There will come a day]* | GER | 1950 | **Rudolf Jugert** | 90(93) |
| 3649 | | | | | |
| 3650 | **One Touch of Venus** | USA | 1948 | **William A. Seiter** | 81 <br> +V |
| 3651 | **Larceny, Inc.** | USA | 1942 | **Lloyd Bacon** | 95 |
| 3652 | **La duda** <br> *(Doubt)* | SP | 1972 | **Rafael Gil** | 92(104) |
| 3653 | **Fortunata y Jacinta** | SP | 1970(69) | **Angelino Fons** | 132(126) |
| 3654 | **Marianela** | SP | 1940 | **Benito Perojo** | 83(88) |
| 3655 | **Marianela** | SP/FR | 1972 | **Angelino Fons** | 111(105) |
| 3656 | **Nazarín** | MEX | 1958 | **Luis Buñuel** | 95 |
| 3657 | **Tormento** | SP | 1974 | **Pedro Olea** | 83(89) <br> +V(85) |
| 3658 | **Tristana** | SP/IT/FR | 1970(69) | **Luis Buñuel** | 102(91) |
| 3659 | **Barbe-bleue** <br> *(Bluebeard)* | FR | 1951 | **Christian-Jaque** | 99 |
| 3660 | **Sleeping Beauty** <br> *{animation}* | USA | 1958 | **Clyde Geronimi** | 75 <br> +V(72) |
| 3661 | **Sleeping Beauty** | USA | 1983 | **Jeremy Kagan** | 58 +V |
| 3662 | **Sleeping Beauty** | USA | 1986 | **David Irving** | 89 +V |
| 3663 | **First Love** | USA | 1939 | **Henry Koster** | 84 |
| 3664 | **Cenerentola** <br> *(Cinderella)* <br> *{musical version}* | IT | 1949(48) | **Fernando Cerchio** | 94 |
| 3665 | **Cinderella** <br> *{animation}* | USA | 1949 | **Wilfred Jackson** <br> **Hamilton Luske** <br> **Clyde Geronomi** | 75 |
| 3666 | **Erase una vez** <br> *{animation}* | SP | 1950 | **Cirici Pellicer** | 86 |
| 3667 | **The Glass Slipper** <br> *{musical version}* | USA | 1955(54) | **Charles Walters** | 94 |
| 3668 | **Cinderella** | GB | 1955 | **Lotte Reiniger** | 10 |
| 3669 | **Grustalni bashmacnok** <br> *(aka: Khrustal'nyi bashmachok)* <br> *(Cinderella)* <br> *(aka: Glass Slipper)* | USSR | 1960 | **Aleksandr Rou** <br> **Rostislav Zakharov** | 80 |
| 3670 | **Cinderella** | USA | 1976 | **Michael Pataki** | 86 |
| 3671 | **The Slipper and the Rose - The Story of Cinderella** <br> *{musical version}* | GB | 1976 | **Bryan Forbes** | 146 <br> +V(136) |
| 3672 | **Pepeljuga** | YUGO | 1979 | **Zlatko Grgić** | 08 |
| 3673 | **Puss in Boots** | USA | 1987 | **Eugene Marner** | 96 <br> +V(93) |
| 3674 | **Peau d'âne** <br> *(Donkey Skin)* <br> *(aka: The Magic Donkey)* | FR | 1971(70) | **Jacques Demy** | 90 |
| 3675 | **Le petit poucet** <br> *(Tom Thumb)* | FR | 1972 | **Michel Boisrond** | 75 |
| 3676 | **Le caporal épinglé** <br> *(The Vanishing Corporal)* <br> *(aka: The Elusive Corporal)* | FR | 1962 | **Jean Renoir** | 106 |

| No. | Author | Nationality | Form | Literary Title | Date |
|-----|--------|-------------|------|----------------|------|
| 3677 | **Perret, Jacques** | French | N | **Ernest le rebelle** | 1937 |
| 3678 | **Peshkov, Alexei Maksimovich** (see: Gorky, Maxim) | Russian | P/N/ SS | | |
| 3679 | **Petersen, Leif** | Danish | P | **Alting og et postnus** | 1969 |
| 3680 | **Peterson, Louis S.** | American(afro) | P | **Take a Giant Step** | 1954 |
| 3681 | **Petőfi Sándor** | Hungarian | V | **János Vitéz** | 1845 |
| 3682 | **Petrescu, Camil** | Romanian | P | **Jocul ielelor** [Dance of the fairies] | 1947 |
| 3683 | **Petrescu, Camil** | Romanian | P | **Mitică Popescu** | 1928 |
| 3684 | **Petrescu, Camil** | Romanian | N | **Ultima noapte de dragoste, întîia noapte de război** [The last night of love, the first night of war] | 1930 |
| 3685 | **Petrescu, Camil** | Romanian | N | **Ultima noapte de dragoste, întîia noapte de război** | 1930 |
| 3686 | **Petrescu, Cezar** | Romanian | N | **Calea Victoriei** | 1932 (1930) |
| 3687 | **Petrescu, Cezar** | Romanian | N | **Fram, ursul polar** (Fram, the Polar Bear) {pt.1, ch.1-7} | 1932 |
| 3688 | **Petrescu, Cezar** | Romanian | N | **Fram, ursul polar** {pt.2, ch.8-16} | 1932 |
| 3689 | **Petrescu, Cezar** | Romanian | N | **Întunecare** (Gathering Clouds) {pts.1-2} | 1927-28 |
| 3690 | **Petrescu, Cezar** | Romanian | SS | **Omul din vis** [The man in the dream] | 1926 |
| 3691 | **Petronius Arbiter** | Latin(anc) | N | **Satyricon** | n.d. |
| 3692 | **Petronius Arbiter** | Latin(anc) | N | **Satyricon** | n.d. |
| 3693 | **Petrov, Evgeny** (joint, see: Ilf, Ilya) | Russian | N | | |
| 3694 | **Peyrefitte, Roger** | French | N | **Les amitiés particulières** (Special Friendships) | 1945 |
| 3695 | **Peyrefitte, Roger** | French | SS | **La maîtresse de piano** [The piano teacher] | 1949 |
| 3696 | **Phillips, David Graham** | American | N | **Susan Lennox, Her Fall and Rise** | 1917 |
| 3697 | **Piḷḷai, Thakazi Sirashankar** (see: Śivaśaṅkara Piḷḷa) | Indian(Mal) | N | | |
| 3698 | **Pillecijn, Filip de** (see: Pillecyn, Filip de) | Belgian(Fle) | SS | | |
| 3699 | **Pillecyn, Filip de** (Filip de Pillecijn) | Belgian(Fle) | SS | **Monsieur Hawarden** | 1935 |
| 3700 | **Pilnyak, Boris** | Russian | SS | **Povest' nepogashenoi luny** (A Tale of the Unextinguished Moon) | 1926 |
| 3701 | **Pincherle, Alberto** (see: Moravia, Alberto) | Italian | SS/N | | |
| 3702 | **Pinero, Arthur Wing** | British | P | **Dandy Dick** | 1893 |
| 3703 | **Pinero, Arthur Wing** | British | P | **The Enchanted Cottage** | 1922 |
| 3704 | **Pinero, Arthur Wing** | British | P | **The Magistrate** | 1892 |
| 3705 | **Pinero, Arthur Wing** | British | P | **The Second Mrs Tanqueray** | 1892 |
| 3706 | **Pinski, David** | Russian | P | **Yenkel de Schmid** [Yankl the smith] | 1908-09 |
| 3707 | **Pinter, Harold** | British | P | **Betrayal** | 1978 |
| 3708 | **Pinter, Harold** | British | P | **The Birthday Party** | 1959 |
| 3709 | **Pinter, Harold** | British | P | **The Caretaker** | 1960 |
| 3710 | **Pinter, Harold** | British | P | **The Dumb Waiter** | 1960 |
| 3711 | **Pinter, Harold** | British | P | **The Homecoming** | 1965 |
| 3712 | **Piovene, Guido** | Italian | N | **Lettere di una novizia** (Confession of a Novice) | 1941 |

| No | Film Title | Country of Production | Date | Director(s) | Duration of Film |
|---|---|---|---|---|---|
| 3677 | Ernest le rebelle | FR | 1938 | Christian-Jaque | 92 |
| 3678 | | | | | |
| | | | | | |
| 3679 | Det er nat med fru Knudsen | DEN | 1970 | Henning Ørnbak | 89 |
| 3680 | Take a Giant Step | USA | 1959 | Philip Leacock | 100 |
| 3681 | János Vitéz (Childe John) (aka: Johnny Corncob) {animation} | HUNG | 1973 | Marcell Jankovics | 81 |
| 3682 | Cei care plătesc cu viaţa [Those who pay with their lives] | ROM | 1989 | Şerban Marinescu | 98 |
| 3683 | Mitică Popescu | ROM | 1984 | Manole Marcus | 91 |
| 3684 | Între oglinzi paralele (Between Facing Mirrors) | ROM | 1979(78) | Mircea Veroiu | 100 |
| | | | | | |
| 3685 | Ultima noapte de dragoste [The last night of love] | ROM | 1980(79) | Sergiu Nicolaescu | 91 |
| 3686 | Calea Victoriei sau cheia visurilor [Victory boulevard, or the key of dreams] | ROM | 1966(65) | Marius Teodorescu | 104 |
| 3687 | Saltimbancii [The jugglers] | ROM/USSR | 1981 | Elisabeta Bostan | 110 |
| 3688 | Un saltimbanc la polul nord [A juggler at the north pole] | ROM/USSR | 1982 | Elisabeta Bostan | 96 |
| 3689 | Întunecare | ROM | 1986 | Alexandru Tatos | 99 |
| | | | | | |
| 3690 | Glissando | ROM | 1984(82) | Mircea Daneliuc | 167 |
| | | | | | |
| 3691 | Satyricon | IT | 1969(68) | Gian Luigi Polidoro | 110(121) |
| 3692 | Fellini Satyricon (aka: Satyricon) | IT/FR | 1969 | Federico Fellini | 129(135) +V(124) |
| 3693 | | | | | |
| | | | | | |
| 3694 | Les amitiés particulières (This Special Friendship) | FR | 1964 | Jean Delannoy | 105 |
| 3695 | Ritratto di borghesia in nero (Nest of Vipers) (aka: Portrait of a Bourgeois in Black) | IT | 1978 | Tonino Cervi | 105 |
| 3696 | Susan Lenox (Her Fall and Rise) (GB: The Rise of Helga) (aka: Rising to Fame) | USA | 1931 | Robert Z. Leonard | 74 |
| 3697 | | | | | |
| | | | | | |
| 3698 | | | | | |
| | | | | | |
| 3699 | Monsieur Hawarden (Mister Hawarden) | BEL/HOLL | 1968 | Harry Kümel | 100 |
| 3700 | Povest' nepogashenoi luny (A Tale of the Unextinguished Moon) | USSR | 1991 | Yevgeny Tsymbal | 84 |
| 3701 | | | | | |
| | | | | | |
| 3702 | Dandy Dick | GB | 1935 | William Beaudine | 72 |
| 3703 | The Enchanted Cottage | USA | 1945 | John Cromwell | 96 +V |
| 3704 | Those Were the Days | GB | 1934 | Thomas Bentley | 80 |
| 3705 | The Second Mrs Tanqueray | GB | 1952 | Dallas Bower | 75 |
| 3706 | Yankel de Schmidt (The Singing Blacksmith) {Yiddish version} | USA | 1938 | Edgar G. Ulmer | 110 |
| 3707 | Betrayal | GB | 1983 | David Jones | 95 +V |
| 3708 | The Birthday Party | GB | 1970(68) | William Friedkin | 126 +V |
| 3709 | The Caretaker (USA: The Guest) | GB | 1963 | Clive Donner | 105 |
| 3710 | The Dumb Waiter | USA | 1987 | Robert Altman | 58 +V |
| 3711 | The Homecoming | GB/CAN | 1976(73) | Peter Hall | 114 |
| 3712 | Lettere di una novizia (Rita) | IT/FR | 1960 | Alberto Lattuada | 95 |

| No. | Author | Nationality | Form | Literary Title | Date |
|---|---|---|---|---|---|
| 3713 | **Pirandello, Luigi** | Italian | P | **Come prima, meglio di prima**<br>*[As well as before, better than<br>before]* | 1921 |
| 3714 | **Pirandello, Luigi** | Italian | P | **Come prima, meglio di prima** | 1921 |
| 3715 | **Pirandello, Luigi** | Italian | P | **Come tu mi vuoi**<br>*(As You Desire Me)* | 1930 |
| 3716 | **Pirandello, Luigi** | Italian | P | **Enrico IV**<br>*(Henry IV)*<br>*(aka: The Emperor)* | 1922 |
| 3717 | **Pirandello, Luigi** | Italian | P | **Enrico IV** | 1922 |
| 3718 | **Pirandello, Luigi** | Italian | N | **Il fu Mattia Pascal**<br>*(The Late Mattia Pascal)* | 1904 |
| 3719 | **Pirandello, Luigi** | Italian | SS | **In silenzio +**<br>**Il gorgo** | 1905+<br>1913 |
| 3720 | **Pirandello, Luigi** | Italian | P | **Liolà** | 1917 |
| 3721 | **Pirandello, Luigi** | Italian | SS-P | **Male di luna** *{ss}* +<br>**L'altro figlio** *{ss-p}* +<br>**La giara** *{ss-p}* +<br>**Requiem æternam dona eis,<br>Domine!** *{ss}* | 1925+<br>1905+<br>1909+<br>1913 |
| 3722 | **Pirandello, Luigi** | Italian | SS-P | **Ma non è una cosa seria**<br>*(aka: Non è una cosa seria)* | 1910{ss}<br>1918{p} |
| 3723 | **Pirandello, Luigi** | Italian | SS-P | **Pensaci, Giacomino!**<br>*[Think, Giacomino!]* | 1910{ss}<br>1917{p} |
| 3724 | **Pirandello, Luigi** | Italian | SS | **Requiem æternam dona eis,<br>Domine!** | 1913(22) |
| 3725 | **Pirandello, Luigi** | Italian | SS-P | **Tutto per bene**<br>*(All For the Best)* | 1906{ss}<br>1920{p} |
| 3726 | **Pirandello, Luigi** | Italian | N | **I vecchi e i giovani**<br>*(The Old and the Young)* | 1909 |
| 3727 | **Pirandello, Luigi** | Italian | P | **Vestire gli ignudi**<br>*(To Clothe the Naked)* | 1937 |
| 3728 | **Pirandello, Luigi** | Italian | SS | **Il viaggio** | 1910(28) |
| 3729 | **Pişculescu, Grigore**<br>*(see: Galaction, Gala)* | Romanian | N | | |
| 3730 | **Plath, Sylvia**<br>*(Victoria Lucas)* | American | N | **The Bell Jar** | 1963 |
| 3731 | **Plenzdorf, Ulrich** | German | P | **Die neuen Leiden des jungen W.**<br>*[The new sorrows of young W.]* | 1972(73) |
| 3732 | **Poe, Edgar Allan** | American | SS | **The Black Cat** | 1843 |
| 3733 | **Poe, Edgar Allan** | American | SS | **The Black Cat** | 1843 |
| 3734 | **Poe, Edgar Allan** | American | SS | **The Black Cat** | 1843 |
| 3735 | **Poe, Edgar Allan** | American | SS | **The Black Cat** | 1843 |
| 3736 | **Poe, Edgar Allan** | American | SS | **The Black Cat** | 1843 |
| 3737 | **Poe, Edgar Allan** | American | V | **City in the Sea**<br>*(aka: The Doomed City)*<br>*(aka: City of Sin)* | 1831 |
| 3738 | **Poe, Edgar Allan** | American | SS | **The Fall of the House of Usher** | 1839(40) |
| 3739 | **Poe, Edgar Allan** | American | SS | **The Fall of the House of Usher** | 1839(40) |
| 3740 | **Poe, Edgar Allan** | American | SS | **Gold Bug +**<br>**The Tell-Tale Heart** | 1843 |
| 3741 | **Poe, Edgar Allan** | American | SS | **Ligeia** | 1838(40) |
| 3742 | **Poe, Edgar Allan** | American | SS | **The Masque of the Red Death +**<br>**Hop-Frog** | 1845+<br>1849 |
| 3743 | **Poe, Edgar Allan** | American | SS | **Metzengerstein +**<br>**William Wilson +**<br>**Never Bet Your Head** | 1840+<br>1839+<br>1841 |
| 3744 | **Poe, Edgar Allan** | American | SS | **Morella +**<br>**The Black Cat +**<br>**The Facts in the Case of M.<br>Valdemar** | 1835+<br>1843+<br>1845 |
| 3745 | **Poe, Edgar Allan** | American | SS | **Murders in the Rue Morgue** | 1841(45) |

| No | Film Title | Country of Production | Date | Director(s) | Duration of Film |
|----|-----------|----------------------|------|-------------|------------------|
| 3713 | **This Love of Ours** | USA | 1945 | **William Dieterle** | 90 |
| 3714 | **Never Say Goodbye** | USA | 1955 | **Jerry Hopper** | 97 |
| 3715 | **As You Desire Me** | USA | 1932 | **George Fitzmaurice** | 71 |
| 3716 | **Enrico IV** <br> *(Henry IV)* | IT | 1943 | **Giorgio Pastina** | 94 |
| 3717 | **Enrico IV** <br> *(Henry IV)* | IT | 1984 | **Marco Bellocchio** | 95 |
| 3718 | **L'homme de nulle part** <br> *(aka: The Late Mathias Pascal)* | FR | 1936 | **Pierre Chenal** | 98 |
| 3719 | **Wir** <br> *[The whirl]* | POL | 1985 | **Henryk Jacek Schoen** | 76 |
| 3720 | **Liolà** <br> *(A Very Handy Man)* | IT/FR | 1964 | **Alessandro Blasetti** | 102 |
| 3721 | **Kaos** | IT | 1984 | **Paolo Taviani** <br> **Vittorio Taviani** | 188 |
| 3722 | **Ma non è una cosa seria** <br> *(But It's Nothing Serious)* <br> *(GER: Der Mann der nicht nein sagen kann)* | IT | 1936 | **Mario Camerini** | 81 |
| 3723 | **Pensaci, Giacomino!** | IT | 1936 | **Gennaro Righelli** | 79 |
| 3724 | **Terra di nessuno** | IT | 1939 | **Mario Baffico** | 97 |
| 3725 | **Todo sea para bien** | ARG | 1957 | **Carlos Rinaldi** | 78 |
| 3726 | **I vecchi e i giovani** | IT | 1978 | **Marco Leto** | 116 |
| 3727 | **Vetir ceux qui sont nus** <br> *(IT: Vestire gli ignudi)* <br> *(Clothe the Naked)* | FR/IT | 1954 | **Marcello Pagliero** | 84 |
| 3728 | **Il viaggio** <br> *(The Voyage)* <br> *(aka: The Journey)* | IT/FR | 1974 | **Vittorio de Sica** | 99(105) |
| 3729 | | | | | |
| 3730 | **The Bell Jar** | USA | 1979 | **Larry Peerce** | 107 +V |
| 3731 | **Die neuen Leiden des jungen W.** | GER | 1975 | **Eberhard Itzenplitz** | 112 |
| 3732 | **The Black Cat** | USA | 1934 | **Edgar G. Ulmer** | 66 |
| 3733 | **The Black Cat** | USA | 1941 | **Albert S. Rogell** | 70 |
| 3734 | **The Black Cat** | USA | 1966 | **Harold Hoffman** | 77 |
| 3735 | **Apokal** | GER | 1971 | **Paul Anczykowski** | 86 |
| 3736 | **Il gatto nero** <br> *(The Black Cat)* | IT | 1981 | **Lucio Fulci** | 88 +V |
| 3737 | **The City Under the Sea** <br> *(USA: War Gods of the Deep)* | GB/USA | 1965 | **Jacques Tourneur** | 84 |
| 3738 | **The Fall of the House of Usher** | GB | 1950 | **George Ivan Barnett** | 70 |
| 3739 | **House of Usher** <br> *(GB: The Fall of the House of Usher)* | USA | 1960 | **Roger Corman** | 85 +V(76) |
| 3740 | **Manfish** | USA | 1956 | **W. Lee Wilder** | 76 |
| 3741 | **The Tomb of Ligeia** | GB | 1964 | **Roger Corman** | 81 |
| 3742 | **The Masque of the Red Death** | GB/USA | 1964 | **Roger Corman** | 84 |
| 3743 | **Histoires extraordinaires** <br> *(IT: Tre passi nel delirio)* <br> *(Spirits of the Dead)* | FR/IT | 1968 | **Roger Vadim** <br> **Louis Malle** <br> **Federico Fellini** | 120 |
| 3744 | **Tales of Terror** <br> *(aka: Poe's Tales of Terror)* | USA | 1962(61) | **Roger Corman** | 88 +V |
| 3745 | **Murders in the Rue Morgue** | USA | 1932 | **Robert Florey** | 62 +V |

| No. | Author | Nationality | Form | Literary Title | Date |
|-----|--------|-------------|------|----------------|------|
| 3746 | Poe, Edgar Allan | American | SS | Murders in the Rue Morgue | 1841(45) |
| 3747 | Poe, Edgar Allan | American | SS | Murders in the Rue Morgue | 1841(45) |
| 3748 | Poe, Edgar Allan | American | SS | The Mystery of Marie Rogêt | 1842(45) |
| 3749 | Poe, Edgar Allan | American | SS | The Oblong Box | 1844(45) |
| 3750 | Poe, Edgar Allan | American | SS+V | The Pit and the Pendulum *(aka: The Gift) {ss} +* The Raven *(v)* | 1845 (aka:1843) |
| 3751 | Poe, Edgar Allan | American | SS | The Pit and the Pendulum | 1845 |
| 3752 | Poe, Edgar Allan | American | SS | The Pit and the Pendulum | 1845 |
| 3753 | Poe, Edgar Allan | American | SS | The Pit and the Pendulum | 1845 |
| 3754 | Poe, Edgar Allan | American | SS | The Premature Burial | 1944(45) |
| 3755 | Poe, Edgar Allan | American | SS | The Premature Burial | 1844(45) |
| 3756 | Poe, Edgar Allan | American | V | The Raven | 1845 |
| 3757 | Poe, Edgar Allan | American | SS | The System of Dr Tarr and Prof Fether | 1845 |
| 3758 | Poe, Edgar Allan | American | SS | The System of Dr Tarr and Prof Fether | 1845 |
| 3759 | Poe, Edgar Allan | American | SS | The Tell-Tale Heart | 1843(45) |
| 3760 | Poe, Edgar Allan | American | SS | The Tell-Tale Heart | 1843(45) |
| 3761 | Poe, Edgar Allan | American | SS | The Tell-Tale Heart | 1843(45) |
| 3762 | Poe, Edgar Allan | American | SS | The Tell-Tale Heart | 1843(45) |
| 3763 | Pogodin, Nikolay *(N.F. Stukalov)* | Russian | P | Chelovek s ruzhyom *(The Man With the Gun)* | 1937 |
| 3764 | Pogodin, Nikolay | Russian | P | Kremlyovskie kuranty *(Kremlin Chimes)* *(aka: The Chimes of the Kremlin)* | 1941 |
| 3765 | Polevoy, Boris Nikolaevich | Russian | N | Doktor Vyera *[Doctor Vera]* | 1966 |
| 3766 | Polevoy, Boris Nikolaevich | Russian | N | Na dikom beregye *(On the Wild Shore)* | 1962 |
| 3767 | Polgar, Alfred | Austrian | P | Die Defraudanten | 1931 |
| 3768 | Popescu, Dumitru Radu | Romanian | SS | Căruţa cu mere *[The apple cart]* | 1962 |
| 3769 | Popescu, Dumitru Radu | Romanian | SS | Duios Anastasia trecea | 1967 |
| 3770 | Popescu, Dumitru Radu | Romanian | SS | Pădurea *[The forest]* | 1962 |
| 3771 | Popov, Aleksandr *(see: Serafimovich, Aleksandr)* | Russian | SS | | |
| 3772 | Popovici, Titus | Romanian | SS | Moartea lui Ipu *[Ipu's death]* | 1970 |
| 3773 | Popovici, Titus | Romanian | N | Setea *[The thirst]* | 1958 |
| 3774 | Popovici, Titus | Romanian | N | Străinul *(The Stranger)* | 1955 |
| 3775 | Poquelin, Jean-Baptiste *(see: Molière)* | French | P | | |
| 3776 | Porter, Katherine Anne | American | SS | The Jilting of Granny Weatherall | 1930 |
| 3777 | Porter, Katherine Anne | American | N | Ship of Fools | 1962 |
| 3778 | Porter, William Sydney *(see: Henry, O.)* | American | SS | | |
| 3779 | Postelnicu, Ioana | Romanian | N | Întoarcerea Vlaşinilor *[The return of the Vlaşin family]* | 1979 |
| 3780 | Postelnicu, Ioana | Romanian | N | Plecarea Vlaşinilor *[The departure of the Vlaşin family]* | 1964 |
| 3781 | Potocki, Jan | Polish(Fr) | N | Le manuscrit trouvé à Saragosse. Dix journées de la vie d'Alphonse van Worden *(The Saragossa Manuscript)* | 1815 |
| 3782 | Potter, Dennis | British | P(TV) | Brimstone and Treacle | 1978 |
| 3783 | Potter, Dennis | British | P(TV) | Pennies From Heaven | 1981 |
| 3784 | Pratolini, Vasco | Italian | N | La costanza della ragione *(Bruno Santini)* | 1963 |
| 3785 | Pratolini, Vasco | Italian | N | Cronaca familiare *(Two Brothers)* | 1947 |
| 3786 | Pratolini, Vasco | Italian | N | Cronache di poveri amanti *(A Tale of Poor Lovers)* | 1947 |

| No | Film Title | Country of Production | Date | Director(s) | Duration of Film |
|---|---|---|---|---|---|
| 3746 | Phantom of the Rue Morgue | USA | 1954 | Roy Del Ruth | 84 |
| 3747 | Murders in the Rue Morgue | USA | 1971 | Gordon Hessler | 87 |
| 3748 | Mystery of Marie Roget | USA | 1942 | Phil Rosen | 61 |
| 3749 | The Oblong Box | GB | 1969 | Gordon Hessler | 91 +V |
| 3750 | The Raven | USA | 1935 | Lew Landers (Louis Friedlander) | 61 |
| 3751 | Pit and the Pendulum | USA | 1961 | Roger Corman | 80 +V |
| 3752 | Die Schlangengrube und das Pendel | GER | 1967 | Harald Reinl | 85 |
| 3753 | The Pit and the Pendulum | USA | 1990 | Stuart Gordon | 92 +V |
| 3754 | The Crime of Dr Crespi | USA | 1935 | John H. Auer | 64 |
| 3755 | The Premature Burial | USA | 1962 | Roger Corman | 81 +V |
| 3756 | The Raven | USA | 1963 | Roger Corman | 86 +V |
| 3757 | System | POL | 1971 | Janusz Majewski | 28 |
| 3758 | Dr Tarr's Torture Dungeon | MEX | 1972 | Juan L. Moctezuma | 88 |
| 3759 | The Tell-Tale Heart (aka: Bucket of Blood) | GB | 1934 | Brian Desmond Hurst | 49 |
| 3760 | Bucket of Blood | USA | 1959 | Roger Corman | 65 |
| 3761 | The Tell-Tale Heart (aka: The Hidden Room of 1,000 Horrors) | GB | 1960 | Ernest Morris | 78 |
| 3762 | The Tell-Tale Heart | USA | 1973 | Steve Carver | 26 +V |
| 3763 | Chelovek s ruzhyom (Man With a Gun) | USSR | 1938 | Sergei Yutkevich | 102 |
| 3764 | Kremlevskie kuranti (Kremlin Chimes) | USSR | 1970 | Viktor Georgiev | 99 |
| 3765 | Doktor Vyera | USSR | 1968 | Damir Vyatich-Berezhnyhk | 89 |
| 3766 | Na dikom beregye {2 - parts} | USSR | 1967 | Anatoli Granik | Pt.1, 79 Pt.2, 73 |
| 3767 | Bei Pichler stimmt die Kasse nicht | GER | 1961 | Hans Quest | 94 |
| 3768 | Căruţa cu mere | ROM | 1983 | George Cornea | 102 |
| 3769 | Duios Anastasia trecea (Anastasia Passed By) | ROM | 1980(79) | Alexandru Tatos | 97 |
| 3770 | Un surîs în plină vară [A midsummer smile] | ROM | 1963 | Geo Saizescu | 100 |
| 3771 | | | | | |
| 3772 | Atunci i-am condamnat pe toţi la moarte [Then we condemned them all to death] | ROM | 1971(70) | Sergiu Nicolaescu | 100 |
| 3773 | Setea | ROM | 1961(60) | Mircea Drăgan | 120 |
| 3774 | Străinul (The Stranger) | ROM | 1964(63) | Mihai Iacob | 106 |
| 3775 | | | | | |
| 3776 | The Jilting of Granny Weatherall | USA | 1980 | Randa Haines | 57 +V |
| 3777 | Ship of Fools | USA | 1965 | Stanley Kramer | 144 |
| 3778 | | | | | |
| 3779 | Întoarcerea Vlaşinilor | ROM | 1984 | Mircea Drăgan | 108 |
| 3780 | Plecarea Vlaşinilor | ROM | 1983 | Mircea Drăgan | 112 |
| 3781 | Rekopis znaleziony w Saragossie (Manuscript Found in Saragossa) | POL | 1965(64) | Wojciech Jerzy Has | 180 |
| 3782 | Brimstone and Treacle | GB | 1982 | Richard Loncraine | 87 +V |
| 3783 | Pennies From Heaven | USA | 1982 | Herbert Ross | 108 +V |
| 3784 | La constanza della ragione (aka: Heart in Mouth) | IT/FR | 1965(64) | Pasquale Festa Campanile | 86(120) |
| 3785 | Cronaca familiare (Family Diary) | IT | 1962 | Valerio Zurlini | 122 |
| 3786 | Cronache di poveri amanti (Stories of Poor Lovers) | IT | 1954(53) | Carlo Lizzani | 102 |

| No. | Author | Nationality | Form | Literary Title | Date |
|-----|--------|-------------|------|----------------|------|
| 3787 | **Pratolini, Vasco** | Italian | N | **Metello** | 1955 |
| 3788 | **Pratolini, Vasco** | Italian | SS | **Le ragazze di Sanfrediano** | 1949 |
| 3789 | **Preda, Marin** | Romanian | SS | **Albastra zare a morţii**<br>*[The blue horizon of death]* | 1948 |
| 3790 | **Preda, Marin** | Romanian | SS | **Desfăşurarea**<br>*(In a Village)* | 1952 |
| 3791 | **Preda, Marin** | Romanian | SS | **Întîlnirea din pămînturi**<br>*[Encounter in the fields]* | 1948 |
| 3792 | **Preda, Marin** | Romanian | N | **Intrusul**<br>*[The intruder]* | 1968 |
| 3793 | **Preda, Marin** | Romanian | N | **Marele singuratic**<br>*[The lonely man]* | 1972 |
| 3794 | **Preda, Marin** | Romanian | N | **Moromeţii**<br>*(vol.1: The Morometes)* | 1955 |
| 3795 | **Premchand**<br>*(Dhanpat Rai Śrīvāstav)* | Indian<br>(Urd/Hin) | SS | **Do bailon kī kathā**<br>*(Story of Two Bulls)* | 1936 |
| 3796 | **Premchand** | Indian | SS | **Do bailon kī kathā**<br>*(TEL: Oka oorie katha)* | 1936 |
| 3797 | **Premchand** | Indian | N | **Godān**<br>*(aka: Go-dana)*<br>*(Godan: a Novel of Peasant India)*<br>*(aka: The Gift of a Cow)* | 1936 |
| 3798 | **Premchand** | Indian | SS | **Sadgati**<br>*(Deliverance)* | 1931 |
| 3799 | **Premchand** | Indian | SS | **Śatranj ke khilāri**<br>*(The Chess Players)* | 1935 |
| 3800 | **Prévost, Abbé**<br>*(see: Prévost d'Exiles,*<br>*Antoine-François)* | French | N | | |
| 3801 | **Prévost d'Exiles,**<br>**Antoine-François**<br>*(Abbé Prévost)* | French | N | **Manon Lescaut**<br>*(aka: L'Histoire du Chevalier Des*<br>*Grieux et de Manon Lescaut)* | 1731(33) |
| 3802 | **Prévost d'Exiles,**<br>**Antoine-François** | French | N | **Manon Lescaut** | 1731(33) |
| 3803 | **Prévost d'Exiles,**<br>**Antoine-François** | French | N | **Manon Lescaut** | 1731(33) |
| 3804 | **Prévost d'Exiles,**<br>**Antoine-François** | French | N | **Manon Lescaut** | 1731(33) |
| 3805 | **Priestley, J. B.** | British | N | **Benighted**<br>*(USA: The Old Dark House)* | 1927 |
| 3806 | **Priestley, J. B.** | British | N | **Benighted** | 1927 |
| 3807 | **Priestley, J. B.** | British | P | **Dangerous Corner** | 1932 |
| 3808 | **Priestley, J. B.** | British | N | **The Good Companions** | 1929 |
| 3809 | **Priestley, J. B.** | British | N | **The Good Companions** | 1929 |
| 3810 | **Priestley, J. B.** | British | P | **An Inspector Calls** | 1945 |
| 3811 | **Priestley, J. B.** | British | P | **Laburnum Grove** | 1934 |
| 3812 | **Priestley, J. B.** | British | N | **Let the People Sing** | 1939 |
| 3813 | **Priestley, J. B.** | British | P | **The Scandalous Affair of Mr**<br>**Kettle and Mrs Moon** | 1956 |
| 3814 | **Priestley, J. B.** | British | P | **They Came to a City** | 1943 |
| 3815 | **Priestley, J. B.** | British | P | **Time and the Conways** | 1937 |
| 3816 | **Priestley, J. B.** | British | P | **When We Are Married** | 1938 |
| 3817 | **Priestley, J. B.**<br>*(see also: Murdoch, Iris)* | British | P/N | | |
| 3818 | **Proust, Marcel** | French | N | **Á la recherche du temps perdu**<br>*(Remembrance of Things Past)*<br>*(vol 1: Du côté de chez Swann)*<br>*(Swann's Way)* | 1913 |
| 3819 | **Prus, Bolesław** | Polish | N | **Emancypantki**<br>*[The emancipationists]* | 1894 |
| 3820 | **Prus, Bolesław** | Polish | N | **Faraon**<br>*(The Pharoah and the Priest)* | 1897 |
| 3821 | **Prus, Bolesław** | Polish | SS | **Grzechy dzieciństwa**<br>*[Sins of childhood]* | 1883(96) |
| 3822 | **Prus, Bolesław** | Polish | N | **Lalka**<br>*(The Doll)* | 1890 |

| No | Film Title | Country of Production | Date | Director(s) | Duration of Film |
|----|-----------|----------------------|------|-------------|------------------|
| 3787 | **Metello** | IT | 1970 | **Mauro Bolognini** | 112 |
| 3788 | **Le ragazze di San Frediano** (The Girls of San Frediano) | IT | 1954 | **Valerio Zurlini** | 102 |
| 3789 | **Porţile albastre ale oraşului** [The blue gates of the city] | ROM | 1974(73) | **Mircea Mureşan** | 101 |
| 3790 | **Desfăşurarea** [The display] | ROM | 1955(54) | **Paul Călinescu** | 73 |
| 3791 | **Întîlnirea din pămînturi** | ROM | 1983 | **Dumitru Dinulescu** | 27 |
| 3792 | **Imposibila iubire** [Impossible love] | ROM | 1984 | **Constantin Vaeni** | 166 |
| 3793 | **Marele singuratic** | ROM | 1977(76) | **Iulian Mihu** | 108 |
| 3794 | **Morometii** (The Morometes) | ROM | 1986 | **Stere Gulea** | 109 |
| 3795 | **Hira moti** | IND (HIN) | 1959 | **Kishen Chopra** | 131 |
| 3796 | **Oka oorie katha** | IND (TEL) | 1977 | **Mrinal Sen** | 117 |
| 3797 | **Godän** (aka: Godaan) | IND (HIN) | 1963 | **R. Jetley** | 110 |
| 3798 | **Sadgati** | IND (HIN) | 1981 | **Satyajit Ray** | 50 |
| 3799 | **Shatranj ke khilari** (The Chess Players) | IND (HIN) | 1977 | **Satyajit Ray** | 133(124) |
| 3800 | | | | | |
| 3801 | **Manon Lescaut** | IT | 1939 | **Carmine Gallone** | 95 |
| 3802 | **Manon** | FR | 1948 | **Henri-Georges Clouzot** | 96(100) |
| 3803 | **Gli amori di Manon Lescaut** (FR: Les amours de Manon Lescaut) | IT/FR | 1955(54) | **Mario Costa** | 97 |
| 3804 | **Manon '70** (aka: Perverse Manon) (GER: Hemmungslose Manon) [Manon, woman without scruples] | FR/GER/ IT | 1968 | **Jean Aurel** | 110(90) |
| 3805 | **The Old Dark House** | USA | 1932 | **James Whale** | 71 +V |
| 3806 | **The Old Dark House** | USA/GB | 1963(62) | **William Castle** | 86 |
| 3807 | **Dangerous Corner** | USA | 1934 | **Phil Rosen** | 67 |
| 3808 | **The Good Companions** | GB | 1933 | **Victor Saville** | 113 |
| 3809 | **The Good Companions** | GB | 1957(56) | **J. Lee Thompson** | 104 |
| 3810 | **An Inspector Calls** | GB | 1954 | **Guy Hamilton** | 79 +V |
| 3811 | **Laburnum Grove** | GB | 1936 | **Carol Reed** | 73 |
| 3812 | **Let the People Sing** | GB | 1942 | **John Baxter** | 105 |
| 3813 | **...Und das am Montagmorgen** [...and on Monday morning, at that] | GER | 1959 | **Luigi Comencini** | 92 |
| 3814 | **They Came to a City** | GB | 1944 | **Basil Dearden** | 77 |
| 3815 | **Die glücklichen Jahre der Thorwalds** [The happy year of the Thorwald family] | GER | 1962 | **Wolfgang Staudte John Olden** | 89 |
| 3816 | **When We Are Married** | GB | 1943 | **Lance Comfort** | 98 |
| 3817 | | | | | |
| 3818 | **Un amour de Swann** (GER: Eine Liebe von Swann) (Swann in Love) | FR/GER | 1984(83) | **Volker Schlöndorff** | 110 |
| 3819 | **Pensja pani latter** [Emancipated women] | POL | 1983 | **Stanisław Różewicz** | 104 |
| 3820 | **Faraon** (The Pharaoh) | POL | 1966(65) | **Jerzy Kawalerowicz** | 183(150) |
| 3821 | **Grzechy dzieciństwa** | POL | 1984 | **Krzysztof Nowak** | 73 |
| 3822 | **Lalka** (The Doll) | POL | 1968 | **Wojciech Jerzy Has** | 158 |

| No. | Author | Nationality | Form | Literary Title | Date |
|-----|--------|-------------|------|----------------|------|
| 3823 | **Pushkin, Alexander** | Russian | P | **Boris Godunov** | 1831 |
| 3824 | **Pushkin, Alexander** | Russian | SS | **Dubrovsky** | 1841 |
| 3825 | **Pushkin, Alexander** | Russian | SS | **Dubrovsky** | 1841 |
| 3826 | **Pushkin, Alexander** | Russian | SS | **Dubrovsky** | 1841 |
| 3827 | **Pushkin, Alexander** | Russian | SS | **Dubrovsky** | 1841 |
| 3828 | **Pushkin, Alexander** | Russian | SS | **Kapitanskaya dochka** <br> *(The Captain's Daughter)* | 1836 |
| 3829 | **Pushkin, Alexander** | Russian | SS | **Kapitanskaya dochka** | 1836 |
| 3830 | **Pushkin, Alexander** | Russian | SS | **Kapitanskaya dochka** | 1836 |
| 3831 | **Pushkin, Alexander** | Russian | SS | **Metel'** <br> *(The Snowstorm)* <br> *(aka: The Blizzard)* | 1831 |
| 3832 | **Pushkin, Alexander** | Russian | SS | **Metel'** | 1831 |
| 3833 | **Pushkin, Alexander** | Russian | SS | **Metel'** | 1831 |
| 3834 | **Pushkin, Alexander** | Russian | SS(V) | **Motsart i Saleri** <br> *(Mozart and Salieri)* | 1830 |
| 3835 | **Pushkin, Alexander** | Russian | SS | **Pikovaya dama** <br> *(The Queen of Spades)* | 1834 |
| 3836 | **Pushkin, Alexander** | Russian | SS | **Pikovaya dama** | 1834 |
| 3837 | **Pushkin, Alexander** | Russian | SS | **Pikovaya dama** | 1834 |
| 3838 | **Pushkin, Alexander** | Russian | SS | **Pikovaya dama** | 1834 |
| 3839 | **Pushkin, Alexander** | Russian | V | **Ruslan i Lyudmila** <br> *(Ruslan and Liudmila)* | 1820 |
| 3840 | **Pushkin, Alexander** | Russian | V | **Ruslan i Lyudmila** | 1820 |
| 3841 | **Pushkin, Alexander** | Russian | V | **Skazka o mertvoy tsarevne i o semi bogatyryakh** <br> *(The Tale of the Dead Princess and the Seven Champions)* | 1833 |
| 3842 | **Pushkin, Alexander** | Russian | SS | **Skazka o Pope i o rabotnike ego Balde** <br> *(Tale of the Pope and His Workman Balda)* | 1831 |
| 3843 | **Pushkin, Alexander** | Russian | SS | **Skazka o Pope i o rabotnike ego Balde** | 1831 |
| 3844 | **Pushkin, Alexander** | Russian | V | **Skazka o rybake i rybke** <br> *(The Tale of the Fisherman and the Fish)* | 1833 |
| 3845 | **Pushkin, Alexander** | Russian | V | **Skazka o rybake i rybke** | 1833 |
| 3846 | **Pushkin, Alexander** | Russian | V | **Skazka o Tsare Saltane o syne ego slarnom i moguchen bogatyre knyaze gridone...** <br> *(Tale of Csar Saltane, his son Prince G..)* | 1831 |
| 3847 | **Pushkin, Alexander** | Russian | V | **Skazka o Tsare Saltane** | 1831 |
| 3848 | **Pushkin, Alexander** | Russian | V | **Skazka o Tsare Saltane** | 1831 |
| 3849 | **Pushkin, Alexander** | Russian | SS | **Skazka o zolotom petukhe** <br> *(Tale of the Golden Cockerel)* | 1834 |
| 3850 | **Pushkin, Alexander** | Russian | SS | **Stantsionny smotritel** <br> *(The Postmaster)* <br> *(aka: The Stationmaster)* | 1831 |
| 3851 | **Pushkin, Alexander** | Russian | SS | **Stantsionny smotritel** | 1831 |
| 3852 | **Pushkin, Alexander** | Russian | SS | **Stantsionny smotritel** | 1831 |
| 3853 | **Pushkin, Alexander** | Russian | SS | **Stantsionny smotritel** | 1831 |

| No | Film Title | Country of Production | Date | Director(s) | Duration of Film |
|---|---|---|---|---|---|
| 3823 | **Boris Godunov** *(2 - parts)* | USSR | 1986 | **Sergei Bondarchuk** | Pt.1, 74 Pt.2, 72 |
| 3824 | **Dubrovsky** | USSR | 1935 | **Alexander Ivanov** | 77 |
| 3825 | **Aquila Nera** *(The Black Eagle)* | IT | 1946 | **Riccardo Freda** | 91 |
| 3826 | **Il vendicatore** *(Revolt on the Volga) (aka: Dubrovsky)* | IT/YUGO | 1959(58) | **William Dieterle** | 110 |
| 3827 | **Blagorodnie razboinik Vladimir Dubrovsky** | USSR | 1989 | **Vyatcheslar Nikiforov** | 103 |
| 3828 | **La figlia del capitano** *(The Captain's Daughter)* | IT | 1947 | **Mario Camerini** | 75 |
| 3829 | **Kapitanskaya dochka** *(The Captain's Daughter)* | USSR | 1958 | **Vladimir Kaplunovski** | 86 |
| 3830 | **La tempesta** *(Tempest)* | IT/FR/ YUGO | 1958 | **Alberto Lattuada** | 122 |
| 3831 | **Metel'** *(Blizzard)* | USSR | 1964 | **Vladimir Basov** | 82 |
| 3832 | **Und der Regen verwischt jede Spur** *[And the rain erases all traces]* | GER/FR | 1973(72) | **Alfred Vohrer** | 98 |
| 3833 | **Esli eto ne lyubov' to tchto zhe...?** | USSR | 1974 | **Daria Gurina** | 21 |
| 3834 | **Legenda o Salieri** *{animation}* | USSR | 1986 | **Vadim Kurtchersky** | 19 |
| 3835 | **La dame de pique** *(The Queen of Spades)* | FR | 1937 | **Fyodor Otsep** | 87 |
| 3836 | **The Queen of Spades** | GB | 1948 | **Thorold Dickinson** | 95 +V |
| 3837 | **La dame de pique** *(The Queen of Spades)* | FR | 1965 | **Léonard Keigel** | 90(94) |
| 3838 | **Eti...tri vernye karty** | USSR | 1988 | **Alexander Orlov** | 86 |
| 3839 | **Ruslan i Lyudmila** | USSR | 1938 | **Ivan Nikitchenko Viktor Nevezhin** | 52 |
| 3840 | **Ruslan i Lyudmila** *(Ruslan and Liudmila)* | USSR | 1970 | **Aleksander Ptushko** | 105 |
| 3841 | **Skazka o mertvoy tsarevne i o semi bogatyryakh** *{animation}* | USSR | 1951 | **Ivan Ivanov-Vano** | 32 |
| 3842 | **Skazka o Pope i o rabotnike ego Balde** *{animation}* | USSR | 1939 | **Piotr Sazonov** | 22 |
| 3843 | **Skazka o Pope i o rabotnike ego Balde** *{animation}* | USSR | 1956 | **Anatoly Karanovich** | 25 |
| 3844 | **Skazka o rybake i rybke** *{animation}* | USSR | 1937 | **Aleksander Ptushko** | 28 |
| 3845 | **O zlaté rybce** *(The Tale of the Fisherman and the Fish) (aka: The Golden Fish) {animation}* | CZ | 1951 | **Jiři Trnka** | 15 |
| 3846 | **Skazka o Tsare Saltane** *{animation}* | USSR | 1943 | **Valentina Brumberg Zinaïda Brumberg** | 37 |
| 3847 | **Skazka o Tsare Saltane** *(The Tale of Czar Saltan)* | USSR | 1966 | **Aleksander Ptushko** | 108 |
| 3848 | **Skazka o Tsare Saltane** *{animation}* | USSR | 1984 | **Ivan Ivanov-Vano Lev Milchin** | 56 |
| 3849 | **Skazka o zolotom petukhe** *{animation}* | USSR | 1967 | **Alexander Snezhko-Blotzkaya** | 32 |
| 3850 | **Nostalgie** *(The Postmaster's Daughter)* | FR | 1937 | **Viktor Tourjansky** | 97 |
| 3851 | **Der Postmeister** | GER | 1940 | **Gustav Ucicky** | 94 |
| 3852 | **Rakkauden risti** *[The cross of love]* | FIN | 1946 | **Teuvo Tulio** | 99 |
| 3853 | **Der Postmeister** *(aka: Dunja)* | AUST | 1955 | **Josef von Baky** | 97 |

**213**

| No. | Author | Nationality | Form | Literary Title | Date |
|---|---|---|---|---|---|
| 3854 | **Pushkin, Alexander** | Russian | V | **Tsygany** <br> *(The Gypsies)* | 1824 |
| 3855 | **Pushkin, Alexander** | Russian | SS | **Vystrel** <br> *(The Shot)* <br> *(aka: The Pistol Shot)* | 1831 |
| 3856 | **Pushkin, Alexander** | Russian | SS | **Vystrel** | 1831 |
| 3857 | **Pushkin, Alexander** | Russian | SS | **Vystrel** | 1831 |
| 3858 | **Quarantotti-Gambini, Pier** | Italian | N | **La calda vita** | 1958 |
| 3859 | **Queirós, Dinah Silveira de** | Brazilian | N | **Floradas na serra** <br> *[Blossoms on the mountain]* | 1939 |
| 3860 | **Queneau, Raymond** | French | N | **Le dimanche de la vie** <br> *(The Sunday of Life)* | 1951 |
| 3861 | **Queneau, Raymond** <br> *(as: Sally Mara)* | French | N | **On est toujours trop bon avec les femmes** <br> *(We Always Treat Women Too Well)* | 1947 |
| 3862 | **Queneau, Raymond** | French | N | **Zazie dans le métro** <br> *(Zazie)* | 1959 |
| 3863 | **Quevedo y Villegas, Francisco Gómez de** | Spanish | N | **La historia de la vida del Buscón** <br> *(The Scavenger)* <br> *(aka: The Swindler)* | 1626 |
| 3864 | **Quiller-Couch** <br> *(joint, see: Stevenson, Robert Louis)* | British | N | | |
| 3865 | **Quiroga, Elena** <br> *(Elena Quiroga de la Válgoma)* | Spanish | N | **Viento del Norte** <br> *[North wind]* | 1951 |
| 3866 | **Quiroga, Horacio** | Uruguay | SS | **Los destiladores de naranja** <br> *(The Orange-Distillers)* + <br> **Una bofetada** <br> *(A Slap in the Face)* | 1923+ <br> 1916 |
| 3867 | **Quiroga de la Válgoma, Elena** <br> *(see: Quiroga, Elena)* | Spanish | N | | |
| 3868 | **Quoirez, Françoise** <br> *(see: Sagan, Françoise)* | French | N/P | | |
| 3869 | **Raabe, Wilhelm** | German | N | **Die schwarze Galeere** <br> *(How the Black Galley Took the Andrea Doria)* | 1902 |
| 3870 | **Racine, Jean** | French | P | **Bérénice** | 1671 |
| 3871 | **Racine, Jean** | French | P | **Phèdre** | 1677 |
| 3872 | **Racine, Jean** | French | P | **Phèdre** | 1677 |
| 3873 | **Radichkov, Yordan** | Bulgarian | N | **Baruten bukvar** <br> *[Gunpowder]* | 1969 |
| 3874 | **Radichkov, Yordan** | Bulgarian | SS | **Goreshto pladne** | 1965 |
| 3875 | **Radichkov, Yordan** | Bulgarian | SS | **Khlyab** <br> *[Bread]* | 1969 |
| 3876 | **Radichkov, Yordan** | Bulgarian | SS | **Privărzaniyat balon** <br> *[The attached balloon]* | 1965 |
| 3877 | **Radichkov, Yordan** | Bulgarian | N | **Vsichki i nikoi** <br> *[Everybody and nobody]* | 1975 |
| 3878 | **Radiguet, Raymond** | French | N | **Le bal du comte d'Orgel** <br> *(Count Orgel)* <br> *(aka: Count d'Orgel Opens the Ball)* | 1924 |
| 3879 | **Radiguet, Raymond** | French | N | **Le diable au corps** <br> *(The Devil in the Flesh)* | 1923 |
| 3880 | **Radványi, Netty** <br> *(see: Seghers, Anna)* | German | N/SS | | |
| 3881 | **Raimund, Ferdinand** | Austrian | P | **Der Bauer als Millionär** | 1868 |
| 3882 | **Raimund, Ferdinand** | Austrian | P | **Der Verschwender** <br> *(The Spendthrift)* | 1868 |
| 3883 | **Ramos, Graciliano** | Brazilian | N | **Memórias do cárcere** <br> *[Memories from prison]* | 1953 |
| 3884 | **Ramos, Graciliano** | Brazilian | N | **São Bernardó** | 1934 |
| 3885 | **Ramos, Graciliano** | Brazilian | N | **Vidãs sêcas** <br> *(Barren Lives)* | 1938 |
| 3886 | **Ramuz, Charles-Ferdinand** | Swiss | N | **Farinet** | 1932 |

| No | Film Title | Country of Production | Date | Director(s) | Duration of Film |
|---|---|---|---|---|---|
| 3854 | **Aleko** | USSR | 1953 | **Sergei Sidelev** | 60 |
| 3855 | **Coups de feu** (Duels) | FR | 1939 | **René Barberis** | 75 |
| 3856 | **Un colpo di pistola** (A Pistol Shot) | IT | 1942(41) | **Renato Castellani** | 95 |
| 3857 | **Vystrel** | USSR | 1967 | **Naum Trakhtenberg** | 78 |
| 3858 | **La calda vita** | IT/FR | 1964(63) | **Florestano Vancini** | 97(110) |
| 3859 | **Floradas na serra** | BRAZ | 1954 | **Luciano Salce** | 98 |
| 3860 | **Le dimanche de la vie** (The Sunday of Life) | FR/IT/GER | 1965 | **Jean Herman** | 100 |
| 3861 | **On est toujours trop bon avec les femmes** | FR | 1971 | **Michel Boisrond** | 77 |
| 3862 | **Zazie dans le métro** (Zazie in the Underground) (aka: Zazie) | FR | 1960 | **Louis Malle** | 88 |
| 3863 | **El buscón** | SP | 1975(74) | **Luciano Berriatúa** | 94(99) |
| 3864 | | | | | |
| 3865 | **Viento del Norte** | SP | 1954 | **Antonio Momplet** | 80 |
| 3866 | **Prisioneros de la tierra** | ARG | 1939 | **Mario Soffici** | 85 |
| 3867 | | | | | |
| 3868 | | | | | |
| 3869 | **Die schwarze Galeere** | GDR | 1962 | **Martin Hellberg** | 95 |
| 3870 | **Bérénice** | FR | 1967(66) | **Pierre-Alain Jolivet** | 90 |
| 3871 | **Au coeur de la Casbah** | FR | 1952 | **Pierre Cardinal** | 96 |
| 3872 | **Phèdre** | FR | 1968 | **Pierre Jourdain** | 92 |
| 3873 | **Baruten bukvar** | BULG | 1977 | **Todor Dinov** | 77 |
| 3874 | **Goreshto pladne** (Hot Noon) | BULG | 1966(64) | **Zako Kheskia** (Zako Heskiya) | 88 |
| 3875 | **Khlyab** | BULG | 1972 | **Naum Shopov** | 43 |
| 3876 | **Privărzaniyat balon** | BULG | 1967 | **Binka Zhelyazkova** | 98 |
| 3877 | **Vsichki i nikoi** | BULG | 1978 | **Krikor Azaryan** | 102 |
| 3878 | **Le bal du comte d'Orgel** | FR | 1970 | **Marc Allégret** | 100 |
| 3879 | **Le diable au corps** (Devil in the Flesh) | FR | 1947 | **Claude Autant-Lara** | 112 |
| 3880 | | | | | |
| 3881 | **Der Bauer als Millionär** | AUST | 1962(61) | **Rudolf Steinböck** | 95 |
| 3882 | **Der Verschwender** | AUST | 1953(52) | **Leopold Hainisch** | 89 |
| 3883 | **Memórias do cárcere** | BRAZ | 1984 | **Nelson Pereira dos Santos** | 193 |
| 3884 | **S Bernardó** (Saint Bernard) | BRAZ | 1973(71) | **Léon Hirszman** | 85 |
| 3885 | **Vidãs sêcas** (Barren Lives) (aka: Sécheresse) | BRAZ | 1964 | **Nelson Pereira dos Santos** | 135 |
| 3886 | **L'or dans la montagne** | SWITZ | 1937 | **Max Haufler** | 91 |

| No. | Author | Nationality | Form | Literary Title | Date |
|-----|--------|-------------|------|----------------|------|
| 3887 | Ramuz, Charles-Ferdinand | Swiss | N | La séparation des races | 1923 |
| 3888 | Rand, Ayn | American/Russ | N | The Fountainhead | 1943 |
| 3889 | Rand, Ayn | American/Russ | P | Night of January 16th | 1936 |
| 3890 | Rand, Ayn | American/Russ | N | We the Living | 1936 |
| 3891 | Raphael, Frederic | British | N | Darling | 1965 |
| 3892 | Raphaelson, Samson | American | P | Accent on Youth (aka: Old Love) | 1935 |
| 3893 | Raphaelson, Samson | American | P | Accent on Youth | 1935 |
| 3894 | Raphaelson, Samson | American | P | Accent on Youth | 1935 |
| 3895 | Raphaelson, Samson | American | SS-P | The Day of Atonement {ss} (The Jazz Singer) {p} | 1922{ss} 1925{p} |
| 3896 | Raphaelson, Samson | American | SS-P | The Day of Atonement {ss} (The Jazz Singer) {p} | 1922{ss} 1925{p} |
| 3897 | Raphaelson, Samson | American | P | Hilda Crane | 1951 |
| 3898 | Raphaelson, Samson | American | P | The Perfect Marriage | 1945 |
| 3899 | Raphaelson, Samson | American | P | Skylark | 1938 |
| 3900 | Rappaport, Shloyme Zanvl (see: An-Ski, Solomon) | Polish | P | | |
| 3901 | Rattigan, Terence | British | P | A Bequest to the Nation | 1970 |
| 3902 | Rattigan, Terence | British | P | The Browning Version | 1949 |
| 3903 | Rattigan, Terence | British | P | The Deep Blue Sea | 1952 |
| 3904 | Rattigan, Terence | British | P | French Without Tears | 1937 |
| 3905 | Rattigan, Terence | British | P | Separate Tables | 1955 |
| 3906 | Rattigan, Terence | British | P | The Sleeping Prince | 1954 |
| 3907 | Rattigan, Terence | British | P | While the Sun Shines | 1944 |
| 3908 | Rattigan, Terence | British | P | Who Is Sylvia? | 1951 |
| 3909 | Rattigan, Terence | British | P | The Winslow Boy | 1946 |
| 3910 | Rawlings, Marjorie K. | American | MEM | Cross Creek | 1942 |
| 3911 | Rawlings, Marjorie K. | American | SS | Gal Young 'Un | 1940 |
| 3912 | Rawlings, Marjorie K. | American | N | The Yearling | 1938 |
| 3913 | Rebelo, Marques (Eddy Dias da Cruz) | Brazilian | N | A estrela sobe [The star rises] | 1939 |
| 3914 | Rebreanu, Liviu | Romanian | N | Ciuleandra [A peasant dance] | 1927 |
| 3915 | Rebreanu, Liviu | Romanian | N | Ciuleandra | 1927 |
| 3916 | Rebreanu, Liviu | Romanian | N | Ion | 1920 |
| 3917 | Rebreanu, Liviu | Romanian | N | Pădurea spînzuraţilor (The Forest of the Hanged) | 1922 |
| 3918 | Rebreanu, Liviu | Romanian | N | Răscoala (The Uprising) | 1932 |
| 3919 | Régio, José (José Maria dos Reis Pereira) | Portuguese | P | Benilde ou a virgem-maē | 1947 |
| 3920 | Régio, José | Portuguese | N | O príncipe com orelhas de burro [The prince with donkey ears] | 1942 |
| 3921 | Régio, José | Portuguese | SS | O vestido cor de fogo | 1946 |
| 3922 | Rego, José Lins do | Brazilian | N | Fogo morto [Dead fire] | 1943 |
| 3923 | Rego, José Lins do | Brazilian | N | Menino de engenho (Plantation Boy)+ Fogo morto | 1932+ 1943 |
| 3924 | Rego, José Lins do | Brazilian | N | Pureza | 1937 |
| 3925 | Reis Pereira, José Maria dos (see: Régio, José) | Portuguese | P/SS | | |
| 3926 | Remarque, Erich Maria | German | N | Arc de Triomphe (Arch of Triumph) | 1946 |
| 3927 | Remarque, Erich Maria | German | N | Arc de Triomphe | 1946 |
| 3928 | Remarque, Erich Maria | German | N | Der Himmel kennt keine Günstlinge (Heaven Has No Favourites) | 1961 |

| No | Film Title | Country of Production | Date | Director(s) | Duration of Film |
|---|---|---|---|---|---|
| 3887 | **Rapt** *(aka: Zweikampf der Geschlechter) (The Magic Mountain)* | SWITZ | 1934 | **Dimitri Kirsanoff** | 102 |
| 3888 | **The Fountainhead** | USA | 1949(48) | **King Vidor** | 114 |
| 3889 | **The Night of January 16th** | USA | 1941 | **William B.Clemens** | 79 |
| 3890 | **Noi vivi** *(We the Living)* | IT | 1942 | **Goffredo Allessandrini** | 174(270) |
| 3891 | **Darling** | GB | 1965 | **John Schlesinger** | 127 |
| 3892 | **Accent on Youth** | USA | 1935 | **Wesley Ruggles** | 77 |
| 3893 | **Mr Music** | USA | 1950 | **Richard Haydn** | 113 |
| 3894 | **But Not For Me** | USA | 1959 | **Walter Lang** | 105 |
| 3895 | **The Jazz Singer** | USA | 1953 | **Michael Curtiz** | 107 |
| 3896 | **The Jazz Singer** | USA | 1980 | **Richard Fleischer** | 115 +V |
| 3897 | **Hilda Crane** | USA | 1956 | **Philip Dunne** | 87 |
| 3898 | **The Perfect Marriage** | USA | 1946 | **Lewis Allen** | 87 |
| 3899 | **Skylark** | USA | 1941 | **Mark Sandrich** | 94 |
| 3900 | | | | | |
| 3901 | **Bequest to the Nation** *(USA: The Nelson Affair)* | GB | 1973 | **James Cellan Jones** | 116 |
| 3902 | **The Browning Version** | GB | 1951 | **Anthony Asquith** | 89 +V |
| 3903 | **The Deep Blue Sea** | GB | 1955 | **Anatole Litvak** | 99 |
| 3904 | **French Without Tears** | GB | 1939 | **Anthony Asquith** | 85 |
| 3905 | **Separate Tables** | USA | 1958 | **Delbert Mann** | 98 |
| 3906 | **The Prince and the Showgirl** | GB | 1957 | **Laurence Olivier** **Anthony Bushell** | 114 +V |
| 3907 | **While the Sun Shines** | GB | 1947 | **Anthony Asquith** | 81 |
| 3908 | **The Man Who Loved Redheads** | GB | 1955(54) | **Harold French** | 90 |
| 3909 | **The Winslow Boy** | GB | 1948 | **Anthony Asquith** | 117 +V |
| 3910 | **Cross Creek** | USA | 1983 | **Martin Ritt** | 122 +V |
| 3911 | **Gal Young Un** | USA | 1979 | **Victor Nunez** | 105 |
| 3912 | **The Yearling** | USA | 1946 | **Clarence Brown** | 135 |
| 3913 | **A estrela sobe** | BRAZ | 1974 | **Bruno Barreto** | 90 |
| 3914 | **Verklungene Träume** | GER/ROM | 1930 | **Martin Berger** | 90 |
| 3915 | **Ciuleandra** | ROM | 1985 | **Sergiu Nicolaescu** | 124 |
| 3916 | **Ion - blestemul pămîntului, blestemul iubirii** *[Ion - The curse of property, the curse of love]* | ROM | 1980(79) | **Mircea Mureşan** | 210 |
| 3917 | **Pădurea spînzuraţilor** *(The Forest of the Hanged) (aka: The Lost Forest)* | ROM | 1965(64) | **Liviu Ciulei** | 160(157) |
| 3918 | **Răscoala** | ROM | 1966 | **Mircea Mureşan** | 108 |
| 3919 | **Benilde ou a virgem-maē** *(Benilde: Virgin and Mother)* | PORT | 1975 | **Manoel de Oliveira** | 110 |
| 3920 | **O príncipe com orelhas de burro** | PORT | 1979 | **António de Macedo** | 105 |
| 3921 | **O vestido cor de fogo** | PORT | 1985 | **Lauro António** | 92 |
| 3922 | **Fogo morto** | BRAZ | 1976 | **Marcos Farias** | 90 |
| 3923 | **Menino de engenho** *(The Boy From the Plantation) (aka: Plantation Boy)* | BRAZ | 1966 | **Walter Lima, Jr.** | 86 |
| 3924 | **Pureza** | BRAZ | 1940 | **Chianca de Garcia** | 140(90) |
| 3925 | | | | | |
| 3926 | **Arch of Triumph** | USA | 1948 | **Lewis Milestone** | 120 +V |
| 3927 | **Arch of Triumph** | USA | 1984 | **Waris Hussein** | 120 |
| 3928 | **Bobby Deerfield** | USA | 1977 | **Sydney Pollack** | 123 +V |

| No. | Author | Nationality | Form | Literary Title | Date |
|-----|--------|-------------|------|----------------|------|
| 3929 | **Remarque, Erich Maria** | German | N | **Im Westen nichts Neues** <br> *(All Quiet on the Western Front)* | 1929 |
| 3930 | **Remarque, Erich Maria** | German | N | **Im Westen nichts Neues** | 1929 |
| 3931 | **Remarque, Erich Maria** | German | N | **Strandgut** <br> *(Flotsam)* | 1940 |
| 3932 | **Remarque, Erich Maria** | German | N | **Three Comrades** <br> *(aka: Drei Kamaraden)* | 1937(38) |
| 3933 | **Remarque, Erich Maria** | German | N | **Der Weg zurück** <br> *(The Road Back)* | 1931 |
| 3934 | **Remarque, Erich Maria** | German | N | **Zeit zu Leben und Zeit zu Sterben** <br> *(A Time to Live and a Time to Die)* <br> *(aka: A Time to Love and a Time to Die)* | 1954 |
| 3935 | **Remenyik Zsigmond** | Hungarian | N | **Mese habbal** | 1934 |
| 3936 | **Renard, Jules** | French | N+P | **Poil de carotte** {n} <br> *(Carrots)*+ <br> **La bigote** {p} | 1894{n} <br> 1900{p} |
| 3937 | **Renard, Jules** | French | N | **Poil de carotte** | 1894 |
| 3938 | **Reuter, Fritz** | German | V | **Kein Hüsung** | 1858 |
| 3939 | **Reuter, Fritz** | German | N | **Ut mine Stromtid** <br> *(Seedtime and Harvest)* <br> *(aka: An Old Story of My Farming Days)* | 1862-64 |
| 3940 | **Reuter, Fritz** | German | N | **Ut mine Stromtid** | 1862-64 |
| 3941 | **Reve, Gerard Kornelis van Het** | Dutch | N | **De taal der liefde** <br> *[The language of love]* + <br> **Lieve jongens** <br> *[Dear boys]* + <br> **Het lieve leven** | 1971+ <br> 1972+ <br> 1974 |
| 3942 | **Reve, Gerard Kornelis van Het** | Dutch | N | **De vierde man** | 1981 |
| 3943 | **Rey, Marcos** | Brazilian | N | **O enterro da cafetina** <br> *[The bawd's burial]* | 1967 |
| 3944 | **Rey, Marcos** | Brazilian | N | **Memórias de um gigolo** <br> *[Memoirs of a gigolo]* | 1968 |
| 3945 | **Reymont, Władysław Stanisław** | Polish | N | **Chłopi** <br> *(The Peasants)* <br> *(aka: Autumn, Winter, Spring, Summer)* | 1902-09 |
| 3946 | **Reymont, Władysław Stanisław** | Polish | N | **Komediantka** <br> *(The Comédienne)*+ <br> **Fermenty** <br> *[Fermentation]* | 1896+ <br> 1897 |
| 3947 | **Reymont, Władysław Stanisław** | Polish | N | **Ziemia obiecana** <br> *(The Promised Land)* | 1899 |
| 3948 | **Rhys, Jean** | British | N | **Quartet** <br> *(aka: Postures)* | 1929 <br> (aka:1928) |
| 3949 | **Ribeiro, Júlio** <br> *(Júlio César Ribeiro Vaughan)* | Brazilian | N | **A carne** | 1888 |
| 3950 | **Rice, Elmer** | American | P | **The Adding Machine** | 1923 |
| 3951 | **Rice, Elmer** | American | P | **Counsellor at Law** | 1931 |
| 3952 | **Rice, Elmer** | American | P | **Dream Girl** | 1946 |
| 3953 | **Rice, Elmer** | American | P | **On Trial** | 1919 |
| 3954 | **Rice, Elmer** | American | P | **See Naples and Die** | 1930 |
| 3955 | **Rice, Elmer** | American | P | **Street Scene** | 1929 |
| 3956 | **Richardson, Ethel Florence** <br> *(Henry Handel Richardson)* | Australian | N | **The Getting of Wisdom** | 1910 |
| 3957 | **Richardson, Ethel Florence** | Australian | N | **Maurice Guest** | 1908 |
| 3958 | **Richardson, Henry Handel** <br> *(see: Richardson, Ethel Florence)* | Australian | N | | |
| 3959 | **Richardson, Samuel** | British | N | **Pamela** | 1740 |
| 3960 | **Richler, Mordecai** | Canadian | N | **The Apprenticeship of Duddy Kravitz** | 1959 |
| 3961 | **Richler, Mordecai** | Canadian | N | **Jacob Two-Two Meets the Hooded Fang** | 1975 |

| No | Film Title | Country of Production | Date | Director(s) | Duration of Film |
|----|-----------|----------------------|------|-------------|------------------|
| 3929 | All Quiet on the Western Front | USA | 1930 | Lewis Milestone | 127 +V(103) |
| 3930 | All Quiet on the Western Front | USA | 1979 | Delbert Mann | 150(180) +V(103) |
| 3931 | So Ends Our Night | USA | 1941 | John Cromwell | 120(117) |
| 3932 | Three Comrades | USA | 1938 | Frank Borzage | 98 |
| 3933 | The Road Back | USA | 1937 | James Whale | 97(92) |
| 3934 | A Time to Love and a Time to Die | USA | 1958 | Douglas Sirk | 131 |
| 3935 | Mese habbal (It's All Moonshine) | HUNG | 1979 | István Bácskai-Lauro | 88 |
| 3936 | Poil de carotte (The Redhead) | FR | 1932 | Julien Duvivier | 94(80) |
| 3937 | Poil de carotte | FR | 1952(51) | Paul Mesnier | 100 |
| 3938 | Kein Hüsung | GDR | 1954 | Arthur Pohl | 93 |
| 3939 | Onkel Bräsig | GER | 1936 | Erich Waschneck | 88 |
| 3940 | Livet på landet [Life in the country] (aka: Onkel Bräsig) | SWE | 1943 | Bror Bügler | 105 |
| 3941 | Lieve jongens (Dear Boys) | HOLL | 1980 | Paul de Lussanet | 88 |
| 3942 | De vierde man (The Fourth Man) | HOLL | 1983(79) | Paul Verhoeven | 104 |
| 3943 | O enterro da cafetina | BRAZ | 1971 | Antonio Pieralisi | 90 |
| 3944 | Memórias de um gigolo | BRAZ | 1970 | Alberto Pieralisi | 80 |
| 3945 | Chłopi (The Peasants) (Pt.1: Boryna) (Pt.2: Jagna) | POL | 1973 | Jan Rybkowski | Pt.1, 100 Pt.2, 100 |
| 3946 | Komediantka | POL | 1987 | Jerzy Sztwiertnia | 112 |
| 3947 | Ziemia obiecana (The Promised Land) (aka: Land of Promise) | POL | 1975(74) | Andrzej Wajda | 178(150) (223) |
| 3948 | Quartet | GB/FR | 1981 | James Ivory | 101 +V |
| 3949 | A carne | BRAZ | 1976 | J. Marreco | 90 |
| 3950 | The Adding Machine | GB | 1969(68) | Jerome Epstein | 99 |
| 3951 | Counsellor at Law | USA | 1933 | William Wyler | 78 |
| 3952 | Dream Girl | USA | 1947 | Mitchell Leisen | 86 |
| 3953 | On Trial | USA | 1939 | Terry Morse | 60 |
| 3954 | Oh Sailor Behave! | USA | 1930 | Archie Mayo | 68 |
| 3955 | Street Scene | USA | 1931 | King Vidor | 80 |
| 3956 | The Getting of Wisdom | AUSTL | 1977 | Bruce Beresford | 103 +V |
| 3957 | Rhapsody | USA | 1954(53) | Charles Vidor | 116 |
| 3958 | | | | | |
| 3959 | Mistress Pamela | GB | 1973 | Jim O'Connolly | 91 |
| 3960 | The Apprenticeship of Duddy Kravitz | CAN | 1974 | Ted Kotcheff | 121 +V |
| 3961 | Jacob Two-Two Meets the Hooded Fang | CAN | 1977 | Theodore J. Flicker | 80 |

| No. | Author | Nationality | Form | Literary Title | Date |
|---|---|---|---|---|---|
| 3962 | **Richler, Mordecai** | Canadian | SS | **The Summer My Grandma Was Supposed to Die** | 1969 |
| 3963 | **Richter, Conrad** | American | N | **The Light in the Forest** | 1953 |
| 3964 | **Richter, Conrad** | American | N | **The Sea of Grass** | 1936 |
| 3965 | **Richter, Conrad** | American | N | **Tacey Cromwell** | 1942 |
| 3966 | **Rifbjerg, Klaus** | Danish | N | **Den kroniske uskyld** | 1958 |
| 3967 | **Rigby, Ray** | British | N | **The Hill** | 1965 |
| 3968 | **Riggs, Lyn** | American | P | **Green Grow the Lilacs** | 1931 |
| 3969 | **Rilke, Rainer Maria** | Austrian | V | **Die Weise von Liebe und Tod des Cornets Christoph Rilke** (Tale of Love and Death of Cornet Christopher Rilke) | 1906 |
| 3970 | **Robbe-Grillet, Alain** | French | N | **Les gommes** (The Erasers) | 1953 |
| 3971 | **Roberts, Elizabeth Madox** | American | N | **The Great Meadow** | 1930 |
| 3972 | **Roberts, Kenneth Lewis** | American | N | **Captain Caution** | 1934 |
| 3973 | **Roberts, Kenneth Lewis** | American | N | **Lydia Bailey** | 1947 |
| 3974 | **Roberts, Kenneth Lewis** | American | N | **Northwest Passage** | 1937 |
| 3975 | **Robertson, T. W.** | British | P | **Caste** | 1876 |
| 3976 | **Roblès, Emmanuel** | French | N | **Cela s'appelle l'aurore** (Dawn On Our Darkness) | 1952 |
| 3977 | **Roché, Henri-Pierre** | French | N | **Deux anglaises et le continent** | 1956 |
| 3978 | **Roché, Henri-Pierre** | French | N | **Jules et Jim** (Jules and Jim) | 1953 |
| 3979 | **Rochefort, Christiane** | French | N | **Le repos du guerrier** (Warrior's Rest) | 1958 |
| 3980 | **Rochefort, Christiane** | French | N | **Les stances à Sophie** (Cats Don't Care For Money) | 1964 |
| 3981 | **Rodrigues, Nelson** | Brazilian | N | **Asfalto selvagem** {livro I} | 1960 |
| 3982 | **Rodrigues, Nelson** | Brazilian | N | **Asfalto selvagem** {livro II} | 1960 |
| 3983 | **Rodrigues, Nelson** | Brazilian | P | **O beijo no asfalto** [The kiss on the asphalt] | 1961 |
| 3984 | **Rodrigues, Nelson** | Brazilian | P | **O beijo no asfalto** | 1961 |
| 3985 | **Rodrigues, Nelson** | Brazilian | P | **Bôca de ouro** [Gold mouth] | 1959-60 |
| 3986 | **Rodrigues, Nelson** | Brazilian | P | **Bonitinha, mas ordinária** [Cute but vulgar] | 1961 |
| 3987 | **Rodrigues, Nelson** | Brazilian | P | **Bonitinha, mas ordinária** | 1961 |
| 3988 | **Rodrigues, Nelson** | Brazilian | N | **O casamento** (The Wedding) (aka: The Marriage) | 1966 |
| 3989 | **Rodrigues, Nelson** | Brazilian | P | **A falecida** | 1953 |
| 3990 | **Rodrigues, Nelson** | Brazilian | N | **Meu destino é pecar** [My destiny is to sin] | 1944 |
| 3991 | **Rodrigues, Nelson** | Brazilian | P | **Os sete gatinhos** [The seven kittens] | 1958 |
| 3992 | **Rodrigues, Nelson** | Brazilian | P | **Tôda nudez será castigada** | 1965-66 |
| 3993 | **Rodríguez Álvarez, Alejandro)** (see: Casona, Alejandro) | Spanish | P | | |
| 3994 | **Rohmer, Eric** | French | F-SS | **L'amour, l'après-midi** (Love in the Afternoon) | 1974 |
| 3995 | **Rohmer, Eric** | French | F-SS | **La boulangère de Monceau** (The Baker's Girl) | 1974 |
| 3996 | **Rohmer, Eric** | French | F-SS | **La carrière de Suzanne** (Suzanne's Career) | 1974 |
| 3997 | **Rohmer, Eric** | French | F-SS | **La collectionneuse** (The Collector) | 1974 |
| 3998 | **Rohmer, Eric** | French | F-SS | **Le genou de Claire** (Claire's Knee) | 1974 |

| No | Film Title | Country of Production | Date | Director(s) | Duration of Film |
|---|---|---|---|---|---|
| 3962 | **The Street** <br> {animation} | CAN | 1976 | **Caroline Leaf** | 10 |
| 3963 | **The Light in the Forest** | USA | 1958 | **Herschel Daugherty** | 92 +V |
| 3964 | **The Sea of Grass** | USA | 1946 | **Elia Kazan** | 131 |
| 3965 | **One Desire** | USA | 1955(54) | **Jerry Hopper** | 94 |
| 3966 | **Den kroniske uskyld** <br> (Chronic Innocence) <br> (aka: Everlasting Innocence) | DEN | 1985 | **Edward Fleming** | 100 |
| 3967 | **The Hill** | GB/USA | 1965 | **Sidney Lumet** | 123 |
| 3968 | **Oklahoma!** <br> {musical version} | USA | 1955 | **Fred Zinnemann** | 145 |
| 3969 | **Der Cornet** <br> [The cornet] | GER | 1955 | **Walter Reisch** | 106 |
| 3970 | **Les gommes** | BEL/FR | 1969(68) | **Lucian Deroisy** | 90 |
| 3971 | **The Great Meadow** | USA | 1931 | **Charles J. Brabin** | 80 |
| 3972 | **Captain Caution** | USA | 1940 | **Richard Wallace** | 85 |
| 3973 | **Lydia Bailey** | USA | 1952 | **Jean Negulesco** | 89 |
| 3974 | **Northwest Passage** | USA | 1940 | **King Vidor** | 126 |
| 3975 | **Caste** | GB | 1930 | **Campbell Gullan** | 70 |
| 3976 | **Cela s'appelle l'aurore** <br> (IT: Gli amanti di domani) | FR/IT | 1955 | **Luis Buñuel** | 108(88) |
| 3977 | **Les deux anglaises et le continent** <br> (aka: Anne and Muriel) <br> (USA: Two English Girls) | FR | 1971 | **François Truffaut** | 108 |
| 3978 | **Jules et Jim** <br> (Jules and Jim) | FR | 1961 | **François Truffaut** | 105 |
| 3979 | **Le repos du guerrier** <br> (IT: Il riposo del guerriero) <br> (Warrior's Rest) | FR/IT | 1962 | **Roger Vadim** | 101(98) |
| 3980 | **Les stances à Sophie** | FR | 1971(70) | **Moshe Mizrahi** | 90 |
| 3981 | **Asfalto selvagem** | BRAZ | 1964 | **J. B. Tanko** | 100 |
| 3982 | **Engraçadinha depois dos 30** | BRAZ | 1966 | **J. B. Tanko** | 96 |
| 3983 | **O beijo** <br> (The Kiss) | BRAZ | 1965(64) | **Flavio Tambellini** | 82 |
| 3984 | **O beijo no asfalto** | BRAZ | 1981(80) | **Bruno Barreto** | 90 |
| 3985 | **O bôca de ouro** | BRAZ | 1962 | **Nelson Pereira dos Santos** | 103(85) |
| 3986 | **Bonitinha, mas ordinária** | BRAZ | 1963 | **J. P. de Carvalho** | 100 |
| 3987 | **Bonitinha, mas ordinária** | BRAZ | 1981 | **Braz Chediak** | 103 |
| 3988 | **O casamento** | BRAZ | 1975 | **Arnaldo Jabor** | 100 |
| 3989 | **A falecida** <br> (The Death) | BRAZ | 1965 | **Léon Hirszman** | 98 |
| 3990 | **Meu destino é pecar** | BRAZ | 1952 | **Manuel Peluffo** | 90 |
| 3991 | **Os setes gatinhos** | BRAZ | 1980 | **Neville d'Almeida** | 95 |
| 3992 | **Tôda nudez será castigada** <br> (All Nudity Will Be Punished) | BRAZ | 1973(72) | **Arnaldo Jabor** | 90 |
| 3993 | | | | | |
| 3994 | **L'amour, l'après-midi** <br> (Love in the Afternoon) <br> (aka: Chloe in the Afternoon) | FR | 1972 | **Eric Rohmer** | 97 <br> +V |
| 3995 | **La boulangère de Monceau** | FR | 1962 | **Eric Rohmer** | 47 <br> +V |
| 3996 | **La carrière de Suzanne** <br> (Suzanne's Profession) | FR | 1963 | **Eric Rohmer** | 60 <br> +V |
| 3997 | **La collectionneuse** | FR | 1966 | **Eric Rohmer** | 90 |
| 3998 | **Le genou de Claire** <br> (Claire's Knee) | FR | 1970 | **Eric Rohmer** | 106 <br> +V |

| No. | Author | Nationality | Form | Literary Title | Date |
|-----|--------|-------------|------|----------------|------|
| 3999 | **Rohmer, Eric** | French | F-SS | **Ma nuit chez Maud** *(My Night With Maud)* | 1974 |
| 4000 | **Rojas, Fernando de** | Spanish | P | **La Celestina** *(aka: La tragicomedia de Calisto y Melibea) (aka: The Spanish Bawd)* | 1500 |
| 4001 | **Rojas, Fernando de** | Spanish | P | **La Celestina** | 1500 |
| 4002 | **Rojas, Fernando de** | Spanish | P | **La Celestina** | 1500 |
| 4003 | **Rolland, Romain** | French | N | **Pierre et Luce** | 1920 |
| 4004 | **Romains, Jules** | French | N | **Les copains** *(The Boys in the Back Room)* | 1913 |
| 4005 | **Romains, Jules** | French | SS-P | **Donogoo-Tonka, ou les miracles la science** *{ss}* *(Donagoo) {p}* | 1920{ss} 1931{p} |
| 4006 | **Romains, Jules** | French | P | **Knock, ou le triomphe de la médecine** *(Doctor Knock)* | 1924 |
| 4007 | **Romains, Jules** | French | P | **Knock, ou le triomphe de la médecine** | 1924 |
| 4008 | **Romains, Jules** | French | P | **Knock, ou le triomphe de la médecine** | 1924 |
| 4009 | **Romero, José Rubén** | Mexican | N | **Rosenda** | 1946 |
| 4010 | **Rooney, Frank** | American | SS | **The Cyclist's Raid** | 1951 |
| 4011 | **Rosa, Guimarães** | Brazilian | N | **Grande sertão: veredas** *(The Devil to Pay in the Backlands)* | 1956 |
| 4012 | **Rosa, Guimarães** | Brazilian | SS | **A hora e vez de Augusto Matraga** *(Augusto Matraga's Hour and Turn)* | 1946 |
| 4013 | **Rosário, António Martinho do** *(see: Santareno, Bernardo)* | Portuguese | P | | |
| 4014 | **Rose, Reginald** | American | P(TV) | **Crime in the Streets** | 1955 |
| 4015 | **Rose, Reginald** - *{tvp}* **Sergel, Kristin** - *{p}* | American | P(TV)-P | **Dino** | 1956 |
| 4016 | **Rose, Reginald; Sergel, Sherman L.** | American | P | **Twelve Angry Men** | 1955 |
| 4017 | **Rosegger, Peter** | Austrian | SS | **Die Fahnelträgerin** | 1913 |
| 4018 | **Rosegger, Peter** | Austrian | N | **Die Försterbuben** | 1908 |
| 4019 | **Rosny, J. H.** *(aîné) (Joseph-Henri Honoré Boëx-Borel)* | French | N | **La guerre du feu** | 1911 |
| 4020 | **Rostand, Edmond** | French | P | **L'aiglon** | 1900 |
| 4021 | **Rostand, Edmond** | French | P | **Cyrano de Bergerac** | 1898 |
| 4022 | **Rostand, Edmond** | French | P | **Cyrano de Bergerac** | 1898 |
| 4023 | **Rostand, Edmond** | French | P | **Cyrano de Bergerac** | 1898 |
| 4024 | **Rostand, Edmond** | French | P | **Cyrano de Bergerac** | 1898 |
| 4025 | **Rosten, Leo** | American | N | **Captain Newman, M. D.** | 1961 |
| 4026 | **Rosten, Leo** | American | SS | **Dark Corner** | 1945 |
| 4027 | **Rosten, Leo** | American | N | **Sleep My Love** | 1946 |
| 4028 | **Roth, Joseph** | Austrian | N | **Das falsche Gewicht** | 1937 |
| 4029 | **Roth, Joseph** | Austrian | N | **Hiob** *(Job: the Story of a Simple Man)* | 1930 |
| 4030 | **Roth, Joseph** | Austrian | N | **Die Kapuzinergruft** | 1938 |
| 4031 | **Roth, Joseph** | Austrian | N | **Die Legende vom heiligen Trinker** *(The Legend of the Holy Drinker)* | 1939 |
| 4032 | **Roth, Joseph** | Austrian | N | **Die Legende vom heiligen Trinker** | 1939 |
| 4033 | **Roth, Joseph** | Austrian | SS | **Die Rebellion** *[The rebellion]* | 1924 |
| 4034 | **Roth, Philip** | American | SS | **Goodbye, Columbus** | 1959 |
| 4035 | **Roth, Philip** | American | N | **Portnoy's Complaint** | 1969 |
| 4036 | **Rou Shi** *(see: Zhao Pingfu)* | Chinese | SS | | |

| No | Film Title | Country of Production | Date | Director(s) | Duration of Film |
|---|---|---|---|---|---|
| 3999 | **Ma nuit chez Maud** *(My Night With Maud)* *(USA: My Night at Maud's)* | FR | 1969 | **Eric Rohmer** | 113(105) |
| 4000 | **La Celestina P...R...** *(aka: La Celestina)* | IT/FR | 1965(64) | **Carlo Lizzani** | 105 |
| 4001 | **La Celestina** *(aka: The Wanton of Spain - La Celestina)* | SP/GER | 1969(68) | **César Fernández Ardavín** | 126(123) |
| 4002 | **Celestina** | MEX | 1977 | **Miguel Sabido** | 88 |
| 4003 | **Mata au hi made** *(Until the Day We Meet Again)* *(aka: Until We Meet Again)* | JAP | 1950 | **Tadashi Imai** | 111 |
| 4004 | **Les copains** | FR | 1965(64) | **Yves Robert** | 95 |
| 4005 | **Donogoo Tonka** | GER | 1936 | **Reinhold Schünzel** | 100 |
| 4006 | **Knock, ou le triomphe de la médecine** *(aka: Knock)* | FR | 1933 | **Louis Jouvet** **Roger Goupillières** | 95 |
| 4007 | **Knock** | FR | 1951(50) | **Guy Lefranc** | 98 |
| 4008 | **Ana al doctor** *[I...the doctor]* | EGY | 1968 | **Abbas Kamel** | 102 |
| 4009 | **Rosenda** | MEX | 1948 | **Julio Bracho** | 103 |
| 4010 | **The Wild One** | USA | 1954(53) | **Laslo Benedek** | 79 +V |
| 4011 | **Grande sertão** | BRAZ | 1964 | **José Geraldo Santos Pereira** **José Renato Santos Pereira** | 90 |
| 4012 | **A hora e vez de Augusto Matraga** *(The Time and Hour of Augusto Matraga)* *(aka: The Hour and Turn of Augusto Matraga)* | BRAZ | 1966(65) | **Roberto Santos** | 105 |
| 4013 | | | | | |
| 4014 | **Crime in the Streets** | USA | 1956 | **Don Siegel** | 80 |
| 4015 | **Dino** | USA | 1957 | **Thomas Carr** | 94 |
| 4016 | **Twelve Angry Men** | USA | 1957(56) | **Sidney Lumet** | 96 +V |
| 4017 | **Die fröhliche Wallfahrt** | GER | 1956 | **Ferdinand Dörfler** | 92 |
| 4018 | **Die Försterbuben** | GER | 1955 | **Robert A. Stemmle** | 102 |
| 4019 | **Quest For Fire** *(FR: La guerre du feu)* | CAN/FR | 1981 | **Jean-Jacques Annaud** | 100 +V |
| 4020 | **Der Herzog von Reichstag** *(FR: L'aiglon)* | GER/FR | 1931 | **Viktor Tourjansky** | 109 |
| 4021 | **Cyrano de Bergerac** | FR | 1946 | **Fernand Rivers** | 100 |
| 4022 | **Cyrano de Bergerac** | USA | 1950 | **Michael Gordon** | 113 |
| 4023 | **Roxanne** | USA | 1987 | **Fred Schepisi** | 107 |
| 4024 | **Cyrano de Bergerac** | FR | 1990 | **Jean-Paul Rappeneau** | 138 +V |
| 4025 | **Captain Newman, M. D.** | USA | 1963 | **David Miller** | 126 |
| 4026 | **The Dark Corner** | USA | 1946 | **Henry Hathaway** | 99 |
| 4027 | **Sleep My Love** | USA | 1948(47) | **Douglas Sirk** | 97 +V |
| 4028 | **Das falsche Gewicht** *(Short Weights)* | GER | 1971 | **Bernhard Wicki** | 131(146) |
| 4029 | **Sins of Man** | USA | 1936 | **Gregory Ratoff** **Otto Brower** | 78 |
| 4030 | **Trotta** | GER | 1971 | **Johannes Schaaf** | 95(105) |
| 4031 | **Die Legende vom heiligen Trinker** | GER | 1963 | **Franz Josef Wild** | 166 |
| 4032 | **Le leggenda del santo bevitore** *(The Legend of the Holy Drinker)* *(aka: La legende du Saint Buveur)* | IT | 1988 | **Ermanno Olmi** | 125 +V |
| 4033 | **Die Rebellion** | GER | 1962 | **Wolfgang Staudte** | 70 |
| 4034 | **Goodbye Columbus** | USA | 1969 | **Larry Peerce** | 102 |
| 4035 | **Portnoy's Complaint** | USA | 1972 | **Ernest Lehman** | 99 +V |
| 4036 | | | | | |

| No. | Author | Nationality | Form | Literary Title | Date |
|-----|--------|-------------|------|----------------|------|
| 4037 | Rousseau, Jean-Jacques | French | N | Émile; ou, de l'éducation *(Émile; or, Education)* | 1762 |
| 4038 | Roussin, André | French | P | Bobosse | 1951 |
| 4039 | Roussin, André | French | P | Une grande fille toute simple | 1943 |
| 4040 | Roussin, André | French | P | Lorsque l'enfant paraît | 1952 |
| 4041 | Roussin, André | French | P | Nina | 1951 |
| 4042 | Roussin, André | French | P | Les oeufs de l'autruche | 1955 |
| 4043 | Roussin, André | French | P | La petite hutte *(The Little Hut)* | 1948 |
| 4044 | Rozov, Victor S. | Russian | P | Vechno zhivye *(Alive Forever)* | 1956 |
| 4045 | Rud, Nils Johan | Norwegian | N | Ettersøkte er atten år | 1958 |
| 4046 | Ruiz, Juan *(Arcipreste de Hita)* | Spanish | V | Libro de buen amor *(The Book of Good Love)* | 1330(43) |
| 4047 | Ruiz Iriarte, Víctor | Spanish | P | La guerra empieza en Cuba | 1957 |
| 4048 | Ruiz Iriarte, Víctor | Spanish | P | Juego de niños *[Children's game]* | 1951 |
| 4049 | Rulfo, Juan | Mexican | N | Pedro Páramo | 1955 |
| 4050 | Rulfo, Juan | Mexican | N | Pedro Páramo | 1955 |
| 4051 | Runyon, Damon | American | SS | Bloodhounds of Broadway | 1931 |
| 4052 | Runyon, Damon | American | SS | Butch Minds the Baby | 1931 |
| 4053 | Runyon, Damon | American | SS | Butch Minds the Baby | 1931 |
| 4054 | Runyon, Damon | American | SS | A Call on The President | 1938 |
| 4055 | Runyon, Damon | American | SS | Gentlemen, The King | 1931 |
| 4056 | Runyon, Damon | American | SS | Hold 'em Yale! | 1934 |
| 4057 | Runyon, Damon | American | SS | The Idyll of Miss Sarah Brown | 1944 |
| 4058 | Runyon, Damon | American | SS | Johnny One-Eye | 1944 |
| 4059 | Runyon, Damon | American | SS | The Lemon Drop Kid | 1934 |
| 4060 | Runyon, Damon | American | SS | The Lemon Drop Kid | 1934 |
| 4061 | Runyon, Damon | American | SS | Little Miss Marker | 1934 |
| 4062 | Runyon, Damon | American | SS | Little Miss Marker | 1934 |
| 4063 | Runyon, Damon | American | SS | Little Miss Marker | 1934 |
| 4064 | Runyon, Damon | American | SS | Little Pinks | 1940 |
| 4065 | Runyon, Damon | American | SS | Madame La Gimp | 1931 |
| 4066 | Runyon, Damon | American | SS | Madame La Gimp | 1931 |
| 4067 | Runyon, Damon | American | SS | Money From Home | 1935 |
| 4068 | Runyon, Damon | American | SS | The Old Doll's House | 1934 |
| 4069 | Runyon, Damon | American | SS | Princess O'Hara | 1934 |
| 4070 | Runyon, Damon | American | SS | Princess O'Hara | 1934 |
| 4071 | Runyon, Damon | American | SS | Three Wise Guys | 1934 |
| 4072 | Runyon, Damon | American | SS | Tight Shoes | 1938 |
| 4073 | Runyon, Damon | American | SS | A Very Honorable Guy | 1931 |
| 4074 | Runyon, Damon; Lindsay, H. | American | P | A Slight Case of Murder | 1940 |
| 4075 | Runyon, Damon; Lindsay, H. | American | P | A Slight Case of Murder | 1940 |
| 4076 | Rusiñol, Santiago | Spanish | N-P | L'auca del senyor Esteve *[Mr Esteve's praise]* | 1907{n} 1929{p} |
| 4077 | Russell, Willy | British | P | Educating Rita | 1981 |
| 4078 | Russell, Willy | British | P | Shirley Valentine | 1988 |
| 4079 | Saba, Umberto | Italian | N | Ernesto | 1975 |
| 4080 | Sábato, Ernesto | Argentine | N | El túnel *(The Outsider)* | 1948 |
| 4081 | Sábato, Ernesto | Argentine | N | El túnel | 1948 |
| 4082 | Sabino, Fernando Tavares | Brazilian | N | A faca de dois gumes *[Two-edged knife]* | 1985 |
| 4083 | Sabino, Fernando Tavares | Brazilian | N | O grande mentecapto *[The great insane]* | 1979 |
| 4084 | Sabino, Fernando Tavares | Brazilian | SS | O homen nú | 1960 |

| No | Film Title | Country of Production | Date | Director(s) | Duration of Film |
|----|-----------|----------------------|------|-------------|------------------|
| 4037 | Le gai savoir (aka: The Joyful Wisdom) | FR/GER | 1968 | Jean-Luc Godard | 95 |
| 4038 | Bobosse | FR | 1959 | Étienne Périer | 88 |
| 4039 | Une grande fille toute simple | FR | 1948(47) | Jaques Manuel | 100 |
| 4040 | Lorsque l'enfant paraît | FR | 1956 | Michel Boisrond | 85 |
| 4041 | Nina | FR | 1958 | Jean Boyer | 88 |
| 4042 | Les oeufs de l'autruche (The Ostrich Has Two Eggs) | FR | 1957 | Denys de la Patellière | 82 |
| 4043 | The Little Hut | USA | 1957(56) | Mark Robson | 90 |
| 4044 | Letyat zhuravli (The Cranes Are Flying) | USSR | 1957 | Mikhail Kalatozov | 94 |
| 4045 | Ung flukt (The Wayward Girl) | NOR | 1959 | Edith Carlmar | 95(91) |
| 4046 | Libro de buen amor | SP | 1975(74) | Tomás Aznar | 85(94) |
| 4047 | La guerra empieza en Cuba | SP | 1957 | Manuel Mur Oti | 107(104) |
| 4048 | Juego de niños | SP | 1952 | Enrique Cahen Salaberry | 85(83) |
| 4049 | Pedro Páramo | MEX | 1967 | Carlos Velo | 108 |
| 4050 | Pedro Páramo | MEX | 1976 | Jose Bolanos | 112(173) |
| 4051 | Bloodhounds of Broadway | USA | 1952 | Harmon Jones | 90 |
| 4052 | Butch Minds the Baby | USA | 1942 | Albert S. Rogell | 75 |
| 4053 | Butch Minds the Baby | GB | 1979 | Peter Webb | 32 |
| 4054 | Joe and Ethel Turp Call on The President | USA | 1939 | Robert B. Sinclair | 70 |
| 4055 | Professional Soldier | USA | 1936 | Tay Garnett | 75 |
| 4056 | Hold 'em Yale! | USA | 1935 | Sidney Lanfield | 61 |
| 4057 | Guys and Dolls {musical version} | USA | 1955 | Joseph L. Mankiewicz | 150 +V |
| 4058 | Johnny One-Eye | USA | 1950(49) | Robert Florey | 80 |
| 4059 | The Lemon Drop Kid | USA | 1934 | Marshall Neilan | 60(71) |
| 4060 | The Lemon Drop Kid | USA | 1951 | Sidney Lanfield | 91 |
| 4061 | Little Miss Marker (GB: The Girl in Pawn) | USA | 1934 | Alexander Hall | 80 +V |
| 4062 | Sorrowful Jones | USA | 1949(48) | Sidney Lanfield | 88 |
| 4063 | Little Miss Marker | USA | 1980 | Walter Bernstein | 103 +V |
| 4064 | The Big Street | USA | 1942 | Irving Reis | 89 |
| 4065 | Lady For a Day | USA | 1933 | Frank Capra | 95(88) |
| 4066 | Pocketful of Miracles | USA | 1961 | Frank Capra | 136 |
| 4067 | Money From Home | USA | 1953 | George Marshall | 100 |
| 4068 | Midnight Alibi | USA | 1934 | Alan Crosland | 59 |
| 4069 | Princess O'Hara | USA | 1935 | David Burton | 79 |
| 4070 | It Ain't Hay (GB: Money For Jam) | USA | 1943 | Erle C. Kenton | 80 |
| 4071 | Three Wise Guys | USA | 1936 | George B. Seitz | 74 |
| 4072 | Tight Shoes | USA | 1941 | Albert S. Rogell | 68 |
| 4073 | A Very Honorable Guy | USA | 1934 | Lloyd Bacon | 62 |
| 4074 | A Slight Case of Murder | USA | 1938(37) | Lloyd Bacon | 85 |
| 4075 | Stop, You're Killing Me | USA | 1953(52) | Roy Del Ruth | 86 |
| 4076 | El señor Esteve | SP | 1948 | Edgar Neville | 108(92) |
| 4077 | Educating Rita | GB | 1983 | Lewis Gilbert | 110 +V |
| 4078 | Shirley Valentine | USA | 1989 | Lewis Gilbert | 108 |
| 4079 | Ernesto | IT/SP/GER | 1978 | Salvatore Samperi | 98(95) |
| 4080 | El túnel | ARG | 1952 | León Klimovsky | 94 |
| 4081 | El túnel (The Tunnel) | SP | 1987 | Antonio Drove | 110 +V |
| 4082 | Faca de dois gumes | BRAZ | 1989 | Murilo Salles | 97 |
| 4083 | O grande mentecapto | BRAZ | 1989 | Osvaldo Caldeira | 103 |
| 4084 | O homen nú (The Naked Man) | BRAZ | 1968(67) | Roberto Santos | 118 |

| No. | Author | Nationality | Form | Literary Title | Date |
|-----|--------|-------------|------|----------------|------|
| 4085 | **Sackler, Howard** | American | P | **The Great White Hope** | 1968 |
| 4086 | **Sade, Donatien** <br> *(Marquis de)* | French | N | **Les 120 journées de Sodome,** <br> **ou l'école du libertinage** <br> *(The 120 Days of Sodom)* | 1904 <br> 1931-35 |
| 4087 | **Sade, Donatien** <br> *(Marquis de)* | French | N | **Justine, ou les malheurs de la** <br> **vertu** <br> *(Justine, or the Misfortunes of* <br> *Virtue) +* <br> **Juliette; ou les prospérités du** <br> **vice** | 1791+ <br> 1797 |
| 4088 | **Sade, Donatien** <br> *(Marquis de)* | French | N | **Justine +** <br> **Juliette** | 1791+ <br> 1797 |
| 4089 | **Sade, Donatien** <br> *(Marquis de)* | French | N | **Justine** | 1791 |
| 4090 | **Sade, Donatien** <br> *(Marquis de)* | French | N | **Justine** | 1791 |
| 4091 | **Sade, Donatien** <br> *(Marquis de)* | French | N | **Justine** | 1791 |
| 4092 | **Sadleir, Michael** | British | N | **Fanny by Gaslight** | 1940 |
| 4093 | **Sadoveanu, Mihail** | Romanian | N | **Baltagul** <br> *(The Hatchet)* | 1930 |
| 4094 | **Sadoveanu, Mihail** | Romanian | SS | **Dumbrava minunată** <br> *(The Wonderful Grove)* <br> *(aka: The Magic Grove)* | 1926 <br> (rev.1950) |
| 4095 | **Sadoveanu, Mihail** | Romanian | N | **Fraţii Jderi** <br> *[The Jder brothers]* <br> *(vol 1)* | 1935 |
| 4096 | **Sadoveanu, Mihail** | Romanian | N | **Locul unde nu s-a întîmplat nimic** <br> *[The place where nothing* <br> *happened]* | 1933 |
| 4097 | **Sadoveanu, Mihail** | Romanian | N | **Mitrea Cocor** | 1949 |
| 4098 | **Sadoveanu, Mihail** | Romanian | SS | **Nada florilor** <br> *[The flower bait]* <br> *(aka: Amintirile unui pescar cu* <br> *undiţa)* <br> *[Memories of a fisherman]* | 1951 |
| 4099 | **Sadoveanu, Mihail** | Romanian | N | **Neamul Şoimăreştilor** <br> *[The Şoimar lineage]* | 1915 |
| 4100 | **Sadoveanu, Mihail** | Romanian | SS | **Ochi de urs** <br> *[A bear's eye]* | 1938 |
| 4101 | **Sagan, Françoise** <br> *(Françoise Quoirez)* | French | N | **Aimez-vous Brahms...?** | 1959 |
| 4102 | **Sagan, Françoise** | French | N | **Bonjour tristesse** | 1954 |
| 4103 | **Sagan, Françoise** | French | N | **Un certain sourire** <br> *(A Certain Smile)* | 1956 |
| 4104 | **Sagan, Françoise** | French | N | **La chamade** | 1965 |
| 4105 | **Sagan, Françoise** | French | P | **Château en Suède** <br> *[Chateau in Sweden]* | 1960 |
| 4106 | **Sagan, Françoise** | French | N | **Un peu de soleil dans l'eau froide** <br> *(Sunlight on Cold Water)* | 1969 |
| 4107 | **Sahia, Alexandru** | Romanian | SS | **Întoarcerea tatii din război +** <br> **Moartea tînărului cu termen** <br> **redus +** <br> **În cîmpia de sînge a Mărăşeştilor** | 1934+ <br> 1933+ <br> 1934 |
| 4108 | **Sahia, Alexandru** | Romanian | SS | **Moartea înghiţitorului de săbii** <br> *[The death of the sword swallower]* | 1934 |
| 4109 | **Saiko, George Emmanuel** | Austrian | N | **Der Mann im Schilf** <br> *[The man in the rushes]* | 1955 |
| 4110 | **Saint-Exupéry, Antoine de** | French | N | **Courrier sud** <br> *(Southern Mail)* | 1929 |
| 4111 | **Saint-Exupéry, Antoine de** | French | N | **Le petit prince** <br> *(The Little Prince)* | 1943 |
| 4112 | **Saint-Exupéry, Antoine de** | French | N | **Le petit prince** | 1943 |

**226**

| No | Film Title | Country of Production | Date | Director(s) | Duration of Film |
|---|---|---|---|---|---|
| 4085 | **The Great White Hope** | USA | 1970 | **Martin Ritt** | 103 +V |
| 4086 | **Saló o le centoventi giornate di sodoma** (Saló or the 120 Days of Sodom) (aka: Pasolini's 120 Days of Sodom) | IT/FR | 1975 | **Pier Paolo Pasolini** | 117 |
| 4087 | **Le vice et la vertu** (IT: Il vizio e la virtù) (Vice and Virtue) | FR/IT | 1963(62) | **Roger Vadim** | 100(117) |
| 4088 | **Justine,das Sexgeschöpf des Marquis de Sade** (IT: Justine ovvero le disavventure della virtù) (aka:Marquis de Sade:Justine) | GER/IT | 1968 | **Jesús Franco** (Jess Franco) | 90 +V(104) |
| 4089 | **Justine de Sade** (The Violation of Justine) | FR/IT | 1972(71) | **Claude Pierson** | 110(85) +V(85) |
| 4090 | **Justine** | GB | 1976 | **Stuart Mackinnon Clive Myers Nigel Perkins** | 90 |
| 4091 | **Cruel Passion** (aka: Justine) (aka: Marquis de Sade's Justine) | GB | 1978(77) | **Chris Boger** | 97 +V(92) |
| 4092 | **Fanny by Gaslight** (USA: Man of Evil) | GB | 1944 | **Anthony Asquith** | 108 +V |
| 4093 | **Baltagul** (The Axe) | ROM/IT | 1969 | **Mircea Mureşan** | 108(100) |
| 4094 | **Dumbrava minunată** | ROM | 1980 | **Gheorghe Naghi** | 86 |
| 4095 | **Fraţii Jderi** | ROM | 1974 | **Mircea Drăgan** | 111 |
| 4096 | **Noiembrie, ultimul bal** [November, the last ball] | ROM | 1989 | **Dan Piţa** | 110 |
| 4097 | **Mitrea Cocor** | ROM | 1952 | **Victor Iliu Marietta Sadova** | 105 |
| 4098 | **Vacanţă tragică** [Tragic holiday] | ROM | 1978(79) | **Constantin Vaeni** | 87 |
| 4099 | **Neamul Şoimăreştilor** | ROM | 1965(64) | **Mircea Drăgan** | 100 |
| 4100 | **Ochi de urs** | ROM | 1983 | **Stere Gulea** | 100 |
| 4101 | **Aimez-vous Brahms?** (USA: Goodbye Again) | FR/USA | 1961 | **Anatole Litvak** | 120 |
| 4102 | **Bonjour tristesse** | GB | 1958(57) | **Otto Preminger** | 93 |
| 4103 | **A Certain Smile** | USA | 1958 | **Jean Negulesco** | 105 |
| 4104 | **La chamade** (Heartbeat) | FR/IT | 1968 | **Alain Cavalier** | 105(99) |
| 4105 | **Château en Suède** (IT: Il castello in Svezia) (Nutty, Naughty Chateau) | FR/IT | 1963 | **Roger Vadim** | 110 |
| 4106 | **Un peu de soleil dans l'eau froide** (Sunlight on Cold Water) | FR | 1971 | **Jacques Deray** | 110 |
| 4107 | **Viaţa nu iartă** [Pitiless life] | ROM | 1959(58) | **Iulian Mihu Manole Marcus** | 61 |
| 4108 | **Înghiţitorul de săbii** [The sword swallower] | ROM | 1982 | **Alexa Visarion** | 113 |
| 4109 | **Der Mann im Schilf** | GER | 1978 | **Manfred Purzer** | 113 |
| 4110 | **Courrier sud** | FR | 1936 | **Pierre Billon** | 95 |
| 4111 | **Malenky prince** | USSR | 1967 | **Arunas Zebriunas** | 68 |
| 4112 | **The Little Prince** | GB/USA | 1975(74) | **Stanley Donen** | 89 |

| No. | Author | Nationality | Form | Literary Title | Date |
|---|---|---|---|---|---|
| 4113 | **Saint-Exupéry, Antoine de** | French | SS | **Vol de nuit**<br>*(Night Flight)* | 1931 |
| 4114 | **Saint-Laurent, Cécil**<br>*(see: Stendhal)* | French | N | | |
| 4115 | **Salacrou, Armand** | French | P | **Histoire de rire** | 1940 |
| 4116 | **Sales, Herberto** | Brazilian | N | **Cascalho**<br>*[Gravel]* | 1944 |
| 4117 | **Salinger, J. D.** | American | SS | **Uncle Wiggily in Connecticut** | 1948 |
| 4118 | **Salminen, Sally** | Swedish/Finnish | N | **Katrina** | 1936 |
| 4119 | **Sandeau, Jules**<br>*(joint, see: Augier, Émile)* | French | P | | |
| 4120 | **Sandel, Cora**<br>*(Sara Fabricius)* | Norwegian | N | **Kranes konditori. Interior med figurer**<br>*(Krane's Café. An Interior With figures)* | 1945 |
| 4121 | **Sandel, Cora** | Norwegian | SS | **Nina** | 1949 |
| 4122 | **Sandemose, Aksel** | Norwegian | N | **Klabautermannen**<br>*[The klabauter man]* | 1927 |
| 4123 | **Sandgren, Gustav** | Swedish | N | **Maria** | 1942 |
| 4124 | **Sandgren, Gustav** | Swedish | N | **...som havets nakna vind**<br>*(As the Naked Wind From the Sea...)* | 1965 |
| 4125 | **Sánta Ferenc** | Hungarian | N | **Húsz óra** | 1964 |
| 4126 | **Sánta Ferenc** | Hungarian | N | **Az ötödik pecsét** | 1963 |
| 4127 | **Santareno, Bernardo**<br>*(António Martinho do Rosário)* | Portuguese | P | **A promessa**<br>*[The promise]* | 1957 |
| 4128 | **Santos, João Felício dos** | Brazilian | N | **Cristo na lama** | 1964 |
| 4129 | **Santos, João Felício dos** | Brazilian | N | **Ganga Zumba, rei dos Palmares** | 1961 |
| 4130 | **Sardou, Victorien** | French | P | **L'affaire des poisons** | 1908 |
| 4131 | **Sardou, Victorien** | French | P | **L'espionne**<br>*(aka: Dora)* | 1936 |
| 4132 | **Sardou, Victorien** | French | P | **Fédora** | 1908 |
| 4133 | **Sardou, Victorien** | French | P | **Fédora** | 1908 |
| 4134 | **Sardou, Victorien** | French | P | **Fernande** | 1870 |
| 4135 | **Sardou, Victorien** | French | P | **Fernande** | 1870 |
| 4136 | **Sardou, Victorien** | French | P | **Fernande** | 1870 |
| 4137 | **Sardou, Victorien** | French | P | **Odette** | 1936 |
| 4138 | **Sardou, Victorien** | French | P | **Odette** | 1936 |
| 4139 | **Sardou, Victorien** | French | P | **Paméla, marchande de frivolités** | 1936 |
| 4140 | **Sardou, Victorien** | French | P | **Les pattes de mouche**<br>*(A Scrap of Paper)* | 1860 |
| 4141 | **Sardou, Victorien** | French | P | **Théodora** | 1907 |
| 4142 | **Sardou, Victorien** | French | P | **La Tosca** | 1909 |
| 4143 | **Sardou, Victorien** | French | P | **La Tosca** | 1909 |
| 4144 | **Sardou, Victorien;**<br>**Gallet, Louis** | French | P | **Patrie!** | 1869 |
| 4145 | **Sardou, Victorien;**<br>**Moreau, Émile** | French | P | **Madame Sans-Gêne**<br>*(Madame Devil-may-care)* | 1907 |
| 4146 | **Sardou, Victorien;**<br>**Moreau, Émile** | French | P | **Madame Sans-Gêne** | 1907 |
| 4147 | **Sardou, Victorien;**<br>**Najac, Émile de** | French | P | **Divorçons**<br>*(Let's Get a Divorce)* | 1883 |
| 4148 | **Sarkadi Imre** | Hungarian | P | **Az elveszett paradicsom** | 1962 |
| 4149 | **Sarkadi Imre** | Hungarian | SS | **Kútban**<br>*(In the Well)* | 1971<br>(coll) |

| No | Film Title | Country of Production | Date | Director(s) | Duration of Film |
|----|-----------|----------------------|------|-------------|-----------------|
| 4113 | **Night Flight** | USA | 1933 | **Clarence Brown** | 84 |
| 4114 | | | | | |
| 4115 | **Histoire de rire** <br> (Foolish Husbands) | FR | 1941 | **Marcel L'Herbier** | 117 |
| 4116 | **Cascalho** | BRAZ | 1950 | **Léo Marten** | 86 |
| 4117 | **My Foolish Heart** | USA | 1949 | **Mark Robson** | 98 +V |
| 4118 | **Katrina** | SWE | 1943 | **Gustaf Edgren** | 102 |
| 4119 | | | | | |
| 4120 | **Kranes konditori** <br> (Krane's Bakery Shop) | NOR | 1951 | **Astrid Henning-Jensen** | 104 |
| 4121 | **Høysommer** | NOR | 1958 | **Arild Brinchmann** | 99 |
| 4122 | **Klabautermanden** <br> (aka: Klabavtermanden) <br> (We Are All Demons) | DEN/SWE/ <br> NOR | 1969 | **Henning Carlsen** | 102 |
| 4123 | **Maria** | SWE | 1947 | **Gösta Folke** | 87 |
| 4124 | **Som havets nakna vind** <br> (As the Naked Wind From the Sea) | SWE | 1968 | **Gunnar Höglund** | 103 |
| 4125 | **Húsz óra** <br> (Twenty Hours) | HUNG | 1964 | **Zoltán Fábri** | 118 |
| 4126 | **Az ötödik pecsét** <br> (The Fifth Seal) | HUNG | 1976 | **Zoltán Fábri** | 116 |
| 4127 | **A promessa** | PORT | 1972 | **António de Macedo** | 102 |
| 4128 | **Cristo na lama** <br> (a história do Aleijadinho) <br> [Christ in the mud (life of Aleijadinho)] | BRAZ | 1968(67) | **Wilson Silva** | 90 |
| 4129 | **Ganga Zumba** | BRAZ | 1963 | **Carlos Diegues** | 100 |
| 4130 | **L'affaire des poisons** <br> (IT: Il processo dei veleni) | FR/IT | 1955 | **Henri Decoin** | 103(110) |
| 4131 | **Dora la espia** | SP/IT | 1943 | **Raffaello Matarazzo** | 95 |
| 4132 | **Fédora** | FR | 1934 | **Louis J. Gasnier** | 75 |
| 4133 | **Fédora** | IT | 1942 | **Camillo Mastrocinque** | 95 |
| 4134 | **Der Bettelstudent** <br> [The pauper student] <br> {musical version} | GER | 1931 | **Viktor Janson** | 92 |
| 4135 | **Der Bettelstudent** <br> {musical version} | GER | 1936 | **Georg Jacoby** | 90 |
| 4136 | **Der Bettelstudent** <br> {musical version} | GER | 1956 | **Werner Jacobs** | 97 |
| 4137 | **Odette** <br> (FR: Déchéance) | IT/FR | 1935(34) | **Jacques Houssin** | 73 |
| 4138 | **Désarroi** | FR | 1946 | **Robert-Paul Dagan** | 85 |
| 4139 | **Paméla** | FR | 1945(44) | **Pierre de Hérain** | 109 |
| 4140 | **Les pattes de mouche** | FR | 1936 | **Jean Grémillon** | 85 |
| 4141 | **Teodora, Imperatrice di Bisanzio** <br> (Theodora, Slave Empress) | IT/FR | 1954(53) | **Riccardo Freda** | 88(92) |
| 4142 | **Tosca** | IT | 1941(40) | **Carlo (Karl) Koch** | 91(105) |
| 4143 | **La Tosca** | IT | 1973 | **Luigi Magni** | 103 |
| 4144 | **Patrie!** | FR | 1946(45) | **Louis Daquin** | 95 |
| 4145 | **Madame Sans-Gêne** | FR | 1941 | **Richard Richebé** | 100 |
| 4146 | **Madame Sans-Gêne** <br> (Madame) | FR/IT/SP | 1961 | **Christian-Jaque** | 102(118) |
| 4147 | **That Uncertain Feeling** | USA | 1941 | **Ernst Lubitsch** | 86 |
| 4148 | **Elveszett paradicsom** <br> (The Lost Paradise) <br> (aka: Paradise Lost) | HUNG | 1962 | **Károly Makk** | 98 |
| 4149 | **Körhinta** <br> (Merry-Go-Round) | HUNG | 1955 | **Zoltán Fábri** | 101 |

| No. | Author | Nationality | Form | Literary Title | Date |
|---|---|---|---|---|---|
| 4150 | Sarkadi Imre | Hungarian | SS | Tanyasi dúvad<br>[Rural brute] | 1953 |
| 4151 | Sarment, Jean<br>(Jean Bellemère) | French | P | Léopold le bien-aimé | 1927 |
| 4152 | Sarment, Jean | French | P | Mamouret | 1943 |
| 4153 | Sarment, Jean | French | P | Le voyage à Biarritz | 1936 |
| 4154 | Saroyan, William | American | N | The Human Comedy | 1943 |
| 4155 | Saroyan, William | American | P | The Time of Your Life | 1939 |
| 4156 | Sarrazin, Albertine | French(Alg) | N | L'astragale<br>(Astragal) | 1965 |
| 4157 | Sarrazin, Albertine | French | N | La cavale<br>(The Runaway) | 1965 |
| 4158 | Sartre, Jean-Paul | French | P | Huis clos<br>(In Camera)<br>(aka: No Exit) | 1947 |
| 4159 | Sartre, Jean-Paul | French | P | Huis clos | 1947 |
| 4160 | Sartre, Jean-Paul | French | P | Les mains sales<br>(Crime Passionel) | 1948 |
| 4161 | Sartre, Jean-Paul | French | SS | Le mur<br>(The Wall) | 1939 |
| 4162 | Sartre, Jean-Paul | French | P | La putain respectueuse<br>(aka: La p... respectueuse) | 1946 |
| 4163 | Sartre, Jean-Paul | French | P | Les sequestrés d'Altona<br>(The Condemned of Altona)<br>(aka: Loser Wins) | 1959 |
| 4164 | Sastre, Alfonso | Spanish | P | La cornada<br>(Death Thrust) | 1960 |
| 4165 | Satomi Ton | Japanese | SS | Akibiyori | 1960 |
| 4166 | Satomi Ton | Japanese | SS | Higanbana<br>(Daughter's Marriage) | 1958 |
| 4167 | Sayers, Dorothy L. | British | N | Busman's Honeymoon | 1937 |
| 4168 | Schade, Jens August | Danish | N | Mennesker mødes og sød musik<br>opstår i hjertet | 1944 |
| 4169 | Schaefer, Jack | American | SS | The Big Range | 1953 |
| 4170 | Schaefer, Jack | American | N | Company of Cowards | 1957 |
| 4171 | Schaefer, Jack | American | N | Monte Walsh | 1963 |
| 4172 | Schaefer, Jack | American | N | Shane | 1949 |
| 4173 | Scherfig, Hans | Danish | N | Den forsvundne fuldmægtig<br>[Head clerk disappeared] | 1938 |
| 4174 | Schiller, Friedrich von | German | P | Die Braut von Messina<br>(The Bride of Messina) | 1803 |
| 4175 | Schiller, Friedrich von | German | P | Don Carlos | 1787 |
| 4176 | Schiller, Friedrich von | German | P | Don Carlos | 1787 |
| 4177 | Schiller, Friedrich von | German | P | Don Carlos | 1787 |
| 4178 | Schiller, Friedrich von | German | P | Kabale und Liebe<br>(Intrigue and Love)<br>(aka: The Minister: a tragedy) | 1784 |
| 4179 | Schiller, Friedrich von | German | P | Maria Stuart | 1801 |
| 4180 | Schiller, Friedrich von | German | P | Wallenstein | 1800 |
| 4181 | Schiller, Friedrich von | German | P | Wilhelm Tell | 1804 |
| 4182 | Schiller, Friedrich von | German | P | Wilhelm Tell | 1804 |
| 4183 | Schiller, Friedrich von | German | P | Wilhelm Tell | 1804 |
| 4184 | Schiller, Friedrich von | German | P | Wilhelm Tell | 1804 |
| 4185 | Schmid, Eduard<br>(see: Edschmid, Kasimir) | German | N | | |
| 4186 | Schmidt, Afonso | Brazilian | SS | A carantonha | 1804 |

| No | Film Title | Country of Production | Date | Director(s) | Duration of Film |
|---|---|---|---|---|---|
| 4150 | **Dúvad** (The Brute) | HUNG | 1959 | Zoltán Fábri | 90 |
| 4151 | **Léopold le bien-aimé** | FR | 1933 | Arno-Charles Brun | 102 |
| 4152 | **Le briseur de châines** | FR | 1941 | Jacques Daniel-Norman | 117 |
| 4153 | **Le voyage à Biarritz** | FR | 1963 | Gilles Grangier | 92 |
| 4154 | **The Human Comedy** | USA | 1943 | Clarence Brown | 117 |
| 4155 | **The Time of Your Life** | USA | 1948 | H. C. Potter | 109 |
| 4156 | **L'astragale** (GER: Astragal) | FR/GER | 1968 | Guy Casaril | 103 |
| 4157 | **La cavale** | FR | 1971 | Michel Mitrani | 100 |
| 4158 | **Huis clos** (No Exit) | FR | 1954 | Jacqueline Audry | 99 |
| 4159 | **No Exit** | USA/ARG | 1962 | Tad Danielewski | 88 |
| 4160 | **Les mains sales** (Dirty Hands) | FR | 1951 | Fernand Rivers | 103 |
| 4161 | **Le mur** | FR | 1967 | Serge Roullet | 90 |
| 4162 | **La p... respectueuse** (aka: La putain respectueuse) (The Respectful Prostitute) | FR | 1952 | Charles Brabant Marcello Pagliero | 95 |
| 4163 | **I sequestrati di Altona** (FR: Les séquestrés d'Altona) (The Condemned of Altona) | IT/FR | 1962 | Vittorio de Sica | 113(118) |
| 4164 | **A las cinco de la tarde** [At five in the afternoon] | SP | 1960 | Juan Antonio Bardem | 93 |
| 4165 | **Akibiyori** (Late Autumn) | JAP | 1960 | Yasujirō Ozu | 129 |
| 4166 | **Higanbana** (Equinox Flower) | JAP | 1958 | Yasujirō Ozu | 120 |
| 4167 | **Busman's Honeymoon** (USA: Haunted Honeymoon) | GB | 1940 | Arthur Woods | 99 |
| 4168 | **Mennesker mødes og sød musik opstår i hjertet** (People Meet and Sweet Music Fills the Heart) | DEN/SWE | 1967 | Henning Carlsen | 99 |
| 4169 | **The Silver Whip** | USA | 1953 | Harmon Jones | 73 |
| 4170 | **Advance to the Rear** (aka: Company of Cowards) | USA | 1964 | George Marshall | 97 |
| 4171 | **Monte Walsh** | USA | 1970 | William A. Fraker | 108 |
| 4172 | **Shane** | USA | 1953(52) | George Stevens | 118 +V |
| 4173 | **Den forsvundne fuldmægtig** | DEN | 1971 | Gert Fredholm | 101 |
| 4174 | **Chamsin** | GER | 1972(70) | Veit Relin | 86 |
| 4175 | **Don Carlos** | AUST | 1960 | Alfred Stöger Josef Gielen | 105(99) |
| 4176 | **Don Carlos** | GER | 1963 | Franz Peter Wirth | 190 |
| 4177 | **Carlos** | GER | 1972(71) | Hans W. Geissendörfer | 102 |
| 4178 | **Kabale und Liebe** (Intrigue and Love) | GDR | 1959 | Martin Hellberg | 108 |
| 4179 | **Maria Stuart** | AUST | 1959 | Alfred Stöger Leopold Lindtberg | 106 |
| 4180 | **Wallenstein** {2 - parts} | GER | 1962 | Franz Peter Wirth | Pt.1, 87 Pt.2, 158 |
| 4181 | **Wilhelm Tell** | GER | 1934 | Heinz Paul | 99 |
| 4182 | **Guglielmo Tell** | IT | 1948 | Giorgio Pastina | 90 |
| 4183 | **Wilhelm Tell** | AUST | 1956 | Josef Gielen Alfred Stöger | 87(85) |
| 4184 | **Wilhelm Tell - Burgen in Flammen** (aka: Flammende Berge) (aka: Bergfeuer lodern) | SWITZ | 1960 | Michel Dickoff Karl Hartl | 128(91) |
| 4185 | | | | | |
| 4186 | **Cara de fogo** [Face of fire] | BRAZ | 1960(59) | Gallileu Garcia | 93 |

| No. | Author | Nationality | Form | Literary Title | Date |
|---|---|---|---|---|---|
| 4187 | Schnitzler, Arthur | Austrian | SS | Doktor Gräsler<br>(Dr Graesler) | 1917 |
| 4188 | Schnitzler, Arthur | Austrian | SS | Fräulein Else | 1923 |
| 4189 | Schnitzler, Arthur | Austrian | P | Liebelei<br>(Light o' Love)<br>(aka: Playing With Love)<br>(aka: The Reckoning) | 1895 |
| 4190 | Schnitzler, Arthur | Austrian | P | Liebelei | 1895 |
| 4191 | Schnitzler, Arthur | Austrian | P | Der Reigen<br>(La Ronde)<br>(aka: Merry-Go-Round) | 1900 |
| 4192 | Schnitzler, Arthur | Austrian | P | Der Reigen | 1900 |
| 4193 | Schnitzler, Arthur | Austrian | P | Der Reigen | 1900 |
| 4194 | Schnitzler, Arthur | Austrian | P | Der Reigen | 1900 |
| 4195 | Schnitzler, Arthur | Austrian | SS | Spiel im Morgengrauen<br>(Daybreak) | 1926(27) |
| 4196 | Schnitzler, Arthur | Austrian | P | Das weite Land | 1911 |
| 4197 | Schönherr, Karl | Austrian | P | Erde<br>(aka: Erde. Eine Komödie des<br>Lebens) | 1907 |
| 4198 | Schönherr, Karl | Austrian | P | Der Judas von Tirol | 1927 |
| 4199 | Schönherr, Karl | Austrian | P | Der Weibsteufel<br>[Demon woman] | 1914 |
| 4200 | Schönherr, Karl | Austrian | P | Der Weibsteufel | 1914 |
| 4201 | Schulberg, Budd | American | N | The Harder They Fall | 1947 |
| 4202 | Schulberg, Budd | American | F-N | Waterfront<br>(GB: On the Waterfront) | 1955 |
| 4203 | Schulberg, Budd | American | SS | Your Arkansas Traveller | 1953 |
| 4204 | Schulz, Bruno | Polish | SS | Sanatorium pod klepsydrą<br>(Sanatorium Under the Sign<br>of the Hourglass) | 1937 |
| 4205 | Sciasia, Leonardo | Italian | N | A ciascuno il suo<br>(A Man's Blessing) | 1966 |
| 4206 | Sciasia, Leonardo | Italian | SS | L'antimonio<br>(Antimony) | 1958 |
| 4207 | Sciasia, Leonardo | Italian | SS | Un caso di coscienza | 1973(coll) |
| 4208 | Sciasia, Leonardo | Italian | N | Il contesto<br>(Equal Danger) | 1971 |
| 4209 | Sciasia, Leonardo | Italian | N | Il giorno della civetta<br>(Mafia Vendetta) | 1961 |
| 4210 | Sciasia, Leonardo | Italian | N | Porte aperte | 1987 |
| 4211 | Sciasia, Leonardo | Italian | N | Todo modo<br>(One Way or Another) | 1974 |
| 4212 | Scott, Gabriel | Norwegian | N | Fant | 1928 |
| 4213 | Scott, Gabriel | Norwegian | SS . | Tante Pose | 1904 |
| 4214 | Scott, Gabriel | Norwegian | N | De vergeløse; et barns historie | 1938 |
| 4215 | Scott, Walter | British(Scot) | N | Ivanhoe | 1819 |
| 4216 | Scott, Walter | British | N | Ivanhoe | 1819 |
| 4217 | Scott, Walter | British | N | Quentin Durward | 1823 |
| 4218 | Scott, Walter | British | N | The Talisman | 1825 |
| 4219 | Scribe, Eugène Legouvé | French | P | Le verre d'eau, ou, les effets et<br>les causes<br>(The Glass of Water) | 1840 |

| No | Film Title | Country of Production | Date | Director(s) | Duration of Film |
|---|---|---|---|---|---|
| 4187 | **Mio caro dottor Graesler** <br> *(The Bachelor)* | IT | 1990 | **Roberto Faenza** | 111 |
| 4188 | **El angel desnudo** | ARG | 1946 | **Carlos Hugo Christensen** | 85 |
| 4189 | **Liebelei** | GER | 1933 | **Max Ophüls** | 88 |
| 4190 | **Christine** <br> *(IT: L'amante pura)* | FR/IT | 1958 | **Pierre Gaspard-Huit** | 101(109) |
| 4191 | **La ronde** <br> *(The Merry-Go-Round)* | FR | 1950 | **Max Ophüls** | 92(97) +V |
| 4192 | **Das große Liebespiel** <br> *(And So To Bed)* | GER/AUST | 1963 | **Alfred Weidenmann** | 137(115) |
| 4193 | **La ronde** <br> *(IT: Il piacere e l'amore)* <br> *(aka: Circle of Love)* | FR/IT | 1964 | **Roger Vadim** | 110(107) |
| 4194 | **Der Reigen** <br> *(aka: La ronde)* <br> *(Merry Go Round)* <br> *(aka: Dance of Love)* | AUST/GER | 1973 | **Otto Schenk** | 122 +V(104) |
| 4195 | **Daybreak** | USA | 1931 | **Jacques Feyder** | 85 |
| 4196 | **Das weite Land** <br> *(FR: Terre étrange)* <br> *(Undiscovered Country)* | FR/AUST/ GER | 1987 | **Luc Bondy** | 101 |
| 4197 | **Trotzige Herzen** <br> *(aka: Die Erbin vom Alpenhof)* <br> *(aka: Erde)* | AUST/ SWITZ | 1949 | **Leopold Hainisch** | 87 |
| 4198 | **Der Judas von Tirol** <br> *(aka: Der ewige Verrat)* | GER | 1933 | **Franz Osten** | 81 |
| 4199 | **Der Weibsteufel** | AUST | 1951 | **Wolfgang Liebeneiner** | 83 |
| 4200 | **Der Weibsteufel** | AUST | 1966 | **Georg Tressler** | 92 |
| 4201 | **The Harder They Fall** | USA | 1956 | **Mark Robson** | 108 |
| 4202 | **On the Waterfront** | USA | 1954 | **Elia Kazan** | 107 +V |
| 4203 | **A Face in the Crowd** | USA | 1957 | **Elia Kazan** | 126 |
| 4204 | **Sanatorium pod klepsydrą** <br> *(The Sandglass)* | POL | 1973 | **Wojciech Jerzy Has** | 123 |
| 4205 | **A ciascuno il suo** <br> *(aka: We Still Kill the Old Way)* <br> *(aka: To Each His Own)* | IT | 1967(66) | **Elio Petri** | 99(93) |
| 4206 | **Una vita venduta** <br> *(A Life For Sale)* | IT | 1976 | **Aldo Florio** | 107(110) |
| 4207 | **Un caso di coscienza** | IT | 1970(69) | **Gianni Grimaldi** | 103(113) |
| 4208 | **Cadaveri eccellenti** <br> *(aka: Cadavres exquis)* <br> *(Illustrious Corpes)* | IT/FR | 1975 | **Francesco Rosi** | 120 |
| 4209 | **Il giorno della civetta** <br> *(The Day of the Owl)* <br> *(FR: La Mafia fait la lui)* <br> *(aka: Mafia)* | IT/FR | 1968 | **Damiano Damiani** | 112 |
| 4210 | **Porte aperte** <br> *(Open Doors)* | IT | 1989 | **Gianni Amelio** | 108 |
| 4211 | **Todo modo** | IT | 1976(75) | **Elio Petri** | 130(110) |
| 4212 | **Fant** | NOR | 1937 | **Tancred Ibsen** | 96 |
| 4213 | **Tante Pose** | NOR | 1940 | **Leif Sinding** | 92 |
| 4214 | **De vergeløse** | NOR | 1939 | **Leif Sinding** | 74 |
| 4215 | **Ivanhoe** | GB | 1952(51) | **Richard Thorpe** | 106 +V |
| 4216 | **Le revanche d'Ivanhoe** <br> *(IT: La rivincita di Ivanhoe)* | FR/IT | 1965(64) | **Amerigo Anton** <br> *(Tanio Boccia)* | 90 |
| 4217 | **The Adventures of Quentin Durward** <br> *(aka: Quentin Durward)* | GB | 1955 | **Richard Thorpe** | 100 |
| 4218 | **King Richard and the Crusaders** | USA | 1954 | **David Butler** | 113 |
| 4219 | **Das Glas Wasser** <br> *(The Glass of Water)* | GER | 1960 | **Helmut Käutner** | 83 |

| No. | Author | Nationality | Form | Literary Title | Date |
|-----|--------|-------------|------|----------------|------|
| 4220 | Sebastian, Mihail | Romanian | P | Jocul de-a vacanţa<br>*[Playing holiday]* | 1946 |
| 4221 | Sebastian, Mihail | Romanian | P | Steaua fără nume<br>*(A Nameless Star)* | 1946 |
| 4222 | Sebastian, Mihail | Romanian | P | Ultima oră<br>*(Stop News)* | 1956 |
| 4223 | Seghers, Anna<br>*(Netty Radványi)* | German | N | Der Aufstand der Fischer von Santa Barbara<br>*(Revolt of the Fishermen of Santa Barbara)* | 1928 |
| 4224 | Seghers, Anna | German | SS | Das Licht auf dem Galgen<br>*[Light on the gallows]* | 1960 |
| 4225 | Seghers, Anna | German | N | Das siebte Kreuz<br>*(The Seventh Cross)* | 1939 |
| 4226 | Seghers, Anna | German | N | Die Toten bleiben jung<br>*(The Dead Stay Young)* | 1949 |
| 4227 | Seghers, Anna | German | N | Transit<br>*(aka: Transit Visa)* | 1944 |
| 4228 | Selby, Hubert | American | N | Last Exit to Brooklyn | 1964 |
| 4229 | Selimović, Meša | Yugoslav(Serb) | N | Derviš i smrt | 1966 |
| 4230 | Sembène, Ousmane<br>*(see: Ousmane Sembène)* | Senegalese(Fr) | SS/N | | |
| 4231 | Seneca, Lucius Annaeus<br>*(the younger)* | Latin(anc) | P | Phaedra | n.d. |
| 4232 | Serafimovich, Aleksandr<br>*(Aleksandr Popov)* | Russian | SS | Zheleznyi potok<br>*(The Iron Flood)* | 1924 |
| 4233 | Sergel, Kristin<br>*(joint, see: Rose, Reginald)* | American | P(TV)-P | | |
| 4234 | Sergel, Sherman L.<br>*(joint, see: Rose, Reginald)* | American | P | | |
| 4235 | Serrano Poncela, Segundo | Spanish | N | El hombre de la cruz verde<br>*[The man with the green cross]* | 1969 |
| 4236 | Sewell, Anna | British | N | Black Beauty | 1877 |
| 4237 | Sewell, Anna | British | N | Black Beauty | 1877 |
| 4238 | Sewell, Anna | British | N | Black Beauty | 1877 |
| 4239 | Shaffer, Anthony | British | P | Sleuth | 1971 |
| 4240 | Shaffer, Peter | British | P | Amadeus | 1980 |
| 4241 | Shaffer, Peter | British | P | Equus | 1973 |
| 4242 | Shaffer, Peter | British | P | Five Finger Exercise | 1958 |
| 4243 | Shaffer, Peter | British | P | The Private Ear | 1964 |
| 4244 | Shaffer, Peter | British | P | The Public Eye | 1962 |
| 4245 | Shaffer, Peter | British | P | The Royal Hunt of the Sun | 1964 |
| 4246 | Shakespeare, William | British | P | Antony and Cleopatra | 1623 |
| 4247 | Shakespeare, William | British | P | As You Like It | 1623 |
| 4248 | Shakespeare, William | British | P | As You Like It | 1623 |
| 4249 | Shakespeare, William | British | P | The Comedy of Errors | 1623 |
| 4250 | Shakespeare, William | British | P | Coriolanus | 1623 |
| 4251 | Shakespeare, William | British | P | Hamlet | 160323 |
| 4252 | Shakespeare, William | British | P | Hamlet | 160323 |
| 4253 | Shakespeare, William | British | P | Hamlet | 160323 |
| 4254 | Shakespeare, William | British | P | Hamlet | 160323 |
| 4255 | Shakespeare, William | British | P | Hamlet | 160323 |
| 4256 | Shakespeare, William | British | P | Hamlet | 160323 |
| 4257 | Shakespeare, William | British | P | Hamlet | 160323 |
| 4258 | Shakespeare, William | British | P | Hamlet | 160323 |
| 4259 | Shakespeare, William | British | P | Hamlet | 160323 |
| 4260 | Shakespeare, William | British | P | Hamlet | 160323 |
| 4261 | Shakespeare, William | British | P | Hamlet | 160323 |

| No | Film Title | Country of Production | Date | Director(s) | Duration of Film |
|---|---|---|---|---|---|
| 4220 | **Al patrulea stol** <br> *[The fourth flock]* | ROM | 1979(78) | **Timotei Ursu** | 101 |
| 4221 | **Mona - l'étoile sans nom** <br> *(ROM: Steaua fără nume)* | FR/ROM | 1966 | **Henri Colpi** | 83 |
| 4222 | **Afacerea Protar** <br> *(Protar Affair)* | ROM | 1956(55) | **Haralambie Boroş** | 82 |
| 4223 | **Vostaniye rybakov** <br> *(Revolt of the Fishermen)* <br> *(aka: Die Fischer von St. Barbara)* | USSR | 1935(34) | **Erwin Piscator** | 97 |
| 4224 | **Das Licht auf dem Galgen** | GDR | 1976 | **Helmut Nitzschke** | 102 |
| 4225 | **The Seventh Cross** | USA | 1944 | **Fred Zinnemann** | 112 |
| 4226 | **Die Toten bleiben jung** | GDR | 1969(68) | **Joachim Kunert** | 112 |
| 4227 | **Fluchtweg nach Marseille** <br> *(Escape Route to Marseilles)* | GER | 1977 | **Ingemo Engström** <br> **Gerhard Theuring** | Pt.1, 90 <br> Pt.2, 120 |
| 4228 | **Letzte Ausfahrt Brooklyn** <br> *(Last Exit to Brooklyn)* | GER | 1989 | **Ulrich Edel** | 98 |
| 4229 | **Derviš i smrt** <br> *(The Dervish and Death)* | YUGO | 1974 | **Zdravko Velimirović** | 104 |
| 4230 | | | | | |
| 4231 | **Fedra** <br> *(Phaedra)* | SP | 1956 | **Manuel Mur Oti** | 94(98) |
| 4232 | **Zheleznyi potok** | USSR | 1967 | **Efim Dzigan** | 104 |
| 4233 | | | | | |
| 4234 | | | | | |
| 4235 | **El segundo poder** <br> *(Second Power)* | SP | 1977(76) | **José María Forqué** | 110(119) |
| 4236 | **Black Beauty** | USA | 1933 | **Phil Rosen** | 68 |
| 4237 | **Black Beauty** | USA | 1946 | **Max Nosseck** | 74 |
| 4238 | **Black Beauty** | GB/GER/SP | 1971 | **James Hill** | 106+V(84) |
| 4239 | **Sleuth** | GB | 1973(72) | **Joseph L. Mankiewicz** | 138 +V |
| 4240 | **Amadeus** | USA | 1984(83) | **Miloš Forman** | 159 +V |
| 4241 | **Equus** | GB | 1977 | **Sidney Lumet** | 137 +V |
| 4242 | **Five Finger Exercise** | USA | 1962 | **Daniel Mann** | 104 |
| 4243 | **The Pad** <br> *(aka: The Pad (...and How to Use It))* | USA | 1966 | **Brian G. Hutton** | 86 |
| 4244 | **Follow Me!** | GB | 1972(71) | **Carol Reed** | 93 |
| 4245 | **The Royal Hunt of the Sun** | GB/USA | 1969 | **Irving Lerner** | 121 |
| 4246 | **Antony and Cleopatra** | SWITZ/SP/GB | 1972 | **Charlton Heston** | 170 +V |
| 4247 | **As You Like It** | GB | 1936 | **Paul Czinner** | 96 |
| 4248 | **As You Like It** | GB/USA | 1978 | **Basil Coleman** | 150 +V |
| 4249 | **The Boys From Syracuse** <br> *{musical version by George Abbot}* | USA | 1940 | **A. Edward Sutherland** | 74 |
| 4250 | **Coriolano, eroe senza patria** <br> *(Coriolanus, Hero Without a Country)* <br> *(aka: Thunder of Battle)* | IT/FR | 1964(63) | **Giorgio Ferroni** | 101(88) |
| 4251 | **Hamlet** | GB | 1948 | **Laurence Olivier** | 153 +V |
| 4252 | **Hamlet** | IND(HIN) | 1955(54) | **Kishore Sahu** | 127 |
| 4253 | **Der Rest ist Schweigen** <br> *(The Rest is Silence)* | GER | 1959 | **Helmut Käutner** | 105 |
| 4254 | **Hamlet** | GER | 1960(59) | **Franz Peter Wirth** | 130 |
| 4255 | **Ophélia** | FR | 1962 | **Claude Chabrol** | 105 |
| 4256 | **Hamlet** | USA | 1964 | **Bill Colleran** | 199 |
| 4257 | **Hamile** <br> *(Hamlet)* | USSR | 1964 | **Grigori Kozintsev** | 150 |
| 4258 | **Ithele na yini vasilias** <br> *[He wanted to be king]* | GR | 1967 | **Angelos Theodoropoulos** | 90 |
| 4259 | **Hamlet** | GB | 1969 | **Tony Richardson** | 117 <br> +V(114) |
| 4260 | **A herança** <br> *[The inheritance]* | BRAZ | 1970 | **Ozualdo R. Candeias** | 87 |
| 4261 | **Hamlet** | GB | 1976 | **Celestino Coronado** | 67 |

| No. | Author | Nationality | Form | Literary Title | Date |
|---|---|---|---|---|---|
| 4262 | **Shakespeare, William** | British | P | **Hamlet** | 160323 |
| 4263 | **Shakespeare, William** | British | P | **Hamlet** | 160323 |
| 4264 | **Shakespeare, William** | British | P | **Hamlet** | 160323 |
| 4265 | **Shakespeare, William** | British | P | **Henry IV**<br>*{Pts I & II}* +<br>**Richard II** +<br>**Henry V** +<br>**The Merry Wives of Windsor** | 1598-1623 |
| 4266 | **Shakespeare, William** | British | P | **Henry IV**<br>*{Pt.1}* | 1598 |
| 4267 | **Shakespeare, William** | British | P | **Henry V** | 160023 |
| 4268 | **Shakespeare, William** | British | P | **Henry V** | 160023 |
| 4269 | **Shakespeare, William** | British | P | **Henry V** | 160023 |
| 4270 | **Shakespeare, William** | British | P | **Julius Caesar** | 1623 |
| 4271 | **Shakespeare, William** | British | P | **Julius Caesar** | 1623 |
| 4272 | **Shakespeare, William** | British | P | **Julius Caesar** | 1623 |
| 4273 | **Shakespeare, William** | British | P | **Julius Caesar** | 1623 |
| 4274 | **Shakespeare, William** | British | P | **Julius Caesar** | 1623 |
| 4275 | **Shakespeare, William** | British | P | **King Lear** | 1608 |
| 4276 | **Shakespeare, William** | British | P | **King Lear** | 1608 |
| 4277 | **Shakespeare, William** | British | P | **King Lear** | 1608 |
| 4278 | **Shakespeare, William** | British | P | **King Lear** | 1608 |
| 4279 | **Shakespeare, William** | British | P | **King Lear** | 1608 |
| 4280 | **Shakespeare, William** | British | P | **Macbeth** | 1623 |
| 4281 | **Shakespeare, William** | British | P | **Macbeth** | 1623 |
| 4282 | **Shakespeare, William** | British | P | **Macbeth** | 1623 |
| 4283 | **Shakespeare, William** | British | P | **Macbeth** | 1623 |
| 4284 | **Shakespeare, William** | British | P | **Macbeth** | 1623 |
| 4285 | **Shakespeare, William** | British | P | **Macbeth** | 1623 |
| 4286 | **Shakespeare, William** | British | P | **Macbeth** | 1623 |
| 4287 | **Shakespeare, William** | British | P | **Macbeth** | 1623 |
| 4288 | **Shakespeare, William** | British | P | **The Merchant of Venice** | 1600 |
| 4289 | **Shakespeare, William** | British | P | **The Merry Wives of Windsor** | 1602 |
| 4290 | **Shakespeare, William** | British | P | **The Merry Wives of Windsor** | 1602 |
| 4291 | **Shakespeare, William** | British | P | **A Midsummer Night's Dream** | 1600 |
| 4292 | **Shakespeare, William** | British | P | **A Midsummer Night's Dream** | 1600 |
| 4293 | **Shakespeare, William** | British | P | **A Midsummer Night's Dream** | 1600 |
| 4294 | **Shakespeare, William** | British | P | **A Midsummer Night's Dream** | 1600 |
| 4295 | **Shakespeare, William** | British | P | **Much Ado About Nothing** | 1600 |
| 4296 | **Shakespeare, William** | British | P | **Much Ado About Nothing** | 1600 |
| 4297 | **Shakespeare, William** | British | P | **Much Ado About Nothing** | 1600 |
| 4298 | **Shakespeare, William** | British | P | **Much Ado About Nothing** | 1600 |
| 4299 | **Shakespeare, William** | British | P | **Much Ado About Nothing** | 1600 |
| 4300 | **Shakespeare, William** | British | P | **Othello** | 1622 |
| 4301 | **Shakespeare, William** | British | P | **Othello** | 1622 |
| 4302 | **Shakespeare, William** | British | P | **Othello** | 1622 |
| 4303 | **Shakespeare, William** | British | P | **Othello** | 1622 |
| 4304 | **Shakespeare, William** | British | P | **Richard II** | 15971608 |
| 4305 | **Shakespeare, William** | British | P | **Richard III** | 15971623 |
| 4306 | **Shakespeare, William** | British | P | **Romeo and Juliet** | 15971623 |

| No | Film Title | Country of Production | Date | Director(s) | Duration of Film |
|---|---|---|---|---|---|
| 4262 | **Hamlet** | GB/USA | 1980 | **Rodney Bennett** | 210 +V |
| 4263 | **Hamlet liikemaailmassa** (Hamlet Goes to Business) | FIN | 1987 | **Aki Kaurismäki** | 86 |
| 4264 | **Hamlet** | USA | 1990 | **Franco Zeffirelli** | 134 +V |
| 4265 | **Campanadas a medianoche** (Chimes at Midnight) (aka: Falstaff) | SP/SWITZ | 1966(65) | **Orson Welles** | 115 |
| 4266 | **Henry IV** | GB/USA | 1979 | **David Giles** | 155 +V |
| 4267 | **Henry V** | GB | 1945(44) | **Laurence Olivier** | 137 +V |
| 4268 | **Henry V** | GB/USA | 1979 | **David Giles** | 170 +V |
| 4269 | **Henry V** | GB | 1989 | **Kenneth Branagh** | 137 +V |
| 4270 | **Julius Caesar** | USA | 1950 | **David Bradley** | 90 |
| 4271 | **Julius Caesar** | USA | 1953 | **Joseph L. Mankiewicz** | 121 +V |
| 4272 | **An Honourable Murder** | GB | 1960 | **Godfrey Grayson** | 69 |
| 4273 | **Julius Caesar** | GB | 1970(69) | **Stuart Burge** | 116 +V |
| 4274 | **Julius Caesar** | GB/USA | 1979 | **Herbert Wise** | 170 +V |
| 4275 | **King Lear** | GB/DEN | 1970 | **Peter Brook** | 137 +V |
| 4276 | **Korol' Lir** (King Lear) | USSR | 1970 | **Grigori Kozintsev** | 139 |
| 4277 | **King Lear** | GB | 1983 | **Michael Elliott** | 180 +V(157) |
| 4278 | **Ran** | FR/JAP | 1985 | **Akira Kurosawa** | 162 +V |
| 4279 | **King Lear** {modern dress} | FR/USA/SWITZ | 1987 | **Jean-Luc Godard** | 91 |
| 4280 | **Macbeth** | USA | 1948 | **Orson Welles** | 109(89) +V |
| 4281 | **Le rideau rouge** | FR | 1952 | **André Barsacq** | 90 |
| 4282 | **Joe Macbeth** {gangster version} | GB | 1955 | **Ken Hughes** | 90 |
| 4283 | **Kumonosu - jo** (Throne of Blood) (aka: Castle of the Spiders Web) (aka: Cobweb Castle) | JAP | 1957 | **Akira Kurosawa** | 110 +V |
| 4284 | **Macbeth** | GB | 1961(60) | **George Schaefer** | 108 |
| 4285 | **Macbeth** | GB/USA | 1971 | **Roman Polanski** | 140 +V |
| 4286 | **Macbeth** | FIN | 1987 | **Pauli Pentti** | 70 |
| 4287 | **Men of Respect** {gangster version} | USA | 1990 | **William Reilly** | 113 |
| 4288 | **Le marchand de Venise** (IT: Il mercante di Venezia) | FR/IT | 1952 | **Pierre Billon** | 102 |
| 4289 | **Die lustigen Weiber** | GER | 1935 | **Carl Hoffmann** | 88 |
| 4290 | **The Merry Wives of Windsor** | GB | 1964 | **George Tressler** | 97 |
| 4291 | **A Midsummer Night's Dream** | USA | 1935 | **Max Reinhardt** **William Dieterle** | 133 +V(120) |
| 4292 | **Sen noci svatojánské** (A Midsummer Night's Dream) {puppets} | CZ | 1959 | **Jiří Trnka** | 76 |
| 4293 | **A Midsummer Night's Dream** | GB | 1968 | **Peter Hall** | 124 |
| 4294 | **A Midsummer Night's Dream** | GB/SP | 1985 | **Celestino Coronado** | 78 |
| 4295 | **Mnogo shuma iz nichevo** (Much Ado About Nothing) | USSR | 1956 | **Lev Zamkovoy** | 94 |
| 4296 | **Viel Lärm um Nichts** | GER | 1964 | **Martin Hellberg** | 101 |
| 4297 | **Mnogo shuma iz nichevo** (Much Ado About Nothing) | USSR | 1973 | **Samson Samsonov** | 101(81) |
| 4298 | **Much Ado About Nothing** | USA | 1978 | **A. J. Anton** **Nick Havinga** | 180(100) |
| 4299 | **Lyubovyu za lyubov'** | USSR | 1983 | **Tatiana Berezantseva** | 84 |
| 4300 | **Othello** | MOR | 1952 | **Orson Welles** | 91 |
| 4301 | **Otello** (Othello) | USSR | 1955 | **Sergei Yutkevich** | 109 +V |
| 4302 | **Venetsianskiy mavr** (Othello) | USSR | 1961(60) | **Vakhtang Chabukiani** | 95 |
| 4303 | **Othello** | GB | 1965 | **Stuart Burge** | 166 +V |
| 4304 | **Richard II** | GB/USA | 1978 | **David Giles** | 150 +V |
| 4305 | **Richard III** | GB | 1955 | **Laurence Olivier** **Anthony Bushell** | 161 +V(150) |
| 4306 | **Romeo and Juliet** | USA | 1936 | **George Cukor** | 127(124) |

| No. | Author | Nationality | Form | Literary Title | Date |
|-----|--------|-------------|------|----------------|------|
| 4307 | Shakespeare, William | British | P | Romeo and Juliet | 15971623 |
| 4308 | Shakespeare, William | British | P | Romeo and Juliet | 15971623 |
| 4309 | Shakespeare, William | British | P | Romeo and Juliet | 15971623 |
| 4310 | Shakespeare, William | British | P | Romeo and Juliet | 15971623 |
| 4311 | Shakespeare, William | British | P | Romeo and Juliet | 15971623 |
| 4312 | Shakespeare, William | British | V | Sonnets | 1609 |
| 4313 | Shakespeare, William | British | P | The Taming of the Shrew | 1623 |
| 4314 | Shakespeare, William | British | P | The Taming of the Shrew | 1623 |
| 4315 | Shakespeare, William | British | P | The Taming of the Shrew | 1623 |
| 4316 | Shakespeare, William | British | P | The Taming of the Shrew | 1623 |
| 4317 | Shakespeare, William | British | P | The Taming of the Shrew | 1623 |
| 4318 | Shakespeare, William | British | P | The Taming of the Shrew | 1623 |
| 4319 | Shakespeare, William | British | P | The Taming of the Shrew | 1623 |
| 4320 | Shakespeare, William | British | P | The Tempest | 1623 |
| 4321 | Shakespeare, William | British | P | The Tempest | 1623 |
| 4322 | Shakespeare, William | British | P | The Tempest | 1623 |
| 4323 | Shakespeare, William | British | P | The Tempest | 1623 |
| 4324 | Shakespeare, William | British | P | The Tempest | 1623 |
| 4325 | Shakespeare, William | British | P | The Tempest | 1623 |
| 4326 | Shakespeare, William | British | P | Twelfth Night | 1623 |
| 4327 | Shakespeare, William | British | P | Twelfth Night | 1623 |
| 4328 | Shakespeare, William | British | P | Twelfth Night | 1623 |
| 4329 | Shakespeare, William | British | P | Twelfth Night | 1623 |
| 4330 | Shakespeare, William | British | P | The Two Gentlemen of Verona | 1623 |
| 4331 | Shakespeare, William | British | P | The Winter's Tale | 1623 |
| 4332 | Shakespeare, William; Fletcher, John | British | P | Henry VIII | 1623 |
| 4333 | Shaw, George Bernard | Irish | P | Androcles and the Lion | 1914 |
| 4334 | Shaw, George Bernard | Irish | P | Arms and the Man | 1898 |
| 4335 | Shaw, George Bernard | Irish | P | Arms and the Man | 1898 |
| 4336 | Shaw, George Bernard | Irish | P | Caesar and Cleopatra | 1901 |
| 4337 | Shaw, George Bernard | Irish | P | The Devil's Disciple | 1901 |
| 4338 | Shaw, George Bernard | Irish | P | The Doctor's Dilemma | 1908 |
| 4339 | Shaw, George Bernard | Irish | P | Great Catherine | 1914 |
| 4340 | Shaw, George Bernard | Irish | P | Heartbreak House | 1919 |
| 4341 | Shaw, George Bernard | Irish | P | How He Lied to Her Husband | 1907 |
| 4342 | Shaw, George Bernard | Irish | P | How He Lied to Her Husband | 1907 |
| 4343 | Shaw, George Bernard | Irish | P | Major Barbara | 1907 |
| 4344 | Shaw, George Bernard | Irish | P | The Millionairess | 1935 |
| 4345 | Shaw, George Bernard | Irish | P | Mrs Warren's Profession | 1898 |
| 4346 | Shaw, George Bernard | Irish | P | Pygmalion | 1913 |
| 4347 | Shaw, George Bernard | Irish | P | Pygmalion | 1913 |
| 4348 | Shaw, George Bernard | Irish | P | Pygmalion | 1913 |
| 4349 | Shaw, George Bernard | Irish | P | Pygmalion | 1913 |
| 4350 | Shaw, George Bernard | Irish | P | Pygmalion | 1913 |
| 4351 | Shaw, George Bernard | Irish | P | Saint Joan | 1924 |
| 4352 | Shaw, George Bernard | Irish | P | Saint Joan | 1924 |

| No | Film Title | Country of Production | Date | Director(s) | Duration of Film |
|---|---|---|---|---|---|
| 4307 | **Romeo y Julieta** | MEX | 1943 | **Miguel M. Delgado** | 100 |
| 4308 | **Romeo and Juliet**<br>*(IT: Giulietta e Romeo)* | GB/IT | 1954 | **Renato Castellani** | 138<br>+V |
| 4309 | **Giulietta e Romeo**<br>*(Romeo and Juliet)* | IT/SP | 1964 | **Riccardo Freda** | 95 |
| 4310 | **Romeo and Juliet**<br>*(IT: Romeo e Giulietta)* | GB/IT | 1968 | **Franco Zeffirelli** | 139(152)<br>+V |
| 4311 | **Romeo and Juliet** | GB/USA | 1978 | **Alvin Rakoff** | 170 +V |
| 4312 | **The Moods of Love** | GB | 1972 | **David Wickes** | 21 |
| 4313 | **Kiss Me Kate**<br>*{musical version}* | USA | 1953 | **George Sidney** | 110<br>+V |
| 4314 | **La fierecilla domada**<br>*(FR: La mégère apprivoisée)* | SP/FR | 1956(55) | **Antonio Román** | 88(94) |
| 4315 | **Ukroshchenie stroptivoy** | USSR | 1961 | **Sergei Kolosov** | 92 |
| 4316 | **The Taming of the Shrew**<br>*(IT: La bisbetica domata)* | USA/IT | 1967(66) | **Franco Zeffirelli** | 126(120)<br>+V |
| 4317 | **The Taming of the Shrew**<br>*{American Conservatory Theatre}* | USA | 1976 | **William Ball**<br>**Kirk Browning** | 120 |
| 4318 | **The Taming of the Shrew** | GB/USA | 1980 | **Jonathan Miller** | 125 +V |
| 4319 | **The Taming of the Shrew**<br>*{Stratford, Ontario production}* | USA | 1981 | **Peter Dews** | 163 |
| 4320 | **The Tempest** | GB | 1969 | **Nicholas Young**<br>**David Snasdell** | 85 |
| 4321 | **The Tempest** | SWE | 1972(71) | **Mats Lonnerblad** | 80 |
| 4322 | **The Tempest** | GB | 1980(79) | **Derek Jarman** | 95 +V |
| 4323 | **The Tempest** | GB/USA | 1980 | **John Gorrie** | 125 +V |
| 4324 | **The Tempest**<br>*{modern dress}* | USA | 1982 | **Paul Mazursky** | 142 |
| 4325 | **Prospero's Books** | HOLL/FR/IT | 1991 | **Peter Greenaway** | 120 +V |
| 4326 | **Dvenadtsataya noch**<br>*(Twelfth Night)* | USSR | 1955 | **Yan Fried** | 87(90) |
| 4327 | **Nichts als Sünde**<br>*{musical version}* | GER | 1965 | **Hans Burger** | 105 |
| 4328 | **Viola und Sebastian** | GER | 1973(71) | **Ottokar Runze** | 93 |
| 4329 | **Twelfth Night** | GB/USA | 1980 | **John Gorrie** | 128 +V |
| 4330 | **Yi jian mei**<br>*[A branch of mei flowers]* | CHN | 1931 | **Bu Wancang** | 90 |
| 4331 | **The Winter's Tale**<br>*{Edinburgh Festival, 1966}* | GB | 1968(66) | **Frank Dunlop** | 151 |
| 4332 | **Henry VIII** | GB/USA | 1979 | **Kevin Billington** | 160<br>+V |
| 4333 | **Androcles and the Lion** | USA | 1952 | **Chester Erskine** | 96 |
| 4334 | **Arms and the Man** | GB | 1932 | **Cecil Lewis** | 85 |
| 4335 | **Helden**<br>*(Heroes)*<br>*(aka: Arms and the Man)* | GER | 1958 | **Franz Peter Wirth** | 96 |
| 4336 | **Caesar and Cleopatra** | GB | 1946(45) | **Gabriel Pascal** | 135 +V |
| 4337 | **The Devil's Disciple** | GB | 1959 | **Guy Hamilton** | 82 |
| 4338 | **The Doctor's Dilemma** | GB | 1959(57) | **Anthony Asquith** | 99 |
| 4339 | **Great Catherine** | GB | 1967 | **Gordon Flemyng** | 98 |
| 4340 | **Scorbnoye beschuvstvie** | USSR | 1986 | **Alexander Sokurov** | 97 |
| 4341 | **How He Lied to Her Husband** | GB | 1931 | **Cecil Lewis** | 33 |
| 4342 | **Kak on Igal eio muzhu** | USSR | 1956 | **Tatiana Berezantseva** | 29 |
| 4343 | **Major Barbara** | GB | 1941 | **Gabriel Pascal**<br>**Harold French**<br>**David Lean** | 112(90) |
| 4344 | **The Millionairess** | GB | 1960 | **Anthony Asquith** | 90 |
| 4345 | **Frau Warrens Gewerbe** | GER/SWITZ | 1960 | **Ákos von Ráthony** | 102 |
| 4346 | **Pygmalion** | GER | 1935 | **Erich Engel** | 93 |
| 4347 | **Pygmalion** | HOLL | 1937 | **Ludwig Berger** | 102(92) |
| 4348 | **Pygmalion** | GB | 1938 | **Anthony Asquith**<br>**Leslie Howard** | 96<br>+V |
| 4349 | **Pigmalion** | USSR | 1957 | **Sergei Alekseev** | 95 |
| 4350 | **My Fair Lady**<br>*{musical version}* | USA | 1964 | **George Cukor** | 175(164)<br>+V |
| 4351 | **Saint Joan** | GB/USA | 1957 | **Otto Preminger** | 110 |
| 4352 | **Saint Joan** | GB | 1977 | **Steven Rumbelow** | 45 |

| No. | Author | Nationality | Form | Literary Title | Date |
|---|---|---|---|---|---|
| 4353 | **Shaw, Irwin** | American | P | **The Gentle People: a Brooklyn Fable** | 1939 |
| 4354 | **Shaw, Irwin** | American | SS | **In the French Style** | 1957 |
| 4355 | **Shaw, Irwin** | American | SS | **Then There Were Three** (aka: Then We Were Three) | 1961 (aka:1957) |
| 4356 | **Shaw, Irwin** | American | SS | **Tip on a Dead Jockey** | 1955 |
| 4357 | **Shaw, Irwin** | American | N | **Two Weeks in Another Town** | 1960 |
| 4358 | **Shaw, Irwin** | American | N | **The Young Lions** | 1948 |
| 4359 | **Sheldon, Edward Brewster** (see: MacArthur, Charles) | American | P | | |
| 4360 | **Shelley, Mary Wollstonecraft** | British | N | **Frankenstein** (aka: Frankenstein, or the Modern Prometheus) | 1818 |
| 4361 | **Shelley, Mary Wollstonecraft** | British | N | **Frankenstein** | 1818 |
| 4362 | **Shelley, Mary Wollstonecraft** | British | N | **Frankenstein** | 1818 |
| 4363 | **Shelley, Mary Wollstonecraft** | British | N | **Frankenstein** | 1818 |
| 4364 | **Shelley, Mary Wollstonecraft** | British | N | **Frankenstein** | 1818 |
| 4365 | **Shelley, Mary Wollstonecraft** | British | N | **Frankenstein** | 1818 |
| 4366 | **Shelley, Mary Wollstonecraft** | British | N | **Frankenstein** | 1818 |
| 4367 | **Shelley, Mary Wollstonecraft** | British | N | **Frankenstein** | 1818 |
| 4368 | **Shen Congwen** (Shen Ts'ung-wen) | Chinese | SS | **Bian cheng** (aka: Pien-ch'eng) [Frontier city] | 193[?] |
| 4369 | **Shen Congwen** | Chinese | SS | **Xiao Xiao** (aka: Hsiao-Hsiao) | 193[?] |
| 4370 | **Shen Fu** (see: Shen Sanbai) | Chinese | AUT | | |
| 4371 | **Shen Sanbai** (as: Shen Fu) | Chinese | AUT | **Fu sheng liu ji** (aka: Fou sheng liu chi) (Shen Fu, Chapters From a Floating Life) | 18[?] |
| 4372 | **Shen Ts'ung-wen** (see: Shen Congwen) | Chinese | SS | | |
| 4373 | **Shen Yanbing** (Shen Yen-ping) (as: Mao Dun) (Mao Tun) | Chinese | SS | **Chuncan** (aka: Ch'un ts'an) (Spring Silkworms) | 1931 |
| 4374 | **Shen Yanbing** (as: Mao Dun) | Chinese | N | **Fu shi** (aka: Fu-shih) [Corruption] | 1941(43) |
| 4375 | **Shen Yanbing** (as: Mao Dun) | Chinese | SS | **Linjia puzi** (aka: Lin chia p'tzu) (Lin's Store) (aka: The Shop of the Lin Family) | 1932 |
| 4376 | **Shen Yen-ping** (see: Shen Yanbing) | Chinese | N | | |
| 4377 | **Shepard, Sam** | American | P | **Fool For Love** | 1984 |
| 4378 | **Shepard, Sam** | American | P | **Motel Chronicles, Paris, Texas** | 1985 |
| 4379 | **Shepard, Sam** | American | P | **True West** | 1980 |
| 4380 | **Sheridan, Richard Brinsley** | Irish | P | **The School For Scandal** | 1781 |
| 4381 | **Sherriff, R. C.** | British | P | **Badger's Green** | 1930 |
| 4382 | **Sherriff, R. C.** | British | P | **Badger's Green** | 1930 |
| 4383 | **Sherriff, R. C.** | British | P | **Home at Seven** | 1950 |
| 4384 | **Sherriff, R. C.** | British | P | **Journey's End** | 1929 |
| 4385 | **Sherriff, R. C.** | British | P | **Journey's End** | 1929 |
| 4386 | **Sherriff, R. C.** | British | P | **Journey's End** | 1929 |
| 4387 | **Sherwood, R. E.** | American | P | **Abe Lincoln of Illinois** | 1939 |
| 4388 | **Sherwood, R. E.** | American | P | **Idiot's Delight** | 1936 |
| 4389 | **Sherwood, R. E.** | American | P | **The Petrified Forest** | 1935 |
| 4390 | **Sherwood, R. E.** | American | P | **The Petrified Forest** | 1935 |
| 4391 | **Sherwood, R. E.** | American | P | **The Queen's Husband** | 1928 |
| 4392 | **Sherwood, R. E.** | American | P | **Reunion in Vienna** | 1932 |
| 4393 | **Sherwood, R. E.** | American | P | **The Road to Rome** | 1927 |
| 4394 | **Sherwood, R. E.** | American | P | **This Is New York** | 1931 |

| No | Film Title | Country of Production | Date | Director(s) | Duration of Film |
|---|---|---|---|---|---|
| 4353 | Out of the Fog | USA | 1941 | Anatole Litvak | 86 |
| 4354 | In the French Style (FR: A la française) | USA/FR | 1963 | Robert Parrish | 105 |
| 4355 | Three | GB | 1969 | James Salter | 105(95) |
| 4356 | Tip on a Dead Jockey (GB: Time For Action) | USA | 1957 | Richard Thorpe | 99 |
| 4357 | Two Weeks in Another Town | USA | 1962 | Vincente Minnelli | 107 |
| 4358 | The Young Lions | USA | 1958 | Edward Dmytryk | 167 +V |
| 4359 | | | | | |
| 4360 | Frankenstein | USA | 1931 | James Whale | 71 +V |
| 4361 | The Bride of Frankenstein | USA | 1935 | James Whale | 75 |
| 4362 | Son of Frankenstein | USA | 1939 | Rowland V. Lee | 99 |
| 4363 | The Curse of Frankenstein | GB | 1957 | Terence Fisher | 83 |
| 4364 | The Horror of Frankenstein | GB | 1970 | Jimmy Sangster | 95 |
| 4365 | Frankenstein: the True Story | GB | 1973 | Jack Smight | 123 |
| 4366 | Victor Frankenstein | SWE/IRE | 1977 | Calvin Floyd | 91 |
| 4367 | The Bride | GB | 1985 | Franc Roddam | 119 |
| 4368 | Bian cheng | CHN | 1984 | Ling Zifeng | 101 |
| 4369 | Xiang Nu Xiao Xiao [Xiao Xiao, the Hunan girl] | CHN | 1986 | Xie Fei Ulan | 100 |
| 4370 | | | | | |
| 4371 | Fu sheng liu ji | CHN | 1947 | Pei Chong | 110 |
| 4372 | | | | | |
| 4373 | Chuncan (Spring Silkworms) | CHN | 1933 | Cheng Bugao (Cheng Bu-kao) | 108 |
| 4374 | Fu shi | CHN | 1950 | Zuolin (Huang Zuolin) | 119 |
| 4375 | Linjia puzi (aka: Lin chia p'tzu) (The Lin Family Shop) | CHN | 1959 | Shuihua (Zhang Shuihua) | 87(90) |
| 4376 | | | | | |
| 4377 | Fool For Love | USA | 1985 | Robert Altman | 103 +V |
| 4378 | Paris Texas | GER/FR | 1984 | Wim Wenders | 114(150) +V |
| 4379 | True West | USA | 1982 | Alan Goldstein | 120 |
| 4380 | The School For Scandal | GB | 1930 | Maurice Elvey | 76 |
| 4381 | Badger's Green | GB | 1934 | Adrian Brunel | 68 |
| 4382 | Badger's Green | GB | 1949 | John Irwin | 62 |
| 4383 | Home at Seven (USA: Murder on Monday) | GB | 1952 | Ralph Richardson | 85 |
| 4384 | Journey's End | GB/USA | 1930 | James Whale | 120 |
| 4385 | Die Andere Seite | GER | 1931 | Heinz Paul | 107 |
| 4386 | Aces High | GB/FR | 1977(76) | Jack Gold | 114 +V |
| 4387 | Abe Lincoln in Illinois (GB: Spirit of the People) | USA | 1940 | John Cromwell | 110 |
| 4388 | Idiot's Delight | USA | 1939 | Clarence Brown | 105 |
| 4389 | The Petrified Forest | USA | 1936(35) | Archie Mayo | 82 |
| 4390 | Escape in the Desert | USA | 1945 | Edward A. Blatt | 81 |
| 4391 | The Royal Bed (GB: The Queen's Husband) | USA | 1930 | Lowell Sherman | 75 |
| 4392 | Reunion in Vienna | USA | 1933 | Sidney A. Franklin | 100 |
| 4393 | Jupiter's Darling | USA | 1955(54) | George Sidney | 96 |
| 4394 | Two Kinds of Women | USA | 1932 | William C. de Mille | 68 |

| No. | Author | Nationality | Form | Literary Title | Date |
|-----|--------|-------------|------|----------------|------|
| 4395 | **Sherwood, R. E.** | American | P | **Waterloo Bridge** | 1930 |
| 4396 | **Sherwood, R. E.** | American | P | **Waterloo Bridge** | 1930 |
| 4397 | **Sherwood, R. E.** | American | P | **Waterloo Bridge** | 1930 |
| 4398 | **Shevchenko, Taras** | Russian(Ukr) | V | **Lileya** | 1888 |
| 4399 | **Shiga Naoya** | Japanese | N | **Anya kōro**<br>*(A Dark Night's Passing)* | 1922-37 |
| 4400 | **Shiina Rinzō** | Japanese | SS | **Mujakina hitobito** | 1952 |
| 4401 | **Shimazaki Tōson** | Japanese | N | **Hakai**<br>*(The Broken Commandment)* | 1906 |
| 4402 | **Shimazaki Tōson** | Japanese | N | **Hakai** | 1906 |
| 4403 | **Shi Naian**<br>*(Shin Nai- an);*<br>**Luo Guanzhong**<br>*(Lo Kuan-chung)* | Chinese | N | **Shuihu zhuan**<br>*(aka: Shui hu chuan)*<br>*(The Water Margin)*<br>*(aka: All Men Are Brothers)* | c.1500 |
| 4404 | **Shi Naian;**<br>**Luo Guanzhong** | Chinese | N | **Shuihu zhuan** | c.1500 |
| 4405 | **Shi Naian;**<br>**Luo Guanzhong** | Chinese | N | **Shuihu zhuan** | c.1500 |
| 4406 | **Shin Nai-an**<br>*(see: Shi Naian)* | Chinese | N | | |
| 4407 | **Sholokhov, Mikhail** | Russian | SS | **Chuzhaia krov'**<br>*(Alien Blood)* | 1926 |
| 4408 | **Sholokhov, Mikhail** | Russian | SS | **Donskie rasskazy**<br>*[Tales of the Don]* | 1926 |
| 4409 | **Sholokhov, Mikhail** | Russian | SS | **Nakhalenok**<br>*(The Shame Child)*<br>*(aka: The Bastard)* | 1926 |
| 4410 | **Sholokhov, Mikhail** | Russian | SS | **O kolchake, krapive i prochem**<br>*(On Kolchak, Nettles and Other*<br>*Things)* | 1926 |
| 4411 | **Sholokhov, Mikhail** | Russian | N | **Oni srazhalis' za rodinu**<br>*(They Fought for Their Country)* | 1943-44 |
| 4412 | **Sholokhov, Mikhail** | Russian | N | **Podnyataya tselina**<br>*(Virgin Soil Upturned)*<br>*(aka: Seeds of Tomorrow)* | 1932-60 |
| 4413 | **Sholokhov, Mikhail** | Russian | N | **Podnyataya tselina** | 1932-60 |
| 4414 | **Sholokhov, Mikhail** | Russian | SS | **Rodinka**<br>*(The Birthmark)* +<br>**Kolevert'**<br>*[The whirlpool]*<br>*[aka: The red guards]* +<br>**Chervotochina** *(Dry Rot)* +<br>**Prodkomissar**<br>*(Food Commissar)* | 1924+<br>1926+<br>1925 |
| 4415 | **Sholokhov, Mikhail** | Russian | SS | **Shibalkovo semia**<br>*[Shibalok's seed]* | 1926 |
| 4416 | **Sholokhov, Mikhail** | Russian | SS | **Sud'ba cheloveka**<br>*(The Fate of a Man)* | 1956-57 |
| 4417 | **Sholokhov, Mikhail** | Russian | SS | **Sud'ba cheloveka** | 1957 |
| 4418 | **Sholokhov, Mikhail** | Russian | N | **Tikhy Don**<br>*(And Quiet Flows the Don)* | 1929 |
| 4419 | **Sholokhov, Mikhail** | Russian | N | **Tikhy Don** | 1929 |
| 4420 | **Sholokhov, Mikhail** | Russian | SS | **Zherebenok**<br>*(The Foal)*<br>*(aka: The Colt)* | 1926 |

| No | Film Title | Country of Production | Date | Director(s) | Duration of Film |
|----|-----------|----------------------|------|-------------|------------------|
| 4395 | **Waterloo Bridge** | USA | 1931 | **James Whale** | 72 |
| 4396 | **Waterloo Bridge** | USA | 1940 | **Mervyn LeRoy** | 101 |
| 4397 | **Gaby** | USA | 1956 | **Curtis Bernhardt** | 97 |
| 4398 | **Lileya** | USSR | 1959 | **Vakhtang Vronsky** **Vasili Lapoknish** | 88 |
| 4399 | **Anya kōro** *(Pilgrimage at Night)* | JAP | 1959 | **Shirō Toyoda** | 140 |
| 4400 | **Entotsuno mieru basho** *(Four Chimneys)* *(aka: Where Chimneys Are Seen)* | JAP | 1953 | **Heinosuke Gosho** | 108 |
| 4401 | **Hakai** *(Apostasy)* *(aka: The Broken Commandment)* | JAP | 1948 | **Keisuke Kinoshita** | 99 |
| 4402 | **Hakai** *(The Sin)* *(aka: The Broken Commandment)* *(aka: The Outcast)* | JAP | 1962(61) | **Kon Ichikawa** | 119 |
| 4403 | **Wu Song and Pan Jinlian** {episode} | CHN | 1938 | **Wu Cun** | 90 |
| 4404 | **Wu Song** {episode} | CHN | 1963 | **Ying Yunwei** **Yu Zhongying** | 109 |
| 4405 | **Ye zhu lin** [Wild boar forest] {episode} | CHN | 1965 | **Cui Wei** | 109 |
| 4406 | | | | | |
| 4407 | **Neproshennaya lubov'** | USSR | 1964 | **Vladimir Monakhov** | 92 |
| 4408 | **Smertnyi vrag** | USSR | 1971 | **Yevgeny Matveyev** | 86 |
| 4409 | **Nakhalenok** | USSR | 1961 | **Eugene Karelov** | 57 |
| 4410 | **Kogda kazaki plachut** | USSR | 1963 | **Eugene Morgunov** | 28 |
| 4411 | **Oni srazhalis' za rodinu** | USSR | 1975 | **Sergei Bondarchuk** | Pt.1, 82 Pt.2, 77 |
| 4412 | **Podnyataya tselina** *(Virgin Soil Upturned)* *(aka: The Soil Upturned)* | USSR | 1940 | **Yuli Raizman** | 117 |
| 4413 | **Podnyataya tselina** *(Virgin Soil Upturned)* {Pt.1, 1959} {Pt.2-3, 1960} | USSR | 1959-61 | **Alexander Ivanov** | Pt.1, 95 Pt.2, 101 Pt.3, 107 |
| 4414 | **V lazorevoy stepi** | USSR | 1970 | **Valery Lonskoi** **Vladimir Shamshurin** **Vitali Koltzov** **Oleg Bondarev** | 103 |
| 4415 | **Donskaya povest'** | USSR | 1964 | **Vladimir Fetin** | 95 |
| 4416 | **Stranitzy rasskaza** | USSR | 1957 | **Boris Kryzhanovsky** **Mikhail Tereshchenko** | 30 |
| 4417 | **Sud'ba cheloveka** *(Destiny of a Man)* *(aka: The Fate of a Man)* | USSR | 1959 | **Sergei Bondarchuk** | 102(98) |
| 4418 | **Tikhy Don** *(The Quiet Don)* *(aka: Cossacks of the Don)* | USSR | 1931 | **Olga Preobrazhenskaya** | 87 |
| 4419 | **Tikhy Don** *(And Quiet Flows the Don)* {3 - parts} | USSR | 1956-58 | **Sergei Gerasimov** | Pt.1, 110 Pt.2, 117 Pt.3, 123 |
| 4420 | **Zherebenok** | USSR | 1960(59) | **Vladimir Fetin** | 42 |

| No. | Author | Nationality | Form | Literary Title | Date |
|---|---|---|---|---|---|
| 4421 | **Shu Ch'ing-ch'un** (see: Shu Qingchun) | Chinese | P | | |
| 4422 | **Shu Qingchun** (Shu Ch'ing-ch'un) (as: Lao She) (Lau Shaw) | Chinese | P | **Cha guan** (aka: Ch'a-kuan) [The tea-house] | 1964 |
| 4423 | **Shu Qingchun** (as: Lao She) | Chinese | P | **Fang Zhenzhu** [The teahouse singer] | 1950 |
| 4424 | **Shu Qingchun** (as: Lao She) | Chinese | N | **Gu shu yi ren** [The storysinger] | 194[?] |
| 4425 | **Shu Qingchun** (as: Lao She) | Chinese | P | **Longxu gou** (Dragon Beard Ditch) | 1950 |
| 4426 | **Shu Qingchun** (as: Lao She) | Chinese | N | **Lou tuo xiangzi** (The Rickshaw Boy) | 1944 |
| 4427 | **Shu Qingchun** (as: Lao She) | Chinese | SS | **Wo zhe yibeizi** [Such a life as mine] | 1949 |
| 4428 | **Shu Qingchun** (as: Lao She) | Chinese | SS | **Yue yaer** [The crescent] | 194[?] |
| 4429 | **Shute, Nevil** (Nevil Shute Norway) | British | N | **Landfall** | 1940 |
| 4430 | **Shute, Nevil** | British | N | **The Lonely Road** | 1932 |
| 4431 | **Shute, Nevil** | British | N | **No Highway** | 1948 |
| 4432 | **Shute, Nevil** | British | N | **On the Beach** | 1957 |
| 4433 | **Shute, Nevil** | British | N | **The Pied Piper** | 1942 |
| 4434 | **Shute, Nevil** | British | N | **A Town Like Alice** (USA: The Legacy) | 1950 |
| 4435 | **Sienkiewicz, Henryk** | Polish | SS | **Janko muzykant** (Janko the Musician) | 1879(80) |
| 4436 | **Sienkiewicz, Henryk** | Polish | N | **Krzyżacy** (The Knights of the Cross) (aka: The Teutonic Knights) | 1900 |
| 4437 | **Sienkiewicz, Henryk** | Polish | N | **Ogniem i mieczem** (With Fire and Sword) | 1884 |
| 4438 | **Sienkiewicz, Henryk** | Polish | N | **Pan Wołodyjowski** (Pan Michael) | 1887-88 |
| 4439 | **Sienkiewicz, Henryk** | Polish | N | **Potop** (The Deluge) | 1886 |
| 4440 | **Sienkiewicz, Henryk** | Polish | N | **Quo vadis?** | 1896 |
| 4441 | **Sienkiewicz, Henryk** | Polish | SS | **Szkice węglem** (Charcoal Sketches) | 1877(80) |
| 4442 | **Sienkiewicz, Henryk** | Polish | N | **W pustyni i w puszczy** (In Desert and Wilderness) (aka: Through the Desert) | 1911 |
| 4443 | **Sillanpää, Frans E.** | Finnish | N | **Elämä ja aurinko** [Life and the sun] | 1916 |
| 4444 | **Sillanpää, Frans E.** | Finnish | N | **Elokuu** [August] | 1941 |
| 4445 | **Sillanpää, Frans E.** | Finnish | N | **Ihmiselon ihanuus ja kurjuus** [The glory and misery of human life] | 1945 |
| 4446 | **Sillanpää, Frans E.** | Finnish | N | **Ihmiset suviyössä** (People in the Summer Night) | 1934 |
| 4447 | **Sillanpää, Frans E.** | Finnish | N | **Miehen tie** | 1932 |
| 4448 | **Sillanpää, Frans E.** | Finnish | N | **Nuorena nukkunut** (...Fallen Asleep While Young) (aka: The Maid Silja) | 1931 |
| 4449 | **Sillanpää, Frans E.** | Finnish | N | **Nuorena nukkunut** | 1931 |
| 4450 | **Sillitoe, Alan** | British | N | **The General** | 1960 |
| 4451 | **Sillitoe, Alan** | British | SS | **The Loneliness of the Long-Distance Runner** | 1959 |
| 4452 | **Sillitoe, Alan** | British | SS | **The Ragman's Daughter** | 1963 |
| 4453 | **Sillitoe, Alan** | British | N | **Saturday Night and Sunday Morning** | 1958 |

| No | Film Title | Country of Production | Date | Director(s) | Duration of Film |
|----|-----------|----------------------|------|-------------|------------------|
| 4421 | | | | | |
| 4422 | **Cha guan** | CHN | 1982 | **Xie Tian** | 125 |
| 4423 | **Fang Zhenzhu** | CHN | 1952 | **Xu Changlin** | 109 |
| 4424 | **Gu shu yi ren** | CHN | 1988 | **Tian Zhuangzhuang** | 98 |
| 4425 | **Longxu gou** (Dragon Beard Ditch) | CHN | 1952 | **Xian Qun** | 119 |
| 4426 | **Lou tou xiangzi** | CHN | 1982 | **Ling Zifeng** | 119 |
| 4427 | **Wo zhe yibeizi** | CHN | 1950 | **Shi Hui** | 119 |
| 4428 | **Yue yaer** | CHN | 1986 | **Sun Yu** | 93 |
| 4429 | **Landfall** | GB | 1949 | **Ken Annakin** | 87 |
| 4430 | **The Lonely Road** (USA: Scotland Yard Commands) | GB | 1936 | **James Flood** | 80 |
| 4431 | **No Highway** (USA: No Highway in the Sky) | GB | 1951 | **Henry Koster** | 99 |
| 4432 | **On the Beach** | USA | 1959 | **Stanley Kramer** | 134 +V |
| 4433 | **The Pied Piper** | USA | 1942 | **Irving Pichel** | 86 |
| 4434 | **A Town Like Alice** (aka: Rape of Malaya) | GB | 1956 | **Jack Lee** | 117 +V(111) |
| 4435 | **Janko muzykant** | POL | 1930 | **Ryszard Ordyński** | 103 |
| 4436 | **Krzyżacy** (Knights of the Teutonic Order) (USA: Knights of the Black Cross) | POL | 1960 | **Aleksander Ford** | 173 |
| 4437 | **Col ferro e col fuoco** (With Fire and Sword) (aka: Daggers of Blood) | IT/FR | 1962(61) | **Fernando Cerchio** | 100(96) |
| 4438 | **Pan Wołodyjowski** (Colonel Wołodyjowski) | POL | 1969(68) | **Jerzy Hoffman** | 160(155) |
| 4439 | **Potop** (The Deluge) | POL | 1974 | **Jerzy Hoffman** | Pt.1, 168 (211). Pt.2, 146 (182) |
| 4440 | **Quo Vadis** | USA | 1951 | **Mervyn LeRoy** | 166 +V |
| 4441 | **Szkice węglem** | POL | 1957 | **Antoni Bohdziewicz** | 97 |
| 4442 | **W pustyni i w puszczy** (In Desert and Wilderness) | POL | 1973 | **Władysław Ślesicki** | Pt.1, 98 Pt.2, 95 |
| 4443 | **Poika eli kesäänsä** [The boy lived up his summer] | FIN | 1955 | **Roland af Hällström** | 82 |
| 4444 | **Elokuu** (Harvest Month) (USA: Destiny) | FIN | 1956 | **Matti Kassila** | 90 |
| 4445 | **Ihmiselon ihanuus ja kurjuus** | FIN | 1988 | **Matti Kassila** | 95 |
| 4446 | **Ihmiset suviyössä** | FIN | 1948 | **Valentin Vaala** | 66 |
| 4447 | **Miehen tie** (A Man's Way) | FIN | 1940 | **Nyrki Tapiovaara** **Hugo Hytönen** | 93 |
| 4448 | **Nuorena nukkunut** | FIN | 1937 | **Teuvo Tulio** | 96 |
| 4449 | **Silja - nuorena nukkunut** [Silja - fallen asleep when young] | FIN | 1956 | **Jack Witikka** | 91 |
| 4450 | **Counterpoint** | USA | 1967 | **Ralph Nelson** | 99(107) |
| 4451 | **The Loneliness of the Long Distance Runner** | GB | 1962 | **Tony Richardson** | 104 |
| 4452 | **The Ragman's Daughter** (aka: The Tea-Leaf) | GB | 1972 | **Harold Becker** | 94 +V(90) |
| 4453 | **Saturday Night and Sunday Morning** | GB | 1960 | **Karel Reisz** | 89 |

**245**

| No. | Author | Nationality | Form | Literary Title | Date |
|-----|--------|-------------|------|----------------|------|
| 4454 | **Silone, Ignazio** | Italian | N | **Fontamara** | 1930 |
| 4455 | **Silva, Aguinaldo** | Brazilian | N | **República dos assassinos** | 1976 |
| 4456 | **Simenon, Georges** | French | N | **L'affaire Saint-Fiacre** <br> *(The Saint-Fiacre Affair)* <br> *(aka: Maigret Goes Home)* | 1932 |
| 4457 | **Simenon, Georges** | French | N | **L'ainé des Ferchaux** <br> *(Magnet of Doom)* <br> *(aka: The First Born)* | 1945 |
| 4458 | **Simenon, Georges** | French | SS | **Annette et la dame blonde** | 1963 <br> (coll) |
| 4459 | **Simenon, Georges** | French | N | **L'assassin** <br> *(The Murderer)* | 1937 |
| 4460 | **Simenon, Georges** | French | SS | **Le baron de l'écluse** | 1954 |
| 4461 | **Simenon, Georges** | French | SS | **Le bateau d'Émile** | 1954 |
| 4462 | **Simenon, Georges** | French | N | **Betty** | 1961 |
| 4463 | **Simenon, Georges** | French | SS | **Les caves du Majestic** | 1942 |
| 4464 | **Simenon, Georges** | French | SS | **Cécile est morte** | 1942 |
| 4465 | **Simenon, Georges** | French | N | **Le chat** <br> *(The Cat)* | 1967 |
| 4466 | **Simenon, Georges** | French | N | **Le chien jaune** <br> *(A Face For a Clue)* | 1931 |
| 4467 | **Simenon, Georges** | French | N | **La danseuse du Gai-Moulin** <br> *(At the 'Gai-Moulin')* | 1931 |
| 4468 | **Simenon, Georges** | French | N | **En cas de malheur** <br> *(In Case of Emergency)* | 1956 |
| 4469 | **Simenon, Georges** | French | SS | **Les fantômes du chapelier** <br> *(The Hatter's Ghost)* | 1949 |
| 4470 | **Simenon, Georges** | French | N | **Les fiançailles de Mr Hire** <br> *(Mr Hire's Engagement)* | 1933 |
| 4471 | **Simenon, Georges** | French | N | **Les fiançailles de Mr Hire** | 1933 |
| 4472 | **Simenon, Georges** | French | N | **Le fils Cardinaud** <br> *(Young Cardinaud)* | 1942 |
| 4473 | **Simenon, Georges** | French | SS | **Le fond de la bouteille** <br> *(The Bottom of the Bottle)* | 1949 |
| 4474 | **Simenon, Georges** | French | SS | **Les frères Rico** <br> *(The Brothers Rico)* | 1952 |
| 4475 | **Simenon, Georges** | French | N | **L'homme de Londres** <br> *(Newhaven-Dieppe)* | 1934 |
| 4476 | **Simenon, Georges** | French | N | **L'homme de Londres** | 1934 |
| 4477 | **Simenon, Georges** | French | N | **L'homme qui regardait passer les trains** <br> *(The Man Who Watched the Trains Go By)* | 1938 |
| 4478 | **Simenon, Georges** | French | SS | **L'horloger d'Everton** <br> *(The Watchmaker of Everton)* | 1954 |
| 4479 | **Simenon, Georges** | French | N | **Les inconnus dans la maison** <br> *(Strangers in the House)* | 1940 |
| 4480 | **Simenon, Georges** | French | N | **Les inconnus dans la maison** | 1940 |
| 4481 | **Simenon, Georges** | French | N | **Lettre à mon juge** <br> *(Act of Passion)* | 1947 |
| 4482 | **Simenon, Georges** | French | N | **Le locataire** <br> *(The Lodger)* | 1934 |
| 4483 | **Simenon, Georges** | French | N | **Le locataire** | 1934 |
| 4484 | **Simenon, Georges** | French | N | **Maigret au 'Picratt's'** <br> *(Maigret in Montmartre)* | 1951 |
| 4485 | **Simenon, Georges** | French | N | **Maigret, Lognon et les gangsters** <br> *(Inspector Maigret and the Killers)* <br> *(aka: Maigret and the Gangsters)* | 1952 |

| No | Film Title | Country of Production | Date | Director(s) | Duration of Film |
|---|---|---|---|---|---|
| 4454 | **Fontamara** | IT | 1980 | **Carlo Lizzani** | 134(139) |
| 4455 | **República dos assassinos** *(Republic of Assassins)* | BRAZ | 1979 | **Miguel Faria, Jr.** | 100 |
| 4456 | **Maigret et l'affaire Saint-Fiacre** | FR | 1959 | **Jean Delannoy** | 98 |
| 4457 | **L'ainé des Ferchaux** *(IT: Lo sciacallo)* *(Magnet of Doom)* | FR/IT | 1963 | **Jean-Pierre Melville** | 104 |
| 4458 | **Annette et la dame blonde** | FR | 1941 | **Jean Dréville** | 85 |
| 4459 | **Der Mörder** | GER | 1979(78) | **Ottokar Runze** | 107 |
| 4460 | **Le baron de l'écluse** *(IT: Il barone)* | FR/IT | 1960 | **Jean Delannoy** | 95 |
| 4461 | **Le bateau d'Émile** *(IT: Letto, fortuna e femmine)* | FR/IT | 1962 | **Denys de la Patellière** | 98(100) |
| 4462 | **Betty** | FR | 1992 | **Claude Chabrol** | 100 |
| 4463 | **Les caves du Majestic** | FR | 1945 | **Richard Pottier** | 100 |
| 4464 | **Cécile est morte** | FR | 1944(43) | **Maurice Tourneur** | 90 |
| 4465 | **Le chat** *(The Cat)* *(IT: Le chat, l'implacabile uomo di Saint Germain)* | FR/IT | 1971 | **Pierre Granier-Deferre** | 88(94) |
| 4466 | **Le chien jaune** | FR | 1932 | **Jean Tarride** | 88 |
| 4467 | **Maigret und sein größter Fall** *(IT: Il caso difficile del commissario Maigret)* | AUST/IT/ FR | 1967(66) | **Alfred Weidenmann** | 90(93) |
| 4468 | **En cas de malheur** *(IT: La ragazza del peccato)* *(Love Is My Profession)* | FR/IT | 1958 | **Claude Autant-Lara** | 120 |
| 4469 | **Les fantômes du chapelier** *(The Hatter's Ghosts)* *(aka: The Hatmaker)* | FR | 1982 | **Claude Chabrol** | 129 |
| 4470 | **Panique** *(Panic)* | FR | 1946 | **Julien Duvivier** | 98 |
| 4471 | **Monsieur Hire** *(aka: Mr Hire's Engagement)* | FR | 1989 | **Patrice Leconte** | 79 +V |
| 4472 | **Le sang à la tête** | FR | 1956 | **Gilles Grangier** | 83 |
| 4473 | **The Bottom of the Bottle** *(GB: Beyond the River)* | USA | 1956 | **Henry Hathaway** | 88 |
| 4474 | **The Brothers Rico** | USA | 1957 | **Phil Karlson** | 91 |
| 4475 | **L'homme de Londres** | FR | 1943 | **Henri Decoin** | 98 |
| 4476 | **Temptation Harbour** | GB | 1947 | **Lance Comfort** | 104 |
| 4477 | **The Man Who Watched Trains Go By** *(aka: Paris Express)* | GB | 1952 | **Harold French** | 80 |
| 4478 | **L'horloger de Saint-Paul** *(The Watchmaker of Saint-Paul)* *(aka: The Watchmaker)* *(aka: The Clockmaker)* | FR | 1974(73) | **Bertrand Tavernier** | 105 |
| 4479 | **Les inconnus dans la maison** *(Strangers in the House)* | FR | 1942(41) | **Henri Decoin** | 94 |
| 4480 | **Stranger in the House** *(aka: Cop-Out)* | GB | 1967 | **Pierre Rouve** | 104 +V(90) |
| 4481 | **Le fruit défendu** *(Forbidden Fruit)* | FR | 1952 | **Henri Verneuil** | 103 |
| 4482 | **Dernier refuge** | FR | 1947 | **Marc Maurette** | 90 |
| 4483 | **L'étoile du Nord** *(The North Star)* | FR | 1982 | **Pierre Granier-Deferre** | 124 |
| 4484 | **Maigret à Pigalle** | FR/IT | 1966 | **Mario Landi** | 108 |
| 4485 | **Maigret voit rouge** *(IT: Maigret e i gangsters)* | FR/IT | 1963 | **Gilles Grangier** | 90 |

| No. | Author | Nationality | Form | Literary Title | Date |
|-----|--------|-------------|------|----------------|------|
| 4486 | Simenon, Georges | French | N | **Maigret tend un piège** <br> *(Maigret Sets a Trap)* | 1955 |
| 4487 | Simenon, Georges | French | N | **La maison des sept jeunes filles** | 1941 |
| 4488 | Simenon, Georges | French | N | **La maison des sept jeunes filles** | 1941 |
| 4489 | Simenon, Georges | French | N | **La Marie du port** <br> *(The Girl in Waiting)* <br> *(aka: A Chit of a Girl)* | 1938 |
| 4490 | Simenon, Georges | French | N | **Monsieur La Souris** <br> *(The Mouse)* | 1938 |
| 4491 | Simenon, Georges | French | N | **Monsieur La Souris** | 1938 |
| 4492 | Simenon, Georges | French | SS | **La mort de Belle** <br> *(Belle)* | 1952 |
| 4493 | Simenon, Georges | French | N | **La neige était sale** <br> *(The Stain on the Snow)* <br> *(aka: The Snow Was Black)* | 1948 |
| 4494 | Simenon, Georges | French | N | **La nuit du carrefour** <br> *(Maigret at the Crossroads)* <br> *(aka: The Crossroad Murders)* | 1931 |
| 4495 | Simenon, Georges | French | N | **Le passager clandestin** <br> *(The Stowaway)* | 1947 |
| 4496 | Simenon, Georges | French | N | **Le président** <br> *(The Premier)* | 1958 |
| 4497 | Simenon, Georges | French | SS | **Signé Picpus** <br> *(To Any Lengths)* | 1944 |
| 4498 | Simenon, Georges | French | N | **La tête d'un homme** <br> *(A Battle of Nerves)* | 1931 |
| 4499 | Simenon, Georges | French | N | **La tête d'un homme** | 1931 |
| 4500 | Simenon, Georges | French | N | **Le train** <br> *(The Train)* | 1961 |
| 4501 | Simenon, Georges | French | N | **Trois chambres à Manhattan** <br> *(Three Beds in Manhattan)* | 1946 |
| 4502 | Simenon, Georges | French | N | **La vérité sur Bébé Donge** <br> *(The Trial of Bebe Donge)* <br> *(aka: I Take This Woman)* | 1942 |
| 4503 | Simenon, Georges | French | N | **La veuve Couderc** <br> *(Ticket of Leave)* <br> *(aka: The Widow)* | 1942 |
| 4504 | Simenon, Georges | French | N | **Le voyageur de la Toussaint** <br> *(Strange Inheritance)* | 1941 |
| 4505 | Simon, Neil | American | P | **Barefoot in the Park** | 1964 |
| 4506 | Simon, Neil | American | P | **Biloxi Blues** | 1987 |
| 4507 | Simon, Neil | American | P | **Brighton Beach Memoirs** | 1985 |
| 4508 | Simon, Neil | American | P | **Broadway Bound** | 1987 |
| 4509 | Simon, Neil | American | P | **California Suit** | 1977 |
| 4510 | Simon, Neil | American | P | **Chapter Two** | 1978 |
| 4511 | Simon, Neil | American | P | **Come Blow Your Horn** | 1961 |
| 4512 | Simon, Neil | American | P | **The Gingerbread Lady** | 1970 |
| 4513 | Simon, Neil | American | P | **I Ought To Be in Pictures** | 1981 |
| 4514 | Simon, Neil | American | P | **Last of the Red Hot Lovers** | 1970 |
| 4515 | Simon, Neil | American | P | **The Odd Couple** | 1966 |
| 4516 | Simon, Neil | American | P | **Plaza Suite** | 1969 |
| 4517 | Simon, Neil | American | P | **The Prisoner of Second Avenue** | 1972 |
| 4518 | Simon, Neil | American | P | **The Star Spangled Girl** | 1967 |
| 4519 | Simon, Neil | American | P | **The Sunshine Boys** | 1972 |
| 4520 | Simonov, Konstantin | Russian | P | **Chetvyorty** <br> *(The Fourth)* | 1961 |
| 4521 | Simonov, Konstantin | Russian | N | **Dni i nochi** <br> *(Days and Nights)* | 1943-44 |
| 4522 | Simonov, Konstantin | Russian | SS | **Dvadtsat' dnei bez voiny** | 1973 |
| 4523 | Simonov, Konstantin | Russian | P | **Paren iz nashego goroda** | 1941 |
| 4524 | Simonov, Konstantin | Russian | P | **Russkiye lyudi** <br> *(The Russian People)* | 1942 |
| 4525 | Simonov, Konstantin | Russian | P | **Russkiy vopros** <br> *(The Russian Question)* | 1946 |

FILM

| No | Film Title | Country of Production | Date | Director(s) | Duration of Film |
|---|---|---|---|---|---|
| 4486 | Maigret tend un piège (Maigret Sets a Trap) (USA: Inspector Maigret) | FR | 1958 | Jean Delannoy | 119 |
| 4487 | La maison des sept jeunes filles | FR | 1942(41) | Albert Valentin | 100 |
| 4488 | Seven Sweethearts | USA | 1942 | Frank Borzage | 98 |
| 4489 | La Marie du port (USA: Maria of the Port) | FR | 1950 | Marcel Carné | 88 |
| 4490 | Monsieur La Souris (Mr Mouse) (aka: Midnight in Paris) | FR | 1942 | Georges Lacombe | 106 |
| 4491 | Midnight Episode | GB | 1950 | Gordon Parry | 78 |
| 4492 | La mort de Belle (The Passion of Slow Fire) | FR | 1961 | Édouard Molinaro | 100 |
| 4493 | La neige était sale (The Stain on the Snow) (aka: The Snow Was Black) | FR | 1954(52) | Luis Saslavsky | 104 |
| 4494 | La nuit du carrefour (Night at the Crossroads) | FR | 1933(32) | Jean Renoir | 80(75) |
| 4495 | Le passager clandestin (The Stowaway) | FR/ AUSTL | 1958 | Ralph Habib | 98 |
| 4496 | Le président (IT: Il presidente) | FR/IT | 1961 | Henri Verneuil | 108 |
| 4497 | Picpus | FR | 1943(42) | Richard Pottier | 95 |
| 4498 | La tête d'un homme | FR | 1932 | Julien Duvivier | 100 |
| 4499 | The Man on the Eiffel Tower | USA/FR | 1949 | Burgess Meredith | 83 |
| 4500 | Le train (IT: Noi due senza domani) | FR/IT | 1974(73) | Pierre Granier-Deferre | 100 |
| 4501 | Trois chambres à Manhattan | FR | 1965(64) | Marcel Carné | 105(90) |
| 4502 | La vérité sur Bébé Donge | FR | 1952(51) | Henri Decoin | 104 |
| 4503 | La veuve Couderc (The Widow Couderc) | FR | 1971 | Pierre Granier-Deferre | 90 |
| 4504 | Le voyageur de la Toussaint | FR | 1943 | Louis Daquin | 102 |
| 4505 | Barefoot in the Park | USA | 1967 | Gene Saks | 109 +V |
| 4506 | Biloxi Blues | USA | 1988 | Mike Nichols | 107 |
| 4507 | Brighton Beach Memoirs | USA | 1986 | Gene Saks | 110 +V |
| 4508 | Broadway Bound | USA | 1991 | Paul Bogart | 94 |
| 4509 | California Suit | USA | 1978 | Herbert Ross | 103 +V |
| 4510 | Chapter Two | USA | 1979 | Robert Moore | 126 +V |
| 4511 | Come Blow Your Horn | USA | 1963 | Bud Yorkin | 112 |
| 4512 | It Only Hurts When I Laugh (aka: Only When I Laugh) | USA | 1981 | Glenn Jordan | 120 +V |
| 4513 | I Ought To Be in Pictures | USA | 1982 | Herbert Ross | 107 +V |
| 4514 | Last of the Red Hot Lovers | USA | 1972 | Gene Saks | 98 |
| 4515 | The Odd Couple | USA | 1968 | Gene Saks | 105 |
| 4516 | Plaza Suite | USA | 1971(70) | Arthur Hiller | 114 +V |
| 4517 | The Prisoner of Second Avenue | USA | 1975 | Melvin Frank | 98 +V |
| 4518 | Star Spangled Girl | USA | 1971 | Jerry Paris | 92 |
| 4519 | The Sunshine Boys | USA | 1975 | Herbert Ross | 111 +V |
| 4520 | Chetvyorty | USSR | 1972 | Alexander Stolper | 71 |
| 4521 | Dni i nochi (Days and Nights) | USSR | 1944 | Alexander Stolper | 90 |
| 4522 | Dvadtsat' dnei bez voiny | USSR | 1976 | Alexei German | 102 |
| 4523 | Paren iz nashego goroda (A Lad From Our Town) | USSR | 1942 | Alexander Stolper | 93 |
| 4524 | Vo imya rodini (In the Name of the Fatherland) | USSR | 1943 | Vsevolod Pudovkin Dmitri Vasiliev | 96 |
| 4525 | Russkiy voproz (The Russian Question) (aka: The Russian Problem) | USSR | 1947 | Mikhail Romm | 91 |

**249**

| No. | Author | Nationality | Form | Literary Title | Date |
|---|---|---|---|---|---|
| 4526 | **Simonov, Konstantin** | Russian | SS | **Sluchai s Polynnym** <br> *[Accident with Polynim]* | 1969 |
| 4527 | **Simonov, Konstantin** | Russian | N | **Soldatami ne rozhdayutsya** | 1964 |
| 4528 | **Simonov, Konstantin** | Russian | V | **Zhdi menya** <br> *(Wait For me)* | 1941 |
| 4529 | **Simonov, Konstantin** | Russian | N | **Zhiviye i myortviye** <br> *(The Living and the Dead)* | 1959 |
| 4530 | **Simpson, Helen** | Australian | N | **Saraband For Dead Lovers** | 1935 |
| 4531 | **Simpson, Helen** | Australian | N | **Under Capricorn** | 1937 |
| 4532 | **Simpson, Helen** <br> *(see also: Dane, Clemence)* | Australian | N/P | | |
| 4533 | **Simpson, N. F.** | British | P | **One Way Pendulum** | 1960 |
| 4534 | **Sinclair, Upton** | American | N | **The Gnomobile. A gnice gnew gnarrative with gnonsense, but gnothing gnaughty...** | 1936 |
| 4535 | **Sinclair, Upton** | American | N | **The Wet Parade** | 1931 |
| 4536 | **Singer, Isaac Bashevis** | American (Yiddish) | SS | **The Beard** | 1973 |
| 4537 | **Singer, Isaac Bashevis** | American | SS | **The Cafeteria** | 1970 |
| 4538 | **Singer, Isaac Bashevis** | American | N | **The Magician of Lublin** | 1960(59) |
| 4539 | **Singer, Isaac Bashevis** | American | N | **Sonim, di Geschichte fun a liebe** <br> *(Enemies: a Love Story)* | 1966 |
| 4540 | **Singer, Isaac Bashevis** | American | SS-P | **Yentl the Yeshiva Boy** *{ss}* <br> *(Yentl) {p}* | 1964{ss} <br> 1977{p} |
| 4541 | **Sirin, Vladimir** <br> *(see: Nabokov, Vladimir)* | Russian/ American | N | | |
| 4542 | **Sitwell, Osbert** | British | SS | **A Place of One's Own** | 1916 |
| 4543 | **Śivaśaṅkara Piḷḷa,Takazi** <br> *(Thakazi Sirashankar Pillai)* | Indian(Mal) | N | **Cemmin** <br> *[Shrimps]* <br> *(HIN: Camin)* <br> *(Chemmeen)* | 1956 |
| 4544 | **Siwertz, Sigfrid** | Swedish | SS | **Enhörningen** | 1939 |
| 4545 | **Siwertz, Sigfrid** | Swedish | P | **Ett brott** | 1938 |
| 4546 | **Siwertz, Sigfrid** | Swedish | N | **Hem från Babylon** | 1923 |
| 4547 | **Siwertz, Sigfrid** | Swedish | N | **Mälarpirater** | 1905 |
| 4548 | **Sjöberg, Birger** | Swedish | V | **Fridas bok +** <br> **Fridas andra bok** | 1922+ <br> 1929 |
| 4549 | **Sjöberg, Birger** | Swedish | N | **Kvartetten som sprängdes** <br> *[The dispersed quartet]* | 1924 |
| 4550 | **Sjöberg, Birger** | Swedish | N | **Kvartetten som sprängdes** | 1924 |
| 4551 | **Skelton, John** | British | V | **The Tunnynge of Elynoure Rummyng** <br> *(The Tunning of Elinour Rumming)* | c.1520 |
| 4552 | **Skouen, Arne** | Norwegian | N | **Gategutter** <br> *[Street urchins]* | 1948 |
| 4553 | **Skram, Amalie** | Norwegian | N | **Lucie** | 1888 |
| 4554 | **Skram, Amalie** | Norwegian | N | **Professor Hieronimus +** <br> **På Sct. Jørgen** <br> *[At St. Jorgens]* | 1895 |
| 4555 | **Slavici, Ioan** | Romanian | N | **Mara** | 1906 |
| 4556 | **Slavici, Ioan** | Romanian | SS | **Moara cu noroc** <br> *[The lucky inn]* | 1881 |
| 4557 | **Slavici, Ioan** | Romanian | SS | **Pădureanca** <br> *[The woodlanders]* | 1884 |
| 4558 | **Slowacki, Juliusz** | Polish | P | **Mazepa** <br> *(Mazeppa)* | 1840 |
| 4559 | **Slowacki, Juliusz** | Polish | P | **Mazepa** | 1840 |
| 4560 | **Smith, Betty** | American | N | **Joy in the Morning** | 1963 |
| 4561 | **Smith, Betty** | American | N | **A Tree Grows in Brooklyn** | 1943 |
| 4562 | **Smith, Thorne** | American | N | **The Night Life of The Gods** | 1931 |
| 4563 | **Smith, Thorne** | American | N | **The Passionate Witch** | 1941 |

| No | Film Title | Country of Production | Date | Director(s) | Duration of Film |
|----|-----------|----------------------|------|------------|------------------|
| 4526 | **Sluchai s Polynnym** | USSR | 1970 | **Alexei Sakharov** | 98 |
| 4527 | **Vozmerdie** <br> *(aka: Soldatami ne rozhdaivtsia)* <br> *(Soldiers Aren't Born)* | USSR | 1968 | **Alexander Stolper** | Pt.1, 69 <br> Pt.2, 70 |
| 4528 | **Zhdi menya** <br> *(Wait For Me!)* | USSR | 1943 | **Alexander Stolper** <br> **Boris Ivanov** | 82 |
| 4529 | **Zhivye i mertvye** <br> *(The Living and the Dead)* | USSR | 1964 | **Alexander Stolper** | 210(130) |
| 4530 | **Saraband For Dead Lovers** | GB | 1948 | **Basil Dearden** <br> **Michael Relph** | 96 |
| 4531 <br> 4532 | **Under Capricorn** | GB | 1949 | **Alfred Hitchcock** | 117 +V |
| 4533 | **One Way Pendulum** | GB | 1964 | **Peter Yates** | 85 |
| 4534 | **The Gnome Mobile** | USA | 1967(66) | **Robert Stevenson** | 90 <br> +V |
| 4535 | **The Wet Parade** | USA | 1932 | **Victor Fleming** | 122 |
| 4536 | **Isaac Singer's Nightmare and Mrs Pupko's Beard** | USA | 1973 | **Bruce Davidson** | 30 |
| 4537 | **The Cafeteria** | USA | 1981 | **Amram Nowak** | 60 |
| 4538 | **Der Magier** <br> *(The Magician of Lublin)* | GER/IS | 1978 | **Menahem Golan** | 114 <br> +V(101) |
| 4539 | **Enemies: a Love Story** | USA | 1989 | **Paul Mazursky** | 120 |
| 4540 <br> 4541 | **Yentl** | GB | 1984(83) | **Barbra Streisand** | 133 <br> +V |
| 4542 | **A Place of One's Own** | GB | 1945(44) | **Bernard Knowles** | 92 |
| 4543 | **Chemeen** | IND | 1965 | **Ramu Kariatt** | 147 |
| 4544 | **Enhörningen** <br> *(The Unicorn)* | SWE | 1955 | **Gustaf Molander** | 98 |
| 4545 | **Ett brott** <br> *(A Crime)* | SWE | 1940 | **Anders Henrikson** | 92 |
| 4546 | **Hem från Babylon** <br> *(Home From Babylon)* | SWE | 1941 | **Alf Sjöberg** | 106 |
| 4547 | **Mälarpirater** | SWE | 1959 | **Per G. Holmgren** | 113 |
| 4548 | **Fridas visor** <br> *(Frida's Songs)* | SWE | 1931(30) | **Gustaf Molander** | 81 |
| 4549 | **Kvartetten som sprängdes** | SWE | 1936 | **Arne Bornebusch** | 104 |
| 4550 | **Kvartetten som sprängdes** <br> *(The Quartet That Split Up)* | SWE | 1950 | **Gustaf Molander** | 100 |
| 4551 | **Tunnyng of Elinour Rummyng** | GB | 1976 | **Julien Temple** | 33 |
| 4552 | **Gategutter** | NOR | 1949 | **Arne Skouen** <br> **Ulf Greeber** | 78 |
| 4553 | **Lucie** | NOR | 1979 | **Jan Erik Düring** | 100(96) |
| 4554 | **Formynderne** <br> *(The Guardians)* | NOR | 1978 | **Nicole Macé** | 104 |
| 4555 | **Dincolo de pod** <br> *[Beyond the bridge]* | ROM | 1976(75) | **Mircea Veroiu** | 98 |
| 4556 | **Moara cu noroc** <br> *(The Mill of Luck and Plenty)* | ROM | 1957(56) | **Victor Iliu** | 116 |
| 4557 | **Pădureanca** | ROM | 1987 | **Nicolae Mărgineanu** | 112 |
| 4558 | **Blanche** | FR | 1971 | **Walerian Borowczyk** | 90 |
| 4559 | **Mazepa** | POL | 1976(75) | **Gustaw Holoubek** | 115 |
| 4560 | **Joy in the Morning** | USA | 1965(64) | **Alex Segal** | 103 |
| 4561 | **A Tree Grows in Brooklyn** | USA | 1945 | **Elia Kazan** | 128 |
| 4562 | **Night Life of The Gods** | USA | 1935 | **Lowell Sherman** | 75 |
| 4563 | **I Married a Witch** | USA | 1942 | **René Clair** | 76 |

| No. | Author | Nationality | Form | Literary Title | Date |
|-----|--------|-------------|------|----------------|------|
| 4564 | Smith, Thorne | American | N | Topper | 1926 |
| 4565 | Smith, Thorne | American | N | Topper | 1926 |
| 4566 | Smith, Thorne | American | N | Topper Takes a Trip | 1932 |
| 4567 | Smith, Thorne | American | N | Turnabout | 1931 |
| 4568 | Sneider, Vern (joint, see: Patrick, John) | American | N-P | | |
| 4569 | Söderberg, Hjalmar | Swedish | N | Den allvarsamma leken [The serious game] | 1912 |
| 4570 | Söderberg, Hjalmar | Swedish | N | Den allvarsamma leken | 1912 |
| 4571 | Söderberg, Hjalmar | Swedish | N | Doktor Glas (Doctor Glas) | 1905 |
| 4572 | Söderberg, Hjalmar | Swedish | N | Doktor Glas | 1905 |
| 4573 | Söderberg, Hjalmar | Swedish | P | Gertrud | 1906 |
| 4574 | Soldati, Mario | Italian | SS | I due maestri | 1957 |
| 4575 | Soldati, Mario | Italian | SS | La giacca verde | 1961 |
| 4576 | Solzhenitsyn, Alexander | Russian | N | Odin den' Ivana Denisovicha (One Day in the Life of Ivan Denisovich) | 1962 |
| 4577 | Solzhenitsyn, Alexander | Russian | N | V kruge pervom (The First Circle) | 1968 |
| 4578 | Somogyi Tóth Sándor | Hungarian | N | A gyerekek kétszer születnek [Children are born twice] | 1973 |
| 4579 | Somogyi Tóth Sándor | Hungarian | N | Gyerektükör [A child's mirror] | 1963 |
| 4580 | Somogyi Tóth Sandor | Hungarian | N | Próféta voltál, szivem | 1965 |
| 4581 | Sønderby, Knud | Danish | N-P | En kvinde er overflødig {n-p} (A Woman Too Many) {p} | 1935{n} 1942{p} |
| 4582 | Sønderby, Knud | Danish | N | Midt i en jazztid [In the middle of a jazz age] | 1931 |
| 4583 | Sono Ayako | Japanese | N | Satōgashi ga kowareru toki | 1965 |
| 4584 | Sono Ayako | Japanese | N | Waga koi no bohyo | 1959 |
| 4585 | Sophocles | Greek(anc) | P | Antigone | c.441 BC |
| 4586 | Sophocles | Greek(anc) | P | Antigone | c.441 BC |
| 4587 | Sophocles | Greek(anc) | P | Electra | c.409 BC |
| 4588 | Sophocles | Greek(anc) | P | Oedipus Rex (aka: Oedipus Tyrannus) (Oedipus the King) | c.420 BC |
| 4589 | Sophocles | Greek(anc) | P | Oedipus Rex | c.420 BC |
| 4590 | Sophocles | Greek(anc) | P | Oedipus Rex + Oedipus at Colonus | c.420+ 401 BC |
| 4591 | Sørensen, Villy | Danish | SS | De forsvundne breve | 1955 |
| 4592 | Sousândrade (Joaquim de Sousa Andrade) | Brazilian | V | Guesa errante (aka: O Guesa) | 1868-77 |
| 4593 | Southern, Terry | American | N | The Magic Christian | 1959 |
| 4594 | Southern, Terry; Hoffenberg, M. | American | N | Candy | 1964 |
| 4595 | Soya, Carl Erik | Danish | P | Bare en tagsten | 1959 |
| 4596 | Soya, Carl Erik | Danish | P | Efter [Afterwards] | 1947 |
| 4597 | Soya, Carl Erik | Danish | N | Sytten | 1953 |
| 4598 | Soyinka, Wole | Nigerian | P | Kongi's Harvest | 1967 |
| 4599 | Spark, Muriel | British(Scot) | N | The Abbess of Crewe: a Modern Morality Tale | 1974 |
| 4600 | Spark, Muriel | British | N | The Driver's Seat | 1970 |
| 4601 | Spark, Muriel | British | N | The Prime of Miss Jean Brodie | 1961 |
| 4602 | Spender, Stephen | British | SS | The Fool and the Princess | 1946(58) |

| No | Film Title | Country of Production | Date | Director(s) | Duration of Film |
|----|-----------|----------------------|------|-------------|------------------|
| 4564 | **Topper** | USA | 1937 | **Norman Z. McLeod** | 97 |
| 4565 | **Topper Returns** | USA | 1941 | **Roy Del Ruth** | 88 |
| 4566 | **Topper Takes a Trip** | USA | 1939 | **Norman Z. McLeod** | 85 |
| 4567 | **Turnabout** | USA | 1940 | **Hal Roach** | 83 |
| 4568 | | | | | |
| 4569 | **Den allvarsamma leken** | SWE | 1945 | **Rune Carlsten** | 105 |
| 4570 | **Den allvarsamma leken** (Games of Love and Loneliness) | SWE/NOR | 1977 | **Anja Breien** | 99 |
| 4571 | **Doktor Glas** | SWE | 1942 | **Rune Carlsten** | 89 |
| 4572 | **Doktor Glas** (Doctor Glass) | DEN | 1968 | **Mai Zetterling** | 83 |
| 4573 | **Gertrud** | DEN | 1964 | **Carl Th. Dreyer** | 115 |
| 4574 | **Il maestro** | BEL | 1989 | **Marion Hänsel** | 90 |
| 4575 | **La giacca verde** (The Green Jacket) | IT | 1979 | **Franco Giraldi** | 120 |
| 4576 | **En dag i Ivan Denisovitsj' liv** (One Day in the Life of Ivan Denisovich) | NOR/GB/ USA | 1970 | **Casper Wrede** | 105 |
| 4577 | **Den forste kreds** (The First Circle) | DEN/GER | 1972 | **Aleksander Ford** | 95 |
| 4578 | **Vállald önmagadat!** (Be Yourself!) | HUNG | 1975 | **Frigyes Mamcserov** | 88 |
| 4579 | **Hogy állunk, fiatalember?** (Well, Young Man?) | HUNG | 1964(63) | **György Révész** | 85 |
| 4580 | **Próféta voltál, szivem** (You Were a Prophet, My Dear) | HUNG | 1967 | **Pál Zolnay** | 86 |
| 4581 | **En kvinde er overflødig** | DEN | 1957 | **Gabriel Axel** | 90 |
| 4582 | **Midt i en jazztid** | DEN | 1969 | **Knud Leif Thomsen** | 100 |
| 4583 | **Satõgashi ga kazureru toki** (When the Cookie Crumbles) | JAP | 1967 | **Tadashi Imai** | 96 |
| 4584 | **Waga koi no tabiji** (Epitaph to My Love) | JAP | 1961 | **Masahiro Shinoda** | 92 |
| 4585 | **Antigone** | GR | 1961 | **George Tzavellas** | 93 |
| 4586 | **I cannibali** (The Cannibals) | IT | 1970(69) | **Liliana Cavani** | 86 |
| 4587 | **Elektra** (aka: Electra) | GR | 1962 | **Takis Mouzenidis** | 110 |
| 4588 | **Oedipus Rex** (King Oedipus) | CAN | 1956 | **Tyrone Guthrie** | 75(87) |
| 4589 | **Oedipus the King** | GB | 1967 | **Philip Saville** | 97 |
| 4590 | **Edipo re** (Oedipus Rex) | IT/MOR | 1967 | **Pier Paolo Pasolini** | 104 +V |
| 4591 | **De forsvundne breve** | DEN | 1967 | **Annelise Hovmand** | 15 |
| 4592 | **O Guesa** | BRAZ | 1969 | **Sérgio Santeiro** | 12(19) |
| 4593 | **The Magic Christian** | GB | 1970(69) | **Joseph McGrath** | 95 +V |
| 4594 | **Candy** (IT: Candy e il suo pazzo mondo) | USA/IT/ FR | 1968 | **Christian Marquand** | 124(108) |
| 4595 | **Soyas tagsten** | DEN | 1966 | **Annelise Meineche** | 90 |
| 4596 | **Tre aar efter** | DEN | 1948 | **Johan Jacobsen** | 104 |
| 4597 | **Sytten** (Seventeen) (aka: Eric Soya's 17) | DEN | 1965 | **Annelise Meineche** | 87 +V |
| 4598 | **Kongi's Harvest** | NIG/SWE/USA | 1970 | **Ossie Davis** | 85 |
| 4599 | **Nasty Habits** (aka: The Abbess) | GB | 1977(76) | **Michael Lindsay-Hogg** | 92 +V(88) |
| 4600 | **Identikit** (The Driver's Seat) (aka: Killing Games) | IT | 1974(73) | **Giuseppe Patroni Griffi** (Patroni Griffi, Giuseppe) | 101 |
| 4601 | **The Prime of Miss Jean Brodie** | GB | 1969(68) | **Ronald Neame** | 116 +V(99) |
| 4602 | **The Fool and the Princess** | GB | 1948 | **William C. Hammond** | 72 |

| No. | Author | Nationality | Form | Literary Title | Date |
|-----|--------|-------------|------|----------------|------|
| 4603 | **Sremac, Stevan** | Yugoslav (Serb) | N | **Pop Ćira i pop Spira** *[Father Ćira and father Spira]* | 1898 |
| 4604 | **Śrīvāstav, Dhanpat Rai** *(see: Premchand)* | Indian (Urd/Hin) | SS | | |
| 4605 | **Stallings, L.** *(joint, see; Anderson, Maxwell)* | American | P | | |
| 4606 | **Stamatov, Georgi** | Bulgarian | N | **Vestovoi Dimo** | 1929 |
| 4607 | **Stancu, Zaharia** | Romanian | N | **Jocul cu moartea** *[A game with death]* | 1962 |
| 4608 | **Stancu, Zaharia** | Romanian | N | **Pădurea nebună** *[The mad woods]* | 1963 |
| 4609 | **Stanev, Emilian** | Bulgarian | N | **Ivan Kondarev** | 1958-64 |
| 4610 | **Stanev, Emilian** | Bulgarian | N | **Kradetsăt na praskovi** | 1948 |
| 4611 | **Stanev, Emilian** | Bulgarian | N | **Tărnovskata tsaritsa** *[The queen of Tarnovo]* | 1973 |
| 4612 | **Stanev, Emilian** | Bulgarian | N | **V tikha vecher** *[On a quiet evening]* | 1948 |
| 4613 | **Stanković, Borislav** | Yugoslav (Serb) | N | **Nečista krv** *[Tainted blood]* | 1911 |
| 4614 | **Stawiński, Jerzy Stefan** | Polish | SS | **Kanał** | 1956 |
| 4615 | **Stawiński, Jerzy Stefan** | Polish | SS | **Sześć wcielen Jańa Piszczyka** *[The six incarnations of Jan Piszczyk]* | 1951 |
| 4616 | **Stawiński, Jerzy Stefan** | Polish | SS | **Wegrzy** *[Hungarians]* + **Ucieczka** *[Escape]* | 1956+ 1958 |
| 4617 | **Stein, Gertrude** | American | N | **Things as They Are** *(aka: Q.E.D.)* | 1950 |
| 4618 | **Steinbeck, John** | American | N | **Cannery Row** + **Sweet Thursday** | 1945+ 1954 |
| 4619 | **Steinbeck, John** | American | N | **East of Eden** | 1952 |
| 4620 | **Steinbeck, John** | American | SS | **Flight** | 1945 |
| 4621 | **Steinbeck, John** | American | N | **The Grapes of Wrath** | 1939 |
| 4622 | **Steinbeck, John** | American | SS | **The Long Valley** | 1939 |
| 4623 | **Steinbeck, John** | American | SS | **The Long Valley** | 1939 |
| 4624 | **Steinbeck, John** | American | N-P | **The Moon Is Down** | 1942{n} 1943{p} |
| 4625 | **Steinbeck, John** | American | N-P | **Of Mice and Men** | 1937 |
| 4626 | **Steinbeck, John** | American | N-P | **Of Mice and Men** | 1937 |
| 4627 | **Steinbeck, John** | American | N | **The Pearl** *(aka: The Pearl of the World)* | 1945 |
| 4628 | **Steinbeck, John** | American | N | **Tortilla Flat** | 1935 |
| 4629 | **Steinbeck, John** | American | N | **The Wayward Bus** | 1947 |
| 4630 | **Stendhal** *(Marie Henri Beyle)* | French | N | **La chartreuse de Parme** *(The Charterhouse of Parma)* | 1839 |
| 4631 | **Stendhal** | French | N | **La chartreuse de Parme** | 1839 |
| 4632 | **Stendhal** | French | SS | **Le coffre et le revenant** | 1867 |
| 4633 | **Stendhal** | French | | **De l'amour** *(Love)* *(aka: On Love)* | 1822 |
| 4634 | **Stendhal** | French | SS | **Mina de Vanghel** | 1855 |
| 4635 | **Stendhal** | French | FD | **Promenades dans Rome** *(A Roman Journal)* | 1829 |
| 4636 | **Stendhal** | French | N | **Le rouge et le noir** *(The Red and the Black)* | 1830 |
| 4637 | **Stendhal** | French | N | **Le rouge et le noir** | 1830 |
| 4638 | **Stendhal** | French | SS | **Vanina Vanini** | 1855 |
| 4639 | **Stendhal** - {n} **Saint-Laurent, Cécil** - {n} | French | N | **Lamiel** + **La fin de Lamiel** | 1889+ 1966 |

| No | Film Title | Country of Production | Date | Director(s) | Duration of Film |
|----|-----------|----------------------|------|-------------|------------------|
| 4603 | Pop Ćira i pop Spira | YUGO | 1957 | Soja Jovanović | 81 |
| 4604 | | | | | |
| 4605 | | | | | |
| 4606 | Sluzhebno polozhenie - ordinarets [Official status - orderly] | BULG | 1978 | Kiran Kolarov | 80 |
| 4607 | Prin cenuşa imperiului [Through the ashes of the empire] | ROM | 1976(75) | Andrei Blaier | 105 |
| 4608 | Pădurea nebună | ROM | 1982 | Nicolae Corjos | 98 |
| 4609 | Ivan Kondarev | BULG | 1974 | Nikolai Korabov | 168 |
| 4610 | Kradetsăt na praskovi (The Peach Thief) | BULG | 1964 | Vălo Radev (Vulo Radev) | 87 |
| 4611 | Tărnovskata tsaritsa | BULG | 1981 | Yanko Yankov | 97 |
| 4612 | V tikha vecher | BULG | 1960 | Borislav Sharaliev | 89 |
| 4613 | Sofka | YUGO | 1948 | Radoš Novaković | 98 |
| 4614 | Kanał (aka: They Loved Life) | POL | 1957(56) | Andrzej Wajda | 95 +V |
| 4615 | Zezowate szczęście (Bad Luck) | POL | 1960(59) | Andrzej Munk | 114 |
| 4616 | Eroica (Heroism) (aka: Eroica - Polen 44) | POL | 1958(57) | Andrzej Munk | 86(83) |
| 4617 | Quest For Love | S.AFR | 1987 | Helena Nogueira | 93 |
| 4618 | Cannery Row | USA | 1982 | David S. Ward | 120 +V |
| 4619 | East of Eden | USA | 1955(54) | Elia Kazan | 114 +V |
| 4620 | Flight | USA | 1960 | Louis Bispo | 91 |
| 4621 | The Grapes of Wrath | USA | 1940 | John Ford | 129 |
| 4622 | The Red Pony | USA | 1949 | Lewis Milestone | 88 +V |
| 4623 | The Red Pony | USA | 1973 | Robert Totten | 68(100) |
| 4624 | The Moon Is Down | USA | 1943 | Irving Pichel | 90 |
| 4625 | Of Mice and Men | USA | 1940 | Lewis Milestone | 106 |
| 4626 | Of Mice and Men | USA | 1992 | Gary Sinise | 110 |
| 4627 | La perla (The Pearl) | MEX/USA | 1948(46) | Emilio Fernández | 72 |
| 4628 | Tortilla Flat | USA | 1942 | Victor Fleming | 106 |
| 4629 | The Wayward Bus | USA | 1957 | Victor Vicas | 89 |
| 4630 | La chartreuse de Parme (IT: La certosa di Parma) | FR/IT | 1947 | Christian-Jaque | 170 |
| 4631 | Prima della rivoluzione (Before the Revolution) | IT | 1964 | Bernardo Bertolucci | 115 +V |
| 4632 | Les amants de Tolède (IT: Gli amanti di Toledo) (Lovers of Toledo) | FR/IT | 1953(52) | Henri Decoin | 86 |
| 4633 | De l'amour (IT: La calda pelle) (All About Loving) | FR/IT | 1965(64) | Jean Aurel | 90 |
| 4634 | Les crimes de l'amour (Pt.1: Mina de Vanghel) | FR | 1953 | Maurice Clavel Maurice Barry | Pt.1, 47 |
| 4635 | L'interno di un convento (Behind Convent Walls) | IT | 1977 | Walerian Borowczyk | 96 +V |
| 4636 | Il corriere del re | IT | 1950(48) | Gennaro Righelli | 91 |
| 4637 | Le rouge et le noir (Scarlet and Black) (IT: L'uomo e il diavolo) | FR/IT | 1954 | Claude Autant-Lara | 146(170) |
| 4638 | Oltre l'amore (aka: Per te ho tradito) | IT | 1940 | Carmine Gallone | 100 |
| 4639 | Lamiel | FR/IT | 1968(67) | Jean Aurel | 95 |

| No. | Author | Nationality | Form | Literary Title | Date |
|---|---|---|---|---|---|
| 4640 | **Stenvall, Aleksis** (see: Kivi, Aleksis) | Finnish | P/N | | |
| 4641 | **Stevenson, Robert Louis** | British(Scot) | N | **Black Arrow** (aka: The Black Arrow: a Tale of the Two Roses) | 1888 |
| 4642 | **Stevenson, Robert Louis** | British | N | **Black Arrow** | 1888 |
| 4643 | **Stevenson, Robert Louis** | British | SS | **The Body Snatcher** | 1894 |
| 4644 | **Stevenson, Robert Louis** | British | N | **The Bottle Imp** | 1891 |
| 4645 | **Stevenson, Robert Louis** | British | N | **Dr Jekyll and Mr Hyde** (aka: The Strange Case of Dr Jekyll and Mr Hyde) | 1886 |
| 4646 | **Stevenson, Robert Louis** | British | N | **Dr Jekyll and Mr Hyde** | 1886 |
| 4647 | **Stevenson, Robert Louis** | British | N | **Dr Jekyll and Mr Hyde** | 1886 |
| 4648 | **Stevenson, Robert Louis** | British | N | **Dr Jekyll and Mr Hyde** | 1886 |
| 4649 | **Stevenson, Robert Louis** | British | N | **Dr Jekyll and Mr Hyde** | 1886 |
| 4650 | **Stevenson, Robert Louis** | British | N | **Dr Jekyll and Mr Hyde** | 1886 |
| 4651 | **Stevenson, Robert Louis** | British | N | **Dr Jekyll and Mr Hyde** | 1886 |
| 4652 | **Stevenson, Robert Louis** | British | V | **Heather Ale: a Galloway Legend** | 1890 |
| 4653 | **Stevenson, Robert Louis** | British | N | **Kidnapped** | 1886 |
| 4654 | **Stevenson, Robert Louis** | British | N | **Kidnapped** | 1886 |
| 4655 | **Stevenson, Robert Louis** | British | N | **Kidnapped** | 1886 |
| 4656 | **Stevenson, Robert Louis** | British | N | **Kidnapped** + **Catriona** (USA: David Balfour) | 1886+ 1892; 1893 |
| 4657 | **Stevenson, Robert Louis** | British | N | **Kidnapped** + **Catriona** | 1886+ 1892 |
| 4658 | **Stevenson, Robert Louis** | British | N | **The Master of Ballantrae** | 1888 |
| 4659 | **Stevenson, Robert Louis** | British | N | **The Master of Ballantrae** | 1888 |
| 4660 | **Stevenson, Robert Louis** | British | SS | **Silverado Squatters** | 1883 |
| 4661 | **Stevenson, Robert Louis** | British | SS | **The Sire de Maletroit's Door** | 1878 |
| 4662 | **Stevenson, Robert Louis** | British | SS | **The Suicide Club** | 1882 |
| 4663 | **Stevenson, Robert Louis** | British | SS | **The Suicide Club** | 1882 |
| 4664 | **Stevenson, Robert Louis** | British | N | **Treasure Island** | 1883 |
| 4665 | **Stevenson, Robert Louis** | British | N | **Treasure Island** | 1883 |
| 4666 | **Stevenson, Robert Louis** | British | N | **Treasure Island** | 1883 |
| 4667 | **Stevenson, Robert Louis** | British | N | **Treasure Island** | 1883 |
| 4668 | **Stevenson, Robert Louis** | British | N | **Treasure Island** | 1883 |
| 4669 | **Stevenson, Robert Louis** | British | N | **Treasure Island** | 1883 |
| 4670 | **Stevenson, Robert Louis** | British | N | **Treasure Island** | 1883 |
| 4671 | **Stevenson, Robert Louis** | British | SS | **Treasure of Franchard** | 1887 |
| 4672 | **Stevenson, Robert Louis; Osbourne, Lloyd** | British | N | **The Ebb Tide** | 1894 |
| 4673 | **Stevenson, Robert Louis; Osbourne, Lloyd** | British | N | **The Ebb Tide** | 1894 |
| 4674 | **Stevenson, Robert Louis; Osbourne, Lloyd** | British | N | **The Wrecker** | 1892 |
| 4675 | **Stevenson, Robert Louis; Osbourne, Lloyd** | British | N | **The Wrong Box** | 1889 |
| 4676 | **Stevenson, Robert Louis; Quiller-Couch, Arthur** | British | N | **St Ives** | 1898 |
| 4677 | **Stifter, Adalbert** | Austrian | SS | **Bergkristall** (Rock Crystal) (aka: Mount Gars; or, Marie's Christmas-Eve) (aka: Der Heilige Abend) | 1853 |
| 4678 | **Stifter, Adalbert** | Austrian | SS | **Der Hochwald** (The Hochwald) | 1841 |
| 4679 | **Stigen, Terje** | Norwegian | N | **Elskere** | 1960 |

| No | Film Title | Country of Production | Date | Director(s) | Duration of Film |
|---|---|---|---|---|---|
| 4640 | | | | | |
| 4641 | The Black Arrow<br>(GB: The Black Arrow Strikes) | USA | 1948 | Gordon Douglas | 76 |
| 4642 | Chernaya strela | USSR | 1985 | Sergei Tarasov | 113 |
| 4643 | The Body Snatcher | USA | 1945 | Robert Wise | 77 +V |
| 4644 | Liebe, Tod und Teufel | GER | 1934 | Heinz Hilpert<br>Reinhart Steinbicker | 104 |
| 4645 | Dr Jekyll and Mr Hyde | USA | 1932(31) | Rouben Mamoulian | 98(82)<br>+V |
| 4646 | Dr Jekyll and Mr Hyde | USA | 1941 | Victor Fleming | 122(114) |
| 4647 | The Ugly Duckling | GB | 1959 | Lance Comfort | 84 |
| 4648 | The Two Faces of Dr Jekyll<br>(aka: House of Fright) | GB | 1960(59) | Terence Fisher | 88 |
| 4649 | Le testement du Docteur Cordelier<br>(The Testament of Doctor Cordelier)<br>(USA: Experiment in Evil) | FR | 1961(59) | Jean Renoir | 100(95) |
| 4650 | I, Monster | GB | 1971 | Stephen Weeks | 75 +V |
| 4651 | Strannaya istoria doctora Dzhekila<br>i mistera Khayda | USSR | 1985 | Alexander Orlov | 92 |
| 4652 | Vereskovyi myod<br>{animation} | USSR | 1974 | Irina Gurvitch | 09 |
| 4653 | Kidnapped | USA | 1938 | Alfred Werker | 80(93) |
| 4654 | Kidnapped | USA | 1948 | William Beaudine | 80 |
| 4655 | Kidnapped | GB | 1960 | Robert Stevenson | 95 +V |
| 4656 | Schüsse unterm Galgen<br>[Shots under the gallows] | GDR | 1968 | Horst Seemann | 107 |
| 4657 | Kidnapped | GB | 1972(71) | Delbert Mann | 107<br>+V |
| 4658 | The Master of Ballantrae | GB | 1953(52) | William Keighley | 88 |
| 4659 | El Señor de Osanto | MEX | 1972 | Jaime H. Hermosillo | 108 |
| 4660 | Adventures in Silverado | USA | 1948 | Phil Karlson | 75 |
| 4661 | The Strange Door | USA | 1951 | Joseph Pevney | 81 |
| 4662 | Trouble For Two<br>(GB: The Suicide Club) | USA | 1936 | J. Walter Ruben | 75 |
| 4663 | The Suicide Club | USA | 1987 | James Bruce | 90 |
| 4664 | Treasure Island | USA | 1934 | Victor Fleming | 105 |
| 4665 | Ostrov sokrovishch | USSR | 1937 | Vladimir Vainshtok | 92 |
| 4666 | Treasure Island | GB/USA | 1950 | Byron Haskin | 96 +V |
| 4667 | Ostrov sokrovishch<br>(Treasure Island) | USSR | 1971 | Eugen Fridman | 76 |
| 4668 | Treasure Island<br>(SP: La isla del tesoro) | GB/GER/<br>FR/SP | 1973(72) | John Hough | 95(77)<br>+V(85) |
| 4669 | Treasure Island<br>{musical version} | GB | 1982 | Dave Heather | 118<br>+V(100) |
| 4670 | Treasure Island | USA | 1990 | Fraser C. Heston | 132 |
| 4671 | The Treasure of Lost Canyon | USA | 1951 | Ted Tetzlaff | 82 |
| 4672 | Ebb Tide | USA | 1937 | James Hogan | 92 |
| 4673 | Adventure Island | USA | 1947 | Peter Stewart<br>(Sam Newfield) | 67 |
| 4674 | Tainata na Apolonia<br>(Apollonia's secret)<br>(CZ: The Derelict) | BULG/CZ | 1984 | Ivo Toman | 95 |
| 4675 | The Wrong Box | GB | 1966 | Bryan Forbes | 110(105)<br>+V(102) |
| 4676 | The Secret of St Ives | USA | 1949 | Phil Rosen | 76 |
| 4677 | Bergkristall<br>(aka: Der Wildschütz von Tirol)<br>(Rock Crystal) | GER/AUST | 1949 | Harald Reinl | 87 |
| 4678 | Die Flucht<br>[The flight] | GER | 1978 | Hajo Baumgärtner | 110 |
| 4679 | Elskere | NOR | 1963 | Nils R. Müller | 103 |

| No. | Author | Nationality | Form | Literary Title | Date |
|-----|--------|-------------|------|----------------|------|
| 4680 | **Stigen, Terje** | Norwegian | N | **Min Marion** | 1972 |
| 4681 | **Stoker, Bram** | Irish | N | **Dracula** | 1897 |
| 4682 | **Stoker, Bram** | Irish | N | **Dracula** | 1897 |
| 4683 | **Stoker, Bram** | Irish | N | **Dracula** | 1897 |
| 4684 | **Stoker, Bram** | Irish | N | **Dracula** | 1897 |
| 4685 | **Stoker, Bram** | Irish | N | **Dracula** | 1897 |
| 4686 | **Stoker, Bram** | Irish | N | **Dracula** | 1897 |
| 4687 | **Stoker, Bram** | Irish | N | **Dracula** | 1897 |
| 4688 | **Stoker, Bram** | Irish | N | **Dracula** | 1897 |
| 4689 | **Stoker, Bram** | Irish | N | **The Jewel of the Seven Stars** (aka: The Jewel of Seven Stars) | 1903 |
| 4690 | **Stoker, Bram** | Irish | N | **The Jewel of the Seven Stars** | 1903 |
| 4691 | **Stoker, Bram** | Irish | N | **The Jewel of the Seven Stars** | 1903 |
| 4692 | **Stoker, Bram** | Irish | N | **The Lair of the White Worm** | 1911 |
| 4693 | **Stone, Robert** | American | N | **Dog Soldiers** | 1974 |
| 4694 | **Stone, Robert** | American | N | **A Hall of Mirrors** | 1968 |
| 4695 | **Stong, Philip Duffield** | American | N | **Career** | 1936 |
| 4696 | **Stong, Philip Duffield** | American | N | **The Farmer in the Dell** | 1935 |
| 4697 | **Stong, Philip Duffield** | American | N | **State Fair** | 1932 |
| 4698 | **Stong, Philip Duffield** | American | N | **State Fair** | 1932 |
| 4699 | **Stong, Philip Duffield** | American | N | **State Fair** | 1932 |
| 4700 | **Stong, Philip Duffield** | American | N | **Stranger's Return** | 1933 |
| 4701 | **Stong, Philip Duffield** | American | N | **A Village Tale** | 1934 |
| 4702 | **Stoppard, Tom** | British | P | **Rosencrantz and Guildenstern Are Dead** | 1968 |
| 4703 | **Storey, David** | British | P | **In Celebration** | 1969 |
| 4704 | **Storey, David** | British | N | **This Sporting Life** | 1960 |
| 4705 | **Storm, Theodor** | German | N | **Aquis submersus** [Beneath the flood] | 1877 |
| 4706 | **Storm, Theodor** | German | SS | **Ein Doppelgänger** | 1887 |
| 4707 | **Storm, Theodor** | German | N | **Immensee** (Immensee: a Dream of Youth) | 1852 |
| 4708 | **Storm, Theodor** | German | N | **Immensee** | 1852 |
| 4709 | **Storm, Theodor** | German | SS | **Pole Poppenspäler** | 1874 |
| 4710 | **Storm, Theodor** | German | SS | **Pole Poppenspäler** | 1874 |
| 4711 | **Storm, Theodor** | German | SS | **Der Schimmelreiter** (The White Horseman) (aka: The Rider on the White Horse) | 1888 |
| 4712 | **Storm, Theodor** | German | SS | **Der Schimmelreiter** | 1888 |
| 4713 | **Storm, Theodor** | German | N | **Viola Tricolor** | 1874 |
| 4714 | **Storm, Theodor** | German | N | **Viola Tricolor** | 1874 |
| 4715 | **Stowe, Harriet Beecher** | American | N | **Uncle Tom's Cabin; or, Life Among the Lowly** (aka: Uncle Tom's Cabin; or, Negro Life in the Slave States of America) | 1852 |
| 4716 | **Stratiev, Stanislav** | Bulgarian | N | **Diva patitsa mezhdu dărvetata** | 1972 |
| 4717 | **Stratiev, Stanislav** | Bulgarian | N | **Divi pcheli** | 1978 |
| 4718 | **Stratiev, Stanislav** | Bulgarian | N | **Kratko slăntse** [Short sun] | 1978 |
| 4719 | **Strauß, Botho** | German | P | **Gross und Klein** (Big and Little) | 1980 |
| 4720 | **Strauß, Botho** | German | P | **Trilogie des Wiedersehens** [Trilogy of farewell] | 1976 |
| 4721 | **Streeter, Edward** | American | N | **Father of the Bride** | 1949 |
| 4722 | **Streeter, Edward** | American | N | **Father of the Bride** | 1949 |

| No | Film Title | Country of Production | Date | Director(s) | Duration of Film |
|---|---|---|---|---|---|
| 4680 | **Min Marion** | NOR | 1975 | **Nils R. Müller** | 107 |
| 4681 | **Dracula** | USA | 1931 | **Tod Browning** | 76(84) +V |
| 4682 | **Dracula** (USA: Horror of Dracula) | GB | 1958 | **Terence Fisher** | 82 |
| 4683 | **Jonathan** | GER | 1969 | **Hans W. Geissendörfer** | 100(103) |
| 4684 | **El conde Dracula** (IT: Il conte Dracula) (GER: Nachts, wenn Dracula erwacht) (Count Dracula) | SP/GER/IT/ LIECH | 1970(69) | **Jesús Franco** (Jess Franco) | 98(90) |
| 4685 | **Blacula** | USA | 1972 | **William Crain** | 92 |
| 4686 | **Dracula** | GB | 1974(73) | **Dan Curtis** | 98 +V |
| 4687 | **Dracula** | USA | 1979 | **John Badham** | 112 +V |
| 4688 | **Nosferatu- Phantom der Nacht** (aka: Nosferatu) (aka: Nosferatu - The Vampire) | GER/FR | 1979 | **Werner Herzog** | 107 +V(96) |
| 4689 | **Blood From the Mummy's Tomb** | GB | 1971 | **Seth Holt** **Michael Carreras** | 94 +V |
| 4690 | **The Awakening** | GB | 1980 | **Mike Newell** | 105 +V |
| 4691 | **The Tomb** | USA | 1985 | **Fred Olen Ray** | 89(84) +V |
| 4692 | **The Lair of the White Worm** | GB | 1988 | **Ken Russell** | 93 +V |
| 4693 | **Who'll Stop the Rain?** (GB: Dog Soldiers) | USA | 1978 | **Karel Reisz** | 126 +V |
| 4694 | **W USA** | USA | 1970 | **Stuart Rosenberg** | 115 |
| 4695 | **Career** | USA | 1939 | **Leigh Jason** | 80 |
| 4696 | **The Farmer in the Dell** | USA | 1936 | **Ben Holmes** | 67 |
| 4697 | **State Fair** | USA | 1933 | **Henry King** | 96 |
| 4698 | **State Fair** (aka: It Happened One Summer) {musical version} | USA | 1945 | **Walter Lang** | 100 |
| 4699 | **State Fair** | USA | 1962 | **José Ferrer** | 118 |
| 4700 | **The Stranger's Return** | USA | 1933 | **King Vidor** | 89 |
| 4701 | **A Village Tale** | USA | 1935 | **John Cromwell** | 79 |
| 4702 | **Rosencrantz and Guildenstern Are Dead** | USA | 1990 | **Tom Stoppard** | 118 |
| 4703 | **In Celebration** | GB/CAN | 1976(74) | **Lindsay Anderson** | 131 |
| 4704 | **This Sporting Life** | GB | 1963 | **Lindsay Anderson** | 134 +V |
| 4705 | **Unsterbliche Geliebte** [Immortal lover] | GER | 1951(50) | **Veit Harlan** | 106 |
| 4706 | **John Glückstadt** | GER | 1975 | **Ulf Miehe** | 94 |
| 4707 | **Immensee** | GER | 1943 | **Veit Harlan** | 94 |
| 4708 | **Unsterbliche Liebe** (aka: Was die Schwalbe sang) | GER | 1956 | **Geza von Bolvary** | 104 |
| 4709 | **Pole Poppenspäler** | GER | 1935 | **Curt Oertel** | 40 |
| 4710 | **Pole Poppenspäler** | GDR | 1956 | **Arthur Pohl** | 87 |
| 4711 | **Der Schimmelreiter** (The Rider on the White Horse) | GER | 1934 | **Curt Oertel** **Hans Deppe** | 85 |
| 4712 | **Der Schimmelreiter** | GER | 1978(77) | **Alfred Weidenmann** | 96 +V |
| 4713 | **Serenade** | GER | 1937 | **Willi Forst** | 109 |
| 4714 | **Ich werde dich auf Händen tragen** [I'll carry you in my arms] | GER | 1958 | **Veit Harlan** | 89(91) |
| 4715 | **Onkel Toms Hütte** (IT: La capanna dello zio Tom) (Uncle Tom's Cabin) | GER/IT/ YUGO | 1965 | **Geza von Radvanyi** | 116(126) |
| 4716 | **Pazachăt na krepostta** [Warder of the fortress] | BULG | 1974 | **Milen Nikolov** | 75 |
| 4717 | **Ravnovesie** [Balance] | BULG | 1983 | **Lyudmil Kirkov** | 107 |
| 4718 | **Kratko slăntse** | BULG | 1979 | **Lyudmil Kirkov** | 106 |
| 4719 | **Gross und Klein** | GER | 1980 | **Peter Stein** | 270 |
| 4720 | **Trilogie des Wiedersehens** | GER | 1978 | **Peter Stein** | 128 |
| 4721 | **Father of the Bride** | USA | 1950 | **Vincente Minnelli** | 93 |
| 4722 | **Father of the Bride** | USA | 1991 | **Charles Shyer** | 105 |

| No. | Author | Nationality | Form | Literary Title | Date |
|-----|--------|-------------|------|----------------|------|
| 4723 | **Streeter, Edward** | American | N | **Mr Hobbs's Vacation** | 1954 |
| 4724 | **Streuvels, Stijn**<br>*(see: Lateur, Frank)* | Belgian(Fle) | N | | |
| 4725 | **Strindberg, August** | Swedish | SS | **Ett dockhem**<br>*[The doll's house]* | 1884 |
| 4726 | **Strindberg, August** | Swedish | P | **Dödsdansen**<br>*(The Dance of Death)*<br>*(aka: Facing Death)* | 1901 |
| 4727 | **Strindberg, August** | Swedish | P | **Dödsdansen** | 1901 |
| 4728 | **Strindberg, August** | Swedish | P | **Dödsdansen** | 1901 |
| 4729 | **Strindberg, August** | Swedish | P | **Erik XIV** | 1899 |
| 4730 | **Strindberg, August** | Swedish | P | **Fadren**<br>*(The Father)* | 1887 |
| 4731 | **Strindberg, August** | Swedish | P | **Fröken Julie**<br>*(Miss Julie)* | 1888 |
| 4732 | **Strindberg, August** | Swedish | P | **Fröken Julie** | 1888 |
| 4733 | **Strindberg, August** | Swedish | P | **Fröken Julie** | 1888 |
| 4734 | **Strindberg, August** | Swedish | N | **Hemsöborna**<br>*(The People of Hemsö)*<br>*(aka: The Natives of Hemsö)* | 1887 |
| 4735 | **Strindberg, August** | Swedish | N | **Hemsöborna** | 1887 |
| 4736 | **Strindberg, August** | Swedish | SS | **Mot betalning**<br>*(For Payment)* | 1886 |
| 4737 | **Strindberg, August** | Swedish | P | **Den starkare**<br>*(The Stronger)* | 1890 |
| 4738 | **Strong, L. A. G.** | British | N | **The Brothers** | 1931 |
| 4739 | **Strug, Andrzej** | Polish | N | **Dzieje jednego pocisku**<br>*[A story of one bomb]* | 1910 |
| 4740 | **Strug, Andrzej** | Polish | N | **Fortuna kasjera Śpiewankiewicza**<br>*[Cashier Śpiewankiewicz's fortune]* | 1928 |
| 4741 | **Strugatsky, Arkadi;**<br>**Strugatsky, Boris** | Russian | SS | **Piknik na obochine**<br>*(Roadside Picnic)* | 1972 |
| 4742 | **Stukalov, N. F.**<br>*(see: Pogodin, Nikolay)* | Russian | P | | |
| 4743 | **Styron, William** | American | N | **Sophie's Choice** | 1979 |
| 4744 | **Suárez y Romero, Anselmo** | Cuban | N | **Francisco** | 1880 |
| 4745 | **Suassuna, Ariano** | Brazilian | P | **Auto da compadecida**<br>*(The Rogues' Trial)* | 1959 |
| 4746 | **Sudermann, Hermann** | German | P | **Heimat**<br>*[Homeland]*<br>*(Magda)* | 1893 |
| 4747 | **Sudermann, Hermann** | German | N | **Das hohe Lied**<br>*(The Song of Songs)* | 1908 |
| 4748 | **Sudermann, Hermann** | German | P | **Johannisfeuer**<br>*(St John's Fire)*<br>*(aka: Fires of St. John)* | 1900 |
| 4749 | **Sudermann, Hermann** | German | P | **Johannisfeuer** | 1900 |
| 4750 | **Sudermann, Hermann** | German | SS | **Jolanthes Hochzeit**<br>*(Iolanthe's Wedding)* | 1892 |
| 4751 | **Sudermann, Hermann** | German | SS | **Jons und Erdme**<br>*(Jons and Erdme)* | 1917 |
| 4752 | **Sudermann, Hermann** | German | N | **Der Katzensteg**<br>*(Regine)* | 1889 |
| 4753 | **Sudermann, Hermann** | German | SS | **Die Reise nach Tilsit**<br>*(The Excursion to Tilsit)* | 1917 |
| 4754 | **Sudraka** | Indian | P | **Mrichakkatika**<br>*(The Little Clay Cart)* | c.400-<br>500 |

| No | Film Title | Country of Production | Date | Director(s) | Duration of Film |
|----|-----------|----------------------|------|-------------|------------------|
| 4723 | **Mr Hobbs Takes a Vacation** | USA | 1962 | **Henry Koster** | 116 |
| 4724 | | | | | |
| 4725 | **Ett dockhem** | SWE | 1956 | **Anders Henrikson** | 78 |
| 4726 | **La danse de morte** (IT: La danza della morte) (aka: La prigioniera dell'isola) (The Dance of Death) | FR/IT | 1946 | **Marcel Cravenne** | 88 |
| 4727 | **Paarungen** (Dance of Death) | GER | 1967 | **Michael Verhoeven** | 83 |
| 4728 | **The Dance of Death** | GB | 1969(68) | **David Giles** | 149 |
| 4729 | **Karin Mänsdotter** (Karin Daughter of Man) | SWE | 1954 | **Alf Sjöberg** | 108 |
| 4730 | **Fadren** (The Father) | SWE | 1969 | **Alf Sjöberg** | 100 |
| 4731 | **El pecado de Julia** | ARG | 1947 | **Mario Soffici** | 95 |
| 4732 | **Fröken Julie** (Miss Julie) | SWE | 1950 | **Alf Sjöberg** | 90(87) |
| 4733 | **Miss Julie** | GB | 1972 | **Robin Phillips** **John Glenister** | 105 |
| 4734 | **Hemsöborna** | SWE | 1944 | **Sigurd Wallén** | 109 |
| 4735 | **Hemsöborna** (The People of Hemsö) | SWE | 1955 | **Arne Mattsson** | 111 |
| 4736 | **Giftas** (Married Life) (aka: Of Love and Lust) | SWE | 1957 | **Anders Henrikson** | 73 |
| 4737 | **The Stronger** | GB | 1980 | **Ian Knox** | 18 |
| 4738 | **The Brothers** | GB | 1947 | **David MacDonald** | 95 |
| 4739 | **Gorączka** [The fever] | POL | 1981 | **Agnieszka Holland** | 115 |
| 4740 | **Niebezpieczny romans** [A dangerous love affair] | POL | 1930 | **Michaeł Waszynsky** | 98 |
| 4741 | **Stalker** | USSR/GER | 1979 | **Andrei Tarkovsky** | 160 |
| 4742 | | | | | |
| 4743 | **Sophie's Choice** | USA | 1982 | **Alan J. Pakula** | 151 +V |
| 4744 | **El otro Francisco** [The other Francisco] | CB | 1974 | **Sergio Giral** | 100 |
| 4745 | **A compadecida** (Our Lady of Compassion) (aka: Rogues Trial) | BRAZ | 1969 | **George Jones** | 104 |
| 4746 | **Heimat** (aka: Magda) | GER | 1938 | **Carl Froelich** | 101(94) |
| 4747 | **The Song of Songs** | USA | 1933 | **Rouben Mamoulian** | 89(100) |
| 4748 | **Johannisfeuer** | GER | 1939 | **Arthur Maria Rabenalt** | 82 |
| 4749 | **...und ewig bleibt die Liebe** (And Love Lasts Forever) | GER | 1954 | **Wolfgang Liebeneiner** | 96 |
| 4750 | **Hochzeit auf Bärenhof** | GER | 1942 | **Carl Froelich** | 105(92) |
| 4751 | **Jons und Erdme** (aka: Die Frau des Anderen) (IT: La donna dell'altro) [Another's wife] | GER/IT | 1959 | **Victor Vicas** | 100 |
| 4752 | **Der Katzensteg** (The Cat's Path) | GER | 1938(37) | **Fritz Peter Buch** | 87 |
| 4753 | **Die Reise nach Tilsit** (The Journey to Tilsit) (aka: The Trip to Tilsit) | GER | 1939 | **Veit Harlan** | 93 |
| 4754 | **Utsav** (Festival of Love) | IND (HIN) | 1984 | **Girish Karnad** | 140(116) |

| No. | Author | Nationality | Form | Literary Title | Date |
|-----|--------|-------------|------|----------------|------|
| 4755 | **Sue, Eugène** | French | N | **Le juif errant** *(The Wandering Jew)* | 1844-45 |
| 4756 | **Sue, Eugène** | French | N | **Les mystères de Paris** *(The Mysteries of Paris)* | 1842-43 |
| 4757 | **Sue, Eugène** | French | N | **Les mystères de Paris** | 1842-43 |
| 4758 | **Sue, Eugène** | French | N | **Les mystères de Paris** | 1842-43 |
| 4759 | **Sue, Eugène** | French | N | **Les mystères de Paris** | 1842-43 |
| 4760 | **Sueiro, Daniel** | Spanish | N | **Solo de moto** *[Motorbike solo]* | 1967 |
| 4761 | **Sukhovo-Kobylin, Aleksandr** | Russian | P | **Smert' Tarelkina** *(The Death of Tarelkin)* *(aka: Rasplyuevskie veselye)* | 1869 |
| 4762 | **Sullivan, Vernon** *(see: Vian, Boris)* | French | N | | |
| 4763 | **Sütő András** | Hungarian (Rom) | P | **Csillag a máglyán** | 1976 |
| 4764 | **Sütő András** | Hungarian | SS | **Félrejáró Salamon** *[The wanderings of Salamon]* | 1955 |
| 4765 | **Sütő András** | Hungarian | SS | **Zászlós Demeter** *[Demeter the standard bearer]* | 1960 |
| 4766 | **Svevo, Italo** | Italian | N | **Senilità** *(As a Man Grows Older)* | 1898 |
| 4767 | **Swift, Jonathan** | Irish | N | **Gulliver's Travels** | 1726 |
| 4768 | **Swift, Jonathan** | Irish | N | **Gulliver's Travels** | 1726 |
| 4769 | **Swift, Jonathan** | Irish | N | **Gulliver's Travels** | 1726 |
| 4770 | **Swift, Jonathan** | Irish | N | **Gulliver's Travels** *{pt.3}* | 1726 |
| 4771 | **Swift, Jonathan** | Irish | N | **Gulliver's Travels** | 1726 |
| 4772 | **Swift, Jonathan** | Irish | N | **Gulliver's Travels** *{pt.2}* | 1726 |
| 4773 | **Synge, John Millington** | Irish | P | **The Playboy of the Western World** | 1907 |
| 4774 | **Synge, John Millington** | Irish | P | **Riders to the Sea** | 1905 |
| 4775 | **Synge, John Millington** | Irish | P | **Riders to the Sea** | 1905 |
| 4776 | **Szabó Pál** | Hungarian | N | **Lakodalom** *[The wedding]* + **Keresztelő** *[Christening]* + **Bölcső** *[Cradle]* | 1942+ 1943 |
| 4777 | **Szép Ernő** | Hungarian | P | **Aranyóra** | 1931 |
| 4778 | **Szép Ernő** | Hungarian | SS | **Lila ákác** *[Wistaria]* | 1919 |
| 4779 | **Szép Ernő** | Hungarian | SS | **Lila ákác** | 1919 |
| 4780 | **Szép Ernő** | Hungarian | P | **Vőlegény** | 1922 |
| 4781 | **Szerb Antal** | Hungarian | N | **A Pendragon-legenda** *(The Pendragon Legend)* | 1934 |
| 4782 | **Szigligeti Ede** | Hungarian | P | **Liliomfi** | 1849 |
| 4783 | **Tagore, Rabīndranāth** *(Rabīndranātha Ṭhākura)* | Indian (Ben) | SS | **Atithi** *(The Runaway)* *(aka: The Wandering Guest)* | 1895 |
| 4784 | **Tagore, Rabīndranāth** | Indian | N | **Ghare bāire** *(The Home and the World)* | 1916 |
| 4785 | **Tagore, Rabīndranāth** | Indian | SS | **Kabulibālā** *(The Cabuliwallah - the Fruitseller From Kabul)* *(aka: The Fruit Seller)* | 1892 |
| 4786 | **Tagore, Rabīndranāth** | Indian | SS | **Kshudhita pāśān** *(The Hungry Stones)* | 1910 |
| 4787 | **Tagore, Rabīndranāth** | Indian | SS | **Mālyadān** *[The garlanding]* | 1903 |

| No | Film Title | Country of Production | Date | Director(s) | Duration of Film |
|----|-----------|----------------------|------|-------------|------------------|
| 4755 | The Wandering Jew | GB | 1933 | Maurice Elvey | 111 |
| 4756 | Les mystères de Paris | FR | 1935 | Félix Gandéra | 110 |
| 4757 | Les mystères de Paris | FR | 1943 | Jacques de Baroncelli | 89 |
| 4758 | I misteri di Parigi (FR: Les mystères de Paris) | IT/FR | 1957(52) | Fernando Cerchio | 80(95) |
| 4759 | Les mystères de Paris (IT: I misteri di Parigi) | FR/IT | 1962 | André Hunebelle | 110(94) |
| 4760 | El puente (aka: The Long Weekend) | SP | 1977(76) | Juan Antonio Bardem | 108(99) |
| 4761 | Veselye Raspliuyevskie dni (Rasplyuyev's Gay Days) | USSR | 1968(66) | Ernst Garin | 89 |
| 4762 | | | | | |
| 4763 | Czillag a máglyán (Bright Star at the Stake) | HUNG | 1978 | Ottó Ádám | 101 |
| 4764 | O mică întîmplare [An unimportant event] | ROM | 1957 | Gheorghe Turcu | 68 |
| 4765 | Doi bărbaţi pentru o moarte [Two men for one death] | ROM | 1970 | Gheorghe Naghi | 107 |
| 4766 | Senilità | IT/FR | 1962(61) | Mauro Bolognini | 110(115) |
| 4767 | Novyi Gulliver (New Gulliver) | USSR | 1935 | Aleksander Ptushko | 85(70) |
| 4768 | Gulliver's Travels {animation} | USA | 1939 | Dave Fleischer | 85(76) +V |
| 4769 | The 3 Worlds of Gulliver | USA/GB/SP | 1960 | Jack Sher | 99 |
| 4770 | Případ pro začinajícío kata (A Case For the New Hangman) | CZ | 1969 | Pavel Juráček | 100 |
| 4771 | Gulliver's Travels {live-action + animation} | GB | 1977(76) | Peter Hunt | 81 +V |
| 4772 | Los viajes de Gulliver (Gulliver's Travels Part 2) (aka: Land of the Giants: Gulliver's Travels Part 2) {animation} | SP | 1983 | Cruz Delgado | 90 +V(77) |
| 4773 | The Playboy of the Western World | IRE | 1962 | Brian Desmond Hurst | 100(96) +V |
| 4774 | Riders to the Sea | GB | 1935 | Brian Desmond Hurst | 40 |
| 4775 | Riders to the Sea | IRE | 1987 | Ronan O'Leary | 46 |
| 4776 | Talpalatnyi föld (The Soil Under Your Feet) (aka: Treasured Earth) | HUNG | 1948 | Frigyes Bán | 105(84) |
| 4777 | Az aranyóra (The Gold Watch) | HUNG | 1946(45) | Ákos von Ráthony | 91 |
| 4778 | Lila ákác (The Girl Who Liked Purple Flowers) | HUNG | 1934 | István Székely (Steve Sekely) | 76 |
| 4779 | Lila ákác (The Girl Who Liked Purple Flowers) | HUNG | 1974(72) | István Székely (Steve Sekely) | 89 |
| 4780 | Võlegény (The Bridegroom) | HUNG | 1982 | László Vámos | 92 |
| 4781 | A Pendragon-legenda (The Pendragon Legend) | HUNG | 1974 | György Révész | 101 |
| 4782 | Liliomfi | HUNG | 1954 | Károly Makk | 125 |
| 4783 | Atithi (Runaway) | IND(BEN) | 1966(65) | Tapan Sinha | 112(103) |
| 4784 | Ghare bāire (The Home and the World) | IND (BEN) | 1984(82) | Satyajit Ray | 140 |
| 4785 | Kabuliwallah (The Man From Kabul) | IND (BEN) | 1956 | Tapan Sinha | 155(90) |
| 4786 | Kshudita pashan (The Hungry Stones) | IND (BEN) | 1960 | Tapan Sinha | 120(110) |
| 4787 | Mālyadān | IND (BEN) | 1970 | Ajoy Kar | 113 |

| No. | Author | Nationality | Form | Literary Title | Date |
|-----|--------|-------------|------|----------------|------|
| 4788 | Tagore, Rabīndranāth | Indian | N | Nastanir<br>(The Broken Nest) | 1901 |
| 4789 | Tagore, Rabīndranāth | Indian | N | Naukā dubi<br>(The Wreck) | 1919 |
| 4790 | Tagore, Rabīndranāth | Indian | SS | Postamāstar<br>(Postmaster) +<br>Monihārā<br>(The Lost Jewels) +<br>Samāpti<br>(The Conclusion) | 1891 |
| 4791 | Tagore, Rabīndranāth | Indian | SS | Strir patra | c.1916 |
| 4792 | Takayama Michio | Japanese | N | Biruma no tategoto<br>(The Harp of Burma)<br>(aka: Harp of Burma) | 1948 |
| 4793 | Takeda Taijun | Japanese | SS | Hakuchū no torima | 1960 |
| 4794 | Takeda Taijun | Japanese | SS | Runinto nite | 1953 |
| 4795 | Talev, Dimităr | Bulgarian | N | Zhelezniyat svetilnik<br>(The Iron Candlestick) | 1952 |
| 4796 | Tamási Áron | Hungarian | P | Tündöklő Jeromos | 1941 |
| 4797 | Tamayo y Baus, Manuel | Spanish | P | Un drama nuevo<br>(A New Drama) | 1867 |
| 4798 | Tamayo y Baus, Manuel | Spanish | P | La locura de amor<br>[Love madness] | 1855 |
| 4799 | Tamiya Torahiko | Japanese | SS | Ibo kyōdai | 1957 |
| 4800 | Tang Xianzu<br>(Tang Yinai) | Chinese | P | Mudan ting<br>(aka: Mu-dan ting)<br>[Peony pavilion] | 1598 |
| 4801 | Tang Yinai<br>(see: Tang Xianzu) | Chinese | P | | |
| 4802 | Tanizaki Jun'ichirō | Japanese | P | Aisureba koso<br>[Because of love] | 1923 |
| 4803 | Tanizaki Jun'ichirō | Japanese | N | Ashikari | 1932 |
| 4804 | Tanizaki Jun'ichirō | Japanese | N | Chijin no ai | 1924 |
| 4805 | Tanizaki Jun'ichirō | Japanese | N | Kagi<br>(The Key) | 1956 |
| 4806 | Tanizaki Jun'ichirō | Japanese | N | Kagi | 1956 |
| 4807 | Tanizaki Jun'ichirō | Japanese | N | Manji<br>(Manji: the Swastika) | 1928 |
| 4808 | Tanizaki Jun'ichirō | Japanese | N | Neko to Shōzō to futari no onna | 1937 |
| 4809 | Tanizaki Jun'ichirō | Japanese | P | Okuni to Gohei<br>(Okuni and Gohei) | 1922 |
| 4810 | Tanizaki Jun'ichirō | Japanese | N | Sasame yuki<br>(The Makioka Sisters)<br>(aka: The Firefly Hunt) | 1942-48 |
| 4811 | Tanizaki Jun'ichirō | Japanese | N | Shunkin-shō<br>(The Story of Shunkin)<br>(aka: A Portrait of Shunkin) | 1933 |
| 4812 | Tarassov, Lev<br>(see: Troyat, Henri) | French/<br>Russian | N | | |
| 4813 | Tarkington, Booth | American | N | Alice Adams | 1921 |
| 4814 | Tarkington, Booth | American | P | Clarence | 1921 |
| 4815 | Tarkington, Booth | American | SS | The Flirt | 1913 |
| 4816 | Tarkington, Booth | American | N | Gentle Julia | 1922 |
| 4817 | Tarkington, Booth | American | N | Little Orvie | 1934 |
| 4818 | Tarkington, Booth | American | N | The Magnificent Ambersons | 1918 |
| 4819 | Tarkington, Booth | American | P | Magnolia | 1924 |

| No | Film Title | Country of Production | Date | Director(s) | Duration of Film |
|----|-----------|----------------------|------|-------------|------------------|
| 4788 | **Chārulatā** (The Lonely Wife) | IND (BEN) | 1964 | **Satyajit Ray** | 124 |
| 4789 | **Milan** (BEN: Naukā ḍubi) | IND (HIN) | 1946 | **Nitin Bose** | 136 |
| 4790 | **Teen kanyā** (Two Daughters) (aka: Monihera) (aka: Samapti) | IND (BEN) | 1961 | **Satyajit Ray** | 174(110) |
| 4791 | **Strir patra** (Letter From the Wife) | IND | 1974 | **Purendu Pattrea** | 98 |
| 4792 | **Biruma no tategoto** (The Burmese Harp) (USA: Harp of Burma) | JAP | 1956 | **Kon Ichikawa** | 116 |
| 4793 | **Hakuchū no torima** (Violence at Noon) | JAP | 1966 | **Nagisa Ōshima** | 99 |
| 4794 | **Shokei no shima** (Punishment Island) (aka: Captive's Island) | JAP | 1966 | **Masahiro Shinoda** | 87 |
| 4795 | **Ikonostasăt** (The Iconostasis) | BULG | 1969 | **Todor Dinov** **Khristo Khristov** | 96 |
| 4796 | **Mezei próféta** (The Prophet of the Fields) | HUNG | 1947 | **Frigyes Bán** | 90 |
| 4797 | **Un drama nuevo** | SP | 1946 | **Juan de Orduña** | 92(86) |
| 4798 | **La locura de amor** | SP | 1948 | **Juan de Orduña** | 120(112) |
| 4799 | **Ibo kyōdai** (Brothers Born of Different Mothers) | JAP | 1957 | **Miyoji Ieki** | 110 |
| 4800 | **You yuan jing meng** [Dreams in the spring garden] {episode} | CHN | 1960 | **Xu Ke** | 80 |
| 4801 | | | | | |
| 4802 | **Daraku sura onna** (A Fallen Woman) | JAP | 1967 | **Kōzaburō Yoshimura** | 100 |
| 4803 | **Oyu-sama** (Miss Oyu) | JAP | 1951 | **Kenji Mizoguchi** | 95 |
| 4804 | **Chijin no ai** (An Idiot in Love) | JAP | 1967 | **Yasuzō Masumura** | 92 |
| 4805 | **Kagi** (Odd Obsession) (aka: The Key) | JAP | 1959 | **Kon Ichikawa** | 96(107) |
| 4806 | **La chiave** (The Key) | IT | 1983 | **Tinto Brass** | 116 +V(109) |
| 4807 | **Interno Berlinele** (Berlin Interior) (GER: Leidenschaften) (aka: Affaire Berlinese) (The Berlin Affair) | IT/ GER | 1985 | **Liliana Cavani** | 121 +V(96) |
| 4808 | **Neko to Shōzō to futari no onna** (A Cat, Shozo and Two Women) (aka: A Cat and Two Women) | JAP | 1956 | **Shirō Toyoda** | 107 |
| 4809 | **Okuni to Gohei** (Okuni and Gohei) | JAP | 1952 | **Mikio Naruse** | 91 |
| 4810 | **Sasame yuki** (The Makioka Sisters) (aka: Gentle Snow) | JAP | 1983 | **Kon Ichikawa** | 140 |
| 4811 | **Shunkin monogatari** (The Story of Shunkin) | JAP | 1954 | **Daisuke Itō** | 110 |
| 4812 | | | | | |
| 4813 | **Alice Adams** | USA | 1935 | **George Stevens** | 100 |
| 4814 | **Clarence** | USA | 1937 | **George Archainbaud** | 64 |
| 4815 | **The Bad Sister** | USA | 1931 | **Hobart Henley** | 71 |
| 4816 | **Gentle Julia** | USA | 1936 | **John Blystone** | 62 |
| 4817 | **Little Orvie** | USA | 1940 | **Ray McCarey** | 66 +V |
| 4818 | **The Magnificent Ambersons** | USA | 1942 | **Orson Welles** | 88 +V |
| 4819 | **Mississippi** | USA | 1935 | **A. Edward Sutherland** | 80 |

| No. | Author | Nationality | Form | Literary Title | Date |
|-----|--------|-------------|------|----------------|------|
| 4820 | Tarkington, Booth | American | SS | Monsieur Beaucaire (aka: Beaucaire) | 1900 |
| 4821 | Tarkington, Booth | American | SS | Monsieur Beaucaire | 1900 |
| 4822 | Tarkington, Booth | American | N | Penrod | 1914 |
| 4823 | Tarkington, Booth | American | N | Penrod | 1914 |
| 4824 | Tarkington, Booth | American | N | Penrod | 1914 |
| 4825 | Tarkington, Booth | American | N | Penrod | 1914 |
| 4826 | Tarkington, Booth | American | N | Penrod, His Complete Story (Penrod + Penrod and Sam + Penrod Jashber) | 1931 |
| 4827 | Tarkington, Booth | American | N | Penrod, His Complete Story | 1931 |
| 4828 | Tarkington, Booth | American | N | The Plutocrat | 1927 |
| 4829 | Tarkington, Booth | American | N | Presenting Lily Mars | 1933 |
| 4830 | Tarkington, Booth | American | N | Seventeen | 1915 |
| 4831 | Tasso, Torquato | Italian | V | Gerusalemme liberata (Jerusalem Delivered) | 1581 |
| 4832 | Taunay, Alfredo d'Escragnolle (as: Sylvio Dinarte) | Brazilian | N | Inocência [Innocence] | 1872 |
| 4833 | Taunay, Alfredo d'Escragnolle | Brazilian | N | Inocência | 1872 |
| 4834 | Távora, Franklin | Brazilian | N | O cabeleira | 1876 |
| 4835 | Teichmann, Howard (joint, see: Kaufman, George S.) | American | P | | |
| 4836 | Teirlinck, Herman | Belgian(Fle) | N | Rolande met de bles (aka: De xxxx brieven aan Rolande door Renier Joskin de Lamarche) | 1944 |
| 4837 | Tennyson, Alfred | British | V | The Charge of the Light Brigade | 1854 |
| 4838 | Tennyson, Alfred | British | V | The Charge of the Light Brigade | 1854 |
| 4839 | Tersánszky Józsi Jenő | Hungarian | N | Kakuk Marci (Martin Cuckoo) | 1950 |
| 4840 | Tersánszky Józsi Jenő | Hungarian | N | Legenda a nyúlpaprikásról | 1936 |
| 4841 | Tersánszky Józsi Jenő | Hungarian | N | Misi Mókus kalandjai | 1953 |
| 4842 | Tervapää, Juhani (see: Wuolijoki, Hella) | Finnish(Est) | P | | |
| 4843 | Testori, Giovanni | Italian | SS | Il ponte della Ghisolfa [The Ghisolfa bridge] | 1958 |
| 4844 | Tevis, Walter S. | American | N | The Color of Money | 1984 |
| 4845 | Tevis, Walter S. | American | N | The Hustler | 1959 |
| 4846 | Tevis, Walter S. | American | N | The Man Who Fell to Earth | 1963 |
| 4847 | Tevis, Walter S. | American | N | The Man Who Fell to Earth | 1963 |
| 4848 | Thackeray, William Makepeace | British | N | Barry Lyndon (aka: The Memoirs of Barry Lyndon Esq.) | 1856 |
| 4849 | Thackeray, William Makepeace | British | SS | The Rose and the Ring | 1855 |
| 4850 | Thackeray, William Makepeace | British | N | Vanity Fair | 1848 |
| 4851 | Thackeray, William Makepeace | British | N | Vanity Fair | 1848 |
| 4852 | Ṭhākura, Rabīndranātha (see: Tagore, Rabīndranáth) | Indian(Ben) | SS/N/P | | |
| 4853 | Theroux, Paul | American | N | Dr Slaughter | 1984 |
| 4854 | Theroux, Paul | American | N | The Mosquito Coast | 1981 |
| 4855 | Theroux, Paul | American | N | Saint Jack | 1973 |
| 4856 | Thiele, Colin | Australian | N | Blue Fin | 1969 |
| 4857 | Thiele, Colin | Australian | N | Storm Boy | 1963 |
| 4858 | Thiery, Herman (see: Daisne, John) | Belgian | N | | |
| 4859 | Thomas, Dylan | British(Welsh) | SS | The Mouse and the Woman | 1936 |
| 4860 | Thomas, Dylan | British | P(R)-P | Under Milk Wood | 1954 |
| 4861 | Thorup, Kirsten | Danish | N | Himmel og helvede | 1982 |
| 4862 | Thurber, James | American | SS | The Catbird Seat | 1943 |
| 4863 | Thurber, James | American | SS | My Life and Hard Times | 1933 |

| No | Film Title | Country of Production | Date | Director(s) | Duration of Film |
|----|-----------|----------------------|------|-------------|------------------|
| 4820 | **Monte Carlo** {musical version} | USA | 1930 | Ernst Lubitsch | 90 |
| 4821 | **Monsieur Beaucaire** | USA | 1946 | George Marshall | 93 |
| 4822 | **Penrod and Sam** | USA | 1931 | William Beaudine | 70 |
| 4823 | **Penrod and Sam** | USA | 1937 | William McGann | 68 |
| 4824 | **Penrod's Double Trouble** | USA | 1938 | Lewis Seiler | 61 |
| 4825 | **By the Light of the Silvery Moon** {musical version} | USA | 1953 | David Butler | 101 |
| 4826 | **Penrod and His Twin Brother** | USA | 1938 | William McGann | 63 |
| 4827 | **On Moonlight Bay** {musical version} | USA | 1951 | Roy Del Ruth | 95 |
| 4828 | **Business and Pleasure** | USA | 1932(31) | David Butler | 76 |
| 4829 | **Presenting Lily Mars** | USA | 1943 | Norman Taurog | 104 |
| 4830 | **Seventeen** | USA | 1940 | Louis King | 76 |
| 4831 | **Gerusalemme liberata** (The Mighty Crusaders) | IT | 1957 | Carlo Ludovico Bragaglia | 87 |
| 4832 | **Inocência** | BRAZ | 1949 | Luis de Barros Fernando de Barros | 71(90) |
| 4833 | **Inocência** | BRAZ | 1983 | Walter Lima, Jr. | 120 |
| 4834 | **O cabeleira** | BRAZ | 1962 | Milton Amaral | 90 |
| 4835 | | | | | |
| 4836 | **Rolande met de bles** (Roland or Chronicle of Passion) | BEL | 1972 | Roland Verhavert | 126 |
| 4837 | **Balaclava** (USA: Jaws of Hell) | GB | 1930(28) | Maurice Elvey Milton Rosmer | 95 |
| 4838 | **The Charge of the Light Brigade** | USA | 1936 | Michael Curtiz | 116 |
| 4839 | **Kakuk Marci** (Martin Cuckoo) | HUNG | 1973 | György Révész | 101 |
| 4840 | **Legenda a nyúlpaprikásról** (The Rabbit Stew) | HUNG | 1975 | Barna Kabay | 94 |
| 4841 | **Misi Mókus kalandjai** (Adventures of Sam the Squirrel) {puppet version} | HUNG | 1984(80) | Ottó Foky | 72 |
| 4842 | | | | | |
| 4843 | **Rocco e i suoi fratelli** (Rocco and His Brothers) | IT/FR | 1960 | Luchino Visconti | 180 +V |
| 4844 | **The Color of Money** | USA | 1986 | Martin Scorsese | 119 |
| 4845 | **The Hustler** | USA | 1961 | Robert Rossen | 135 +V |
| 4846 | **The Man Who Fell to Earth** | GB | 1976 | Nicolas Roeg | 140 +V |
| 4847 | **The Man Who Fell to Earth** | USA | 1987 | Robert J. Roth | 100 +V |
| 4848 | **Barry Lyndon** | GB | 1975 | Stanley Kubrick | 187 +V |
| 4849 | **Pierscień i róza** [The ring and the rose] | POL | 1987 | Jerzy Gruza | 104 |
| 4850 | **Vanity Fair** | USA | 1932 | Chester M. Franklin | 78 |
| 4851 | **Becky Sharp** | USA | 1935 | Rouben Mamoulian | 83 |
| 4852 | | | | | |
| 4853 | **Half Moon Street** | USA | 1986 | Bob Swaim | 89 +V |
| 4854 | **The Mosquito Coast** | USA | 1986 | Peter Weir | 119 +V |
| 4855 | **Saint Jack** | USA | 1979 | Peter Bogdanovich | 115 |
| 4856 | **Blue Fin** | AUSTL | 1978 | Carl Schultz | 95 |
| 4857 | **Storm Boy** | AUSTL | 1976 | Henri Safran | 87 |
| 4858 | | | | | |
| 4859 | **The Mouse and the Woman** (aka: In the Afternoon of War) | GB | 1981(80) | Karl Francis | 105 +V |
| 4860 | **Under Milk Wood** | GB | 1971 | Andrew Sinclair | 88 +V |
| 4861 | **Himmel og helvede** | DEN | 1988 | Morten Arnfred | 121 |
| 4862 | **The Battle of the Sexes** | GB | 1960(59) | Charles Crichton | 84 |
| 4863 | **Rise and Shine** | USA | 1941 | Allan Dwan | 93 |

| No. | Author | Nationality | Form | Literary Title | Date |
|---|---|---|---|---|---|
| 4864 | Thurber, James | American | SS | The Night the Ghost Got In | 1945 |
| 4865 | Thurber, James | American | SS | The Secret Life of Walter Mitty | 1945 |
| 4866 | Thurber, James; Nugent, Elliot | American | P | The Male Animal | 1941 |
| 4867 | Thurber, James; Nugent, Elliot | American | P | The Male Animal | 1941 |
| 4868 | Thurzó Gábor | Hungarian | N | A szent [The Saint] | 1966 |
| 4869 | Tian Han | Chinese | P | Guan Hanqing | 1958 |
| 4870 | Tian Han | Chinese | P | Liren xing [The fate of three women] | 1945 |
| 4871 | Tieck, Ludwig | German | SS | Des Lebens Überfluß | 1871 |
| 4872 | Timmermans, Felix | Belgian(Fle) | N | Pallieter | 1916 |
| 4873 | Ting Yi (see: He Jingzhi) | Chinese | P | | |
| 4874 | Tobino, Mario | Italian | N | Per le antiche scale | 1972 |
| 4875 | Tokuda Shusei | Japanese | N | Arakure [Tough as nails] | 1915 |
| 4876 | Tolkien, J. R. R. | British | N | Lord of the Rings | 1954-55 |
| 4877 | Toller, Ernst | German | P | Pastor Hall | 1937 |
| 4878 | Tolstoy, Alexsey Nikolayevich | Russian | SS | Gadyuka | 1929 |
| 4879 | Tolstoy, Alexsey Nikolayevich | Russian | N | Giperboloid inzhenera Garina (The Garin Death Ray) (aka: The Death Box) | 1926 |
| 4880 | Tolstoy, Alexsey Nikolayevich | Russian | N | Khozhdeniye po mukam {pt.1} (The Road to Calvary) (aka: Ordeal) | 1922-45 |
| 4881 | Tolstoy, Alexsey Nikolayevich | Russian | N | Khozhdeniye po mukam {pt.2} | 1922-45 |
| 4882 | Tolstoy, Alexsey Nikolayevich | Russian | N | Khozhdeniye po mukam {pt.3} | 1922-45 |
| 4883 | Tolstoy, Alexsey Nikolayevich | Russian | SS | Pokhozdenya grafa Nevzorova, ili Ybikus [The adventures of Nevzorov; or Ibikus] | 1925 |
| 4884 | Tolstoy, Alexsey Nikolayevich | Russian | N | Pyotr pervy (Peter the Great) (aka: Peter the First) | 1929- |
| 4885 | Tolstoy, Alexsey Nikolayevich | Russian | N | Pyotr pervy | 1929-45 |
| 4886 | Tolstoy, Alexsey Nikolayevich | Russian | P | Zolotoy klyuchik; ili, priklyuchenya Buratino (The Golden Key or the Adventures of Buratino) | 1936 |
| 4887 | Tolstoy, Alexsey Nikolayevich | Russian | SS | Zolotoy klyuchik; ili, priklyuchenya Buratino | 1936 |
| 4888 | Tolstoy, Leo (see: Tolstoy, Lev Nikolayevich) | Russian | N/SS/P | | |
| 4889 | Tolstoy, Lev Nikolayevich (Leo Tolstoy) | Russian | N | Anna Karenina | 1875-77 |
| 4890 | Tolstoy, Lev Nikolayevich | Russian | N | Anna Karenina | 1875-77 |
| 4891 | Tolstoy, Lev Nikolayevich | Russian | N | Anna Karenina | 1875-77 |
| 4892 | Tolstoy, Lev Nikolayevich | Russian | N | Anna Karenina | 1875-77 |
| 4893 | Tolstoy, Lev Nikolayevich | Russian | N | Anna Karenina | 1875-77 |
| 4894 | Tolstoy, Lev Nikolayevich | Russian | N | Anna Karenina | 1875-77 |
| 4895 | Tolstoy, Lev Nikolayevich | Russian | SS | Chem liudi zhivy (What Men Live By) (aka: Life Is Worth Living) | 1882 |
| 4896 | Tolstoy, Lev Nikolayevich | Russian | SS | Fal'shivyi kupon (The False Note) (aka: The Forged Coupon) (aka: The Lost Coupon) (aka: The Forged Note) | 1911 |

| No | Film Title | Country of Production | Date | Director(s) | Duration of Film |
|----|-----------|----------------------|------|-------------|------------------|
| 4864 | James Thurber's: The Night the Ghost Got In | USA | 1977 | Robert Stitzel | 16 |
| 4865 | The Secret Life of Walter Mitty | USA | 1947 | Norman Z. McLeod | 110 +V |
| 4866 | The Male Animal | USA | 1942 | Elliott Nugent | 101 |
| 4867 | She's Working Her Way Through College | USA | 1952 | Bruce Humberstone | 101 |
| 4868 | Bekötött szemmel (Blindfold) (aka: With Bound Eyes) | HUNG | 1974 | András Kovács | 85 |
| 4869 | Guan Hanqing | CHN | 1960 | Xu Tao | 138 |
| 4870 | Liren xing | CHN | 1949 | Chen Liting | 90 |
| 4871 | Des Lebens Überfluß | GER | 1950 | Wolfgang Liebeneiner | 83 |
| 4872 | De pallieter | BEL/HOLL | 1975 | Roland Verhavert | 90 |
| 4873 | | | | | |
| 4874 | Per le antiche scale (Down the Ancient Stairs) | IT/FR | 1975 | Mauro Bolognini | 102 |
| 4875 | Arakure (Untamed) (aka: Untamed Woman) | JAP | 1957 | Mikio Naruse | 121 |
| 4876 | The Lord of the Rings {animation} | USA | 1978 | Ralph Bakshi | 133 +V(60) |
| 4877 | Pastor Hall | GB | 1940 | Roy Boulting | 97 |
| 4878 | Gadyuka | USSR | 1966 | Victor Ivchenko | 105 |
| 4879 | Giperboloid inzhenera Garina | USSR | 1966(65) | Alexander Ginzburg | 96 |
| 4880 | Sestry (The Sisters) | USSR | 1957 | Grigori Roshal | 111 |
| 4881 | Vosemnadtsaty god (1918) | USSR | 1958 | Grigori Roshal | 97 |
| 4882 | Khuroye utro (Gray Dawn) | USSR | 1959 | Grigori Roshal | 104 |
| 4883 | Pokhozdenya grafa Nevzorova | USSR | 1982 | Alexander Pankratov-Tchiorny | 78 |
| 4884 | Piotr pervyi (Pt.1: Peter the Great) (aka: Peter the First) (Pt.2: The Conquests of Peter the Great) | USSR | 1937-38 | Vladimir Petrov | Pt.1, 102 Pt.2, 124 |
| 4885 | Yunost' Petra {2 - parts} | USSR/GDR | 1980 | Sergei Gerasimov | Pt.1, 72 Pt.2, 69 |
| 4886 | Zolotoi klutchik (The Golden Key) {live-action + puppets} | USSR | 1939(38) | Aleksander Ptushko | 70 |
| 4887 | Priklyuchenya Buratino {animation} | USSR | 1959 | Dmitri Babichenko Ivan Ivanov-Vano | 68 |
| 4888 | | | | | |
| 4889 | Anna Karenina | USA | 1935 | Clarence Brown | 95 |
| 4890 | Anna Karenina | GB | 1948(47) | Julien Duvivier | 123(139) +V |
| 4891 | Anna Karenina {2 - parts} | USSR | 1953 | Tatiana Lukashevitch | Pt.1, 83 Pt.2, 82 |
| 4892 | Amor prohibido | ARG | 1958 | Luís César Amadori | 99 |
| 4893 | Anna Karenina | USSR | 1967 | Alexander Zarkhi | 135 |
| 4894 | Anna Karenina | USSR | 1975 | Margarita Pilikhina | 85 |
| 4895 | What Men Live By | GB | 1939 | Donald Taylor | 42 |
| 4896 | L'argent (Money) | SWITZ/FR | 1983 | Robert Bresson | 85 |

| No. | Author | Nationality | Form | Literary Title | Date |
|---|---|---|---|---|---|
| 4897 | **Tolstoy, Lev Nikolayevich** | Russian | N | **Khadzh-Murat** <br> *(Hadji Murat)* <br> *(aka: Hadji Murad)* | 1911 |
| 4898 | **Tolstoy, Lev Nikolayevich** | Russian | N | **Khadzh-Murat** | 1911 |
| 4899 | **Tolstoy, Lev Nikolayevich** | Russian | N | **Kazaki** <br> *(The Cossacks)* | 1863 |
| 4900 | **Tolstoy, Lev Nikolayevich** | Russian | N | **Kazaki** | 1863 |
| 4901 | **Tolstoy, Lev Nikolayevich** | Russian | SS | **Kreytserova sonata** <br> *(The Kreutzer Sonata)* | 1889 |
| 4902 | **Tolstoy, Lev Nikolayevich** | Russian | SS | **Kreytserova sonata** | 1889 |
| 4903 | **Tolstoy, Lev Nikolayevich** | Russian | SS | **Kreytserova sonata** | 1889 |
| 4904 | **Tolstoy, Lev Nikolayevich** | Russian | SS | **Kreytserova sonata** | 1889 |
| 4905 | **Tolstoy, Lev Nikolayevich** | Russian | SS | **Mnogo li chelovka zemli nuzno?** <br> *(How Much Land Does a Man Need?)* | 1885 |
| 4906 | **Tolstoy, Lev Nikolayevich** | Russian | SS | **Otets Sergei** <br> *(Father Sergius)* | 1898 |
| 4907 | **Tolstoy, Lev Nikolayevich** | Russian | SS | **Otets Sergei** | 1898 |
| 4908 | **Tolstoy, Lev Nikolayevich** | Russian | SS | **Otets Sergei** | 1898 |
| 4909 | **Tolstoy, Lev Nikolayevich** | Russian | SS | **Polikushka** | 1863 |
| 4910 | **Tolstoy, Lev Nikolayevich** | Russian | SS | **Smert Ivana Ilicha** <br> *(The Death of Ivan Ilyica)* | 1886 |
| 4911 | **Tolstoy, Lev Nikolayevich** | Russian | SS | **Tri medvedya** | 1875 |
| 4912 | **Tolstoy, Lev Nikolayevich** | Russian | N | **Voskreseniye** <br> *(Resurrection)* <br> *(aka: The Awakening)* | 1899 |
| 4913 | **Tolstoy, Lev Nikolayevich** | Russian | N | **Voskreseniye** | 1899 |
| 4914 | **Tolstoy, Lev Nikolayevich** | Russian | N | **Voskreseniye** | 1899 |
| 4915 | **Tolstoy, Lev Nikolayevich** | Russian | N | **Voskreseniye** | 1899 |
| 4916 | **Tolstoy, Lev Nikolayevich** | Russian | N | **Voskreseniye** | 1899 |
| 4917 | **Tolstoy, Lev Nikolayevich** | Russian | N | **Voskreseniye** | 1899 |
| 4918 | **Tolstoy, Lev Nikolayevich** | Russian | N | **Voskreseniye** | 1899 |
| 4919 | **Tolstoy, Lev Nikolayevich** | Russian | N | **Voyna i mir** <br> *(War and Peace)* | 1863-69 |
| 4920 | **Tolstoy, Lev Nikolayevich** | Russian | N | **Voyna i mir** | 1863-69 |
| 4921 | **Tolstoy, Lev Nikolayevich** | Russian | N | **Voyna i mir** | 1863-69 |
| 4922 | **Tolstoy, Lev Nikolayevich** | Russian | P | **Zhivoi trup** <br> *(The Living Corpse)* <br> *(aka: The Live Corpse)* | 1911 |
| 4923 | **Tolstoy, Lev Nikolayevich** | Russian | P | **Zhivoi trup** | 1911 |
| 4924 | **Tolstoy, Lev Nikolayevich** | Russian | P | **Zhivoi trup** | 1911 |
| 4925 | **Topelius, Zachris** | Finnish(Swe) | N | **Gröna kammarn på Linnais gård** | 1859 |
| 4926 | **Topelius, Zachris** - *{p};* <br> **Grimm, J. & W.** - *{ss}* | Finnish | SS-P | **Prinsessan Törnrosa** *{p}* <br> **Dornröschen** *{ss}* <br> *(Little Briar Rose)* | 1870+ <br> 1812 |
| 4927 | **Torberg, Friedrich** <br> *(Friedrich Kantor-Berg)* | Austrian | N | **Der Schüler Gerber hat absolviert** <br> *(aka: Der Schüler Gerber)* <br> *(The Examination)* | 1930 |
| 4928 | **Trakl, Georg** | Austrian | V | **Die junge Magd** | 1913 |

| No | Film Title | Country of Production | Date | Director(s) | Duration of Film |
|---|---|---|---|---|---|
| 4897 | **Der Weiße Teufel** (The White Devil) | GER | 1930 | **Alexandre Volkoff** | 110 |
| 4898 | **Agi Murad, il diavolo bianco** (The White Warrior) | IT/YUGO | 1959 | **Riccardo Freda** | 91(86) |
| 4899 | **I cosacchi** (The Cossacks) | IT/FR | 1959 | **Giorgio Rivalta** **Viktor Tourjansky** | 114 |
| 4900 | **Khazakki** (The Cossacks) | USSR | 1962(61) | **Vasili Pronin** | 96 |
| 4901 | **Die Kreutzersonate** (The Kreutzer Sonata) | GER | 1937 | **Veit Harlan** | 84 |
| 4902 | **Les nuits blanches de Saint-Pétersbourg** | FR | 1938(37) | **Jean Dréville** | 97 |
| 4903 | **Celos** [Jealousy] | ARG | 1946 | **Mario Soffici** | 100 |
| 4904 | **Kreytserova sonata** (The Kreutzer Sonata) | USSR | 1987 | **Mikhail Schweitzer** **Sofia Milkina** | 158(135) |
| 4905 | **Scarabea - Wieviel Erde braucht der Mensch?** (Scarabea - How Much Land Does a Man Need?) | GER | 1968 | **Hans-Jürgen Syberberg** | 130(90) |
| 4906 | **Le père Serge** | FR | 1945 | **Lucien Ganier-Raymond** | 105 |
| 4907 | **Otets Sergii** (Father Sergius) (aka: Father Serge) | USSR | 1978 | **Igor Talankin** | 95 |
| 4908 | **Il sole anche di notte** (Night Sun) | IT/FR/ GER | 1990 | **Paolo Taviani** **Vittorio Taviani** | 113 |
| 4909 | **Polikuschka** (IT: Polikuska) | GER/IT/ FR | 1958 | **Carmine Gallone** | 79(88) |
| 4910 | **Prostaya smert** | USSR | 1985 | **Alexander Kaidanovsky** | 68 |
| 4911 | **Tri medvedya** {animation} | USSR | 1958 | **Roman Davydov** | 13 |
| 4912 | **Resurrection** | USA | 1931(30) | **Edwin Carewe** | 81 |
| 4913 | **We Live Again** (aka: Resurrection) | USA | 1934 | **Rouben Mamoulian** | 85 |
| 4914 | **Fu huo** [Resurrection] | CHN | 1941 | **Mei Qian** | 90 |
| 4915 | **Resurrección** | MEX | 1943 | **Gilberto Martínez Solares** | 92 |
| 4916 | **Fukkatsu** (aka: Maslova) | JAP | 1950 | **Akira Nobuchi** | 93 |
| 4917 | **Auferstehung** (IT: Resurrezione) (Resurrection) | GER/FR/ IT | 1958 | **Rolf Hansen** | 106(121) |
| 4918 | **Voskreseniye** (Resurrection) | USSR | 1960-62 | **Mikhail Shveytzer** | Pt.1, 101 Pt.2, 108 |
| 4919 | **War and Peace** (IT: Guerra e pace) | USA/IT | 1956 | **King Vidor** **Mario Soldati** | 211(240) +V(208) |
| 4920 | **Tozhe lyudi** | USSR | 1959 | **Georgi Danelia** | 14 |
| 4921 | **Voyna i mir** (War and Peace) {4 - parts} | USSR | 1963-67 | **Sergei Bondarchuk** | 507(434) (373) +V |
| 4922 | **Redemption** | USA | 1930 | **Fred Niblo** | 82(67) |
| 4923 | **Nuits de feu** (Nights of Fire) (aka: The Living Corpse) | FR | 1937 | **Marcel L'Herbier** | 98 |
| 4924 | **Zhivoi trup** (The Living Corpse) | USSR | 1969(68) | **Vladimir Vengerov** | 135(141) |
| 4925 | **Linnaisten vihreä kamari** [The green chamber of Linnainen] | FIN | 1945 | **Valentin Vaala** | 91 |
| 4926 | **Prinsessa Ruusunen** (Sleeping Beauty) | FIN | 1949 | **Edvin Laine** | 99 |
| 4927 | **Der Schüler Gerber** [Student Gerber] | GER/AUST | 1980 | **Wolfgang Glück** | 99 |
| 4928 | **An diesen Abenden** | AUST | 1951 | **Herbert Vesely** | 10 |

| No. | Author | Nationality | Form | Literary Title | Date |
|-----|--------|-------------|------|----------------|------|
| 4929 | **Traven, Ben** (Bruno Traven) | American(Ger) | N | **Die Brücke im Dschungel** (The Bridge in the Jungle) | 1929 |
| 4930 | **Traven, Ben** | American | N | **Macario** (aka: The Healer) | 1950 |
| 4931 | **Traven, Ben** | American | N | **Die Rebellion der Gehenkten** (The Rebellion of the Hanged) | 1936 |
| 4932 | **Traven, Ben** | American | N | **Der Schatz der Sierra Madre** (The Treasure of the Sierra Madre) | 1927 |
| 4933 | **Traven, Ben** | American | N | **Das Totenschiff** (The Death Ship) | 1926 |
| 4934 | **Traven, Ben** | American | N | **Die weisse Rose** (The White Rose) | 1929 |
| 4935 | **Traven, Bruno** (see: Traven, Ben) | American(Ger) | N | | |
| 4936 | **Trenyov, Konstantin** | Russian | P | **Lyubov' Yarovaya** | 1926 |
| 4937 | **Trenyov, Konstantin** | Russian | P | **Lyubov' Yarovaya** | 1926 |
| 4938 | **Trevor, William** | Irish | SS | **Attracta** | 1978 |
| 4939 | **Trevor, William** | Irish | N | **Fools of Fortune** | 1983 |
| 4940 | **Trifonov, Yurri Valentinovich** | Russian | N | **Utolyeniye zhazhdy** [Quenching thirst] | 1963 |
| 4941 | **Trigo, Felipe** | Spanish | N | **Jarrapellejos** | 1914 |
| 4942 | **Trollope, Anthony** | British | SS | **Malachi's Cove** | 1864 |
| 4943 | **Troyat, Henri** (Lev Tarassov) | French/ Russian | N | **Grandeur nature** (One Minus Two) | 1936 |
| 4944 | **Troyat, Henri** | French/ Russian | N | **La neige en deuil** (The Mountain) | 1952 |
| 4945 | **Troyat, Henri** | French/ Russian | N | **Tendre et violente Elisabeth** (Tender and Violent Elizabeth) | 1957 |
| 4946 | **Ts'ao Chan** (see: Cao Zhan) | Chinese | N | | |
| 4947 | **Ts'ao Hsüeh-ch'in** (see: Cao Zhan) | Chinese | N | | |
| 4948 | **Ts'ao Yu** (see: Wan Jiabao) | Chinese | P | | |
| 4949 | **Tsuboi Sakae** | Japanese | N | **Nijūshi no hitomi** (Twenty-Four Eyes) | 1952 |
| 4950 | **Tsuruya Nanboku, IV** | Japanese | P(K) | **Tōkaidō Yotsuya kaidan** (aka: Yotsuya kaidan) {pts.1-2} | 1825 |
| 4951 | **Tsuuchi Hanjūrō** | Japanese | P(K) | **Narukami** [Saint Narukami] | 1742 |
| 4952 | **Tucholsky, Kurt** | German | SS | **Rheinsberg, ein Bilderbuch für Verliebte** | 1912 |
| 4953 | **Tucholsky, Kurt** | German | N | **Schloß Gripsholm** (Gripsholm Palace) | 1931 |
| 4954 | **Turgenev, Ivan** | Russian | SS | **Asya** (aka: Assya) (aka: Acia) | 1858 |
| 4955 | **Turgenev, Ivan** | Russian | SS | **Biryuk** (The Lone Wolf) | 1852 |
| 4956 | **Turgenev, Ivan** | Russian | N | **Dvoryanskoe gnezdo** (Home of the Gentry) (aka: A House of Gentlefolk) | 1859 |
| 4957 | **Turgenev, Ivan** | Russian | N | **Dvoryanskoe gnezdo** | 1859 |
| 4958 | **Turgenev, Ivan** | Russian | P | **Mesyats v derevne** (A Month in the Country) | 1855 |
| 4959 | **Turgenev, Ivan** | Russian | P | **Mesyats v derevne** | 1855 |
| 4960 | **Turgenev, Ivan** | Russian | SS | **Mumu** | 1854 |
| 4961 | **Turgenev, Ivan** | Russian | SS | **Mumu** | 1854 |
| 4962 | **Turgenev, Ivan** | Russian | N | **Nakanune** (On the Eve) | 1860 |

| No | Film Title | Country of Production | Date | Director(s) | Duration of Film |
|----|-----------|----------------------|------|-------------|------------------|
| 4929 | The Bridge in the Jungle | USA/MEX | 1971 | Pancho Kohner | 85 |
| 4930 | Macario<br>*(aka: Le destin)* | MEX | 1960 | Roberto Gavaldón | 90 |
| 4931 | La rebelión de los colgados | MEX | 1954 | Alfredo B. Crevenna | 83 |
| 4932 | The Treasure of the Sierra Madre | USA | 1948 | John Huston | 126<br>+V(121) |
| 4933 | Das Totenschiff | GER | 1959 | Georg Tressler | 97 |
| 4934 | La Rosa Blanca | MEX | 1961 | Roberto Gavaldón | 100 |
| 4935 | | | | | |
| 4936 | Lyubov' Yarovaya<br>*{2 - parts}* | USSR | 1953 | Ian Frid | Pt.1, 84<br>Pt.2, 70 |
| 4937 | Lyubov' Yarovaya | USSR | 1970 | Vladimir Fetin | 100 |
| 4938 | Attracta | IRE | 1983 | Kieran Hickey | 55 |
| 4939 | Fools of Fortune | GB | 1990 | Pat O'Connor | 109 +V |
| 4940 | Utolyeniye zhazhdy | USSR | 1968 | Bulat Mansurov | 83 |
| 4941 | Jarrapellejos | SP | 1987 | Antonio Giménez Rico | 108 |
| 4942 | Malachi's Cove<br>*(aka: The Seaweed Children)* | GB | 1973 | Henry Herbert | 89<br>+V(75) |
| 4943 | Le feu de paille<br>*(Fire in the Straw)*<br>*(aka: L'enfant prodige)* | FR | 1939 | Jean Benoit-Lévy | 117(89) |
| 4944 | The Mountain | USA | 1956 | Edward Dmytryk | 105 |
| 4945 | Tendre et violente Elisabeth<br>*(aka: Passionate Affair)* | FR | 1960 | Henri Decoin | 105 |
| 4946 | | | | | |
| 4947 | | | | | |
| 4948 | | | | | |
| 4949 | Nijūshi no hitomi<br>*(Twenty Four Eyes)* | JAP | 1954 | Keisuke Kinoshita | 154(105) |
| 4950 | Yotsuya kaidan<br>*(aka: Shinshaku Yotsuya kaidan)*<br>*(The Yotsuya Ghost Story)*<br>*(aka: Illusion of Blood)* | JAP | 1949 | Keisuke Kinoshita | Pt.1, 85<br>Pt.2, 73 |
| 4951 | Bijo to kaī-ryū<br>*(Beauty and the Dragon)* | JAP | 1955 | Kōzaburō Yoshimura | 99 |
| 4952 | Rheinsberg | GER | 1967 | Kurt Hoffmann | 88 |
| 4953 | Schloß Gripsholm<br>*(Gripsholm Palace)* | GER | 1963 | Kurt Hoffmann | 99 |
| 4954 | Asya<br>*(aka: Love Should Be Guarded)* | USSR | 1977 | Iosif Heifitz | 96 |
| 4955 | Birjuk<br>*(Lone Wolf)* | USSR | 1977 | Roman Balaian | 76 |
| 4956 | Chun can meng duan<br>*[Dream broken in late spring]* | CHN | 1947 | Sun Jing | 100 |
| 4957 | Dvorianskoe gnezdo<br>*(A Nest of Gentlefolk)* | USSR | 1969 | Andrei Mikhalkov-Konchalovsky | 106 |
| 4958 | Secrets | FR | 1943(42) | Pierre Blanchar | 100 |
| 4959 | A Month in the Country | USA | 1985 | Quentin Lawrence | 90 +V |
| 4960 | Mumu | USSR | 1960(59) | Anatoli Bobrovsky<br>Yevgeni Teterin | 71 |
| 4961 | Mumu<br>*{animation}* | USSR | 1987 | V. Karavaev | 20 |
| 4962 | Nakanunye<br>*(BULG: V navecherieto)*<br>*(On the Eve)* | USSR/BULG | 1959 | Vladimir Petrov | 88(97) |

| No. | Author | Nationality | Form | Literary Title | Date |
|-----|--------|-------------|------|----------------|------|
| 4963 | **Turgenev, Ivan** | Russian | P | **Nakhlebnik**<br>*(A Poor Gentleman)*<br>*(aka: The Family Charge)*<br>*(aka: Chuzhoy khleb)*<br>*[Alien bread]* | 1869<br>(aka:1857) |
| 4964 | **Turgenev, Ivan** | Russian | N | **Ottsy i dety**<br>*(Fathers and Sons)*<br>*(aka: Fathers and Children)* | 1862 |
| 4965 | **Turgenev, Ivan** | Russian | SS | **Pervaya lyubov'**<br>*(First Love)* | 1860 |
| 4966 | **Turgenev, Ivan** | Russian | SS | **Pervaya lyubov'** | 1860 |
| 4967 | **Turgenev, Ivan** | Russian | N | **Rudin** | 1856 |
| 4968 | **Turgenev, Ivan** | Russian | SS | **Veshniye vody**<br>*(Torrents of Spring)*<br>*(aka: Spring Floods)* | 1872 |
| 4969 | **Turgenev, Ivan** | Russian | SS | **Veshniye vody** | 1872 |
| 4970 | **Turgenev, Ivan** | Russian | SS | **Veshniye vody** | 1872 |
| 4971 | **Turgenev, Ivan** | Russian | P | **Zavtrak u predvoditelya**<br>*(An Amicable Settlement)* | 1856 |
| 4972 | **Tuuri, Antti** | Finnish | N | **Pohjanmaa**<br>*[Plainlands]* | 1982 |
| 4973 | **Tuuri, Antti** | Finnish | N | **Talvisota**<br>*[The winter war]* | 1984 |
| 4974 | **Twain, Mark**<br>*(Samuel Clemens)* | American | SS | **The Celebrated Jumping Frog of Calaveras County**<br>*(aka: The Jumping Frog)* | 1867 |
| 4975 | **Twain, Mark** | American | N | **A Connecticut Yankee in King Arthur's Court** | 1889 |
| 4976 | **Twain, Mark** | American | N | **A Connecticut Yankee in King Arthur's Court** | 1889 |
| 4977 | **Twain, Mark** | American | N | **A Connecticut Yankee in King Arthur's Court** | 1889 |
| 4978 | **Twain, Mark** | American | N | **Huckleberry Finn, the Adventures of** | 1884 |
| 4979 | **Twain, Mark** | American | N | **Huckleberry Finn, the Adventures of** | 1884 |
| 4980 | **Twain, Mark** | American | N | **Huckleberry Finn, the Adventures of** | 1884 |
| 4981 | **Twain, Mark** | American | N | **Huckleberry Finn, the Adventures of** | 1884 |
| 4982 | **Twain, Mark** | American | N | **Huckleberry Finn, the Adventures of** | 1884 |
| 4983 | **Twain, Mark** | American | SS | **Is He Living or Is He Dead?** | 1900 |
| 4984 | **Twain, Mark** | American | SS | **The Man That Corrupted Hadleyburg** | 1900 |
| 4985 | **Twain, Mark** | American | SS | **The £1,000,000 Bank-Note** | 1893 |
| 4986 | **Twain, Mark** | American | N | **The Prince and the Pauper** | 1881 |
| 4987 | **Twain, Mark** | American | N | **The Prince and the Pauper** | 1881 |
| 4988 | **Twain, Mark** | American | N | **The Prince and the Pauper** | 1881 |
| 4989 | **Twain, Mark** | American | N | **Tom Sawyer, Adventures of** | 1876 |
| 4990 | **Twain, Mark** | American | N | **Tom Sawyer, Adventures of** | 1876 |
| 4991 | **Twain, Mark** | American | N | **Tom Sawyer, Adventures of**<br>*{pt.1}* | 1876 |
| 4992 | **Twain, Mark** | American | N | **Tom Sawyer, Adventures of**<br>*{pt.2}* | 1876 |
| 4993 | **Twain, Mark** | American | N | **Tom Sawyer, Adventures of** | 1876 |
| 4994 | **Twain, Mark** | American | N | **Tom Sawyer, Adventures of** | 1876 |
| 4995 | **Twain, Mark** | American | SS | **Tom Sawyer, Detective** | 1897 |
| 4996 | **Tyler, Anne** | American | N | **The Accidental Tourist** | 1985 |

| No | Film Title | Country of Production | Date | Director(s) | Duration of Film |
|---|---|---|---|---|---|
| 4963 | **Nakhlebnik** | USSR | 1953 | **Vladimir Basov**<br>**Mstislav Kortchagin** | 100 |
| 4964 | **Ottsy i deti**<br>*(Fathers and Sons)* | USSR | 1958 | **Adolf Bergunker**<br>**Natalia Rashevskaya** | 102 |
| 4965 | **Primer amor**<br>*(First Love)* | SP | 1942(41) | **Claudio de la Torre** | 92 |
| 4966 | **Erste Liebe**<br>*(First Love)* | GER/SWITZ/<br>HUNG | 1970 | **Maximilian Schell** | 89(96)<br>+V |
| 4967 | **Rudin** | USSR | 1976 | **Konstantin Voinov** | 94 |
| 4968 | **Jarní vody**<br>*(Spring Floods)* | CZ | 1968 | **Václav Krška** | 93 |
| 4969 | **Poezdka v Visbaden** | USSR | 1989 | **Eugenie Gerasimov** | 86 |
| 4970 | **Acque di primavera**<br>*(Torrents of Spring)* | IT/FR | 1989 | **Jerzy Skolimowski** | 101 |
| 4971 | **Zavtrak u predvoditelya** | USSR | 1953 | **Anatoly Rybakov** | 55 |
| 4972 | **Pohjanmaa** | FIN | 1988 | **Pekka Parikka** | 129 |
| 4973 | **Talvisota** | FIN | 1989 | **Pekka Parikka** | 199 |
| 4974 | **The Best Man Wins** | USA | 1948 | **John Sturges** | 75 |
| 4975 | **A Connecticut Yankee** | USA | 1931 | **David Butler** | 96 |
| 4976 | **A Connecticut Yankee in King Arthur's Court**<br>*(aka: A Connecticut Yankee)*<br>*(aka: A Yankee in King Arthur's Court)* | USA | 1949(48) | **Tay Garnett** | 107 |
| 4977 | **The Spaceman and King Arthur**<br>*(aka: Unidentified Flying Oddball)* | USA | 1979 | **Russ Mayberry** | 93<br>+V |
| 4978 | **Huckleberry Finn** | USA | 1931 | **Norman Taurog** | 78 |
| 4979 | **The Adventures of Huckleberry Finn** | USA | 1939 | **Richard Thorpe** | 90 |
| 4980 | **The Adventures of Huckleberry Finn** | USA | 1960 | **Michael Curtiz** | 107 |
| 4981 | **Huckleberry Finn**<br>{musical version} | USA | 1974 | **J. Lee Thompson** | 114 |
| 4982 | **Sovsem propashtshiy**<br>*(The Adventures of Huckleberry Finn)* | USSR | 1974 | **Georgi Danelia** | 95 |
| 4983 | **Det er ikke appelsiner - det er heste**<br>*[It is not oranges - but horses]* | DEN | 1967 | **Ebbe Langberg** | 95 |
| 4984 | **The Man That Corrupted Hadleyburg** | USA | 1980 | **Ralph Rosenblum** | 40 |
| 4985 | **The Million Pound Note**<br>*(USA: Man With a Million)* | GB | 1954(53) | **Ronald Neame** | 91<br>+V(85) |
| 4986 | **The Prince and the Pauper** | USA | 1937 | **William Keighley** | 118 +V |
| 4987 | **The Prince and the Pauper** | GB | 1962 | **Don Chaffey** | 93 +V |
| 4988 | **The Prince and the Pauper**<br>*(aka: Crossed Swords)* | PAN | 1977 | **Richard Fleischer** | 121 |
| 4989 | **Tom Sawyer** | USA | 1930 | **John Cromwell** | 86 |
| 4990 | **The Adventures of Tom Sawyer** | USA | 1938(37) | **Norman Taurog** | 93 +V(76) |
| 4991 | **Aventurile lui Tom Sawyer** | ROM/FR | 1968 | **Wolfgang Liebeneiner**<br>**Mihai Iacob** | 96 |
| 4992 | **Moartea lui Joe Indianul**<br>*[The death of Joe, the indian]* | ROM/FR | 1969(68) | **Wolfgang Liebeneiner**<br>**Mihai Iacob** | 80 |
| 4993 | **Tom Sawyer**<br>{musical version} | USA | 1973 | **Don Taylor** | 103<br>+V(95) |
| 4994 | **Páni Kluci**<br>*(Tom Sawyer)* | CZ | 1976 | **Věra Plívová-Šimková** | 90 |
| 4995 | **Tom Sawyer, Detective** | USA | 1938 | **Louis King** | 68 |
| 4996 | **The Accidental Tourist** | USA | 1988 | **Lawrence Kasdan** | 121 +V |

| No. | Author | Nationality | Form | Literary Title | Date |
|---|---|---|---|---|---|
| 4997 | **Ueda Akinari** | Japanese | SS | **Asaji ga yado** (House Amid the Thickets)+ **Jasei no in** (The Lust of the White Serpent) | c.1768 |
| 4998 | **Uhry, Alfred** | American | P | **Driving Miss Daisy** | 1987 |
| 4999 | **Unamuno, Miguel de** (Miguel de Unamuno y Jugo) | Spanish | N | **Abel Sanchez: una historia de pasión** | 1917 |
| 5000 | **Unamuno, Miguel de** | Spanish | SS | **Nada menos que todo un hombre** (Nothing Less Than a Whole Man) | 1916 |
| 5001 | **Unamuno, Miguel de** | Spanish | SS | **Nada menos que todo un hombre** | 1916 |
| 5002 | **Unamuno, Miguel de** | Spanish | SS | **Nada menos que todo un hombre** | 1916 |
| 5003 | **Unamuno, Miguel de** | Spanish | SS | **Nada menos que todo un hombre** | 1916 |
| 5004 | **Unamuno, Miguel de** | Spanish | N | **Niebla** (Mist) | 1914 |
| 5005 | **Unamuno, Miguel de** | Spanish | N | **La tia Tula** [Aunt Tula] | 1921 |
| 5006 | **Unamuno y Jugo, Miguel de** (see: Unamuno, Miguel de) | Spanish | N/SS | | |
| 5007 | **Updike, John** | American | SS | **The Music School** | 1966 |
| 5008 | **Updike, John** | American | N | **Rabbit, Run** | 1960 |
| 5009 | **Updike, John** | American | N | **The Witches of Eastwick** | 1984 |
| 5010 | **Uppdal, Kristofer** | Norwegian | N | **Dansen gjenom skuggeheim** [The dance through the world of shadows] | 1911-24 |
| 5011 | **Usigli, Rodolfo** | Mexican | N | **Ensayo de un crimen** [Trial of a crime] | 1944 |
| 5012 | **Vailland, Roger** | French | N | **Beau masque** [Beautiful mask] | 1954 |
| 5013 | **Vailland, Roger** | French | N | **Drôle de jeu** (Playing With Fire) | 1945 |
| 5014 | **Vailland, Roger** | French | N | **La loi** (The Law) | 1957 |
| 5015 | **Vailland, Roger** | French | N | **Les mauvais coups** (Turn of the Wheel) | 1948 |
| 5016 | **Vailland, Roger** | French | N | **La truite** (The Trout) (aka: A Young Trout) | 1964 |
| 5017 | **Valera, Juan** (Juan Valera y Alcalá Galiano) | Spanish | N | **Pepita Jiménez** | 1874 |
| 5018 | **Valera y Alcalá Galiano, Juan** (see: Valera, Juan) | Spanish | N | | |
| 5019 | **Valle-Inclán, Ramón María del** | Spanish | SS | **Femeninas +** **Mi hermana Antonia** (My Sister Antonia) | 1895+ 1909 |
| 5020 | **Valle-Inclán, Ramón María del** | Spanish | N | **Flor de santidad** | 1904 |
| 5021 | **Vālmīki** | Indian(Sans) | V | **Ramayana** (aka: Valmiki-Ramayana) | n.d. |
| 5022 | **Vālmīki** | Indian | V | **Ramayana** | n.d. |
| 5023 | **Vančura, Vladislav** | Czech | N | **Konec starých časů** (The End of Our Times) | 1934 |
| 5024 | **Vančura, Vladislav** | Czech | N | **Markéta Lazarová** | 1931 |
| 5025 | **Vančura, Vladislav** | Czech | N | **Rozmarné léto** (Capricious Summer) | 1926 |
| 5026 | **Van der Post, Laurens** | South African | N | **The Seed and the Sower** | 1963 |
| 5027 | **Van Druten, John** (see: Isherwood, Christopher) | British/ American | P/SS | | |
| 5028 | **Vargas Llosa, Mario** | Peruvian | N | **La tía Julia y el escribidor** (Aunt Julia and the Scriptwriter) | 1977 |
| 5029 | **Värnlund, Rudolf** | Swedish | P | **U 39** | 1939 |
| 5030 | **Vassilikos, Vassilis** | Greek | N | **Z** | 1966 |
| 5031 | **Vazov, Ivan** | Bulgarian | SS | **Edna balgarka** (A Bulgarian Woman) | 1899 |

| No | Film Title | Country of Production | Date | Director(s) | Duration of Film |
|---|---|---|---|---|---|
| 4997 | **Ugetsu monogatari** *(Tales of the Pale and Silvery Moon After the Rain)* *(aka: Ugetsu)* | JAP | 1953 | **Kenji Mizoguchi** | 89(96) |
| 4998 | **Driving Miss Daisy** | USA | 1989 | **Bruce Beresford** | 99 |
| 4999 | **Abel Sanchez** | SP | 1946 | **Carlos Serrano de Osma** | 67 |
| 5000 | **Todo un hombre** | ARG | 1943 | **Pierre Chenal** | 94 |
| 5001 | **La entrega** | MEX | 1954 | **Julián Soler** | 110 |
| 5002 | **Nada menos que todo un hombre** | SP | 1972(71) | **Rafael Gil** | 132(123) +V |
| 5003 | **Todo un hombre** | SP/MEX | 1983(81) | **Rafael Villaseñor** | 91(98) |
| 5004 | **Las cuatro novias de Augusto Pérez** | SP | 1975 | **José Jara** | 101 |
| 5005 | **La tia Tula** | SP | 1964(63) | **Miguel Picazo** | 109(114) |
| 5006 | | | | | |
| 5007 | **The Music School** | USA | 1977 | **John Korty** | 30 |
| 5008 | **Rabbit, Run** | USA | 1970 | **Jack Smight** | 94 |
| 5009 | **The Witches of Eastwick** | USA | 1987 | **George Miller** | 118 +V |
| 5010 | **Rallarblod** | NOR | 1979 | **Erik Solbakken** | 123 |
| 5011 | **Ensayo de un crimen** *(aka: La vida criminal de Archibaldo de la Cruz)* *(The Criminal Life of Archibaldo de la Cruz)* | MEX | 1955 | **Luis Buñuel** | 92 |
| 5012 | **Beau masque** | FR/IT | 1972 | **Bernard Paul** | 100 |
| 5013 | **Drôle de jeu** | FR | 1968 | **Pierre Kast** | 90 |
| 5014 | **La legge** *(FR: La loi)* *(Where the Hot Wind Blows)* *(aka: The Law)* | IT/FR | 1959(58) | **Jules Dassin** | 126 |
| 5015 | **Les mauvais coups** *(Naked Autumn)* | FR | 1960 | **François Leterrier** | 103 |
| 5016 | **La truite** *(The Trout)* | FR | 1982 | **Joseph Losey** | 105 |
| 5017 | **Pepita Jiménez** *(Bride to Be)* | SP/USA | 1975 | **Rafael Moreno Alba** | 108(99) +V(106) |
| 5018 | | | | | |
| 5019 | **Beatriz** | SP | 1976 | **Gonzalo Suárez** | 84(99) |
| 5020 | **Flor de santidad** *(Flowers of Holiness)* | SP | 1973(72) | **Adolfo Marsillach** | 105(109) |
| 5021 | **Lab kush** | IND (BEN) | 1967 | **Ashoke Chatterjee** | 140 |
| 5022 | **Ram Rajya** *[The kingdom of Ram]* | IND (HIN) | 1967 | **Vijay Bhatt** | 175 |
| 5023 | **Konec starých časů** *(The End of Old Times)* | CZ | 1989 | **Jiří Menzel** | 97 |
| 5024 | **Markéta Lazarová** | CZ | 1967 | **František Vláčil** | 162 |
| 5025 | **Rozmarné léto** *(Capricious Summer)* | CZ | 1968 | **Jiří Menzel** | 75 |
| 5026 | **Merry Christmas Mr Lawrence** | GB | 1983 | **Nagisa Ōshima** | 123 |
| 5027 | | | | | |
| 5028 | **Aunt Julia and the Scriptwriter** *(aka: Tune in Tomorrow)* | USA | 1990 | **Jon Amiel** | 104 |
| 5029 | **Ubåt 39** *(U-Boat 39)* | SWE | 1952 | **Erik 'Hampe' Faustman** | 85 |
| 5030 | **Z** | FR/ALG | 1968 | **Constantin Costa-Gavras** | 125 |
| 5031 | **Edna balgarka** *(A Bulgarian Woman)* | BULG | 1956 | **Nikolai Borovishki** | 22 |

| No. | Author | Nationality | Form | Literary Title | Date |
|-----|--------|-------------|------|----------------|------|
| 5032 | **Vazov, Ivan** | Bulgarian | V | **Gramada** | 1880 |
| 5033 | **Vazov, Ivan** | Bulgarian | N | **Pod igoto**<br>*(Under the Yoke)* | 1889-90 |
| 5034 | **Vega, Lope de**<br>*(Lope de Vega Carpio)* | Spanish | P | **Fuenteovejuna**<br>*(aka: Fuente ovejuna)*<br>*(The Sheep-Well)*<br>*(aka: All Citizens Are Soldiers)* | 1619 |
| 5035 | **Vega, Lope de** | Spanish | P | **El mejor alcalde, el rey**<br>*(The King, the Greatest Alcalde)* | 1620-23 |
| 5036 | **Vega, Lope de** | Spanish | P | **La moza del cántaro** | 1646 |
| 5037 | **Vega, Ventura de la** | Spanish | P | **El hombre de mundo** | 1845 |
| 5038 | **Vélez de Guevara, Luis** | Spanish | N | **El diablo cojuelo**<br>*(The Limping Devil)* | 1641 |
| 5039 | **Verbitsky, Bernardo** | Argentine | N | **Calles de tango** | 1953 |
| 5040 | **Vercors**<br>*(Jean Bruller)* | French | N | **Le silence de la mer**<br>*(Put Out the Light)* | 1942(43) |
| 5041 | **Verga, Giovanni** | Italian | SS | **L'amante di Gramigna**<br>*[Gramigna's lover]* | 1880 |
| 5042 | **Verga, Giovanni** | Italian | SS-P | **Cavalleria rusticana**<br>*(Rustic Chivalry)* | 1880 |
| 5043 | **Verga, Giovanni** | Italian | SS-P | **Cavalleria rusticana** | 1880 |
| 5044 | **Verga, Giovanni** | Italian | SS-P | **La lupa**<br>*(The She-Wolf)* | 1880{ss}<br>1896{p} |
| 5045 | **Veríssimo, Érico** | Brazilian | SS | **Um certo capitão Rodrigo**<br>*(from: O tempo e o vento)*<br>*(Time and the Wind)* | 1949 |
| 5046 | **Veríssimo, Érico** | Brazilian | N | **Noite**<br>*(Night)* | 1954 |
| 5047 | **Veríssimo, Érico** | Brazilian | N | **Olhai os lírios do campo**<br>*(Consider the Lilies of the Field)* | 1937 |
| 5048 | **Veríssimo, Érico** | Brazilian | SS | **O sobrado**<br>*(from: O tempo e o vento)* | 1949 |
| 5049 | **Veríssimo, Érico** | Brazilian | SS | **O sobrado +**<br>**Um certo capitão Rodrigo +**<br>**Ana Terra** *[Ann Land]* | 1949 |
| 5050 | **Verne, Jules** | French | N | **Un capitaine de quinze ans**<br>*(Dick Sands, the Boy Captain)* | 1878 |
| 5051 | **Verne, Jules** | French | N | **Le château des Carpathes**<br>*(Castle of the Carpathians)* | 1892 |
| 5052 | **Verne, Jules** | French | N | **Le château des Carpathes** | 1892 |
| 5053 | **Verne, Jules** | French | N | **Cinq semaines en ballon**<br>*(Five Weeks in a Balloon)* | 1863 |
| 5054 | **Verne, Jules** | French | N | **De la terre à la lune: trajet**<br>**direct en 97 heures**<br>*(From the Earth to the Moon*<br>*Direct in 97 hours 20 Minutes)* | 1865 |
| 5055 | **Verne, Jules** | French | N | **De la terre à la lune: traget**<br>**direct en 97 heures** | 1865 |
| 5056 | **Verne, Jules** | French | N | **Deux ans de vacances**<br>*(Two Years Holiday)*<br>*(aka: Long Vacation)* | 1888 |
| 5057 | **Verne, Jules** | French | N | **Les enfants du Capitaine Grant**<br>*(Captain Grant's Children)*<br>*(aka: Voyage Round the World)* | 1867-68 |
| 5058 | **Verne, Jules** | French | N | **L'étoile du Sud**<br>*(The Vanished Diamond)*<br>*(aka: Southern Star Mystery)* | 1884 |
| 5059 | **Verne, Jules** | French | N | **Face au drapeau**<br>*(For the Flag)* | 1896 |
| 5060 | **Verne, Jules** | French | N | **Hector Servadac** | 1878 |
| 5061 | **Verne, Jules** | French | N | **L'île mystérieuse**<br>*(The Mysterious Island)* | 1874-75 |
| 5062 | **Verne, Jules** | French | N | **L'île mystérieuse** | 1874-75 |

| No | Film Title | Country of Production | Date | Director(s) | Duration of Film |
|---|---|---|---|---|---|
| 5032 | **Gramada**<br>*(Cairn)* | BULG | 1936 | **Aleksandăr Vazov** | 91 |
| 5033 | **Pod igoto**<br>*(Under the Yoke)* | BULG | 1952 | **Dako Dakovski** | 123 |
| 5034 | **Fuenteovejuna** | SP | 1947(45) | **Antonio Román** | 99(103) |
| 5035 | **El mejor alcalde, el rey** | SP/IT | 1973 | **Rafael Gil** | 105(103) |
| 5036 | **La moza del cántaro** | SP | 1953 | **Florián Rey** | 72(88) |
| 5037 | **Un hombre de mundo** | SP | 1949(48) | **Manuel Tamayo** | 100 |
| 5038 | **El diablo cojuelo** | SP | 1971(70) | **Ramón Fernández** | 104 |
| 5039 | **Una cita con la vida** | ARG | 1958 | **Hugo del Carril** | 89 |
| 5040 | **Le silence de la mer** | FR | 1948 | **Jean-Pierre Melville** | 86 |
| 5041 | **L'amante di Gramigna**<br>*(BULG: Lyubovnitsata na Graminya)* | IT/BULG | 1969(68) | **Carlo Lizzani** | 100(108) |
| 5042 | **Cavalleria rusticana** | IT | 1940(39) | **Amleto Palermi** | 77 |
| 5043 | **Cavalleria rusticana**<br>*(USA: Fatal Desire)* | IT | 1953 | **Carmine Gallone** | 83 |
| 5044 | **La lupa**<br>*(The She-Wolf)* | IT | 1953 | **Alberto Lattuada** | 90 |
| 5045 | **Um certo capitão Rodrigo**<br>*(That Certain Captain Rodrigo)* | BRAZ | 1971 | **Anselmo Duarte** | 100 |
| 5046 | **Noite** | BRAZ | 1984 | **Gilberto Loureiro** | 85 |
| 5047 | **Mirad los lirios del campo** | ARG | 1947 | **Ernesto Arancibia** | 109 |
| 5048 | **O sobrado** | BRAZ | 1956 | **Walter George Durst**<br>**Cassiano Gabus Mendes** | 110 |
| 5049 | **Ana Terra** | BRAZ | 1972 | **Durval Gomes Garcia** | 100 |
| 5050 | **Pyatnadtzatiletny kapitan** | USSR | 1945 | **Vasili Zhuravlov** | 82 |
| 5051 | **Castelul din Carpaţi** | ROM | 1981 | **Stere Gulea** | 103 |
| 5052 | **Tajemstvi hradu v Karpatech**<br>*(The Mysterious Castle in the Carpathians)* | CZ | 1981 | **Oldřich Lipský** | 97 |
| 5053 | **Five Weeks in a Balloon** | USA | 1962 | **Irwin Allen** | 101 |
| 5054 | **From the Earth to the Moon** | USA | 1958 | **Byron Haskin** | 100 +V |
| 5055 | **Jules Verne's Rocket to the Moon**<br>*(USA: Those Fantastic Flying Fools)*<br>*(aka: Blast Off)* | GB | 1967 | **Don Sharp** | 101 |
| 5056 | **Insula comorilor**<br>*[Treasure island]*<br>*(aka: Piratti din Pacific)* | FR/ROM | 1975 | **Gilles Grangier**<br>**Sergiu Nicolaescu** | 124(74) |
| 5057 | **In Search of the Castaways** | GB | 1962 | **Robert Stevenson** | 100 +V |
| 5058 | **L'étoile du Sud**<br>*(The Southern Star)* | FR/GB | 1969(68) | **Sidney Hayers** | 105 |
| 5059 | **Vynález zkázy**<br>*(An Invention For Destruction)*<br>*(aka: The Fabulous World of Jules Verne)*<br>*{live-action + animation}* | CZ | 1958 | **Karel Zeman** | 86 |
| 5060 | **Na komete**<br>*(On the Comet)* | CZ | 1970 | **Karel Zeman** | 85 |
| 5061 | **Tainstvenny ostrov** | USSR | 1941 | **Eduard Pentzlin** | 92 |
| 5062 | **Mysterious Island**<br>*(aka: Jules Verne's Mysterious Island)* | GB | 1962(61) | **Cyril Endfield** | 100 +V |

| No. | Author | Nationality | Form | Literary Title | Date |
|-----|--------|-------------|------|----------------|------|
| 5063 | **Verne, Jules** | French | N | **L'île mystérieuse** | 1874-75 |
| 5064 | **Verne, Jules** | French | N | **La jangada**<br>*(The Giant Raft)* | 1881 |
| 5065 | **Verne, Jules** | French | N | **Mathias Sandorf** | 1885 |
| 5066 | **Verne, Jules** | French | N | **Michel Strogoff**<br>*(Michel Strogoff, the Courier of the Czar)* | 1876 |
| 5067 | **Verne, Jules** | French | N | **Michel Strogoff** | 1876 |
| 5068 | **Verne, Jules** | French | N | **Michel Strogoff** | 1876 |
| 5069 | **Verne, Jules** | French | N | **Michel Strogoff** | 1876 |
| 5070 | **Verne, Jules** | French | N | **Michel Strogoff** | 1876 |
| 5071 | **Verne, Jules** | French | N | **Michel Strogoff** | 1876 |
| 5072 | **Verne, Jules** | French | N | **Le phare du bout du monde**<br>*(The Lighthouse at the End of the World)* | 1905 |
| 5073 | **Verne, Jules** | French | N | **Le pilote du Danube**<br>*(The Danube Pilot)* | 1908 |
| 5074 | **Verne, Jules** | French | N | **Robur le conquérant**<br>*(Robur the Conqueror)*<br>*(aka: The Clipper of the Clouds)+*<br>**Maître du monde**<br>*(Master of the World)* | 1886+<br>1904 |
| 5075 | **Verne, Jules** | French | N | **Le tour du monde en quatre-vingt jours**<br>*(Around the World in Eighty Days)* | 1873 |
| 5076 | **Verne, Jules** | French | N | **Les tribulations d'un chinois en Chine**<br>*(Tribulations of a Chinaman)* | 1879 |
| 5077 | **Verne, Jules** | French | N | **Vingt mille lieues sous les mers**<br>*(Twenty Thousand Leagues Under the Seas)* | 1870 |
| 5078 | **Verne, Jules** | French | N | **Vingt mille lieues sous les mers** | 1870 |
| 5079 | **Verne, Jules** | French | N | **Voyage au centre de la terre**<br>*(Journey to the Centre of the Earth)* | 1864 |
| 5080 | **Verne, Jules** | French | N | **Voyage au centre de la terre** | 1864 |
| 5081 | **Verne, Jules** | French | N | **Voyage au centre de la terre** | 1864 |
| 5082 | **Verne, Jules** | French | N | **Voyage au centre de la terre** | 1864 |
| 5083 | **Vesaas, Tarjei** | Norwegian | N | **Brannen**<br>*[The fire]* | 1961 |
| 5084 | **Vesaas, Tarjei** | Norwegian | N | **Dei svarte hestane** | 1928 |
| 5085 | **Vesaas, Tarjei** | Norwegian | N | **Fuglane**<br>*[The birds]* | 1957 |
| 5086 | **Vesaas, Tarjei** | Norwegian | N | **Is-slottet**<br>*(The Ice Palace)*<br>*(aka: Palace of Ice)* | 1963 |
| 5087 | **Vesaas, Tarjei** | Norwegian | N | **Kimen**<br>*(The Seed)* | 1940 |
| 5088 | **Vesaas, Tarjei** | Norwegian | N | **Vårnatt**<br>*(Spring Night)* | 1954 |
| 5089 | **Vestdijk, Simon** | Dutch | N | **Pastorale 1943** | 1967 |
| 5090 | **Vezhinov, Pavel** | Bulgarian | N | **Barierata** | 1977 |
| 5091 | **Vezhinov, Pavel** | Bulgarian | N | **Chovekât v syanka**<br>*[The man in the shadow]* | 1965 |

| No | Film Title | Country of Production | Date | Director(s) | Duration of Film |
|---|---|---|---|---|---|
| 5063 | L'isola misteriosa e il Capitano Nemo (SP: La isla misteriosa) (The Mysterious Island of Captain Nemo) | IT/FR/SP | 1973(72) | Juan Antonio Bardem Henri Colpi | 96(104) |
| 5064 | Ochocientas leguas por el Amazonas (aka: La Jangada) | MEX | 1958 | Emilio Gómez Muriel | 106 |
| 5065 | Mathias Sandorf (SP: El conde Sandorf) (IT: Il grande ribelle) | FR/SP/IT | 1963(62) | Georges Lampin | 105(85) |
| 5066 | Michel Strogoff | FR/GER | 1936(35) | Jaques de Baroncelli | 100 |
| 5067 | Der Kurier des Zaren [The Czar's courier] | GER/FR | 1936 | Richard Eichberg | 93 |
| 5068 | The Soldier and the Lady (GB: Michael Strogoff) | USA | 1937 | George Nicholls, Jr. | 86 |
| 5069 | Miguel Strogoff (aka: El correo del zar) | MEX | 1943 | Miguel M. Delgado | 98 |
| 5070 | Michel Strogoff (IT: Michele Strogoff) | FR/IT/ YUGO | 1956 | Carmine Gallone | 111 |
| 5071 | Strogoff (GER: Der Kurier des Zaren) | FR/IT/GER/ BULG | 1970 | Eriprando Visconti | 109(94) (117) |
| 5072 | The Light at the Edge of the World (SP: La luz del fin del mundo) | USA/SP/ LIECH | 1971 | Kevin Billington | 119 123 +V |
| 5073 | A dunai hajós (Danube Pilot) (aka: Boatman on the Danube) | HUNG | 1974 | Miklós Markos | 106 |
| 5074 | Master of the World | USA | 1961 | William Witney | 104 +V(98) |
| 5075 | Around the World in Eighty Days | USA | 1956 | Michael Anderson | 175 (167) +V |
| 5076 | Les tribulations d'un chinois en Chine (IT: L'uomo di Hong Kong) (Up to His Ears) | FR/IT | 1965 | Philippe de Broca | 110(94) |
| 5077 | Twenty Thousand Leagues Under the Sea (aka: 20,000 Leagues Under the Sea) | USA | 1954 | Richard Fleischer | 122 +V |
| 5078 | Twenty-Thousand Leagues Under the Sea (aka: 20,000 Leagues Under the Sea) {animation} | USA | 1973 | William Hanna Joseph Barbera | 60 +V(48) |
| 5079 | Journey to the Centre of the Earth | USA | 1959 | Henry Levin | 129 (132) +V |
| 5080 | Journey to the Centre of the Earth {animation} | AUSTL | 1976 | Richard Slapczynski | 49 +V |
| 5081 | Viaje al centro de la tierra (Where Time Began) | SP | 1978 | Piquer Simon (Juan Piquer) | 107 (86) +V |
| 5082 | Journey to the Centre of the Earth | USA | 1988 | Rusty Lemorande | 77(86) +V |
| 5083 | Brannen | NOR | 1973 | Haakon Sandøy | 75 |
| 5084 | Dei svarte hestane | NOR | 1951 | Hans Jacob Nilsen Sigval Maartmann-Moe | 85 |
| 5085 | Żywot Mateusza (The Life of Matthew) (aka: The Days of Matthew) | POL | 1968(67) | Witold Leszczyński | 79 |
| 5086 | Is-slottet (The Ice-Palace) | NOR | 1988(87) | Per Blom | 76 |
| 5087 | Kimen (The Seed) | NOR | 1974 | Erik Solbakken | 93 |
| 5088 | Vårnatt | NOR | 1976 | Erik Solbakken | 99 |
| 5089 | Pastorale 1943 | HOLL | 1978 | Wim Verstappen | 127 |
| 5090 | Barierata (The Barrier) | BULG | 1979 | Khristo Khristov | 113 |
| 5091 | Chovekăt v syanka | BULG | 1967 | Yakim Yakimov | 97 |

| No. | Author | Nationality | Form | Literary Title | Date |
|-----|--------|-------------|------|----------------|------|
| 5092 | Vezhinov, Pavel | Bulgarian | N | Proizshestvie na tikhata ulitsa | 1960 |
| 5093 | Vezhinov, Pavel | Bulgarian | N | Sinite peperudi | 1968 |
| 5094 | Vezhinov, Pavel | Bulgarian | N | Sledite ostavat<br>*[The traces remain]* | 1954 |
| 5095 | Vian, Boris | French | N | L'écume des jours<br>*(Froth on the Daydream)* | 1947 |
| 5096 | Vian, Boris<br>(as: Vernon Sullivan) | French | N | J'irai cracher sur vos tombes<br>*(I Spit on Your Grave)* | 1946 |
| 5097 | Vidal, Gore | American | P | The Best Man: a Play About Politics | 1960 |
| 5098 | Vidal, Gore | American | N | Myra Breckinridge | 1968 |
| 5099 | Vidal, Gore | American | P(TV) | Visit to a Small Planet | 1956 |
| 5100 | Villaverde, Cirilo | Cuban | N | Cecilia Valdés ó la loma del angel | 1839(82) |
| 5101 | Villaverde, Cirilo | Cuban | SS | Palenques de negros cimarrones | 1890 |
| 5102 | Virgil<br>*(Vergilius)* | Latin(anc) | V | Aeneid | c.20 BC |
| 5103 | Vishnevsky, Vsevolod | Russian | P | Nezabyvayemyi 1919 god<br>*[The unforgettable year 1919]* | 1949 |
| 5104 | Vishnevsky, Vsevolod | Russian | P | Optimisticheskaya tragediya<br>*(An Optimistic Tragedy)* | 1933 |
| 5105 | Vittorini, Elio | Italian | N | Uomini e no | 1945 |
| 5106 | Vojnović, Ivo | Yugoslav<br>(Cro) | P | Ekvinocij<br>*(The Equinox)* | 1895 |
| 5107 | Volodin, Alexander | Russian | P | Moya starshaya sestra | 1961 |
| 5108 | Volodin, Alexander | Russian | P | Pyat' vecherov<br>*(Five Evenings)* | 1959 |
| 5109 | Voltaire, François-Marie Arouet de | French | SS | Babouc, ou le monde comme il va<br>*(Babouc; or, the World as it Goes)* | 1750 |
| 5110 | Voltaire, François-Marie Arouet de | French | SS | Candide<br>*(aka: Candide, ou l'optimisme)*<br>*(Candide: or Optimism)* | 1759 |
| 5111 | Voltaire, François-Marie Arouet de | French | SS | Candide | 1759 |
| 5112 | Voltaire, François-Marie Arouet de | French | SS | L'ingénu<br>*(The Pupil of Nature)* | 1767 |
| 5113 | Vonnegut, Kurt | American | P | Happy Birthday, Wanda June | 1971 |
| 5114 | Vonnegut, Kurt | American | SS | Next Door | 1968 |
| 5115 | Vonnegut, Kurt | American | N | Slapstick, or, Lonesome No More! | 1976 |
| 5116 | Vonnegut, Kurt | American | N | Slaughterhouse Five<br>*(aka: Slaughterhouse Five or The Children's Crusade)* | 1969 |
| 5117 | Vonnegut, Kurt | American | SS | Who Am I This Time? | 1968 |
| 5118 | Wägner, Elin | Swedish | N | Vändkorset<br>*[The turnstile]* | 1935 |
| 5119 | Wägner, Elin | Swedish | N | Vansklighetens land<br>*(aka: Åsa-Hanna)* | 1917(18) |
| 5120 | Wagoner, David | American | N | The Escape Artist | 1965 |
| 5121 | Walker, Alice | American(afro) | N | The Color Purple | 1983 |
| 5122 | Wallace, Lew | American | N | Ben Hur | 1880 |
| 5123 | Wallant, Edward Lewis | American | N | The Pawnbroker | 1961 |
| 5124 | Walpole, Hugh | British | N | Mr Perrin and Mr Traill | 1911 |
| 5125 | Walpole, Hugh | British | N | Vanessa | 1933 |
| 5126 | Walpole, Hugh - {ss}<br>Chodorov, Edward - {p} | British | SS-P | The Silver Mask {ss}<br>*(Kind Lady) {p}* | 1933{ss}<br>1936{p} |
| 5127 | Walser, Martin | German | N | Das Einhorn<br>*(The Unicorn)* | 1966 |
| 5128 | Walser, Martin | German | N | Der Sturz | 1973 |
| 5129 | Waltari, Mika | Finnish | N | Ei koskaan huomispäivää<br>*(Never a Tomorrow)* | 1942 |

| No | Film Title | Country of Production | Date | Director(s) | Duration of Film |
|---|---|---|---|---|---|
| 5092 | **Pohishtenie v zhălto** [Crime in yellow] | BULG | 1981 | **Mariana Evstatieva** | 74 |
| 5093 | **Treta sled slăntseto** [The birth of man] | BULG | 1972 | **Georgi Stoyanov** | 124 |
| 5094 | **Sledite ostavat** | BULG | 1956 | **Petăr Vasilev** (Peter Vassilev) | 98 |
| 5095 | **L'écume des jours** (The Froth of Time) | FR | 1968(67) | **Charles Belmont** | 115 |
| 5096 | **J'irai cracher sur vos tombes** (I Spit on Your Grave) | FR | 1959 | **Michel Gast** | 107 |
| 5097 | **The Best Man** | USA | 1964 | **Franklin J. Schaffner** | 104 |
| 5098 | **Myra Breckinridge** | USA | 1970 | **Mike Sarne** | 91 +V |
| 5099 | **Visit to a Small Planet** | USA | 1960(59) | **Norman Taurog** | 101 |
| 5100 | **Cecilia** (aka: Cecilia Valdés) | CB/SP | 1982 | **Humberto Solás** | 247(120) |
| 5101 | **Rancheadór** [Slave-hunter] | CB | 1976 | **Sergio Giral** | 95 |
| 5102 | **La legenda di Enea** | IT/FR | 1962 | **Giorgio Rivalta** | 86 |
| 5103 | **Nezabyvayemyi 1919 god** (The Unforgettable Year 1919) | USSR | 1952(51) | **Mikhail Chiaureli** | 108 |
| 5104 | **Optimisticheskaya tragediya** (The Optimistic Tragedy) | USSR | 1963 | **Samson Samsonov** | 112 |
| 5105 | **Uomini e no** (Men and Not Men) (aka: Men and Others) | IT | 1980 | **Valentino Orsini** | 102 |
| 5106 | **Nevjera** (Equinox) | YUGO | 1953 | **Vladimir Pogaćić** | 80 |
| 5107 | **Starshaya sestra** [The elder sister] | USSR | 1967 | **Georgi Natanson** | 102 |
| 5108 | **Pyat' vecherov** (Five Evenings) | USSR | 1980(78) | **Nikita Mikhalkov** | 101 |
| 5109 | **L'or et le plomb** (aka: Paris comme il va) | FR | 1966 | **Alain Cuniot** | 80 |
| 5110 | **Candide ou l'optimisme au XX.e siècle** | FR | 1960 | **Norbert Carbonnaux** | 86 |
| 5111 | **Mondo candido** | IT | 1975 | **Gualtiero Jacopetti** **Franco Prosperi** | 118(110) |
| 5112 | **L'ingénu** | FR | 1972(71) | **Norbert Carbonnaux** | 80 |
| 5113 | **Happy Birthday, Wanda June** | USA | 1971 | **Mark Robson** | 105 |
| 5114 | **Next Door** | USA | 1975 | **Andrew Silver** | 24 |
| 5115 | **Slapstick of Another Kind** (aka: Slapstick (of another kind)) | USA | 1982 | **Steven Paul** | 94 +V(82) |
| 5116 | **Slaughterhouse Five** | USA | 1972 | **George Roy Hill** | 104 +V(99) |
| 5117 | **Who Am I This Time?** | USA | 1982 | **Jonathan Demme** | 60 |
| 5118 | **Vändkorset** | SWE | 1944 | **Rune Carlsten** **Lauritz Falk** | 95 |
| 5119 | **Åsa-Hanna** | SWE | 1946 | **Anders Henrikson** | 108 |
| 5120 | **The Escape Artist** | USA | 1982 | **Caleb Deschanel** | 96 +V |
| 5121 | **The Color Purple** | USA | 1985 | **Steven Spielberg** | 154 +V |
| 5122 | **Ben Hur** | USA | 1959 | **William Wyler** | 209 +V |
| 5123 | **The Pawnbroker** | USA | 1965(64) | **Sidney Lumet** | 114 +V |
| 5124 | **Mr Perrin and Mr Traill** | GB | 1948 | **Lawrence Huntington** | 92 |
| 5125 | **Vanessa** (aka: Vanessa: Her Love Story) | USA | 1935 | **William K. Howard** | 76 |
| 5126 | **Kind Lady** | USA | 1951 | **John Sturges** | 78 |
| 5127 | **Das Einhorn** | GER | 1978 | **Peter Patzak** | 111 |
| 5128 | **Der Sturz** (The Fall) | GER | 1979 | **Alf Brustellin** | 101 |
| 5129 | **Ingen morgondag** (No Tomorrow) | SWE | 1957 | **Arne Mattsson** | 105 |

| No. | Author | Nationality | Form | Literary Title | Date |
|-----|--------|-------------|------|----------------|------|
| 5130 | Waltari, Mika | Finnish | N | Ei koskaan huomispäivää | 1942 |
| 5131 | Waltari, Mika | Finnish | SS | Jokin ihmisessä<br>(Something in People) | 1944 |
| 5132 | Waltari, Mika | Finnish | N | Komisario Palmun erehdys<br>[Police Inspector Palmu's mistake] | 1940 |
| 5133 | Waltari, Mika | Finnish | N | Kuka murhasi rouva Skrofin? | 1939 |
| 5134 | Waltari, Mika | Finnish | P | Kuriton sukupolvi<br>[The wild generation] | 1937 |
| 5135 | Waltari, Mika | Finnish | P | Kuriton sukupolvi | 1937 |
| 5136 | Waltari, Mika | Finnish | P | Noita palaa elämään<br>[The witch came back to life] | 1947 |
| 5137 | Waltari, Mika | Finnish | N | Sinuhe, egyptiläinen<br>(Sinuhe the Egyptian)<br>(aka: The Egyptian) | 1946 |
| 5138 | Waltari, Mika | Finnish | N | Suuri illusioni<br>[Grand illusion] | 1928 |
| 5139 | Waltari, Mika | Finnish | N | Tanssi yli hautojen | 1944 |
| 5140 | Waltari, Mika | Finnish | N | Vieras mies tuli taloon<br>(A Stranger Came to the Farm) | 1937 |
| 5141 | Waltari, Mika | Finnish | N | Vieras mies tuli taloon | 1937 |
| 5142 | Wan Chia-pao<br>(see: Wan Jiabao) | Chinese | P | | |
| 5143 | Wan Jiabao<br>(Wan Chia-pao)<br>(as: Cao Yu)<br>(Ts'ao Yu) | Chinese | P | Lei yu<br>[Thunderstorm] | 1934 |
| 5144 | Wan Jiabao<br>(as: Cao Yu) | Chinese | P | Lei yu | 1934 |
| 5145 | Wan Jiabao<br>(as: Cao Yu) | Chinese | P | Ri chu<br>(aka: Jih ch'u)<br>(Sunrise) | 1936 |
| 5146 | Wan Jiabao<br>(as: Cao Yu) | Chinese | P | Ri chu | 1936 |
| 5147 | Wan Jiabao<br>(as: Cao Yu) | Chinese | P | Yuan ye<br>[The wild country]<br>[aka: Savage plains] | 1939 |
| 5148 | Wan Jiabao<br>(as: Cao Yu) | Chinese | P | Yuan ye | 1939 |
| 5149 | Warren, Robert Penn | American | N | All the King's Men | 1946 |
| 5150 | Warren, Robert Penn | American | N | Band of Angels | 1955 |
| 5151 | Wassermann, Jakob | German | N | Der Fall Maurizius<br>(The Maurizius Case) | 1928 |
| 5152 | Waterhouse, Keith - {n-p}<br>Hall, Willis - {p} | British | N-P | Billy Liar | 1959{n}<br>1960{p} |
| 5153 | Watkins, Peter | British | P(TV) | The War Game | 1967 |
| 5154 | Watson, John<br>(as: Ian Maclaren) | British(Scot) | N | Doctor of the Old School | 1895 |
| 5155 | Waugh, Alec | British | N | Guy Renton | 1952 |
| 5156 | Waugh, Alec | British | N | Island in the Sun | 1955 |
| 5157 | Waugh, Evelyn | British | N | Decline and Fall | 1928 |
| 5158 | Waugh, Evelyn | British | N | A Handful of Dust | 1934 |
| 5159 | Waugh, Evelyn | British | N | The Loved One | 1948 |
| 5160 | Webb, Charles | American | N | The Graduate | 1963 |
| 5161 | Webb, Charles | American | N | The Marriage of a Young Stockbroker | 1970 |
| 5162 | Webb, Mary | British | N | Gone to Earth | 1917 |
| 5163 | Wedekind, Frank | German | P | Die Büchse der Pandora<br>(Pandora's Box)+<br>Der Erdgeist<br>(Earth-Spirit) | 1904+<br>1895 |
| 5164 | Wedekind, Frank | German | P | Die Büchse der Pandora | 1904 |
| 5165 | Wedekind, Frank | German | P | Die Büchse der Pandora +<br>Der Erdgeist | 1904+<br>1895 |

| No | Film Title | Country of Production | Date | Director(s) | Duration of Film |
|---|---|---|---|---|---|
| 5130 | **Verta käsissmääme** [Blood on our hands] | FIN | 1958 | **William Markus** | 83 |
| 5131 | **Jokin ihmisessä** | FIN | 1956 | **Aarne Tarkas** | 75 |
| 5132 | **Komisario Palmun erehdys** | FIN | 1960 | **Matti Kassila** | 108 |
| 5133 | **Kaasua, komisario Palmu!** [Step on the gas, Inspector Palmu!] | FIN | 1961 | **Matti Kassila** | 98 |
| 5134 | **Kuriton sukupolvi** | FIN | 1937 | **Wilho Ilmari** | 109 |
| 5135 | **Kuriton sukupolvi** | FIN | 1957 | **Matti Kassila** | 93 |
| 5136 | **Noita palaa elämään** | FIN | 1952 | **Roland af Hällström** | 80 |
| 5137 | **The Egyptian** | USA | 1954 | **Michael Curtiz** | 140 |
| 5138 | **Suuri illusioni** | FIN | 1985 | **Tuija-Maija Niskanen** | 95 |
| 5139 | **Tanssi yli hautojen** (Dance Over the Graves) | FIN | 1950 | **Toivo Särkkä** | 100 |
| 5140 | **Vieras mies tuli taloon** | FIN | 1938 | **Wilho Ilmari** | 106 |
| 5141 | **Vieras mies** [The stranger] | FIN | 1957 | **Hannu Leminen** | 104 |
| 5142 | | | | | |
| 5143 | **Lei yu** | CHN | 1938 | **Fang Peilin** | 98 |
| 5144 | **Lei yu** | CHN | 1984 | **Sun Daolin** | 120 |
| 5145 | **Ri chu** (Sunrise) | CHN | 1938 | **Yue Feng** (Yueh Feng) | 106 |
| 5146 | **Ri chu** | CHN | 1985 | **Yu Benzheng** | 159 |
| 5147 | **Shenlin enchou ji** [Love and revenge in the black forest] | CHN | 1941 | **Yue Feng** (Yueh Feng) | 118 |
| 5148 | **Yuan ye** | CHN | 1980 | **Ling Zi** | 109 |
| 5149 | **All the King's Men** | USA | 1949 | **Robert Rossen** | 109 |
| 5150 | **Band of Angels** | USA | 1957 | **Raoul Walsh** | 127 |
| 5151 | **L'affaire Maurizius** (IT: Il caso Maurizius) (On Trial) | FR/IT | 1954(53) | **Julien Duvivier** | 110(99) |
| 5152 | **Billy Liar** | GB | 1963 | **John Schlesinger** | 98 +V |
| 5153 | **The War Game** | GB | 1966(65) | **Peter Watkins** | 50 +V |
| 5154 | **Hills of Home** | USA | 1948 | **Fred M. Wilcox** | 97 |
| 5155 | **Circle of Deception** | GB | 1960 | **Jack Lee** | 110 |
| 5156 | **Island in the Sun** | GB | 1957 | **Robert Rossen** | 123 |
| 5157 | **Decline and Fall ... of a Birdwatcher!** (aka: Decline and Fall) | GB | 1968 | **John Krish** | 113 |
| 5158 | **A Handful of Dust** | GB | 1987 | **Charles Sturridge** | 118 +V |
| 5159 | **The Loved One** | USA | 1965 | **Tony Richardson** | 117 |
| 5160 | **The Graduate** | USA | 1967 | **Mike Nichols** | 105 +V |
| 5161 | **The Marriage of a Young Stockbroker** | USA | 1971 | **Lawrence Turman** | 95 |
| 5162 | **Gone to Earth** (USA: The Wild Heart) | GB | 1950 | **Michael Powell** **Emeric Pressburger** | 110 +V(82) |
| 5163 | **Lulu** (aka: No Orchids For Lulu) | AUST | 1962 | **Rolf Thiele** | 100 |
| 5164 | **Lulu** | USA | 1977 | **Ronald Chase** | 96 |
| 5165 | **Lulu** | GER | 1980(79) | **Walerian Borowczyk** | 86 |

| No. | Author | Nationality | Form | Literary Title | Date |
|-----|--------|-------------|------|----------------|------|
| 5166 | Wedekind, Frank | German | P | Frühlings Erwachen<br>(The Awakening of Spring)<br>(aka: Spring Awakening) | 1891 |
| 5167 | Wedekind, Frank | German | P | Tod und Teufel<br>(Death and Devil)<br>(aka: Totentanz)<br>(Damnation) | 1909<br>(aka:1906) |
| 5168 | Weidman, Jerome | American | N | I Can Get It for You Wholesale | 1937 |
| 5169 | Weisenborn, Günter | German | N | Das Mädchen von Fanö | 1935 |
| 5170 | Weiss, Peter | German | P | Die Verfolgung und Ermordung<br>Jean Paul Marats<br>(The Persecution and Assassination<br>of Jean-Paul Marat) | 1964 |
| 5171 | Wells, H. G. | British | SS | The Door in the Wall | 1911 |
| 5172 | Wells, H. G. | British | SS | Empire of the Ants | 1913 |
| 5173 | Wells, H. G. | British | N | The First Men in the Moon | 1901 |
| 5174 | Wells, H. G. | British | SS | The Food of the Gods and How<br>It Came to Earth | 1904 |
| 5175 | Wells, H. G. | British | N | The History of Mr Polly | 1910 |
| 5176 | Wells, H. G. | British | N | The Invisible Man | 1897 |
| 5177 | Wells, H. G. | British | N | The Invisible Man | 1897 |
| 5178 | Wells, H. G. | British | N | The Island of Dr Moreau | 1896 |
| 5179 | Wells, H. G. | British | N | The Island of Dr Moreau | 1896 |
| 5180 | Wells, H. G. | British | N | Kipps | 1905 |
| 5181 | Wells, H. G. | British | N | Kipps | 1905 |
| 5182 | Wells, H. G. | British | SS | The Magic Shop | 1905 |
| 5183 | Wells, H. G. | British | SS | The Man Who Could Work<br>Miracles | 1899 |
| 5184 | Wells, H. G. | British | N | The Passionate Friends | 1913 |
| 5185 | Wells, H. G. | British | N | The Shape of Things to Come | 1933 |
| 5186 | Wells, H. G. | British | N | The Time Machine | 1895 |
| 5187 | Wells, H. G. | British | N | War of the Worlds | 1897 |
| 5188 | Wells, H. G. | British | N | The Wonderful Visit | 1895 |
| 5189 | Weöres Sándor | Hungarian | N(V) | Psyché: egy hajdani költőnő<br>írásai<br>[Psyche: writings of a poetess<br>of yore] | 1972 |
| 5190 | Werfel, Franz | Austrian | P | Jacobowsky und der Oberst<br>(Jacobowsky and the Colonel) | 1944 |
| 5191 | Werfel, Franz | Austrian | P | Juarez und Maximilian<br>(Juan and Maximilian) | 1924 |
| 5192 | Werfel, Franz | Austrian | N | Das Lied von Bernadette<br>(The Song of Bernadette) | 1941 |
| 5193 | Werfel, Franz | Austrian | N | Verdi. Roman der oper<br>(Verdi: a Novel of the Opera) | 1924 |
| 5194 | Werfel, Franz | Austrian | N | Der veruntreute Himmel<br>(Embezzled Heaven) | 1948 |
| 5195 | Wesker, Arnold | British | P | The Kitchen | 1960 |
| 5196 | West, Jessamyn | American | N | The Friendly Persuasion | 1945 |
| 5197 | West, Nathanael | American | N | The Day of the Locust | 1939 |
| 5198 | West, Nathanael | American | SS | Miss Lonelyhearts | 1933 |
| 5199 | West, Nathanael | American | SS | Miss Lonelyhearts | 1933 |
| 5200 | West, Rebecca | British | SS | Abiding Vision | 1935 |
| 5201 | West, Rebecca | British | N | The Return of the Soldier | 1918 |
| 5202 | Wexley, John | American | P | The Last Mile<br>(aka: All the World Wondered) | 1930 |
| 5203 | Wexley, John | American | P | The Last Mile | 1930 |
| 5204 | Weyssenhoff, Józef | Polish | N | Soból i panna<br>(The Sable and the Girl) | 1912 |
| 5205 | Wharton, Edith | American | N | The Age of Innocence | 1920 |
| 5206 | Wharton, Edith | American | N | The Children | 1928 |

| No | Film Title | Country of Production | Date | Director(s) | Duration of Film |
|---|---|---|---|---|---|
| 5166 | **Warm in the Bud** | USA | 1970(69) | **Rudolph Caringi** | 60 |
| 5167 | **Death and the Devil** | GER/GB | 1976(73) | **Steve Dwoskin** | 90(92) |
| 5168 | **I Can Get It for You Wholesale** <br> (aka: This Is My Affair) <br> (aka: Only the Best) | USA | 1951 | **Michael Gordon** | 90 |
| 5169 | **Das Mädchen von Fanö** | GER | 1941(40) | **Hans Schweikart** | 97 |
| 5170 | **The Marat/Sade** <br> (aka: The Persecution and Assassination of Jean-Paul Marat as Performed by the Inmates of the Asylum of Charenton Under the Direction of the Marquis de Sade) | GB | 1966 | **Peter Brook** | 116 |
| 5171 | **The Door in the Wall** | GB | 1956 | **Glenn H. Alvey, Jr.** | 29 |
| 5172 | **Empire of the Ants** | USA | 1977 | **Bert I. Gordon** | 90 +V |
| 5173 | **First Men in the Moon** | GB | 1964 | **Nathan Juran** | 103 +V(99) |
| 5174 | **The Food of the Gods** | USA | 1976 | **Bert I. Gordon** | 88 +V(84) |
| 5175 | **The History of Mr Polly** | GB | 1949(48) | **Anthony Pélissier** | 94 |
| 5176 | **The Invisible Man** | USA | 1933 | **James Whale** | 71 |
| 5177 | **The Invisible Man Returns** | USA | 1940 | **Joe May** | 81 |
| 5178 | **Island of Lost Souls** | USA | 1932 | **Erle C. Kenton** | 74 |
| 5179 | **The Island of Dr Moreau** | USA | 1977 | **Don Taylor** | 98 +V |
| 5180 | **Kipps** <br> (USA: The Remarkable Mr Kipps) | GB | 1941 | **Carol Reed** | 112 |
| 5181 | **Half a Sixpence** <br> {musical version} | GB/USA | 1967 | **George Sidney** | 146 |
| 5182 | **The Magic Shop** | GB | 1982 | **Ian Eames** | 23 |
| 5183 | **The Man Who Could Work Miracles** | GB | 1936 | **Lothar Mendes** | 80 |
| 5184 | **The Passionate Friends** <br> (aka: One Woman's Story) | GB | 1949(48) | **David Lean** | 91 |
| 5185 | **Things to Come** | GB | 1936 | **William Cameron Menzies** | 108 +V(89) |
| 5186 | **The Time Machine** | USA | 1960 | **George Pal** | 101 +V |
| 5187 | **War of the Worlds** | USA | 1953(52) | **Byron Haskin** | 85 +V |
| 5188 | **La merveilleuse visite** <br> (USA: The Wonderful Visit) | FR | 1974 | **Marcel Carné** | 102 |
| 5189 | **Nárcisz és Psyché** <br> (Narcissus and Psyche) | HUNG | 1980 | **Gábor Bódy** | 140 |
| 5190 | **Me and the Colonel** <br> (aka: The Best of Enemies) | USA | 1958 | **Peter Glenville** | 109 +V |
| 5191 | **Juarez** | USA | 1939 | **William Dieterle** | 128(132) |
| 5192 | **The Song of Bernadette** | USA | 1943 | **Henry King** | 156 |
| 5193 | **Verdi** <br> (aka: Giuseppe Verdi) | IT | 1953 | **Raffaello Matarazzo** | 105(120) |
| 5194 | **Der veruntreute Himmel** <br> (Embezzled Heaven) | GER | 1958 | **Ernst Marischka** | 102 |
| 5195 | **The Kitchen** | GB | 1961 | **James Hill** | 74 |
| 5196 | **Friendly Persuasion** | USA | 1956 | **William Wyler** | 140 |
| 5197 | **The Day of the Locust** | USA | 1975(74) | **John Schlesinger** | 143 |
| 5198 | **Advice to the Lovelorn** | USA | 1933 | **Alfred Werker** | 62 |
| 5199 | **Lonelyhearts** | USA | 1958 | **Vincent J. Donehue** | 103 |
| 5200 | **A Life of Her Own** | USA | 1950 | **George Cukor** | 108 |
| 5201 | **The Return of the Soldier** | GB | 1983(82) | **Alan Bridges** | 102 +V |
| 5202 | **The Last Mile** | USA | 1932 | **Sam Bischoff** | 84 |
| 5203 | **The Last Mile** | USA | 1959 | **Howard W. Koch** | 81 |
| 5204 | **Soból i panna** | POL | 1984 | **Hurbert Drapella** | 92 |
| 5205 | **The Age of Innocence** | USA | 1934 | **Philip Moeller** | 71 |
| 5206 | **The Children** | GB | 1990 | **Tony Palmer** | 115 |

| No. | Author | Nationality | Form | Literary Title | Date |
|-----|--------|-------------|------|----------------|------|
| 5207 | **Wharton, Edith** | American | N | **The Old Maid** | 1924 |
| 5208 | **White, Lionel** | American | N | **Clean Break**<br>(aka: The Killing) | 1955 |
| 5209 | **White, Lionel** | American | N | **The Money Trap** | 1963 |
| 5210 | **White, Lionel** | American | N | **Obsession** | 1962 |
| 5211 | **White, Patrick** | Australian | SS | **The Night the Prowler** | 1974 |
| 5212 | **White, T. H.** | British | N | **The Sword in the Stone** | 1938 |
| 5213 | **Whiting, John** | British | P | **The Devils** | 1961 |
| 5214 | **Whittier, John Greenleaf** | American | V | **The Barefoot Boy** | 1856 |
| 5215 | **Wiechert, Ernst** | German | SS | **Regina Amstetten** | 1936 |
| 5216 | **Wied, Gustav** | Danish | N+P | **Livsens ondskab** {n}<br>[Life's malice] +<br>**Thummelumsen** {p} | 1899+<br>1901 |
| 5217 | **Wied, Gustav** | Danish | N | **Slægten**<br>[Kin] | 1898 |
| 5218 | **Wiers-Jenssen, Hans** | Norwegian | P | **Anne Pedersdotter**<br>(aka: The Witch) | 1917 |
| 5219 | **Wilbur, Richard** | American | SS | **A Game of Catch** | 1954 |
| 5220 | **Wilde, Oscar** | Irish | V | **The Ballad of Reading Gaol** | 1898 |
| 5221 | **Wilde, Oscar** | Irish | SS | **The Birthday of the Infanta** | 1891 |
| 5222 | **Wilde, Oscar** | Irish | SS | **The Canterville Ghost** | 1891 |
| 5223 | **Wilde, Oscar** | Irish | SS | **The Canterville Ghost** | 1891 |
| 5224 | **Wilde, Oscar** | Irish | SS | **The Happy Prince** | 1888 |
| 5225 | **Wilde, Oscar** | Irish | P | **An Ideal Husband** | 1899 |
| 5226 | **Wilde, Oscar** | Irish | P | **An Ideal Husband** | 1899 |
| 5227 | **Wilde, Oscar** | Irish | P | **An Ideal Husband** | 1899 |
| 5228 | **Wilde, Oscar** | Irish | P | **The Importance of Being Ernest** | 1899 |
| 5229 | **Wilde, Oscar** | Irish | P | **The Importance of Being Ernest** | 1899 |
| 5230 | **Wilde, Oscar** | Irish | P | **Lady Windermere's Fan** | 1893 |
| 5231 | **Wilde, Oscar** | Irish | P | **Lady Windermere's Fan** | 1893 |
| 5232 | **Wilde, Oscar** | Irish | P | **Lady Windermere's Fan** | 1893 |
| 5233 | **Wilde, Oscar** | Irish | P | **Lady Windermere's Fan** | 1893 |
| 5234 | **Wilde, Oscar** | Irish | P | **Lady Windermere's Fan** | 1893 |
| 5235 | **Wilde, Oscar** | Irish | SS | **The Nightingale and the Rose** | 1888 |
| 5236 | **Wilde, Oscar** | Irish | N | **The Picture of Dorian Gray** | 1891 |
| 5237 | **Wilde, Oscar** | Irish | N | **The Picture of Dorian Gray** | 1891 |
| 5238 | **Wilde, Oscar** | Irish | N | **The Picture of Dorian Gray** | 1891 |
| 5239 | **Wilde, Oscar** | Irish | P | **Salomé** | 1893 |
| 5240 | **Wilde, Oscar** | Irish | P | **Salomé** | 1893 |
| 5241 | **Wilde, Oscar** | Irish | P | **Salomé** | 1893 |
| 5242 | **Wilde, Oscar** | Irish | P | **Salomé** | 1893 |
| 5243 | **Wilde, Oscar** | Irish | P | **A Woman of No Importance** | 1894 |
| 5244 | **Wilde, Oscar** | Irish | P | **A Woman of No Importance** | 1894 |
| 5245 | **Wilder, Thornton** | American | N | **The Bridge of San Luis Rey** | 1927 |
| 5246 | **Wilder, Thornton** | American | P | **The Matchmaker** | 1957 |
| 5247 | **Wilder, Thornton** | American | P | **Our Town** | 1938 |
| 5248 | **Wilder, Thornton** | American | N | **Theophilus North** | 1973 |
| 5249 | **Wildgans, Anton** | Austrian | V | **Kirbisch** | 1927 |
| 5250 | **Williams, Emlyn** | British(Welsh) | P | **The Corn Is Green** | 1938 |
| 5251 | **Williams, Emlyn** | British | N | **Headlong** | 1981 |
| 5252 | **Williams, Emlyn** | British | P | **Light of Heart** | 1940 |
| 5253 | **Williams, Emlyn** | British | P | **Night Must Fall** | 1935 |
| 5254 | **Williams, Emlyn** | British | P | **Night Must Fall** | 1935 |
| 5255 | **Williams, Emlyn** | British | P | **Someone Waiting** | 1954 |

| No | Film Title | Country of Production | Date | Director(s) | Duration of Film |
|----|-----------|----------------------|------|-------------|------------------|
| 5207 | The Old Maid | USA | 1939 | Edmund Goulding | 95 |
| 5208 | The Killing | USA | 1956 | Stanley Kubrick | 83 |
| 5209 | The Money Trap | USA | 1966(65) | Burt Kennedy | 92 |
| 5210 | Pierrot le fou<br>(IT: Il bandito delle undici) | FR/IT | 1965 | Jean-Luc Godard | 110 |
| 5211 | The Night the Prowler | AUSTL | 1978 | Jim Sharman | 89 |
| 5212 | The Sword in the Stone<br>{animation} | USA | 1963 | Wolfgang Reitherman | 75<br>+V |
| 5213 | The Devils | GB | 1971 | Ken Russell | 111 +V |
| 5214 | Barefoot Boy | USA | 1938 | Karl Brown | 67 |
| 5215 | Regina Amstetten | GER | 1954(53) | Kurt Neumann | 97 |
| 5216 | Thummelumsen | DEN | 1941 | Emanuel Gregers | 95 |
| 5217 | Slægten | DEN | 1978 | Anders Refn | 119 |
| 5218 | Vredens dag<br>(Day of Wrath) | DEN | 1943 | Carl Th. Dreyer | 97 |
| 5219 | A Game of Catch | USA | 1974 | Steven K. Witty | 07 |
| 5220 | The Ballad of Reading Gaol | GB | 1988 | Richard Kwietniowski | 12 |
| 5221 | Black and Silver | GB | 1981 | William Raban<br>Merilyn Raban | 75 |
| 5222 | The Canterville Ghost | USA | 1944 | Jules Dassin | 95 |
| 5223 | O caçador de fantasma | BRAZ | 1975 | Flávio Migliaccio | 86 |
| 5224 | Prinţul fericit<br>[The happy prince] | ROM | 1968 | Aurel Miheleş | 26 |
| 5225 | Ein Idealer Gatte | GER | 1935 | Herbert Selpin | 85 |
| 5226 | An Ideal Husband | GB | 1948(47) | Alexander Korda | 96 +V |
| 5227 | Idealny muzh | USSR | 1981 | Viktor Georgiev | 92 |
| 5228 | Liebe, Scherz und Ernst<br>(aka: Bunbury) | GER | 1932 | Franz Wenzler | 91 |
| 5229 | The Importance of Being Ernest | GB | 1952 | Anthony Asquith | 96 +V |
| 5230 | Lady Windermeres Fächer | GER | 1935 | Heinz Hilpert | 95 |
| 5231 | Shao nainai de shanzi<br>[The young lady's fan] | CHN | 1938 | Li Pingqian | 90 |
| 5232 | El abanico de Lady Windermere | MEX | 1944 | Juan J. Ortega | 89 |
| 5233 | Historia de una male mujer<br>(aka: Lady Windermere's Fan) | ARG | 1948 | Luis Saslavsky | 90 |
| 5234 | The Fan<br>(GB: Lady Windermere's Fan) | USA | 1949 | Otto Preminger | 79 |
| 5235 | The Nightingale and the Rose<br>{animation} | USA | 1967 | Joseph Karbert | 14 |
| 5236 | The Picture of Dorian Gray | USA | 1945 | Albert Lewin | 111 |
| 5237 | Das Bildnis des Dorian Gray<br>(IT: Il dio chiamato Dorian)<br>(The Evils of Dorian Gray)<br>(aka: Dorian Gray) | GER/IT | 1970 | Massimo Dallamano | 93(104)<br>+V(86) |
| 5238 | The Picture of Dorian Gray | USA | 1973 | Glenn Jordan | 180 |
| 5239 | Salomé | GER | 1971 | Werner Schroeter | 81 |
| 5240 | Salomé | IT | 1972 | Carmelo Bene | 75 |
| 5241 | Salomé | FR/IT | 1985 | Claude D'Anna | 95 +V |
| 5242 | Salome's Last Dance | GB | 1988(87) | Ken Russell | 89 +V |
| 5243 | Eine Frau ohne Bedeutung | GER | 1936 | Hans Steinhoff | 81 |
| 5244 | Une femme sans importance | FR | 1937 | Jean Choux | 90 |
| 5245 | The Bridge of San Luis Rey | USA | 1944 | Rowland V. Lee | 85 |
| 5246 | The Matchmaker | USA | 1958(57) | Joseph Anthony | 101 |
| 5247 | Our Town | USA | 1940 | Sam Wood | 90 |
| 5248 | Mr North | USA | 1988 | Danny Huston | 93 +V |
| 5249 | Cordula | AUST | 1950 | Gustav Ucicky | 97 |
| 5250 | The Corn Is Green | USA | 1945 | Irving Rapper | 118 |
| 5251 | Headlong | USA | 1991 | David S. Ward | 97 |
| 5252 | Life Begins at Eight-Thirty<br>(aka: Light of Heart) | USA | 1942 | Irving Pichel | 85 |
| 5253 | Night Must Fall | USA | 1937 | Richard Thorpe | 117 |
| 5254 | Night Must Fall | GB | 1964 | Karel Reisz | 101 |
| 5255 | Time Without Pity | GB | 1957 | Joseph Losey | 88 |

| No. | Author | Nationality | Form | Literary Title | Date |
|-----|--------|-------------|------|----------------|------|
| 5256 | **Williams, John A.** | American(afro) | N | **Night Song** | 1961 |
| 5257 | **Williams, Tennessee** | American | P | **Cat On a Hot Tin Roof** | 1955 |
| 5258 | **Williams, Tennessee** | American | P | **The Glass Menagerie** | 1945 |
| 5259 | **Williams, Tennessee** | American | P | **The Glass Menagerie** | 1945 |
| 5260 | **Williams, Tennessee** | American | P | **The Glass Menagerie** | 1945 |
| 5261 | **Williams, Tennessee** | American | P+SS | **The Milk Train Doesn't Stop Here Any More** {p} + **Man Bring This Up Road** {ss} | 1964+ 1966 |
| 5262 | **Williams, Tennessee** | American | P | **The Night of the Iguana** | 1962 |
| 5263 | **Williams, Tennessee** | American | P | **Orpheus Descending** | 1958 |
| 5264 | **Williams, Tennessee** | American | P | **Period of Adjustment** | 1960 |
| 5265 | **Williams, Tennessee** | American | N | **The Roman Spring of Mrs Stone** | 1950 |
| 5266 | **Williams, Tennessee** | American | P | **The Rose Tattoo** | 1951 |
| 5267 | **Williams, Tennessee** | American | P | **The Seven Descents of Myrtle** (aka: Kingdom of Earth) | 1968 |
| 5268 | **Williams, Tennessee** | American | P | **A Streetcar Named Desire** | 1947 |
| 5269 | **Williams, Tennessee** | American | P | **Suddenly Last Summer** | 1958 |
| 5270 | **Williams, Tennessee** | American | P | **Summer and Smoke** | 1948 |
| 5271 | **Williams, Tennessee** | American | P | **Sweet Bird of Youth** | 1959 |
| 5272 | **Williams, Tennessee** | American | P | **This Property Is Condemned** | 1958 |
| 5273 | **Williams, Tennessee** | American | P | **27 Wagons Full of Cotton** + **The Long Stay Cut Short; or, The Unsatisfactory Supper** | 1945+ 1948 |
| 5274 | **Williamson, David** | Australian | P | **The Club** | 1978 |
| 5275 | **Williamson, David** | Australian | P | **The Coming of Stork** | 1974 |
| 5276 | **Williamson, David** | Australian | P | **Don's Party** | 1973 |
| 5277 | **Williamson, David** | Australian | P | **The Removalists** | 1972 |
| 5278 | **Williamson, David** | Australian | P | **Travelling North** | 1980 |
| 5279 | **Willis, Ted** | British | P(TV)-P | **Woman in a Dressing Gown** | 1959 |
| 5280 | **Wilson, John** - {p} **Hodson, James L.** - {n} | British | N+P | **Hamp** {p} + **Return to the Wood** {n} | 1966+ 1955 |
| 5281 | **Wilson, Sloan** | American | N | **The Man in the Gray Flannel Suit** | 1955 |
| 5282 | **Wilson, Sloan** | American | N | **A Summer Place** | 1958 |
| 5283 | **Wister, Owen** | American | N | **The Virginian, a Horseman of the Plains** | 1902 |
| 5284 | **Wodehouse, P. G.** | British | N | **A Damsel in Distress** | 1919 |
| 5285 | **Wodehouse, P. G.** | British | N | **The Girl on the Boat** | 1922 |
| 5286 | **Wodehouse, P. G.** | British | N | **Piccadilly Jim** | 1917 |
| 5287 | **Wodehouse, P. G.** | British | N | **Summer Lightning** | 1929 |
| 5288 | **Wodehouse, P. G.** | British | N | **Summer Lightning** | 1929 |
| 5289 | **Wodehouse, P. G.** | British | N | **Thank You, Jeeves!** | 1934 |
| 5290 | **Wolf, Christa** | German | N | **Der geteilte Himmel** (Divided Heaven) (aka: Divided Sky) | 1964 |
| 5291 | **Wolfe, Tom** | American | N | **The Bonfire of the Vanities** | 1989 |
| 5292 | **Wolfe, Tom** | American | N | **The Right Stuff** | 1979 |
| 5293 | **Wolkers, Jan Hendrick** | Dutch | N | **Kort amerikaans** | 1964 |
| 5294 | **Wolkers, Jan Hendrick** | Dutch | N | **Turks fruit** (Turkish Delight) | 1970 |
| 5295 | **Woolf, Leonard** | British | N | **The Village in the Jungle** | 1913 |
| 5296 | **Woolf, Virginia** | British | N | **The Waves** | 1931 |
| 5297 | **Woolrich, Cornell** (see: Hopley-Woolrich, Cornell George) | American | N/SS | | |
| 5298 | **Wouk, Herman** | American | N | **The Caine Mutiny** | 1951 |
| 5299 | **Wouk, Herman** | American | N | **The City Boy** | 1948 |
| 5300 | **Wouk, Herman** | American | N | **Marjorie Morningstar** | 1955 |
| 5301 | **Wouk, Herman** | American | F-N | **Slattery's Hurricane** | 1956 |
| 5302 | **Wouk, Herman** | American | N | **Youngblood Hawke** | 1962 |

| No | Film Title | Country of Production | Date | Director(s) | Duration of Film |
|----|-----------|----------------------|------|-------------|------------------|
| 5256 | Sweet Love, Bitter (aka: Black Love, White Love) | USA | 1967(66) | Herbert Danska | 92 |
| 5257 | Cat On a Hot Tin Roof | USA | 1958 | Richard Brooks | 108 +V |
| 5258 | The Glass Menagerie | USA | 1950 | Irving Rapper | 107 |
| 5259 | The Glass Menagerie | USA | 1973 | Anthony Harvey | 112(100) |
| 5260 | The Glass Menagerie | USA | 1987 | Paul Newman | 135 +V |
| 5261 | Boom! | GB | 1968 | Joseph Losey | 113 |
| 5262 | The Night of the Iguana | USA | 1964 | John Huston | 118(125) |
| 5263 | The Fugitive Kind | USA | 1959 | Sidney Lumet | 121(135) |
| 5264 | Period of Adjustment | USA | 1962 | George Roy Hill | 122(110) |
| 5265 | The Roman Spring of Mrs Stone | GB/USA | 1962 | José Quintero | 104 |
| 5266 | The Rose Tattoo | USA | 1955 | Daniel Mann | 117(114) |
| 5267 | Last of the Mobile Hot- Shots (aka: Blood Kin) | USA | 1970(69) | Sidney Lumet | 108 |
| 5268 | A Streetcar Named Desire | USA | 1951 | Elia Kazan | 122 +V |
| 5269 | Suddenly, Last Summer | GB | 1960(59) | Joseph L. Mankiewicz | 114 +V |
| 5270 | Summer and Smoke | USA | 1961 | Peter Glenville | 118 |
| 5271 | Sweet Bird of Youth | USA | 1962(61) | Richard Brooks | 120(88) |
| 5272 | This Property Is Condemned | USA | 1966 | Sydney Pollack | 110 +V |
| 5273 | Baby Doll | USA | 1956 | Elia Kazan | 114 |
| 5274 | The Club (aka: Players) | AUSTL | 1980 | Bruce Beresford | 102 +V(90) |
| 5275 | Stork | AUSTL | 1971 | Tim Burstall | 90 |
| 5276 | Don's Party | AUSTL | 1976 | Bruce Beresford | 90 +V |
| 5277 | The Removalists | AUSTL | 1975 | Tom Jeffrey | 93 |
| 5278 | Travelling North | AUSTL | 1988 | Carl Schultz | 97 +V |
| 5279 | Woman in a Dressing Gown | GB | 1957 | J. Lee Thompson | 94 |
| 5280 | King & Country | GB | 1964 | Joseph Losey | 86 +V |
| 5281 | The Man in the Gray Flannel Suit | USA | 1956 | Nunnally Johnson | 152 |
| 5282 | A Summer Place | USA | 1959 | Delmer Daves | 130 |
| 5283 | The Virginian | USA | 1946 | Stuart Gilmore | 90 |
| 5284 | A Damsel in Distress {musical version} | USA | 1937 | George Stevens | 101 +V(87) |
| 5285 | The Girl on the Boat | GB | 1961 | Henry Kaplan | 91 |
| 5286 | Piccadilly Jim | USA | 1936 | Robert Z. Leonard | 100 |
| 5287 | Summer Lightning | GB | 1933 | Maclean Rogers | 78 |
| 5288 | Blixt och dunder [Thunder and lightning] | SWE | 1938 | Anders Henrikson | 91 |
| 5289 | Thank You, Jeeves! (aka: Thank You, Mr Jeeves) | USA | 1936 | Arthur Greville Collins | 68 |
| 5290 | Der geteilte Himmel (Divided Sky) | GDR | 1964 | Konrad Wolf | 110(118) |
| 5291 | The Bonfire of the Vanities | USA | 1990 | Brian De Palma | 125 +V |
| 5292 | The Right Stuff | USA | 1983 | Philip Kaufman | 192 +V |
| 5293 | Kort amerikaans (Crew Cut) | HOLL | 1979 | Guido Pieters | 100(97) |
| 5294 | Turks fruit (Turkish Delight) (aka: The Sensualist) | HOLL | 1973(72) | Paul Verhoeven | 110 +V(106) |
| 5295 | Baddegama (Village in the Jungle) | SL | 1981(80) | Lester J. Peries | 130 |
| 5296 | Golven (The Waves) | HOLL | 1982 | Annette Apon | 92 |
| 5297 | | | | | |
| 5298 | The Caine Mutiny | USA | 1954 | Edward Dmytryk | 124 +V |
| 5299 | Her First Romance | USA | 1951 | Seymour Friedman | 73 |
| 5300 | Marjorie Morningstar | USA | 1958 | Irving Rapper | 122 |
| 5301 | Slattery's Hurricane | USA | 1949 | André de Toth | 83 |
| 5302 | Youngblood Hawke | USA | 1964(63) | Delmer Daves | 137 |

| No. | Author | Nationality | Form | Literary Title | Date |
|-----|--------|-------------|------|----------------|------|
| 5303 | Wren, P. C. | British | N | Beau Geste | 1924 |
| 5304 | Wren, P. C. | British | N | Beau Geste | 1924 |
| 5305 | Wren, P. C. | British | N | Beau Ideal | 1928 |
| 5306 | Wright, Richard | American(afro) | SS | The Man Who Was Almost a Man *(aka: Almos' a Man)* | 1961 |
| 5307 | Wright, Richard | American | N | Native Son | 1940 |
| 5308 | Wright, Richard | American | N | Native Son | 1940 |
| 5309 | Wu Che'eng-en *(see: Wu Chengen)* | Chinese | N | | |
| 5310 | Wu Chengen *(Wu Che'eng-en)* | Chinese | N | Xi you ji *(aka: Hsi-yu chi)* *(Monkey)* | 1592 |
| 5311 | Wu Chengen | Chinese | N | Xi you ji | 1592 |
| 5312 | Wuolijoki, Hella *(Juhani Tervapää)* | Finnish(Est) | P | Entäs nyt, Niskavuori? | 1953 |
| 5313 | Wuolijoki, Hella | Finnish | P | Justiina | 1937 |
| 5314 | Wuolijoki, Hella | Finnish | P | Juurakon Hulda *[Hulda of Juurakko]* | 1937 |
| 5315 | Wuolijoki, Hella | Finnish | P | Juurakon Hulda | 1937 |
| 5316 | Wuolijoki, Hella | Finnish | P | Niskavuoren Heta | 1953 |
| 5317 | Wuolijoki, Hella | Finnish | P | Niskavuoren leipä | 1939 |
| 5318 | Wuolijoki, Hella | Finnish | P | Niskavuoren naiset *[The women of Niskavuori]* | 1936 |
| 5319 | Wuolijoki, Hella | Finnish | P | Niskavuoren naiset | 1936 |
| 5320 | Wuolijoki, Hella | Finnish | P | Niskavuoren naiset + Niskavuoren leipä | 1936+ 1938 |
| 5321 | Wuolijoki, Hella | Finnish | P | Niskavuoren nuori emäntä | 1940 |
| 5322 | Wuolijoki, Hella | Finnish | P | Vihreä kulta *[Green gold]* | 1938 |
| 5323 | Wuolijoki, Hella *(see also: Brecht, Bertolt)* | Finnish(Est) | P | | |
| 5324 | Wyndham, John *(John Beynon Harris)* | British | N | The Day of the Triffids *(USA: Revolt of the Triffids)* | 1951 |
| 5325 | Wyndham, John | British | N | The Midwich Cuckoos | 1957 |
| 5326 | Wyndham, John | British | N | The Midwich Cuckoos | 1957 |
| 5327 | Wyndham, John | British | SS | Random Quest | 1961 |
| 5328 | Wyspiański, Stanisław | Polish | P | Wesele *(The Wedding)* | 1901 |
| 5329 | Wyss, Johann David | German | N | Der schweizerische Robinson *(The Swiss Family Robinson)* | 1812-27 |
| 5330 | Wyss, Johann David | German | N | Der schweizerische Robinson | 1812-27 |
| 5331 | Xu Dishan *(Hsü Ti-shan)* *(as: Luo Huasheng)* *(Lo Hua-sheng)* | Chinese | SS | Chun Tao *(aka: Ch'un-T'ao)* | 1927 |
| 5332 | Yādav, Rājendra | Indian(Hin) | N | Sārā ākās *[The whole sky]* | 1960 |
| 5333 | Yanagawa Shun'yō | Japanese | N | Nasanu naka | 1912-13 |
| 5334 | Yeats, William Butler | Irish | P | The Only Jealousy of Emer | 1919 |
| 5335 | Yerby, Frank | American(afro) | N | The Foxes of Harrow | 1946 |
| 5336 | Yerby, Frank | American | N | The Golden Hawk | 1948 |
| 5337 | Yerby, Frank | American | N | The Saracen Blade | 1952 |
| 5338 | Yordan, Philip | American | P | Anna Lucasta | 1945 |
| 5339 | Yordan, Philip | American | P | Anna Lucasta | 1945 |
| 5340 | Yordan, Philip | American | N | Man of the West | 1955 |
| 5341 | Yoshikawa Eiji | Japanese | N | Miyamoto Musashi | 1936 |

| No | Film Title | Country of Production | Date | Director(s) | Duration of Film |
|---|---|---|---|---|---|
| 5303 | **Beau Geste** | USA | 1939 | William A. Wellman | 114(120) |
| 5304 | **Beau Geste** | USA | 1966 | Douglas Heyes | 105 |
| 5305 | **Beau Ideal** | USA | 1931(30) | Herbert Brenon | 81(76) |
| 5306 | **Almos' a Man** | USA | 1977 | Stan Lathan | 39 |
| 5307 | **Sangre negra** *(aka: Native Son)* | ARG | 1951 | Pierre Chenal | 91 |
| 5308 | **Native Son** | USA | 1986 | Jerrold Freedman | 112 +V |
| 5309 | | | | | |
| 5310 | **Sun wukong san da baigujing** *[The holy monkey fights the white boned devil three times]* | CHN | 1960 | Yang Xiaozhong Yu Zhongying | 90 |
| 5311 | **Da nao tian gong** *[Revolt of the holy monkey in the heavenly palace]* | CHN | 1964 | Wu Yingju | 69 |
| 5312 | **Niskavuori taistelee** *[Niskavuori fights]* | FIN | 1957 | Edvin Laine | 86 |
| 5313 | **Eteenpäin-elämään** *[Forward-toward life]* | FIN | 1939 | Toivo Särkkä Yrjo Norta | 109 |
| 5314 | **Juurakon Hulda** | FIN | 1937 | Valentin Vaala | 87 |
| 5315 | **The Farmer's Daughter** | USA | 1947(46) | H. C. Potter | 96 +V |
| 5316 | **Niskavuoren Heta** *(Heta of Niskavuori)* | FIN | 1952 | Edvin Laine | 95 |
| 5317 | **Niskavuoren Aarne** *[Aarne of Niskavuori]* | FIN | 1954 | Edvin Laine | 91 |
| 5318 | **Niskavuoren naiset** | FIN | 1938 | Valentin Vaala | 84 |
| 5319 | **Niskavuoren naiset** | FIN | 1958 | Valentin Vaala | 80 |
| 5320 | **Niskavuori** | FIN | 1984 | Matti Kassila | 120 |
| 5321 | **Loviisa** | FIN | 1946 | Valentin Vaala | 91 |
| 5322 | **Vihreä kulta** | FIN | 1939 | Valentin Vaala | 85 |
| 5323 | | | | | |
| 5324 | **The Day of the Triffids** | GB | 1962 | Steve Sekely | 94 +V |
| 5325 | **Village of the Damned** | GB | 1960 | Wolf Rilla | 77 |
| 5326 | **Children of the Damned** | GB | 1963 | Anton M. Leader | 90 |
| 5327 | **Quest For Love** | GB | 1971 | Ralph Thomas | 91 +V |
| 5328 | **Wesele** *(The Wedding)* | POL | 1973(72) | Andrzej Wajda | 105 |
| 5329 | **Swiss Family Robinson** | USA | 1940 | Edward Ludwig | 93 |
| 5330 | **Swiss Family Robinson** | GB | 1960 | Ken Annakin | 126(104) +V |
| 5331 | **Chun Tao** | CHN | 1987 | Ling Zifeng | 90 |
| 5332 | **Sārā ākās** | IND (HIN) | 1970(69) | Basu Chatterjee | 100 |
| 5333 | **Nasanu naka** *(Not Blood Relations) {silent}* | JAP | 1932 | Mikio Naruse | 105 |
| 5334 | **The Only Jealousy of Emer** | IRE | 1980 | John McCormick Alan Stamford | 26(vo) |
| 5335 | **The Foxes of Harrow** | USA | 1947 | John M. Stahl | 117 |
| 5336 | **The Golden Hawk** | USA | 1952 | Sidney Salkow | 83 |
| 5337 | **The Saracen Blade** | USA | 1954 | William Castle | 76 |
| 5338 | **Anna Lucasta** | USA | 1949 | Irving Rapper | 86 |
| 5339 | **Anna Lucasta** | USA | 1958 | Arnold Laven | 97 |
| 5340 | **Gun Glory** | USA | 1957 | Roy Rowland | 89 |
| 5341 | **Miyamoto Musashi** *(aka: Musashi Miyamoto)* | JAP | 1945(44) | Kenji Mizoguchi | 60 |

| No. | Author | Nationality | Form | Literary Title | Date |
|---|---|---|---|---|---|
| 5342 | Yoshikawa Eiji | Japanese | N | Shin Heike monogatari<br>(The Heike Story) | 1950-57 |
| 5343 | Yourcenar, Marguerite | French | N | Le coup de grâce | 1939 |
| 5344 | Yovkov, Yordan<br>(Iordan Iovkov) | Bulgarian | SS | Chastniyat uchitel<br>[The private teacher] | 1922 |
| 5345 | Yovkov, Yordan | Bulgarian | N | Chiflikăt kray granitsata<br>[The farm near the frontier] | 1933-34 |
| 5346 | Yovkov, Yordan | Bulgarian | SS | Shibil | 1925(27) |
| 5347 | Zamfirescu, Duiliu | Romanian | N | Tănase Scatiu | 1885-86<br>(1907) |
| 5348 | Zamfirescu, George Mihail | Romanian | P | Domnişoara Nastasia<br>[Miss Nastasia] | 1928 |
| 5349 | Zapolska, Gabriela | Polish | P | Moralność pani Dulskiej<br>(The Morals of Mrs Dulska) | 1907 |
| 5350 | Zapolska, Gabriela | Polish | P | Moralność pani Dulskiej | 1907 |
| 5351 | Zapolska, Gabriela | Polish | N | O czym sie nie mówi<br>[What one doesn't talk about] | 1909 |
| 5352 | Zegadłowicz, Emil | Polish | N | Zmory<br>[Incubi] | 1936(35) |
| 5353 | Żeromski, Stefan | Polish | N | Dzieje grzechu | 1908 |
| 5354 | Żeromski, Stefan | Polish | N | Dzieje grzechu | 1908 |
| 5355 | Żeromski, Stefan | Polish | N | Ludzie bezdomni<br>[Homeless people] | 1899 |
| 5356 | Żeromski, Stefan | Polish | N | Popióły<br>(Ashes) | 1904 |
| 5357 | Żeromski, Stefan | Polish | P | Róża<br>[The rose] | 1909 |
| 5358 | Żeromski, Stefan | Polish | N | Uroda życia<br>[The beauty of life] | 1912 |
| 5359 | Żeromski, Stefan | Polish | N | Wierna rzeka<br>(The Faithful River) | 1912 |
| 5360 | Żeromski, Stefan | Polish | N | Wierna rzeka | 1912 |
| 5361 | Zhao Pingfu<br>(Chao P'ing-fu)<br>(as: Rou Shi)<br>(Jou Shih) | Chinese | SS | Er yue<br>[February] | 1930 |
| 5362 | Zhao Shuli<br>(Chao Shu-li) | Chinese | SS | Xiao Erhei jiehun<br>(aka: Hsiao Erh-Hei chieh-hun)<br>[The marriage of Hsiao Erh-hei] | 1945 |
| 5363 | Zhong Ahcheng<br>(as: Ahcheng) | Chinese | SS | Hai zi wang<br>[Children's king] | 1982 |
| 5364 | Zhong Ahcheng<br>(as: Ahcheng) | Chinese | SS | Qi wang<br>[The chess king] | 1982 |
| 5365 | Zhong Ahcheng; - {ss}<br>Chang Chang Hsi-Kuo - {n} | Chinese<br>Taiwanese | SS+N | Qi wang {ss}<br>Qi wang {n} | 1982 |
| 5366 | Zhou Lipo<br>(Chou Li-po) | Chinese | N | Bao feng zhou yu<br>(The Hurricane) | 1948 |
| 5367 | Zhou Shuren<br>(Chou Shu-jen)<br>(as: Lu Xun)<br>(Lu Hsün) | Chinese | SS | Ah Q zheng zhuan<br>(aka: Ah Q cheng ch'uan)<br>(The Tragedy of Ah Q)<br>(aka: The True Story of Ah Q) | 1921 |
| 5368 | Zhou Shuren<br>(as: Lu Xun) | Chinese | SS | Ah Q zheng zhuan | 1921 |
| 5369 | Zhou Shuren<br>(as: Lu Xun) | Chinese | SS | Shang shi<br>[Regret for things past] | 1925 |
| 5370 | Zhou Shuren<br>(as: Lu Xun) | Chinese | SS | Yao<br>[Remedy] | 1923 |
| 5371 | Zhou Shuren<br>(as: Lu Xun) | Chinese | SS | Zhu fu | 1925 |
| 5372 | Zidarov, Kamen<br>(Todor Sŭbev Manev) | Bulgarian | P | Tsar Ivan Shishman<br>(aka: Ivan Shishman) | 1962(59) |
| 5373 | Zidarov, Kamen | Bulgarian | P | Tsarska milost | 1949 |

| No | Film Title | Country of Production | Date | Director(s) | Duration of Film |
|----|-----------|----------------------|------|-------------|------------------|
| 5342 | **Shin Heike monogatari** (New Tales of the Taira Clan) (aka: The Taira Clan) | JAP | 1955 | **Kenji Mizoguchi** | 107 |
| 5343 | **Der Fangschuß** (aka: Coup de grâce) | GER/FR | 1976 | **Volker Schlöndorff** | 95 |
| 5344 | **24 chassa duzhd** (24 Hours of Rain) | BULG | 1982 | **Vladislav Ikonomov** | 86 |
| 5345 | **Nona** | BULG | 1973 | **Grisha Ostrovski** | 86 |
| 5346 | **Shibil** | BULG | 1968 | **Zahari Zhandov** | 89 |
| 5347 | **Tănase Scatiu** (Summer Tale) | ROM | 1976 | **Dan Piţa** | 124 |
| 5348 | **Dincolo de barieră** [Beyond the barrier] | ROM | 1965 | **Francisc Munteanu** | 85 |
| 5349 | **Moralność pani Dulskiej** (The Morals of Mrs Dulska) | POL | 1930 | **Bolesław Newolin** | 91 |
| 5350 | **Dulscy** [The Dulski's] | POL | 1976(75) | **Jan Rybkowski** | 86 |
| 5351 | **O czym sie nie mówi** | POL | 1939 | **Mieczysław Krawicz** | 101 |
| 5352 | **Zmory** (Nightmares) | POL | 1979(78) | **Wojciech Marczewski** | 104 |
| 5353 | **Dzieje grzechu** (The Story of Sin) | POL | 1933 | **Henryk Szaro** | 97 |
| 5354 | **Dzieje grzechu** (The Story of Sin) | POL | 1975 | **Walerian Borowczyk** | 129 |
| 5355 | **Doktor Judym** | POL | 1975 | **Włodzimierz Haupe** | 95 |
| 5356 | **Popióły** (Ashes) (aka: The Lost Army) | POL | 1965 | **Andrzej Wajda** | 233 |
| 5357 | **Róża** | POL | 1936 | **Jósef Lejtes** | 95 |
| 5358 | **Uroda życia** | POL | 1930(29) | **Juliusz Gardan** | 124 |
| 5359 | **Wierna rzeka** (Baltic Rhapsody) | POL | 1936 | **Leonard Buczkowski** | 89 |
| 5360 | **Wierna rzeka** | POL | 1987(83) | **Tadeusz Chmielewski** | 137 |
| 5361 | **Zao chun er yue** (Early Spring) | CHN | 1963 | **Xie Tieli** | 107 |
| 5362 | **Xiao Erhei jiehun** | CHN | 1964 | **Gan Xuewei** **Shi Yifu** | 90 |
| 5363 | **Hai zi wang** | CHN | 1987 | **Chen Kaige** | 90 |
| 5364 | **Qi wang** | CHN | 1988 | **Teng Wenji** | 168 |
| 5365 | **King of Chess** | HK | 1991 | **Yim Ho** **Tsui Hark** | 111 |
| 5366 | **Bao feng zhou yu** (Hurricane) | CHN | 1961 | **Xie Tieli** | 120 |
| 5367 | **Ah Q zheng zhuan** (The True Story of Ah Q) | HK | 1958 | **Yuen Yang-an** | 107 |
| 5368 | **Ah Q zhen zhuan** (aka: The True Story of Ah Q) (aka: The Story of Ah Q) | CHN | 1982 | **Chen Fan** | 124(115) |
| 5369 | **Shang shi** | CHN | 1981 | **Shuihua** (Zhang Shuihua) | 103 |
| 5370 | **Yao** | CHN | 1981 | **Yu Yanfu** | 89 |
| 5371 | **Zhu fu** (New Year Sacrifice) | CHN | 1956 | **Sang Hu** | 90 |
| 5372 | **Tsar Ivan Shishman** | BULG | 1969 | **Yuri Arnaudov** | 80 |
| 5373 | **Tsarska milost** (Royal Mercy) | BULG | 1962 | **Stefan Sărchadzhiev** (Stefan Surchadjiev) | 89 |

| No. | Author | Nationality | Form | Literary Title | Date |
|-----|--------|-------------|------|----------------|------|
| 5374 | **Zilahy Lajos** | Hungarian | P | **A tábornok**<br>*(The General)* | 1928 |
| 5375 | **Zilahy Lajos** | Hungarian | P | **A tábornok** | 1928 |
| 5376 | **Zilahy Lajos** | Hungarian | P | **Tűzmadár**<br>*(Firebird)* | 1932 |
| 5377 | **Zilahy Lajos** | Hungarian | N | **Valamit visz a víz**<br>*[Something is adrift in the water]* | 1928 |
| 5378 | **Zindel, Paul** | American | P | **The Effect of Gamma Rays on Man-in-the-Moon Marigolds** | 1970 |
| 5379 | **Zola, Émile** | French | N | **L'argent**<br>*(Money)* | 1891 |
| 5380 | **Zola, Émile** | French | N | **L'assommoir**<br>*(The Dram Shop)*<br>*(aka: The Drunkard)* | 1877 |
| 5381 | **Zola, Émile** | French | N | **L'assommoir** | 1877 |
| 5382 | **Zola, Émile** | French | SS | **L'attaque du moulin**<br>*(The Attack on the Mill)* | 1880 |
| 5383 | **Zola, Émile** | French | N | **Au bonheur des dames**<br>*(Ladies Delight)*<br>*(aka: The Ladies Paradise)* | 1883 |
| 5384 | **Zola, Émile** | French | N | **La bête humaine**<br>*(The Beast in Man)*<br>*(aka: The Human Beast)* | 1890 |
| 5385 | **Zola, Émile** | French | N | **La bête humaine** | 1890 |
| 5386 | **Zola, Émile** | French | N | **La curée**<br>*(The Kill)*<br>*(aka: The Rush For the Spoil)* | 1872 |
| 5387 | **Zola, Émile** | French | N | **La faute de l'abbé Mouret**<br>*(Abbé Mouret's Sin)*<br>*(aka: The Sin of Father Mouret)* | 1875 |
| 5388 | **Zola, Émile** | French | N | **Germinal**<br>*(aka: Germinal: or, Master and Man)* | 1885 |
| 5389 | **Zola, Émile** | French | SS | **Naïs Micoulin** | 1884 |
| 5390 | **Zola, Émile** | French | N | **Nana** | 1880 |
| 5391 | **Zola, Émile** | French | N | **Nana** | 1880 |
| 5392 | **Zola, Émile** | French | N | **Nana** | 1880 |
| 5393 | **Zola, Émile** | French | N | **Nana** | 1880 |
| 5394 | **Zola, Émile** | French | N | **Nana** | 1880 |
| 5395 | **Zola, Émile** | French | N | **Pot-Bouille**<br>*(Piping Hot)*<br>*(aka: Restless House)* | 1882 |
| 5396 | **Zola, Émile** | French | SS | **Pour une nuit d'amour**<br>*(For One Night of Love)* | 1882 |
| 5397 | **Zola, Émile** | French | SS | **Pour une nuit d'amour** | 1882 |
| 5398 | **Zola, Émile** | French | SS | **Pour une nuit d'amour** | 1882 |
| 5399 | **Zola, Émile** | French | N | **Le rêve**<br>*(The Dream)* | 1888 |
| 5400 | **Zola, Émile** | French | N | **Thérèse Raquin** | 1867 |
| 5401 | **Zorrilla y Moral, José** | Spanish | V | **A buen juez mejor testigo** | 1837 |
| 5402 | **Zorrilla y Moral, José** | Spanish | P | **Don Juan Tenorio** | 1844 |
| 5403 | **Zuckmayer, Carl** | German | N | **Engele von Löewen** | 1952 |
| 5404 | **Zuckmayer, Carl** | German | SS | **Die Fastnachtsbeichte**<br>*(Carnival Confession)* | 1959 |
| 5405 | **Zuckmayer, Carl** | German | P | **Der fröhliche Weinberg** | 1925 |
| 5406 | **Zuckmayer, Carl** | German | P | **Der Hauptmann von Köpenick**<br>*(The Captain of Köpenick)* | 1930 |

| No | Film Title | Country of Production | Date | Director(s) | Duration of Film |
|----|-----------|----------------------|------|-------------|------------------|
| 5374 | **The Virtuous Sin** (GB: Cast Iron) | USA | 1930 | **Louis J. Gasnier** **George Cukor** | 81 |
| 5375 | **Die Nacht der Entscheidung** | GER | 1931 | **Dimitri Buchowetzki** | 76 |
| 5376 | **The Firebird** | USA | 1934 | **William Dieterle** | 75 |
| 5377 | **Hrst plná vody** (Adrift) | CZ/USA | 1969 | **Ján Kádár** | 108 |
| 5378 | **The Effect of Gamma Rays on Man-in-the-Moon Marigolds** | USA | 1972 | **Paul Newman** | 101 |
| 5379 | **L'argent** | FR | 1936 | **Pierre Billon** | 107 |
| 5380 | **L'assommoir** | FR | 1933 | **Gaston Roudès** | 105 |
| 5381 | **Gervaise** | FR/IT | 1956 | **René Clément** | 115(102) |
| 5382 | **Noc póslubna** (FIN: Hääyö) (Wedding Night) | POL/FIN | 1959(58) | **Erik Blomberg** | 75 |
| 5383 | **Au bonheur des dames** (Shop-Girls of Paris) | FR | 1943 | **André Cayatte** | 88 |
| 5384 | **La bête humaine** (Human Beast) (aka: Judas Was a Woman) | FR | 1938 | **Jean Renoir** | 104(88) |
| 5385 | **Human Desire** | USA | 1954 | **Fritz Lang** | 91 |
| 5386 | **La curée** (IT: La calda preda) (aka: The Game Is Over) | FR/IT | 1966 | **Roger Vadim** | 95 |
| 5387 | **La faute de l'abbé Mouret** (The Sin of Father Mouret) (IT: L'amante del prete) (USA: The Demise of Father Mouret) | FR/IT | 1970 | **Georges Franju** | 93(91) |
| 5388 | **Germinal** (IT: La furia degli uomini) | FR/HUNG/ IT | 1963 | **Yves Allégret** | 110 |
| 5389 | **Naïs** | FR | 1945 | **Raymond Leboursier** | 127(120) |
| 5390 | **Nana** (GB: Lady of the Boulevards) | USA | 1934 | **Dorothy Arzner** | 87 |
| 5391 | **Nana** | MEX | 1943 | **Celestino Gorostiza** | 87 |
| 5392 | **Nana** | FR/IT | 1955(54) | **Christian-Jaque** | 100(120) |
| 5393 | **Ta mej - älska mej** (FR: Nana) (Take Me to God) (aka: Take Me, Love Me) | SWE/FR | 1970 | **Mac Ahlberg** (Bert Torn) | 97(110) |
| 5394 | **Nana** | IT | 1982 | **Dan Wolman** | 100 +V |
| 5395 | **Pot Bouille** (IT: Le donne degli altri) (The House of Lovers) (aka: Lovers of Paris) | FR/IT | 1957 | **Julien Duvivier** | 118(115) |
| 5396 | **Pour une nuit d'amour** (aka: Passionnelle) | FR | 1946 | **Edmond T. Gréville** | 95 |
| 5397 | **La petición** (The Request) (aka: The Engagement Party) | SP | 1976 | **Pilar Miró** | 92(88) +V |
| 5398 | **Manifesto** (aka: For a Night of Love) | USA/ YUGO | 1988 | **Dusan Makavejev** | 93(96) |
| 5399 | **Le rêve** | FR | 1931(30) | **Jacques de Baroncelli** | 73 |
| 5400 | **Thérèse Raquin** (USA: The Adulteress) | FR | 1953 | **Marcel Carné** | 108 |
| 5401 | **El milagro del Cristo de la Vega** | SP | 1940 | **Adolfo Aznar** | 99(96) |
| 5402 | **Don Juan Tenorio** | SP | 1952(51) | **Alejandro Perla** | 110(90) |
| 5403 | **Ein Mädchen aus Flandern** (A Girl From Flanders) | GER | 1956 | **Helmut Käutner** | 101 |
| 5404 | **Die Fastnachtsbeichte** (The Lenten Confession) | GER | 1960 | **William Dieterle** | 99 |
| 5405 | **Der fröhliche Weinberg** (The Happy Vineyard) (aka: The Merry Vineyard) | GER | 1952 | **Erich Engel** | 91 |
| 5406 | **Der Hauptmann von Köpenick** (The Captain of Köpenick) | GER | 1931 | **Richard Oswald** | 107(85) |

| No. | Author | Nationality | Form | Literary Title | Date |
|---|---|---|---|---|---|
| 5407 | **Zuckmayer, Carl** | German | P | **Der Hauptmann von Köpenick** | 1930 |
| 5408 | **Zuckmayer, Carl** | German | P | **Der Hauptmann von Köpenick** | 1930 |
| 5409 | **Zuckmayer, Carl** | German | N | **Herr über Leben und Tod** *[Lord of life and death]* | 1938 |
| 5410 | **Zuckmayer, Carl** | German | P | **Katharina Knie** | 1928 |
| 5411 | **Zuckmayer, Carl** | German | SS | **Eine Liebesgeschichte** *[A love story]* | 1934 |
| 5412 | **Zuckmayer, Carl** | German | P | **Schinderhannes** | 1927 |
| 5413 | **Zuckmayer, Carl** | German | N | **Der Seelenbräu** | 1945 |
| 5414 | **Zuckmayer, Carl** | German | P | **Des Teufels General** | 1945 |
| 5415 | **Żukrowski, Wojciech** | Polish | SS | **Lotna** | 1946 |
| 5416 | **Zunzunegui, Juan Antonio de** | Spanish | N | **Dos hombres y dos mujeres en medio** | 1944 |
| 5417 | **Zunzunegui, Juan Antonio de** | Spanish | N | **El mundo sigue** *[Life goes on]* | 1960 |
| 5418 | **Zweig, Arnold** | German | N | **Das Beil von Wandsbek** *(The Axe of Wandsbek)* | 1947 |
| 5419 | **Zweig, Arnold** | German | N | **Das Beil von Wandsbek** | 1947 |
| 5420 | **Zweig, Arnold** | German | N | **Der Streit um den Sergeanten Grischa** *(The Case of Sergeant Grischa)* | 1927 |
| 5421 | **Zweig, Stefan** | Austrian | SS | **Amok** | 1922 |
| 5422 | **Zweig, Stefan** | Austrian | SS | **Amok** | 1922 |
| 5423 | **Zweig, Stefan** | Austrian | SS | **Die Angst** | 1920 |
| 5424 | **Zweig, Stefan** | Austrian | SS | **Die Angst** | 1920 |
| 5425 | **Zweig, Stefan** | Austrian | SS | **Brennendes Geheimnis** *(The Burning Secret)* | 1929 |
| 5426 | **Zweig, Stefan** | Austrian | SS | **Brennendes Geheimnis** | 1929 |
| 5427 | **Zweig, Stefan** | Austrian | SS | **Brief einer Unbekannten** *(Letter From an Unknown Woman)* | 1922 |
| 5428 | **Zweig, Stefan** | Austrian | SS | **Brief einer Unbekannten** | 1922 |
| 5429 | **Zweig, Stefan** | Austrian | BIO | **Marie Antoinette, Bildnis eines mittleren Charakters** *(Marie Antoinette, the Portrait of an Average Woman)* | 1932 |
| 5430 | **Zweig, Stefan** | Austrian | SS | **Schachnovelle** *(The Royal Game)* | 1942 |
| 5431 | **Zweig, Stefan** | Austrian | N | **Ungeduld des Herzens** *(Beware of Pity)* | 1938 |
| 5432 | **Zweig, Stefan** | Austrian | N | **Vierundzwanzig Stunden aus dem Leben einer Frau** *(Four and Twenty Hours in a Woman's Life)* | 1926 |
| 5433 | **Zweig, Stefan** | Austrian | N | **Vierundzwanzig Stunden aus dem Leben einer Frau** | 1926 |
| 5434 | **Zweig, Stefan** | Austrian | N | **Vierundzwanzig Stunden aus dem Leben einer Frau** | 1926 |
| 5435 | **Zweig, Stefan** | Austrian | N | **Vierundzwanzig Stunden aus dem Leben einer Frau** | 1926 |

| No | Film Title | Country of Production | Date | Director(s) | Duration of Film |
|----|-----------|----------------------|------|-------------|-----------------|
| 5407 | **The Captain of Koepenick** *(aka: I Was a Criminal)* | USA | 1946 | **Richard Oswald** | 71 |
| 5408 | **Der Hauptmann von Köpenick** *(The Captain From Koepenick)* | GER | 1956 | **Helmut Käutner** | 93 |
| 5409 | **Herr über Leben und Tod** | GER | 1955 | **Victor Vicas** | 87 |
| 5410 | **Menschen, die vorüberziehen** *(aka: Gens, qui passent)* | SWITZ | 1942 | **Max Haufler** | 104 |
| 5411 | **Eine Liebesgeschichte** | GER | 1954 | **Rudolf Jugert** | 95 |
| 5412 | **Schinderhannes** | GER | 1958 | **Helmut Käutner** | 115 |
| 5413 | **Der Seelenbräu** | AUST | 1950 | **Gustav Ucicky** | 98 |
| 5414 | **Das Teufels General** *(The Devil's General)* | GER | 1955 | **Helmut Käutner** | 120(115) |
| 5415 | **Lotna** | POL | 1959 | **Andrzej Wajda** | 89 |
| 5416 | **Dos hombres... y, en medio, dos mujeres** | SP | 1977(76) | **Rafael Gil** | 101(96) |
| 5417 | **El mundo sigue** | SP | 1965(63) | **Fernando Fernán-Gomez** | 124 |
| 5418 | **Das Beil von Wandsbek** *(The Axe of Wandsbek)* | GDR | 1951 | **Falk Harnack** | 111 |
| 5419 | **Das Beil von Wandsbek** *(The Axe of Wandsbeck)* | GDR | 1983 | **Falk Harnack** | 90 |
| 5420 | **The Case of Sergeant Grischa** | USA | 1930 | **Herbert Brenon** | 82(89) |
| 5421 | **Amok** | FR | 1934 | **Fédor Ozep** | 92 |
| 5422 | **Amok** | MEX | 1944 | **Antonio Momplet** | 106 |
| 5423 | **La peur** *(aka: Vertige d'un soir)* | FR | 1936 | **Viktor Tourjansky** | 90 |
| 5424 | **Die Angst** *(IT: Paura)* *(aka: Incubo)* *(aka: Non credo più al l'amore)* *(Fear)* | GER/IT | 1954 | **Roberto Rossellini** | 82(75) |
| 5425 | **Brennendes Geheimnis** *(Burning Secret)* | GER | 1933 | **Robert Siodmak** | 93 |
| 5426 | **Burning Secret** *(GER: Brennendes Geheimnis)* | GB/USA/ GER | 1988 | **Andrew Birkin** | 105 +V |
| 5427 | **Valkoiset ruusut** *[The white roses]* | FIN | 1943 | **Hannu Leminen** | 102(106) |
| 5428 | **Letter From an Unknown Woman** | USA | 1948 | **Max Ophüls** | 87(90) |
| 5429 | **Marie Antoinette** | USA | 1938 | **W. S. Van Dyke** | 142 |
| 5430 | **Die Schachnovelle** *(The Royal Game)* *(aka: Brainwashed)* | GER | 1960 | **Gerd Oswald** | 103 |
| 5431 | **Beware of Pity** | GB | 1946 | **Maurice Elvey** | 106(102) |
| 5432 | **Vierundzwanzig Stunden aus dem Leben einer Frau** *(FR: Vingt-quatre heures dans la vie d'une femme)* | GER/FR | 1931 | **Robert Land** | 73 |
| 5433 | **24 horas en la vida de una mujer** | ARG | 1944 | **Carlos Borcosque** | 90 |
| 5434 | **Twenty-Four Hours of a Woman's Life** *(aka: Affair in Monte Carlo)* | GB | 1952 | **Victor Saville** | 90(75) |
| 5435 | **Vingt-quatre heures dans la vie d'une femme** *(Twenty Four Hours in a Woman's Life)* | FR/GER | 1968 | **Dominique Delouche** | 84 |

# Index of Film Titles

| | | | | |
|---|---|---|---|---|
| 3200 | Carmen proibita | *IT/SP* | *1952* | |
| 3949 | Carne, a | *BRAZ* | *1976* | |
| 2987 | Carnival | *GB* | *1946* | |
| 3433 | Carnival of Sinners | *FR* | *1942* | |
| 768 | Carnival Scenes | *ROM* | *1959(58)* | |
| 1881 | Carolina | *USA* | *1934* | |
| 1756 | Caro Michele | *IT* | *1976* | |
| 3306 | Carousel | *USA* | *1956* | |
| 1339 | Carrie | *USA* | *1952(51)* | |
| 3996 | Carrière de Suzanne, la | *FR* | *1963* | |
| 3208 | Carrosse d'or, la | *IT/FR* | *1953* | |
| 3208 | Carrozza d'oro, la | *IT/FR* | *1953* | |
| 233 | Cartomante, a | *BRAZ* | *1974* | |
| 3768 | Căruţa cu mere | *ROM* | *1983* | |
| 789 | Casa assassinada, a | *BRAZ* | *1971* | |
| 1719 | Casa de Bernarda Alba, la | | | |
| | | *SP* | *1987 (86)* | |
| 1556 | Casa de la lluvia, la | *SP* | *1943* | |
| 2316 | Casa de muñecas | *ARG* | *1943* | |
| 3988 | Casamento, o | *BRAZ* | *1975* | |
| 807 | Casanova | *IT* | *1969* | |
| 808 | Casanova | *IT* | *1976* | |
| 808 | Casanova di Federico Fellini, il | | | |
| | | *IT* | *1976* | |
| 4116 | Cascalho | *BRAZ* | *1950* | |
| 3364 | Case For the Jury, a | *GB* | *1962* | |
| 4770 | Case For the New Hangman, a | *CZ* | *1969* | |
| 5420 | Case of Sergeant Grischa, the | | | |
| | | *USA* | *1930* | |
| 3180 | Caso Claudia, a | *BRAZ* | *1979* | |
| 4207 | Caso di coscienza, un | *IT* | *1970(69)* | |
| 4467 | Caso difficile del commissario Maigret, | | | |
| | il | *AUST/IT/FR* | *1967(66)* | |
| 5151 | Caso Maurizius, il | *FR/IT* | *1954(53)* | |
| 1841 | Casse, le | *FR/IT* | *1971* | |
| 2824 | Cass Timberlane | *USA* | *1947* | |
| 3975 | Caste | *GB* | *1930* | |
| 4105 | Castello in Svezia, il | *FR/IT* | *1963* | |
| 5051 | Castelul din Carpaţi | *ROM* | *1981* | |
| 5374 | Cast Iron | *USA* | *1930* | |
| 2482 | Castle, the | *GER/SWITZ* | *1968* | |
| 2483 | Castle, the | *FIN* | *1986* | |
| 1446 | Castle Keep | *USA* | *1969* | |
| 3101 | Castle of Crimes | *GB* | *1940* | |
| 2769 | Castle of Doom | *GER/FR* | *1932* | |
| 4283 | Castle of the Spiders Web | *JAP* | *1957* | |
| 4465 | Cat, the | *FR/IT* | *1971* | |
| 1877 | Cat and Mouse | *GER/POL* | *1967(66)* | |
| 4808 | Cat and Two Women, a | *JAP* | *1956* | |
| 3503 | Catch, the | *JAP* | *1961* | |
| 2102 | Catch-22 | *USA* | *1970* | |
| 869 | Catered Affair, the | *USA* | *1956* | |
| 5257 | Cat On a Hot Tin Roof | *USA* | *1958* | |
| 3536 | Cats Game | *HUNG* | *1974* | |
| 4808 | Cat, Shozo and Two Women, a | | | |
| | | *JAP* | *1956* | |
| 4752 | Cat's Path, the | *GER* | *1938(37)* | |
| 3536 | Catsplay | *HUNG* | *1974* | |
| 3537 | Catsplay | *GER* | *1983* | |
| 1076 | Cavalcade | *USA* | *1933* | |
| 1077 | Cavalcade | *USA* | *1955* | |
| 4157 | Cavale, la | *FR* | *1971* | |
| 1349 | Cavaliere di Maison Rouge, il | *IT* | *1953* | |
| 732 | Cavaliere inesistente, il | *IT* | *1970(69)* | |
| 1380 | Cavalieri della regina, i | *IT* | *1954* | |
| 2979 | Cavalinho azul, o | *BRAZ* | *1985* | |
| 5042 | Cavalleria rusticana | *IT* | *1940(39)* | |
| 5043 | Cavalleria rusticana | *IT* | *1953* | |
| 4463 | Caves du Majestic, les | *FR* | *1945* | |
| 4464 | Cécile est morte | *FR* | *1944(43)* | |
| 5100 | Cecilia | *CB/SP* | *1982* | |
| 5100 | Cecilia Valdés | *CB/SP* | *1982* | |
| 3151 | Ce cochon de Morin | *FR* | *1933* | |
| 729 | Cedar Madona, the | *BRAZ* | *1968(67)* | |
| 3682 | Cei care plătesc cu viaţa | *ROM* | *1989* | |
| 3976 | Cela s'appelle l'aurore | *FR/IT* | *1955* | |
| 4000 | Celestina, la | *IT/FR* | *1965(64)* | |
| 4001 | Celestina, la | *SP/GER* | *1969(68)* | |
| 4002 | Celestina | *MEX* | *1977* | |
| 4000 | Celestina P...R..., la | *IT/FR* | *1965(64)* | |
| 473 | Cell, the | *GER* | *1971* | |
| 4903 | Celos | *ARG* | *1946* | |
| 2563 | Celui qui doit mourir | *FR/IT* | *1957* | |
| 435 | Cena delle beffe, la | *IT* | *1941* | |
| 3664 | Cenerentola | *IT* | *1949(48)* | |
| 1623 | Cerromaior | *PORT* | *1980* | |
| 4103 | Certain Smile, a | *USA* | *1958* | |
| 5045 | Certo capitão Rodrigo, um | | | |
| | | *BRAZ* | *1971* | |
| 4630 | Certosa di Parma, la | *FR/IT* | *1947* | |
| 1662 | Cervantes | *SP/IT/FR* | *1968(67)* | |

| | | | | | |
|---|---|---|---|---|---|
| 3588 | César | *FR* | *1936* | | |
| 2929 | Cet obscur objet du désir | | | | |
| | | *FR/SP* | *1977* | | |
| 1453 | Chad Hanna | *USA* | *1940* | | |
| 4422 | Cha guan | *CHN* | *1982* | | |
| 1401 | Cha hua nu | *CHN* | *1938* | | |
| 266 | Chalk Garden, the | *GB* | *1963* | | |
| 3322 | Challenge, the | *USA* | *1930* | | |
| 2900 | Challenge to White Fang | | | | |
| | | *IT/SP/FR* | *1974(73)* | | |
| 3546 | Cham | *POL* | *1931* | | |
| 4104 | Chamade, la | *FR/IT* | *1968* | | |
| 3397 | Chambre obscure, la | *GB/FR* | *1969* | | |
| 3016 | Chambre rouge, la | *BEL/FR* | *1972* | | |
| 2401 | Chambre verte, la | *FR* | *1978* | | |
| 2737 | Champ de lin, le | *BEL/HOLL* | *1983* | | |
| 2728 | Champion | *USA* | *1949* | | |
| 4174 | Chamsin | *GER* | *1972(70)* | | |
| 385 | Change | *GER* | *1974* | | |
| 2863 | Changing Trains | *SWE* | *1943* | | |
| 175 | Chanson de Roland, la | *FR* | *1978* | | |
| 1758 | Chant du monde, le | *FR/IT* | *1965* | | |
| 2580 | Chant of Jimmie Blacksmith, | | | | |
| | the | *AUSTL* | *1978* | | |
| 1261 | Chão bruto | *BRAZ* | *1959* | | |
| 1690 | Chapayev | *USSR* | *1934* | | |
| 2688 | Chapeau de paille d'Italie, | | | | |
| | un | *FR* | *1944(40)* | | |
| 4510 | Chapter Two | *USA* | *1979* | | |
| 2378 | Chardons du Baragan, les | | | | |
| | | *ROM/FR* | *1958(57)* | | |
| 4838 | Charge of the Light Brigade, | | | | |
| | the | *USA* | *1936* | | |
| 2704 | Charlotte Löwensköld | *SWE* | *1930* | | |
| 2704 | Charlotte Löwensköld | *SWE* | *1930* | | |
| 2705 | Charlotte Löwensköld | *SWE* | *1979* | | |
| 2709 | Charrette fantôme, la | *FR* | *1939* | | |
| 4630 | Chartreuse de Parme, la | *FR/IT* | *1947* | | |
| 4788 | Chārulatā | *IND(BEN)* | *1964* | | |
| 2231 | Chase, the | *USA* | *1946* | | |
| 1659 | Chasing Yesterday | *USA* | *1935* | | |
| 4465 | Chat, le | *FR/IT* | *1971* | | |
| 3600 | Château de ma mère, le | *FR* | *1990* | | |
| 4105 | Château en Suède | *FR/IT* | *1963* | | |
| 4465 | Chat, l'implacabile uomo di Saint | | | | |
| | Germain, le | *FR/IT* | *1971* | | |
| 880 | Chayka | *USSR* | *1971* | | |
| 1848 | Chelkash | *USSR* | *1956* | | |
| 3763 | Chelovek s ruzhyom | *USSR* | *1938* | | |
| 882 | Chelovek v futlyare | *USSR* | *1939* | | |
| 883 | Chelovek v futlyare | *USSR* | *1983* | | |
| 4543 | Chemeen | *IND* | *1965* | | |
| 251 | Chemin des écoliers, le | *FR/IT* | *1959* | | |
| 1120 | Chère Louise | *FR/IT* | *1972* | | |
| 991 | Chéri | *FR* | *1950* | | |
| 4642 | Chernaya strela | *USSR* | *1985* | | |
| 884 | Chernyi monakh | *USSR* | *1988* | | |
| 3799 | Chess Players, the | *IND(HIN)* | *1977* | | |
| 4520 | Chetvyorty | *USSR* | *1972* | | |
| 1732 | Chevalier de Maupin, le | | | | |
| | | *IT/FR/SP* | *1966(65)* | | |
| 3153 | Chevelure, la | *FR* | *1961* | | |
| 2971 | Cheviot, the Stag and the Black, Black | | | | |
| | Oil, the | *GB* | *1974* | | |
| 207 | Chèvre d'or, la | *FR* | *1943* | | |
| 4806 | Chiave, la | *IT* | *1983* | | |
| 4466 | Chien jaune, le | *FR* | *1932* | | |
| 4804 | Chijin no ai | *JAP* | *1967* | | |
| 948 | Chikamatsu monogatari | *JAP* | *1955* | *(54)* |
| 563 | Child, the | *NOR* | *1938* | | |
| 1597 | Child | *DEN* | *1940* | | |
| 3681 | Childe John | *HUNG* | *1973* | | |
| 1852 | Childhood of Maxim Gorky | | | | |
| | | *USSR* | *1938* | | |
| 5206 | Children, the | *GB* | *1990* | | |
| 3179 | Children of a Lesser God | *USA* | *1986* | | |
| 5326 | Children of the Damned | *GB* | *1963* | | |
| 2105 | Children's Hour, the | *USA* | *1962(61)* | | |
| 4265 | Chimes at Midnight | *SP/SWITZ* | | | |
| | | *1966 (65)* | | | |
| 649 | China Sky | *USA* | *1945* | | |
| 652 | China Story | *GB* | *1962* | | |
| 1040 | Chingachgock - die grosse Schlange | | | | |
| | | *GDR* | *1967* | | |
| 1479 | Chinmoku | *JAP/USA* | *1971* | | |
| 93 | Chiriţa la laşi | *ROM* | *1988* | | |
| 3994 | Chloe in the Afternoon | *FR* | *1972* | | |
| 3945 | Chłopi | *POL* | *1973* | | |
| 3312 | Chocolate Soldier, the | *USA* | *1941* | | |
| 3402 | Chorus Girl | *JAP* | *1957* | | |
| 248 | Chorus of Disapproval, a | *GB* | *1988* | | |

# Guide to Literature on Film

| | | | | |
|---|---|---|---|---|
| 2330 | Dharamveer *IND(MAR)* *1937* | | 450 | Dollar *SWE* *1938* |
| 3879 | Diable au corps, le *FR* *1947* | | 2316 | Doll's House, a *ARG* *1943* |
| 838 | Diablo bajo la almohada, un *SP* *1968* | | 2318 | Doll's House, a *GB* *1973* |
| 5038 | Diablo cojuelo, el *SP* *1971(70)* | | 2319 | Doll's House, a *GB/FR* *1973* |
| 2776 | Dialoghi delle Carmelitane, i *FR/IT* *1960* | | 3280 | Domaren *SWE* *1960* |
| 2776 | Dialogue des Carmélites, le *FR/IT* *1960* | | 3410 | Domingo à tarde *PORT* *1966(64)* |
| | | | 14 | Domino *FR* *1943(42)* |
| 3644 | Diamante bruto *BRAZ* *1977* | | 329 | Domnişoara Aurica *ROM* *1986* |
| 44 | Diamant noir, le *FR* *1940(39)* | | 888 | Dom s mezoninom *USSR* *1960* |
| 2949 | Diao chan *CHN* *1938* | | 1700 | Doña Barbara *MEX* *1943* |
| 3264 | Diario di una cameriera, il *FR/IT* *1964(63)* | | 110 | Dona Flor and Her Two Husbands *BRAZ* *1976* |
| 1794 | Diary *GER* *1975* | | 110 | Dona Flor e seus dois maridos *BRAZ* *1976* |
| 3263 | Diary of a Chambermaid *USA* *1946* | | 3075 | Doña María la Brava *SP* *1948(47)* |
| 3264 | Diary of a Chambermaid, the *FR/IT* *1964(63)* | | 4175 | Don Carlos *AUST* *1960* |
| | | | 4176 | Don Carlos *GER* *1963* |
| 457 | Diary of a Country Priest *FR* *1950* | | 842 | Don Chisciotte *IT* *1984* |
| 3158 | Diary of a Madman *USA* *1962* | | 839 | Don Chisciotte e Sancho Panza *IT* *1968* |
| 1820 | Diary of a Madman *USA* *1967* | | 577 | Don Giovanni in Sicilia *IT* *1967* |
| 542 | Días de odio *ARG* *1954* | | 5402 | Don Juan Tenorio *SP* *1952(51)* |
| 579 | Difficult Years *IT* *1948(47)* | | 3674 | Donkey Skin *FR* *1971(70)* |
| 1426 | Diga sul Pacifico, la *IT/FR* *1957(56)* | | 834 | Don Kikhot *USSR* *1957* |
| 144 | Dikie lebedi *USSR* *1988* | | 1340 | Donna alla finestra, una *FR/IT* *1976* |
| 1847 | Dilemma *DEN* *1962* | | 4751 | Donna dell'altro, la *GER/IT* *1959* |
| 546 | Dimanche à la campagne, un *FR* *1984* | | 3343 | Donna invisibile, la *IT* *1969* |
| 3860 | Dimanche de la vie, le *FR/IT/GER* *1965* | | 5395 | Donne degli altri, le *FR/IT* *1957* |
| | | | 4005 | Donogoo Tonka *GER* *1936* |
| 2167 | Dimboola *AUSTL* *1979* | | 831 | Don Quichotte *GB/FR* *1933(32)* |
| 5348 | Dincolo de barierǎ *ROM* *1965* | | 837 | Don Quichotte *FR/SP/GER* *1966(64)* |
| 3427 | Dincolo de nisipuri *ROM* *1973* | | 835 | Don Quijote *FIN* *1962* |
| 4555 | Dincolo de pod *ROM* *1976(75)* | | 837 | Don Quijote *FR/SP/GER* *1966(64)* |
| 1582 | Dindon, le *FR* *1951* | | 836 | Don Quijote, ayer y hoy *SP* *1964* |
| 2542 | Dinner at Eight *USA* *1933* | | 840 | Don Quijote cabalga de nuevo *MEX/SP* *1974(72)* |
| 4015 | Dino *USA* *1957* | | 832 | Don Quijote de la Mancha *SP* *1948 (47)* |
| 5237 | Dio chiamato Dorian, il *GER/IT* *1970* | | 831 | Don Quixote *GB/FR* *1933(32)* |
| 1488 | Dionysus in 69 *USA* *1970* | | 832 | Don Quixote *SP* *1948(47)* |
| 742 | Diós se lo pague *ARG* *1948* | | 834 | Don Quixote *USSR* *1957* |
| 4160 | Dirty Hands *FR* *1951* | | 842 | Don Quixote *IT* *1984* |
| 3043 | Disorder and Early Suffering *GER* *1977(76)* | | 839 | Don Quixote and Sancho Panza *IT* *1968* |
| 3493 | Displaced Person, the *USA* *1977* | | 840 | Don Quixote Rides Again *MEX/SP* *1974(72)* |
| 3342 | Disprezzo, il *FR/IT* *1963* | | 1947 | Don Segundo Sombra *ARG* *1969* |
| 317 | Distant Thunder *IND(BEN)* *1973* | | 4415 | Donskaya povest' *USSR* *1964* |
| 2175 | Dites-lui que je l'aime *FR* *1977* | | 5276 | Don's Party *AUSTL* *1976* |
| 3447 | Ditta: Child of Man *DEN* *1946* | | 1410 | Don't Look Now *GB/IT* *1973* |
| 3447 | Ditte Menneskebarn *DEN* *1946* | | 1859 | Donzoko *JAP* *1957* |
| 657 | Dit vindarna bär *NOR* *1948* | | 5171 | Door in the Wall, the *GB* *1956* |
| 5290 | Divided Sky *GDR* *1964* | | 188 | Doppelselbstmord *GER* *1937* |
| 993 | Divine *FR* *1935* | | 2512 | Doppelte Lottchen, das *GER* *1950* |
| 4521 | Dni i nochi *USSR* *1944* | | 4131 | Dora la espía *SP/IT* *1943* |
| 1170 | Dobrodružství Robinson Crusoe, namornika z Yorku *CZ/GER* *1982* | | 5237 | Dorian Gray *GER/IT* *1970* |
| | | | 3432 | Dorotej *YUGO* *1981* |
| 2024 | Dobrý voják Švejk *CZ* *1931* | | 2039 | Dorothea Angermann *GER* *1959(58)* |
| 2026 | Dobrý voják Švejk *CZ* *1956* | | 5416 | Dos hombres... y, en medio, dos mujeres *SP* *1977(76)* |
| 2340 | Doce sillas, las *CB* *1962* | | 3064 | Dottor Faustus, il *GB/IT* *1967* |
| 3364 | Dock Brief, the *GB* *1962* | | 770 | Douǎ lozuri *ROM* *1957* |
| 4725 | Dockhem, ett *SWE* *1956* | | 516 | Double Deadly *CAN* *1978* |
| 1092 | Doctor Bull *USA* *1933* | | 1767 | Double destin *FR/GER* *1955(54)* |
| 3064 | Doctor Faustus *GB/IT* *1967* | | 710 | Double Indemnity *USA* *1944* |
| 3038 | Doctor Faustus *GER* *1982* | | 3313 | Double Play *HUNG/USA* *1984* |
| 1887 | Dr Fischer of Geneva *GB* *1984(83)* | | 949 | Double Suicide *JAP* *1969* |
| 4572 | Doctor Glass *DEN* *1968* | | 950 | Double Suicide of Sonezaki *JAP* *1978* |
| 4645 | Dr Jekyll and Mr Hyde *USA* *1932(31)* | | 3307 | Double Wedding *USA* *1937* |
| 4646 | Dr Jekyll and Mr Hyde *USA* *1941* | | 3652 | Doubt *SP* *1972* |
| 529 | Dr Murkes Collected Silences *SWE* *1968* | | 1938 | Dou er yuan *CHN* *1959* |
| | | | 3558 | Dowerless Bride *USSR* *1984* |
| 2136 | Doctor Rhythm *USA* *1938* | | 1515 | Down and Out in Beverly Hills *USA* *1986(85)* |
| 4338 | Doctor's Dilemma, the *GB* *1959(57)* | | | |
| 1743 | Dr Strangelove *GB* *1964(63)* | | 2390 | Downfall, the *JAP* *1935(34)* |
| 1743 | Dr Strangelove: or How I Learned to Stop Worrying and Love the Bomb *GB* *1964(63)* | | 2390 | Downfall of Osen, the *JAP* *1935(34)* |
| | | | 1969 | Downhill Racer *USA* *1969* |
| 3758 | Dr Tarr's Torture Dungeon *MEX* *1972* | | 4874 | Down the Ancient Stairs *IT/FR* *1975* |
| 3634 | Dr Zhivago *USA* *1965* | | 1054 | Doživljaji Nikoletine Bursaća *YUGO* *1964* |
| 2825 | Dodsworth *USA* *1936* | | | |
| 918 | Dogadaj *YUGO* *1969* | | 4681 | Dracula *USA* *1931* |
| 4693 | Dog Soldiers *USA* *1978* | | 4682 | Dracula *GB* *1958* |
| 4765 | Doi bărbaţi pentru o moarte *ROM* *1970* | | 4686 | Dracula *GB* *1974(73)* |
| | | | 4687 | Dracula *USA* *1979* |
| 3038 | Doktor Faustus *GER* *1982* | | 4425 | Dragon Beard Ditch *CHN* *1952* |
| 4571 | Doktor Glas *SWE* *1942* | | 650 | Dragon Seed, the *USA* *1944* |
| 4572 | Doktor Glas *DEN* *1968* | | 2808 | Drama From Olden Times *USSR* *1971* |
| 5355 | Doktor Judym *POL* *1975* | | | |
| 529 | Dr Murkes samlade tystnad *SWE* *1968* | | 2808 | Drama iz starinnoi zhizni *USSR* *1971* |
| | | | 890 | Drama na okhote *USSR* *1978(77)* |
| 3765 | Doktor Vyera *USSR* *1968* | | 4797 | Drama nuevo, un *SP* *1946* |
| 1396 | Dolcezze del peccato, le *GER/IT/FR* *1968* | | | |
| 3822 | Doll, the *POL* *1968* | | | |

**310**

# Guide to Literature on Film

**318**

**335**

**336**

| | | | | |
|---|---|---|---|---|
| 4962 | V navecherieto USSR/BULG 1959 | | 5296 | Waves, the HOLL 1982 |
| 987 | Voce, una IT 1948(47) | | 1761 | Ways of Love FR 1934(33) |
| 2498 | Voice of Bugle Ann, the USA 1936 | | 987 | Ways of Love IT 1948(47) |
| 4524 | Vo imya rodini USSR 1943 | | 2669 | Way to Paradise YUGO 1970 |
| 4780 | Võlegény HUNG 1982 | | 249 | Way Upstream GB 1986 |
| 11 | Voleur de femmes FR 1964(62) | | 4629 | Wayward Bus, the USA 1957 |
| 3573 | Volki i ovtsy USSR 1952 | | 4045 | Wayward Girl, the NOR 1959 |
| 2320 | Volksfeind, ein GER 1937 | | 3348 | Wayward Wife IT 1952 |
| 2466 | Volpone FR 1941(40) | | 1950 | Way West, the USA 1967 |
| 1569 | Volvoreta SP 1976 | | 2742 | Way We Were, the USA 1973 |
| 3641 | Von der Wolke zum Wilderstand | | 4122 | We Are All Demons DEN/SWE/ |
| | IT/FR/GER/GB 1979 | | | NOR 1969 |
| 2045 | Vor Sonnenaufgang GER 1976 | | 2186 | We Are Not Alone USA 1939 |
| 2047 | Vor Sonnenuntergang GER 1956 | | 2777 | Weather in the Streets, the |
| 1937 | Vorstadtkrokodile GER 1978 | | | GB 1984 (83) |
| 4881 | Vosemnadtsaty god USSR 1958 | | 1105 | Web of Evidence GB 1959 |
| 60 | Voskhozhdeniye na Fudziyamu USSR 1988 | | 926 | Wedding USSR 1944 |
| 4918 | Voskreseniye USSR 1960-62 | | 5328 | Wedding, the POL 1973(72) |
| 4223 | Vostaniye rybakov USSR 1935(34) | | 2720 | Wedding, the YUGO/USSR 1973 |
| 3728 | Voyage, the IT/FR 1974 | | 869 | Wedding Breakfast USA 1956 |
| 4153 | Voyage à Biarritz, le FR 1963 | | 5382 | Wedding Night POL/FIN 1959(58) |
| 2691 | Voyage de Monsieur Perrichon, le FR 1934 | | 3193 | Wednesday's Child GB 1971 |
| 1676 | Voyager GER/FR 1991 | | 2622 | Wee Willie Winkie USA 1937 |
| 4504 | Voyageur de la Toussaint, le FR 1943 | | 199 | Weg abwärts, der AUST 1950 |
| 184 | Voyageur sans bagage, le FR 1944 | | 3118 | Weib im Dschungel GER/FR/ |
| 4921 | Voyna i mir USSR 1963-67 | | | USA 1931(30) |
| 4527 | Vozmerdie USSR 1968 | | 4199 | Weibsteufel, der AUST 1951 |
| 3455 | Vozvrashchenie Vasilya Bortnikova | | 4200 | Weibsteufel, der AUST 1966 |
| | USSR 1953 | | 3496 | Weisheit des Blutes, die USA/ |
| 3457 | Vpervye zamuzhem USSR 1980 | | | GER 1979 |
| 3620 | V poiskakh radosti USSR 1940 | | 4897 | Weiße Teufel, der GER 1930 |
| 1863 | Vragi USSR 1938 | | 4196 | Weite Land, das FR/AUST/GER 1987 |
| 940 | Vragi USSR 1960 | | 1258 | Welcome to Hard Times |
| 170 | Vrata raja GB/YUGO 1967 | | | USA 1967 (66) |
| 5218 | Vredens dag DEN 1943 | | 4913 | We Live Again USA 1934 |
| 1263 | Vreme razdelno BULG 1988 | | 4579 | Well, Young Man? HUNG 1964(63) |
| 3877 | Vsichki i nikoi BULG 1978 | | 2736 | Wenn die Sonne wieder scheint GER 1943 |
| 2659 | V stepyakh Ukrayiny USSR 1952 | | 3437 | Wenn Poldi ins Manöver zieht |
| 4612 | V tikha vecher BULG 1960 | | | AUST 1956 |
| 3257 | Vu du pont FR/IT 1961 | | 1895 | Went the Day Well? GB 1942 |
| 5059 | Vynález zkázy CZ 1958 | | 341 | We're Not Dressing USA 1934 |
| 3857 | Vystrel USSR 1967 | | 1787 | Werther FR 1938 |
| | | | 5328 | Wesele POL 1973(72) |
| 3425 | Wagahai wa neko de aru JAP 1975 | | 4205 | We Still Kill the Old Way IT 1967(66) |
| 4584 | Waga koi no tabiji JAP 1961 | | 2743 | West Side Story USA 1961 |
| 219 | Wages of Fear, the FR 1953 | | 334 | Westward Passage USA 1932 |
| 220 | Wages of Fear, the USA 1977 | | 3890 | We the Living IT 1942 |
| 1793 | Wahlverwandtschaften, die GDR 1975 | | 4535 | Wet Parade, the USA 1932 |
| 4528 | Wait For Me! USSR 1943 | | 351 | What Every Woman Knows USA 1934 |
| 2376 | Wakai hito JAP 1937 | | 1090 | What Mad Pursuit? GB 1985 |
| 2377 | Wakai hito JAP 1952 | | 2414 | What Maisie Knew USA 1976 |
| 3419 | Wake Up and Dream USA 1946 | | 4895 | What Men Live By GB 1939 |
| 633 | Walk in the Sun, a USA 1946(45) | | 158 | What Price Glory? USA 1952 |
| 103 | Walk on the Wild Side USA 1962 | | 3628 | What's the Time, Mr Clock? HUNG 1985 |
| 2308 | Walk Proud USA 1979 | | 2969 | Wheels IRE 1976 |
| 4180 | Wallenstein GER 1962 | | 2695 | When a Woman in Love FR 1976 |
| 1777 | Walpurgis Night USA 1932 | | 1674 | When Meadows Bloom SWE 1946 |
| 3044 | Wälsungenblut GER 1964 | | 123 | When Svante Disappeared DEN 1975 |
| 2948 | Waltz of Sex SWE 1968 | | 4583 | When the Cookie Crumbles JAP 1967 |
| 183 | Waltz of the Toreadors GB 1962 | | 3816 | When We Are Married GB 1943 |
| 67 | Wanderer, the FR 1967 | | 1648 | Where Angels Fear to Tread GB 1991 |
| 2058 | Wanderer's Notebook, a JAP 1962 | | 4400 | Where Chimneys Are Seen JAP 1953 |
| 4755 | Wandering Jew, the GB 1933 | | 5014 | Where the Hot Wind Blows |
| 2864 | Wandering With the Moon SWE 1945 | | | IT/FR 1959(58) |
| 1940 | Wang jiang ting CHN 1958 | | 5081 | Where Time Began SP 1978 |
| 753 | Wang Xifeng danao ning-kuofu | | 3248 | Where Was Your Majesty Between |
| | CHN 1939 | | | 3 and 5? HUNG 1965(64) |
| 520 | Wanton Contessa, the IT 1954 | | 3907 | While the Sun Shines GB 1947 |
| 4001 | Wanton of Spain, - La Celestina, the | | 2990 | Whisky Galore! GB 1949(48) |
| | SP 1969(68) | | 51 | White Boat, the USSR 1976 |
| 4919 | War and Peace USA/IT 1956 | | 2862 | White Cat, the SWE 1950 |
| 4921 | War and Peace USSR 1963-67 | | 4897 | White Devil, the GER 1930 |
| 5153 | War Game, the GB 1966(65) | | 757 | White Disease, the CZ 1937 |
| 3737 | War Gods of the Deep GB/USA 1965 | | 2898 | White Fang USA 1936 |
| 1970 | Warlock USA 1959 | | 2900 | White Fang IT/SP/FR 1974(73) |
| 2163 | War Lover, the GB 1962 | | 2901 | White Fang USA 1990 |
| 5166 | Warm in the Bud USA 1970(69) | | 2392 | White Heron, the JAP 1958 |
| 5187 | War of the Worlds USA 1953(52) | | 1267 | White Nights IT/FR 1957 |
| 3979 | Warrior's Rest FR/IT 1962 | | 1268 | White Nights USSR 1960(59) |
| 656 | Warum bellt Herr Bobikow? | | 4898 | White Warrior, the IT/YUGO 1959 |
| | IT/GER 1976 | | 5117 | Who Am I This Time? USA 1982 |
| 4708 | Was die Schwalbe sang GER 1956 | | 4693 | Who'll Stop the Rain? USA 1978 |
| 4478 | Watchmaker, the FR 1974(73) | | 83 | Who's Afraid of Virginia Woolf? |
| 4478 | Watchmaker of Saint-Paul, the | | | USA 1966 |
| | FR 1974(73) | | 966 | Whose Life Is It Anyway? USA 1981 |
| 2110 | Watch on the Rhine USA 1943 | | 1567 | Why Does Your Husband Deceive You? |
| 2609 | Water Babies, the GB/POL 1978 | | | SP 1969(68) |
| 4395 | Waterloo Bridge USA 1931 | | 1126 | Wiatr w oczy POL 1975 |
| 4396 | Waterloo Bridge USA 1940 | | 294 | Wicked Duchess, the FR 1942 |
| 1958 | Watusi USA 1958 | | 4503 | Widow Couderc, the FR 1971 |

# Index of Literary Titles

# Guide to Literature on Film

# Guide to Literature on Film

# Guide to Literature on Film

# BIBLIOGRAPHY AND SOURCES

## Literary Referees

Bédé, Jean-Albert, and William B. Edgerton, eds. *Columbia Dictionary of Modern European Literature*. New York: Columbia UP, 1980.

Beyer, Harald. *A History of Norwegian Literature*. New York: New York UP, 1956.

Bondanella, Peter, and Julia Conaway Bondanella, eds. *The Macmillan Dictionary of Italian Literature*. London: Macmillan, 1979.

Bordman, Gerald, ed. *The Oxford Companion to American Theatre*. New York: Oxford UP, 1984.

Czigány Lóránt. *The Oxford History of Hungarian Literature*. Oxford: Clarendon, 1984.

Daiches, David, ed. *The Penguin Companion to Literature - 1 -: Britain and the Commonwealth*. Harmondsworth: Penguin, 1971.

Downs, Brian W. *Modern Norwegian Literature 1860-1918*. Cambridge: Cambridge UP, 1966.

Drabble, Margaret, ed. *The Oxford Companion to English Literature. (5th. ed.)* Oxford: Oxford UP, 1985.

Dudley, D. R., and D. M. Lang, eds. *The Penguin Companion to Literature - 4 -: Classical and Byzantine, Oriental and African*. Harmondsworth: Penguin, 1969.

Garland, Henry, and Mary, eds. *The Oxford Companion to German Literature*. Oxford: Clarendon, 1976.

Goodwin, Ken. *A History of Australian Literature*. London: Macmillan, 1986.

Gustafson, Alrik. *A History of Swedish Literature*. Minneapolis: Univ. of Minnesota, 1961.

Hart, James D., ed. *The Oxford Companion to American Literature. (4th.ed.)* New York: Oxford UP, 1965.

---. ed. *The Concise Oxford Companion to American LIterature*. Oxford: Oxford UP, 1986.

Hartnoll, Phyllis, ed. *The Concise Companion to the Theatre*. London: Omega, 1988.

Harvey, Paul, ed. *The Oxford Companion to Classical Literature*. Oxford: Oxford UP, 1984.

---. ed. *The Oxford Companion to English Literature. (3rd.ed.)* Oxford: Oxford UP, 1946.

---. and J. E. Heseltine, eds. *The Oxford Companion to French Literature*. Oxford: Oxford UP, 1959.

Hogan, Robert, ed. *The Macmillan Dictionary of Irish Literature*. London: Macmillan, 1980.

Hsia, C. T. *The Classic Chinese Novel: A critical introduction*. Bloomington: Indiana UP, 1980.

---. *A History of Modern Chinese Fiction. (2nd.ed)* New Haven: Yale UP, 1971.

Kirkpatrick, D. L., ed. *Reference Guide to American Literature. (2nd.ed)* Chicago: St James, 1987.

Klein, Leonard S., ed. *African Literatures in the 20th Century: A Guide*. Harpenden: Oldcastle, 1988.

---., ed. *Encyclopedia of World Literature in the 20th Century. (4 vols.)* New York: Ungar, 1971-84.

---., ed. *Far Eastern Literatures in the 20th Century: A Guide*. Harpenden: Oldcastle, 1988.

---., ed. *Latin American Literature in the 20th Century: a Guide*. Harpenden: Oldcastle, 1988.

Kramer, Leonie, ed. *The Oxford History of Australian Literature*. Melbourne: Oxford UP, 1981.

Lang, David Marshall, ed. *A Guide to Eastern Literatures*. London: Weidenfeld, 1971.

Mitchell, P.M. *A History of Danish Literature*. Copenhagen: Gyldendal, 1957.

Miłosz, Czesław. *The History of Polish Literature*. London: Collier, 1969.

Moser, Charles A., ed. *The Cambridge History of Russian Literature*. Cambridge:

Cambridge UP, 1989.

Mottram, Eric., Malcolm Bradbury, and Jean Franco, eds. *The Penguin Companion to Literature - 3 -: U.S.A. & Latin America.* Harmondsworth: Penguin, 1971.

Paes, José Paulo, and Massaud Moisé, eds. *Pequeno Dicionário de Literatura Brasileira.* Saõ Paulo: Cultrix, 1967.

Popa, Marian, ed. *Dicţionar de literatură română contemporană.* Bucureşti: Albatros, 1971.

Pringle, David, ed. *The Ultimate Guide to Science Fiction.* London: Grafton, 1990.

Průšek, Jaroslav, ed. *Dictionary of Oriental Literatures. (3 vols.)* London: Allen, 1974.

Reid, Joyce M. H., ed. *The Concise Oxford Dictionary of French Literature.* Oxford: Oxford UP, 1976.

Rimer, J. Thomas. *Modern Japanese Fiction and Its Traditions.* Princeton: Princeton UP, 1978.

---., ed. *A Reader's Guide to Japanese Literature.* Tokyo: Kodansha, 1988.

Ronconi, Enzo, and Redazione Vallecchi, eds. *Dizionario generale degli autori italiani contemporanei. (2 vols.)* Firenza: Vallecchi, 1974.

Sen'ichi Hisamatsu, ed. *Biographical Dictionary of Japanese Literature.* Tokyo: Kodansha, 1976.

Stephens, Meic, ed. *The Oxford Companion to the Literature of Wales.* Oxford: Oxford UP, 1986.

Stern, Irwin, ed. *Dictionary of Brazilian Literature.* Westport: Greenwood, 1988.

Taylor, John Russell, ed. *The Penguin Dictionary of the Theatre.* Harmondsworth: Penguin, 1979.

Terras, Victor, ed. *Handbook of Russian Literature.* New Haven: Yale UP, 1985.

Thorlby, Anthony, ed. *The Penguin Companion to Literature - 2 -: European.* Harmondsworth: Penguin, 1969.

Vinson, James, ed. *Contemporary Novelists.* London: St James, 1976.

---. *20th-Century American Literature.* London: Macmillan, 1980.

Vinson, James, and D. L. Kirkpatrick, eds. *American Literature to 1900.* London: Macmillan, 1980.

---. *Commonwealth Literature.* London: Macmillan, 1979.

---. *Contemporary Foreign Language Writers.* London: St James, 1984.

---. *Great Foreign Language Writers.* London: St James, 1984.

Ward, Philip, ed. *The Oxford Companion to Spanish Literature.* Oxford: Clarendon, 1978.

Wilde, William H., Joy Hooton, and Barry Andrews, eds. *The Oxford Companion to Australian Literature.* Melbourne: Oxford UP, 1985.

## Literature: General

Alexandrova, Vera, and Mirra Ginsburg, trans. *A History of Soviet Literature 1917-1964: From Gorky to Solzhenitsyn.* New York: Anchor, 1964.

Algulin, Ingemar. *A History of Swedish Literature.* Stockholm: Swedish Institute, 1989.

Barac, Antun. *A History of Yugoslav Literature.* Beograd: 1955.

Bibliotheca Nationalis Hungariae. *Bibliographia Hungarica: 1945-1960. (Vol.iv.).* Budapestini: Bibliotheca Nationalis Hungariae, 1964.

Brée, Germaine; and Louise Guiney, (trans.) *Twentieth-Century French Literature.* Chicago: Univ. of Chicago, 1983(1978).

Brown, Edward J. *Russian Literature Since the Revolution. (rev. ed.)* Cambridge, Mass: Harvard UP, 1982.

Closs, August, ed. *Twentieth Century German Literature.* London: Cresset, 1969.

Clyman, Toby W, ed. *A Chekhov Companion.* Westport: Greenwood, 1985.

Contento, William, ed *Science Fiction: anthologies and collections.* Boston: Hall, 1978.

Cook, D. E., and I. S. Monro, eds. *Short Story Index. (13 vols.)* New York: Wilson, 1923-90.

Czigány Magda, ed. *Hungarian Literature in English Translation, published in Great Britain 1830-1968: A Bibliography.* London: Szepsi Csombor, 1969.

Dolby, William. *A History of Chinese Drama.* London: Elek, 1976.

Domandi, Agnes Körner, ed. *Modern German Literature: A Library of Literary Criticism.* (2 vols.) New York: Ungar, 1972.

Eloesser, Arthur. *Modern German Literature.* London: Hamilton, 1933.

Garten, H. F. *Modern German Drama.* London: Methuen, 1959.

Ghosh, Dipali, ed. *Translations of Bengali Works into English: A bibliography.* London: Mansell, 1986.

Griffiths, Trevor R., and Carole Woddis, eds. *Bloomsbury Theatre Guide.* London: Bloomsbury, 1988.

Guha-Thakurta, P. *The Bengali Drama: its origin and development.* London: Kegan Paul, 1930.

Gunn, Edward M. *Unwelcome Muse: Chinese Literature in Shanghai and Peking: 1937-1945.* New York: Columbia UP, 1980.

Haltsonen, Sulo, and Rauni Puranen, eds. *Kauno-kirjallisuutemme käännöksiä.* Helsinki: Soumalaisen Kirjallisuuden Seura, 1979.

Heifetz, Anna, and Avrahm Yarmolinsky, eds. *Chekhov in English: A List of Works By and About Him.* New York: N.Y. Public Library, 1949.

Holt, Marion P. *The Contemporary Spanish Theatre: (1949-1972).* Boston: Twayne, 1975.

Huebener, Theodore. *The Literature of East Germany.* New York: Ungar, 1970.

Innes, C. D. *Modern German Drama.* Cambridge: Cambridge UP, 1979.

Ireland, Norma Olin, ed. *Index to Full Length Plays 1944 to 1964.* Boston: Faxon, 1965.

Kadić, Ante. *Contemporary Serbian Literature.* The Hague: Mouton, 1964.

Kinkley, Jeffrey C., ed. *After Mao: Chinese Literature and Society 1978-1981.* Cambridge, Mass: Harvard, 1985.

Klaniczay, Tibor, ed. *A History of Hungarian Literature.* Budapest: Corvina, 1982.

Komparu Kunio. *The Noh Theater: Principles and Perspectives.* New York: Weatherhill, 1983.

Kovtun, George J., ed. *Czech and Slovak Literature in English: A Bibliography. (2nd.ed.)* Washington: Library of Congress, 1988.

Kunisch, Hermann, ed. *Handbuch der deutschen Gegenwartsliteratur.* München: Nymphenburger, 1969.

Kunitz, Stanley J., and Howard Hatcraft, eds. *Twentieth Century Authors: A Biographical Dictionary of Modern Literature.* New York: Wilson, 1955.

Landeira, Ricardo. *The Modern Spanish Novel 1898-1936.* Boston: Twayne, 1985.

Leiter, Samuel L., ed. & trans. *Kabuki Encyclopedia: An English-Language Adaptation of Kabuki Jiten.* Westport: Greenwood, 1979.

Lemaître, Henri, ed. *Dictionnaire Bordas de Littérature Française et francophone.* Paris: Bordas, 1985.

Lewanski, Richard C., ed. *The Literatures of the World in English Translation: A Bibliography. Vol. 2: The Slavic Literatures.* New York: Ungar, 1967.

Madison, Charles A. *Yiddish Literature.* New York: Ungar, 1968.

Martins Janeira, Armando. *Japanese and Western Literature: A Comparative Study.* Rutland: Tuttle, 1970.

Mirsky, D. S., Francis J. Whitfield, ed. *A History of Russian Literature.* London: Routledge, 1949.

Moore, Harry T., and Albert Parry. *Twentieth-Century Russian Literature.* London: Heinemann, 1976.

Morgan, Bayard Quincy, ed. *German Literature in English Translation: 1481-1927.* New York: Scarecrow, 1965.

---., ed. *German Literature in English Translation: 1928-1955.* New York: Scarecrow, 1965.

Nienhauser, William H., ed. *The Indiana Companion to Traditional Chinese Literature.* Bloomington: Univ. of Indiana, 1986.

P. E. N., ed. *Japanese Literature in European Languages: A Bibliography.* Tokyo: P.E.N., 1961.

Reilly, John M., ed. *Twentieth-Century Crime and Mystery Writers. (2nd. ed.)* London: St James, 1985.

Roger, Jacques, and Jean-Charles Payen. *Histoire de la Littérature Française: t. 1. Du Moyen Age à la fin du XV11 siècle.* Paris: Colin, 1969.

Roger, Jacques. *Histoire de la Littérature Française: t. 2. Du XV111 siècle à nos jours.* Paris: Colin, 1970.

Rudder, Robert S., ed. *The Literature of Spain in English Translation: A Bibliography.* New York: Ungar, 1975.

Scobbie, Irene, ed. *Aspects of Modern Swedish Literature.* Norwich: Norvik, 1988.

Seymour-Smith, Martin, ed. *Guide to Modern World Literature.* London: Macmillan, 1985.

Slonim, Marc. *The Epic of Russian Literature: From its Origins Through Tolstoy.* New York:

Oxford UP, 1950.

---. *Soviet Russian Literature: Writers and Problems 1917-1977. (2nd. ed.)* New York: Oxford UP, 1977.

Smith, Murray F., ed. *A Selected Bibliography of German Literature in English Translation, 1956-1960.* Metuchen: Scarecrow, 1972.

Steinberg, Jacob. *Introduction to Rumanian Literature.* New York: Twayne, 1966.

Steinberg, S. H., and J. Buchanan-Brown, eds. *Cassell's Encyclopaedia of World Literature. (3 vols.)* London: Cassell, 1973.

Straumanis, Alfreds, ed. *Baltic Drama: A Handbook and Bibliography.* Illinois: Waveland, 1981.

Struve, Gleb. *Russian Literature under Lenin and Stalin 1917-1953.* London: Routledge, 1972.

---. *Soviet Russian Literature 1917-50.* Norman: Univ. of Oklahoma, 1951.

---. *25 Years of Soviet Russian Literature (1918-1943).* London: Routledge, 1944(1935)

Tezla, Albert, ed. *Hungarian Authors: A Bibliographical Handbook.* Cambridge, Mass: Harvard UP, 1970.

Thomson, Peter, and Gāmini Salgādo, eds. *The Everyman Companion to the Theatre.* London: Dent, 1987.

Watson, Roderick. *The Literature of Scotland.* London: Macmillan, 1984.

Wilkins, Ernest Hatch. *A History of Italian Literature.* London: Oxford UP, 1954.

Yachnin, Rissa, and David H. Stam, eds. *Turgenev in English: A Checklist of Works by and about Him.* New York: N.Y. Public Library, 1962.

Yang, Winston L. Y., and Nathan K. Mao, eds. *Modern Chinese Fiction.* Boston: Hall, 1981.

Young, Trudee, ed. *Georges Simenon: A Checklist of His 'Maigret' and other Mystery Novels and Short Stories in French and in English Translations.* Metuchen: Scarecrow, 1976.

Yukio Fujino, ed. *Modern Japanese Literature in Western Translations: A Bibliography.* Tokyo: International House of Japan, 1972.

Zool, M. H., ed. *Bloomsbury Good Reading Guide to Science Fiction and Fantasy.* London: Bloomsbury, 1989.

## Film Sources: Book Materials

Aguilar, Carlos. *Guia del Video-Cine.* Madrid: Cátedra, 1986.

Algar, Nigel, ed. *Films on Offer. (10 vols.)* London: BFI, 1975-90.

anon. *Contemporary Polish Cinematography.* Warsaw: Polonia, 1962.

Arhiva Naţională de Filme, ed. *Filmografia: producţiei cinematografice româneşti 1949-1965: filme artistice şi de animaţie.* Bucureşti: Arhiva Naţională de Filme, 1965.

---; ed. *Caiet de documentare cinematografică: Nr. 3 (16), 1963.* Bucureşti: 1963.

---; ed. *Caiet de documentare cinematografică: Nr. 1-3, 1983.* Bucureşti: 1983.

Bauer, Alfred, ed. *Deutscher Spielfilm Almanach: 1929-1950.* München: Winterberg, 1976.

---., ed. *Deutscher Spielfilm Almanach: band 2 : 1946-1955.* München: Winterberg, 1981.

Bech, Leif-Erik, ed. *Norsk Filmografi, 1908-1979.* Oslo: Norsk Filminstitutt, 1980.

British Film Institute, ed. *Monthly Film Bulletin. (vols. 31-58.)* London: BFI, 1964-91

Browning, Wendy, and Jane Pitcher, eds. *Audio-visual materials on drama 1978.* London: BUFC, 1978.

Centro Cattolico Cinematografica. *Nuova guida cinematografica: I film usciti in italia dal 1928 al 1976. (2 vols.)* Roma: Centro Cattolico, 1977.

---. *Nuova guida cinematografica: Aggiornamento 1977-1980.* Roma: Centro Cattolico, 1981.

Chirat, Raymond, ed. *Catalogue des films français de long metrage: film sonores de fiction 1929-1939.* Brussels: Cinémathèque Royale, 1981.

---. *Catalogue de films français de long metrage: films de fiction 1940-1950.* Luxembourg: Cinémathèque Municipale, 1981.

Chirat, Raymond, and Jean-Claude Romer, eds. *Catalogue des films de fiction: de première partie 1929-1939.* Bois d'Arcy: Film Centre National, 1984.

Cowie, Peter, ed. *World Filmography 1967.* London: Tantivy, 1977.

---; ed. *World Filmography 1968.* London: Tantivy, 1977.

Daisne, Johan, ed. *Dictionnaire filmographique de la littérature mondiale. (3 vols.)* Gand: E. Story-Scientia, 1971-78.

Elliot, John, ed. *Elliot's Guide to Films on Video.* London: Boxtree, 1990.

# Guide to Literature on Film

Emmens, Carol A., ed. *Short Stories on Film and Video. (2nd. edition)* Littleton: Libraries Unlimited, 1985.

Enser, A.G.S., ed. *Filmed Books and Plays.* London: Deutsch, 1975.

Estermann, Alfred. *Die Verfilmung Literarischer Werke.* Bonn: Bouvier, 1965.

---; ed. *Filmobibliografischer Jahrresbericht: 1965-1970 / 1972-1985.* Berlin: Kunst, 1985.

Fuksiewicz, Jacek. *Film and Television in Poland.* Warsaw: Interpress, 1976.

Gencheva, Galina, ed. *Bulgarian Feature Films: Volume two (1948-1970).* Sofia: State, 1988.

Gifford, Denis, ed. *The British Film Catalogue: 1895-1985.* Newton Abbot: David & Charles, 1986.

Givanni, June, ed. *Black & Asian Film / Video List.* London: BFI, 1988.

Gomez Mesa, Luis, ed. *La Literatura Española en el Cine Nacional: 1907-1977.* Madrid: Filmoteca Nacional de España, 1978.

Halliwell, Leslie, ed. *Halliwell's Film Guide. (1st. & 6th. eds.)* London: Granada, 1979;1988.

Heinzlmeier, Adolf, and Berndt Schulz, eds. *Lexikon Filme im Fernsehen.* Hamburg: Rasch und Röhring, 1988.

Helt, Richard C., and Marie E. Helt, eds. *West German Cinema Since 1945: A Reference Handbook.* New Jersey: Scarecrow, 1987.

Holloway, Ronald. *The Bulgarian Cinema.* Cranbury: AUP, 1986.

Johnson, Randel, and Robert Stam. *Brazilian Cinema.* E.Brunswick: AUP, 1982.

Kardzhilov, Peter, ed. *Bulgarian Feature Films: Volume One (1915-1948).* Sofia: State, 1987.

Leyda, Jay. *Kino: A History of the Russian and Soviet Film.* London: Allen, 1960.

McFarlane, Brian. *Words and Images: Australian Novels into Film.* Victoria: Heinemann, 1983.

MacKinnon, Kenneth. *Greek Tragedy into Film.* London: Croom Helm, 1986.

McIlroy, Brian. *World Cinema 4: Ireland.* Trowbridge: Flicks, 1989.

Maltins, Leonard, ed. *Leonard Maltin's TV Movies and Video Guide.* New York: Penguin, 1988.

Measham, Joan. *Henry James: Adaptation of his fiction both by himself and others.* Univ. of Nottingham: (unpublished thesis), 1980.

Nash, Jay Robert, Stanley Ralph Ross, and Robert B. Connelly, eds. *The Motion Picture Guide: 1910-1984. (12 vols)* Chicago: Cinebooks, 1987.

Nemesküty, István. *Word and Image: History of the Hungarian Cinema.* Budapest: Corvina, 1974.

Norsk Filminstitutt, ed. *Knut Hamsun: en filmografi.* Oslo: Norsk Filminstitutt, 1989.

---., ed. *Oskar Braaten 1881-1981: En filmografi.* Oslo: Norsk Filminstitutt, n.d.

Peary, Gerald, and Roger Shatzkin, eds. *The Classic American Novel and the Movies.* New York: Ungar, 1977.

---., eds. *The Modern American Novel and the Movies.* New York: Ungar, 1978.

Pflaum, Hans Günther, and Hans Helmut Prinzler, eds. *Film in der Bundesrepublik Deutschland.* Frankfurt: Fischer, 1982.

Rentschler, Eric, ed. *German Film & Literature: Adaptations and Transformations.* New York: Methuen, 1986.

Salmi, Markku, ed. *Catalogue of Stills, Posters and Designs.* London: BFI, 1982.

Svenska Filminstitutet, ed. *Svensk filmografi: (vol.3) 1930-1939.* Stockholm: Svenska Filminstitutet, 1979.

---., ed. *Svensk filmografi: (vol.4) 1940-1949.* Stockholm: Svenska Filminstitutet, 1980.

---., ed. *Svensk filmografi: (vol.5) 1950-1959.* Stockholm: Svenska Filminstitutet, 1984.

---., ed. *Svensk filmografi: (vol.6) 1960-1969.* Stockholm: Svenska Filminstitutet, 1977.

Terris, Olwen, ed. *Twentieth-Century Dramatists: A list of audio-visual materials available in the UK.* London: BUFC, 1987.

Unifrance Films, ed. *Cinema française: production - 1977-1982.* Paris: Unifrance, 1984.

---., ed. *La production française: 1985-1986.(+ supp.).* Paris: Unifrance, 1986.

---., ed. *Les films français: production - 1987-1990.* Paris: Unifrance, 1987-90.

Van Tieghem, Philippe, ed. *Dictionnaire des littératures. (4 vols.)* Paris: PUF, 1984.

Variety, ed. *Variety Film Reviews 1930-1988. (vols.4-20)* New York: Bowker, 1990.(set)

Wingrove, David, ed. *The Science Fiction Film Source Book.* London: Longman, 1985.

Winquist, Sven G., ed. *Svenska ljudfilmer: 1929-69 och deras regissörer. (2nd. ed.)* Stockholm: Svenska Filminstitutet, 1969.

## Film: General

Anderson, Joseph L., and Donald Richie. *The Japanese Film: Art and Industry.* New Jersey: Princeton UP, 1982.

Bartoskova, Sarka, and Lubos Bartosek. *Filmove profily.* Prague: CS, 1986.

Beja, Morris. *Film & Literature.* New York: Longman, 1979.

Bergan, Ronald, and Robyn Karney, eds. *Bloomsbury Foreign Film Guide.* London: Bloomsbury, 1988.

Besas, Peter. *Behind the Spanish Lens: Spanish Cinema under Fascism and Democracy.* Denver: Arden, 1985.

Björkman, Stig. *Film in Sweden: The New Directors.* London: Tantivy, 1977.

Bluestone, George. *Novels into Film.* Baltimore: John Hopkins, 1957.

Bock, Audie. *Japanese Film Directors. (2nd.ed.)* Tokyo: Kodansha, 1985.

Bordwell, David. *Ozu and the Poetics of Cinema.* London: BFI, 1988.

Boussinot, Roger, ed. *L'encyclopédie du cinéma.:* Bordas, 1967.

Bren, Frank. *World Cinema 1: Poland.* London: Flicks, 1986.

British Film Institute. *Sight and Sound. (vols. 37-60.)* London: BFI, 1967-91

Buache, Freddy. *Le cinéma français des années 60.* Renens: 5 Continents / Hatier, 1987.

---. *Le cinéma italien 1945-1979.* Lausanne: L'age D'homme, 1979.

---. *Le cinéma suisse.* Lausanne: L'age D'homme, 1978.

Burton, Julianne, ed. *The New Latin American Cinema: an annotated bibliography 1960-1980.* New York: Smyrna, 1983.

Caparros Lera, Jose Ma. *El Cine Republicano Español: (1931-1939).* Barcelona: Dopesa, 1977.

Centre Pompidou, ed. *Cinema français: les années 50.* Paris: Centre Pompidou, 1987.

Chanan, Michael. *The Cuban Image.* London: BFI, 1985.

Costa, Alves. *Breve história do cinema português (1896-1962).* Lisboa: Instituto de Cultura Portuguesa, 1978.

Di Núbila, Domingo. *Historia del Cine Argentino.* Buenos Aires: Cruz de Malta, 1959.

Elsaesser, Thomas. *New German Cinema: A History.* Basingstoke: Macmillan, 1989.

Garbicz, Adam, and Jacek Klinowski. *Cinema, The Magic Vehicle: A Guide to Its Achievement, Journey One: The Cinema Through 1949.* New York: Schocken, 1983.

---. *Cinema, The Magic Vehicle: A Guide to Its Achievement, Journey Two: The Cinema in the Fifties.* New York: Schocken, 1983.

Gilson, René; and Ciba Vaughan, (trans.) *Jean Cocteau: An investigation into his films and philosophy.* New York: Crown, 1969.

Goulding, Daniel J. *Liberated Cinema: The Yugoslav Experience.* Bloomington: Indiana UP, 1985.

Hall, Sandra. *Critical Business: The New Australian Cinema in Review.* Adelaide: Rigby, 1985.

Hardy, Phil, ed. *The Encyclopedia of Western Movies.* London: Octopus, 1984.

Hopewell, John. *Out of the Past: Spanish Cinema after Franco.* London: BFI, 1986.

Horton, Andrew S., and Joan Magretta, eds. *Modern European Filmmakers and the Art of Adaptation.* New York: Ungar, 1981.

Johnson, Randal. *Cinema Novo x 5: Masters of Contemporary Brazilian Film.* Austin: Univ. of Texas, 1984.

---. *The Film Industry in Brazil.* Pittsburgh: Univ. of Pittsburgh, 1987.

Jorgens, Jack J. *Shakespeare on Film.* Bloomington: Indiana UP, 1977.

Katz, Ephraim, ed. *The International Film Encyclopedia.* London: Macmillan, 1982.

Kawin, Bruce F. *Faulkner and Film.* New York: Ungar, 1977.

Kittredge, William, and Steven M. Krauzer. *Stories into Film.* New York: Harper, 1979.

Klein, Michael, and Gillian Parker, eds. *The English Novel and the Movies.* New York: Ungar, 1981.

König, Regula, and Marianne Lewinsky, eds. *Keisuke Kinoshita.* Locarno: Editions du Festival, 1986.

Laurence, Frank M. *Hemingway and the Movies.* New York: Da Capo, 1981.

Leprohon, Pierre. *The Italian Cinema.* London: Secker, 1972(1966).

Leyda, Jay. *Dianying: An Account of Films and the Film Audience in China.* Cambridge, Mass: MIT, 1972.

Limbacher, James L., ed. *Feature Films: A Directory of Feature Films on 16mm and Videotape Available for Rental, Sale, and Lease. (8th. ed.)* New York: Bowker, 1985.

Lizzani, Carlo. *Il cinema italiano: Dalle origini agli anni ottanta. (2nd. ed.)* Roma: Riuniti, 1982.

Luhr, William. *Raymond Chandler and Film*. New York: Ungar, 1982.

Lyon, Christopher, ed. *The International Dictionary of Films and Filmmakers: Volume 1, Films*. London: St James, 1984.

---., ed. *The International Dictionary of Films and Filmmakers: Volume 2, Directors / Filmmakers*. London: Macmillan, 1987.

McDonald, Keiko. *Cinema East: A Critical Study of Major Japanese Films*. Toronto: Fairleigh Dickinson UP, 1983.

Marcus, Fred H. *Film and Literature: Contrasts in Media*. Scranton: Chandler, 1971.

---. *Short Story / Short Film*. New Jersey: Prentice-Hall, 1977.

Mesnil, Michel. *Mizoguchi Kenji*. Paris: Seghers, 1965.

Michalczyk, John J. *The French Literary Filmmakers*. Philadelphia: AUP, 1980.

Miller, Gabriel. *Screening the Novel: Rediscovered American Fiction in Film*. New York: Ungar, 1980.

Millichap, Joseph R. *Steinbeck and Film*. New York: Ungar, 1983.

Mora, Carl J. *Mexican Cinema: Reflections of a Society 1896-1980*. Berkeley: Univ. of California, 1982.

Orlandello, John. *O'Neill on Film*. E.Brunswick: AUP, 1982.

Pendo, Stephen. *Raymond Chandler on Screen: His Novels into Film*. New Jersey: Scarecrow, 1976.

Petrie, Graham. *History Must Answer to Man: The Contemporary Hungarian Cinema*. Hungary: Corvina, 1978.

Phillips, Gene D. *Graham Greene: The Films of His Fiction*. New York: Teachers, 1974.

Phillips, Klaus, ed. *New German Filmmakers: from Oberhausen through the 1970s*. New York: Ungar, 1984.

Pines, Jim. *Blacks in Films*. London: Studio Vista, 1975.

Richie, Donald. *The Films of Akira Kurosawa*. Berkeley: Univ. of California, 1984.

---. *Japanese Cinema: Film Style and National Character*. London: Secker, 1972.

Sadoul, Georges, and Peter Morris, eds. *Dictionary of Films*. Berkeley: 1972.

Sandford, John. *The New German Cinema*. London: Methuen, 1981.

Savio, Francesco. *Ma L'Amore No: realismo, formalismo, propaganda e telefoni bianchi nel cinema italiano di regime (1930-1943)*. Milan: Sonzogno, 1975.

Torres, Augusto M., ed. *Cine español 1896-1983*. Madrid: Ministerio de Cultura, 1984.

Vorontsov, Yuri, and Igor Rachuk. *The Phenomenon of the Soviet Cinema*. Moscow: Progress, 1980.

Yacowar, Maurice. *Tennessee Williams and Film*. New York: Ungar, 1977.

Zalman, Jan. *Films and Film-Makers in Czechoslovakia*. Prague: Orbis, 1968.